History of London

LONDON 800–1216:
THE SHAPING OF A CITY

History of London

LONDON
800-1216:
THE SHAPING OF
A CITY

Christopher N. L. Brooke

Assisted by Gillian Keir

LONDON
SECKER & WARBURG

First published in England 1975
by Martin Secker & Warburg Limited
14 Carlisle Street, London W1V 6NN

Copyright © 1975 by Christopher N. L. Brooke and Gillian Keir

436 06920 2

Maps by Gillian Keir and Cartographic Enterprises

Printed in Great Britain by
Richard Clay (The Chaucer Press) Ltd
Bungay, Suffolk

Contents

List of Illustrations

List of Maps

Preface

'IT WAS the best of times, it was the worst of times.' Such is the predicament of anyone now who sets out to write the history of either of Dickens' two cities between the ninth and the thirteenth centuries. London, like many others in western Europe, was conscious of its Roman past. But in the early Middle Ages, though never defunct, it was a shadow of a town. During the centuries covered by this book London again became, in the fullest sense of the word, a greaty city, and in some senses the political capital of England and the commercial capital of a large area of north-western Europe. Here is an exciting subject; but also a sharp challenge, for while some of the story has been told and retold, for the rest the material is unequal and often baffling and demands a long detective enterprise to make sense of it.

Rapid strides have been made in recent years in the study of the cities of Europe at every point in the Middle Ages, and archaeology, topography and numismatics have added new perspectives to the work of reconstruction. To take a fresh look at London in this wider context, and to see what impact modern techniques of research have made, is an urgent need for students of London and of medieval towns; this is the right time, almost the best of times.

Yet in all these fields pioneer research is in progress or yet to begin. We have much recent work to be thankful for: Professor Grimes' *The Excavation of Roman and Mediaeval London* lays out the major discoveries of recent years; Miss Honeybourne's maps and topographical studies have provided essential foundations; the late Eilert Ekwall set the study of street-names on a scientific basis. Archaeological discovery, however, has recently entered a new and crucial phase; the plotting of all the finds and codifying of all the material is being planned, but not yet accomplished; and the publication of *The Future of London's Past* (1973 – see p. 90) has established new hopes and fresh targets in this field. The English Place-Name Society has recently embarked on a new study of London's place-names; the history of the London Mint is still unwritten. In a few years' time these will give us quite a new view of the materials for this book, and perhaps put sections of it quickly out of date. In a vital sense, it is the worst of times to be writing a book on London in the period most likely to be illuminated by these studies.

In planning the book we have had to put together familiar and unfamiliar, to prepare readers instructed and less instructed for a long detective enquiry. This has made any simple, logical or chronological plan of little use; instead we have attempted to develop our themes more on the analogy of a piece of symphonic music. In the first part the themes are declared, but only in small measure developed. The first two chapters explain our approach in a very general way and outline the political history of London in these centuries. There is a continuity in London's history from Roman times; but very great change too, the product of a creative act and a long period of development. The act was Alfred's, the development part of the story of the urban renaissance of the tenth, eleventh and twelfth centuries, a major theme in European history. We conclude Part I by studying these topics (Chapter 3) and by explaining and illustrating some of the materials and methods by which London's place in the urban renaissance can be traced (Chapter 4).

Before the thirteenth century the documentary record is lamentably deficient, yet this was the period when the shape of London was firmly set for many centuries to come. Part II is about this shape and its formation; from the unique and vivid contemporary description written in 1173–4, from the maze of parishes and wards and streets, we trace the pattern and attempt to explain it. There are many gaps; but if the threads we have found are strong and secure, then this part will have provided a frame for the rest of the book. It is evidently true of any great town that the social strata of its ruling classes, the personalities and nature of its government and its place in the larger commercial world of the age are crucial elements in its history. These are the themes of Part III, in which we have tried in particular to trace the elements in London's trade, the links between the money market and the shrievalty, and in which we have laid a special emphasis on the officials who came in our period to be the leaders in city government: the mayor and sheriffs. One special feature of the eleventh and twelfth centuries in urban history is that the Church played a quite exceptional part; its importance to the modern student is greatly enhanced by the survival of ecclesiastical records and the exceptional degree to which remains of churches yield their secrets to the spade. The parish churches have already provided a core to Part II; a full study of the major churches in London, its abbeys, priories and hospitals, provides the core of Part IV, in the course of which many aspects of political and social history are investigated, from social welfare for the poor, through dowries for rich men's daughters in the convents of nuns, to high politics in the palace and abbey of Westminster and the meeting of court, church and city in St Paul's.

Such is the pattern, and it is evident that the book must be a mingling of things old and new. We have been constantly aware of the fundamental work in the political, social and constitutional history of London of J. H. Round and William Page; on the guilds, George Unwin's great book still retains most of its value; the social history is the background to a story made familiar in the more recent works of Gwyn Williams and Sylvia Thrupp. Although the City's own records are not copious before the mid-thirteenth century, all students of its history owe a large debt to the distinguished succession of its archivists, and the *Studies in London History* presented to Philip Jones was not only a fitting tribute to one of the most respected of the line but revealed in its contents the active condition of the subject.

First among our more personal debts must be named the Corporation of London, and its Library Committee, through whose munificence Gillian Keir was able to work for three years in collecting materials for this study; and we owe particular gratitude to successive Secondaries of London, Captain C. B. Saunders and Mr Ralph Snagge, for the initiatives they took and the help they gave in arranging the grant. The original plan had been for a book on the origins of the mayoralty and shrievalty; but it was agreed at the beginning of our involvement in the scheme that the nature of the material made a separate book on this subject impossible. Real progress in this field depends on studying the sheriffs and mayors in the wider contexts of London and urban history, and searching the copious but scattered records of the twelfth century for evidence for every aspect of the city's life. We hope we have made the reasons for this sufficiently plain in the planning of Part III, though it will be seen that mayors and sheriffs impinge on every section, from Chapter 2 to Chapter 12.

C.N.L.B. was invited to write this book by Secker & Warburg six years ago, and he owes much to their help. It was through the publishers that he was first put in touch with the Corporation; but the suggestion that the Corporation's own project should be united with this book was first made by Miss Susan Reynolds. Thus we owe to her a very great debt, and her help, encouragement and advice have been frequently and generously

given. Much of G.K.'s work has consisted in the analysis of documents
and their indexing; she has collaborated with Miss Reynolds in forming
a very substantial corpus of prosopographical material, which the latter
has most generously allowed us freely to use – though much of it is of her
own making, and the conception was entirely hers – in our sections on
London's social and political history; she has also allowed us to use her
list of sheriffs in Appendix II. For all this, and for our joint work on the
Charter of Henry I (see p. 207) we offer her thanks both warm and deep.

Susan Reynolds has also put us yet further in her debt by reading a
substantial part of the book in manuscript and saving us from many errors.
She is one of a numerous band of generous friends who have corrected
the book in draft: Professor Eleanora Carus-Wilson, Mr William Kellaway, Professor Geoffrey Martin, Miss Betty Masters, C.B.'s wife, Dr.
Rosalind Brooke and our General Editor, Mr Francis Sheppard. All
have given us advice and encouragement; Mr Sheppard has done more
than this, in a number of ways, to help and encourage us; Mr Kellaway
has helped us not only from the stores of his knowledge of London history,
but also as Secretary and Librarian of the Institute of Historical Research
– to whose Director and Staff we owe many debts, for most of the fundamental work of the book was conducted there. Of the debt that we owe
to Miss Honeybourne the many references to her maps and topographical
studies give a little indication. Mr Martin Biddle has been generous in
giving his time to showing us, in his trenches and his study, how our
knowledge of early urban history is being transformed under the inspiration of his work at Winchester.

Very generous too has been the help of Mr Ian Stewart, who provided
us with notes and references on which the section on coins in Chapter 4,
and Appendix IV, are based. We are responsible for the presentation, and
for our errors; any virtue these pages has is his.

To a numerous band of librarians and archivists we offer thanks for
liberal and friendly help: and especially to those of the Guildhall and the
Guildhall Library, Mr Philip Jones, Miss Masters and Dr Albert Holl-
aender, and to the Guildhall Librarian, Mr Thompson; to Mr A. R. B.
Fuller at St Paul's, to Dr Nellie Kerling at St Bartholomew's, to Mr
N. H. MacMichael at Westminster Abbey; to Dr Patricia Barnes and Miss
Alexandra Marr at the Public Record Office; and to all who helped us in
the British Museum, the libraries of Oxford and Cambridge, and the
Cathedral Libraries of Canterbury, Gloucester and Peterborough. In
pursuit of documents and comparative material abroad, we have had kind

help from Professor Donald Bullough, Professor E. Cristiani, Dr J. V. Fearns, Professor F.-L. Ganshof, Professor Cinzio Violante; and from Dottoressa M. L. Corsi and a number of other archivists in northern and central Italy. On various points we have had advice and help from Professor Mgr C. D. Fonseca, Dr M. Gervers, Miss Joan Gibbs, Professor Philip Grierson, Dr and Mrs J. B. Hall, Professor Jerzy Kloczowski, Professor R. B. Pugh, Dr R. W. Southern. A special word must be said of the late Miss I. Darlington, who placed her transcripts of the Canterbury rentals at our disposal. We would also like to thank Mr Maurice Temple Smith and the present staff of Secker & Warburg, especially Mr John Blackwell and Mr William Neill-Hall.

For permission to quote a substantial part of C.B.'s inaugural lecture at Westfield College (in Chapter 5) the kind consent of the Principal is acknowledged; and to the College we are also indebted for providing the opportunity for C.B. to become once again a student of London history, and for giving hospitality to G.K. when the Corporation of London made its research grant; to our colleagues in the History Department we owe many debts of help and friendship. To the University of Newcastle-upon-Tyne C.B. owes the opportunity, and the honour, of giving three lectures in 1971 which form the substance of Chapters 1–3.

The authors and publishers would also like to thank the following for permission to reprint copyright material: The Honourable Society of Cymmrodorion – *De nugis curialium* by Walter Map; Professor Dorothy Whitelock and Eyre & Spottiswoode (Publishers) Ltd – 'Anglo-Saxon Chronicle' (version by Professor Dorothy Whitelock) in *English Historical Documents*, Vol. I; Mr K. Potter and Thomas Nelson & Sons Ltd – *Gesta Stephani* (edited and translated by K. Potter), and *The Chronicle of Richard of Devizes* (edited by J. T. Appleby).

It is not easy to disentangle the responsibilities of joint authors who have worked together over a number of years. Roughly speaking, the detailed research in archives and record offices on which Chapters 6, 8, 9 in particular are based, a considerable share of the work on which the whole book is based, the penultimate form of Chapter 6 and the final form of Chapter 2 are G.K.'s; C.B. wrote most of the rest in its final form, and Chapters 11–12 depend mainly on his earlier researches. Chapter 3 is an attempt to express a joint conviction of the context in which such a book should be written; it is partly based on expeditions which G.K. took in 1970 and 1972, C.B. in 1971, mainly to Italy. Finally, we share a particular debt to Dr Rosalind Brooke and Dr Peter Keir, who, apart from specific aid in numerous ways, have cheerfully sustained the numerous inconveniences which a large, obtrusive book cause to those close to its authors.

C.B.
G.K.
November 1973

On rereading our Preface we are aware how many debts have passed inadequately recorded. We would particularly like to thank Dr Caroline Barron, Dr Norman Cook, Mr Ralph Merrifield, Dr John Morris for their help and advice; Miss M. Barber, Mr Geoffrey Bill, Dr N. P. Brooks, Mr A. R. B. Fuller, Professor W. F. Grimes, Frau Barbara Hesse, Mr J. Hopkins, Mr J. Howgego, Mr J. Kenyon, Dr Edmund King, Miss B. Masters, Dr Arthur Owen, Mr Ralph Pinder-Wilson, Mr Ian Stewart, Mr F. H. Thompson, Professor George Zarnecki, the Berkshire Archaeological Society and all those listed on pp. vii–x for generous help with the plates; and Mr Kellaway for adding to our burden of debt by reading the proofs; and we would also like to refer to three recent events of particular note: the formation of the London Archaeological Unit, and the publication of Dr Nellie J. M. Kerling's *Cartulary of St Bartholomew's Hospital* (1973) and Dr C. Barron's *The Medieval Guildhall of London* (1974).

C.B.
G.K.
June 1974

Glossary

ADVOWSON The right to nominate rectors or vicars, to present to an ecclesiastical benefice.

BASTIDE A type of small fortified town, especially common in the south of France: see p. 76.

BURH The Old English word for a town, used especially for the fortified market town of Alfred's time and later. On the continent the similar word 'burgum' was often used for the burgesses' part of the town, in contrast to the 'castrum', the old military centre (but see p. 71 and n.).

CONTADO The country district pertaining to an Italian city.

DAPIFER A royal official, commonly translated sewer or steward; originally one of the heads of the royal pantry and kitchen, but in fact one or a pair or group of senior administrators among the lay royal servants.

DEMESNE Domain, a lord's estate, or the territory which lay immediately under his control.

EALDORMAN The Old English word for a senior official, in origin commonly the chief official of a shire: the word was later converted into the Danish jarl, or earl, and the word ealdorman eventually came to be used of civic officials, hence aldermen.

ENCEINTE The area of a town, city or castle surrounded by its walls.

EYRE Circuit made by royal judges to investigate offences.

FIEF Territory (or in some cases money income) held of a lord for feudal, knight service; unit of land in military tenure in a feudal society.

FOLKMOOT An ancient assembly and court attended by all members of a specific community. The London folkmoot met three times a year in St Paul's churchyard to transact business of general importance to the City.

HUSTING An ancient London court which dealt with civil actions. In the twelfth century it met once a week and was attended by aldermen. Its business included the regulation of commercial practices, the hearing of disputes between Londoners, and men from outside the City and the supervision of property transactions.

JUSTICE, JUSTICIAR A royal officer, appointed to work in a town, shire or group of shires; he combined wide supervisory powers over local administration with a special responsibility for the execution of royal justice. The local justice or justiciar was a shire official in Norman times (down to *c.* 1154), parallel to the sheriff. In this book the word 'justice' is used to avoid confusion with the Justiciar or Chief Justiciar, the head of the king's judicial and administrative organization, centred in the Exchequer in the twelfth century; and often the king's deputy in his absence.

MARTYRIUM (pl MARTYRIA) The tomb of a martyr, especially when placed, as at St Peter's, Rome, under the high altar of a church built in his or her honour.

MESSUAGE A plot of land supporting a dwelling and attendant buildings; often, a house and garden.

MONEYER The official who had the right to strike coins; apparently the moneyer usually employed craftsmen rather than struck coins himself in this period.

MURDRUM A fine originating in post-Conquest times: it was payable by a community unable to produce the slayer of a murdered Norman found in their midst.

PORTREEVE Literally 'town-reeve', the official responsible to the king for the action of the town or city whose government he headed: see pp. 193–7.

PRISAGE A tax upon imported wine.

PURPRESTURE An obstruction in the king's highway: i.e. building, stalls, etc, on the street or projecting into it.

RAPE The rapes of Sussex were the subdivisions of the shire, roughly equivalent to hundreds elsewhere.

SHRIEVALTY   The office of sheriff: see Chap. 8.

SOKE   A private jurisdiction, involving exemption from some customary legal and financial obligations; sometimes the word was used for the area covered by such a jurisdiction. See pp. 156–7.

STALLER   An Anglo-Saxon royal official with various functions, primarily military. See p. 193.

STYCAS   The old English word in the Lindisfarne Gospels for the widow's mite; it has been applied to a type of copper coin of the eighth–ninth centuries. Those found in London are all spurious.

TALLAGE   A due or tax imposed upon the king's estates and upon the towns, etc.

THEGN   In origin a man engaged in military or other forms of personal service to an overlord; in the end, the word was used for any Anglo-Saxon noble or man of any standing in the military, landholding strata of society.

VILL   Approximately, a village; but the word was originally often used of a village centre or nucleus, and came to mean the equivalent of the modern civil parish, the smallest area of secular jurisdiction, the whole extent of a village and its land.

WITAN   The council of prominent ecclesiastics and nobles which in Anglo-Saxon times advised the king and enhanced the authority of his actions; literally, the wise men, or moot of the wise – witenagemot.

Part I

The Approach

1

Prologue: The Approach to Medieval London

IT IS widely held that few institutions of the Middle Ages are more remote today than its cities; and it is the purpose of this chapter to establish that the reverse is true. Yet the approach is not easy; and the first step is the most difficult. To this end we invoke the help of the great chronicler of the Victorian city, Charles Dickens:

London. Michaelmas Term lately over, and the Lord Chancellor sitting in Lincoln's Inn Hall. Implacable November weather. As much mud in the streets, as if the waters had but newly retired from the face of the earth, and it would not be wonderful to meet a Megalosaurus, forty feet long or so, waddling like an elephantine lizard up Holborn Hill. Smoke lowering down from chimney-pots, making a soft black drizzle, with flakes of soot in it as big as full-grown snowflakes – gone into mourning, one might imagine, for the death of the sun. Dogs, undistinguishable in mire. Horses, scarcely better; splashed to their very blinkers. Foot passengers, jostling one another's umbrellas, in a general infection of ill-temper, and losing their foot-hold at street corners, where tens of thousands of other foot passengers have been slipping and sliding since the day broke (if this day ever broke), adding new deposits to the crust upon crust of mud, sticking at those points tenaciously to the pavement, and accumulating at compound interest.[1]

And so on to the fog which grips the whole world of *Bleak House* from its centre in the Court of Chancery to every scene and every character in

[1] *Bleak House* (1853), chap. i.

which and in whom the plot of this most brilliantly constructed novel is going to be played out.

The mud and the fog with which *Bleak House* begins can be taken as symbols of the study of towns in an earlier age. If ever we doubt that this or that in London's early history can really be grasped, we may recall the mud of which at least we can be sure: since the Romans first founded the great city, down to the age of Dickens, mud had been a permanent element in its character. The fog reminds us how difficult it used to seem to penetrate to any real understanding of medieval English towns to a generation bred on the constitutional studies which dissolved the medieval borough inexorably, as so much medieval history has been dissolved, into a rainbow of constitutional abstractions.

A generation of historians mainly bred on documents has given way to a generation leavened by interest in the physical remains of the past; and the study of topography has been called in to blow the dust off the borough charters. First and foremost, any attempt to make a medieval city live depends on whether it can live in its stones, its buildings, its street-plan and its names. Historians must proceed, at every level, from the known to the unknown; and the success of this enterprise depends on whether our imagination is steadily at work as we go back through the London of Dickens, past the London of Langland and Chaucer, to the great, yet modest city in which Thomas Becket was born in the early twelfth century, and beyond.

At first sight London is unpromising material for an approach of this kind: a vast sprawling city of the nineteenth and twentieth centuries with no more than enclaves of remoter days. Nor will it reveal its secrets to the casual visitor. We need first to sharpen our vision in cities which deliver their message in more open fashion; and then, if viewed imaginatively, London can become a rich feast for a historian. Every city is a palimpsest, and its history can only be understood if we are prepared to see its present form as part of a long process; and the first lesson – and one of the most valuable – is to acquire some sense of the time since the city began.

One prescription for this is a visit to Italy, where the whole history of European towns can be seen on a single hill-top. The Italian cities indeed are vital if we wish to gain any understanding of the meaning of city life in western Europe. We may visit Perugia and see the enormous foundations of a great Etruscan gate, surmounted by a Roman arch and a Renaissance loggia, spanning a roadway still very much in use. We may visit Assisi and in the small central piazza contemplate the front of a Roman temple, now turned Christian church. We can pass on to Spoleto and see the foundations of a temple in the heart of a city supporting a Romanesque church; or explore the tumbledown remains of the Roman amphi-theatre converted into very medieval-looking tenements; or discover outside the walls one of the rare surviving churches of late imperial times (Plates 1–2).

Spoleto was always a modest place, save in the darkest of the dark ages, when its citadel was the home of a Lombard duke. But no city in the world, save Rome and Cordova, reveals the continuity of its history over the centuries more convincingly. It is worth dwelling for a moment on the contrast between these places, because it enshrines a great area of history. In Cordova one may see a splendid Roman bridge (many times restored) and a city still medieval in its impact on the eye; a city, for example, where a rich man's palace still lies surrounded by the dwellings of the poor, as in a medieval town. But the visitor to Cordova goes first to the quarter which is swept and garnished, through the Calle Maimonides and the Calle Averroes, through the courtyard of the orange-trees to the mosque which pretends to be a cathedral; and in the mosque – one of the most spectacular monuments of medieval Europe – one feels the presence of the caliphate of Cordova, one sees the way in which Christendom was Islam's poor relation in the eighth, ninth and tenth centuries; one can imagine or deduce, according to one's cast of mind, the way in which the riches of Islam and Christendom – the spices of the east and the slaves of the west – combined to make so rich a city in an age when northern Christendom could hardly remember what a city was.[1]

If Cordova is the most improbable of medieval cities in the west, Rome follows it close. What can one say in a sentence about Rome which is not obvious or absurd? Yet many good historians have written words about cities in the Middle Ages which suggest that they have forgotten that Rome existed or was a city. The saints have made Rome the most sacred, the motor-car has made Rome the most dangerous of European towns; and this is a good introduction to its extraordinary ambivalence. The medieval Romans loved and hated their father the Pope – hated him because every good citizen of every medieval city (like every medieval student) was in a state of rebellion, against authority, against tyranny, against freedom or against rebellion itself. They loved him because he was their father, the earthly presence of their own Apostle, and because his

[1] On Cordova, see E. Lévi-Provençal, *Histoire de l'Espagne musulmane*, vol. iii, Paris, 1967, chap. xiii.

court was the centre of the tourist trade on which the economy of Rome has been securely based since the early Middle Ages. Call them pilgrims, call them suitors, call them ambassadors: without the visitors to the Roman curia the hoteliers of Rome would starve; and so while the Romans drove out the Pope again and again when the call to freedom stirred them, hunger and penitence turned them almost at once to fetch him back.[1]

Two days in Cordova can leave an impression of a deep and powerful kind if we are at all attuned to receive the impression of a medieval city; two years in Rome might enable one to scratch the surface and uncover a little of its message. But the history of medieval towns at large is best read in towns of the second rank, in places like Spoleto and Assisi, and slightly larger cities, Verona, best preserved of medieval towns, or Lucca: and if we visit Lucca or Spoleto, let us remember that they were visited by throngs of English pilgrims in the early and mid-Middle Ages, from the young King Alfred down.[2]

Verona reveals the continuity of its history in the grandest way.[3] The Roman theatre is still open to view, with a little tenth-century chapel in a baroque case keeping an eye on it; the amphitheatre, now in the centre of the city, formerly just outside the main *enceinte*, is Verona's historic hall of assembly. A Roman gate in the ancient walls is still in use. The city's medieval greatness is revealed by the wider *enceinte* of walls and castle; and the Adige reminds us that Verona has always been the key to the approaches to the Brenner, one of the great commercial and strategic centres of north Italy. The throng of Romanesque churches points to a golden age, and invites us to understand the piety, the fashion and the ostentation of the eleventh and twelfth centuries, just as the German craftsmanship of the bronze doors of San Zeno (crude though they are) remind us that this was the gateway to Germany, once indeed a part of the German world, the home in legend of Theodoric the Great, Dietrich von Bern, Theodoric of Verona, who also has his place at San Zeno, in stone.[4]

Yet for the English student of medieval cities the smaller hill-towns have a special piquancy. It is rare in Italy to find a new city of the Middle

[1] P. Partner, *The Lands of St Peter*, London, 1972; P. Llewellyn, *Rome in the Dark Ages*, London, 1971; the classic is still F. Gregorovius, *History of the City of Rome in the Middle Ages*, Eng. trans., 2nd edn, 8 vols, London, 1900-2.

[2] W. Levison, *England and the Continent in the Eighth Century*, Oxford, 1946, pp. 36 ff.; see below, pp. 62-3.

[3] See *Verona e il suo Territorio*, esp. vol. ii, 1964.

[4] Ibid (chap. by A. M. Romanini) and L. Puppi, *Chiesa di San Zeno Verona*, Tesori d'Arte Cristiana, Bologna, 1967.

Ages; Venice is an exception which has never quite lived down its parvenu origin; and even Venice began to be more than a pirates' lair in the seventh century; Assisi and Spoleto are characteristic samples of ancient towns on hill-sides and hill-tops. It has never been convenient to live on a hill-top, as the aqueduct at Spoleto forcibly reminds us. But these places have a magic which makes their design intelligible while one is under the spell. The Mediterranean peoples have a tradition of living in towns older and deeper rooted by far than ours; and the Italian town has been a vivid centre of loyalty in every age of recorded history, above all in the heroic age of the city republics. They passed a message of freedom and civic pride to the rest of urban Europe in the twelfth and thirteenth centuries which has never been entirely lost or forgotten; and interests petty and grand mingled in their nature in a way which we cannot disentangle. The basilica of St Francis of Assisi is a monument to a peace-loving saint of wide appeal; but one has only to look at it to see that this great fortress, set square in the face of the city which looks towards Perugia, is also a monument to a traditional local rivalry which Francis himself had striven to quell.

In these Italian cities the stones cry out even if men are silent; a wander in the streets, prepared by a little instruction, gives a sermon in stone better than any course of reading. When we return to England, are we bound to feel a sense of anti-climax?

In our experience, quite the contrary: the comparison has been a stimulus and a challenge. It is extremely rare in this country to find a city on the site of a prehistoric hill-fort; no certain case is known. The physical facts of life are harder in England, the need for defence less, and English peasants do not live on hill-tops. This does not mean that realism has always conquered – this would be entirely contrary to our experience of life and of history; and St Albans, for instance, is a striking example of the triumph of religion over convenience. The Roman city by the river, plentifully supplied by water and protected by its Roman walls, was abandoned for an inconvenient minor summit near by, entirely (so far as one can tell) for the sake of St Alban, whose relics and whose abbey clung to the spot where it was believed that he had been martyred.[1] A glance at four English towns will make plain how deep and far the contrast with Italy goes.

First, Old Sarum, Old Salisbury, one of the most uncomfortable of sites,

[1] W. Levison, 'St Alban and St Albans', *Antiquity*, vol. xv, 1941, pp. 337-59; cf. S. Frere, *Brittania*, London, 1967, p. 332.

and one of the very few towns based on a prehistoric hill-fort.[1] During the Danish invasions of the early eleventh century the moneyers of Wilton sought for a stronger fortress, and in due course the Normans established a great castle and a cathedral within the ancient ramparts on the summit of Old Sarum Hill. Round the entrances small suburbs sprang up and formed the town where the parents of the eminent scholar John of Salisbury lived in the early twelfth century. Canons, soldiers and towns-folk lived in uneasy proximity. Much the same could be said of Durham, where castle and cathedral still dominate the space on the narrow hill made almost into an island by the river twisting round it. But in Durham the dominance of the bishop made for a measure of harmony between castle and cathedral, and Scottish raids made strong defence a necessity; and, as in Cambridge, an easily accessible bridge linked a transpontine to a cispontine city, thus giving elbow-room to citizens who did not care to live under the immediate eye of bishop and monks.[2] Old Sarum offered little in the way of amenity: there was no convenient site for suburban expansion, and in times of drought water must have been nearly as expensive as wine. The story is told that in 1217 the clergy of the cathedral went on their customary rogationtide procession down to St Martin's church in the bottom of the valley, and on their return they found the city gates closed against them by the castellan and his troops. They indignantly turned to the bishop, Richard Poore, for counsel and support, and so the idea was born of building a new Salisbury down by the river, near St Martin's church, where they felt more welcome and more comfortable than on top of the hostile, windswept hill. New Salisbury is a splendid example of a successful new town, one of a hundred founded in this country in the twelfth and thirteenth centuries.[3] The ample close, on the edge of the watermeadows in the bend of the river, has the best of the site for amenity and comfort; but the town is a model of medieval planning, a tight grid of streets gathered round three sides of the main parish church and the market-place; a pattern of streets convenient to a medieval town, though a nightmare to the modern planner, since it offers him a cross-roads every hundred yards or so.

[1] See Beresford and St Joseph, *Medieval England*, pp. 185–7; *VCH Wilts*, vol. vi, pp. 51 ff. (Sir F. Hill, et al.); *Medieval Archaeology*, vols iii, 1959, p. 314; vi, 1962, pp. 138 f.; vii, p. 330: esp. P. A. Rahtz and J. W. G. Musty in *Wiltshire Archaeological . . . Magazine*, vol. lvii, 1958–60, pp. 353–70. See **Plate 4**.

[2] Beresford and St Joseph, pp. 183–5.

[3] *Historic Towns*, vol. i, ed. M. D. Lobel, Oxford, 1969, article by K. H. Rogers, separately paged: maps by W. H. Johns; *VCH Wilts*, vol. vi, pp. 69 ff. (M. K. Dale).

Old Sarum was a prehistoric hill-fort refurbished; Portchester is the commoner case of Roman walls providing a frame within which town life could be revived.[1] It was one of the towns founded by Alfred and his son – in this case an Edwardian *burh* (see p. xix) of 904 or soon after. Within it a cluster of houses gradually grew up, with a market at hand and walls to keep Vikings and smugglers at bay. The Normans characteristically built a large castle to keep the town under control and expanded the main church into a monastery. Yet the walls and the market were not sufficient by themselves to keep Portchester alive. Newmarket in Suffolk and Newport in Hertfordshire are witnesses that a new market, a new port, of the twelfth century or so can oust and suppress an old; and Portchester was finally killed when Richard I planted Portsmouth near by, to the damage (no doubt) of Portchester's citizens, but to our great benefit, since we may there inspect a Roman fort, a tenth-century *burh* and a twelfth-century town untrammelled by later housing schemes.

In Wallingford one sees a good example of one of Alfred's *burhs* still occupied, yet still revealing much of its early history.[2] Within the ramparts of earth surmounted by wood, later by stone, of which large traces still survive, one may still find the pattern of a ninth–tenth-century town. The relation of river-crossing, church, market and grid of streets makes it an Anglo-Saxon trial run, as it were, for the grander new Salisbury of the thirteenth century. Defence, administration, trade, industry and agriculture were all mingled in Wallingford's birth and early fortunes. The later stage of medieval town-building is represented by Alnmouth in Northumberland, built in the twelfth century by the Lord of Alnwick to provide a harbour and a market where goods coming to supply Alnwick and its garrison might meet the products of his broad estate.

In Alnmouth and Wallingford the message is most easily read from the air, when one is not distracted by later buildings and modern planning schemes. In the greatest of all the Alfredian *burhs* neither from the air nor on the ground, at first sight, can one readily find the traces of its early physiognomy; yet if one can unravel London's history a greater effort, in

[1] B. Cunliffe in *Antiquaries Journal*, vol. xlix, 1969, pp. 62–74; cf. *Medieval Archaeology*, vols. viii, 1964, p. 87 and n. (N. P. Brooks), xii, 1968, p. 157, xiii, 1969, p. 232, xiv, 1970, p. 157. The settlement pattern is still unclear, and the site of the market unknown.

[2] Beresford and St Joseph, pp. 179–81; N. P. Brooks in *Berks. Archaeological Journal*, vol. lxii, 1965–6, pp. 17–21; cf. M. Biddle and D. Hill in *Antiquaries Journal*, vol. li, 1971, pp. 78 ff. See **Plates** 3, 5 (map by N. P. Brooks in art. cit., p. 18).

ordinary historical terms, yields a greater reward than any city so far mentioned save Cordova and Rome.

The shape and structure of medieval London can be approached from two directions, by working forward and by working back. One may strip off the accretion of the centuries, work backwards until the core is reached. This is a necessary part of the exercise. The row of great railway stations from Paddington to King's Cross is a very good rough indication of where London's northern edge stood in the early nineteenth century; and if an objector should say, but what of Liverpool Street? How comes it that the Eastern Counties' line, of all things, should have found its way right into the city?—then we may answer something as follows. The wealth of the city is the permanent fact to which so much in London bears witness. The new buildings which gather round St Paul's bear witness to London's answer to its two greatest fires; and the presence of Fenchurch Street, Cannon Street, Blackfriars, Holborn Viaduct and Liverpool Street is an extraordinary reminder that the railway-builders needed to bring the city men right to its heart if their lines were to pay. Where Liverpool Street now stands there was a tumble of small houses which had replaced a great hospital, long since departed to a better home; yet though it had gone long before the railway came to the city's edge, it must seem to some that the spirit of Bedlam still rules in Liverpool Street.[1]

In such a fashion one can trace the layers in the palimpsest. No city in the world is blessed with a richer store of sixteenth- and seventeenth-century maps and panoramas. Hogenberg's map of 1572 is of special interest, since in all essentials it represents the London of the 1550s,[2] of the moment, that is, before the first great era of expansion. No doubt London was a considerably richer and more populous city in 1550 than in 1150; but the area it covered is precisely that encircled by the ancient city boundaries and the other places included by William FitzStephen in his famous description written in 1173 or 1174: Southwark, Westminster and the 'populous suburb' between Westminster and the City.[3] Hogenberg's map is still a monument to two key moments in the history of London and the kingdom: to the Roman and the Norman Conquests. The line of the walls can be seen clearly in the map, and throughout its length it was built

[1] See Sheppard, chap. 4.

[2] See Darlington and Howgego, pp. 10–12, 51–2: Hogenberg's map was based on an original of *c.* 1553–9 (**Plate 6**).

[3] See below, chap. 5.

on Roman foundations – one can still see part of the superstructure of the wall, of the third to the seventeenth centuries, above ground in St Alphege's churchyard, and a part of its Roman base in an underground car-park near by.[1] At either end of the wall the Normans built great castles to guard, govern and protect the city; and round the bend in the river William the Conqueror was crowned in Edward the Confessor's abbey church and William Rufus rebuilt the great hall of the Confessor's palace, the basic structure of Westminster Hall as it still is (Plate 8). From that day to this London has had, as it were, two centres, two foci, Westminster and the City, the political headquarters of Britain and the commercial capital of north-western Europe. To anyone who thinks of Britain as an island, it must seem strange and unsuitable that its greatest city and its capital should lie in a corner. Politically, this is a symbol of the two ages when England was part of a great continental empire, in the days of the Romans who first planted and defended the city, and of the Normans and Angevins. Commercially, it is a symbol of the fact that London has always been a cosmopolitan, international city. After the Romans left it ceased for many centuries to be a capital in the political sense. Until medieval government ceased to be peripatetic – that is until the late Middle Ages – there could be no political capital in a modern sense. But long before, at least from the early eighth century, it had become once again (in Bede's famous phrase) the 'mart of many peoples'.[2]

The map of 1572 shows the physiognomy of a medieval town, and so in a measure do the early panoramas. But the panoramas show almost as little of the twelfth century as we can see today, and this for two reasons fundamental to the history of the city. First, it has always been a prosperous place, and so has commanded the resources for constant rebuilding. The resources, and the opportunity too, for throughout its recorded history down to 1666 it was a city with many buildings of wood and mud, much of which could be easily cleared and altered, at least in outward show. London, in William FitzStephen's view, had two faults only: 'the immoderate drinking of fools and the frequency of fires'.[3] It is a city far from any good quarries, as the Caen stone of which some of the abbey and most of the White Tower are built reminds us. For these reasons we cannot hope to see as much of London's history on its face as in Verona or

[1] See below, pp. 161–2; Grimes, p. 91.

[2] Bede, *Historia Ecclesiastica*, bk ii, c. 3 (ed. B. Colgrave and R. A. B. Mynors, OMT, 1969, p. 142); our translation.

[3] *MB*, vol. iii, p. 8 (H. E. Butler's translation, Stenton, p. 30).

Assisi. This makes all the more striking the amount which can be discerned with a more penetrating search.

What can we see of eleventh- and twelfth-century London? Of its palaces, Westminster Hall; of its fortresses, the White Tower; of its religious houses, Westminster Abbey and the church of St Bartholomew the Great, and the restored rotunda of the Temple Church, one time home of the royal treasury; of its parish churches, the crypt of St Mary-le-Bow and a few smaller or larger fragments; and some pieces of the wall. The archaeologists have made discoveries of great interest in recent years, and transformed our knowledge of Roman London; they have taught us much of medieval London too – something of its churches, a little of its streets and houses, of its mints and other trades.[1] But they have also taught us that much of the city has been rebuilt below as well as above its Roman level, and so that much of Roman and medieval London has gone beyond recall.

In some parts only a depth of eight feet separates the modern surface from the Roman, and even quite modest Victorian cellars have replaced every archaeological stratum. The recent survey undertaken for *The Future of London's Past*[2] showed that of the 677 acres of land in the city, 559 had been seriously disturbed, and of these 559 nearly one-third – 167 acres – had lost all the strata of interest to the archaeologist. None the less, it has also shown that what remains is likely to be much more extensive than some had feared, especially on and behind the present waterfront, and has given new hope of major finds – on condition that urgent steps are taken to safeguard what remains. When all is said and done, however, little of the past reveals itself to the casual visitor to the city, and less as each year passes.

Far more survives than sits on the face of modern London. The famous ship excavated at Sutton Hoo in Suffolk can be reconstructed in every detail; yet not a scrap of timber remains. In a similar way, the skeleton of medieval London survives, even though most of the flesh has long since gone to dust. The street-plan of the city – leaving aside great sweeps of the sickle associated with the names of King William IV and Queen Victoria, and modern motorways – is the street-plan of medieval London. A large proportion of the street-names are medieval, and twenty or more have not changed since the twelfth century.[3] Of these a certain number go back well before the Norman Conquest when the city formed two modest

[1] See pp. 90–1.   [2] Pp. 28–9.
[3] See p. 89; Ekwall, *passim*.

settlements round the markets of the east and west, the east and west Cheaps; to the days of Ealdred who rebuilt or lived over Aldersgate; to the princes who lived in the two Atheling Streets (now curiously corrupted to Addle and Watling Streets).

If one walks south across the bridge over the new freeway called London Wall, one comes upon a modern terrace surrounded by a group of buildings of the 1960s. Here one meets the legend Basinghall Street, adorning a modern pavement; yet the name harks back to the Hall or Haga of the men of Basing, probably a pre-Conquest enclosure and town house of the folk of Basingstoke.[1] Thus in imagination one can strip the layers off the palimpsest, from the city of 1970 to the map of 1572, through the London of the livery halls to the London of the early cheaps and hagas, though one needs a fair play of historical imagination, and a fair knowledge of medieval towns where stone was more plentiful and prosperity less constant, to dwell in medieval London.

'There are . . . in London and its suburbs,' wrote William FitzStephen, 'thirteen conventual churches and a hundred and twenty-six lesser, parish churches besides . . .'[2]

If one looks at modern Florence, one can see written in stone and paint and metal the pride of the Florentines in their city, the reflection of civic loyalty and Renaissance patronage. In William FitzStephen one hears the same language, and one can in imagination visualize the city which he loved. Thus the numerous great churches remind us of the glory of Romanesque Pisa or Verona. In them one meets the pride of a community at large, and of a few great patrons – their pride and wealth and piety and fear of death. In the 126 parish churches one sees a more complex pattern, not exactly paralleled outside England; among other things a pattern of smaller patronage and smaller loyalties: the loyalty and piety of the haga and the neighbourhood. Thus six churches dedicated to St Olaf (Olave) remind us of the part that Norse and Danes must have played in the creation of medieval London, particularly in the eleventh century; numerous St Botolphs, St Alban, St Swithun and St Alphege (Ælfheah) that it was one of the most English as well as the most cosmopolitan of cities.

At the centre of our story lies the Norman Conquest. Superficially, the Conquest provides us with a paradox. Of all the major elements in English society, the leading citizens of London seem to have been least affected by

[1] Ekwall, p. 94.   [2] *MB*, vol. iii, pp. 2–3.

the Norman invasion; yet of this comparatively peaceful transition, the supreme document is a great fortress, a document so obvious and so universally known that we take it for granted in a way in which the Londoners of the eleventh and twelfth centuries undoubtedly could not. The White Tower was the Conqueror's great stone monument of power (Plate 7). The capture of London was as crucial to the Norman Conquest as the Battle of Hastings;[1] and after 1066, while the Normans stripped the Old English aristocracy of their lands, London and some other towns remained predominantly English. The Norman castles, and especially the Tower, were built to ensure that the citizens recognized their master. It is a symbol in the broader sense of the relationship of love and hate which always existed between the king and the patriciate of London; in a special sense of the presence of the Norman conquerors in the city. When we try to imagine what all the rough and tumble and destruction and effort the building of the Tower meant to late eleventh-century Englishmen, the analogy which springs to mind is the vision in *Dombey and Son* of the railway builders breaking down to Euston, of the earthquake, confusion, noise and chaos, culminating in the 'mounds of ashes' which 'blocked up rights of way, and wholly changed the law and custom of the neighbourhood', and the crashing irony of the conclusion: 'In short, the yet unfinished and unopened railroad was in progress; and, from the very core of all this dire disorder, trailed smoothly away, upon its mighty course of civilization and improvement.'[2]

[1] See pp. 26–9.
[2] *Dombey and Son* (1848), chap. vi, quoted in Sheppard, p. 133.

2

A Sequence of Events

597–899 FROM MELLITUS TO ALFRED

IN THE year 886 'King Alfred occupied London; and all the English people that were not under subjection to the Danes submitted to him. And he then entrusted the borough to the control of Ealdorman Ethelred.'[1] Thus the 'Anglo-Saxon Chronicle' (version A), written at most within half a dozen years of the event, notes one of the central moments of Alfred's career and an event of exceptional significance in the history of London.

It is indeed one of the very few events in London's history recorded at all in this age, and it has invited much comment and many glosses. It is clear that it is a testimony to the importance of London, and also to the fact that it was not a city in Alfred's kingdom of Wessex. In a world in which towns were few and for the most part of little moment, this is surprising; but no better start could be made to a survey of London's history in these centuries than a brief reflection on why it was a city of prestige already in 886, and why it was not in Wessex.

In 596–7 Pope Gregory the Great had sent Augustine to convert the English people, and then and for some years after regarded London as the metropolis of the southern English.[2] In 601 he sent a second group of missionaries, who included Mellitus and Paulinus, and in the letter which came with them he laid down arrangements for two provinces, one centred in London, the other in York. No doubt Gregory had studied

---

[1] *ASC A(EHD*, vol. i, p. 183). For commentary on the event, see Stenton, *Anglo-Saxon England*, pp. 255–6 and n.

[2] On Gregory the Great's intentions see Bede, *Hist. Eccl.*, bk i, c. 29 (ed. B. Colgrave and R. A. B. Mynors, OMT, 1969, pp. 104–7); R. Hill in *History of York Minster* (forthcoming). Some scholars hold that Gregory had more serious knowledge and intent.

lists of the Roman provinces and knew that these had been the major cities of north and south in former centuries; very possibly he had also seen lists of bishops attending fourth-century councils and knew that London and York had once had bishops. But it is unlikely that his plans were wholly based (so to speak) on guide-books belonging to a former epoch, and we may be tolerably sure that London was a place to be reckoned with in 601. Three years later Mellitus was established there as bishop, and from that time on the cathedral of London has been dedicated to St Paul. But Augustine stayed at Canterbury, and although bishops of London complained in the twelfth century that theirs should be the primatial see, and although the archbishops set up their main head-quarters in the same period at Lambeth, Canterbury Cathedral has remained from Augustine's day to this the spiritual home of his successors.

Mellitus' reign in London was brief, and eventually he was compelled to withdraw to Kent, where he later became Archbishop of Canterbury. His mission had been temporarily successful because of the support of Saeberht, king of the East Saxons, or of Essex, at the time a faithful adherent of Ethelbert of Kent, Augustine's patron and the Bretwalda, or chief king, of the island. But in Ethelbert's later years – he died in 616 – his grip over the lesser kings of south-eastern Britain was relaxed and his place as Bretwalda taken by Raedwald of the East Angles, who was never more than a half-hearted Christian, if so much.[1] When Saeberht died he was succeeded by three heathen sons; hence Mellitus' expulsion. It be-came increasingly clear that the permanent success of the mission to England must depend in a substantial degree on happy relations with its rulers. Late in the seventh century the English Church was reorganized by the immensely energetic, elderly Syrian Greek, Theodore of Tarsus, Archbishop of Canterbury from 668 to 690, and some parts of the diocesan structure which he formed survived until the end of the Middle Ages, some even to the present day. Thus the bishoprics of Worcester and Hereford until the age of Henry VIII, and the latter, on its northern frontier, until the present, corresponded to the territories of the Hwicce and the Magonsaetan, people already being absorbed into Mercia in Theodore's time, and by the mid-eighth century virtually forgotten. The precision and persistence of these lost boundaries is very striking; and it strengthens our confidence that the boundaries of the see of London

---

[1] Bede, bk ii, c. 15, pp. 188–91; the Sutton Hoo burial is now once again coming to be attributed to Raedwald (see the official British Museum *Handbook*, by R. Bruce-Mitford, edn of 1972, p. 64).

represent the kingdom of Essex. The old diocese, down to the formation of the see of Chelmsford, comprised Essex, Middlesex – including London – and the south-eastern third of Hertfordshire.[1] The boundary in Hertfordshire may have been disturbed by the great estate or liberty of St Albans Abbey, founded by King Offa, and always part of Mercia, and so of the diocese of Dorchester, later Lincoln. In early days Surrey, or some part of it, was closely linked and probably under the jurisdiction of the Bishop of London. This apart, we may be sure that the diocese and the kingdom of Essex marched together. In or about 675 Theodore placed St Eorconweald as bishop, and he restored the ancient cathedral and established the see of the East Saxons, alias of London.

The curious consequence of the geography of seventh-century Essex was that London, for the rest of the Anglo-Saxon period, was to lie on a frontier. It remained, in some sense, a great city. To Bede, writing in the 730s, and looking back over the previous century, it was 'a mart of many peoples', a trading centre for English merchants and for ships from overseas.[2] Its place at the heart of the system of communications of north-western Europe, between the North Sea, the Channel and the Thames, had already been won in Roman times, and though no doubt its trade had been reduced and interrupted, and was a shadow of its former self, it remained one of the centres of this world in the seventh and eighth centuries, and a place of a certain prestige and power. Partly it owed this power to survive to its line of walls, which must have been in a measure preserved. That there was any large population living within the walls we have no reason to believe. No doubt it was both the prestige which appealed to Gregory the Great and the practical utility of walls in a barbarous age which sent Eorconweald, like Mellitus, to London. Prestigious, defensible, and still (after a fashion) a centre of trade: thus London survived, and even flourished, in the seventh and eighth centuries. Almost certainly there was a community of a kind within the walls. But it was not until the age of Alfred, so far as we can tell, that the community began once more to grow, and the lineaments of a city to re-emerge.[3]

Throughout the centuries from the seventh to the tenth London lay on a frontier. It had not always been so. Even after the fall of the Roman

---

[1] On the boundaries of Hertfordshire, see J. E. B. Gover, A. Mawer, F. M. Stenton, *Place-Names of Herts.*, Cambridge, 1938, pp. xiii ff., esp. xvii f. There appears to be no recent discussion of the frontiers of the diocese (first fully recorded in the *Valuation of Norwich*, pp. 326–62—1254).

[2] Bede, bk ii, c. 3, p. 142.   [3] See below, pp. 58 ff.

Empire in the west, a great river and a great port remained a centre for the Saxons, not a frontier. Round the Thames, as round the rivers of the Wash and Humber, their early settlements sprang up. They may not have made much of London and its district in the earliest phase of the Saxon conquest; but the name of Surrey, the southern district – or the folk of the southern 'gē' or 'Gau' – presupposes, as has often been observed, a northern district now no longer visible.[1] It looks as if London had been the centre of a larger area, of which Middlesex remained the shrivelled remnant when the kingdoms of the seventh century had gathered round it. Surrey was first lorded over by the South Saxons, the men of Sussex, then submerged into the kingdom of the West Saxons, of Wessex. From then on until the tenth century the Thames was the frontier, first between Wessex and Essex – with the Middle Angle kingdom, later Mercia, approaching close to it on the north and west. By the mid-eighth century the kingdom of Essex had become a cipher under the high kings of the land, Æthelbald and Offa of Mercia, and London and Middlesex passed more and more under the sway of Mercia.[2] Æthelbald treated London as a Mercian city; Offa is traditionally supposed to have built the little church of St Alban in Wood Street as well as founding the great abbey of St Alban in Hertfordshire; and there are reasons for believing him also the founder of the first monastery in Westminster, on the isle of Thorney, where the Tyburn divided as it ran into the Thames. Thus London became, in principle at least, a Mercian city, and so it was to his son-in-law Ethelred that Alfred gave it after he had rescued it from the domination of the Danes.

But we do well to emphasize the words 'in principle'. For London still lay on a frontier, and it was still within the see of Essex, with the cathedral of Essex in its midst. As the reign of Offa (757–96) wore on, his authority in almost every part of England seemed established, and the significance of the Thames as the frontier between Mercia and Essex to the north and Wessex and Kent to the south began to diminish; but only for a time. Offa's first effective successor Cenwulf, just before the turn of the century, wrote to the Pope hinting that London might be made the seat of an archbishop.[3] At that epoch, owing to Offa's schemes, there were three

[1] J. E. B. Gover, A. Mawer, F. M. Stenton, *Place-Names of Surrey*, Cambridge, 1934, pp. xii ff.

[2] See p. 92 and n.

[3] The letter is not unambiguous, but was so interpreted by the Pope (A. W. Haddan and W. Stubbs, *Councils and Ecclesiastical Documents*, vol. iii, Oxford, 1871, pp. 521–5; cf. Stenton, *Anglo-Saxon England*, pp. 224–5).

archbishoprics in England, at Canterbury, York and Lichfield. Cenwulf's idea was to restore Gregory the Great's plan, and amalgamate Lichfield and Canterbury in London. The Pope, however, refused, and soon after Cenwulf was sufficiently master in Kent not to be seriously troubled by the authority of a Kentish archbishop over part of his kingdom; in due course the archbishopric of Lichfield was suppressed. But in 821 Cenwulf died, and his successors were harried, defeated and conquered by Egbert of Wessex. Egbert's supremacy was short-lived, and Mercia had staged a revival before his death. Yet his career had emphasized that the Thames was still a frontier and that London did not yet fit into the pattern of political geography of a stable country.

Egbert died in 839, and already from about 830 his grip on London had been relaxed. For a generation Mercia survived, and London remained under Mercian suzerainty. But from the mid-ninth century on, the old political structure of the country, and the survival of English society and culture, were increasingly threatened by the Viking raids and invasions. In 871 Alfred succeeded to the throne of Wessex, and at that moment a large Danish force was lodged in his territory. With it he had many none too successful engagements, and in the end he had to buy peace. The Danes then moved east with their plunder and Alfred's pay, and settled for the winter in London.[1] For the next few years London seems to have been a Danish base, where they minted coins and which they used as a centre and link between their military forces in Kent and East Anglia. Its walls made it a fortress which could house a large army in winter and be garrisoned by a more slender force in the campaigning season; and it seems likely that London was manned by the Danes from 871 until the conquest by Alfred and Ethelred in the 880s.[2] In 878 the Danes made their famous attack in midwinter into the heart of Wessex, which nearly brought Alfred to his knees. But the outcome was his victory at Edington, the siege of Guthrum's camp and the baptism of the Danish leader. From then on Alfred's position grew stronger; he was never secure, but his authority and prestige increased and the fighting took place further east and north. By 883 the submerged kingdom of Mercia began to revive under the ealdorman Ethelred, who then or later married Alfred's daughter Æthelflæd. Ethelred acknowledged Alfred as his overlord, and

---

[1] *ASC* A, 871–2 (*EHD*, vol. i, pp. 177–8).

[2] *ASC* 883 (p. 181) (all versions except A) refers to a siege of London by Alfred in or before 883, and it seems clear that the events of 886 were the culmination of earlier movements.

in return was given full support in his efforts to restore the old territory of Mercia.

In 883 the 'Anglo-Saxon Chronicle' reveals an English army camped outside London, and it may be that it was in that year that the Danish army was forced back behind the Lea. In 886 Alfred concluded his resettlement of Mercia and his eastward drive by formally establishing Ethelred as lord of the City, after a ceremony in which 'all the English people that were not under subjection to the Danes submitted to him'.[1]

Once again the mysterious authority of London, which had impressed Pope Gregory, Bede and Offa, had asserted itself. But once again London was a frontier city. For then, or soon after, Alfred and Guthrum fixed for a space the frontier between them along the Thames and Lea.[2] London and Middlesex stayed firmly attached to Mercia, and the see of London was presumably confined to its western corner, for although the Danish king was nominally a Christian, the conversion of the Danes had hardly begun, and there is no reason to suppose that there was any effective ecclesiastical organization in their kingdom. In any event, the bishops of the see are but shadowy figures until the appearance of Bishop Theodred in the 920s, who not only restored his see, but carried the work of reconversion deep into Danish territory, and founded the church which was to grow in the next century into the abbey of Bury, around the shrine of the last king of East Anglia, who had been killed by the Danes in 870.[3]

899–1066

Ethelred was probably remembered until the twelfth century by the name of one of the chief wharves on the Thames, 'Ethelred's hithe' – renamed in Henry I's time 'Queenhithe'; but in the tenth century the distinction between Mercia and Wessex soon disappeared. In 918 the lady Æthelflæd, Ethelred's widow, died, and her brother King Edward the Elder united Mercia with Wessex. From then on London ceased to be a Mercian, and became an English city; yet it was also a cosmopolitan centre, and in a town dedicated to sea travel and trade the Vikings were no doubt as

---

[1] *ASC* A, s.a. 886 (*EHD*, vol. i, p. 183).

[2] *EHD*, vol. i, pp. 380–1.

[3] Cf. *HSP*, pp. 13, 364; cf. D. Whitelock in *Saga Book of the Viking Soc. for Northern Research*, vol. xii, 1937–45, pp. 159–76, esp. pp. 171–2: Theodred may have been Bishop of East Anglia for a time before or during his tenure of London. See D. Whitelock's forthcoming Chambers Lecture on the early bishops of London.

much at home as the English. But for a time London was spared from war and siege, and the south-east of England became comparatively peaceful. For several decades London almost disappears from the record of events.

Yet this can only be taken to show how inadequate the 'Anglo-Saxon Chronicle' and its lesser rivals are in telling us the story of London. It has little to offer before a great fire in 982 and a siege, nearly followed by another fire, in 994. But all the indications are that the era from King Alfred to King Edgar saw London converted into a City in the full sense of the term. We shall inspect evidence in a later chapter which suggests that much of the pattern of medieval streets, and some of the earlier parish churches, belonged to this epoch, though the main period of growth may have come later, in the eleventh and twelfth centuries.

Two annals late in the century reveal not only that London had become a well-peopled city but also that its citizens were a community to be reckoned with. Under 982 we read: 'In this year three ships of Vikings arrived in Dorset and ravaged in Portland. That same year London was burnt down.' Whether the fire was due to chance or the Danes, the annal does not make entirely clear; but the implication seems to be that the Danes had a hand in it. No such ambiguity attaches to the second entry, 994: 'In this year Olaf [Tryggvason of Norway] and Swein [king of Denmark] came to London on the Nativity of St Mary [8 September] with 94 ships, and they proceeded to attack the city stoutly and wished also to set it on fire; but there they suffered more harm and injury than they ever thought any citizen would do to them. But the holy Mother of God showed her mercy to the citizens on that day and saved them from their enemies.'[1] So the Vikings departed, ravaging as they went in Essex, Kent, Sussex and Hampshire, until King Ethelred II, the 'Unready', paid them off. The raids of Swein continued sporadically during the next decades; in 1013 he came to stay and conquer. At first he failed to capture London. Part of his army was drowned trying to cross the Thames without waiting to find a bridge; and 'when he came to the borough the citizens would not yield, but resisted with full battle, because King Ethelred was inside and Thorkel with him' – Thorkel the Tall was a Viking chieftain who had changed sides. But later in the year the citizens submitted, and eventually Ethelred fled the country for a time. After Swein's death in 1014 and the accession of his son, Cnut, Ethelred formed an alliance with another Olaf, later king of Norway, the future St Olaf; and from Olaf's saga

[1] *ASC* C (*EHD*, vol. i, p. 214).

comes the most familiar incident in London's history before the Conquest.[1]

If the memory of events recorded in the Norse sagas is correct, London was the centre of Ethelred's operations from the moment of his return in 1014. In the early thirteenth century the great antiquary Snorri, in the final version of the Cnut Saga, described how Olaf and Ethelred came up the Thames to London, but found that the bridge was fortified against them, and had been turned into a great defensive work, and that Southwark too was protected by ditches and 'walls of wood, stones and turf'. Olaf sailed through the bridge, tied ropes round the posts supporting it, and hauled them down; the bridge collapsed, the army defending it fled in confusion, many of them falling into the river. The city was captured and became Ethelred's headquarters once again.

How much of this vivid scene belongs to the age of St Olaf, how much to imagination playing on the old wooden bridge in its last days at the turn of the twelfth and thirteenth centuries, is a nice question. What is certain is that Ethelred returned, and that in the confused campaigns which followed London remained the key to his power; it is equally certain that St Olaf's memory was kept alive in London more than that of any other great figure of his age, by the dedication to him of six churches, one, in Southwark, very close to the bridge he is supposed to have pulled down.[2]

In 1014 Ethelred re-established himself in London, and Cnut left England for a space to recruit his strength in his native Denmark. In 1015 he returned, but it was not until 1016 that the decisive events took place which established him as king of the whole of England. In the winter of 1015–16 King Ethelred was still based on London, and his son Edmund Ironside was gathering an army to attack Cnut, who was ravaging in Warwickshire. 'When the army was assembled,' says the Chronicle, 'nothing would satisfy them except that the king should be there with them and they should have the assistance of the citizens of London.'[3] Evidently there was dissension in the ranks, and the army presently melted away. Soon after, the army was ordered out again, 'and

---

[1] M. Ashdown, *English and Norse Documents*, Cambridge, 1930, pp. 154–73; cf. *EHD*, vol. i, pp. 305–6 (and 132, giving references to the original *Heimskringla*); A. Campbell, *Encomium Emmae*, Camden 3rd Series, 1949, pp. 76–82, for the difficulties in accepting the saga as historical narrative. See also M. Honeybourne in *Studies in London History*, pp. 17–18.

[2] See pp. 141–2, and art. by B. Dickins on the cult of St Olaf there cited; also Honeybourne in *Studies in London History*, pp. 34–5.

[3] *ASC* C, s.a. (*EHD*, vol. i, p. 225).

word was sent to the king in London, begging him to come to join the army with the forces which he could muster. When they all came together, it availed nothing, no more than it had often done before. The king was then informed that those who should support him wished to betray him; he then left the army and returned to London.' Edmund Ironside manoeuvred and skirmished, and Cnut on his side gradually extended his sway. In the spring 'the atheling Edmund went to London to his father. And then after Easter, King Cnut turned with all his ships towards London. Then it happened that King Ethelred died before the ships arrived. He ended his days on St George's day [23 April], and he had held his kingdom with great toil and difficulties as long as his life lasted.' The king was buried in St Paul's Cathedral, and his death was followed by a renewal of the schism in the kingdom. A large number of bishops, abbots, ealdormen and leading men of the kingdom went to Southampton and there acknowledged Cnut as king. They 'elected' him, as the medieval texts so often say, describing a process of formal acceptance with hardly any features of a modern election in it. But 'all the councillors who were in London and the citizens chose Edmund as king, and he stoutly defended his kingdom while his life lasted'.[1]

Thus to both Cnut and Edmund London was an important city. It was the chief port of England, the centre of communications with the Continent, on which Ethelred and Edmund greatly depended, the key to the links with Normandy and Flanders which were to dominate England's overseas relations, political and mercantile, for several centuries to come. This gave it military importance as well as economic: and its walls doubtless much reinforced its strategic strength. Even if the main royal treasury was at this time (and until the late twelfth century) at Winchester, London was the centre of the money-markets of England and north-western Europe; and its importance as the hub of the English currency must have been especially crucial at a time when money was very much needed to pay off the Danes with Danegeld as well as to pay troops to fight them. A complex social and political situation evidently lay behind these references to London's citizens, and this earliest indication of the part they played in the choice or acknowledgement of a king.

In the immediate future the support of London was not to avail Edmund Ironside for long. In October 1016 he and Cnut fought an inconclusive engagement at Ashingdon; owing to the treachery of the ealdorman of Herefordshire, Eadric, who evidently had for some years

[1] *ASC* C, s.a. 1016 (*EHD*, vol. i, p. 226).

fancied himself as the king-maker, Cnut was the victor, but it was not a decisive victory, even though the English losses were great. The two kings met and divided England between them, Edmund taking Wessex, Cnut Mercia and with it, London. His army 'went to the ships' with their booty, and came to London, whose citizens 'bought peace for themselves'; and Cnut and his troops took up winter quarters in and around the city.[1] But on 30 November King Edmund died. In the months which followed Cnut became effective ruler of the whole land; and in the course of 1017 the treacherous ealdorman was murdered in London, presumably at Cnut's command; and what was to prove a splendid and peaceful reign began in fear and bloodshed. Not only blood was shed; for in the following year the largest Danegeld ever raised was gathered to pay off some of Cnut's army and provide him with essential means, £82,500 if the Chronicle is to be believed, of which £10,500 came from London alone.

After its violent opening the reign of Cnut came to be an interlude of peace, order and prosperity; the trappings and traditions of the Old English kingdom were revived, and in this peace and prosperity London doubtless shared. But as the monks who wrote the Chronicle only troubled to record the affairs of the Church and the camp, hardly any events relating to the city are described. Though a great fortress and a still greater port and market, London was not a notable ecclesiastical centre before the reign of Edward the Confessor. This is reflected in an event which took place in 1023. In a ceremony in St Paul's Cathedral, Cnut gave his assent for the removal of the relics of St Ælfheah, or Alphege, the Archbishop of Canterbury, to his own cathedral. There seems to have been no powerful community of clerks or canons at St Paul's to resist such a move, but it must have been a serious loss.[2] In an age when relics were coming to be increasingly valued, the Archbishop of Canterbury no doubt suffered from the fact that most of his predecessors were buried in St Augustine's Abbey, which Augustine himself had founded outside the city wall at Canterbury. Of the great archbishops, Dunstan alone lay in Canterbury Cathedral, until Ælfheah, the martyr – murdered by the Danes, drunk with 'wine from the south' which they had found on ships or wharves in the Thames in 1012 – was brought in a great procession in 1023. And there he continued to perform the miracles first reported at his tomb in St Paul's.

[1] *ASC* C, s.a. 1016 (*EHD*, vol. i, p. 227), also s.a. 1018 (p. 228) for what follows; and on the Danegeld, see p. 94.

[2] *ASC* D, also C and E, less fully; *EHD*, vol. i, pp. 229–30.

In 1035 Cnut died, still a comparatively young man. He left two sons, the elder, Harold Harefoot, by his concubine Ælfgifu of Northampton, the younger by his more official wife, the Norman Emma; for Cnut was a Viking, and so not brought up to monogamy; and the Norman Emma was also in a sense a Viking princess and prepared to accept a half share in her husband's marriage, so long as she enjoyed the trappings and privileges of a queen. Though powerful and ambitious, she did not enjoy them long after Cnut's death. Her son Harthacnut was recognized as king in Denmark, and by some of the English leaders. But the majority followed the lead of 'Earl Leofric and almost all the thegns north of the Thames and the shipmen [*lithsmen*] in London' and chose Harold as regent; later he became king, and Emma went overseas.[1] In 1040 Harold died, and Harthacnut became undisputed king, bringing Emma back from her honourable exile at Bruges. His reign, however, was even shorter than that of his half-brother, for in 1042 he went to the wedding-feast of an eminent thegn, Tofi the Proud, at Lambeth – the lambs' hithe across the Thames first named in the sources on this account – and there collapsed and died as he drank. 'And before he was buried, all the people chose Edward as king, in London.'

Thus Edward the Confessor became king by popular acclamation; but his relations with the citizens of London were not to be altogether happy. In 1051 Godwine, the Earl of Wessex, the king's father-in-law, and far the most powerful man in the kingdom after the king, tried to enforce his will on Edward. But he was summoned with his sons to answer charges against him before the *Witan* in London in September. Godwine set up his camp at Southwark and tried to bargain with the king; but to no avail. In this crisis the other leading earls, Leofric of Mercia and Siward of Northumbria, supported the king, and London and the rest of the *Witan* were loyal. Godwine and all his family were sent into exile, and even Queen Edith was dismissed the court. But Edward was not able to sustain the advantage thus gained, and in 1052 Godwine returned, as powerful as ever. The royal fleet, gathered in the south-east to prevent him, presently dispersed, and reinforcements summoned from the north to London to help the king were slow to arrive. In due course Godwine and Harold, the chief of his sons, sailed up the Thames and headed for Southwark, where Wessex and the earl's possessions impinged on London. As he approached the bridge, he waited for the tide. As the tide rose, the ships came up

---

[1] *ASC* E, s.a. 1036 (*EHD*, vol. i, p. 232); for what follows, ib. s.a. 1042 (p. 235). On Lambeth, see below, p. 364.

through the bridge, along the Southwark bank, supported by a large number of Godwine's troops on the shore. Then the ships turned across the river to encircle the king's small fleet. Meanwhile the citizens of London had been in communication with Godwine, who knew that he had their support, or at least the support of a faction among them; and they proceeded to impress upon the king the need for a peaceful settlement. The king gave way; Godwine was restored, and after his death in 1053 his son Harold became the under-king. How happy the arrangement was from Edward's point of view we have no means of knowing. He lived in peace with his brother-in-law and his wife for the rest of his days, contented, so far as the outward appearances recorded by his first biographer can tell us.[1] But he also took the precaution of abandoning his palace in the city and moving to Westminster, where he could concentrate on the rebuilding of his favourite monastery, whose endowment he substantially increased, and on providing Westminster with its first palace. Thus in his later years one and a half miles separated him from the citizens who had forced him to make peace with Godwine, as well as from the noise and the smells of a rapidly growing town.[2]

1066

At the turn of 1065 and 1066 Edward lay dying. The Bayeux Tapestry portrays the drama of his last days with vivid skill. The great new church of Westminster Abbey, built on the continental pattern and strangely vast to English eyes, is shown in all its majesty. At one end a steeplejack is just finishing it for the dedication ceremony of Christmas 1065, which the Confessor was too ill to attend. At the other end comes the funeral of the king, which followed hard upon. The king's deathbed has been turned round so as to portray the speed of events, and also to enable the designer to tell the story of Harold's succession. The king lies on his deathbed, talking to his faithful followers.[3] If we follow the embroidery to the right, we see that the consequence of this speech is the offer of the crown to Harold and his coronation, not more than a day or two after Edward's death; in the same panel as his deathbed colloquy he lies dead, and we

[1] *Vita Ædwardi*, ed. F. Barlow, NMT, 1962, pp. 40 ff. For the events of 1051–2, see *ASC* s.a.; F. Barlow, *Edward the Confessor*, London, 1970, chaps. 5–6.
[2] See pp. 296–9.
[3] Phaidon Press edn (2nd ed., 1965), plates 32 ff.; cf. Brooke, *Saxon and Norman Kings*, London, 1963, pp. 11, 39. See **Plate 11**.

can follow out to the left the funeral cortege to the abbey. This is one of the very few places in which the story is reversed; and it forces us to view as a whole the sequence of events from the placing of the weathercock on the abbey to the acclamation of Harold, King of the English, by the citizens of London. Before the year was out they were acclaiming another king; and the acclamation given to William the Conqueror on Christmas Day 1066 was a fitting symbol of the completion of the Conquest, for the capture of the City earlier in December had been as crucial an event in the conquest as the Battle of Hastings and the death of Harold itself.

Harold won the throne because virtually all the elements in the *Witan* were united in January in their wish to see a native king and avoid the upheaval (as they saw it) of a foreign usurpation. Edward on his deathbed designated him – or so all those present gave out[1] – the *Witan* confirmed, the church anointed and crowned, the people, led by the citizens of London, acclaimed. Later in the year he faced invasion by Harold of Norway; this was effectively defeated at the Battle of Stamford Bridge near York on 25 September, in which Harold Hardrada was killed; but the death of Harold of England three weeks later at Hastings left England again without a king.

After Hastings, the leading men of the realm gathered in London; and the earliest and best account of the events which led to the Conqueror's coronation, the *Song of the Battle of Hastings* by Guy, Bishop of Amiens, shows the importance of London in this crisis.[2] After a month spent in Dover consolidating his position, gathering reinforcements, taking such surrenders as came his way – including the submission of Winchester – and waiting on events, William began a slow march on London, devastating as he went, so that the *Witan* should be under no illusion as to the nature of their enemy. London, Guy tells us, 'is a great city, overflowing with froward inhabitants and richer in treasure than the rest of the kingdom. Protected on the left side by walls, on the right side by the river, it neither fears enemies nor dreads being taken by storm.'[3] Meanwhile in London the only available prince of the Old English royal line, Edgar the Ætheling, had been elected by the *Witan*. Edgar was greatnephew to Edward the Confessor, and brother of St Margaret, Queen of Scotland. But he was very young at the time, and never showed any of his

---

[1] Cf. ib., pp. 31 ff.; *Carmen*, pp. 55 ff.
[2] *Carmen*, esp. pp. 40–8.
[3] *Carmen*, pp. 40–1.

sister's ability or strength; and so it happened that he was allowed to live out his later life unmolested by the ambitious and ruthless Normans who had brushed him aside.

William established himself in the royal palace at Westminster and prepared to besiege the city. 'He built siege-engines and made moles and the iron horns of battering-rams for the destruction of the city; then he thundered forth menaces and threatened war and vengeance, swearing that, given time, he would destroy the walls, raze the bastions to the ground, and bring down the proud tower [whatever that may have been] in rubble.'[1] The defence of the city was in the hands of Ansgar, or Esgar, the Staller, who was carried in a litter on account of the wounds he had received at Hastings, but had lost none of his mental agility. If Guy is to be trusted, however, he was presently outwitted by William, who by promises and bribes won a peaceful surrender. Guy records a procession of the leaders of the *Witan* and the people of London to Westminster Palace; the 'Anglo-Saxon Chronicle' describes how the Archbishop of York, Ealdred, Edgar the Ætheling, and the Earls of Mercia and Northumbria came to William at Berkhamsted with 'all the best men from London' to submit to him. Whatever precisely may have happened, the surrender of London was the crucial event in the Conquest after Hastings, and opened the way for the anointing and coronation of William in Westminster Abbey on Christmas Day.[2]

As the ceremony began, the Conqueror was presented to the people by the Bishop of Coutances, who called on his French-speaking followers in French, and by the Archbishop of York, who spoke in English, to acclaim him king. The strength of the English acclamation was taken by the Norman troops outside the church for a riot, and they set fire to some buildings round the abbey and killed some of the by-standers in the panic which followed. Within the church the anointing and coronation were presently completed, and William was king both by force and by the Church's blessing.

The city of London was too rich, and its share in his winning of the throne too crucial, for William to cause it much damage. He took steps to see that it should remember he was its master; but he did not destroy any large part of it or expropriate the leading citizens. Soon after his coronation he granted the tiny charter which still remains the earliest surviving royal privilege in the City's Records Office, in form an Old English writ com-

[1] *Carmen*, pp. 42–3.
[2] Cf. *Carmen*, pp. liv ff., 48 ff. and references, for what follows.

posed by a native scribe, with the earliest surviving impression of William I's seal upon it:

> William king greets William the bishop and Geoffrey the portreeve and all the citizens [*burhwaru*] in London, French and English, in friendly fashion; and I inform you that it is my will that your laws and customs be preserved as they were in King Edward's day, that every son be his father's heir after his father's death; and that I will not that any man do wrong to you. God yield you.[1]

The writ addresses both French and English; of the two officials named both were French: the bishop had held sway since the days when Edward the Confessor showed special favour to the Normans, the portreeve was a newcomer. They represented the French element in what was already a very cosmopolitan city. Norse and Danes, Germans and Flemings, Jews and Frenchmen mingled with the native English in the late eleventh century in a city which was the *caput* of the Anglo-Norman empire. But the language of the writ is English, and London remained a predominantly English city.[2] By the time of Domesday (1086) all but a tiny handful of the Anglo-Saxon thegns in the country at large had been replaced by Normans and French; all the bishops save one had been brought over by the Conqueror. But the English element among the leading citizens in the towns, and especially in London, remained substantial, and compelled William and his successors to take note of the needs and interests of their English subjects.

1066–1100

William I, and William II after him, kept *en rapport* with London by frequent visits to the Palace of Westminster. When he was in England, in particular, he commonly spent the Whitsun feast there. Only in a limited sense can London-Westminster be spoken of as a political capital;[3] for the small staff the king needed to compose his writs and guard the relics, jewels and cash he carried with him, his *capella*, or chapel as it was grandly called, went with him from place to place. In the eleventh century only a

---

[1] Bishop and Chaplais, no. 15 and Plate xiv; Robertson, *Laws*, pp. 223, 230–1 (with trans. here used). **Plate 9.**

[2] See pp. 99, 146, 342–3, etc.

[3] In the sense of royal city used by Professor C. Brühl in his studies of civitas and palatium in the early Middle Ages for cities with a royal *palatium* within the walls (see Brühl in Fonseca, pp. 157 ff.).

ruler who was also a bishop and head of a city-state, like the Pope in Rome, or a ruler confined to a narrow domain with only one great city in it, like the French king in Paris, could have a capital. But in the broader sense London had long been a capital, as the greatest commercial centre, the largest town in the kingdom, the city with a special role to play in king-making.

Yet it is hardly surprising that William I felt the need to ring London with a group of fortresses. An invader himself, he reckoned that London needed protection against other invaders; and although in fact it stood no siege in the century following the Conquest, it narrowly escaped it on more than one occasion, and there was a threat of Danish attack several times in the Conqueror's reign. Chiefly, however, the fortresses were needed to control the city itself. In almost every English town of any age the Normans laid out a castle and thus converted the Alfredian *burh*, or enclosure of the tenth or eleventh century, into something more resembling the common pattern of a town on the Continent. From these castles the Norman castellan, often a sheriff, could dominate the town, administer its district or shire, and house a garrison against its enemies. The Normans provided London with three. William's first act after his coronation was to spend a few days at Barking while some fortifications – 'firmamenta quaedam' – were made in the city.[1] Doubtless the site of the White Tower was first fortified at this time, and it may not have been much later that the two castles at the west end of the city wall – Baynard's Castle, then, or soon after, the stronghold of the lord who acted as royal standard-bearer when the militia of the city was called out, and Montfichet Castle, whose origin and site are alike obscure, but was a strong defensive work in the twelfth century. In the Conqueror's middle and later years the White Tower itself was built, a remarkable development from the gaunt stone towers of the continent of his age, even more in contrast to the mounds of earth and wood beside a courtyard – motte and bailey – which proliferated in Normandy and England. The White Tower was a palace, of a kind – though never so comfortable as to tempt any king to live there voluntarily for more than a few days – and a fortress of great strength; it was also a magnificent portrait of the Norman image, strong and dour. It was copied elsewhere, and at Colchester an even larger stone keep was begun for the Conqueror and his sheriff; but it was not until the next century that stone keeps became common. Meanwhile, the contrast between the White Tower, largely built of the light-coloured Norman limestone from

[1] William of Poitiers, *Gesta Guillelmi*, ed. R. Foreville (Paris, 1952), p. 236.

Caen, and the wooden houses of the City, must have been very striking. The Tower endured and much of the rest disappeared during fires which swept the City, especially the disastrous fires of 1077 and of 1087, in which 'the holy church of St Paul, the [cathedral] of London, was burnt down, as well as many other churches and the largest and fairest part of the whole city'.[1] The man who organized the building of the Tower, and was evidently William's trusted assistant in large and complex building operations, was Gundulf, Bishop of Rochester. This saintly monk seems to us a strange choice for such a role. But when we bear in mind that he had been a monk of Bec and Caen with the great monk-administrator Lanfranc, and that when Gundulf became Bishop of Rochester he continued to assist his old master, now Archbishop of Canterbury, it becomes intelligible. For the Abbaye-aux-Hommes at Caen was the Conqueror's chief building work before the Tower, and the quarries at Caen a notable source for stone for building in London and elsewhere in south-eastern and southern England. Gundulf also built the castle and cathedral at Rochester, and endowed his church with the church and manor of Lambeth, where already, while Gundulf lived, Archbishop Anselm stayed when he visited Westminster, and which was to remain a favourite home of the archbishops until they bought it outright at the end of the twelfth century.[2]

The Conqueror and his associates built castles; William Rufus rebuilt the great hall of the Palace of Westminster in stone. His hall still stands covered with fourteenth-century carpentry, and heavily restored. Rufus was a man of the camp and hunting-field; but his constant need of money gave him a special interest in cities where money was to be found, and his hearty dislike of everything clerical made it a particular pleasure for him to protect and aid the Jews of Rouen and London, to whom he gave patronage not without hope of return. Westminster Hall no doubt represents William II's concern for good relations with his surviving English subjects, who had helped him in the great rebellion of his opening years; this was to be an alliance even more necessary to his successor.

1100–1135

The first tolerably full list of London aldèrmen belongs to the year 1127, or thereabouts.[3] It shows us that sixty years after the Norman Conquest,

---

[1] *ASC*, C, s.a. 1077, 1087. For later fires, see pp. 207, 212 n.
[2] See p. 364 and n. 1.   [3] See pp. 163, 166–7.

and in a city that had long been cosmopolitan in its nature, a handsome majority of the city patriciate still had English names or were sprung from English parents. Some of this generation had already received French names in baptism, a sign that some reconciliation between English and Norman was under way.[1] No king had more to fear from rebellion than Henry I; at the battle of Tinchebrai in 1106 he captured his elder brother, Robert Curthose, and seized his duchy; yet Robert lived on, a prisoner, until near the end of the reign. If anyone had seriously considered an English restoration, the ex-king Edgar the Ætheling was alive at least until the mid 1120s. Henry kept his Norman subjects loyal by a mixture of patronage, strength and blackmail.[2] He raised many barons and royal servants, many clerks and bishops, a rung or two, or even more, on the ladder of promotion; and they knew that their prosperity, in some cases even their survival, depended on preserving Henry's patronage. Henry wooed his English subjects by marrying an English queen, Edith-Matilda, daughter of St Margaret of Scotland, niece of Edgar the Ætheling. There can be little doubt that this, the traditional explanation of his choice, is the correct one. Contemporaries spoke of love; recent historians have dreamt of a Scottish alliance.[3] But there are strong reasons to believe that she was chosen to legitimize Henry's line and strengthen his hold on his English subjects. London was offered an English queen, and in return she gave the City the latest model in pastoral care and a hospital, Holy Trinity Aldgate and St Giles in the Fields.

Yet we have little reason to suppose that Henry himself greatly loved the cities of his realm. Orderic Vitalis tells us how Henry as a young man had helped his brother William to suppress a rising in Rouen.[4] The young Henry led the richest of the leading citizen rebels to the top of the tower

---

[1] This is made clear by the example on p. 343 of the family of Ralph son of Algod. But there is a danger in this argument. In the nature of the case the evidence for most folk's origin is philological, and once fashion takes hold this can cease to be valid. It is, however, reasonable to infer that the linguistic character of names soon after the Conquest is a fair guide to their origin, and that the survival of English names in a society whose aristocracy was French-speaking betokens the survival of men of partly or largely English descent.

[2] See Southern.

[3] See p. 316; cf. Eadmer, *Historia Novorum*, ed. M. Rule, Rolls Series, 1884, p. 121; but see also R. W. Southern, *St Anselm and his Biographer*, Cambridge, 1963, p. 188.

[4] Orderic Vitalis, ed. and trans. M. Chibnall, OMT, vol. iv, 1973, pp. 224–7.

of the citadel and showed him the fair city of Rouen – not so different from London – lying at his feet between its walls and its great river, the Seine. Then he personally threw the unfortunate burgher to his death. The details have doubtless lost nothing in the telling, but the story makes it very unlikely that Henry had the reputation of being much attached to aspiring townsfolk. Towards the end of his life his intrigues in Flanders strongly suggest that he had failed to appreciate the strength and importance of some of the most flourishing of northern cities, even when they could have been his allies.[1] Perhaps he learned his lesson from the events in Bruges and Ghent; perhaps, in the years which followed, he showed favour to the citizens of London, reduced the annual tax, or farm, he drew from the city and granted them by charter the right to elect their own sheriffs. That he granted them this right for a time about 1130 is recorded in the one surviving Pipe Roll of his reign.[2] The rest of the story depends on his famous charter to the citizens of London; but we have shown elsewhere that this charter cannot be greatly relied on as a guide to the intentions of King Henry I.[3]

In 1133 Henry left London for the last time. Shortly before, in Whit week, one of the most disastrous fires of the century raged in the City. It is possible that it was on this occasion that the fire started in the house of the sheriff or ex-sheriff Gilbert Becket, and destroyed almost all his property, so that his son, the future archbishop, was brought up in an impoverished household.[4]

1135–1154

In 1135 Henry I died and the citizens showed their gratitude to him by ignoring his daughter, the Empress Matilda, and accepting instead his nephew, Stephen of Blois. Doubtless they had reasons both personal and practical. Matilda was for the most part a stranger to them, although she may well have shown signs of that imperious temper which was later her undoing. Stephen, on the other hand, could be counted a local landowner. He was married to Matilda, heiress of Boulogne, and by virtue of his wife's inheritance held extensive property in Essex associated with a soke and a court in London.[5] Even more important, he controlled the ships of

[1] See p. 100.   [2] *PR 31 Henry I*, p. 148.
[3] See Brooke, Keir and Reynolds.
[4] See p. 212.
[5] R. H. C. Davis, *King Stephen*, pp. 8–10; Page, p. 143.

Boulogne which carried some of the English wool to Flanders.[1] Thus his influence over English mercantile fortunes easily outweighed that exercised by Matilda or her unpopular husband, the count of Anjou.

Whatever their motives, the Londoners acted promptly and decisively at a crucial point in national politics. First they welcomed Stephen within their walls; then they set about his election as king in a council attended by 'the elders and those most shrewd in counsel'.[2] From the account of the *Gesta Stephani* it seems that some hard bargaining took place. The path to Westminster was laid open before Stephen and preparations began for a speedy coronation. But in return he had to acknowledge the Londoners' peculiar right, now vigorously asserted, to choose a king. That curious function which we have glimpsed the Londoners, or groups of men meeting in London, exercising from time to time in Anglo-Saxon England thus emerged in December 1135 as an established privilege.[3]

But almost certainly the negotiations which took place at this time involved even more weighty issues. On another occasion the Londoners complained of the severe laws of Henry I,[4] and no doubt like other men they hoped for a return to easier times. More specifically they may have planned to increase their own power and authority. In the political language of the twelfth century this might mean establishing a commune.[5] The word is redolent of municipal independence, and notoriously ambiguous. In origin it seems to have meant any kind of sworn oath supporting a fellowship with a common purpose: first, in the eleventh century, gatherings of clergy and laymen under the Church's patronage to maintain peace or check violence; then sworn associations to which civic privileges might be accorded, or to maintain the peace within a town. In this sense, many towns of northern France and northern Italy in particular – but in other areas too – achieved civic consciousness by forming or receiving a commune in the eleventh and twelfth centuries; in the same epoch many more achieved a similar status without ever using the word or forming quite such a bond. Yet in the eleventh and twelfth centuries the word commune, *communa*, *communia* or *communio*, came to

[1] Davis, *King Stephen*, p. 10, and n. 23.
[2] *Gesta Stephani*, ed. K. R. Potter, NMT, 1955, p. 3.
[3] See M. McKisack, 'London and the succession to the crown during the Middle Ages', in *Studies in Medieval History presented to F. M. Powicke*, ed. R. W. Hunt, W. A. Pantin and R. W. Southern, Oxford, 1948, pp. 76–89.
[4] Florence of Worcester, vol. ii, p. 132.
[5] See below, pp. 45 ff.

have a charisma which might make it sound horrible in the ears of a conservative monk or a king who associated it with civic disorders, but might equally well be unpleasing to a town proletariat, who associated it with the privileges of the rich, and music in the ears of oligarchs and monarchs, who sometimes formed such associations for their mutual profit. All depended on the circumstances in which the commune was formed.

Thus in the late eleventh and twelfth centuries throughout northern France and, more distantly, in northern Italy, ambitious citizens were seizing the opportunities presented by a fractured pattern of lordship to declare the independence of their towns. The revival of trade favoured their cause and self-governing communes made their first impact on the European scene. There was no uniformity in communal institutions as they developed in different areas. But they all expressed a deeply felt desire for liberty and were intended to protect those urban interests which otherwise lacked security. Since the Norman Conquest, which occurred roughly at the same time as the beginnings of this movement, London, by reason of its very pre-eminence, had been subject to strict supervision or 'protection' by the king. It was far too important and wealthy a city to be allowed independence and all three Norman kings were strong enough to dominate urban politics. In 1135, however, the succession problem radically altered the whole situation. Both Stephen and his London supporters took oaths,[1] in itself a step characteristic of the setting up of a commune. The citizens swore to help their king with all the resources at their command. Stephen's promise, as it has come down to us, was vaguer; he undertook to establish peace in the land 'for the benefit of them all'. The reference is oblique and unhelpful. But in view of the striking way in which the Londoners fulfilled their side of the bargain and the full, if brief, emergence of the commune later in the reign, it seems probable that vital concessions to civic ambitions were made in 1135.

That royal protection still meant a great deal to the citizens is vividly illustrated by a lawsuit heard at Westminster a year or so later.[2] Queen Matilda's foundation of Holy Trinity Priory ran into trouble when it tried to secure the large soke outside Aldgate which was among its most important early endowments.[3] No less a person than the Constable of

[1] *Gesta Stephani*, p. 4.

[2] *Regesta*, vol. iii, no. 506; *Cart. Aldgate* nos 960, 963.

[3] For the early history of the Aldgate soke see *Cart. Aldgate*, nos 871–5, Round, *CL*, pp. 99 ff.; and below, pp. 320 ff.

the Tower of London disputed the priory's claim, simply by seizing a great part of the soke for himself. Henry I failed to remedy matters, but his successor appears, somewhat surprisingly in view of his general reputation, to have been more conscientious. Approached on the prior's behalf by his own wife and some eminent citizens, he arranged to hear the dispute himself. Holy Trinity produced a large number of witnesses who swore that the priory owed their claim legitimately to the English Cnihtengild, whose right could be traced back to King Edward's time; the opposite case rested solely upon the bare fact of possession. Stephen then upheld the superiority of tradition over force by pronouncing in favour of the priory. Those who gathered to hear him included a canon of St Paul's, Andrew Buccuinte (Justice of London), a group of aldermen and other prominent city figures.

During the civil wars which followed upon the Empress Matilda's landing in England, London redeemed its promise to help Stephen with its own material resources. But at the Battle of Lincoln in 1141 the king fell into his enemies' hands, leaving his allies in the country temporarily without a leader. The attitude taken by London was all-important in this crisis, for it determined whether Matilda fought her campaigns as former Empress and queen of Germany or as an anointed queen of England. At a church council in Winchester Henry of Blois, Stephen's own brother and one of the most powerful ecclesiastics of the land, urged that the king's misdeeds justified his replacement as ruler.[1] He received a sympathetic hearing, but further business waited until a delegation from London should arrive to add or deny their sanction to the council's proceedings. When at last the Londoners came, they appeared vested with the full authority and dignity of their commune.[2] Their aim was simple; rather than entering into heated debate they intended to plead as strongly as possible for Stephen's release from imprisonment. They were joined in this by a group of barons faithful to the king who had been received within the London commune.

Henry of Blois replied to this challenge with a long and eloquent speech. He flattered the civic dignitaries, acknowledging that they were mighty leaders; and he sought to divide the opposition by arguing that it was unworthy of them to harbour traitors to the king and the Church,

---

[1] William of Malmesbury, *Historia Novella*, ed. K. R. Potter, NMT, 1955, pp. 52-4; for this and what follows see also Davis, *King Stephen*, pp. 57-8, and Page, pp. 87-92.

[2] 'Feria quarta uenerunt Londonienses, et, in concilium introducti, causam suam eatenus egerunt ut dicerent, missos se a communione quam uocant Londoniarum . . .'

men who only made common cause with them in order to tap their wealth. His argument seems to have carried some weight with the Londoners. Before they left they agreed to report Henry's case to their fellow citizens in as favourable a light as possible.[1]

Whatever the course of the negotiations which followed, the Empress' approach to the City in the company of a great army precipitated a decision in her favour. A group of citizens came out to greet her at St Albans and to discuss terms for handing over the City; she was then escorted to Westminster.[2] While preparations were being made for her coronation, Matilda took a step which vividly illustrates her attitude to her new allies. The eminent baron, Geoffrey de Mandeville, had recently been made Earl of Essex by Stephen in recognition of his power and influence in the south east.[3] He appears to have had no respect either for the traditional forms of authority or for the civic ambitions developing within London. In addition, his own father-in-law, Aubrey de Vere, had perished during recent, but obscure, disturbances within the City.[4] Not surprisingly, therefore, he and the citizens were known to be at loggerheads. Yet to Geoffrey Matilda now granted a charter confirming and extending his rights and lands as Earl of Essex and granting, among his new possessions, the Tower of London, which he was freely allowed to fortify.[5] Clearly the Empress was intent on fulfilling two objectives: she had to win the support of a powerful aristocrat, even at the cost of making him more powerful; and she had to dominate those independent citizens who had proved hostile to her in the past. A strong Geoffrey de Mandeville brooding over the City from his embattled refuge in the Tower seemed her best security.

For the citizens worse was to come. Knowing how much they had contributed to her enemies, the Empress peremptorily demanded money from the richest of them.[6] A personal confrontation proved disastrous. When asked to lessen her demands, Matilda flew into a temper which left her audience both discomforted and disillusioned. In the circumstances they could not hope to gain what lay apparently close to their hearts: a restoration of their ancient laws.[7]

[1] *Historia Novella*, p. 55.
[2] Florence of Worcester, vol. ii, p. 131; and for what follows, Round, *GM, passim*, corrected by R. H. C. Davis in *EHR*, vol. lxxix, 1964, pp. 299–307.
[3] *Regesta*, vol. iii, no. 273; on Geoffrey see Round, *GM*, and below, pp. 217–18.
[4] *Complete Peerage*, rev. edn, vol. x, p. 198.
[5] *Regesta*, vol. iii, no. 274.
[6] *Gesta Stephani*, p. 80.
[7] Florence of Worcester, vol. ii, p. 132.

Tension mounted after this rebuff when Stephen's queen appeared with an army to ravage the area about the City. Then, in a spontaneous movement of resistance so like the flashpoint which marked the beginnings of many continental communes, the citizens seized weapons and poured on to the streets 'like thronging swarms from beehives'.[1] Bells set ringing all over the City added to the tumult. The Empress had misjudged the situation and was taken by surprise. 'She, with too much boldness and confidence, was just bent on reclining at a well-cooked feast, but on hearing the frightful noise from the City and getting secret warning from someone about the betrayal on foot against her she with all her retinue immediately sought safety in flight. They mounted swift horses and their flight had hardly taken them farther than the suburbs when, behold, a mob of citizens, great beyond expression or calculation, entered their abandoned lodgings and found and plundered everywhere all that had been left behind in the speed of their unpremeditated departure.'

But the Empress was not a woman to give up the struggle lightly and from a safer refuge at Oxford she continued to display her authority over the capital. To fill the see of London, vacant since 1134, she had drawn a chancery clerk of her father's, Robert de Sigillo, out of his monastic retirement at Reading.[2] Even more important, she reinforced Geoffrey de Mandeville's position with a long string of privileges. As Sheriff and hereditary Justice of London and Middlesex, Essex and Hertfordshire, his control over the home counties was now unrivalled. Underlining this point, the Empress explicitly gave up any right to intervene in relations between the earl and the burgesses of London.[3] It was the most effective blow against civic pretensions which could have been devised.

Nevertheless a turning point in the civil wars had been reached. By refusing to tolerate her arrogant demands, the Londoners defeated the Empress' hope of a coronation at Westminster which would have set the seal on her claims to the throne. The citizens returned enthusiastically to their former allegiance. They opened their gates to Stephen's queen and contributed to the royalist force which took Robert, Earl of Gloucester, the Empress's half-brother and the architect of her fortunes, captive at the siege of Winchester.[4] Thus they helped to make possible Stephen's

[1] For this and what follows, *Gesta Stephani*, p. 82.

[2] Le Neve, p. 2; *Regesta*, vol. iii, pp. x–xi; cf. H. W. C. Davis in *Essays . . . presented to R. L. Poole*, p. 185; Round, *GM*, pp. 117–18.

[3] *Regesta*, vol. iii, no. 275; see pp. 217–18.

[4] *Gesta Stephani*, pp. 83, 85–6, 89–90.

release from custody which took place on 1 November 1141. It was with justice that about this time the Archbishop of Rouen sent his thanks to the noble senators, honoured citizens and whole commune of London for the help and loyalty they had rendered the king.[1]

For the rest of the reign London continued firm in its support of Stephen's cause. At least one of its great citizens, Gervase of Cornhill, lent money to the queen, and probably more did so.[2] Nevertheless they encountered one notable setback. Stephen sought the help of Geoffrey de Mandeville as eagerly as his rival had done. To win that adroit politician to his side he had to do little more than make effective Matilda's grant, but it is hard to see how he could reconcile urban interests which had deserved so well of him with the far-reaching authority generously accorded to such a prominent feudal magnate. As Sheriff of London and Middlesex Geoffrey had to account to the royal exchequer for the modest sum of £300.[3] But when the king himself had difficulty in controlling his depredations the citizens must have been even harder pressed. Holy Trinity Priory certainly suffered. It again lost part of its hardly won land in the Portsoken when a rare flight of fancy led the Constable of the Tower to experiment with growing vines in east Smithfield.[4] However, by 1143 Geoffrey's independence provoked even the tolerant Stephen to action and the earl was driven from his castles. After a brief reign of terror in East Anglia he met a violent death.

Arrangements for London's government after Geoffrey's departure are obscure; but probably as a community accorded a large degree of independence because of its wealth and importance, the City gave Stephen military as well as financial help. Apart from the thousand men it sent to the siege of Winchester, it swelled the royalist forces with which the king took Faringdon in 1145.[5] The tradition of a powerful civic militia, a prominent feature of communes abroad, was recorded a generation later by FitzStephen who proudly assessed its army at this time at 20,000 cavalry and 60,000 footsoldiers.[6]

[1] Round, *GM*, p. 116.

[2] Round, *GM*, pp. 120, 305.

[3] *Regesta*, vol. iii, no. 276.

[4] *Cart. Aldgate*, no. 961.

[5] Henry of Huntingdon, ed. T. Arnold, Rolls Series, 1879, p. 278.

[6] *MB*, vol. iii, p. 4. Needless to say, the figures are not to be taken literally; but even one tenth of such a number would make a formidable contingent.

1154–1189

Stephen's death in 1154 opened a new and apparently quieter era in London's history. Henry II, the Empress's son, came peacefully to the throne in accordance with an agreement made during the previous year, so that the citizens did no more than witness the coronation service, performed at Westminster by Archbishop Theobald. Very early in his reign the new king granted London an important charter.[1] Many of its clauses upheld the City's judicial privileges. Thus, apart from royal officials and moneyers and excepting cases involving property outside, no citizen was obliged to attend courts held beyond the walls; he was exempt from the oppressive *murdrum* fine and was allowed to follow ancient city custom in cases concerned with crown pleas; the Court of Husting was to meet once a week and technical mistakes in pleading were not to provoke penalties in this or any other city court; no citizen was to be fined in excess of the sum allowed in Henry I's time. Other clauses stress financial security as well as judicial privilege. Citizens were not to have men billeted upon them; they were to be free from tolls throughout England and if this regulation was contravened the Sheriff of London was empowered to take reprisals on their behalf; they were placed in full possession of their lands, properties, gages and debts, and all cases arising from these were to be tried in London according to city custom; they were to be free from a number of specified royal exactions. Finally the king confirmed their hunting rights and 'all their liberties and free customs which they had in the time of Henry my grandfather' (**Plate 10**).

Henry made concessions, both in practical detail and in the general security which such a charter gave to the Londoners. But there were limits to his generosity. Some of the laws which prevailed in Henry I's time are described; but many are obscure to us or known only by inference. What appeared to the king as ancient and laudable custom may have seemed both outdated and reactionary to contemporaries. This was certainly true in the case of the Church, where Henry's attempt to put the clock back involved him in one of the bitterest disputes of his reign. The Londoners themselves had earlier deemed Henry I's laws 'oppressive',[2] so there is no need to suppose that the retrospective elements of the charter met with their wholehearted approval. More startling, however, is its

---

[1] *Liber Cust.* pt i, pp. 31–2; cf. Brooke, Keir and Reynolds, pp. 577–8.
[2] Florence of Worcester, vol. ii, p. 132.

silence on the vital issue of the City's government. No subject could have been closer to the citizens' hearts; they had recently experienced both independence and oppression and must have seen the future of their commune in the balance. Their charter in fact marked a compromise. Henry II accepted his predecessors' role as defender of England's largest town. But he refused to allow any independent faction to seize control or, generally, to authorize those institutions which characterized the more independent communes abroad. By avoiding the subject of urban politics in his formal grant, he thus re-established the situation which existed at least in the middle part of his grandfather's reign and possibly also at the end of Stephen's reign.

The years which followed upon the charter saw a working out of this compromise. We know the names of almost all London sheriffs from 1154 onwards and, while it is difficult to get behind the formal list to some sense of the subtleties of the balance of power which it reflects, they are recognizably City folk.[1] We are firmly in the world of the Buccuintes, the Cornhills, the Haverhills, great urban dynasties which, although they have left few traces of their mercantile interests, are still to be found in the property records of the city. Other names more obscure, Ralph the goldsmith, Josce the vintner, suggest a link with the City's crafts and trade.

Every year the sheriffs came before the Exchequer Court at Westminster charged with a debt of some £500.[2] Sometimes they cleared themselves completely, listing the expenses they had met on the king's behalf and proffering the balance in cash. But often they failed to answer for the total sum. In this case the royal clerks entered what was due in every subsequent record until the debt was paid off. There is no doubt that the farm was a large one. In comparison, Lincoln was rendering £180, Winchester, the ancient West Saxon capital, about £150, and the developing port of Southampton between £200 and £300.[3] Moreover, apart from the farm, London sheriffs, as elsewhere, had frequently to account for so-called 'gifts'. In 1159, for example, the king demanded £1,043, in 1161 and 1173, 1,000 marks.[4]

The bare record of annual payments tells us something of London's all-

[1] See below, pp. 218 ff.
[2] On the London farm see Tait, pp. 156–9, 163–9, 180–2; for the farm in Henry II's reign, Reynolds, 'Rulers of London', pp. 343–4.
[3] Tait, pp. 162, 171, 170, 184. The figures have been adjusted to allow for reckoning by tale.
[4] *PR 5 Henry II*, p. 2; *PR 7 Henry II*, p. 18; *PR 19 Henry II*, p. 186 (£666 13s. 4d.).

important relations with the crown. But we may learn more of the feelings current in the city from its reaction to the major political crisis of the reign. In 1173 Henry's eldest son, also King Henry, since his coronation at his father's command in 1170, rose in rebellion against his father. For a time the situation looked extremely serious; for while the king dealt with the threat to his continental lands, William of Scotland crossed the northern border into England and the Earl of Leicester stirred up trouble in East Anglia. From his base in Flanders the young king sounded out the opinions of the Londoners,[1] sending them letters and messengers promising all kinds of rewards in return for their help. Feeling ran high within the City. Gilbert Montfichet, in alliance with the powerful Clare family, was reported to be garrisoning Montfichet castle, near St Paul's, for the rebels; meanwhile the townsfolk were busy arming themselves.[2] The king also sent to find out where their sympathies lay. Learning that the majority were steadfastly loyal to him, he swiftly crossed the Channel and, pausing neither for food nor sleep, made for London. Even before he reached its walls he was met by an impressive host of richly dressed citizens who had ridden out to welcome him.[3] Assuring him of their support, they accompanied him as far as his palace at Westminster. To celebrate his arrival they showered him with gifts, and when news came that night that the Scottish king had been captured they set the City bells ringing in token of their joy. Doubtless sound political thinking led them to reject the rebels' cause, but the enthusiasm with which they welcomed Henry sounds another note. At its most superficial level it contrasts vividly with the truculence they had shown his mother some thirty years before.

'A good city indeed – if it should have a good lord' was FitzStephen's summing up of the situation, made as far as we can tell very close to this particular crisis.[4] As political comment it is scarcely original; in view of the writer's clerical background its emphasis on authority is perhaps entirely predictable. But taken together with the pride, amounting at times to complacence, which informs his description of London in Henry II's reign, it may prompt us to look for signs of developing prosperity within the City during this period of good lordship.

After 1154 the king of England was also ruler of lands across the

[1] Chron. Jordan Fantosme in *Chrons. Stephen etc.*, ed. R. Howlett, Rolls Series, vol. iii, 1886, pp. 280–3.
[2] Fantosme, pp. 338–9.
[3] Fantosme, pp. 362–5.
[4] *MB*, vol. iii, p. 4.

Spoleto (Italy), showing on the right the medieval aqueduct on Roman foundations, in the centre the 'Rocca' or castle, on the left the walls of the medieval town (*see p. 5*)

2. Perugia, Etruscan gate, with Roman arch and Renaissance loggia above (*see p. 4*)

3. Wallingford from the air, showing the rectangle formed, on the left, by earth ramparts of the ninth–tenth centuries, whose line is clearly visible and which remain in the north-west corner, and on the right the river: see the map opposite (*see also p. 9*)

4. Old Sarum from the air, looking north-east, showing the prehistoric ramparts, improved in t eleventh century, with the Norman cathedral to the left and the Norman castle in the centre (*pp. 7–8*)

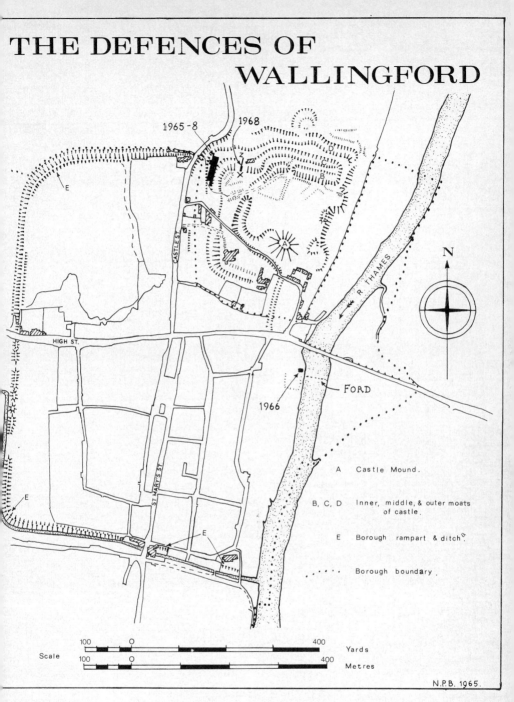

THE DEFENCES OF
WALLINGFORD

1965–8   1968

E

CASTLE ST.

N

R. THAMES

HIGH ST.

FORD

1966

ST. MARY'S ST.

E

E

A   Castle Mound.

B, C, D   Inner, middle, & outer moats
of castle.

E   Borough rampart & ditch.

· · · ·   Borough boundary.

Scale

| 100 | O | | 400 | Yards |
| 100 | O | | 400 | Metres |

N.P.B. 1965.

Plan of Wallingford, by N. P. Brooks; the dates mark the site of recent excavations (*see p. 9 n. 2*)

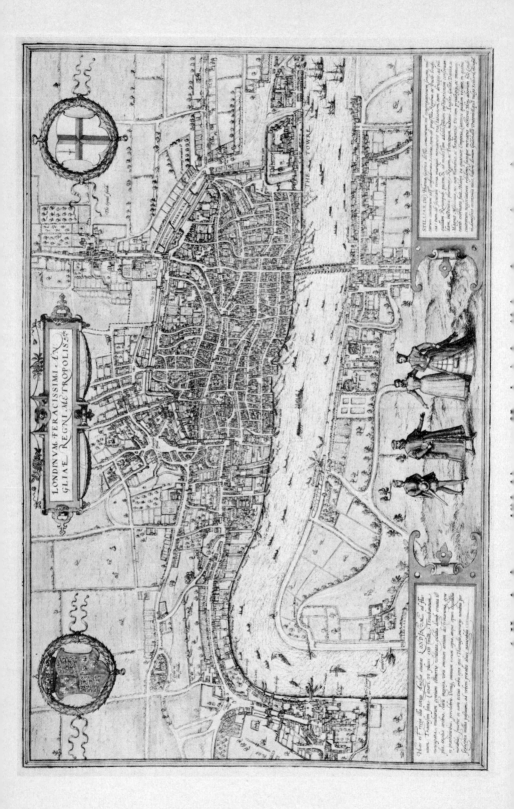

8. The interior of Westminster Hall: the walls are of *c.* 1090–1100, the roof a masterpiece of late-fourteenth-century carpentry (*see p. 11*)

7. The White Tower, chapel

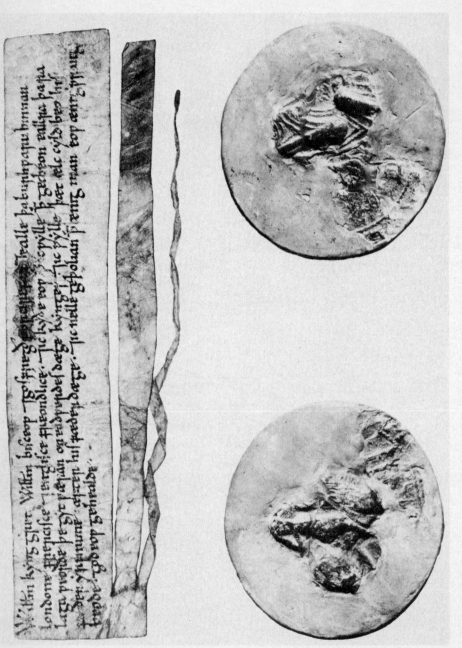

9. William I's writ confirming the rights of the City; the seal (shown both in obverse and reverse) was originally attached to the broad thong. 'William king greets William bishop and Gosfregth the portreeve and all the citizens in London French and English in friendly fashion . . .' (see pp. 78–9)

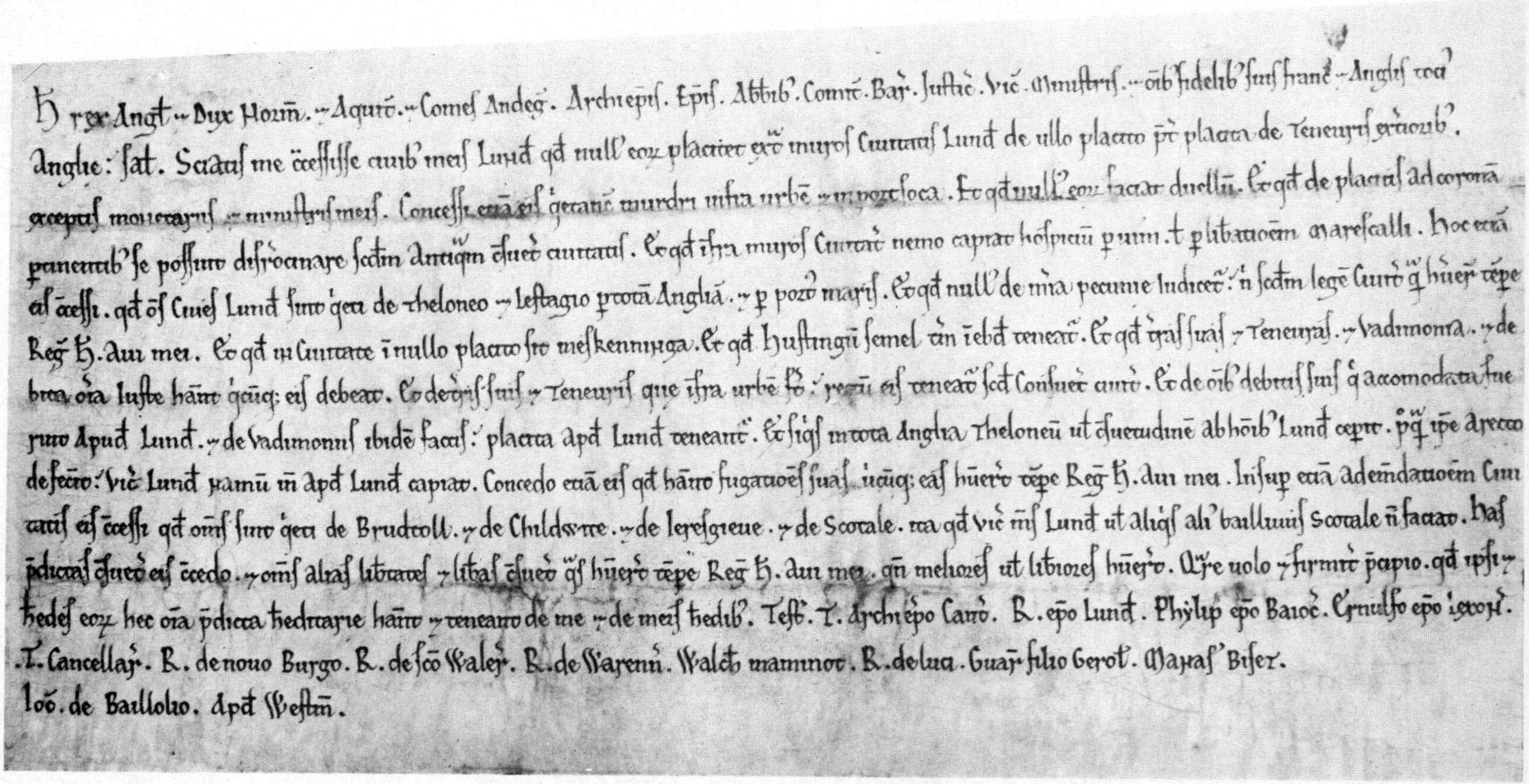

10. The charter of Henry II, 1155–8, probably 1158 (*see p. 40*)

HIC PORTATUR:CORPVS:EADWARDI:REGIS:AD:ECCLESIAM:S[...] PETRI[...] APL[...]

11. The burial of Edward the Confessor in the recently completed Westminster Abbey, from the Bayeux Tapestry. Note the steeple-jack on the left adding the weathercock to the church. Although stylized, the representation probably bears some relation to the large Romanesque church (*see*

Channel sufficiently vast to be termed an empire. Compelled to spend most of his time policing these lands, Henry needed a firm base within England. Thus London tended to become increasingly important as an administrative centre during his reign. Many councils, both secular and ecclesiastical, assembled there. In 1170, for example, following investigations into the activities of his sheriffs, Henry summoned bishops, abbots, earls, barons, sheriffs, reeves and aldermen to the City. They came 'each man fearing as his conscience prompted him'.[1] However, the most important item on the agenda proved to be the knighting and coronation at Westminster of the king's eldest son. Although a convenient meeting place, London was not without its perils for those unused to city life. The author of the *Gesta Henrici Secundi*, the Yorkshireman Roger of Howden, recounts that the sons of influential citizens used to congregate in large gangs at night, making the streets unsafe for the law-abiding and threatening the property of the wealthy.[2] An ugly incident in 1177 led the authorities to hang one of the City's most prominent citizens. Three years later during another council Lord Ferrers, a brother of the Earl of Derby, was murdered on the streets of London.

Nevertheless London continued to act as host to ever-increasing numbers. Besides attending royal assemblies, many came to be within range of the king's court at Westminster and in particular to seek justice before those royal judges who were beginning to make Westminster the permanent centre of their activities. By the middle of Henry's reign it was fast becoming – perhaps had long been – vital for both ecclesiastical and secular lords to maintain households close to these centres of power and influence. As FitzStephen recorded, many built residences in London and thus became, in some sense of the term, 'citizens' of London.[3]

While visitors came thronging to the council chamber and the court, by the river the wharves were no less busy. Henry confirmed the commercial privileges enjoyed in London by the men of Rouen,[4] and there can be no doubt that trade prospered after England and Normandy were once again ruled by the same man. Henry's marriage to Eleanor of Aquitaine also brought new trade in the form of ships laden with the wines of central and

[1] Gervase of Canterbury, ed. W. Stubbs, Rolls Series, 1879, vol. i, p. 219.

[2] For this and for the examples below see *Gesta Henrici II*, ed. W. Stubbs, Rolls Series, vol. i, 1867, pp. 155–6. On Howden's authorship see D. M. Stenton, in *EHR*, vol. lxviii, 1953, pp. 574–82.

[3] *MB*, vol. iii, p. 8: 'quasi cives et municipes sunt urbis Londoniae'.

[4] *Regesta*, vol. iii, no. 729.

southern France. It was by the river that one of the biggest building enterprises of our period took place. The ancient wooden bridge which linked London with Southwark had suffered badly from the river's tidal movement and, more important, from the fires which regularly devastated areas of the city.[1] In the 1170s Peter, priest of St Mary Colechurch, organized a scheme to replace the wooden bridge with a stone structure. The prospect might well have daunted him. The Thames was then considerably wider, if shallower, than it is now, and to the basic problems of engineering were added those of transporting the stone from distant quarries to the site. Moreover, as far as we know the government of the City had no sums of money available to subsidize such a venture. For a time a number of charitable fraternities may have supported the building programme; five Bridge guilds occur in 1179–80 when they owed the king fines totalling 42 marks.[2] Later, in the thirteenth century, responsibility for the fabric of the bridge lay with a trust which received rents from property given by numerous benefactors. It had its headquarters in Bridge House, at the Southwark end of the bridge, and was administered by two wardens, usually chosen from the City's most prominent citizens.

Progress in building was understandably slow. By 1205, when Peter of Colechurch died, the work was still unfinished; but the chapel on the middle of the bridge had been built and dedicated to the greatest of Peter's twelfth-century parishioners, St Thomas Becket.[3] Here, appropriately, Peter was buried. Four years later the bridge, comprising in all nineteen stone arches, stood complete, a worthy memorial to the man who had directed its construction and to the prosperity of early medieval London. It did not survive intact for long.[4] In the later Middle Ages men loved to build shops and dwellings, as well as chapels, on their bridges, and these remained a considerable fire risk. But, patched and repaired many times, Peter's structure was to last into the nineteenth century.

[1] On London Bridge see Gordon Home, *Old London Bridge*, London, 1931; M. B. Honeybourne, 'The Pre-Norman Bridge of London', in *Studies in London History*, pp. 15–39; below, p. 109.

[2] *PR 26 Henry II*, pp. 153–4; *GFL*, no. 418 is an indulgence by Bishop Gilbert Foliot for 'R.' of 1163 x *c.* 1180 (or 1187) – collecting money either to help repair the old bridge (as the phrasing suggests), or else 'R.' hides Peter of Colechurch himself.

[3] According to tradition Thomas Becket was baptized in St Mary Colechurch (*Cal. Patent Rolls, 1446–52*, p. 70); his father's house to the north of Cheapside became first the hospital of St Thomas Acon, and later the Mercers' Hall. Stow, vol. i, p. 264, and below, pp. 334–5.

[4] Below, pp. 109–10.

THE GRANTING OF THE COMMUNE

When Henry II died in 1189 a new phase began in the development of English towns, and particularly of London. Richard I looked to even wider horizons than his father had done and devoted almost his entire reign to crusading in the Holy Land and war in France. He visited England in 1189 to be crowned, and again in 1194, but he left to his administration the problem of finding sufficient money to finance royal adventures. One expedient favoured by the king's officials was to sell charters of privileges. As this became known, more and more boroughs sought to have their own distinctive customs recognized and to secure some measure of self-government. Thus the move towards urban independence, which Henry II had carefully controlled, gradually gained momentum.

Richard of Devizes, a contemporary chronicler with the heartiest distaste for civic ambitions, commented that neither the new king nor his father would willingly have allowed London to become a commune 'for a million silver marks'.[1] But Richard I's attitude was doubtless more flexible; the same chronicler had previously attributed to Richard the remark that he would sell London itself if he could find a bidder.[2]

The first sign of real change within the city was the reduction of the farm from just over £500 to £300 in the course of 1190-1, and its payment at the Exchequer by sheriffs who had apparently been elected by the citizens.[3] We do not know the background of this change; but we are on firmer ground with the political crisis which occurred soon after, in the autumn of 1191. William de Longchamp was justiciar of England in Richard's absence, until the king's secret appointment of Walter of Coutances, Archbishop of Rouen, to succeed him when news reached Richard of troubles in England in 1191. Longchamp was therefore a key figure in royal administration from 1189 to 1191, and had roused the resentment of powerful barons. Chief among these was the king's own brother, John, who, in spite of his closeness to the throne and his extensive landed possessions within the country, had been assigned no particular authority. London was a natural focal point for the conflict which developed. Longchamp, among his other strongholds, controlled the Tower of London, which he strengthened by rebuilding part of its curtain

---

[1] *The Chronicle of Richard of Devizes*, ed. J. T. Appleby, NMT, 1963, p. 49.
[2] Richard of Devizes, p. 9.
[3] Tait, pp. 181-2; Reynolds, 'Rulers of London', p. 348.

wall and attempting to flood the surrounding ditch.[1] To the Tower he
fled as his enemies united against him. John himself had briefly owned a
block of city property connected with the Peverel honour in Nottingham-
shire and was financially involved with the prominent FitzReiner family.[2]
As he advanced upon London the citizens had once again to decide where
their loyalties should lie. An assembly met at the Guildhall and heard
strong arguments by Henry of Cornhill in favour of supporting Longchamp.[3] But these were countered by Richard FitzReiner, who pointed
out that to bar the City's gates against the king's brother and heir might
have dangerous consequences. FitzReiner offered to negotiate with John
and in the end his advice was taken. During the night of 7–8 October John
entered the City, welcomed by at least a section of the population who
came to meet him with lanterns and torches.[4] The next day a great con-
course, made up of prominent ecclesiastics and nobles as well as citizens,
crowded into St Paul's. They decided to deprive Longchamp of all
authority and accepted as justiciar in his stead Walter of Coutances, the
Archbishop of Rouen, who had now arrived and revealed the king's
nomination.[5] John seems to have claimed for himself the title 'supreme
governor of the whole realm'. Then followed the dramatic political climax
to years of development within the City. John and Walter of Coutances,
together with a number of other justices, granted the commune to the
citizens, while bishops and secular magnates swore that they would
maintain it, as long as it pleased the king. In return, the citizens promised
the king and his heir faithful service; they agreed, if Richard died without
children, to accept John as king, and in token of this they swore, saving
their loyalty to Richard, to support him against all men. Thus it seems
that the Londoners, perhaps FitzReiner himself, had struck a bargain
with John: they would further his cause and use their influence to secure
the crown for him. The price paid was their commune.

FitzReiner did not live long to enjoy this triumph but the office of
Mayor which emerged about this time symbolized the continuing development of his city.[6] Based on French precedents but having its roots deep

[1] Colvin, vol. ii, London, 1963, pp. 708–9.

[2] Page, pp. 109, 149.

[3] Giraldus, *Opera*, vol. iv, pp. 404–5.

[4] Richard of Devizes, p. 46.

[5] For varying accounts of this meeting see Richard of Devizes, pp. 48–9; Giraldus,
Opera, vol. iv, pp. 404–5; *Gesta Henrici II*, vol. ii, pp. 213–14 (cf. Howden, vol. iii,
pp. 140–1).

[6] On the mayoralty, see chap. 9; on FitzAilwin see pp. 245 ff.

in European history, it gave the citizens an administrative head and a say in national affairs. Henry FitzAilwin filled this position until his death in 1212 and thus guided it through its early, critical years. We do not know that he took any important initiative in the crisis of 1191, but if not this may, in fact, have strengthened his control over city politics. For the outstanding duty which faced the mayor was to make his commune respectable. If he could prove that, despite its revolutionary name, it was entirely loyal to the throne and ready to co-operate in royal service then Richard was unlikely to upset a fait accompli.

Consistently with this policy the mayor is found in the spring of 1193 acting as one of the treasurers responsible for collecting a ransom to free King Richard, then a prisoner in Germany.[1] When John raised the standard of rebellion against his brother early in the following year the mayor again acted with the strictest propriety. He arrested an envoy from John who was found boasting incautiously of his master's prospects, and handed him over to Hubert Walter, the king's justiciar.[2] The sentence of dispossession subsequently passed upon John was openly published in London. After Richard had returned and personally re-established his position in England, the Londoners offered him 1500 marks.[3] The sum was partly a contribution to his ransom money; but partly also a *douceur* intended to strengthen the king's goodwill towards the city and to prompt a confirmation of their liberties.

Such efforts did not go entirely unrewarded. Before he left to continue his foreign adventures Richard allowed them a charter which repeated the terms of his father's grant.[4] Of the commune there was no mention at all. It was not until the first year of the following reign that the key privilege of appointing their own sheriffs was formally acknowledged, while the office which FitzAilwin held so long with distinction only received formal royal authorization in 1215. But the granting of charters often followed actual concessions at some distance. In practice Richard allowed the mayor to continue in office and the sheriffs to pay the reduced farm of £300. Thus he tacitly allowed London to keep the privileges it had won in the crisis of 1191.

[1] Howden, vol. iii, p. 212. Those within the commune also took an oath of loyalty at this time to Richard I and to the Mayor and his associates, Page, pp. 281–2; Round, *CL*, pp. 235–6.

[2] Howden, vol. iii, p. 236.

[3] *PR 6 Richard I*, p. 182; Tait, p. 182.

[4] *Liber Cust.* pt i, pp. 248–9.

UNREST WITHIN THE CITY

In the course of Richard's reign two incidents occurred which show how close to the surface violence lay in the medieval community. The crusading movement from its very beginning had exerted a powerful influence upon popular feelings. Late in the twelfth century the hatred which it generated against the infidels occupying the Holy Land spilled over into resentment of unbelievers closer to hand.[1] The Jews had always been vulnerable. Their manners and beliefs prompted suspicion while their business abilities excited envy, and the king, although he protected them in his own interests, could not or did not always hold such feelings in check. An episode during Richard's coronation acted as a signal for the release of these feelings. Misunderstanding the motives of a Jewish deputation who brought gifts for the king, a crowd of citizens set upon them.[2] The violence spread quickly from Westminster to the City where Jews were murdered and their property plundered and burnt in a riotous outbreak which the authorities were powerless to control. In many other cities this appalling example was followed and Jewish communities suffered gravely at the hands of fanatical, outraged citizens.

A second popular disturbance in London centred on the unusual person and career of William FitzOsbert. A citizen of this name is first found among a group of Londoners who set off together for the Holy Land.[3] On their way a great storm arose which threatened their lives, but after the miraculous intervention of St Edmund, St Nicholas and St Thomas of Canterbury they came safely to harbour in Portugal. This William Fitz-Osbert is most likely the same man who in 1194 brought his own brother to court, accusing him, together with some of his friends, of speaking treacherously about the king.[4] FitzOsbert possessed remarkable talents, in particular a flair for eloquence. In 1196 he embarked upon a well-nigh revolutionary course.[5] Apparently for some years the wealthy citizens had been in the habit of passing on to their poorer brethren the main burden of the heavy taxes which often fell upon the City. FitzOsbert championed the cause of the oppressed majority and built up a large following for

[1] C. Roth, *A History of the Jews in England*, 3rd edn, Oxford, 1964, chap. 2; on the Jews in London, see below, pp. 222–7.

[2] C. Roth, pp. 19–20; William of Newburgh, ed. R. Howlett, *Chrons. Stephen etc.*, vol. i, 1884, pp. 294–7.

[3] On William FitzOsbert, see Page, pp. 105, 117–18.

[4] See p. 247 n. 6.

[5] Howden, vol. iv, pp. 5–6; William of Newburgh, vol. ii, pp. 466–71.

himself which amounted, according to the inflated estimate of one contemporary, to 52,000. He soon found it necessary to visit the king abroad to obtain protection for himself; the two seem to have been on good terms, possibly because of FitzOsbert's record as a Crusader. But he had aroused the intense hostility not only of his colleagues in London, but of Hubert Walter, the king's justiciar.[1] After killing one man who was sent to arrest him, FitzOsbert fled for safety to the church of St Mary-le-Bow. His enemies then set fire to the church and he was forced to surrender to them. Carried off to the Tower, he was tried with nine of his associates, condemned to death and promptly hanged at Smithfield. But even this ignominious end did not immediately solve the problem he had created for the civic authorities. The site of his death became a centre of pilgrimage for many travelling to London on business from distant parts of the country, and it was some years before his cult lost its appeal. FitzOsbert interested religious chroniclers because they felt bound to reject the claims to sanctity made for him, and also because to them he represented a supremely wicked type of person: the man who betrayed his own class. He is interesting to us, partly because of the basic conflicts inherent in his career; partly because as London's first known demagogue he played upon resentments and tensions within the City which have otherwise gone completely unrecorded.

1199–1216

In April 1199 King Richard received a fatal wound while besieging the castle of Chalus in northern France. John, his nominated heir, acted quickly, fearing that his enemies might help his principal rival for the throne, Arthur of Brittany, nephew of Richard and John. He took formal possession of Normandy and then crossed to England. On 27 May he was crowned at Westminster by the Archbishop of Canterbury, Hubert Walter. Thus, without undue difficulty, he achieved the aim which seems to have lain behind his negotiations with the Londoners in 1191.

Shortly after his coronation John granted the city three charters.[2] The first merely repeated the terms of his father's charter and thus confirmed privileges long enjoyed. The second, abolishing weirs on the River Thames

[1] C. R. Cheney, *Hubert Walter*, London, 1967, pp. 93–4.
[2] *Rotuli Chartarum*, ed. T. D. Hardy, Record Commission, 1837, p. xl; W. de Gray Birch, *The Historical Charters of the City of London*, London, 1887, pp. 13–14 (in translation); *Liber Cust.* pt i, pp. 249–51.

and the River Medway, was couched in the same terms as a royal charter issued two years previously. The third, however, marked the king's personal acceptance of recent and possibly controversial customs. John formally allowed the citizens to appoint their own sheriffs at the modest farm of £300. Men who held such office, it was emphasized, were answerable to the Exchequer judges, but they retained the rights of London citizens. Thus if they committed crimes punishable by the loss of life or limbs, they were to be tried according to city law. On the other hand they might be liable for fines as high as £20, a sum apparently four times greater than that usually accorded to citizens.[1]

John was careful about the privileges he granted to the City. He was also careful to get something in return. The Londoners agreed to pay him 3,000 marks,[2] a considerable sum for a charter which said nothing about the mayoralty and the commune – surely more vital issues in 1199 than the shrievalty. It took four years before this debt was paid.[3] Meanwhile, in 1200 the sheriffs admitted among the citizens' unpaid debts over £167 and an additional £278, both owed to the king and representing 'gifts'.[4] Five years later the citizens were saddled with a £1,000 fine; before this was eventually paid another for the same sum was imposed and this in turn was replaced in the Exchequer accounts by a 'gift' of 2,000 marks.[5]

John had embarked upon an expensive policy aimed at recovering his lands in France at a time when steeply rising prices were diminishing his own resources. To allow the sheriffs of London to pay a farm lower than that which had existed in his father's day might seem in the circumstances a piece of folly only to be redeemed by the imposition of additional taxes. London no doubt enjoyed large and growing profits as her trade expanded. When the king imposed a customs duty of a fifteenth upon goods passing in or out of England, London's sheriffs accounted for over £836.[6] But to

---

[1] 100 shillings is the sum mentioned in both the *Libertas Londoniensis* (Liebermann, vol. i, pp. 673–5) and in Henry I's charter to London (Brooke, Keir and Reynolds, p. 575).

[2] *PR 2 John*, p. 153; the grant of the charter was made conditional upon this payment, *Rotuli de Oblatis et Finibus in Turri Londinense*, ed. T. D. Hardy, Record Commission, 1835, p. 11.

[3] *PR 5 John*, p. 9; a substantial part of the remainder was paid in 1208, *PR 10 John*, p. 167.

[4] *PR 2 John*, pp. 150, 152.

[5] *PR 7 John*, p. 9; *PR 10 John*, p. 167; *PR 13 John*, pp. 133, 135.

[6] *PR 6 John*, p. 218. It is doubtful, however, if this whole sum was paid. In 1206 the citizens offered 200 marks to be quit of the fifteenth and even this debt was not cleared until 1211; *Rotuli de Oblatis*, p. 341; *PR 13 John*, p. 133.

lay hands upon civic wealth was, as John discovered, a tricky and dangerous business. In 1206 he had to intervene in the City's internal affairs,
ordering its barons to elect twenty-four citizens; the committee so formed
was to look into the collection of the revenue known as tallage, which had
hitherto been born by the ordinary townspeople rather than the wealthy
minority.[1] This tax, together with aids and 'gifts' arbitrarily required,
roused strong resentment within London and any popularity John may
have had quickly disappeared. The tradition he left behind him was an
evil one. Matthew Paris in the middle of the thirteenth century recorded
the opinion that he had contravened the ancient liberties of the City and
reduced its inhabitants 'almost to the condition of slaves'.[2] The first part
of the charge was embroidered by a slightly later writer who pictured John
personally consigning the City's charters to the flames.[3]

Throughout the kingdom resistance to the king's demands and suspicion
of his motives were growing. For all the ingenuity of his financial ex-
pedients, John could show little direct gain. Within five years of his
accession Maine, Anjou and Normandy had all fallen to the king of
France. He quarrelled bitterly with some of his barons who were unwilling
to embark on extensive campaigns abroad. From 1205 onwards John had
to deal with plots against him. At first he faced casual alliances between
barons who were brought together by an immediate grievance and soon
divided. But as the reign wore on they accumulated political experience
and saw the need, if they were ever to place effective restraint upon the
king, to widen their ranks and popularize their objectives.

In one particular way we can test, if not the general temper of London,
at least the interests and some of the activities of her government. During
this period an unknown writer put together, or copied, a collection of
national and civic laws, adding in random form jottings on various aspects
of civic administration.[4] The result is a strange patchwork yielding
valuable information on specific topics but strangely incoherent in general
layout. The author's legal antiquarianism is of more than passing interest.
He wrote out at length the laws of Henry I, which became political

[1] Page, pp. 282-3.

[2] Matthew Paris, *Abbreviatio Chronicorum Anglaie*, p. 232.

[3] *Chronicles of the reigns of Edward I and Edward II*, ed. W. Stubbs, Rolls Series,
vol. i, 1882, p. 14.

[4] Now divided into two MSS: John Rylands MS Lat. 155 and British Museum Add. MS
14252. The latter was analysed and partly edited by M. Bateson in *EHR*, vol. xvii,
1902, pp. 480–511, 707–730; on the former cf. Liebermann, *EHR*, vol. xxviii, 1913,
pp. 732–45, and Brooke, Keir and Reynolds, pp. 572–3.

dynamite in the hands of the barons early in 1215; and near the beginning
of these laws he inserted what is our earliest copy of the London charter
of liberties attributed to Henry I.

We do not know the exact date when this manuscript was compiled and
it is possible that it was the barons who influenced its contents rather than
vice versa. But the general link between London and the baronial opposition to the king is clear. There are other parallels. The City's communal
organization formed a precedent, if not the model, for the *conjuratio*, or
sworn company of barons, who led the struggle against the king; and it
seems likely, in view of their relative inexperience in constitutional
affairs, that when they sought some means of enforcing Magna Carta the
barons took from London the idea of a committee of twenty-five.[1] It has
even been argued that they were self-consciously attempting to turn the
whole kingdom into a commune.[2]

On the City's own problems the London manuscript throws some light.[3]
Active measures were being taken for its defence, which included a
special tax levied upon both citizens and foreign merchants. The aldermen were ordered – who by, does not appear – to survey the arms borne
by those living in their wards and check that they were able to defend the
City. Every alderman was to possess a banner behind which parish
contingents might assemble. Most important, however, there survives a
list of nine brief headings which apparently summarize the City's political
objectives towards the end of John's reign.[4] They included demands that
all evil taxes should be abolished and that no tallage should be taken
without the agreement of both kingdom and City; the mint was to belong
to the City as in former years; foreign merchants should come and go
freely and responsibility for the River Thames should rest entirely with
London. Most of these articles suggest that the citizens resented changes
the king had introduced, and wanted a return to the situation which had
prevailed at an earlier time. The most startling exception was an article
which called for a mayor to be elected annually in the folkmoot. Clearly it
was time that the head of the commune, who had been addressed and
therefore acknowledged in royal documents, should receive full official
recognition; but the provisions for his election point to a radical strain
within city politics. Not only do they imply resistance to FitzAilwin's

---

[1] J. C. Holt, *Magna Carta*, Cambridge, 1965, p. 48.
[2] Holt, pp. 48–9.
[3] Bateson, pp. 726–8.
[4] Ibid., p. 726.

long term as mayor, but they ignore the smaller, more efficient City courts, like the Husting Court, in favour of the old-fashioned and rather cumbersome popular assembly.

If London had some cause for siding with those organizing resistance to John, she also had personal links with some of the barons involved. Robert FitzWalter, lord of Dunmow in Essex, fell foul of John as early as 1203.[1] In 1212 plots were uncovered in which he was deeply implicated and to save his life he fled straight to John's chief enemy, the king of France. Restored to his English property in the following year he played a leading part in the struggles which forced John to grant the Great Charter. FitzWalter was lord of Baynard's Castle, one of the few great fortifications in London, and by virtue of this possession acted as the *procurator* of the City and leader of its forces in time of war.[2] He had therefore some influence within the city. Another rebellious baron interested in London was the Earl of Gloucester and Essex, who bore the same name as his redoubtable predecessor, Geoffrey de Mandeville. Alienated by John, he joined forces with FitzWalter, hoping to lay hands upon the Tower of London which he regarded as a family property.[3]

The year 1212 saw a number of significant events within London. A fire which broke out in Southwark had unusually devastating results. It spread to the bridge where a large crowd, attracted by the size of the calamity, became trapped between the flames and the river.[4] Many lost their lives in the panic which followed, while the fire, having demolished the bridge chapel, swept over to the northern bank and caused widespread damage. In the autumn, after long years of service, Henry FitzAilwin died. We know very little about the political sympathies of those who followed him as mayor; but it may well be that with his death the tradition of co-operation with the crown which he seems so carefully to have maintained, came to an end. Finally, while FitzWalter was in France King John took what revenge was possible by razing Baynard's Castle to the ground.[5]

Any hopes which the king may have had of quelling opposition, however, fell victim to his continental ambitions. When he left England in 1214

[1] On FitzWalter, see *DNB*.

[2] See p. 216.

[3] Walter of Coventry, ed. W. Stubbs, Rolls Series, vol. ii, 1873, p. 221.

[4] Walter of Coventry, vol. ii, pp. 205–6; Matthew Paris, *Hist. Anglorum*, vol. ii, p. 131; Annals of Waverley, *Ann. Mon.*, vol. ii, p. 268 (*LAL*, p. 3, has 1211, evidently in error).

[5] *Chronicles of the reigns of Edward I and Edward II*, vol. i, p. 15, where the year is incorrectly given.

a small nucleus of powerful and discontented barons remained behind. Critical of his campaigns and of the way money was raised to finance them, they may well have enjoyed the sympathy of the Londoners who were looking for ways of paying the tallage of 2,000 marks recently levied upon them.[1] Then the coalition of interests which John had carefully built up abroad collapsed on the field of Bouvines. With the triumph of the French king he lost all opportunity of recovering his continental dominions. After he himself had suffered a humiliating defeat in Poitou, he returned to face hostility which could no longer be restrained.

Early in 1215 the king met his barons at London. Intent on obtaining safeguards for his future conduct, they demanded that he should confirm the laws of Edward the Confessor and the laws and a charter of Henry I.[2] John played for time and appealed to the Pope for judgement on the issue. At last he seems to have appreciated the temper of the Londoners, for on 9 May he granted them a charter. The citizens were permitted to elect a mayor every year, choosing different men or re-electing the same man, as they saw fit. In addition all their accustomed liberties were confirmed to them.[3]

But the Londoners were not conciliated. Both king and barons had armed themselves and the baronial contingent, led by Robert FitzWalter, who styled himself Marshal of the Army of God and the Holy Church, was now approaching the city. They encountered no resistance, entered the city and fortified it. Such an easy victory puzzled many who chronicled it. Walter of Coventry stated that most of the citizens were at church at the time and that the better part of them knew nothing of a plot which gave the City into the barons' hands.[4] Another version suggested that while the rich actively favoured the barons, the poor were too frightened to oppose them.[5] But it is unlikely that the whole conflict took the citizens by surprise. John's efforts at conciliation probably came too late to win back the loyalty of men whom he had long antagonized.

It is clear that the leading citizens of London hoped to exact their own share of concessions from the king. The articles which the barons submitted to John for his approval early in June reflected their interests.[6] While

[1] *PR 16 John*, p. 81.

[2] Holt, pp. 135–6.

[3] W. Stubbs, *Select Charters*, 9th ed., 1913, pp. 311–12.

[4] Walter of Coventry, vol. ii, p. 220.

[5] Roger of Wendover, *Flores Historiarum*, ed. H. G. Hewlett, Rolls Series, 1886–9, vol. ii, pp. 116–17.

[6] Holt, pp. 304–12, esp. ch. 32.

the barons wished John to accept the principle that extraordinary taxes required their own consent, the Londoners tried to apply this principle both to the aids and tallages taken from their city. In addition they wanted their ancient liberties confirmed to them.

Forced into an impasse by his loss of London, John negotiated with his enemies. The result, wrung from him in a moment of strategic weakness, was the Great Charter, to which the king agreed that his seal should be attached in June 1215. However important the document was to be in the wider context, its practical concessions to the City of London were only moderate.[1] Her ancient liberties and rights on land and water were confirmed but not specified. Clauses which abolished fishweirs on all rivers, including the Thames, and guaranteed freedom of movement to merchants protected her interests. Aids might be taken from London, as from the rest of the realm, only in certain circumstances and under stated conditions. But of tallage – the tax which the king levied arbitrarily upon his own estates and upon the towns – there was no mention.

In the months that followed the City's loyalties were of crucial concern. The mayor was appointed one of the twenty-five barons, selected from both sides of the dispute, whose task it was to see that the charter was implemented. At first it looked as if London might occupy a neutral position,[2] but the barons acted quickly to maintain their interests in the capital. John was forced to agree that Robert FitzWalter and his associates should hold the City until 15 August, provided that he himself continued to receive his accustomed dues and that civic liberties were not contravened.[3] He also promised not to fortify the City, or the Tower, which passed temporarily into the hands of the Archbishop of Canterbury. The sting of the agreement lay in its final conditions. If steps were taken by 15 August to fulfil the terms of the Great Charter then both the City and the Tower were to be returned to the king; if they were not then the barons and archbishop were to remain in control for as long as that situation prevailed. FitzWalter well appreciated how vital London was to the baronial cause. Writing to William de Albini, he described the city as a haven and warned of the dangers of losing it. Other forces, he wrote, were only waiting to find London left unprotected, to move in themselves.[4]

[1] Holt, pp. 221–2, 320–1.
[2] C. R. Cheney, 'The Twenty-Five Barons of Magna Carta', *Bulletin of the John Rylands Library*, vol. l, 1967–8, pp. 292–3, 307.
[3] Holt, Appendix VII (1), pp. 342–3.
[4] Holt, p. 250.

While king and barons remained intensely suspicious of one another, difficulties arose about implementing the Great Charter. King John soon gave up his attempts at a compromise and in September papal letters were published which first of all attacked the barons' cause and then annulled the Charter in its entirety. Once again both sides took up arms. The rebel barons, with the possession of London as their chief asset, met to decide on their next action. They concluded that only if John was replaced as king could they hope to achieve their objectives. Consequently they invited Prince Louis of France to fight with their help for the English throne.

The moving force behind this decision may well have been Robert FitzWalter himself, who had links with the French court. But London and its citizens continued to play an important part in this last campaign. Serlo the mercer, recently mayor, and four other citizens who held responsible office in this period personally raised the sum of 1,000 marks, which they supplied to Prince Louis.[1] When he landed in England in May 1216 Louis made straight for London. On 2 or 3 June in St Paul's churchyard the citizens, led by Robert FitzWalter and William Hardel, the mayor, rendered homage to the French prince.[2] For a while it looked as if London's traditional claim to elect a king was again to influence national politics.

But in the autumn of 1216 John became ill and died. The whole situation was transformed. The king's heir, Henry, was only nine years of age and feeling in England ran against visiting the sins of the father upon his son. Moreover Louis, as a French prince, commanded little popularity outside his limited circle of baronial and civic allies. Defeated by royalist forces at Lincoln, Louis made the Treaty of Kingston whereby he agreed to abandon his claims to the English throne in return for a substantial payment. In the autumn of 1217 he left England for good. The civil war was at an end and London opened its gates to the young king and his supporters.

[1] *Eyre*, nos 195, 316.
[2] M. Tyson, 'The Annals of Southwark and Merton', *Surrey Archaeological Collections*, vol. xxxvi, 1925, pp. 50–1.

3

Early Medieval Towns and the Urban Renaissance

I THE ENGLISH BACKGROUND

LET US glance at a few of the large questions which have fascinated historians of medieval towns in recent generations. Why did Europe see so marked a renaissance of town life in the tenth, eleventh and twelfth centuries? Is there some universal explanation, or must we look for a multiplicity of causes in different centuries and different regions? Were the towns in their origin and their essence military or mercantile, made for war or for peace? Did they prosper under the benevolent eye of kings and noblemen, or were they enclaves of capitalism in a hostile, feudal world?

There have been heroic attempts to find a single answer to some of these questions, to cut a clear, narrow path through the jungle of diverse opinions and theories. They have failed; but their failure need not leave us hopeless of finding large causes: the phenomenon was too large, too widespread, too general to be due to chance. Yet it is all too easy, by playing with the word 'town', to gather quite different problems under a common umbrella, to create a fictitious appearance of simplicity in a rich and complex world.

In this country the town had first appeared in prehistoric times, shortly before the arrival of the Romans. The great hill-top forts, like the Wrekin or Maiden Castle or St Catherine's Hill, which were originally enclosures into which the local tribes could drive their wives and their cattle in dangerous times, were presently converted into places of settlement.[1]

[1] See the recent symposium on the early hill-forts of Britain, *The Iron Age and its Hill Forts: Papers presented to Sir M. Wheeler*, ed. M. Jesson and D. Hill, Southampton, 1971.

Most of these primitive settlements were moved into the plains, and replaced by much more sophisticated, planned towns when the Romans came. Obviously enough, they brought a full grown idea of what a town should be, with temples and baths and threatres and town houses for the local gentry or chieftains or whatever one likes to call them. At a somewhat more barbarous level the rise of the medieval town in this country was not so different. Before the late ninth century there were two kinds of town, if they may be graced with so lofty a title. There were the decaying shells of Roman towns, whose walls still afforded shelter within which cathedrals might be built, mints established, royal reeves hold sway, and a few people squat. These were hardly towns by our standards, though they were coming to play an increasingly notable part in the life of their neighbourhoods. Thus Canterbury was a flourishing place, with cathedral, market, mint, royal palace – everything, in fact, a town might have save a substantial population; not of course that it was uninhabited, but that the settlement within it was scattered and small, so far as we can tell, and neither numerous nor prosperous enough to sustain anything recognizable as urban life. So too was Winchester, where cathedral, bishop, clergy, king and moneyers might safely dwell behind the city wall; but it was the community of traders and fishers at Hamwih or Southampton, who gave their name to Hampshire, and formed a much more active body down to the ninth century, even though they had no Roman past worth the name, and no walls at all.[1] Historical evidence from Bede's time on suggests that London in some measure combined the roles of Winchester and Hamwih; but so far archaeological finds suggest rather the slender population of Winchester than anything truly approaching an urban centre. More may yet be found, and there seems little doubt that London was both a place to reckon with and far from uninhabited in the eighth and ninth centuries; but it is very doubtful whether it had many of the characteristics of an urban community.

THE ALFREDIAN *Burg*

Late in the ninth century all this was changed by an astonishing, and indeed highly improbable act of creation.[2] The formation of the first

[1] See P. V. Addyman and D. H. Hill, 'Saxon Southampton: a review of the evidence', *Proc. of the Hants. Field Club*, vols. xxv, 1968, pp. 61–93, xxvi, 1969, pp. 61–96.

[2] For recent studies of the Alfredian *burh*, and of town planning in the ninth and tenth centuries, see M. Biddle and D. Hill in *Antiquaries Journal*, vol. li, 1971, pp. 70–85. On the general problems of late Old English towns, see H. Loyn in *England*

boroughs, the *burhs*, by Alfred of Wessex was a characteristic act of insight and imagination. All the indications are that Alfred was a man who came slowly to any sort of realization of his talents and opportunities. His early life, apart from the remarkable episode of his visits to Italy, was mainly filled with conventional, and only very moderately successful, warfare against the Danes. The crisis of 878, however, brought about by the Danish invasion of Wessex, seems to have driven him to look for new methods of warfare, and the last twenty years of his reign witnessed a flowering of imaginative schemes – the reorganization of the army; the design of new ships for sea warfare; the foundation of the *burhs* as centres for defence in depth; the compilation of laws; the formation of his seminar of learned men (learned at least by ninth-century standards) to help him translate a group of major works into the vernacular; and finally the inspiration of court propaganda on the Carolingian model, which led to the writing of Asser's *Life* and the 'Anglo-Saxon Chronicle'. Alfred was a heroic warrior who barely succeeded in saving the last old English kingdom from the Viking onslaught. But he was more than this: and we owe it largely to his court propaganda that we discern how he paved the way for the creation of a new English kingdom in the tenth century.[1] He was perfectly aware of the constant danger of his life, the uncertainty of his own and his kingdom's future which made the *Consolations of Philosophy*, originally written by Boethius when under the threat of death, seem to fit Alfred's circumstances sufficiently to merit a translation; yet many of his acts, his laws and his translations show an intense vision of a happier, more settled, more peaceful and prosperous future. But it must be admitted that the ponderous Asser shows little comprehension of the meaning of some of his hero's activities. ' . . . I may tell of fortresses ordered by him and still not begun, or begun too late to be brought to completion . . .' so that the enemy arrived while the walls were still building, and those who had ignored or openly resisted Alfred's instructions were ashamed of their folly[2] – yet he has little to tell us of the *burhs*,

---

before the Conquest: Studies in Primary Sources presented to Dorothy Whitelock, Cambridge, 1971, pp. 115–28. Both these papers have valuable references. On the Burghal Hidage and its relation to the Alfredian and post-Alfredian towns, see N. P. Brooks in *Medieval Archaeology*, vol. viii, 1964, pp. 74–90; D. Hill, ib., vol. xiii, 1969, pp. 84–92. It is a singular misfortune that the Burghal Hidage omits London.

[1] See recent discussions by R. H. C. Davis in *History*, vol. lvi, 1971, pp. 169–82; Brooke in *La Storiografia altomedievale*, vol. i, 223 ff.

[2] Asser, c. 91, ed. W. H. Stevenson, Oxford, 1904, p. 78, trans. D. Whitelock, *EHD*, vol. i, p. 273.

no description of what the king had in mind, no clear statement of their nature.

There was nothing new in using the shells of Roman towns or fortresses as enclosures for defence, and some have supposed that this was all that was involved in the foundation of the Alfredian *burhs*. It is clear that places like Winchester and London had had a considerable prestige and a life of a kind for centuries; and London may have had inhabitants from Roman times without a break. But if so, they were squatters in the great city, for the spade has unearthed exceedingly little evidence of real settlement between the fifth century and Alfred's time;[1] and London, like many other cities, was used by the Danes as a convenient fortress in which to spend a month or two, or even a whole winter. If all that Alfred had attempted was to organize local militias to provide garrisons for a group of such fortresses – and to build a few more, with earth ramparts and stockades – then we might perceive that he had learned an important lesson from the Danish attacks, but not regard it as showing exceptional vision. But it seems clear that more was involved, and more of a kind wholly characteristic of Alfred. Some of the *burhs* disappeared in the tenth or eleventh centuries, one or two even later; none survived which did not prosper in the eleventh and twelfth centuries as a market-town, an administrative centre and a place of trade and industry as well as a fortress. Effective settlement of these towns – whether they were revivals or new creations – must have been a slow process, and taken several generations. But it seems clear Alfred intended them (or some of them at least) to become towns in a fairly sophisticated sense of the term. Recent study of the topography and archaeology of Alfred's *burhs* is slowly revealing the way in which he tried to provide not only walls and security, but a street-plan and the basis of settlement.[2] The evidence recently collected for town planning in the late ninth and early tenth centuries is very impressive. He cannot have hoped himself to see flourishing town life revive in England, yet here again, and here in particular, he had a vision beyond what the present could conceivably offer. He seems to have seen in a town

[1] In spite of many discoveries in recent years, the picture is still much as presented in Sir R. E. M. Wheeler's *London and the Saxons*, which made the most of evidence of continuity between Roman and Saxon London; see also the articles by Wheeler and J. N. L. Myres in *Antiquity*, vol. viii, 1934, pp. 290–302, 437–42 and Wheeler's reply, pp. 443–7. That the origin of London's street-plan is to be seen in the Alfredian revival is briefly argued in Biddle and Hill, art. cit., p. 83.

[2] Biddle and Hill, art. cit.

a place where great men had town houses, a place with large churches and small, with a market and merchants, or groups of tradesmen, gathered in orderly houses in streets laid out in a simple grid; above all, perhaps, a place in some measure under the control of the king's reeve.[1] It is reasonable to suppose that this idea did not step out of his imagination – or that of his courtiers – unaided by the world in which they lived. But it is not easy to determine what sources he had for his notions of what a town could be.

In the translation of Orosius, once attributed to Alfred himself, now thought to have come from the hands of a subject and admirer of the king, there is interpolated a famous account of the visit to England of two Scandinavian seafarers, and of some of the places they had visited in the Baltic and the Viking world.[2] It names one major town of the northern world, the Danish market settlement at Hedeby, but shows no special interest in it; and the chief other northern town of which we have some knowledge, Birka, is not mentioned.[3] The Viking treatment of English towns may have helped Alfred to see the benefits and dangers of surviving town walls, and to convince him that they needed permanent garrisons; but the passage in the Orosius tells us little or nothing positively of the sources available to Alfred and his circle for their idea of a town.

Details of the Viking and the Baltic world were noted because they were relatively unfamiliar; no doubt Alfred and his colleagues knew more of France, Germany and the Low Countries. His seminar of learned men included John the Old Saxon from northern Germany and Grimbald from Flanders. It is likely enough that he knew something of Frisian and Flemish towns of the age – of Duurstede and Quentavic, Ghent and Bruges. But the Flemish castra were hardly towns at this time. The enclosure at Ghent measured $4\frac{3}{4}$ hectares, that at Bruges no more than $1\frac{1}{2}$.[4] They were enclosures in which a count and his administrative headquarters – grand words for a garrison and a chapel – and a market could live in uneasy proximity, and which could serve as refuges in hard times. In this sense

[1] See pp. 194 ff.

[2] 'Alfred's Orosius', ed. H. Sweet, Early English Text Soc., part i, 1873, pp. 17–21; on the authorship see D. Whitelock, in *Continuations and Beginnings*, ed. E. G. Stanley, pp. 70, 73–4, 89–94; J. M. Bately, in *Anglia*, vol. lxxxviii, 1970, pp. 433–60; E. M. Liggins, ibid., pp. 289–322.

[3] On these towns, see P. G. Foote and D. M. Wilson, *Viking Achievement*, London, 1970, pp. 203 ff.; P. Sawyer, *Age of the Vikings*, 2nd edn, 1971, chap. 8.

[4] Ganshof, p. 17. On Bruges see also Galbert, ed. Ross, pp. 52 ff., and references.

they were far smaller, and probably less like our idea of a town than London itself before Alfred took the town in 886. Some larger communities could no doubt be found here and there in northern Europe; Paris and Verdun, for instance, must have been closer to Alfred's conception than anything in Flanders at the time.[1] Nearer still, probably, were Quentavic and Duurstede, the great emporia of Frisian merchants, the trading capitals of northern Europe before the Viking onslaught. Quentavic was the home of many of the merchants who plied the north sea and the English Channel; Duurstede commanded an extensive trade (as archaeology has shown) throughout the northern part of the Carolingian empire.[2] In Alfred's time they were in decline, but Alfred seems to have visited Quentavic and may well have learned from it; it is not, however, likely to have played a vital part in his vision of what a town could be.

Quentavic and Duurstede were the homes and bases of communities of merchants. The Alfredian *burhs* were hardly designed to play so large a part in trade; we can scarcely credit Alfred with a prophetic vision of the commercial renaissance of the eleventh and twelfth centuries. Yet in a way they were more sophisticated towns, in conception, than those of Frisia (Friesland). They had walls and large enclosed areas to provide shelter; many of them had the buildings needed to provide headquarters for ealdorman and bishop, houses for reeves and clergy. They also had a grid of little streets for houses; above all, they had market-places. They were market-towns and country-towns: centres of the communities which they served and which served them. When another great Saxon warlord imitated Alfred's *burhs* a generation later, he imitated the fortress and the enclosure, but did not create embryo towns: Henry the Fowler's Saxony was not ripe, or his vision did not include, the idea of a town in this fuller sense.[3]

The only part of Alfred's world where real towns with any serious pretension to the name could really be found in any profusion, was northern and central Italy. In some measure, it seems very likely that the Italian cities had entered Alfred's dreams; how precisely we shall never know.[4] The idea is not so fantastic as it seems. No generation passed without a posse of English pilgrims taking the path to Rome. Already in

[1] Cf. Ganshof, pp. 30 ff., 37. On early medieval towns see esp. Ganshof, and E. Ennen, *Frühgeschichte der Europäischen Stadt*, Bonn, 1953.

[2] See p. 262 n.; Ganshof, p. 22 and n.

[3] Ennen, pp. 49 f.; C. Erdmann in *Deutsches Archiv*, vol. vi, 1943, pp. 59–101.

[4] See p. 63 and n. 3.

the eighth century St Boniface had noted sadly how widely spread in Lombardy as well as in northern Europe were the lady pilgrims from England who had found their journey's end in a continental brothel.[1] Early in the ninth century already the English in Rome called their quarter a *burh*, and to it in the mid-ninth century came many English visitors, including Alfred himself. At any meeting of the West Saxon *Witan* when Alfred was king there would very likely have been a few at least who knew the Italian cities on the pilgrim route[2] – Milan, Pavia, Piacenza, Pisa, Lucca, Perugia, Spoleto, Viterbo and Rome herself – from personal experience. Alfred had visited Italy twice, and on the second occasion he spent a year in the eternal city.[3] But he was only six or seven at the time of his departure, and so we must be for ever tantalized by the speculation as to how much he really remembered of what he had seen.

THE ELEVENTH CENTURY

An observer of the English scene at the end of the ninth century, however percipient, could hardly have forecast the growth of the English kingdom of Edgar or Cnut; nor could he have foreseen with any clarity the pattern of towns in northern Europe a century-and-a-half later. This was to owe something to Alfred's vision, something to the survival and development of Old English arrangements for shire government, something to such continuity as there was in military necessities and techniques before and after the Norman Conquest; but more than all these to the growth in European wealth and commerce in the eleventh century and to the shape this growth assumed. Of this there are two outstanding monuments: in the Flemish towns, especially Ghent, Bruges and Arras, and in 'Domesday Book'.[4] The marriage of William the Conqueror with Matilda of Flanders may serve as a symbol of the union of the northern plutocracies

---

[1] *Epistola* 78, ed. M. Tangl, p. 169, cited by W. Levison, *England and the Continent in the Eighth Century*, Oxford, 1946, p. 39; cf. ib. pp. 37 ff. for links between England and Italy.

[2] See references in Levison, esp. p. 41; the accounts of Alfred's visits (next note) suggest that he and his father went with a substantial following. On the Italian routes, see P. Rajna in *Atti della Società Italiana per il progresso delle scienze*, vol. v, Rome, 1911, pp. 99–118.

[3] Asser, cc. 8, 11 (ed. Stevenson, pp. 7, 9); *ASC* A, C (etc.) s.a. 853, 855–8. Cf. J. Nelson in *Journal of Ecclesiastical History*, vol. xviii, 1967, pp. 145–63.

[4] See pp. 268 ff.; P. Sawyer, 'The wealth of England in the eleventh century', *TRHS*, 5th Series, vol. xv, 1965, pp. 145–64.

of the eleventh century, and the political involvement of kings and princes played its part in the story, especially in Flanders. But it is primarily a story of trade and industry.

Once a group of huts round a great monastery, Arras was already in the early eleventh century on the way to becoming one of the great cloth-towns of Europe, renowned by the twelfth century at least as far as Italy. The little enclosure at Ghent and the tiny enclosure at Bruges had grown into flourishing industrial and commercial towns. Although London was probably at this time a larger town than either, and could be regarded as the commercial capital of Flanders from certain viewpoints for two centuries to come,[1] the Flemish towns grew from smaller beginnings with greater rapidity than the English, and by that token the more rapidly than the French or German. The formation of these islands of industrial and commercial growth in the eleventh century is in fact of great significance in the European history of the day. Contemporaries may well have observed it more clearly than many modern historians; for William the Conqueror seems to have grasped that the Conquest of England should begin in Flanders, and it was not for nothing that he defied the papal ban for ten years and insisted on marrying his Flemish bride.[2] Modern economic historians have indeed given considerable weight to the patronage of the counts of Flanders among the explanations of the rise of Flanders; yet this must not hide from us that the story on which we have embarked has a very large economic element in it, and that the key to it is the large wealth of England and the even larger wealth of Flanders in the mid-eleventh century.[3]

The English towns of the late eleventh and twelfth centuries form part of the outstanding evidence of England's wealth – comparative wealth, one should rather say, since they were small towns and even England a country of very modest resources by modern standards. Yet the eleventh century was an age crucial in England's economic development, since it was then that Alfred's towns really determined to be towns and not market enclosures, refuges for country-folk or (save for a few) mere vestiges of former glory.

The other notable witness is 'Domesday Book'. In manor after manor, all over England, Domesday confidently records the manor's money

[1] See p. 270.
[2] On the Conqueror's marriage, see D. C. Douglas, *William the Conqueror*, London, 1964, pp. 391–5; *Carmen*, p. 63 and n. 3.
[3] See pp. 268 ff.

value – what it was worth in 1066, what it was worth when the present lord received it, what it was worth in 1086. We may find many reasons why England and no other land should have its Domesday: the need to define the holdings after the chaos of the Norman Conquest; the exceptional, ruthless determination of the king; the Old English organization of hundred and shire; the special genius of the clerk or clerks who planned it, perhaps, in particular (as Galbraith has argued) of the man whose hand wrote 'Domesday Book', volume I.[1] Yet at the end of the day it is hard to believe that there were many parts of Europe where a book whose structure is essentially tenurial could reveal so sophisticated a knowledge of economic values. What is most striking is the penetration of pounds, shillings and pence into the calculations. If almost every manor can be assessed in coin, this can only mean (as has come in recent years to be increasingly appreciated) that such assessments were common in practice – that manors were let for rent; that peasants and middling farmers had ready access to silver pennies in considerable quantities – hardly perhaps a surprise in a country which had paid out such enormous quantities of silver pennies in Danegeld for two or three generations at least, yet an impressive indication of the degree to which money had penetrated the economy, and of the central place of markets, and so of market-towns, in English life. Yet the men who planned Domesday also knew that money and values so expressed did not reveal the whole story. And so they assessed plough-teams and oxen, not to mention the half-ox, the *semi-bos*, who portrays so vividly this premature passion for statistics; they totted up woodland (by pigs per wood), and sometimes also knights and churches. Yet in the end they could not entirely reconcile their tenurial, feudal interest, with a purely economic calculation. As the survey was reduced to its final state, the pigs were eliminated, and with them what may well have been the chief source of England's wealth, the sheep;[2] and London was eliminated too. Thus we are left with a remarkable irony. Domesday is in many ways the supreme witness to England's wealth. Yet most of what was special to England – the export of wool and also (perhaps) of cloth, of slaves and other commodities – can only be glimpsed occasionally between

[1] V. H. Galbraith, *The Making of Domesday Book*, Oxford, 1961, esp. chap. xiii, pp. 198 ff.; supplemented in 'Notes on the career of Samson, Bishop of Worcester', *EHR*, vol. lxxxii, 1967, pp. 86–101.

[2] See Sawyer, *TRHS*, 5th Series, vol. xv, 1965, p. 162. The failure of Domesday to record sheep is indeed a major puzzle which has never been adequately grasped by those who reckon England's wealth lay largely in wool already in 1086.

its lines. It even recorded very unevenly the supreme symbol to the modern historian of England's spare resources, its churches.[1]

The obscure story of the growth of English and continental towns in this age must be reconstructed from every vestige: from the chronicles, charters, laws; from the archaeologist's finds; from the topography and street-names. The chief sources not yet adequately collected or interpreted are the churches, and especially the parish churches of the cities.[2] There can be little doubt that the proliferation of parish churches in English towns, which far exceeded any comparable movement on the Continent, was especially characteristic of the eleventh and early twelfth centuries. Wealth cannot simply be measured in terms of numbers – it is not impossible that the money Edward the Confessor put into Westminster Abbey, or the money Henry I put into the great third church at Cluny,[3] would have paid for two or three score of city churches. But the eighty churches of York, the fifty in Lincoln and Norwich and Winchester, and close on a hundred within the city walls of London – in Winchester and London not less than one per 3½ acres – all reflect a society with money to spare for earthly stone or timber, and treasure in heaven.

II The Urban Renaissance

We have spoken of the urban renaissance, and it is the heart of our story: the cities of Europe were the arteries which it supplied. But what was it and whence did it grow? The question is not easily answered. Between the tenth century and the early thirteenth towns grew and multiplied in every part of western Europe. In Italy, where there were always towns, the city-states flourished until they became as characteristic of the society and culture of the Mediterranean world in the later Middle Ages as they had been in the heyday of ancient Greece and Rome. In northern Europe towns had been a mere shadow or skeleton; nowhere in these centuries did they achieve the independence of their Italian colleagues, but everywhere they became again a characteristic expression of European life, and in a different way they enjoyed their heroic age and their maturity in the same period as did the Italian. The differences between north and south have sometimes been much exaggerated.[4] The northern communes first appeared in the same age as the southern, in the second half of the eleventh

[1] See F. Barlow, *The English Church 1000–1066*, pp. 183 ff.

[2] See chap. 6   [3] See p. 321 and ref. in n. 2.

[4] As, for instance, in the classical English account by M. V. Clarke, *The Medieval City State*, London, 1926. This chapter owes much to Waley; *Cambridge Economic*

century; the earliest consuls in Pisa are recorded in the 1080s, the first hint of a civic oligarchy in London in the same decade. The first Italian chief magistrate or podestà occurs not long before 1150; the first French mayors of consequence are revealed to us in the 1160s or 1170s, and by 1193 at latest London too had a mayor.

Two types of community were especially characteristic expressions of the nature of life in the eleventh and twelfth centuries: monasteries and towns. The monastic growth we can in a measure quantify. Thus in England alone the number of monasteries grew from about sixty to about 500 between the Conquest and the accession of Henry II in 1154, and the number of religious (so far as we can compute them) five or sixfold.[1] No such figures can be produced for the towns. In England, indeed, we can count the towns which were revived in Alfred's day and under his successors, and make some calculation – never wholly satisfactory or precise – of the newcomers of the eleventh and early twelfth centuries; new towns in England and southern France in the period 1150–1250, the highwatermark of the renaissance, have been the subject of a special study by Professor Beresford.[2] Yet these are but the limbs and outer flourishes of the movement; for in Italy, its centre, new towns were rare.

Nor is the documentary record very helpful. Even in the south, municipal records rarely begin before the thirteenth century. Many Italian cities and churches rejoice in collections of charters which are far more copious than the exiguous documents of Anglo-Saxon England.[3] But they are land transactions for the most part, with little to tell us directly of the life, the commerce or the society of the towns. We could wish that we

---

History, vol. iii, ed. M. M. Postan, E. E. Rich and E. Miller, Cambridge, 1963; G. Fasoli, *Dalla 'civitas' al comune nell'Italia settentrionale*, Bologna, 1969; and to the histories of individual cities cited below. On Pisa, see Waley, pp. 56 ff.; G. Volpe, *Studi sulle istituzioni comunali di Pisa*, Pisa, 1902, rev. edn with a valuable introduction by C. Violante, 1970 (for our knowledge of this, and much other help, we are greatly indebted to Professor Violante); see also E. Tolaini, *Forma Pisarum*, Pisa, 1967. On podestà and mayors, see chap. 9. See now also J. K. Hyde, *Society and Politics in Medieval Italy*, London, 1973.

[1] KH, esp. Appendix II, pp. 488 ff.
[2] M. Beresford, *New Towns of the Middle Ages*.
[3] Lucca and Pisa are good examples. In 1970 G. K. undertook a journey to Italy to check the possibility of finding evidence of links with London and England in this period in Italian archives (see below, pp. 270, 274). From this visit, and visits by C. N. L. B. in 1969 and 1971, sprang many of the ideas developed in this chapter.

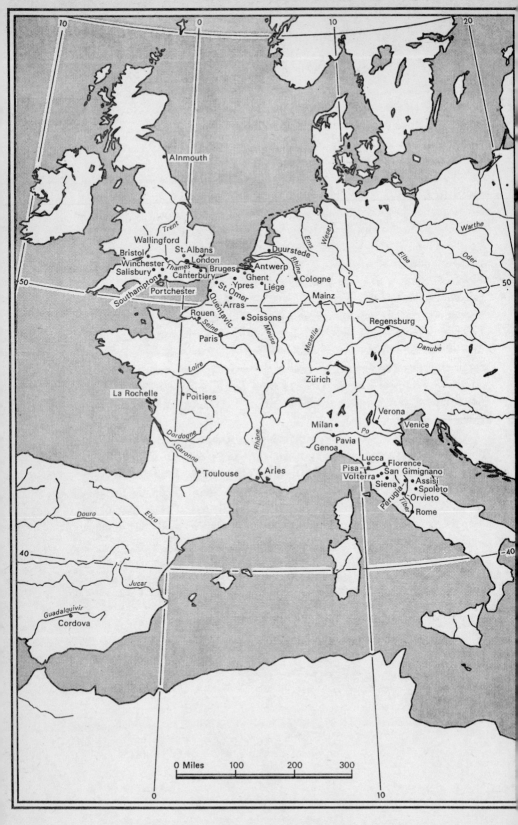

European towns, 800–1216

knew far more of the early sheriffs and mayors of London than we do, yet they are among the best documented of any set of major officials of any city in western Christendom in the twelfth century.

Thus many town histories contain only a threadbare account of the early medieval history of the town, perhaps a discussion of its nature in the ninth or tenth century, lip-service to the critical importance of the eleventh and twelfth, a few stray illustrations of how the patriciate was recruited in that era, or how the city's merchants made their fortune, and then a swift transition to the age when the city's archives become rich and copious. There are, indeed, many exceptions,[1] and historians have not failed to notice the importance of this period; but it is easy to understand why the urban renaissance still waits for its historian.

Heroic attempts have sometimes been made to judge the growth of cities in the Middle Ages from the successive extensions of the city walls. The layout, topography and the physical remains of the cities are indeed the major source for modern study, and investigation of their *enceintes* stems from a genuine recognition of this fact. But simple studies of size are of little use. Especially characteristic of this period is the way in which (as in Greece in the sixth and fifth centuries BC) modest towns flourished alongside the great and enjoyed a measure of independence. The fact that a number of Italian towns prospered exceedingly in the twelfth and thirteenth centuries and were then halted in their tracks by more powerful neighbours helps to explain why their physical appearance is still today exceptionally clear evidence of civic aspiration in this period; and the contrasts – and similarities, equally, though easily and often overlooked – make them ideal subjects for comparison with London, and for sharpening our focus on the aspirations of northern cities.

In few towns can one learn more about this period from their stones than in San Gimignano, famous for its feudal towers, and its neighbour Volterra, which boasts an exceptionally early town hall.[2] Yet San Gimignano's walls lie mainly (so far as is at present known) on Etruscan and Roman foundations, and Volterra never in the Middle Ages came near its ancient size. At the other extreme, the citizens of Florence undertook in the fourteenth century an enormous extension of their *enceinte*. Much of this still survives and encloses ample gardens and parks at its periphery;

[1] See pp. 66–7 n.

[2] See E. Fiumi, *Storia economica e sociale di San Gimignano*, Florence, 1961. The early history of Volterra is conveniently summarized in H. H. Scullard, *The Etruscan Cities and Rome*, London, 1967, pp. 146 ff., 299.

and it is clear that it has always done so.[1] London is unusual among the great cities of the Middle Ages in that it remained content with a line of walls only slightly changed at the two points where it met the river.[2] Yet already by 1100 it had spilt beyond its gates and formed faubourgs, which were to be protected by bars on the main roads, but never by defences; and even so it was possible for the space within the walls to hold a far higher population in later centuries than the whole of London in the Middle Ages. In the late seventeenth century, it has been calculated, London within the walls housed some 70,000 people. Its population in the Middle Ages can only be conjectured, and the guesses for its peak, presumably about 1300, have ranged from 20,000 to 50,000; even if one supposes[3] that the latter figure is nearer the truth, perhaps even itself a slight underestimate, it seems clear that the Roman walls were capable of housing the whole medieval population and more. When the *enceinte* of a great city was extended, we may be sure that it is a sign of prosperity and confidence; but no defined proportion to the size of its expanding population can be presumed, nor does it follow that a city content with its traditional walls was any less prosperous.

This comparison, however, points one contrast between England and the Continent. Though London's walls were used for defence, it was not expected that they would often have to stand a siege; the assumption of most citizens and all kings of the twelfth century, no doubt, was that it was a city of peace in a land normally peaceful.[4] The walls and towers of San

---

[1] Cf. Y. Renouard, *Les Villes d'Italie*, nouv. édn, 1969, vol. ii, pp. 269 ff., with map (see also Waley, p. 36); Renouard, *Hist. de Florence*, 2nd edn, Paris, 1967; R. Davidsohn, *Geschichte von Florenz*, vol. iv, pt 3, (edn of Berlin, 1927), esp. pp. 247 ff. On the architectural history of Tuscan towns, see W. Braunfels, *Mittelalterliche Stadtbaukunst in der Toskana*, 3rd edn, Berlin, 1966.

[2] Contrast Trier, where the medieval *enceinte* never expanded to more than about half that of the Roman city, or Paris, which grew in a series of concentric circles from a small core. These are characteristic examples: see Ganshof, plates 28, 34, and *passim* for many similar cases.

[3] Broadly speaking, all estimates of medieval population are supposition, although fourteenth- and fifteenth-century taxation records sometimes give a basis for calculation, and there is copious evidence for shifts in population. The figures which have been suggested for the population of London in the twelfth and thirteenth centuries have no such basis. For the seventeenth century calculations (almost 70,000 within and 54,000 without the walls) see P. E. Jones and A. V. Judges in *EcHR*, 1st Series, vol. vi, 1935-6, pp. 45–63, esp. p. 54; D. V. Glass, introd. to *London Inhabitants within the Walls, 1695*, LRS, 1966, p. xx.

[4] But see pp. 37 ff.

Gimignano and Volterra are witness to an assumption entirely different. Every Italian city aspired to have its independence, and in the twelfth and thirteenth centuries this meant a private army and private warfare against its neighbours.[1]

Yet most of the time it was not the difference but the similarities of which the walls of Volterra and London were the symbols. Of power and prestige, of might if need be, of the great markets publicly protected from thieves and smugglers, of the deep aspiration of the citizens to be free: all this we may read in the walls of medieval cities, and much more. It is reasonable, therefore, to go on and look at the other aspirations of a medieval city revealed by the copious remains that one can see in north and central Italy, to enquire what they tell us of the image that a city wished to reveal to the world, and of its inner life.

THE IDEA OF THE CITY

We must not look for any idea too simple or monolithic. The monastic and civic chroniclers of the twelfth century talked of cities, towns and villages as we do, but the words show an astonishing instability in their use.[2] In Latin a city might be *urbs*, *civitas* or *castrum*; a town might be *castrum*, *castellum*, *oppidum*, *burgus* or *vicus*; a village *vicus* or *villa*. Any possibility of a serious semantic discussion is happily destroyed by the vagueness of the central, key word *castrum*, which can mean indifferently castle, fortified town, fortified centre or quarter of a town, or just town or city. It can be the other half of a *burgus* – *castrum* being the royal or noble headquarters, *burgus* the merchants' quarter; or they can be synonymous. Yet there were in our period many people who used the words *urbs* and *civitas* – as did FitzStephen in his description of London – and knew that they had been used for many great cities of the ancient world, Greek cities, Roman cities, Rome and new Rome, Jerusalem old and new, St Augustine's City of God and earthly, or devilish, city. In a similar way the

---

[1] See Waley, chaps 4 and 6. A good example is the warfare between Assisi and Perugia, which led to the imprisonment of the young St Francis *c.* 1204–5 (Thomas de Celano, *Vita secunda S. Francisci*, pt i, c. 4, ed. in *Analecta Franciscana*, vol. x, Quaracchi, 1926–41, p. 132).

[2] See Ennen, *passim*, esp. pt 2, chap. 1, pp. 124 ff., 130 ff., 152 ff.; Fasoli (pp. 66–7 n. 4), pp. 15 ff.; J. J. Verbruggen in *Revue Belge de philologie et d'histoire*, vol. xxviii, 1950, pp. 147–55 (on 'castrum'): *Mittellateinisches Wörterbuch*, ed. O. Prinz and J. Schneider, vol. i, cols 1622–4 (burgus), vol. ii, pp. 338–9, 347–50 (castellum, castrum).

outward form of a medieval city could be used to stress its ancient lineage and continuity, its new-found military glory and strength, its power, prestige and wealth, and, above all, God's blessing on it in an age which lavished its surplus wealth on churches and cathedrals. No single idea and aim could define the philosophy of medieval cities, nor the reasons which made men seek them out. There was much variety. Yet nearly all had walls to keep enemies at bay and reveal their earthly power and their relation to the heavenly city; they had markets and quarters for artisans and for industry and commonly for peasants as well; a town hall and other guildhalls; and a multitude of churches. The medieval city was the home of a community at once military and mercantile, practical and ideal, gracious and squalid, commercial, agricultural, administrative and social – or, to adapt Polonius' words, tragical, comical, historical and pastoral.

CONTINUITY

Of continuity the Italian cities all speak with accents clear or muffled according to the degree of modern rebuilding. We may study Etruscan gates at Volterra, Orvieto and Perugia – Perugia above all, where the massive piers support a Roman arch and a Renaissance loggia, and tell the whole story of the city's greatness; and numerous hill-forts carry the physiognomy still of Etruscan towns, with Roman features, medieval streets, houses, town halls and especially churches.[1] The cities of the plain still show the rigid grid of the Roman town planners. Thus Verona (see **Plate 12**) is set in a bend of the Adige, roughly pear-shaped; and many a visitor has tried to walk from the Roman gate near the stalk of the pear to the centre of the river bend, to find himself frustrated by a fixed pattern of streets which always carries him a little to the right of where he wishes, or expects, to go. This represents the Roman pattern laid down, according to a formula which paid no attention to the shape of the site, in the first century BC.[2] For all the ebb and flow of life between, for all the revivals and rebuildings, Verona's pattern has remained substantially unaltered. The same is true of many Roman towns of the Mediterranean world. In Gaul and Britain, however, it is exceedingly rare to find a Roman town preserving the pattern of its streets: the line of walls and the site of gates may influence a town plan to this day, as in Trier, Chester, Chichester or

---

[1] See **Plates** 1–2, 13–15.
[2] See *Verona e il suo territorio*, vol. i, esp. pp. 186 ff.

York, and (less obviously) in the City of London;[1] occasionally a major cross-roads may survive, as in Carfax at Oxford and in the centre of Gloucester. But the pattern of streets is usually of the age of Alfred or soon after. Even in Provence, where theatres and amphitheatres still proclaim the Roman presence, and Romanesque artists and architects studied Roman architecture and imitated it, the pattern of Roman streets has usually disappeared. From the summit of the arena at Arles one may look across the town to the Rhone, and the contrast between the order of the Roman arena and the disorder of the streets beyond is striking. In the planned towns of the Middle Ages, whether planned by Alfred and his successors or by the prospectors of the twelfth and thirteenth centuries, a grid is common; but it is never rigid in form, always flexible to the land and to the needs of markets and churches. New Salisbury to this day remains a striking illustration, a true grid, set beside the larger rectangle of the cathedral close; but no angles in the town plan are exact right-angles.[2]

CHANGE AND GROWTH

The relation of continuity and change in northern cities is especially clear in modern Zürich, where the power of tradition has forbidden the erasure of the past in spite of the great prosperity of the modern burghers.[3] The result is that in the heart of a present-day conurbation one finds a sprawling town of the nineteenth century, and within that town a tight medieval core with much of the City's history written on its face. The centre of modern Zürich lies where the Zürchersee and the rivers Limmat and Sihl meet, and its ancient heart lies by the Limmat. Here is a little hill on which the Romans planted the first citadel, later to be replaced by the early medieval castle. In the thirteenth century the citizens of Zürich freed themselves from the Zähringen dukes, and in the fourteenth levelled the castle and planted lime trees; to this day the Lindenhof proudly declares the fact that no tyrant's castle lords it over the town, and is the symbol of civic freedom. From the little hill of the Lindenhof the town spread in the

---

[1] See p. 111.

[2] See *Historic Towns*, vol. i, fasc. on Salisbury; and, in general, Beresford, *New Towns of the Middle Ages*.

[3] For what follows, see K. Dändliker, *Geschichte der Stadt und des Kantons Zürich*, vol. i (to 1400), Zürich, 1908, esp. pp. 37 ff., 43, 61, 65–71; more briefly in A. Largiadér, *Geschichte von Stadt und Landschaft Zürich*, 2 vols, Erlenbach-Zürich, 1945 (with useful bibliography). See Plates 16–18.

early Middle Ages towards the lake; and also beyond the Limmat, out
from the bridge head on the river's northern bank. Three great churches
symbolize this expansion. The old city church, St Peter's, lies near the
Lindenhof. Across the Limmat, in the early Middle Ages, were discovered
or invented the tombs of two Roman martyrs, St Felix and St Regula,
near the place assigned by tradition to their martyrdom. Their authenticity is more than doubtful, but the part they played in the growth of
Zürich was none the less significant. Here the Carolingian rulers of the
mid and late ninth century planted what seems to have been a double
monastery for clerks or canons and nuns. On the same site in the twelfth
century grew up the fine Romanesque church, the Grossmünster as it is
today, though adapted to suit the eloquence of Zwingli and much restored.
The nuns meanwhile, in accordance with normal twelfth-century opinions,
had the width of the Limmat put between them and the canons, and were
settled on their present site on reclaimed land towards the lake – the
chronology is far from certain, but this seems the best received opinion –
some time in the twelfth century. Thus the architecture and the sculpture
of the Grossmünster, and the site of the Fraumünster, are major monuments of Zürich's first age of prosperity and documents of considerable
importance, for written records of twelfth-century Zürich are scanty,[1] and
in a town which has prospered as continuously as London major early
monuments are rare survivals. In and after the twelfth century the *enceinte*
continued to grow in all directions from the Lindenhof, but especially
along the banks of the Limmat, and beyond the Grossmünster up the
the northern slope, where the Neumarkt, or new market, which is so
common a feature of Swiss and German towns, still shows the limit of
Zürich's medieval growth. Finally, in the sixteenth–seventeenth centuries
the great bastions were thrown out beyond the medieval walls, whose lines
may still be traced in the pleasant meandering stream which follows the
scientifically designed firing lines of the bastions' ditches.

[1] See *Urkundenbuch der Stadt und Landschaft Zürich*, ed. J. Escher and P. Schweizer,
vol. i, Zürich, 1888. The fullest discussion of the origin of the Grossmünster and Fraumünster is by E. Egloff, *Der Standort des Monasteriums Ludwigs des Deutschen in
Zürich*, Zürich, (1949); cf. R. Folz, *Le souvenir et la légende de Charlemagne . . .*, Paris,
1950, pp. 344–7. It is probable that both minsters were founded where the Grossmünster now stands – the traditional site of the martyrdom of St Felix and St Regola
– in the mid-ninth century, the Fraumünster crossing the river in the twelfth century.
But St Peter's church is the old chapel of the palace and probably the main parish
church in early times (cf. Dändliker, vol. i, p. 43). The Neumarkt is referred to in a
document of 1145 (*Urkundenbuch*, vol. i, no. 288; cf. Dändliker, vol. i, pp. 70 f.).

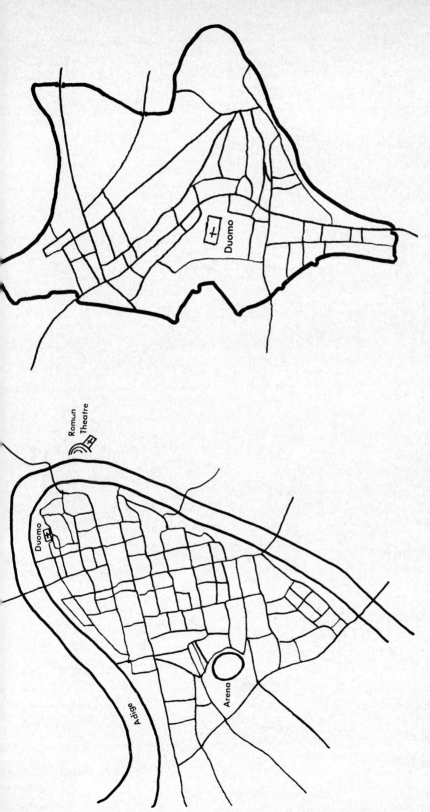

12. Plan of Verona, showing the way in which the remains of the Roman grid
fit into the bend of the River Adige (*see p. 72*)

13. Plan of San Gimignano: an Etruscan hill-top town, in which
the streets meander as fancy and the contours decided

11 San Gimignano, still displaying the image of an Italian hill city of the twelfth–thirteenth centuries (*see pp. 78–9*)

15. San Gimignano. The tower immediately right of centre, with the tiny dome, was one of those built by the noble family of the Gregorii, sprung from a rich merchant of the mid-twelfth century

16. From the Lindenhof looking east and north-east, left, across the River Limatt to the Grossmünster, with the lake and the Alps in the distance. By R. Bodmer, after J. J. Meyer, *c.* 1830

17. Plan by Joseph Murer, 1576, looking north across the Limatt, showing the late-medieval *enceinte*: on the south bank, right, is the Fraumünster

18. Plan by Heinrich Vogel, 1705, showing the same plan with the sixteenth–seventeenth-century bastions added. 'Grundriss der Statt Zürich samt deroselben Fortifications-werken Anno 1705'

16.

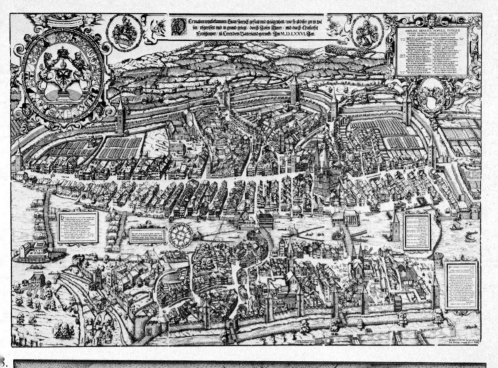

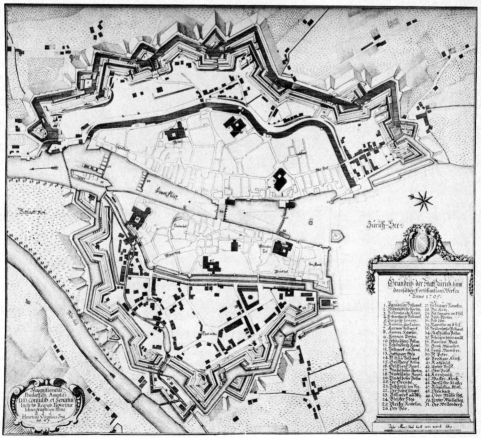

19. Egbert, 829–30, the first coin after 800 with mint name LVNDONIA CIVIT(AS), probably to celebrate West Saxon control of the city

20. Alfred, *c.* 886, with a portrait of the king, evidently copied from fourth-century Roman portraits, on the obverse, and the monogram of 'Londonia' on the reverse. Alfred may have celebrated the events of 886 by issuing coins with London named on them in imitation of Egbert, his grandfather

21. A short-cross coin of Henry II of 1180 by Philip Aimer. The reduction of the mints in 1180 increased the dominance of London. Philip Aimer of Tours was brought to London by Henry II to administer the recoinage; he was the first of a long line of continental moneyers at the Tower

19.

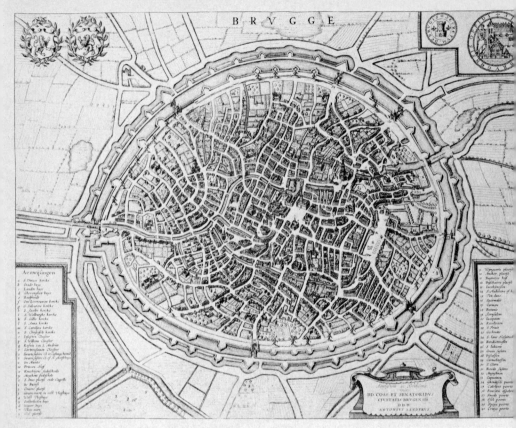

22. Bruges, from A. Sanderus, *Flandria Illustrata* (1641), vol. i, pp. 182–3; the top of the pla
roughly south-east; the main *enceinte* late thirteenth century, with sixteenth–seventeenth-cen
bastions. In the centre the white space is the old market-place; to its left the great church o
Donatian, the centre of a small rectangle of buildings which marks the old *castrum*. Round
central area can be seen the rough rectangle of the ditch which approximately marked the i
enceinte of 1127—the line of the river, from left to right, defines two sides of this rectangle,
a third is marked by the long white space of the later cattle-market (*see pp. 76 & 269*)

Zürich has always been a city of traders and bankers, and for many centuries the capital of a fiercely independent canton. The river, the bridges, the markets, the churches and the walls make its history, and the formless pattern of its ancient streets reveals its piecemeal growth. There is enough to show that the twelfth century marked an epoch in its story; nothing like enough to tell us how marked it was.

The Italian cities, by and large, tell their story more completely than their northern sisters, partly because their prosperity was (for the most part) more pronounced in this period, their pride in it more ostentatious, their addiction to durable materials, brick and stone, greater than in the north; and some of the Italian cities have not prospered in more recent centuries as they did in the twelfth and thirteenth.[1] None of these factors should be too greatly stressed. FitzStephen's rhapsody on London goes far beyond any literary record of civic pride from twelfth-century Italy; there are many towns in northern Europe with stone houses of this age,[2] and few which cannot show some trace of their stone churches; and though Siena may proclaim that its great days came at the turn of the thirteenth and fourteenth centuries, and Florence that its heyday was later still, it is striking how some even of the most prosperous cities still have much of this age to show us.

Milan had already replaced Pavia as the capital of Lombardy, and was one of the largest towns of Europe, before the expansion of the late eleventh and twelfth centuries. It has flourished so often since that we cannot expect to find large traces of this particular epoch, but in the area round the Basilica of Sant'Ambrogio one may see the way in which the ancient Roman *enceinte* was expanded to include what had been the region of cemeteries and of *martyria*.[3] The main body of the Basilica itself reveals the lavish expense on the beautification of this quarter in the late eleventh and twelfth centuries, and immediately outside it the twelfth-century gateway rebuilt in the fourteenth, the *Pusterla* of Sant'Ambrogio, tells the same story. The tale is also told by traces of the new *enceintes* of many towns widely scattered, and in particular by the visible witness of the gates

---

[1] Note the contrast between San Gimignano, so little altered since the fourteenth century, and Milan, a city of the nineteenth and twentieth centuries with much that is ancient hidden in it.

[2] In England they are rare (see **Plates 32–3**); the houses in Lincoln are the best surviving examples, but there are fine cellars in Canterbury and elsewhere.

[3] See *Storia di Milano*, vols iii and iv, Milan, 1954.

and walls of Lucca and Mainz;[1] elsewhere, as at Bruges (**Plate 22**), Ghent and Liège, the plans of these *enceintes* can still be traced.

Although the literature of the twelfth and thirteenth centuries has much to say of cities – descriptions of fine towns in the romantic, courtly vernacular literature, discussions of divine and earthly cities in philosophical and theological literature – the authors who discussed the value, use or nature of contemporary cities in this age were surprisingly few. The city in the works of John of Salisbury or St Thomas Aquinas, townsmen both, is essentially the ancient city of the Greeks or Romans, an academic city. Yet it is implicit in their writings,[2] and explicit in the monuments of these centuries, that clear and forceful ideas of considerable variety were held on the place of the city in human affairs. The outstanding evidence, paradoxically, lies in the foundation of new towns in the north and the destruction of old in the south. The city-states of Italy became larger and more self-conscious in the twelfth and thirteenth centuries. Their increase partly reflects growing population and wealth; but it was also due to deliberate concentration.[3] The nobles of the *contado* and dwellers in the smaller towns and villages were encouraged, cajoled or compelled to move into the city; and in due course wealth and power came to be concentrated in fewer and fewer large centres; hence the survival, so little altered, of San Gimignano. Thus towns were fossilized as cities grew. In the north, on the other hand, this period saw the formation of many new settlements.[4] Most notable patrons of these were the English nobility and the Angevin kings: one hundred new towns sprang up in England *c.* 1150–1250; more than three hundred *bastides* were founded in Gascony and Aquitaine. Some of the English planned towns, like Salisbury or Hull, grew into places of substance; most of the *bastides* were modest, military enclosures for markets and small groups of people. But they all represent a philosophy of towns surprisingly self-conscious. The towns of Wales represent the last phase of this movement: Edward I's attempt to implant Anglo-French patterns of living and trafficking on the conquered Welsh. But

---

[1] On Mainz, see Ganshof, *passim*, esp. pp. 34, 54 and n. (destruction of walls in 1163, reconstruction in 1200), **Plate 22**.

[2] On John of Salisbury see esp. H. Liebeschütz, *Mediaeval Humanism in the life and writings of John of Salisbury*, London, 1951, pp. 97–8, commenting on his lack of interest in the contemporary commune, in contrast to his strong academic interest in Athens and Rome.

[3] Waley, pp. 110 ff.

[4] For what follows, see Beresford, *New Towns of the Middle Ages*.

perhaps its most vivid monument is Aigues-Mortes, St Louis' crusading port amid the infested, dead waters of the Camargue, a wonderfully preserved example of a medieval community which could only have expected to survive by divine intervention.[1]

These planned towns were built round ample market-places; and the growth of towns provided many others apart from Zürich with a Neumarkt. The spread of these markets even in remote country districts reflects the economic basis of the urban renaissance, which was the fructification by selling and trading of the wealth of communities still in most areas mainly agricultural. Even at the height of their prosperity, one of the chief concerns of the most industrial of cities, be it Florence, Milan, Arras, Bruges or London, was its food market. In the course of the thirteenth century initiative and control in most prosperous cities fell increasingly into the hands of a mercantile oligarchy, who earned and held their place in civic society by their contribution to its long-distance trade. No doubt there had long been places of which this was true, such as Duurstede and Quentavic in the eighth and ninth centuries,[2] and Venice throughout the Middle Ages. But the city aristocracies of the eleventh and twelfth centuries were for the most part composed of a wider variety of social types, rural and urban, landed and mercantile; epitomes of the economic life of their *contadi*. The local landowners, the feudal nobility, acquired town houses, and jostled in the courts and the communes with men whose first interest lay in the counting house.

THE PATRICIATE

It has long been disputed whether the patricians who came to rule the cities of Europe in the central Middle Ages (to adapt Lady Bracknell's words) were born in the purple of commerce, or had risen from the ranks of the aristocracy – or, as the problem was more commonly phrased, were sons of the feudal nobility or self-made merchants. For two reasons, the problem thus stated is now seen to be quite unreal. First of all, we only know the origin of a tiny percentage of the patricians of the crucial period between 1050 and 1250, and these mainly from a few cities, possibly not typical. We must be resigned to ignorance. Secondly, it takes too little

[1] Cf. C. Petit-Dutaillis, *Les communes françaises*, Paris, 1947, pp. 135-6; Beresford pp. 111, 140.
[2] See p. 262.

account of the pattern of economic life in this age. The twelfth-century merchant was an adventurer who took enormous risks. If he succeeded, he could grow rich very fast, and in many places, may be, his sons could mingle with the landed gentry and melt into the landscape. There were such adventurers who rose from poverty to wealth, probably a great number of them, since enterprise was the chief quality needed and investment by men of established wealth in such adventures already common by the mid-twelfth century.[1] This we can assert, without entering into the ancient dispute as to how typical was the career of the beachcomber (or wrecker) turned monk and hermit, St Godric of Finchale, or the more mundane version represented by the story of the two Italian self-made merchants Sceva and Ollo told by Walter Map.[2] These two 'boys of low birth, acquired at the same time a small capital, and in our days became first hawkers of small commodities, and then by continued success of large ones. From packmen they rose to be carriers, from being carriers to be masters of many waggoners and always remained trusty partners. With the growth of their trade . . . the love of money grew as great as grew the wealth. The bond of partnership and the joint union of stock now became irksome, and separate ownership was agreed upon.' Hence the quarrel which is the subject of Map's tale. How common this kind of progress was we can never know. Beside such men sat the landowners, or younger sons of landowners, turned merchants. This is not a simple story: some Italian cities compelled them to come in, others ejected them; in some there was endemic conflict between peaceful merchants and warlike feudatories; in more the factions followed families and groups, not classes or interests – as in the Verona of Romeo and Juliet.[3] The towers of San Gimignano and the prose of William FitzStephen declare the presence of great men's houses within the walls of cities moderate and large.[4] In most

---

[1] See esp. Y. Renouard, *Les Hommes d'affaires italiens*, nouv. edn, 1968, esp. pp. 69 ff.; A. Sapori, *Le Marchand italien au moyen âge*, Paris 1952, has excellent general bibliography.

[2] *De nugis curialium*, dist. iv, c. 16 (ed. M. R. James, pp. 197 ff.; trans. James, pp. 218 ff.).

[3] Cf. Waley, pp. 110 ff.; chap. 6.

[4] E. Fiumi, *Storia economica e sociale di S. Gimignano*, pp. 45 ff., shows that the *torri* of San Gimignano were not built by an established feudal aristocracy, but by men who had risen to be *boni homines* by acquiring mercantile and landed wealth. Thus one of the finest surviving towers was owned by Gregorio di Gregorio, three times podestà in the early thirteenth century, whose family cannot be traced back much behind the mid-twelfth century. The splendid absurdity of these *torri* may in part

an alliance between aspiring merchants and established landed wealth was probably a necessity; for the landowners provided money for investment and officered the armies which were felt on all hands to be somehow an essential ornament of every civic community. To the eye untrained in medieval warfare the towers appear militarily useless,[1] and one is perhaps not wholly mistaken in assuming that they were more symbols of status than weapons of war. They certainly represent an extraordinarily active, aspiring, belligerent, creative society.

THE URBAN RENAISSANCE

At the end of the day it is the creativity of this society which the cities help to prove and which in its turn explains them. The growth of cities in this period doubtless reflects a general rise in population. As with the monasteries, it is almost certain that growth of cities far outstripped the general expansion; some cities suffered slimming exercises, more gathered their people in. In a host of ways the age of the twelfth-century renaissance saw new beginnings and a large extension of the opportunities open to men. Many thousands found peace in a monastic life, or if not peace, a warfare at any rate partly spiritual;[2] yet for those who sought peace the alternatives became much more numerous and more attractive: the secular church gained several new dimensions, with the development of schools and universities, of the clerical staffs of kings and bishops; industry and trade took on a new complexion. The enterprise of farming and land-management, farming of tithes and all manner of taxes greatly increased; beside the merchants grew up bankers and moneylenders.[3] In the late twelfth century the growing specialization of the academic schools, with their immensely complex structures of legal and theological *summae*, was not the only evidence of increasing sophistication. In many ways the evidence

reflect the parvenu origin of their builders. But there is danger of confusion of terms here, for Gregorio di Gregorio was a patrician of the third generation, a man of similar background both to Henry FitzAilwin and to Henry of Cornhill, that is, a man with a fortune based as much in land and office as in mercantile wealth, so far as we know. See Plates 13–15.

[1] As is true of quite a number of apparently fortified medieval buildings. Cf. C. Hohler, in *Flowering of the Middle Ages*, ed. J. Evans, London, 1966, p. 162 for examples of fanciful castles.

[2] Even monks were sometimes involved in warfare, and monastic officials constantly in other affairs of the world.

[3] See pp. 222 ff.

of vernacular literature, art and architecture is even more striking. The simple idiom and monolithic world of sentiment of the 'Song of Roland' was replaced by a literature of much greater variety and sophistication, especially in French and German, written by a wide variety of folk: minstrels, knights, barons, even kings, and above all clerks of very various education.[1] Though little of this reflects the inner life of the cities, it helps us to understand the world of hectic creativity and the bewildering variety that we find in every sphere of life in the late twelfth century.

In many cities, the sworn commune, the militant patrician oligarchy gathering and preserving its privileges, was turned against the established order, king, great nobles and bishops. In the south of France and northern Italy especially, many members of the communes seem to have been anti-clerical and to have sympathized with heresy and heretics. Some historians have seen evidence here of class conflict or fundamental divergences of interest. This is simply a mistake. Many patricians were related to the aristocracy they fought; many, perhaps most, bishops had family ties within the communes of their own or neighbouring towns. The characteristic status symbols of the city patriciate, even before walls, gates and towers, were the churches they endowed and enriched. No doubt there was great variety of interest, aspiration and outlook; for variety is the keynote of the urban renaissance. But the typical city father of the twelfth century was fervently anti-clerical and a princely benefactor to the Church.

A stroll in the streets of Lucca reveals some twenty Romanesque churches, those that survive from a far larger number, not boxes like those of London, but ample in size and rich in ornament, however monotonous the repetition of a single design.[2] In contrast, the monastic complex of Santo Stefano in Bologna contains seven churches all quite different, most built or rebuilt in this same period, monuments to a range of local cults.[3] Both reflect the assumption that earthly treasure is ephemeral and some permanent memorial in stone is its natural destiny; or that stone churches make good weight in the recording angel's scale; or else, quite simply, sheer delight in the creation of beautiful buildings. In many cities the

---

[1] See Brooke, *Twelfth Century Renaissance*, London, 1969, chap. VI.

[2] A convenient guide is I. B. Barsali, *Guida di Lucca*, 2nd edn, Lucca, 1970.

[3] See G. Aprato, *Bologna, complesso di S. Stefano*, Tesori d'Arte Cristiana, Bologna, 1966. The seven churches of the eleventh–thirteenth centuries were reduced to four in nineteenth–twentieth-century restorations.

churches have endured while secular buildings and rich men's houses have left little trace; this may lead us to exaggerate the concentration of resources in church building from this epoch. Oddly enough, historians have tended to lay more stress on the anti-clericalism of the age. The churches could also lead us to exaggerate the novelty, for church building has been in a measure a feature of many different centuries, from the fourth to the nineteenth; yet not greatly, for wealth and artistic creation were concentrated in the most striking manner in the expression of creative piety, and if the fashion is as manifest in *trecento* Siena and *quattrocento* Florence, it is but the continuation of what one can see most visibly in Pisa and Assisi.[1]

These two cities reflect in a quite ironical way the ambiguous relations of God and Mammon between the eleventh and thirteenth centuries. The prosperity of Pisa was established in a great piratical expedition in the 1060s in which (to put it another way) the cross triumphed over the crescent, and the rich booty was largely invested in founding a new cathedral. A whole quarter of the city was set aside as a thank-offering to God, and there the foundations of a new cathedral and baptistery were laid. Both were 200 years in the building, and finally adorned in the thirteenth century with pulpits by Pisa's most famous artists, the sculptors Nicola and Giovanni Pisano. Meanwhile the fair field set aside for these churches was also provided with a hospital and other charitable institutions, and with the famous twelfth-century campanile, the *Torre pendente*, or leaning tower; later, too, with a cloister which is frankly and solely commemorative in character. The baptistery was the symbol of the religious and parochial unity of many Italian cities, in Pisa as in Florence. In Assisi, meanwhile, the addiction to wealth and secular values of Pietro Bernardone had led his son Francesco, or Francis, to search for a life more romantic or more spiritual, and ultimately to found the Order of Friars Minor and to become the apostle of poverty. After his death the citizens conspired with his followers and the Church's hierarchy to build a splendid monument to him. The only podestà of Assisi who are more than names to us from Francis' lifetime were a heretic and an anti-clerical, but from that day to this Assisi has been rich in beautiful churches and in pilgrims to the Poverello's shrine.

To the outward eye, London has shed most of the visible evidence of the urban and cultural renaissances of the twelfth century; yet not all, for Hollar's drawings, the crypt of St Mary-le-Bow[2] and archaeological

[1] See p. 7 (Assisi), 66–7 and n. (Pisa).   [2] See **Plate 42**.

reconstruction enable us to visualize twelfth-century St Paul's and the throng of lesser churches; and London has preserved one of the most striking witnesses of the close relation between these movements in the description of London by William FitzStephen.

4

The Materials: How much can be known?[1]

THE SOURCES

Chronicles

ON 1 DECEMBER 1135, King Henry I was alive and dead, and within a few days his nephew Count Stephen had crossed the channel:

And after landing with a very small retinue, as was stated above, he journeyed hastily to London, the capital, the queen of the whole kingdom. At his arrival the town was immediately filled with excitement and came to meet him with acclamation, and whereas it had been sadly mourning the grievous death of its protector Henry, it revelled in exultant joy as though it had recovered him in Stephen. So the elders and those most shrewd in counsel summoned an assembly, and taking prudent forethought for the state of the kingdom, on their own initiative, they agreed unanimously to choose a king. For, they said, every kingdom was exposed to calamities from ill-fortune when a representative of the whole government and a fount of justice was lacking. It was therefore worth their while to appoint as soon as possible a king who, with a view to re-establishing peace for the benefit of all, would meet the insurgents of the kingdom in arms

[1] This chapter surveys the field, but does not attempt a systematic cataloguing of sources: for those in print, see J. M. Sims, *London and Middlesex published Records, a handlist*, LRS, 1970; for unprinted, see Bibliography. For records in the Guildhall and Guildhall Library, see P. E. Jones and R. Smith, *A Guide to the Records in the Corporation of London Guildhall Records Office and the Guildhall Library Muniment Room*, 1951.

and would justly administer the enactments of the laws. Moreover, they said, it was their own right and peculiar privilege that if their king died from any cause a successor should immediately be appointed by their own choice; and they had no one at hand who could take the king's place and put an end to the great dangers threatening the kingdom except Stephen, who, they thought, had been brought among them by Providence; all regarded him as suited to the position on account both of his high birth and of his good character. So, when these arguments had been heard and favourably received by all without any open objection, they made out a general resolution admitting him to the sovereignty and appointed him king with universal approval, though a mutual compact was previously made and an oath taken on both sides, as was commonly asserted, that as long as he lived the citizens would aid him with their resources and protect him with their power, while he would gird himself with all his might to pacify the kingdom for the benefit of them all.[1]

At the opening of any study of the sources for London's history in the central Middle Ages must stand the chronicles, for on them we have already heavily relied; they are the traditional basis for the historian at work in the period, and the eleventh and twelfth centuries were the golden age of medieval literary history. Terse annals, like the 'Anglo-Saxon Chronicle', more leisurely and reflective chronicles or histories, like the works of William of Malmesbury, and biographies, like the Life of St Thomas of Canterbury to which William FitzStephen attached his *Description*, have much to tell us of London's history.[2] The *Description* apart, they have uses and limitations well illustrated in this passage from the *Gesta Stephani*, a chronicle with some elements of biography, since it deals essentially with the reign of a single king, its hero. The *Gesta* was probably written by Robert, bishop of Bath, a protégé and admirer of Stephen, who later changed sides and had become a fervent supporter of Henry II by the time he completed the book, early in Henry's reign. Robert was not a Londoner, and the place he allots to the city, 'the capital, the queen of the whole kingdom', is not due to civic pride, but partly a reflection of London's actual importance, partly of the happy part

---

[1] *Gesta Stephani*, ed. and trans. K. R. Potter, NMT, 1955, pp. 3–4; on the *Gesta*, see R. H. C. Davis in *EHR*, vol. lxxvii, 1962, pp. 209–32 and in *Gesta*, 2nd edn by Potter and Davis, OMT, forthcoming.

[2] See pp. 112 ff.

(as the author saw it) that she played in the making of Stephen. The trouble is, however, that Stephen was in some senses a usurper, and it is extremely probable that the author exaggerated the citizens' claim in order to boost his hero's standing as king; it is also probable that he tampered with the passage in later years so as to eradicate elements in Stephen's claim injurious to Henry II.[1] It is noticeable, furthermore, that in a political chronicle London only plays a conspicuous part when she impinges on such events as these, that the author is not interested in telling us who the Londoners were, nor in the citizens as individuals, nor in defining the oath and 'mutual compact' which is the first adumbration of the city's commune. There are no civic chronicles from this period,[2] and so it is by such incidental notices, by providing the political framework of London's history, that the narrative sources illuminate our subject.

FitzStephen's *Description* must have a chapter to itself; the other helpful literary sources are mainly annals and chronicles of London's religious houses. High among these must come the brief chronicle which prefaces the cartulary of Holy Trinity, Aldgate, revealing the religious and social purpose of the house and opening the window to a whole chapter on social welfare and ecclesiastical observance; and the curiously similar document which describes the foundation of St Bartholomew's.[3]

Documents

For the secular life of the City, and the large area where the church and lay society met, we look to accounts, surveys, legal records and charters. From about 1250 on, these are very copious; in our period much less profuse, and therefore demanding a proportionately thorough and careful sifting. Thus for the period 800–1066, apart from charters endowing St

[1] Cf. Brooke, *Saxon and Norman Kings*, London, 1963, p. 53.

[2] There are a number of later chronicles, of which the late thirteenth-century *Liber de Antiquis Legibus* by the city magnate Arnald FitzThedmar is the most important (ed. T. Stapleton, Camden Society, vol. xxxiv, 1846, henceforth *LAL*). For a list of London chronicles, see R. Flenley (ed.), *Six Town Chronicles of England*, Oxford, 1911, pp. 96–8. Most were composed in the fifteenth century and their early entries, often beginning in 1189, are sparse and derivative. Apart from the *Ann. Londonienses* (1195–1330, a major source for the early fourteenth century, ed. W. Stubbs, *Chrons. of . . . Edward I and Edward II*, Rolls Series, 1882–3, vol. i) the main exception is Brit. Mus. Harl. Roll C. 8, which Stow consulted and which is closely related to the brief chronicle in *Cart. Aldgate*, nos 1072–3. See also C. L. Kingsford, *Chronicles of London, English Historical Literature of the Fifteenth Century*, pp. 70–112, 292–8.

[3] See pp. 326 ff.

Paul's Cathedral and Westminster Abbey with country properties, less than twenty charters survive with any significant bearing on London's history, and of these at least three are spurious, and several more are hardly in their pristine form.[1] The earliest is a grant by Burgred, king of Mercia, of a haga, or enclosure,[2] in London to the Bishop of Worcester; this is a useful epilogue to four charters earlier than 800 which show the Mercian kings assuming sway in London in the age of Mercian supremacy. The charters between the time of Alfred and the Conquest tell us a little about hagas and sokes and wharves;[3] a little – but that of great importance – about the boundary of the City;[4] they show us the religious houses of the area, the abbeys of Chertsey, Barking, St Albans and Westminster, as well as the Bishop of Worcester and the abbey of St Peter's Ghent, acquiring land there. Among the most interesting are the documents which show the Cathedral Priory of Christ Church, Canterbury, acquiring city lands and churches.[5] But the total they represent is very modest, and exceeded by the resources of several lesser English cities, including Winchester and Worcester, and by many abroad.

After the Conquest charters multiplied, and the number which survives relevant to London's history is numerous already in the twelfth century, legion in the thirteenth. They include the early charters of the City's own liberties and privileges, sedulously preserved. From the Husting Rolls and other collections of deeds something approaching the systematic recording of conveyances in the City can be traced between the second half of the thirteenth century and the end of the Middle Ages;[6] this evidence will one day be put together with other topographical and archaeological evidence to tell us much more than we at present know of the way London was settled in the late Middle Ages. Before the mid-thirteenth century this can only be done in the most fragmentary way. Surveys and accounts are none the less important to us. One early survey of St Paul's, of *c.* 1127, is our chief source for the early history of wards and aldermen, and for the assertion that the City patriciate, as late as the second quarter of the twelfth century, was still predominantly English not Norman.[7] Two Canterbury rentals of the late twelfth and early thirteenth centuries are very helpful in describing the pattern of settlement in the City, though

---

[1] See Appendix I.   [2] See p. 367.
[3] See pp. 150 ff., 158.   [4] See p. 169.   [5] See pp. 135–6.
[6] See G. H. Martin in *The Study of Medieval Records: Essays in Honour of Kathleen Major*, ed. D. A. Bullough and R. L. Storey, Oxford, 1971, pp. 151–73.
[7] See pp. 163 n., 166–7.

pitifully inadequate compared with the earlier, fuller and more detailed surveys for Winchester.[1] Much of what we know of the government of London, and of its money market and trade, comes from the central records of the royal Exchequer, the Pipe Rolls.[2] The roll of 1129–30 shows us the sheriffs in action at a moment of particular interest and change; those from 1155–6 on give us a more consistent picture of the workings of the farm, of the shape of the shrievalty, of the involvement of London citizens in royal administration and supply, and a variety of other topics otherwise wholly obscure.[3] In finance and trade, they lift the corner of a curtain; they tantalize; they suggest numerous questions we cannot answer; and although we can do something to reconstruct the nature of the markets in money and land, and the trade far and near of which London was the centre,[4] our impression in the end must be of the obscurity of the history of London's markets in a very creative period.

The pre-Conquest legal codes contain some statements of custom of London and its region, and of the great peace-guild of the tenth century;[5] and from the twelfth century we have substantial statements of London customs and laws. These were first enshrined, very briefly, in the document we know as the charter of Henry I. Its authenticity and date are doubtful, but it comprises, without much doubt, a genuine account of the citizens' more cherished privileges of the 1130s and 1140s.[6] At the turn of the century, perhaps in the reign of John, a London lawyer of antiquarian turn of mind put together a large assemblage of legal customs, traditions, and other matters which is our chief source for London's customs before the thirteenth century;[7] and shortly after the end of our period there was

[1] Three versions of a late twelfth-century rental appear in Canterbury, Dean and Chapter, Literary MSS B 14, 15 and 16. Canterbury, Dean and Chapter, Register K, ff. 66v–69 contains a fuller list of the priory's London properties which dates from the second or third decade of the thirteenth century; Register B ff. 248–260 contains the same rental and some additions slightly later in date.

[2] See pp. 222 ff.

[3] These have been closely studied by Miss Susan Reynolds: see pp. xv–xvi and her 'Rulers of London'.

[4] See chap. 10.

[5] See pp. 195–6.

[6] See pp. 207 ff.

[7] Now British Museum Addit. MS 14252 and Manchester, John Rylands Library MS Lat. 155: see M. Bateson in *EHR*, vol. xvii, 1902, pp. 480–511, 707–30; F. Liebermann in *EHR*, vol. xxviii, 1913, pp. 732–45; many of the texts are ed. M. Weinbaum in *London unter Eduard I.*, vol. ii.

compiled the first surviving major legal record, of the Eyre of 1244, which reveals in great detail much of the structure of London law and custom, and much else besides of value for its social history and topography.[1]

Of all these documents, the charters are far and away the most numerous; and any attempt to reconstruct the topography and social structure of the City must have at its base an analysis and index of the surviving charters. Much that we say is based on this analysis, and the index which Miss Susan Reynolds and one of us (Mrs Keir) have been engaged in compiling. From these indexes much can be learned of the people who counted in London society and of the structure of its government and customs, and Miss Reynolds is continuing her studies of the City families and of the social roots from which they sprang. What we offer below is in the nature of an interim report; but a large amount of the detail on which many passages in this book are founded have their origin in the index or in the researches it involved.[2]

Topography

The sources for London's history have often been pillaged for the study of its street-names, of its wards and churches. First in time and honour must be named the great Elizabethan antiquary, John Stow, whose *Survey* enshrined the first edition of FitzStephen's *Description* and much information still constantly consulted by students of London.[3] In recent times the

[1] For our use of *Eyre*, see esp. pp. 163 ff.

[2] See esp. chaps 8–9, Appendix II. We are especially indebted to Miss Reynolds for her fundamental work and help in this index, and for permission to use it.

[3] The MSS of FitzStephen's *Description* are listed and discussed by H. E. Butler in Stenton, p. 34. Of these Bodl. Douce 287 (incomplete, but early, prob. twelfth century) and Brit. Mus. Lansdowne 398 are copies of the *Vitae S. Thomae* in full; the Bodl. Marshall MS 75 (early thirteenth century) and Guildhall *Liber Custumarum* (early fourteenth) contain the *Description* alone. The Marshall MS has been shown by A. G. Watson to have belonged to Stow (*The Manuscripts of Henry Savile of Banke*, London, 1969, p. 56, no. 200) and must undoubtedly be the basis of his edition. The readings which caused Butler to deny this are probably due to Stow's knowledge of the *Liber Custumarum*. Stow's text is in his *Survey*, edn of 1598, pp. 474–83, 1603, pp. 570–9; a study of the copies in the British Museum Library suggests that these were not clear-cut editions, but a fount of type set up in 1598 and gradually altered as necessary. The *Description* has been many times printed since; we refer to the edition in *MB*, though we have used Butler's notes and looked at all the MSS ourselves. A fuller account of the MSS and editions will appear in *Councils and Synods*, vol. i, and a new study of Fitz-Stephen's *Life* is being undertaken by Mrs M. G. Cheney.

topographical evidence has been laid out in comprehensive fashion by an amateur scholar of great devotion and learning, H. A. Harben, in his *Dictionary of London*, and the street-names have been systematically studied by the eminent philologist Eilert Ekwall;[1] even as we write the English Place-Name Society has in hand a volume to replace his pioneer study. The well-known maps and articles by Miss Honeybourne have made plain the lines of the City's topographical history.[2] The written evidence is exceptionally rich, for the names of streets survived for centuries in spite of the frequent fires and rebuilding; many twelfth-century names are still in use. Thus London, in common with many English towns, can trace the pattern of its streets with tolerable completeness back to late Old English times.

What is quite exceptional, however, is the antiquity of London's ward and parish boundaries.[3] It is not uncommon both in England and on the Continent for the history of parish boundaries to be fairly well known where parishes were few and large. But it is characteristic of a number of English towns – York, Lincoln, Norwich and Winchester are good examples to set beside London – to have numerous and tiny parishes; those of the City within the walls were on average not more than three and a half acres in extent. London is unique in that we can trace the pattern of the parish boundaries to a comparatively early date, also unique in that the same is true of the boundaries of her civic units or wards. The student of early Cambridge or Huntingdon can conjecture with a certain freedom (as some have done) where the wards noted in 'Domesday Book' lay; for their boundaries there is no evidence of any solidity.[4] The reasons for believing that the ward boundaries, still the basis for local government in the City in the 1970s, were formed within the period of this book must provide an important part of our argument in later chapters. The pattern of city streets bears only the most incidental relation to the Roman street pattern, even though walls and gates owed much to Roman foundations.

[1] Harben; Ekwall; see also Ekwall's *Studies on the Population of Medieval London*, Stockholm, 1956.

[2] See Bibliography and below, pp. 147, 169, etc. Her published maps are of London under Henry II (in Stenton) and under Richard II (London Topographical Soc. no. 93, 1960; cf. *LTR*, vol. xxii, 1965, pp. 29–76). Our debt to Miss Honeybourne's maps and studies is substantial, as will be clear in chapters 5–7.

[3] See pp. 165 ff., 129 ff.

[4] Cf. esp. *VCH Cambs*, vol. iii, pp. 111 ff. (H. M. Cam; cf. C. Stephenson, *Borough and Town*, Cambridge, Mass., 1933, pp. 200 ff., and rejoinder by H. M. Cam, *Liberties and Communities in Medieval England*, Cambridge, 1944, pp. 11 ff.).

London was a considerable place between the departure of the Romans and the urban renaissance, but not a settled or populous city. The process by which it became such is one of our central themes, and the tight grid of boundaries laid by the parishes and wards upon the street-plan is one of the most crucial pieces of evidence for this story.

Archaeology

Topography is evidently enough much helped by the spade, and the history of London has been illuminated at innumerable points by archaeological finds. We have observed how the obscurity of the literary evidence for the tenth and eleventh centuries in particular makes this contribution especially welcome; and the history of early medieval cities is being transformed by the systematic work of the current generation of archaeologists;[1] since this chapter was written, a new perspective has opened with the publication of *The Future of London's Past*.[2] The recording of finds by the staffs of London's two museums (now in process of amalgamation) is one major base for its history as a place of settlement and trade; the investigation of the walls by Professor Grimes and his Excavation Committee has revealed much, not only of their early history in Roman times, but throughout the period when London was in a state of active defence, right down to the seventeenth century.[3] To take a point of detail, the line of the Walbrook divided the City between east and west in Roman times and in the early Middle Ages; thereafter it suffered the supreme indignity and became first a sewer then a memory. The ward boundaries still suggest the line it took, but crucial confirmation of this has come from a series of digs at various points along its course.[4]

Professor Grimes's work has been especially fruitful in the history of the City churches. Seven have been excavated with great precision since the Second World War, four of them under his direction.[5] Beneath Wren's

[1] Especially, in England, by the work of Mr Biddle and his colleagues in Winchester, and of Mr Addyman and his colleagues in Southampton and York: see Bibliography under Addyman, Biddle. See also now C. Platt, *Medieval Southampton*, London, 1973.

[2] By M. Biddle, D. Hudson and C. Heighway, Worcester, 1973.

[3] See Grimes, and the annual reports of finds by the staff of the Guidhall Museum in *LMAS*. The major collections are in the Guildhall and London Museums, shortly to be amalgamated in a new Museum of London near the Guildhall.

[4] Grimes, pp. 92 ff.; Merrifield, *Roman City of London*, esp. the map in folder and pp. 264–7.

[5] St Bride's Fleet St, St Swithun, London Stone, St Alban Wood St (Grimes, pp. 182–209), St Mary Aldermanbury (see brief account in *Medieval Archaeology*,

foundations, in nearly every case,[1] has appeared a complex of walls of varying date, with a small stone box of the Romanesque period at its core. It is rarely possible to be absolutely certain that this was the first church on the site, for over the centuries of rebuilding the post-holes of a primitive wooden chapel might easily have disappeared; but it is rare even for such structures to leave no trace at all, and it is probable in every case that the excavators have found the framework at least of the whole story. For one church they were able to be more precise. Under the earliest nucleus of St Nicholas Acon there was found a secular rubbish pit not sealed until the eleventh century was well under way. The documents forbid a date later than 1084 for its foundation, and we shall see in a later chapter how in this case dedication and cognomen – Christian name and surname – combine with the message in stone and vellum to assure us of a mid-eleventh century date for the church's foundation.[2]

Only in one case out of seven are we so well provided; and only for seven out of nearly one hundred churches within London's boundaries has the archaeologist yet anything of substance to tell us. Nor will the case ever be greatly different. In a number of churches Wren's superstructure survives to make investigation virtually impossible; in an even greater number rebuilding after the Great Fire has made the site inaccessible or barren.[3] Substantial areas of the City have been rendered immune to archaeology by later building, and especially by Victorian cellars and modern basements.[4] The pace of modern building, and road schemes, tend to make the time allotted to the archaeologists desperately short, and under these conditions the achievement is impressive. The spade has a great deal more to tell us still, but we cannot expect miracles.

---

vol. xiii, 1969, p. 251) by Professor Grimes; also St Pancras, St Nicholas Acon and St Michael Bassishaw (*LMAS*, vols xxi, 1963–7, pp. 217–18, 218–20, xxii, pt i, 1968, pp. 14–16) by P. R. V. Marsden. See below, pp. 137 ff.

[1] St Alban Wood St, is the only one of certainly early origin – i.e. early rather than late Saxon; for St Bride's, where a sixth-century origin has been claimed – though not by Prof. Grimes – see below, pp. 139 f. The word 'Romanesque' used below is extremely imprecise; in this context it means probably of eleventh–twelfth century date.

[2] See p. 138.
[3] See p. 136.
[4] See *Future of London's Past*, chap. 5; Grimes, esp. pp. 4 ff.

Coins[1]

In particular, we can hope to know something more when all the host of tiny finds in London and immediately round the old City have been mapped and studied in bulk, and all objects found elsewhere of London provenance have been sifted. Of outstanding importance are coins, for they can commonly be dated and their history reconstructed with far more precision than other surviving objects, and they can tell us something directly of material wealth and trade.

They reveal to us, above all, the way in which London became, by the eleventh and twelfth centuries, one of the monetary capitals of Europe. The silver currency on which the English economy was based, like all those of northern Europe, began in the eighth century; before that, since the Romans departed, there had been occasional coins, but no currency in the effective sense of the term. The early history of the London mint is extremely obscure. Its name first appears on gold coins of the seventh century, but the history of medieval currency really begins in the eighth, with the revival of silver coins, that is of a medium of exchange which was small enough to be generally useful. Offa of Mercia launched the silver penny, the basic English coin for centuries to come, when he was lord of most of England; pennies were minted in his time in Canterbury, and at least one other centre which was evidently in Mercia and has been presumed to have been in London.[2] Under his successors minting was carried on in Canterbury, at Rochester, somewhere in East Anglia, and at two other centres, presumed to be in Winchester and London. But the name of London only appeared on coins when it was conquered by the kings of Wessex – first, briefly, under Egbert (829–30), then under his grandson, Alfred. Thus London may have been an important mint under the Mercian supremacy; but we cannot be sure, and any argument either that London was essentially a Mercian city[3] or that it was a place of great

[1] This section is in large measure based on notes generously provided by Mr Ian Stewart; a chronology and bibliography are given in Appendix IV below, both for the London mint and for hoards found in and near the City. See **Plates 19–21**.

[2] See C. E. Blunt, C. S. S. Lyon and B. H. I. H. Stewart in *BNJ*, vol. xxxii, 1963, pp. 1–74, esp. pp. 5–8, 30–43; H. E. Pagan in *BNJ*, vol. xxxiv, 1965, pp. 8–10. For Egbert, see **Plate 19**.

[3] The evidence for the influence of Mercia in London depends, so far as we know, entirely on charters and on the events of 886 (see pp. 15, 20). The charters show Æthelbald and Offa of Mercia granting land in Middlesex (Sawyer, nos 100, 106, 119, 132;

moment under Offa and his successors, cannot be based on the evidence
of coins.

Under Alfred the name of the city appears with the king's head, very
likely a deliberate celebration of Alfred's success in conquering the city.
From then on, the mint in all probability had a continuous history,
though it was still not commonly named on coins. From the reign of Edgar,
at least from the 970s, the mint is normally named, and it becomes
apparent that it had come to assume the place it never subsequently lost
as the home of the largest mint and the largest team of moneyers in the
country. From the 970s, both the city and the moneyer are normally
specified on the coins; and on them we can read the names of a very high
proportion of the few London citizens whose names are known before the
twelfth century.

In the tenth and early eleventh centuries the English currency became
the most highly organized and centralized of any European monarchy of
the age; and after the Norman Conquest it became the most stable in
weight. This stability, granted to it, so it would appear, by William I and
Henry I, was remarked on at the time and gave it the reputation and the
name of being of sterling quality.[1] But the central organization is really its
most unusual feature. In the late tenth century dies were cut at several
centres, including London, on which the moneyers could strike their
coins; in the early eleventh century the number of centres declined, and
by the reign of Edward the Confessor (1042–66) London had achieved a
virtual monopoly. From then on, whenever a new issue of coin was made,
all the moneyers had to receive from London, from the London goldsmith
who was (as we should say) controller of the mint, the dies for the new
coinage. By the late twelfth century the current William son of Otto, or
Otto son of William, was not only a goldsmith, but a hereditary royal
servant with his headquarters in or near London and a substantial country

see Appendix I), but Offa also granted land in Kent (Sawyer, nos 123, 125, etc.) and
Surrey (Sawyer, no. 127), and was more nearly king of the whole of England than any
later monarch until the tenth century. Thus it may well be that London was essentially
Mercian in the eighth–ninth centuries, but at present the evidence must be treated with
caution (but cf. F. M. Stenton, *Anglo-Saxon England*, Oxford, 1943, pp. 56–7, 203;
linguistic evidence from place-names may also confirm Mercian influence, or it may
only help to establish that London was 'a mart of many peoples').

[1] See P. Grierson, 'Sterling', in *AS Coins*, pp. 266–83. For what follows see H. R.
Loyn in *AS Coins*, pp. 124–5; C. S. S. Lyon in H. R. Mossop, *The Lincoln Mint*, pp.
11–12; and in *BNJ*, vol. xxxix, 1970, pp. 200 ff.

estate.[1] In earlier days, his ancestors had been (so far as we can tell) essentially leading city craftsmen in the necessary skill; rich men furnished with ability. It is likely that it was the nature of London as a centre of international commerce in the tenth and eleventh centuries that dictated to the English kings the use of its goldsmiths for this purpose. But there was also a large element of politics in the process, for it was precisely under Ethelred the Unready, when enormous Danegelds had to be collected and paid, that the system reached its first perfection:[2] from this time, from about the year 1000, date both the beginnings of London's monopoly and the effective prohibition of the import of foreign currency.

This prohibition is the other chief indication of the effectiveness of central control over English coinage.[3] In hoards of coins dug up in England, consequently, that date from about 1000 to at least 1200, coins from overseas are exceedingly rare: evidently in practice as well as in theory they were gathered at the ports and exchanges and translated into English. Only in an island could such a rule have been enforced; yet it is extraordinary even so that it was effective. This has the fortunate consequence of teaching us that English royal administration, even before the Conquest, could be more effective than we would have dared to imagine. But it also has the unfortunate consequence that coin hoards found in England are of no use as evidence of the range and quantity of foreign trade. Coins from London and England as a whole have been found in many parts of the Continent, and tell us something of the spread of English links abroad. The evidence of coins always needs a certain delicacy in interpretation. The largest hoards of English coins are in Scandinavia: nearly 1,500 pennies minted in London in the reigns of Æthelred II and Cnut are now in the Copenhagen Museum, and even more in Stockholm.[4] No doubt this partly represents Viking trade and plunder; in the main it is part of the remnant, now spread all over the museums of the north, of the Danegeld.

[1] See esp. D. F. Allen, pp. cxii, cxiii and references, for Otto, who made William I's shrine, his son William and grandson Otto (cf. esp. *Regesta*, vol. ii, nos 760, 1524; *PR 30 Henry I*, p. 145, *2–4 Henry II*, pp. 3, etc., *16 Henry II*, p. 16, cf. also *Eccles. Hist. of Orderic Vitalis*, ed. and trans. M. Chibnall, vol. iv, Oxford, 1973, pp. 110–11 and n.; Gibbs, no. 177 and n.).

[2] The contrast between the political failure and administrative success of Ethelred the Unready's government is very striking and, so far, wholly unexplained.

[3] Liebermann, vol. i, pp. 158–9. On its success see esp. Dolley in *LMAS*, vol. xx, 1959–61, pp. 40, 49 n. 19.

[4] *Sylloge of Coins of the British Isles*, Copenhagen Museum, vols iiib and iv, British Academy, London, 1970–2.

For the late eleventh and twelfth centuries, we might hope that the coins would reflect the pattern of trade, and in a measure they do. English coins have been found in hoards in Germany and along the Baltic coast, and in Normandy and the adjacent areas of France.[1] Hoards of various dates on the roads to Italy seem to reflect ecclesiastical tribute en route for Rome rather than trade, and English coins in southern Europe are otherwise scarce.[2] But the greatest surprise is that Flanders, from all other evidence the chief centre of trade with England, has a very slight yield of English coins. This has been taken to indicate that the balance of trade was steadily in England's favour: it suggests that from the eleventh century English wool was paying for the silver flowing from the Continent, and this in its turn helps to answer the question where the silver came for the excellent English currency.[3] But the absence of Flemish coins in England and of English coins in Flanders is a sharp reminder of the limits of this type of evidence; and collateral evidence on the balance of trade is almost non-existent.

If we set aside a pile of lead 'stycas' found in Fore Street, and probably of the nineteenth century rather than the ninth, we can count about twelve hoards of coins which have been found in London and its immediate neighbourhood, and which were probably buried between 800 and 1200.[4] This is quite a handsome total, showing in very broad terms that London was a centre of bullion. But this impression is somewhat blurred on a closer look; for peaceful prosperity produces few or no hoards – coins circulate and are returned to the mints to make new

[1] See S. E. Rigold in *BNJ*, vol. xxvi, 1949–51, pp. 31–55, esp. pp. 37–8 (showing English influence to and along the Baltic, and evidence of imitations; suggesting a break in the Norman period and resumption in the thirteenth century – the break is, however, doubtful); cf. ibid. p. 55; *Sylloge* (vol. xi), Royal Coin Cabinet, Stockholm, Anglo-Norman Series, pp. 45 ff., showing Norman coins still travelling to Sweden. Movement further east is represented by a hoard of late Norman coins now in Moscow (F. Elmore Jones and C. E. Blunt in *BNJ*, vol. xxxvi, 1967, pp. 86–92 [after 1158]). Circulation in north-western France (esp. Normandy, Maine, Anjou and Brittany) is shown by J. Yvon in *BNJ*, vol. xxxix, 1970, pp. 24–60.

[2] Cf. *AS Coins*, pp. 50 (C. E. Blunt) and 82 (R. H. M. Dolley and Blunt) and references for a Swiss hoard of *c.* 790–2 and the Vatican and Forum (*c.* 945) hoards. M. A. O'Donovan in *BNJ*, vol. xxxiii, 1964, pp. 7–29, suggests very tentatively that the Vatican hoard of 517 pennies may have been intended as a payment by Archbishop Wulfhelm for the pallium in 927.

[3] Cf. P. Sawyer, *Age of the Vikings*, 2nd edn, pp. 198–9; and in *TRHS*, 5th Series, vol. xv, 1965, pp. 145–64, esp. pp. 161 ff.

[4] See Appendix IV, pp. 377–8.

currency; buried hoards are recovered. It is the hoards whose owners were never able to reclaim which were left for us to find, and it is not surprising that many of these hoards can be associated with particular moments of crisis. A group from the ninth century suggest the first age of Viking attacks; a large hoard of *c.* 1015 the siege and counter-siege of Ethelred II's final years. Two more may be associated with the rebellion and Danish threat of 1075; one even with the troubles of 1190–1.[1] But far and away the most dramatic is the collection of several thousand coins dug up near the Walbrook and evidently buried in 1066.[2] They even include a coin from Byzantium, another from Germany and one from Denmark, rare exceptions to the rule that only English coins appear in these hoards, and may possibly represent the bullion of a moneyer. In any event the hoard seems likely to have been buried in panic as William the Conqueror approached the City.

The study of early medieval coinage is a highly technical and abstruse skill; a maze, full of hopeful paths and blind alleys, which every student of medieval London must attempt to penetrate, since in the dies and mints of London, and in the hoards of coins found in and around the city, lie such answers as we can give to the major questions as to London's prosperity and commercial prowess in this age.

KNOWLEDGE AND IGNORANCE

1 An example of our knowledge : The Cnihtengild

We have often in this chapter lamented the areas of our ignorance, or the failings of the evidence, and it is right that before it is concluded we should give an illustration of the way in which a small piece of evidence – in this case a leaf of parchment of very modest size – can illuminate large areas of our field. We have indicated the importance of parishes, wards and sokes, and among the most interesting of these was and is the Portsoken, originally the space east of the walls where the Cnihtengild held sway.

King Edward sends friendly greetings to Bishop Ælfweard and Wulfgar my portreeve and all the citizens in London. And I inform you that my will is that my men in the guild of English *cnihtas* shall be entitled to their sake and their soke within borough and without over

---

[1] See pp. 22 ff., 45 ff. for these events.
[2] See p. 377.

their lands and over their men. And my will is that they shall enjoy as good laws as they enjoyed in the days of King Edgar and in my father's days and similarly in Cnut's. And I will moreover augment its benefits. And I will not permit anyone to do them any wrong, but [on the contrary] may they all prosper! And God keep you all.[1]

The document is well known; but its fascination has certainly not been exhausted. It reveals to us an institution of a very curious kind. It is likely enough that the *guild* was formed, as the writ and later tradition agree, in the days of Edgar the Peaceable; and it certainly had a peaceful demise in the reign of Henry I, when its rights and properties were handed over to the great foundation of Henry's first wife, the late Queen Matilda, Holy Trinity Priory, Aldgate. All the indications are that a guild so well endowed was of major consequence; and the writ makes it abundantly clear that this was so – Edward has an apologetic tone which can hardly be understood unless he was dealing with important people. One puzzling feature of it is the emphatic word *English*; as some commentators have observed, there must be a contrast here with foreigners whose privileges had presumably aroused the jealousy of the natives. The men of Rouen and of the Emperor are known to have had privileges at this time, and Edward's continental background and foreign friends may already have aroused jealousy in the first years of his reign.[2] Here are puzzles which need unravelling; and the first, immediately suggested by the reference to English *cnihtas*, is that the foreigners with whom they are contrasted would have been, one might reasonably presume, merchants, which at first sight is not likely to be the meaning of *cnihtas*. *Cniht*, indeed, can mean almost anything except merchant;[3] it has so broad a variety of meanings that a guild of *cnihtas* might well have merchants in its midst; and in its latter days it doubtless had a cross-section of the city patriciate of whatever occupation. But the word itself seems, in the context of the eleventh century, to carry two connotations in particular: in its native meaning, it represents a servant or retainer – not a menial necessarily, far from it, indeed; but someone who was in some measure at least beholden to a greater than himself. After the Norman Conquest this simple English

---

[1] Harmer, no. 51, pp. 234–5; cf. pp. 231 ff., 466 ff., with references to the copious literature. See esp. Unwin, pp. 23 ff.; Stenton, pp. 13–14.

[2] See pp. 265–7.

[3] For what follows see Stenton, pp. 13–14; idem, *The First Century of English Feudalism*, 2nd edn, Oxford, 1961, pp. 132 ff.

word survived, to conquer its French rivals, and attach itself to that most Norman and French of characters, the knight.[1] This is inconceivable unless the *cnihtas* of the mid-eleventh century were frequently military, and we know from other evidence that many were. One should never be happy about a definition of the Cnihtengild in Edward the Confessor's time which makes it wholly peaceable in its nature.

Later tradition asserted that the Cnihtengild not only had properties within the walls and the Portsoken without, but rights over land as far south of the river as they could throw their lances.[2] Whatever the true meaning of this absurd rigmarole the combination of precise rights over a well-defined strip of land marking the eastern boundary of the City with some less well-defined rights across the river strongly suggests that their original function was to defend the City against attack from the east. If this is so, we can readily understand why they became first entirely peaceful, and then quite extinct, after the Norman Conquest. The Normans could not leave the city's defence in the hands of English burghers; nor did they. The Conqueror's Tower defended the city from the east and kept the city under the strong hand of its Norman castellan. The military role of the Cnihtengild had gone.

This is not to say that the guild was ever purely military in character. That is most improbable. It seems always to have been of the nature of medieval societies of this kind that they were from the outset, or rapidly became, charitable, religious and social, whether the specific function which set them apart from other guilds was the pursuit of entertainment, peace or lucre. Much of the difficulty, indeed, in interpreting the Cnihtengild has lain in the wide stretch of different meanings to which the word guild could be attached; in other words, to the difficulty of detaching the Cnihtengild from the later London companies. What was a guild? An association; a vehicle of privileges? A company for mutual profit, in this world or the next? The eleventh- and early twelfth-century texts are only quite specific on two points: it was something you paid for, and something you drank.[3]

---

[1] See S. Harvey in *Past and Present*, no. 49, Nov. 1970, pp. 3–43 for an interesting study of the growth in status of knights in the eleventh and twelfth centuries which may help to explain this development.

[2] *Cart. Aldgate*, no. 871, p. 167; also in *Cal. Letter Book C*, pp. 216 ff.

[3] See pp. 278 ff., esp. 280.

2 An area of knowledge: Church, Society and Queen Matilda

The clearest evidence of the religious and charitable character of the Cnihtengild lies in its demise. In 1125, under pressure, we may assume, from the king, the guild wound up its affairs, and laid them all at the feet of the prior and canons of Holy Trinity, Aldgate.[1] The foundation of Holy Trinity Priory by Queen Matilda in 1107–8 and its subsequent progress are central events in the ecclesiastical history of the city in this century; they were also important political events. It is a curious fact that no aspect of urban history has been so much neglected until recent years as its ecclesiastical history. It is not that the history of the churches in our great cities has itself been neglected; and there are significant and distinguished exceptions. But there has been a tendency to relegate the churches to a separate compartment, and to see the history of the city as a branch of secular, economic, social or constitutional history. For two reasons, this is a form of heresy: first, because before 1200 the vast majority of our documents for the history of English towns are ecclesiastical in origin, and we must be prepared willy-nilly to see the cities, part of the time at least, through spiritual eyes; and secondly, because the relation of town and church is much tighter, more subtle, more sophisticated even, than we naturally assume or readily accept. In the foundation of Holy Trinity by Henry's English wife, and in its endowment with the rights and properties of the English Cnihtengild, something hard to grasp, yet obviously very near the political, spiritual and social centre of London's life was accomplished.

Thus Matilda's work reveals the way in which the religious and social aspects of London's history mingle with high politics; and further reflection on her role suggests the importance of continental evidence and analogy in understanding the native history of an English city. She was evidently a considerable personality in her own right; yet her involvement in a city still very English in some ways – if very cosmopolitan in others – illustrates the reason why Henry married her.[2] She was an English princess, and her first and major task was to bear Henry a legitimate heir. No king is so sensitive about legitimacy as a usurper; and Henry lived all his reign until its final year under the shadow of his elder brother, however securely Robert might be locked in his last years in Cardiff Castle. Robert's presence was always a threat, for a successful rebellion, however ephemeral, had in him a natural centre; and Robert's son, William Clito, was at

[1] *Cart. Aldgate*, no. 871, p. 168. For what follows, see pp. 315 ff.   [2] See ibid.

large on the Continent. In 1118 Matilda died, and in 1120 her only son, William, was drowned in the wreck of the *White Ship*. In 1127 the Count of Flanders was brutally murdered in the church of St Donatian in Bruges, and for a time William Clito was established as count – not by the murderers, but by Louis VI of France, always anxious for a stick with which to beat Henry.[1] It was a curious commentary on the Norman marriage policies, for William's right came from another Matilda, the Conqueror's wife, a Flemish princess. While Louis and William triumphed, and Henry fumed and intrigued, a new power arose to destroy the calculations of both. By bold political action, and a series of alliances among themselves and with a section of the nobility, the cities of Flanders combined to challenge Count William (who shortly afterwards died) and to replace him with a candidate of their own chosing. The great dynasts were suddenly compelled to take notice of the political power of the cities of Europe, and we may be sure that Henry I, little as he may have anticipated the denouement, did not fail to learn a lesson.

Henry's first wife, Matilda, had helped to secure his legitimacy and had helped to secure his hold on London and to sustain the religious life and social welfare of the city. But she had failed to provide him with a male heir who survived him. From 1127 on Henry's schemes were centred in the attempt to secure the throne for yet another Matilda, their daughter, and her heirs. In 1129–30 we find Henry engaged in enlarging the privileges of the City of London; not so much as was supposed when his charter was accepted as genuine, but in some measure at least.[2] Was he deliberately fostering the goodwill of a city about to play a crucial role in the election of his successor? We have, unfortunately, no means of knowing.

3 Our ignorance

The extent of our ignorance, here and everywhere, is very great, and there are many questions to which we cannot hope to know the answer. We do not know the population of London with any sort of precision in this period; we have no idea how much it grew. We know perilously little about the ingredients of its trade, and we have no statistics. There are worse cases. At some date unknown the men of Chester enlarged their walls in the expectation, evidently, of a thriving city with a growing population. The indications are that this was never fulfilled,[3] but we do

[1] Galbert of Bruges, *passim*.
[2] See pp. 207 ff. and Brooke, Keir and Reynolds.
[3] From the remarkable dearth of medieval finds over substantial areas of the City.

not know the date of the extension, nor the reason why it was thought necessary and proved not so. One might conjecture that a substantial ingredient in the story was the rise of Bristol,[1] the success of the Irish slave-trade in the tenth and eleventh centuries, and its decline thereafter. It is likely enough that Chester was a major entrepôt for Irish slaves (and English slaves going to Ireland) in the tenth and eleventh centuries, and that the poverty of its hinterland, and its distance from the south-east, prevented it from forging ahead as Bristol was able to do after the collapse of one of its original pillars. All this is likely; but there is not a single document to prove that slaves were ever sold in Chester in Christian times. In this respect, London is one up on Chester: there is a single well-documented case of a slave sold and bought in London.[2] For obvious reasons, the slave-trade is ill-documented to a degree which is remarkable even in a period when trade as a whole is hidden by our sources. We know that England lay on one of the major routes from the Slav world to the western Mediterranean by which slaves were moved through the early and central Middle Ages, so that the words slav and slave are identical in almost every west European language; and we know that slavery itself survived in England until the Norman Conquest (and see p. 263), long after it had disappeared in most of northern Europe. But that is all: the details escape us.

Yet in spite of difficulties of this character which afflict the students of early medieval trade, markets and towns, our final impression is not of scepticism or despair. For through the half-light of our sources we can discern with some clarity the outlines of a pattern; we can be sure that it was between the age of Alfred and the late twelfth century that London became a great city, as it had not been since the Romans departed. However much it grew and flourished in the thirteenth century,[3] the pattern of the city – walls, wards, parishes and streets – had been established well before 1200.

[1] See E. M. Carus-Wilson in *Historic Towns*, vol. ii, forthcoming; William of Malmesbury, *Vita Wulfstani*, ed. R. R. Darlington, Camden 3rd Series, vol. xl, 1928, pp. 43–4.

[2] Bede, *Hist. Ecclesiastica*, bk iv, c. 22 (ed. Colgrave and Mynors, pp. 404–5), tells the story of a young king's retainer from Northumbria, taken prisoner by a Mercian *gesith* in 679, and sold to a Frisian in London. On the slave-trade, see below, pp. 263–4.

[3] See G. Williams, esp. pp. 17 ff.: 'Within the walls, deed after deed testifies to the intensification of settlement'. But this is not argued in detail, and in view of the difficulty of interpreting evidence of this kind, it is unlikely that it could be. In our view, it is probable that Prof. Williams has exaggerated the growth in population and prosperity of London in the thirteenth century. That some growth and great changes took place in the thirteenth century is not in doubt, and so much Prof. Williams has brilliantly demonstrated.

Part II

The Shape of London

5

London in the 1170s

THIS BOOK is written in the faith that it is possible to penetrate to
the heart of London's history in the eleventh and twelfth centuries;
a faith in the first instance not supported by documentary evidence,
for documents, though profuse, are scattered, and their message far from
clear. Thus it has long been recognized that the earliest survey of City rents
and houses, the list of city properties of St Paul's Cathedral of *c.* 1127,
has much to tell us of the structure of the City at that date, of wards, sokes
and aldermen in their prime.[1] It tells of a city already divided into wards,
approximately twenty-four of them, and it gives us a jumble of names of
leading city magnates. It shows us a city in which the hold of the Church
seems at first sight stronger than in later times – one of the wards is in the
hands of the bishop, another in those of a canon, Ralph, son of Algod. It
shows us a city bristling with sokes. But as to what a ward was or where
most of them lay, it tells us nothing at first reading: nor again much about
sokes. Only after a long exploration of the topographical and personal or
prosopographical evidence can we hope to make sense of this document;
and then we shall find that it helps to unveil large areas of hidden territory.

THE PLACE OF THE CITY IN LONDON AND BRITAIN

Our first task is to explore the City and the surrounding territory which is
essential to its understanding. Those who came along the Roman road
from the west or over Highgate Hill in the early Middle Ages, as today,
presently found themselves on roads which led them to the City, the river
and the Bridge. From the Bridge one may look west to Westminster or
east to the port of London; and by 1100 the City, the port and the palace

[1] See pp. 163 n., 166–7. The section of this chapter on FitzStephen's *Description* is
based on C. N. L. B.'s Inaugural Lecture at Westfield College, *Time the Archsatirist*,
1968.

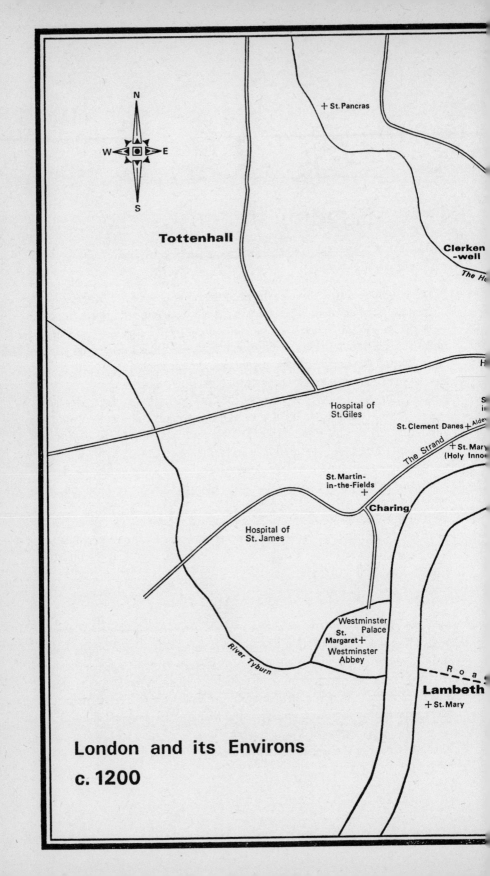

N
W E
S

+ St. Pancras

Tottenhall

Clerken -well

The He

Hospital of
St. Giles

H

S
i

St. Clement Danes + *Alde*

The Strand + St. Mary
(Holy Inno

St. Martin-
in-the-Fields
+

Charing

Hospital of
St. James

Westminster
Palace
St.
Margaret +
Westminster
Abbey

River Tyburn

R o a
Lambeth
+ St. Mary

London and its Environs
c. 1200

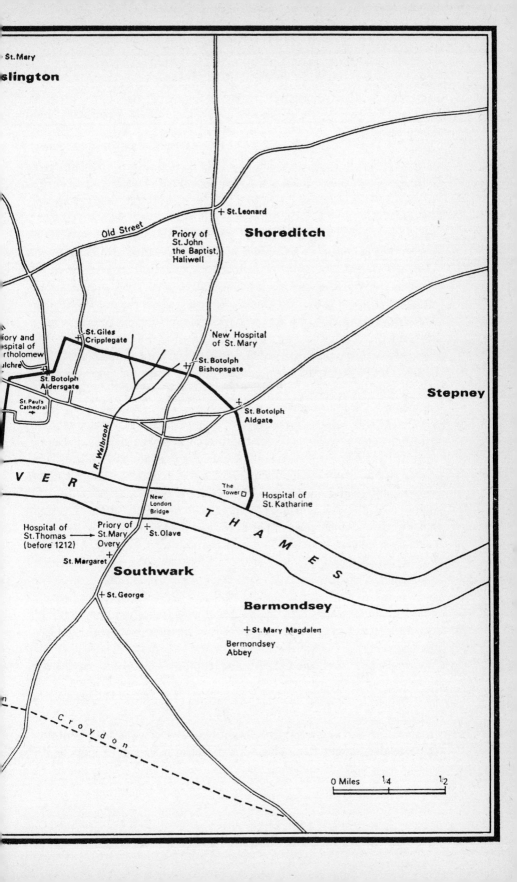

St. Mary

slington

Old Street

✝ St. Leonard

Shoreditch

Priory of
St. John
the Baptist,
Haliwell

St. Giles
Cripplegate

ory and
spital of
rtholomew
ulchre

'New' Hospital
of St. Mary

✝ St. Botolph
Bishopsgate

St. Botolph
Aldersgate

St. Paul's
Cathedral

✝ St. Botolph
Aldgate

Stepney

R. Walbrook

The
Tower ▫

Hospital of
St. Katharine

V E R

New
London
Bridge

T H
A M
E S

Hospital of
St. Thomas ⟶
(before 1212)

Priory of
St. Mary
Overy

✝ St. Olave

✝
St. Margaret

Southwark

✝ St. George

Bermondsey

✝ St. Mary Magdalen

Bermondsey
Abbey

Croydon

0 Miles   ¼   ½

and abbey of Westminster were firmly established as the chief centres of trade and the court in the south-east of England, in some respects for the whole island.

In earlier centuries the richest city in western Europe had been Cordova, set, like London, by an ancient bridge over a great river in the south-east of the country whose capital it was. Cordova was the headquarters of the Moslem caliphs, lords of an empire covering most of Spain, yet always with close links in the Mediterranean and north Africa. Spain is a country whose core consists of mountain ranges and plateaux; it has no natural centres, but the position of Cordova in the heyday of Islam in the western Mediterranean is intelligible enough. In a similar way London owed its foundation to the Romans: it was an ideal place for the major political and commercial centre of Roman Britain, for it lay where the great navigable river of the south-east, the Thames, met the chief overland road coming up from the south and east: port and bridge and a network of roads mainly Roman but partly pre-Roman made a centre in London attractive. So long as the North Sea and the rivers flowing into it remained the main centres of communication in the island, so long as Britain's links with continental Europe were of consequence, London was likely to be a convenient centre of commercial activity; and after the Norman Conquest it resumed its situation as intermediary between the main expanse of England and the lines of communication essential to an empire with a strong foothold on the Continent; more concretely, it was conveniently placed for an English king who was also Duke of Normandy, as well as the natural centre for a system of trade whose main routes lay between England and Flanders – though also to the Rhine and the Garonne. In one respect London is much better placed for its purpose than Cordova. Britain is roughly divided into a lowland and a highland zone, and the former covers almost the whole of the south-east and midlands; thus London lies near enough to the centre of a wheel whose spokes spread over the lowland zone and out to sea over the main lines of communication by water. The landward spokes follow the Roman roads of the first century AD, and also the main railway lines of the nineteenth and twentieth.

We may now enter the City and unravel the medieval town under the palimpsest of later changes. Little that belongs to the twelfth century is now visible; but a great deal of the structure of medieval London can be found by careful enquiry into its boundaries and street-lines, into the many traces of its early topography which survived into later centuries, some to the present day. Those which are especially revealing for the

history of the eleventh and twelfth centuries are the site, and the boundaries, of the old parish churches – most now departed and gone, but
leaving many indications in the current topography of the City; and the
boundaries of wards, still very much a feature of modern local government,
even if alderman and wardmote are rarely called out to face a siege. More
visible than these are the lines of the roads, many of them still in general
following the pattern of the twelfth century, and the site of London
Bridge itself. In a sense, these should be our chief guides to London's
topography; but in the present state of knowledge too much is still
conjecture which will presently be made plain. We walk the streets,
therefore, with a wary tread; then follow FitzStephen in his *Description*
with somewhat greater confidence, and give our closest attention to those
characteristic creations of our period, the wards and parishes.

London Bridge[1]

No one doubts that the Romans built the first London Bridge, nor that it
lay approximately where the present bridge now runs; nor that the meeting
of river and bridge determined the site of the first port of London. In a
characteristically careful and penetrating study, Miss Honeybourne has
argued that the Roman bridge ran a little to the east of the line to which we
are accustomed; that the Roman bridge was of wood and survived, however many times repaired and even rebuilt, down to the twelfth century.
To this doctrine the archaeologists have taken some exception, based on
archaeological traces in Southwark and the history of the road-lines in the
City, which suggest a more complex history. It seems that the richest
prospects for new discoveries by the spade lie along the river bank north
of the Thames, and it is reasonable to hope that in the next few years
traces may be found of roads and footings for successive bridges, if such

---

[1] On London Bridge, see G. Home, *Old London Bridge*, London, 1931; M. B. Honeybourne, in *Studies in London History*, pp. 17–39; G. Dawson and R. Merrifield in
London Archaeologist, vol. i, pts 5–14, 1969–72, pp. 114–17, 156–60, 186–7, 224,
330–2; *Future of London's Past*, pp. 12, 23, 81; see also J. G. Broodbank, *History of the
Port of London*, 2 vols, London, 1921. Some of the Bridge House Deeds in the Corporation Records Office were described and illustrated in *To God and the Bridge*
(Catalogue of Exhibition in Guildhall Art Gallery, 1972): see esp. F23, no. 1 in
Catalogue, grant by Peter the Priest of *c*. 1200 or before. The Ann. Waverley (*Ann
Mon.*, vol. ii, 240, 256–7) give the dates 1176, 1205; for 1209, Ann. Bermondsey (ib. vol.
iii, 451). The fire of 1212 is noted by Ann. Waverley, p. 268; Ann. Worcester (ib.
vol. iv), p. 400; etc. *LAL*, p. 3, is probably in error in dating it 1211.

there were. Meanwhile, there is no topic on which it is more essential to be cautious than on the approach to London Bridge. It is likely that the Roman bridge survived into the early Middle Ages, though there may well have been periods when its line was cut. It is likely too that its continuous history begins again in Alfred's time or thereabouts; that the revival of London as a major centre of population was encouraged by the repair, renewal or rebuilding of the bridge. The most probable view at present seems to be that Miss Honeybourne was right to set this bridge a little to the east of the present bridge; though it cannot be ruled out of court that the last wooden bridge, of late Saxon and Norman times, lay exactly on the present line, and was replaced piecemeal by the stone bridge in the late twelfth century. All this is doubtful; firm ground comes again only in 1176, when the annals of Waverley tell us that Peter, chaplain of Colechurch – presumably, as we should say, vicar of St Mary Colechurch – began the building of the stone bridge.[1] What he seems to have done is to form the first of a series of confraternities and guilds which raised the money as a pious, charitable work; and he seems to have founded the chapel in honour of St Thomas Becket, then recently martyred, which was the first of the bridge's many buildings. By the time that he died in 1205 the work was doubtless virtually complete; if we may trust the annals of Bermondsey, it was finished in 1209. These annals are among the most unreliable of such records; but they occasionally deviate into accuracy, and this date cannot be far wrong, for the deeds of the Bridge House Trust, which has administered the Bridge from that day to this, show it as a going concern in the opening years of the thirteenth century, or even a little earlier, and it was sufficiently in being in 1212 to be severely damaged by fire.

The City Streets[2]

The road line which runs down from Bishopsgate, through Gracechurch Street, to Fish Street Hill and the river evidently formed the main line from north to south through the medieval City, and is a major route,

---

[1] For what follows, see previous note.
[2] See below, pp. 171 ff.; Ekwall; Harben; and for recent studies, J. Haslam in *London Archaeologist*, vol. ii, no. 1, 1972, pp. 3–8 (citing excavations revealing Aldermanbury, Aldersgate Street, St Paul's Wharf, St Paul's Hill, Bosse Lane and Trig Lane); *Future of London's Past*, pp. 14, 16, 21, 23, 81. See also the important comparative study, M. Biddle and D. Hill, in *Antiquaries Journal*, vol. li, 1971, pp. 70–85.

characteristic of the main City streets, in that it neither conforms to the Roman pattern nor to the needs of the modern City. The modern City has played havoc with the small roads and lanes which it inherited. In the nineteenth century a few sabre cuts were made in the pattern, of which King William Street (begun in 1829) and Queen Victoria Street (1871) are monuments; and a few before that – but very few – after the Great Fire of 1666, such as Queen Street and Prince's Street. But the main structure can be shown to be of the twelfth century or earlier by the evidence of street-names and documents; the age of a few, but so far of only a few, has been revealed by the spade. There is little doubt that this structure is the product partly of planning, partly of self-help: a glance at the map shows how some streets meander, some form blocks and grids. More precise than this one cannot be until the archaeologists have had more chance to check what still survives under the modern road surfaces: this is one area of City archaeology whose future seems distinctly hopeful. Yet already a few points seem tolerably clear. As in most cities north of the Alps whose foundation was Roman, the line of the Roman walls has made a permanent contribution to London's history, the lines of the Roman streets very little.

Yet there are three remarkable indications that the Roman pattern has had some permanent influence on this structure. First of all, in the north-west, where the line of the walls still shows the outline of the Cripplegate fort, the earliest of the Roman defensive works; here the grid pattern of the streets owes something to the survival of Roman streets; here thirteenth-century tradition placed the old royal palace; and here has been supposed the greatest measure of continuity in London settlement.[1] The second link is in the line of the great market-places of west and east, the West Cheap or Cheapside, and Eastcheap, part of which follow Roman roads; and the third is in the line of Upper Thames Street, which apparently conforms in part of its length to the original river frontage of Roman times. The placing of the two cheaps reflects something of the division between east and west which appears to be characteristic both of the first Roman

[1] See esp. *Future of London's Past*, pp. 20–1. The tradition first appears in Matthew Paris's *Gesta Abbatum S. Albani* (cf. Rolls Series ed., vol. i, p. 55; and for authorship and texts see R. Vaughan, *Matthew Paris*, Cambridge, 1958, pp. 182 ff.). Unfortunately the context is a tendentious account of the origin of St Alban's Wood Street, which is said to have been a chapel built by Offa adjacent to his palace and originally given to the abbey of St Albans; and it may be that the whole story was invented to bolster this tale. In any event the unsupported word of Matthew Paris is poor evidence for traditions of a much earlier period.

settlements and of the early Saxon settlements in the City. The two markets probably formed the nuclei round which London grew in late Saxon times; but the details are still very obscure. We shall presently see reason to suppose that the east and north-east of the City revived more slowly than the west and south; and the pattern of the streets certainly conforms with such a view. For over most of the western half of the City, barring the area immediately round St Paul's, there is still visible a rough grid of medieval streets of the kind which one finds in smaller towns more certainly re-planned or planned in and after the age of Alfred.[1] Such a pattern can be seen equally along the river bank, as it then was, and round Eastcheap. But from Aldgate and Bishopsgate major roads have been driven in sweeping curves at variance with the Roman structure, and of these Fenchurch Street at least was wide enough in the central Middle Ages for the church of All Hallows to sit in its midst.[2]

Along these lines we may see in the structure of the City in recent centuries a great deal of its history indicated or hinted at; and to make these hints more audible we must invoke the aid of FitzStephen and other contemporary witnesses.

WILLIAM FITZSTEPHEN'S *Description*

On 29 December 1170, as darkness fell over Canterbury and its cathedral, the archbishop's companions, monks and clerks, fled from him, and only three remained by his side to face his murderers. One of these, William, son of Stephen, or FitzStephen, as he is commonly called, sat down three or four years later to write what is still one of the best lives of Thomas Becket that we have, though written in a rhetorical Latin below the best the twelfth century could achieve.[3]

FitzStephen had two notable qualities: a capacity for pithy dialogue, and an eye for colour, for a man's dress, for the scene. This is a quality we particularly prize in these centuries; three hundred years later the Renaissance cult of precise representation can bring us face to face, so to speak, with the men of the fifteenth and sixteenth centuries, and with their

---

[1] See p. 110 n. 2 above, esp. article by Biddle and Hill.

[2] *Eyre*, no. 276.

[3] On FitzStephen, see p. 88 n., and references there cited. The extracts are our own translation from *MB*, vol. iii, pp. 2–13, though we have benefited from H. E. Butler's translation and notes in Stenton, and have ourselves studied all the surviving MSS. For other extracts, see pp. 13, 42, 288–9.

physical surroundings, in a way in which we can only in a very exceptional
case know those of the twelfth. It is a singular misfortune that the railway
builders of the nineteenth century flattened Northampton Castle to make
Northampton Castle station, for it would be peculiarly valuable to be able
to compare FitzStephen's precise, yet elusive, description of the setting
of the Council of Northampton in October 1164, when Becket and the
king finally parted company, with a castle still in being.[1] Yet we can in a
measure still do this with his most famous description, his account of
London, in which both he and Becket were born, at the beginning of his
book:

> Plato sketched the shape of a Republic in a discourse; Sallust des-
> cribed the situation of Africa in his History on account of the
> Carthaginian rebellion against the Romans ... and I shall now
> describe the site and commonwealth of London on account of St
> Thomas.
>
> Amid the noble cities of the world, the City of London, throne of
> the English kingdom, is one which has spread its fame far and wide,
> its wealth and merchandise to great distances, raised its head on high.
> It is blessed by a wholesome climate, blessed too in Christ's religion,
> in the strength of its fortifications, in the nature of its site, the repute
> of its citizens, the honour of its matrons; happy in its sports, prolific
> in noble men. Let us take each of these points in turn.

What follows by no means fulfils the programme, but we are given much
precise – sometimes inflated, always optimistic, but rarely entirely
fanciful – information about the London of FitzStephen's day. 'On the
east lies the royal citadel, of very notable size and strength; its court and
wall rise from very deep foundations, where mortar mingles with animal's
blood.'[2] This is a nice example of the mingling of precise description and
fragments of mythology; and this is one of the few points where Fitz-
Stephen's description and the modern City meet. In FitzStephen's time
the Tower consisted of the Conqueror's great keep, the familiar White
Tower, and a modest *enceinte*, wholly within the circuit of the walls.
Outside the wall at this point lay the southern end of the Portsoken and
parish of St Botolph without Aldgate, which ran down to the river; and

[1] Cf. D. Knowles, *Episcopal Colleagues of Archbishop Thomas Becket*, Cambridge,
1951, pp. 169–70.
[2] It is just possible that it is more than coincidence that foreign butchers were centred
in East Smithfield in the later Middle Ages.

the hospital of St Katharine founded in Stephen's reign by Stephen's queen. The Tower began to extend beyond the wall in the late twelfth century, and reached its present extent, with its great concentric defences and moats, in the reign of Edward I. In the course of this process it became a Liberty independent of the City, and played curious tricks with the boundaries of parishes, the Portsoken and the City itself at this point.

'On the west are two keeps strongly fortified' – the castles of Baynard and Montfichet,[1] both of which fell into disuse in the thirteenth century, since City, Holborn and Westminster had become by then one urban complex, and were absorbed late in the thirteenth century into the Blackfriars, the great enclosure of the Dominican Convent. 'The whole way round the north of the city the wall, tall and wide, strengthened with turrets at intervals, links the seven gates of the city, each double-faced' – which we may recognize now as a reference to Ludgate, Newgate, Cripplegate, Aldersgate, Bishopsgate, Aldgate and presumably the Tower postern; for Moorgate was an addition of the fifteenth century, when the City and the moor were first linked.[2] Though none of the six main gates, nor any fragment above ground, now survives, all have left their mark on the City's topography, and provided it with some of its most ancient and long-lived names.

Once London was walled and towered on the south side too; but that great river, the Thames, well-stocked with fish, with tidal flow and ebb, has lapped against the walls over the years and undermined and destroyed them.

This passage has caused historians and archaeologists quite a search; but it is now established that the southern wall of the city was a fiction; that in Roman times as later the river was the boundary.[3] Some pieces of

[1] See pp. 214–15; Brooke, Keir and Reynolds, pp. 565–6 and notes; Kingsford in *LTR*, vols x, pp. 59–64, xi, pp. 46–7. The association of Montfichet with the castle bearing his name is first definitely recorded in 1173 (Jordan Fantosme in *Chrons. of the reigns of Stephen etc.*, ed. R. Howlett, Rolls Series, London, 1884–9, vol. iii, p. 338); but there are grounds for supposing it at least a generation earlier. Baynard Castle must have acquired its name before the forfeiture of the last Bainard in 1110–11. Both were probably in origin late eleventh century. Both disappeared under the Black Friars' new house in the late thirteenth century (*c*. 1275), and Castle Baynard was rebuilt in the early fourteenth century on the site recently excavated.

[2] On the gates, see Stow, vol. i, pp. 27 ff., vol. ii, pp. 274 ff. Cf. Harben, s.v. Aldersgate, Aldgate, etc.

[3] See R. Merrifield, *Roman City of London*, pp. 48, 221 ff.; Grimes, p. 56.

wall were built in Roman times, and surviving fragments inspired the imagination of the first medieval age seriously to indulge in archaeological research – or rather fancy; and so FitzStephen extended them into a complete circuit.

Two miles to the west of the City, with a populous faubourg in between, the royal palace [of Westminster] rises on the bank, a building of the greatest splendour with outwork and bastions. Everywhere without their houses are the citizens' gardens, side by side yet spacious and splendid, and set about with trees. To the north lie arable fields, pasture land and lush, level meadows, with brooks flowing amid them, which turn the wheels of watermills with a happy sound. Close by is the opening of a mighty forest, with well-timbered copses, lairs of wild beasts, stags and does, wild boars and bulls.

We seem to be stretching our eyes here far to the north-east, to Middlesex and to Essex, to the hunting-grounds that began at or about Highgate whose chief remnant today is Epping Forest.[1]

There are also in the northern suburbs of London splendid wells and springs, with sweet, healing, clear water . . . Holywell, Clerkenwell and St Clement's Well are especially famous and often visited; and crowds of schoolboys and students and young men of the City take the air there on summer evenings. A good city indeed – if it should have a good lord . . .

The citizens of London are universally held up for admiration and renown for the elegance of their manners and dress, and the delights of their tables. Other cities have citizens, London's are called Barons.[2] Among them an oath-swearing ends every dispute. The matrons of the City are very Sabines.

FitzStephen briefly mentions the churches of London, and not so briefly the schools where he himself had evidently learned the art of rhetoric. Next follow the retail trades, wine-cellars, the public kitchen, described in detail, not without reference to the *Gorgias* of Plato; the Smithfield horse-market and the races by which the horses show their worth; the cattle-market; the long-distance trade in luxuries, including

---

[1] *VCH Essex*, vol. ii, pp. 615 ff.; cf. ib., Bibliography, pp. 22 ff. The whole county of Essex was under forest law in the twelfth century.

[2] See p. 258.

gold from Arabia, oil from Egypt, silk from China and furs from Norway and Russia.[1]

London, as the chroniclers have shown, is far older than Rome. For owing its birth to the same Trojan ancestors, it was founded by Brutus before Rome was founded by Romulus and Remus. Hence both still use the same laws and common institutions. London like Rome is divided into wards [*regionibus*]; has sheriffs annually appointed for consuls; has a senatorial order, and lesser magistracies; sewers and aqueducts in its streets; deliberative, demonstrative, judicial cases have their distinct places, their individual courts; London has its assemblies on fixed days. I can think of no city with customs more admirable, in the visiting of churches, ordaining of festivals to God's honour and their due celebration, in almsgiving, in receiving guests, in concluding betrothals, contracting marriages, celebrating weddings, laying on ornate feasts and joyful occasions, and also in caring for the dead and burying them. The only plagues of London are the immoderate drinking of fools and the frequency of fires. Added to all this almost all the bishops, abbots and great men of England are as it were citizens and dwellers in the City of London, having their own noble edifices, where they stay, lay out lavish expenditure, when they are summoned to the City by the king or their archbishop to councils or other large gatherings, or to attend to their own affairs.

In this passage is distilled much that will form the theme of later chapters. The citizens of London, the barons – who were they, with their Sabine wives? In what sense were the great men of the realm citizens of London? What consequences flowed from this? Again, the account of city government and laws, and the attempt to draw analogies with Rome, will help us in our enquiry into the history of London's 'magistrates'.[2] Let us observe, meanwhile, that the reference to wards and to the citizens' Trojan ancestors mark the opposite ends of the spectrum in FitzStephen, of fact and fiction.

In the late Middle Ages the central assemblies of City Government were (as they still are) the Court of Common Council and the Court of Aldermen. Of these, the former is a development of the late Middle Ages, and falls quite outside our period; but in some sense the Court of Aldermen is undoubtedly more ancient. The aldermen were in later and better

---

[1] See pp. 258 ff.   [2] See chaps 8–9.

documented centuries the leading officials of the twenty-four wards (ultimately twenty-six) into which the City was divided; and it is as such that they make their debut, so far as the documents are concerned, in the twelfth century. For the study of City government, and many other aspects of the City's history, it is of quite peculiar importance to work back behind FitzStephen's text, to the origins of wards and aldermen. Here we shall find the St Paul's survey of the 1120s and the topography of the wards the crucial evidence; and we may also learn something from the history of the word 'alderman' itself.[1]

FitzStephen concluded his portrait of the City with a long account of its sports, and a short mention of its notable worthies, from the Emperor Constantine[2] to the blessed Thomas, 'Christ's glorious martyr'. And so he is back where he began, and can embark on his hero's life; a shapely book, with a shapely introduction; yet the two are hardly in accord. For if we look at the end for a panegyric on Canterbury, where Becket's relics lay and already gathered the pilgrims when FitzStephen wrote, we look in vain. Becket's citizenship was a shallow pretext for a rhapsody which the author wished in any case to write on the City he loved.

Yet it remains in many ways a puzzling document. There is only one medieval analogy known to us from FitzStephen's day or earlier for a description of a city prefixing a biography: a ninth- or tenth-century description of Milan prefacing some lives of its archbishops;[3] and it is not at all probable that the book was known to FitzStephen. It is very likely that he knew the contemporary guide-books to Rome and Jerusalem which were the most popular descriptions of cities produced before the Renaissance.[4] The Roman guide-book of the 1140s bears a superficial resemblance to FitzStephen on London in that it shows a markedly secular interest in a supposedly religious setting; and it may have influenced

[1] See p. 155.

[2] This seems to be based on Geoffrey of Monmouth, *Hist. Regum Britanniae*, bk v, c. 6, who tells us Constantine was born in England, though he does not specify London.

[3] For possible analogies see the interesting study by J. K. Hyde, 'Medieval Descriptions of Cities', *Bulletin of the John Rylands Library*, vol. xlviii, 1966, pp. 308–40; the Milanese description was ed. G. B. Pighi in *Versus de Verona, Versus de Mediolano Civitate*, Bologna, 1960 (cf. Hyde, p. 339, and pp. 338–40 for a list of these descriptions). See also A. Gransden in *Speculum*, vol. xlvii, 1972, pp. 44 ff.

[4] See Hyde, art. cit.; Master Gregory, *De mirabilibus urbis Rome*, ed. R. Valentini and G. Zucchetti, *Codice topografico della città di Roma*, vol. iii, *Fonti per la Storia d'Italia*, Rome, 1946, with bibliography. For descriptions of Jerusalem, see Hyde, p. 339.

his references to Rome. But there the resemblance ends: the colour and life of the streets of London, the sports and games of its people, the pageantry and show were what chiefly attracted FitzStephen's eye; in the Roman guide-book it was the pagan antiquities which particularly delighted the author. We may well believe that if FitzStephen had visited Rome, his observant eye would also have been struck by the remains of antiquity, as its literary remains clearly fascinated him. We must not be misled by his citations: his pretentious references to Plato and Sallust at the outset are pure bravado. It is clear that he knew little or nothing at first hand of either. Plato was a name to conjure with, and the ultimate source of much which was most characteristic of the scholastic thought of the eleventh and twelfth centuries. But apart from the *Timaeus* his writings were only known in FitzStephen's youth from quotations in Latin authors; a thin stream of his other writings began to come through Sicily in this age.[1] Sallust was widely read and much influenced twelfth-century historians; but if FitzStephen knew him at first-hand, he had forgotten Sallust's text when he referred to him.[2] His copious quotations from Horace, Virgil and Lucan show similarly that he took his learning from garbled anthologies, or quoted from a rather distant memory of the days when he had been judged happy in the flow of words with the best of his fellow students. In this respect he is a fine sample of the twelfth-century renaissance: fascinated by the pagan classics, but with an ear really tuned to the theatrical prose of late Roman rhetoric, and to the verse of his own day, and so prepared to maul and mutilate the subtle rhythms and sophisticated obscurities of classical Latin literature.

As to the physical remains of the Roman world, London had nothing to show save the line of her walls. FitzStephen displays an antiquarian, but hardly an archaeological, interest. The present in fair measure blotted out the past. It was very different in the little ruined fortress of Caerleon 'situated in a passing pleasant position on the river Usk in Glamorgan, not far from the Severn sea', as Geoffrey of Monmouth describes it in his *History of the Kings of Britain* (*c.* 1138).[3] Caerleon had caught

---

[1] See the series of *Plato Latinus*, publ. by the Warburg Institute ed. R. Klibawsky (vol. i– , 1940–).

[2] Since Sallust's *Jugurtha* does not in fact begin with the description of Africa FitzStephen attributes to it; this is a surprising error since most twelfth-century historians had read Sallust or knew something of him, and it may be a failure of memory. For classical and other allusions, see Butler in Stenton, p. 33.

[3] Geoffrey of Monmouth, *Historia Regum Brittaniae*, bk ix, cc. 12–15 (ed. A. Griscom, New York, 1929, pp. 451 ff.). On Geoffrey see Brooke in *Studies in the Early*

Geoffrey's eye and stirred his imagination; and he made it the setting for the central scene of his book, the crown-wearing of King Arthur and Queen Guinevere. He does not give a formal description of Caerleon, but its site, its walls, its streets, its churches lift from the page as effectively as FitzStephen's London. There is copious evidence that FitzStephen had read Geoffrey, and we need not doubt that Geoffrey's Caerleon, King Arthur's capital, was one of the inspirations of FitzStephen's London, throne of the Angevin kings. Certainly Arthur's crown-wearing was calculated to bring the reigning king to mind, since it is the best description we have of this ceremony in the twelfth century, though fiction as applied to King Arthur. There are other links between Geoffrey and William. The Trojan origin of Britain was invented by Geoffrey after equally fantastic, but much more ancient, Frankish legends. Perhaps the closest link is in the account of the great churches of the two cities:

> It was also famous for its two churches, [writes Geoffrey of Monmouth of Caerleon], one built in honour of the martyr Julius, charmingly adorned by a choir of virgins dedicated to God's service, and the second dedicated to the blessed Aaron, his companion, served by a community of canons – and this was the cathedral of the third metropoliton see of Britain. It had, in addition, a school of two hundred philosophers, skilled in astronomy and the other arts, who diligently observed the course of the stars, and accurately foretold the wonders that were shortly to befall King Arthur. Such was the City, famous for abundance of everything delightful, which was now preparing for the festival [of Pentecost].[1]

Behind this claim for Caerleon to be the third metropolitan see lies a curious story. Disputes over primacy were wholly characteristic of eleventh- and twelfth-century Europe; in this island at that time York was disputing Canterbury's claim to primacy of all England; Scotland and Wales were both seeking to escape from English jurisdiction; and the bishop of Llandaff was claiming equality at least with St David, the protagonist of Welsh independence.[2] Geoffrey of Monmouth made merry with his friends by appointing St David himself to succeed St Dubricius

---

British Church, ed. N. K. Chadwick, Cambridge, 1958, pp. 202 ff.; J. S. P. Tatlock, *The Legendary History of Britain*, Univ. of California, 1950.

[1] Geoffrey of Monmouth, loc. cit.
[2] See summary and references in *GF*, pp. 153 ff.; for Geoffrey's influence on Gilbert Foliot, *GF*, pp. 151 ff.

(the legendary founder of Llandaff) as archbishop of a see of his own devising – that of Caerleon – at the end of the Pentecostal celebrations; and thus he set the Welsh clergy the task of rewriting their legends and started a fuse which nearly exploded under the throne of Canterbury itself.

> . . . The bishop's see [wrote FitzStephen[1]] is in the church of St Paul. It was once a metropolitan see, and will be so again – so it is thought – if 'the citizens return to the island'. But perchance the title of archbishop which Thomas the blessed martyr held, and the presence of his body, may keep that dignity for ever in Canterbury, where he lies. But since St Thomas glorified both these cities – London by his rise and Canterbury by the setting of his sun – by that same token the one might claim his merit with greater justice than the other.
>
> There are also . . . in London and its suburbs thirteen conventual churches and a hundred and twenty-six lesser, parish churches besides . . . The three principal churches have famous schools of ancient dignity and privilege;

and he goes on – not to claim two hundred philosophers – but to boast of the skill in rhetoric of the London schoolboys. This passage brings us face to face with striking examples of the way in which both legend and precise fact entered into FitzStephen's calculations.

The little piece of gibberish at the outset – 'if the citizens return to the island' – has for the most part passed unnoticed by FitzStephen's numerous editors and commentators. Samuel Pegge, in the eighteenth century, observed it and gave an explanation which is entirely improbable; more recently, an attempt was made to translate it intelligibly, but by violence to the Latin.[2] It is in fact an echo of the 'Prophecies of Merlin', which are a part of Geoffrey's *History*.[3] The prophecy is attributed to the period of Uther Pendragon, Arthur's father, and this makes possible the familiar technique of prophecy after the event; the first third of the Prophecies take us in an odd, allusive way, through history (as Geoffrey viewed it) from the fifth to the twelfth centuries; there is then a brief vision of the immediate future, and a very long vision of the more distant future which is entirely unintelligible. In the passage describing the immediate future

---

[1] *MB*, vol. iii, p. 2.

[2] S. Pegge's edition of the *Description* (1772), pp. 15–16; Brooke in *HSP*, p. 30.

[3] Geoffrey of Monmouth, op. cit., bk vii, c. 3, ed. Griscom, p. 388.

there is a description of a great empire, which has been variously interpreted as the vision of a pan-Celtic revival and as a forecast of the Angevin
empire; no doubt its ambiguity was intended. Part of the preparation for
this is the return of the citizens to the island; and all that FitzStephen
probably meant was 'if the millennium arrives' London will become once
again the seat of the primate. Geoffrey was glossing a genuine piece of
ancient history whose memory had recently been revived by a bishop of
London of the early twelfth century, Richard de Belmeis I; and Geoffrey
in his turn was used by FitzStephen's bishop, Gilbert Foliot, Becket's
chief episcopal opponent, as a stick with which to beat the archbishop;
for Gilbert Foliot reckoned that Geoffrey's book provided evidence that
Foliot and not Becket should be archbishop.[1]

One hundred and twenty-six parish churches is a high figure; but if it
is taken to include a fair part of Middlesex (which is not unreasonable)
it could be precisely correct.[2] What is very strange to us looking back is
that the overwhelming majority of these churches lay within the walls of
the City. Such a number, at such a date, within the walls of a city, is
the largest recorded in western Europe. Comparable figures can be found
in much smaller towns in England, no figures truly comparable can be
detected on the Continent. The outcome, furthermore, was the formation
of a structure of parish boundaries covering the City like a net with a
small mesh; if it can be shown that this mesh is as old as the churches,
then we have a most unusually precise piece of evidence for the structure
and layout of the City.

Indeed, boundaries have even more to teach us than this; for wards have
boundaries as well as parishes. Sometimes the two sets of boundaries
marched together, equally often, they diverged, sometimes much, sometimes little. The dialectic between the two is most instructive; and from it
we can hope to penetrate deeper into the origins of the wards, and with
them into the whole nature of City government.

[1] *GF*, pp. 151 ff.
[2] See next chapter; Brooke in *Studies in Church History*, vol. vi, pp. 59–83.

6

On Parishes

B Y THE mid-thirteenth century, and probably by 1200, the tale of small churches, and the parish map, were complete.[1] The enormous number of parish churches within and without the City walls – and especially within – compels us to enquire how such a proliferation could ever have been possible: and this in its turn takes us to the heart of a series of intriguing problems of religious sentiment and law and economics. It is the first and major key to the growth of London in this period.

THE ORIGIN OF CHURCHES AND PARISHES

In the building of large churches the Norman Conquest marked an epoch: in the building of small, it was much less of a breach. The Normans built and rebuilt cathedrals and large abbey churches of a size and number unprecedented in pre-Conquest England. The Confessor's abbey church at Westminster anticipated this change, and perhaps may indicate that it would have come (in a measure at least) in any event, but hardly on the scale of many Norman buildings. Nonetheless, the Normans, like the

[1] On churches and church building in England in the eleventh century, see H. M. and J. Taylor, *Anglo-Saxon Architecture*, 2 vols, Cambridge, 1965; A. W. Clapham, *English Romanesque Architecture before the Conquest* and *English Romanesque Architecture after the Conquest*, Oxford, 1930, 1934. Recent excavations have increased our knowledge of the lay-out and furnishing of parish churches: see M. Biddle, 'Excavations at Winchester, 1966', pp. 262-3; '1967', pp. 263-5; '1968', pp. 305-8; '1969', pp. 302-5; '1970', pp. 104 ff., 111 ff.

This chapter is based on extensive notes and an unpublished paper by G. K.; we hope to publish a detailed account of the early evidence for the parish churches elsewhere. A general survey of the background was given in Brooke, 'The Missionary at Home . . .', in *Studies in Church History*, vol. vi.

We are greatly indebted to much earlier work, from Stow and Newcourt on; and to the lists by Miss Jeffries Davis and Miss Honeybourne in Stenton, Map.

This map is based upon the parish boundaries before the Union of Parishes Act 1907 as shown in the Ordnance Survey, 1878 (repr. London Topog. Soc. 1959). Ogilby's map of c. *1676 has prompted a few alterations, but there is no evidence of major change over the period.*

The letters on the map refer to changes which took place c. *1216–1676:*

A   The parish boundaries of St Audoen and St Nicholas Shambles were obliterated after the Grey Friars established their house and precinct near Newgate.

B   St Anne Blackfriars was built after the Black Friars settled in this area.

C   St Mary Monthaw was founded in the course of the thirteenth century.

D   St Olaf Broad Street and its parish disappeared after the Augustinian Friars settled close by.

E   The parish of St Mary Axe was united to that of St Andrew Cornhill in 1565.

F   The parish of St Augustine on the Wall was united to that of All Hallows on the Wall in the fifteenth century.

G   The recent parish of St James Duke's Place occupies the site and precinct of Holy Trinity Priory Aldgate.

H   A chapel of St Katherine seems to have existed from the early twelfth century. It was rebuilt late in the thirteenth century and subsequently obtained a parish.

Key to London Churches

1   St (Anne and St) Agnes
2   St Alban Wood Street
3   All Hallows Barking
4   All Hallows Bread Street
5   All Hallows Colemanchurch (later St Katherine)
6   All Hallows Fenchurch (later St Gabriel)
7   All Hallows Gracechurch
8   All Hallows the Great
9   All Hallows Honey Lane
10   All Hallows the Less
11   All Hallows Staining
12   All Hallows on the Wall
13   St Alphege (Ælfheah)
14   St Andrew Castle Baynard (by the Wardrobe)
15   St Andrew Cornhill (Undershaft)
16   St Andrew at Eastcheap (Hubberd)
17   St Antonin
18   St Audoen
19   St Augustine by St Paul
20   St Augustine on the Wall (Papey)
21   St Bartholomew
22   St Benet Fink
23   St Benet Gracechurch
24   St Benet Sherehog
25   St Benet on Thames (Algar; Paul's Wharf)

26   St Botolph Aldersgate
27   St Botolph Aldgate
28   St Botolph Billingsgate
29   St Botolph Bishopsgate
30   St Christopher
31   St Clement Candlewick Street (Eastcheap)
32   St Dionis (Denis) Backchurch
33   St Dunstan towards the Tower (in the East)
34   St Edmund
35   St Ethelburga
36   St Faith
37   St George
38   St Giles Cripplegate
39   St Gregory
40   St Helen
41   St James Garlickhithe
42   St John upon Walbrook (the Baptist)
43   St John Zachary (the Baptist)
44   St Katherine Christchurch (Cree)
45   St Lawrence Jewry
46   St Lawrence on Thames (Pountney)
47   St Leonard Eastcheap
48   St Leonard Foster Lane
49   St Magnus the Martyr
50   St Margaret towards the Bridge
51   St Margaret Friday Street
52   St Margaret Lothbury

53   St Margaret Pattens (Patin)
54   St Martin Jewry
55   St Martin Ludgate
56   St Martin Orgar
57   St Martin Ottewich
58   St Martin on Thames
59   St Mary Abchurch
60   St Mary Aldermanbury
61   St Mary Aldermary
62   St Mary Axe
63   St Mary Bothaw
64   St Mary-le-Bow
65   St Mary Colechurch
66   St Mary at Hill
67   St Mary Magdalen in the Fishmarket
68   St Mary Magdalen Milk Street
69   St Mary Somerset
70   St Mary Staining
71   St Mary Woolchurch
72   St Mary Woolnoth
73   St Matthew
74   St Michael Bassishaw
75   St Michael towards the Bridge
76   St Michael Cornhill
77   St Michael Cornmarket (le Querne)
78   St Michael Paternoster
79   St Michael Queenhithe
80   St Michael Wood St
81   St Mildred Bread Street

82   St Mildred Walbrook
83   St Nicholas Acon
84   St Nicholas Shambles (Aldred)
85   St Nicholas West Fishmarket (Coldabbey)
86   St Olaf (Olave) Bread Street (St Nicholas Olaf)
87   St Olaf Broad Street
88   St Olaf Jewry
89   St Olaf Monkwell Street
90   St Olaf towards the Tower (Hart St)
91   St Pancras
92   St Peter in the Bailey
93   St Peter Broad Street (the Poor)
94   St Peter Cornhill
95   St Peter the Little (Paul's Wharf)
96   St Peter West Cheap
97   St Sepulchre (Newgate)
98   St Stephen Coleman Street
99   St Stephen Walbrook
100   St Swithin
101   St Thomas the Apostle
102   Holy Trinity the Little (or Less)
103   St Vedast
104   St Werburga (later St John the Evangelist)

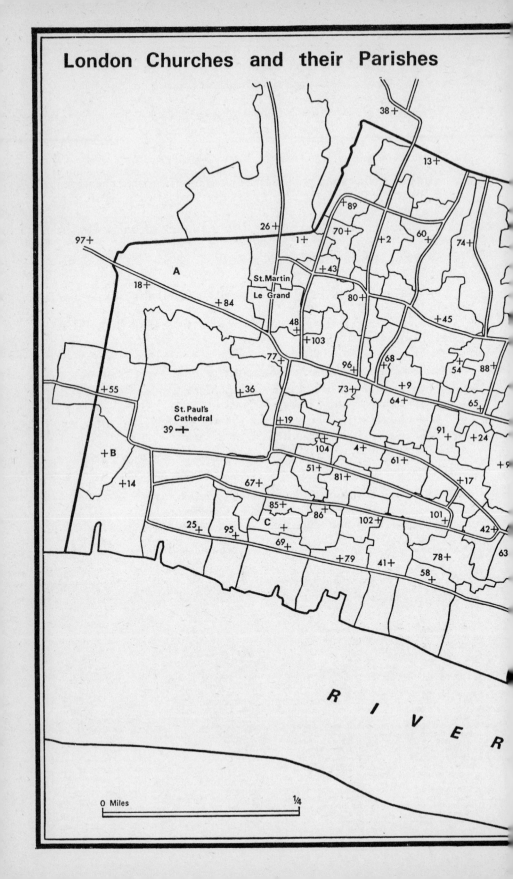

London Churches and their Parishes

38 +

13 +

+ 89

26 +

97 +

1 +

70 +

60

2 +

74 +

A

+ 43

18 +

St. Martin
Le Grand

80 +

+ 84

+ 45

48 +

+ 103

68 +

77 +

96 +

+ 9

54

88

+ 55

+ 36

73 +

64 +

65 +

St. Paul's
Cathedral

+ 19

91 +

+ 24

39 +

104 +

4 +

61 +

+ B

51 +

81 +

+ 17

+ 9

+ 14

67 +

85 +

102 +

101 +

86 +

42 +

25 +

95 +

C +

69 +

78 +

63

+ 79

41 +

58 +

O Miles   ¼

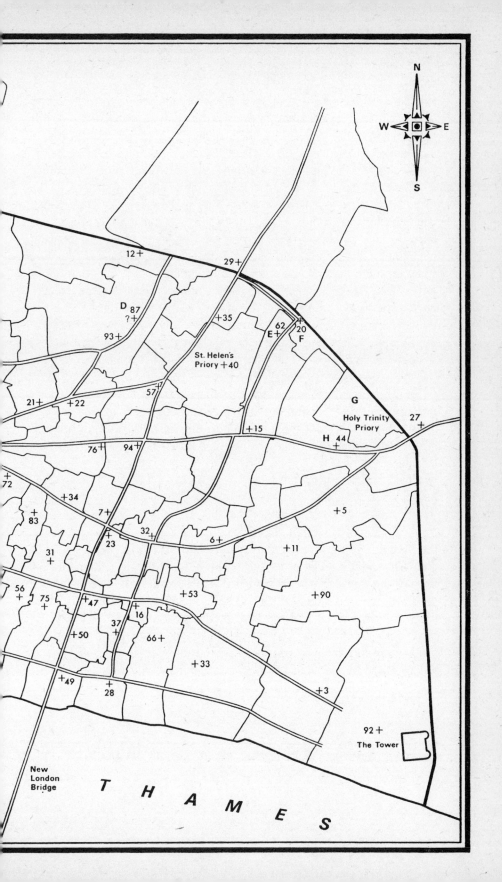

N
W E
S

12 +

29 +

D 87
? +

93 +

+ 35

62
E + 62
+ 20
F

St. Helen's
Priory + 40

57 +

G

Holy Trinity
Priory

27 +

21 +   + 22

+ 15

H 44 +

76 +   94 +

+
72

+ 34

7 +

+
83

32 +

+
23

+ 5

31
+

6 +

+ 11

56
+   75
+

+ 47

+ 53

+ 90

37 +
+ 16

+ 50

66 +

+ 33

+ 49

+
28

+ 3

92 +
The Tower

New
London
Bridge

T H A M E S

English and other peoples all over Christendom, seem on the whole to have preferred tiny churches for everyday use and normal worship. While the cathedrals doubled and trebled in area and tremendous provision was made in their naves for occasional visits by throngs of laymen, the parish churches and oratories remained tiny. There are some exceptions, of which St Mary-le-Bow was evidently one of the most striking in the City, as its crypt still bears witness. But on the whole the large parish church reflects the fashion of the late twelfth and thirteenth centuries and later. It may have been due in part, and in some places, to growing population. But it commonly affected the chancel (at least in the first instance) more than the nave; and it seems much more likely that it was in the main due to changes in religious sentiment and liturgical arrangements, and to increasing use of furniture, even in the end of benches for the laity, rather than increasing numbers. In any event, larger numbers can hardly account for most of such rebuilding as took place in London, since one would suppose that nearly one hundred churches within the walls would satisfy the piety of any age.

Thus the tiny churches and their profusion represent a world in which the laity wished to worship normally in small congregations close to their priests; the tiny parish church was almost as intimate as the house church of the Roman Empire in times of persecution. How they were supported is a puzzle. It is generally reckoned that the prosperity of London had reached a peak by the mid-thirteenth century beyond anything dreamed of before.[1] Yet when the papal tax gatherers went round in 1254 or thereabouts assessing the churches of the City and the diocese for taxation, they sadly noted of church after church in the City that it was not worth the fleecing: and a number they simply left out.[2] They were assessing their tithes and dues in order to tax them. Unfortunately the nature of tithe in the eleventh, twelfth and thirteenth centuries is a very obscure problem: and it is difficult for us to know whether the assessments were likely to have represented the facts of the situation at all precisely. In theory, tithe could be raised from agricultural land, from rents, from craftsmanship, from mercantile profit – from everything under the sun. That it was so raised in practice in these early centuries is more than doubtful.[3]

---

[1] See pp. 360–1.

[2] *Valuation of Norwich*, pp. 326–33 (from a register of *c.* 1262–3); on the date, cf. pp. 178–81.

[3] The early history of tithe in urban churches is extremely obscure. In theory tithe was payable on anything and everything, but what actually happened may well be

In any case, we may take comfort from the tax-assessors' discomfort: if they could find nothing to tax, we may be sure there was no large hidden wealth.

How then, did the City clergy live? Behind this question there lies a deeper, harder question: how could these churches ever have been built and kept in repair? From the thirteenth century at latest the lion's share of any parish church's income came from tithes. If we may be confident of anything, it is that these churches were not built – and were never expected to live – on tithes alone. To this problem there can be only one general answer, though no doubt particular circumstances affected numerous special cases: they were built from the offerings of the faithful. They represent something very familiar to students of church-building on the large scale: the tremendous concentration of resources into church offerings at certain moments in the Middle Ages. At certain moments – in a sense this is too confined. Offerings were part of the scene from the days of St Augustine to the Reformation, and beyond. But there is one period of the Middle Ages when they fundamentally affected the finances of the Church, and the whole nature of society as well; and that was in the eleventh and early twelfth centuries. This can be illustrated from two very well-known continental examples. It used to puzzle historians how the abbey of Cluny could afford to build one of the most extravagant churches in Christendom in the late eleventh and early twelfth centuries, and yet hardly had the resources to feed its own monks a generation later. This was explained in a famous paper by Georges Duby, who showed how the wealth of the abbey had been vastly expanded for a time by tribute, by gifts and by offerings from far and near: and how after a while the flow ceased, and they were left once more to rely on their own estates.[1] The story can be paralleled many times over, though rarely on anything like the scale of Cluny, for the kings of Castile and England (Henry I) were among her most princely benefactors at the height of her prosperity, and many others contributed from an equal distance.[2] At a middle point in the period of Cluny's prosperity, in 1098, Pope Urban II had to intervene in the affairs of the great Basilica of Sant'Ambrogio, St Ambrose, at Milan.

---

quite a different story (cf. G. Constable, *Monastic Tithes from their Origins to the Twelfth Century*, Cambridge, 1964, esp. p. 268 n.; and references there cited).

[1] *Annales*, vol. vii, 1952, pp. 155–71; see also his paper in *Petrus Venerabilis, 1156–1956*, ed. G. Constable and J. Kritzeck, Rome, 1956, pp. 128–40.

[2] See Brooke in *Il monachesimo e la riforma ecclesiastica*, Milan, 1971, p. 137; for Sant' Ambrogio, idem, *Monastic World 1000–1300*, London, 1974, pp. 219 ff.

To this day it has a Romanesque tower on either side – with a large Renaissance cloister beyond each – as witness that two communities, one of canons, the other of monks, served the basilica from the eighth to the nineteenth centuries. The faithful meanwhile laid their offerings on the altars in the church to such good purpose that most of it could be rebuilt and most of what we see today is a splendid monument to that golden age. As the faithful laid their offerings, they were watched with jealous eyes by the canons on this side, the monks on that; and in 1098 the monks burst in with soldiers at their back, and seized offerings the canons thought were theirs. We cannot now tell where right lay (if anywhere), but only wonder at the imprudence of the archbishop who had placed two communities in this ambiguous station. He acted thus in the eighth century, little knowing what was to come.

The groups of folk who seem to have lived in London before the tenth century no doubt had other oratories beside St Paul's; and we shall count a small number of them presently. It is inconceivable that they could have paid to build, or could have supported, one hundred or any figure near it. The full number must reflect an age of gold, or at least profuse in silver; and even so it is not very easy to imagine medieval London affording on its own resources so gargantuan a feast of the spirit. The spread may well have started in the tenth century and before; but the greater number can hardly, as a simple piece of economics, be reckoned older than the eleventh and twelfth centuries.

There is indeed a danger that the argument will turn in a circle. Among the most dramatic evidences of London's wealth in the central Middle Ages the parish churches stand supreme. They do not stand alone: the documents, archaeological finds, the numismatic evidence, all that we know of the general history of England and Europe at this time co-operate to make it clear that London became a great city in the period between the tenth and twelfth centuries. But all the evidence is crowned by the proliferation of the small churches, followed by the large – for the epoch from Edward the Confessor's first rebuilding of Westminster Abbey to Henry III's second saw every old church rebuilt and many new conventual churches established. If we say of the parish churches that they could not have been built in such profusion before London was rich enough, and that we know it was rich in the eleventh and twelfth centuries because so many parish churches were built, we are in a circle: but our case is not desperate, for the other evidence would make any suggestion that London was clothed with a mantle of churches before the year 1000 frankly absurd. Yet we shall do well to look very closely at all the other evidence about the growth of small churches before we accept the economic evidence as wholly binding.[1]

In the end we shall find a striking coherence between types and items of evidence not always individually cogent or obviously representative. Thus the archaeological evidence relates only to a small sample of the churches; but it shows that while a few were very ancient, some, perhaps many, were newcomers in the eleventh and twelfth centuries; and an exploration of the whole range of the evidence strongly indicates that the sample is more representative than one might have feared. The legal evidence helps to make clear why the pattern grew stable in the twelfth century and to explain the movements in the tenth and eleventh which made so large a number of churches and parishes conceivable. The close study of boundaries and settlement patterns shows that the full growth of the parish churches belongs to the era when London finally became a great city once again. The documentary evidence is hazardous: many churches may be much older than the earliest evidence for their existence. But in a few cases, the pen, like the spade, reveals a church and a parish in the act of creation. The study of dedications has been treated in the past with uncritical abandon; discreetly handled, the dedications and the surnames of churches – such as the Haakon who gave his name to St Nicholas Acon, and the Danes of St Clement – help to fix the proliferation in the late Viking era and the age of the proprietary church, that is, in the late tenth, eleventh and twelfth centuries.

THE PARISHES AND THEIR BOUNDARIES

In law a parish was a bundle of rights, in which the rights to baptize, to bury and to tithe were paramount. So much is clear and certain, and tolerably simple. But we know this from reading the authorities of canon law, and we know that those authorities were not fully enforced before the thirteenth century, and many did not exist before the twelfth. To put the matter in its simplest frame, parish rights came to be fully defined in western Christendom from about the middle of the twelfth century. Before 1100 there was much diversity in practice as to how tithes were paid and to whom, and the shifting of parish boundaries was a comparatively simple matter. After 1200 parish rights were clearly defined, and although changes were made – in many towns, substantial changes – they

[1] See p. 143.

required due process, careful organization, sometimes elaborate litigation.

It is known that the City parishes were still being defined in the early twelfth century, and perhaps later; but it is very rare to find evidence of the re-drawing of a boundary, or of litigation on a boundary, after 1200. We have references, furthermore, to all but a handful of the churches, and to a large number of parishes specifically as such, earlier than 1200.[1] The presumption is therefore very strong that in their main lines the parish boundaries of later times were the parish boundaries of 1200 – though more cogently for the parishes within the walls than without, a distinction to which we shall return.

But this immediately raises a curious and baffling difficulty. How did boundaries come to be defined in these early days – and what did they mean? Let us take the second question first. We are told quite categorically that London citizens had the privilege to be buried where they liked;[2] burial privileges were therefore not of the essence of London's parochial rights. It must be admitted that this did not prevent disputes on burial rights from occurring, and it may well be that the simple doctrine hid a much more complex situation. Yet it is probable that most of the parish churches in the mid- or late Middle Ages had a cemetery or burial ground; it is certain that many existed in the twelfth century.[3] Anyone who has visited Poitiers, Florence, Pisa or the Lateran is familiar with the great baptisteries, which still bear witness that from early days all or a large part of the population were actually carried to the cathedral baptistery for christening.[4] This practice continued in many Italian cities right down to the nineteenth century: and in Italian cities one can trace at various dates

---

[1] See above, p. 122 n. and map; and for a provisional list, Stenton, Map (by Miss Honeybourne and Miss E. Jeffries Davis). There is an example of an alteration (at least, of one alleged) in *London Possessory Assizes*, ed. H. M. Chew, London Rec. Soc., 1965 p. 80.

[2] *Regesta*, vol. ii, no. 1774 = no. cclxxi.

[3] The best twelfth-century evidence is in the visitation of St Paul's churches of *c.* 1181 (Liber L, St Paul's W.D.4, ff. 86–8; *Archaeologia*, vol. lvii, pp. 283–300; for date see Hale, p. cii; Gibbs, no. 180 confirms that it must be before 1184). Of fifteen churches this specifies whether they had cemeteries: nine had, six had not. Mr W. Kellaway has generously provided us with copious evidence of very numerous cemeteries in later centuries, and has pointed out that even parishes without cemeteries could have used the churches themselves for a modest number of burials: he suggests that burial within the parish may always have been normal in London.

[4] See the catalogue of Italian baptisteries by E. Cattaneo in *Miscellanea G. G. Meersseman*, Padua, 1970, vol. i, pp. 171–95.

customs as to burial similar to those of London. In Italy it appears to have been common to regard the cathedral as the sole parish church – however many oratories may have sprung up around it – down to the twelfth century; and although the formation of parishes from that date forward defined the distribution of tithe, it did not necessarily affect the customs governing the new-born and the dying.[1] Whatever canon law may wear on its face, there was one law for the country, another for the town.

Thus we may be tolerably sure that in London, as elsewhere, the definition of the parish from the twelfth century on referred to tithe more than to burial or baptism, though these were also involved. But we have often wondered by what practical arrangement the gradual division into numerous small parishes could take place. Where ecclesiastical authority or canon law were strong, effective sub-division on this scale would have been inconceivable. There is evidently here a considerable measure of give-and-take, of common understanding; and a legal situation in which whatever was locally arranged was accepted. We are evidently in the world of the 'proprietary' church.[2] Let us imagine two circumstances. A man builds a church on his own property, his own soke; it is in the first instance a personal possession, its priest his chaplain; his tenants, the men under the jurisdiction of his soke – whatever that means[3] – will naturally worship in his church, perhaps have an obligation to do so; and he will expect them to contribute to its building fund and to help him keep it in repair. The other case is of a group of pious craftsmen, living in the same neighbourhood, who decide to build themselves a little church for their own use and support a priest in it. The Church and the priest will serve a community which may from the first be quite clearly defined; but it is of its nature (unlike the first example) a voluntary community, not a conscript congregation.

PARISH CHURCH AND PROPRIETARY CHURCH

We may observe, first of all, that parallels can be found in many parts of Europe in the tenth, eleventh and twelfth centuries for such foundations,

[1] See C. Boyd, *Tithes and parishes in Medieval Italy*, Ithaca, 1952; Brooke in *Studies in Church History*, vol. vi, pp. 64 ff., esp. 68 ff.

[2] See esp. F. Barlow, *The English Church 1000–1066*, London, 1963, pp. 186 ff., and p. 186 n. for references; Brooke, art. cit., pp. 71 ff. (esp. p. 71 n. 2).

[3] See p. 156. The sokes of London have been described more often than defined. Page, pp. 127–58, lists some of the most important sokes, but his topographical reconstructions must be treated with the greatest caution.

and especially in the eleventh century, the heyday of the proprietary church; and we may also take note that the essence of these arrangements is that the upkeep of the church depends on the offerings of a group of citizens who can be either loosely or closely defined.[1] Under these circumstances it is the proprietary nature of the churches and the central importance of offerings that make their building, and their proliferation, practicable. The history of law confirms what the economics of the situation seemed to dictate, that most of these churches were built, and their parishes first defined, between the tenth and the twelfth centuries. We must look more closely at the nature of the proprietary church and at the nature of these offerings if we are to penetrate to the heart of the problem.

We possess one deed which seems to take us very close to the origin of a parish.[2] In 1148 the canons of St Paul's granted the church of St Augustine to Edward the priest for a high rent of 20s per annum which Edward the priest was to pay for six years. In the course of this period the money was to be spent on building the church of St Augustine (at the corner of Watling Street and Old Change, close to the east end of St Paul's), which Edward was to hold thereafter for one mark a year. 'The limits of this parish,' the canons thoughtfully added, 'are the dwellings of Alfred of Windsor, Nicholas Parvus and Hugh le Noreis.' The individual witnesses were reinforced by 'tota parochia'. Archaeological evidence confirms a twelfth-century building, though other evidence suggests that in fact it was a rebuilding.[3] In any event we witness here the crystallization of a parish, and, we may be sure, the firm assertion of who was responsible for its upkeep. In 1254 the papal tax-gatherers observed that the income of St Augustine's 'does not suffice to support it'.[4] It is clear that if the three

---

[1] See Brooke, *Time the Archsatirist*, pp. 20 ff.; P. Johansen, 'Die Kaufmanskirche im Ostseegebiet', in *Studien zu den Anfängen des europäischen Städtewesens*, Vorträge und Forschungen, ed. T. Mayer, Lindau-Constance, 1958, pp. 499–525. The church built by a group of neighbours has interesting connections in parts of the continent with the practice (of which no trace has been found in this country) of electing parish priests; see D. Kurze, *Pfarrerwahlen im Mittelalter: Ein Beitrag zur Geschichte der Gemeinde und des Niederkirchenwesens*, Cologne-Graz, 1966, esp. pp. 308–9.

[2] *HMC, 9th Report*, p. 63; St Paul's W.D.4, f. 31v.

[3] *LMAS*, vol. xxii, pt. i, 1968, p. 11, for a preliminary survey of the site; *Essays . . . presented to T. F. Tout*, p. 59; *HMC, 9th Report*, *p.* 61b = St Paul's W.D.4, f. 22v, have persons named 'of St Augustine' and 'ante ecclesiam S. Augustini' in a context which may suggest that the parish already existed before 1148.

[4] *Valuation of Norwich*, p. 332.

parishioners of 1148 formed the whole parish and not just the boundary-marks, they were tolerably well-to-do and more than tolerably generous; for if so, it must have been mainly out of their offerings that the church was built and Edward the priest maintained; and it is to be observed that the later parish of St Augustine did consist, almost entirely, of three blocks of territory, one south of Cannon Street, one between Cannon Street and Watling Street, the third to the north of Watling Street. In any case, there is no word of tithes in the charter; its finances must be based on offerings, on an early example of a stewardship campaign.

That many parishes were formed – and churches built or at least maintained – by groups of neighbours, is strongly confirmed by the layout of parishes and boundaries. The boundaries are first defined for us by Ogilby's map of *c.* 1676;[1] with all the uncertainties already outlined, we may take it that most of the boundaries shown are those of the twelfth century – or at least of the late twelfth century. The variations in shape and size, and irregular outline, suggest that they are related to the boundaries of property; but not to large units of property. For their most conspicuous feature is that in every case a major thoroughfare runs through their midst; sometimes an important cross-roads forms their centre. They are thus natural units, not formed by artificial frontiers.

An analogy will help to make clear the force of this argument. The River Duddon in the Lake District is the boundary between Lancashire and Cumberland, and was, till 1974, an ancient frontier of great significance. For many centuries down to the eleventh it was the frontier of Scotland (or Strathclyde) and England. Yet it flows down the middle of a small, long valley, cut off from the world; and for the people who lived there it can never have been a frontier. It was the centre of their life. So it was with the London thoroughfares. If ecclesiastical authority had drawn the boundaries, then the pattern would be as it is in New Salisbury, where tidy, or moderately tidy lines, often following main streets, divide the comparatively modest number of parishes formed there in the thirteenth and fourteenth centuries under the benevolent but watchful eyes of bishop and archdeacon.[2] The contrast is striking and eloquent.

No doubt in some cases there were special reasons for the site of the church. The doubts about rights to city churches were remarkably illustrated as late as 1244 by the statement in the record of the Eyre that:

---

[1] See Darlington and Howgego, pp. 22 ff., 65; a Facsimile was issued by the London and Middlesex Arch. Soc. in 1895.

[2] See *Historic Towns*, vol. i, Salisbury, esp. general map and map of parishes.

'The City answers saying that the churches of St Paul London [the cathedral] and St Martin le Grand and St Peter in the Bailey and the chapel of the Blessed Mary in Jewry [St Mary Aldermanbury] are in the king's gift, and further it seems to them that the churches of All Hallows Fenchurch and St Magnus the Martyr and St Audoen and St Michael le Querne and St Peter Paul's Wharf and St Alphege which are situated on the king's highway and the church of All Hallows London Wall and St Augustine [Papey] which are situated on the City Wall ought to belong to the king and be in his gifts.'[1] St Michael le Querne stood in the midst of the cornmarket at the western end of the great West Cheap (now Cheapside). Attached to it was an ancient cross;[2] and we may reasonably suppose that the cross had been there, and a centre of worship or of reverence at least for a while before the church was built. The same seems likely outside the City at St Clement Danes, where an ancient cross stood by the church. This helps to explain why these churches were built in a situation so unlikely, and there may have been other cases where churches were built near a cross at a cross-roads. It is not perfectly clear that all these churches actually stood with the road lapping round them, like St Clement Danes and St Michael le Querne, and now St Mary le Strand; but presumably some of them did. The two in the Strand lie in the midst of a great highway outside the City; we may assume that the Strand for many centuries remained broad and straddling and muddy. St Magnus at the Bridge Head was there before the Bridge – that is, before the stone bridge of the late twelfth century – and presumably jutted into the road running to the Bridge, as it did in later times.[3] This may be all that is meant: but it is clear that St Audoen sat in the wide section of Newgate Street later known as the Newgate market and All Hallows (later St Gabriel's) in Fenchurch Street. Yet however we may explain individual sites, the general pattern is of groups small and large – but never very large – of neighbours gathering round a small church in which they worshipped, to which they paid their dues, and so they formed its parish. In many cases, we may presume that they or their forebears had paid to build it too.

By the late twelfth century the Church had asserted its rights over these churches. In canon law they were no one's property; in many cases the right to present to them – the advowson – had been granted to a religious

---

[1] *Eyre*, no. 276.

[2] Stow, vol. i, p. 267, who says that it was taken down in 1390 when St Michael's church was enlarged.

[3] See M. Honeybourne in *Studies in London History*, pp. 22 ff.

house, and in quite a few the religious house drew a pension or some portion of the tithe from them.[1] The implication of the City fathers of 1244 that the king ought to have the advowson on account of his property rights in the king's highway was old-fashioned, an echo of the doctrine which had enabled these churches to grow. They were many of them impoverished by the thirteenth century because they had become (in one sense) too spiritual: the Church had abolished the confusion of spiritual and temporal which gave them birth.

In the eleventh century, and in a measure in the twelfth, these tiny churches had been pieces of property. It was often unclear whose property they were. They might be spoken of as belonging to the owner of the property or soke in which they stood, to the man who built it, to the community which contributed to it, to the parish priest or to the patron saint. The eminent Norman baron Eudo Dapifer built St Stephen Walbrook shortly after the Conquest to serve (so it seems) his City estate in the Walbrook ward.[2] Shortly before the Conquest Brihtmær of Gracechurch presented the church of All Hallows Gracechurch to Canterbury Cathedral.[3] It seems likely that he had actually built the church for All Saints – a common Anglo-Saxon dedication – and covered it with the roof of thatch or 'grass' which gave the church, himself and his street their names. In any event, he was only one of a group of men endowing Canterbury Cathedral with churches at this time.[4] The rest were priests, and we have a fascinating list of London clergy who gave their churches to Canterbury in the early and mid-eleventh century. They claimed as priests full ownership of the churches, and their claims were accepted and upheld as such claims were not always upheld. They became monks, and the Cathedral community presented their successors. Such at least was the theory. What actually happened we cannot be sure. In some cases arrangements of this kind were a sort of pension-scheme: the priest may even have stayed in his parish, though clothed now as a monk.[5] In the end

---

[1] Both patrons and pensions are listed in many cases (not invariably) in *Valuation of Norwich*, pp. 326–33.

[2] See *Cart. Colchester*, vol. i, pp. 3, 62, 87; cf. vol. ii, p. 294.

[3] *Anglo-Saxon Charters*, ed. A. J. Robertson, Cambridge, 1956, no. 116, pp. 216–17, 468–9.

[4] B. W. Kissan in *LMAS*, New Series, vol. viii, 1940, pp. 57–69, esp. pp. 57–8; *EHD*, vol. ii, pp. 954–6.

[5] We have found no direct evidence of such a practice. But this is the period when monks justified drawing tithes by engaging in pastoral work – even though the nature and extent of the practice is still controversial (see esp. G. Constable, *Monastic Tithes*

he will have retired to the Cathedral priory; and in some cases it may well have been accepted that his son would succeed him as rector. In the short run, a suitable family settlement was achieved; in the long run the Cathedral priory acquired a church.

Thus we may investigate the history of a few sample churches, and from them gain an insight into the processes which explain their dramatic growth. If we enlarge the question and ask now in what measure can we corroborate the evidence already cited that in bulk the churches were of the eleventh and twelfth centuries, we must turn from the documents to the evidence of the spade and of the dedications of the churches. The documents tell us when the church is first recorded; and if we consider how numerous they were, and how insignificant, it is remarkable how early is the first mention of most of them. But documents before 1100 relating to London are very scarce, and will only help to isolate a few really ancient foundations.[1] The spade is more helpful, though its evidence is hampered by a difficulty which afflicts all archaeological evidence from the City. The long prosperity of the area, and in earlier centuries the frequency of fires, have meant that most of the City has been many times rebuilt. In the last hundred years this rebuilding had commonly been conducted below as well as above ground to the point that every level, from Roman strata up, has been cleared away. Over roughly one quarter of the City, no archaeological enquiry can throw light earlier than the nineteenth century.

The churches have been relatively fortunate; but even here we are unlikely ever to have the chance for a detailed investigation of a large number. More than half the medieval churches disappeared in the Great Fire of 1666 and their sites have been swallowed. Of those which Wren rebuilt, a number still stand, and his building keeps the archaeologist at bay. There remain a certain number of cases in which the damage wrought in the Second World War levelled a church and gave the opportunity for full enquiry and excavation; and a few more which have always preserved some sign or segment of their medieval past.[2]

---

from their Origins to the Twelfth Century, Cambridge, 1964, chaps 3–6, esp. pp. 165 ff.; cf. Brooke in *Studies in Church History*, vol. vi, p. 82 n. 1).

[1] Such as St Alban Wood St (see p. 139) and the churches granted to Canterbury Cathedral. A series of writs bearing William I's name refer to a number of London churches in the gift of Westminster Abbey, but these were forged in the middle of the twelfth century (see p. 369).

[2] See pp. 90–1 and n.

Most splendid of these is St Mary-le-Bow, with its magnificent Norman crypt (**Plate 42**). Nothing is visible of an earlier epoch; but it is clear that this was the mother of the Canterbury churches in the City – hence its later fame as centre of the Court and Deanery of Arches; and the documents take it back at least to the early eleventh century.[1] It may well be much older. Of two City churches we may confidently assert that they were. St Alban Wood Street has yielded archaeological evidence which places it fairly definitely in the eighth or ninth centuries (**Plate 26**). Tradition associated it with King Offa of Mercia, whose devotion to the ancient martyr led him to found St Alban's abbey.[2] Perhaps he built St Alban Wood Street too, though we cannot now be sure; in any event it belongs, very roughly, to his age. The church of Barking Abbey, All Hallows 'Barkingchurch' as it was originally called, was equally ancient, and no doubt served the town properties of Barking Abbey, founded in the seventh century by St Eorcenweald, Bishop of London, whose relics were among the chief glories of St Paul's.[3] Excavation has revealed an ancient church of considerable size; and the splendid eleventh-century sculptures still in its crypt (**Plates 28–9**) show that it prospered in late Saxon times as well as early. Outside the City walls the documents show St Andrew's Holborn to be of the ninth century, or very early tenth at latest – and it may be earlier still; the spade cannot help us. At St Bride's it has given fascinating but ambiguous evidence.[4] It is clear that St Bride's sits on an ancient cemetery beside one of the main western thoroughfares out of the City. It began as a pagan Roman cemetery, and may have had a continuous history through the Saxon conquest; and the presence of the cemetery may well account for the church. But the age of the church itself is far from clear. Claims that it is of the sixth century in origin are not substantiated by Professor Grimes' admirably cautious statement of what he actually found; and the dedication to an Irish saint of the sixth century, which has caused much speculation, actually points in quite a different direction, as we shall see.[5] It remains very possible that there was an early cemetery chapel, of which a

[1] Kissan in *LMAS*, New Series, vol. viii, 1940, pp. 57 ff.

[2] See p. 111 n.

[3] In 1086 Barking Abbey possessed half a church in London, presumed to be All Hallows. In the twelfth century the other half seems to have been owned first by the Cathedral Priory of Canterbury and then by Rochester Cathedral Priory: cf. Kissan, pp. 65–6; B. M. Cotton Charter vii, 7. On the cult of St Eorconweald, see *HSP*, pp. 5–6; *GF*, p. 198 and references.

[4] W. F. Grimes, *Excavation of Roman and Mediaeval London*, pp. 182 ff.

[5] See pp. 139–40.

fragment may now survive; it is likely that the church was rebuilt in the eleventh century and that it was then that it acquired its parish (**Plate 27**).

The other churches which have been excavated seem to belong to the eleventh or twelfth centuries. So it is with St Mary Aldermanbury, so too with St Swithun London Stone.[1] The most interesting case is that of St Nicholas Acon.[2] 'Acon' is a corruption of Haakon, and is one of a number of 'surnames' by which various of the City churches have been distinguished at one time or another. The majority of these surnames name the streets in which the churches lie; a few, like Gracechurch, note some conspicuous feature. A few – the number was formerly much greater – bear a man's name: St Nicholas Haakon, St Nicholas Aldred, St Benet Algar, St Mary Woolnoth, St Mary Ailward (? the later St Mary Aldermary), St Martin Orgar, St Denis Backchurch, St Nicholas Bernard and St Andrew Hubberd evidently enshrine the names of Haakon, Ealdred, Ælfgar, Wulfnoth, Ælfward, Orgar (the deacon), Bernard and Hubert, who built or owned them at an early date; and to these we could add a posse of surnames, some of them like Bokerel and Patin well known in the City's history.[3] Haakon is a Norse name, and we might guess that he belonged to the heyday of Viking settlement in London, the early eleventh century (or the late tenth). The dedication suggests a date not earlier than the mid-eleventh century, when the cult of St Nicholas first appears to have spread in western Europe, and the saint first appears in English calendars.[4] We know that it cannot be later than 1084, when it first impinges on the documents;[5] and the spade has unearthed a secular pit beneath it which shows that it was not consecrated to ecclesiastical use until after about the first quarter of the eleventh century. In this case all the possible types of evidence – dedication, surname, documents and archaeology – conspire

---

[1] Grimes, pp. 199–203.

[2] See p. 91. The church was granted to Malmesbury Abbey in 1084 by Godwin and his wife Turgund: *Reg. Malmesbury*, vol. i, p. 328.

[3] For a full study, see G. Keir's forthcoming article on the origin of the City churches; many of these surnames are in the *Valuation of Norwich*, pp. 326 ff., and a number are noted in Harben; cf. Ekwall, *Early London Personal Names*, esp. pp. 56, 198. For St Martin Orgar, see **Plate 31**; *HMC, 9th Rept*, p. 63a.

[4] Before, and not after, the translation of St Nicholas to Bari in 1087 (as is often stated): cf. P. Hodges' unpublished study on Church dedications in the diocese of Lichfield-Coventry; F. Wormald, *English Kalendars before A.D. 1100*, Henry Bradshaw Soc., London, 1934, pp. 41, 55, etc., showing the feast on 6 Dec. coming into English calendars in the (mid-) eleventh cent., but not earlier.

[5] See above, n. 2.

NDON, THE CITY WALL. MOST OF
E WALL IS ON ROMAN FOUNDATIONS,
STORED AT MANY DIFFERENT PERIODS
e pp. 160–2)

In St Alphege's churchyard we can
see the Roman core surmounted by
medieval stonework, a fourteenth-
century rubble repair, and, top left,
a section of fifteenth-century brick

Near the Tower, showing Roman
foundations

25. Old St Pancras' Church, by Jonathan Skelton, 1755, Victoria and Albert Museum, R. H. Stephenson Bequest, P. 117-1929. Though much altered the basic structure gives a good idea still of a small extra-mural Norman parish church

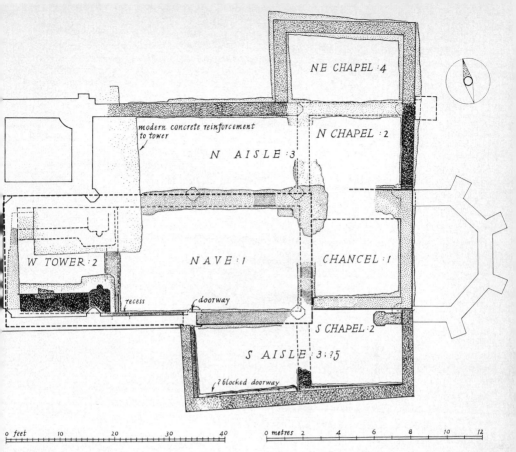

St Alban's Wood Street. 1—the first church; 2, 3, 4—the medieval church (fourteenth–fifteenth century); ?5—south aisle, ?Inigo Jones (1633–4). Wren's work (north-west tower, west nave 1682–7) in outline; also apse (1858). Plan by Professor W. F. Grimes (see his *Excavation of Roman and Mediaeval London*, pl. 50, p. 205)

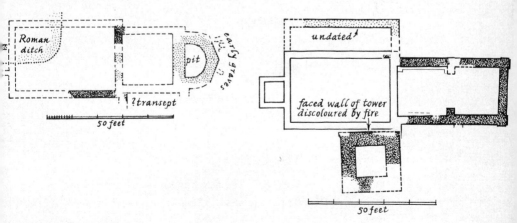

St Bride's Fleet Street. Left—the first church; right—the twelfth-century church. Plans by W. F. Grimes (see his *Excavation of Roman and Mediaeval London*, pls 42 and 44, pp. 185 and 188)

28–29. All Hallows' Barking, remains of an Anglo-Saxon cross of *c*. 1030–50, showing two views of the substantial fragment (*see* *p. 137*)

Viking relief, early eleventh century, in the 'Ringerike' style, fragment of a sarcophagus found in St Paul's churchyard, now in the Guildhall Museum

An original charter of early-mid-twelfth century describing an arrangement between the citizen Orgar and the chapter of St Paul's about the church of St Martin Orgar, still in the Cathedral Archives (A15/1376) (see p. 138)

32–33. Porch and undercroft of the Prior of Lewes' house in Southwark, originally built perhaps for the Earl de Warenne in the mid-late twelfth century, later occupied by the prior; it was destroyed c. 1830 for the approaches to the new London Bridge, but these sepia wash sketches by J. C. Buckler of c. 1830 give the best surviving impression of a great town house of the period. Society of Antiquaries, Surrey Red Portfolio, S–Z, p. 8; see *Archaeologia*, vol. xxiii, 1831 (1830), pp. 299ff. and pls XXIII–IV; also vol. xxv, pp. 604–6

shown, the two patron saints, St Thomas of Canterbury (above) and St Paul (below) preside over the city

35. Edward the Confessor at Mass; he is in a thirteenth-century artist's impression of Westminster Palace. Cambridge University Library, MS Ee. 3.59, f. 27v

36. Bond of William Cade, 1163, by which Roger d'Oilli pledges himself to repay his debt in the Exchequer, Public Record Office, E210/5199 (*see p. 229*)

37. Oath of the Commune, 1193; see p. 236 British Museum Addit. M 14252, f. 112v, reduced

together to a happy result. If this happened more often, we could be a great deal more categorical in our conclusions.

St Nicholas Acon has provided a very good example of the possibilities of dedications. Let St Bride speak for the dangers. St Bride is a form of St Brigit or Bridget, the Irish saint of the sixth century; and her name is exceedingly rare among English dedications, and equally rare in calendars. When traces, however faint, of a very early church were found on the site, the temptation to link a church perhaps of the sixth century with a saint undoubtedly of the sixth century was very great. Unfortunately, such evidence as we have of the way in which churches were dedicated in early times makes an early dedication to an Irish saint extremely improbable. Neither in the Celtic nor in the Anglo-Saxon church is there any evidence that churches were dedicated to recent, local saints before the eighth and ninth centuries;[1] nor any that the practice was common before the tenth and eleventh centuries, which were its heyday. From very early times English dedications were made to the Blessed Virgin most frequently of all – in principle, a dedication to the Virgin may belong to any period from the Conversion to the present. Next most common were dedications to the Apostles, especially (in early days) Peter, Paul and Andrew; St Paul's Cathedral is the lasting witness to this practice in London and far and away the earliest recorded dedication.[2] Roman martyrs were also of the band from early days, and there is no difficulty in supposing that his church in Wood Street has always been dedicated to St Alban, though we cannot prove it.[3] St Bride was an Irish saint, and the researches of Mr Paul Hodges have revealed a striking analogy.[4] On the Wirral peninsula in Cheshire, Norsemen settled thick in the tenth and eleventh centuries, and have scored their mark deep in the local place-names. 'By' is well known to be the Viking word for a village or settlement, and the association of the Norse with Ireland, from which the Wirral settlers (in large measure) immediately came, is fossilized in the name of Irby, the 'by' of the Irish. The whole of the north-western corner of the peninsula formed for many centuries the parish of West Kirby, the 'by' with the kirk or church; and

[1] See O. Chadwick in H. M. Chadwick *et al.*, *Studies in Early British History*, Cambridge, 1954, pp. 173–88.

[2] Bede, *Hist. Eccl.*, bk iii, c. 3, ed. Colgrave and Mynors, pp. 142–3. On early dedications, see W. Levison, *England and the Continent in the Eighth Century*, Oxford, 1946, pp. 259–65.

[3] See above, p. 137; and Grimes, pp. 203–9.

[4] See Hodges (above, p. 138 n.); J. M. Dodgson, *Place-Names of Cheshire*, vol. iv, esp. pp. 229 ff., 264 ff., 273, 291 ff.; vol. v, introd.

the church of West Kirby is dedicated to St Bride. If we turn back to London we find that her church there sits not far from St Clement of the Danes, and that both are in the space west of the City over which settlement was spreading fastest in the Viking period, in the late tenth and eleventh centuries, that is. We may be tolerably confident that the dedication is due to the Irish Norse settlers of this period, who doubtless provided for the eleventh-century reconstruction. They may well have rebuilt an earlier chapel, for it was not uncommon to give a church a new dedication when it was rebuilt. Beyond St Clement's lies St Mary le Strand, originally the chapel of the Holy Innocents;[1] there may well be other examples of which we are not informed.[2]

Yet all this should not make us unduly sceptical of the cumulative evidence of dedications, for even so tricky a case as St Bride's can reveal a surprisingly satisfactory result. We cannot hope for much from eight churches dedicated to the Blessed Virgin or five to St Peter, though we may be grateful that the common Christian name stimulated a number of interesting surnames. But many of the names of the saints are more revealing.

We have observed that the multitudinous churches of London spread all over the surface of the city. If we look at the face of some continental cities, such as Poitiers, where we can discern the physiognomy of much earlier centuries, we find a quite different pattern.[3] The small churches of early days tend to be tiny oratories clustering round the cathedral or a great relic church or abbey – in Poitiers round the cathedral, St-Porchaire and the abbey of St-Hilaire-le-Grand. It has been pointed out in the past that St Gregory and St Augustine cluster close to St Paul's in London; and it has been suggested that these were early oratories close to the

---

[1] FitzStephen, *MB* vol. iii, p. 17, calls it 'ecclesiam . . . beatae Mariae Littoream'; in earlier charters, from 1085–6 to 1156 it is the church of the Holy Innocents, but in the mid- and late twelfth century normally called the Church of St Mary. The moment of change seems to be between 1146 and 1152 (*Chron. Abingdon*, vol. ii, pp. 15–16, 192 [Holy Innocents, 1085–6 and 1146], 197 [St Mary, 1152]; *Cart. of Worcester Priory*, ed. R. R. Darlington, Pipe Roll Soc., 1968, nos. 53, 71–2; Lees, *Templars*, p. 13 and n.).

[2] Thus it seems that All Hallows Gracechurch was called St Peter's when given to Canterbury Cathedral, and St Pancras Soper Lane is also called St Benet's in Kissan, loc. cit. (see also p. 135 n. on Gracechurch). We know of four other churches whose dedications were changed in later centuries, and three to which an additional dedication was added.

[3] D. Claude, *Topographie und Verfassung der Städte Bourges und Poitiers bis in das 11. Jahrhundert*, Lübeck and Hamburg, 1960, esp. map facing p. 196.

cathedral whose foundation Pope Gregory the Great and St Augustine, the apostle of the English, inspired.[1] This is quite possible, though it cannot be proved; and beyond that point, dedications help us very little to identify early churches, for reasons already made apparent – early dedications were usually to saints who never lost their popularity. Nor is the occasional unusual saint unduly helpful. St Augustine on the wall bore the surname Papey, evidently 'of Pavia', which shows that he was not Augustine of Canterbury but the older, greater saint of Hippo, whose relics were preserved at Pavia;[2] and we may conjecture that it was the arrival of some relics from Italy which led to the building of the church. But this could have happened at almost any date. What is really significant is the battalion of Viking saints, the platoon of English, and the small contingents from Normandy and Flanders.

Five churches in the City were dedicated to St Olaf of Norway, and one in Southwark. This makes him one of the most popular, close on the heels of St Mary, St Michael and All Hallows. Since Olaf only died in 1030, these dedications cannot be earlier than the mid-eleventh century; they are indeed unlikely to be earlier than the death of Olaf's conqueror, King Cnut, in 1035.[3] Two of the churches are recorded in the eleventh century, and we may be tolerably sure that they represent the Viking settlement which seems likely in the main to be pre-Conquest, though some of the churches may be somewhat later. To St Olaf we may possibly add St Clement, who has been claimed as a favourite Viking saint,[4] as is still remembered in St Clement Danes, and St Bride. These churches are scattered all over the City, but with a concentration in the western suburb, and a bridgehead across the Thames, which seem to point very clearly to Viking settlement in the growing western and southern suburbs in the eleventh century. Here is very strong evidence of the spread of churches in the eleventh century. No church could be dedicated to St Olaf before the mid-eleventh century, and the Viking settlement which

[1] R. E. M. Wheeler, *London and the Saxons*, London Museum, 1935, pp. 100 ff.

[2] St Augustine of Hippo became known in northern Europe as Augustine of Pavia after the translation of his relics to Pavia from Sardinia in ?726 (see D. A. Bullough, 'Urban Change in early medieval Italy', p. 120).

[3] Bruce Dickins, in *Saga-Book of the Viking Society*, vol. xii, 1937–45, pp. 53–80.

[4] The source of the common belief that Clement was a favourite Viking dedication seems to be the name of the London church, St Clement 'of the Danes'. To be sure, there was a church of St Clement in Oslo (H. Christie in *Medieval Archaeology*, vol. x, 1966, p. 48) and a high proportion of English dedications to St Clement are found in the area of the Danelaw. The matter needs further investigation.

these dedications must reflect cannot have been substantial before the reign of Cnut; for the list of moneyers of Ethelred II's period strongly suggests that the Viking element in the middling ranks of Londoners was negligible down to 1016.[1]

After the Viking element, the English is an anticlimax. We might expect to find a crop of English saints of the same era; but that is hardly the case. St Alban, as we have seen, is probably more ancient; and St Swithun is almost certainly post-Conquest, and probably twelfth century in foundation. St Alphege (Ælfheah) cannot have received his dedication before the saint's martyrdom in 1012; but we cannot date those to St Dunstan (of the East and West), St Edmund and St Mildred, although no doubt the eleventh and twelfth centuries saw the heyday of their cults. St Botolph is more interesting, and to him we must presently return.

By comparison with the Norse and English elements, the Norman and Flemish are extremely modest. St Audoen reminds us of Rouen, also of the Norman canon of St Paul's who became Bishop of Evreux.[2] St Vedast reminds us of Arras and of London's vital Flemish links. But why have the Normans contributed so little to the total? The answer must surely be found in two facts: first, that London remained a predominantly English city for a generation or two after the Conquest; and that by the time the Normans had effectively infiltrated into the City, the task of dedicating the parish churches was accomplished.

The study of church dedications in a wider field might well suggest that a saint's cult tended to be associated with the extent of his property. Thus churches belonging to a great abbey or cathedral dedicated to St Martin were often dedicated to their saintly owner. In the case of the teeming and tiny parish churches of the larger English towns this can rarely have been the case. For the great majority seem evidently to have been dedicated before they came into the hands of any religious community. To put it another way, it is now widely recognized that the proliferation of churches in English towns presupposes a world in which ecclesiastical authority, and especially the authority of large local communities, was weak. The London churches were proprietary, whether built by particular rich land-

---

[1] The lists in Mrs Smart's paper (below, pp. 379–80) are very striking: whereas York yields a substantial majority of Viking names, London has an overwhelming majority of English. Since mint names only appear on Edgar's coins at the end of the reign, the names of moneyers, though very interesting, are not so revealing as under Ethelred: see O. von Feilitzen and C. E. Blunt, 'Personal names on the coinage of Edgar'.

[2] Le Neve, p. 36.

holders or by groups of citizens, whether Eigenkirchen or Kaufmann-kirchen (literally, private or proprietary churches and merchants' churches). Their dedication must reflect the personal tastes of their founders, or, in some cases, of whoever owned them at the moment when they received their present dedication.

Thus if we set together all the economic, legal, documentary, archaeo-logical evidence with the indications of the church's Christian and surnames, there is a convergence of testimony that the eleventh century was the epoch of most rapid growth in parish churches, though it was still in progress in the twelfth. But we have still to consider the two most striking facts about the shape of the parish boundaries. First, they bore some relation, very difficult to define, to the boundaries of the wards; and second, at almost every point where the City wall impinged on a parish, it formed its boundary. Here is a point of striking contrast with the wards. In Ogilby's map of *c.* 1676 the wall was never the boundary of a ward, almost invariably of a parish. This divergence surely demands an explana-tion. For the wall was originally set there for defence, and the wards were in part defensive institutions; whereas the parishes (in principle) were dedicated to the God of peace. The key to this lies in a close inspection of the suburbs.

OUTSIDE THE WALLS

If we inspect the pattern of churches outside the City walls, we have the best chance now available both to reconstruct the age and development of the suburbs, and also to determine the period when the wall itself was most likely to have become the boundary of so many parishes. In the far west lies the ancient church of St Peter of Westminster; much nearer to the gates, and within the boundaries of the City, another ancient church, St Andrew's Holborn. The age of the other churches depends on a variety of factors, documentary and archaeological; but largely on dedications. It is in this region that the history of dedications is most crucial.

State the case that a man sets out from Westminster in the mid-twelfth century to walk east along the Strand and Fleet Street, skirt round the City wall, and come down to the Thames beside the Tower. He will pass churches dedicated to St Peter and St Margaret, leave St Giles and his lepers well to his north,[1] walk near the Holy Innocents (later St Mary le Strand, then a little south of where it now stands), St Clement of the

[1] See p. 334.

Danes, St Dunstan in the West, St Bride; then, as he turns left, he may see over his left shoulder the ancient church of St Andrew in Holborn, and he presently passes one by one the extra-mural parish churches of the City: St Sepulchre by Newgate, the hospital and priory of St Bartholomew, St Botolph Aldersgate, St Giles without Cripplegate, St Botolph again, by Bishopsgate and by Aldgate, and so, down to the new hospital of St Katharine by the river, not without a glance at Holy Trinity Priory just inside Aldgate and St Peter in the Bailey inside the postern gate beside the Tower.[1] An intriguing jumble of saints, but can it be more? If correctly interpreted, and fitted into the other evidence, these saints may provide the key to London's extra-mural history from the eighth to the twelfth centuries.

None of these saints came to London so early as St Paul, who presided over the City from the early seventh century. But already by the end of the eighth century St Peter had joined his fellow-apostle on the banks of the Thames, at Westminster; and from the mid-eleventh he presided in Westminster over a great abbey and the greatest of the English royal palaces. Peter's brother, Andrew, was certainly in Holborn by the tenth century. It would be nice to think that St Margaret Westminster commemorated the Queen of Scotland, whose daughter, Henry I's Queen Matilda, founded St Giles's hospital in the fields outside Holborn, and Holy Trinity Priory within the Wall. But St Margaret's was in Westminster while Queen Margaret was still in the prime of her life, and it is undoubtedly the more ancient lady with the name of 'pearl' – *margarita* – who was honoured in the oratory, later the parish church, under the abbey's shadow. St Clement of the Danes and St Bride have already given their witness that Viking settlers and Viking trade played a crucial part in the development of this western suburb in the eleventh century.

But the extra-mural churches from St Sepulchre to the ultimate St Botolph seem to belong rather to the twelfth century than to the eleventh. Devotion to the Holy Sepulchre in this country (where it can be dated) belongs to the era of the Crusades; the earliest datable examples are St Sepulchre at Cambridge, *c.* 1130, and St Sepulchre at Northampton, first built by Henry I *c.* 1110.[2] St Sepulchre Newgate was apparently built by one or a group of the circle which gathered round Rahere, the

[1] See p. 145.

[2] See M. Gervers, 'Rotundae Anglicanae', *Actes du xxiie Congrès International d'Histoire de l'Art*, Budapest . . . 1969 (Budapest, 1972), pp. 359–76, esp. pp. 363, 370–1; cf. Brooke in *Il monachesimo* (p. 321 n.), p. 139 and n.

courtier turned secular canon turned Augustinian, who founded St Bartholomew's Hospital and Priory in a large and insalubrious open space in 1123.[1] The dedication of St Bartholomew's reflects private, personal devotion to a saint who called on Rahere in a dream and instructed him to found the hospital and priory; and continued long after to signify his approval of the project by performing numerous miracles of healing, events which have never entirely ceased in Rahere's precinct. Among Rahere's friends was one Ælfwine or Aelmund, who built St Giles, Cripplegate, thus showing (in spite of his English name) the same devotion to this definitely French saint that the English Queen Matilda also showed.[2] Three Botolphs, each guarding a gate – four, if we add St Botolph of the water gate, of Billingsgate – can hardly have happened by pure coincidence. Two at least were there by the 1120s or 1130s, yet Aldgate's was not much older.

A series of lawsuits from *c.* 1130 to the 1160s show that St Botolph's Aldgate was no ancient foundation.[3] About 1130 one Deorman, 'the priest of the Tower' – evidently the rector of St Peter in the Bailey – tried to exercise rights over the space outside the walls, over a part, that is, of the Portsoken. Norman, the first prior of Holy Trinity Aldgate, fought him in a meeting of the chapter of St Paul's at which the Archbishop of Canterbury was present and a group of the local City clergy, the priests of St Benet (probably Fink), of St Nicholas Coldabbey, St Margaret and others. The outcome was that Prior Norman received confirmation of the parish of St Botolph, and it is clear that at this date it was co-terminous with the ward of Portsoken, and ran down to the river. Yet this was not the end of the matter. In 1157 another rector of St Peter's carried off the body of Bodlune wife of Eilric 'rusticus' of East Smithfield; Ailward claimed her as his parishioner although Withulf, the priest of St Botolph, had already performed the last rites. An appeal was lodged, but the archdeacon allowed Ailward to bury the body in St Peter's cemetery. The whole dispute is an interesting commentary on the doctrine enshrined in Henry I's charter to the priory, granted between 1108 and 1133, that the citizens could be buried where they wished.[4] Perhaps the difference in this case was that Eilric was a peasant; indeed the whole issue reveals that the Portsoken

---

[1] See p. 326; Norman Moore, vol. i, p. 26.

[2] St Bartholomew's *FB*, p. 24 (Moore), p. 23 (Webb), where he is called 'Alfun', but in St Paul's W.D.4, f. 25 = *HMC, 9th Report*, p. 62a, he is Aelmund.

[3] *Cart. Aldgate*, nos 964–9; cf. *GFL*, pp. 514–15.

[4] *Regesta*, vol. ii, no. 1774 = no. cclxxi.

was still very rural. The entire area, including East Smithfield, was adjudged to be in the parish of St Botolph. Even this did not end the matter. In 1166 Robert 'the Philosopher', yet another rector of St Peter's, complained that when he was abroad with the king in the Toulouse campaign of 1159, he had been cheated of three sheep from his extra-mural parishioners. On this occasion the archdeacon testified without more ado that the evidence of the earlier suits established that East Smithfield was a part of St Botolph's parish, and there the case at last rested. This recital of litigious rectors and sheep has a crucial interest for our story. It is the nearest that we come to the process by which the parish boundaries were fixed and then fossilized in the era of the rise of canon law and of archdeacon's courts. It shows the difference between well-populated areas where the people, on the whole, seem to have shuffled the thing about among themselves by a series of understandings and arrangements, and sparsely populated areas where customs could be forgotten and peasants bullied.

Prior Norman, whom Queen Matilda summoned to be first prior of Holy Trinity, was already a Canon Regular of considerable experience when he arrived in London. He had travelled on the Continent to study the new ideas of the Canons Regular; he had served his apprenticeship at what was perhaps the first Augustinian house in England, the priory of St Julian and St Botolph outside the south gate of Colchester.[1] It cannot be proved, but it seems highly probable, that it was from Colchester Priory that the canons took the dedication of their extra-mural church to this East Anglian saint,[2] and from Aldgate that Botolph spread to the other gates of London still untenanted, perhaps also to his very similar situation by the south gate of Cambridge. His cult bears witness to the Englishness of London still in the first half of the twelfth century.

[1] *Cart. Aldgate*, pp. 226 ff.; cf. pp. 322 ff.

[2] This argument raises a difficulty, since Henry I's charter (*Regesta*, vol. ii, no. 1467; *Cart. Aldgate*, no. 875) talks of the church of St Botolph as if already built and decicated before the Cnihtengild handed over its rights. If this, the surface interpretation of the document, is correct, the reconstruction in the text must fail – and we are left with a striking coincidence between the St Botolph churches in London and Colchester, and an unexplained link through the early community of Holy Trinity, Aldgate. On the other hand, the purpose of Henry's charter was to establish rights to an identifiable church and parish, and there are parallel cases in which grants were made of churches which might subsequently be built (cf. *GFL*, p. 392). In any event the grant of the Cnihtengild is likely to have been the culmination of a period in which it had a close liaison with Holy Trinity.

It also helps us to come to grips with the significance of the wall in the story of the boundaries. In the Portsoken, ward and parish were identical; hence here alone the wall was a boundary for both. Elsewhere the wall bounded the parishes, save for St Stephen's, which spilt over into the Moor. But it is unlikely that this was really a part of the parish in the twelfth century, since before the opening of Moorgate in the fifteenth century there was no direct access from the main part of the parish to the Moor. No doubt it was at that time simply a pleasure-ground and bog.[1] The probability that new parishes could still be formed along the north and east of London suggests how little these suburbs had developed by the early twelfth century, in contrast to the western suburb. These facts give us crucial help in interpreting the history of the wards.

Our last word, for the time being, on the parish boundaries, must be on the consequence of Miss Honeybourne's brilliant investigation of the precinct of St Martin le Grand.[2] St Martin's was a collegiate church founded by one of Edward the Confessor's chaplains in the mid-eleventh century, who provided its precinct with powerful liberties; and Miss Honeybourne has shown that the precinct was placed across the boundaries of three parishes already defined. When Henry VIII swept St Martin's away, the parish boundaries arose, crumpled but intact, and resumed their sway for several generations more. In this part of London, whatever may be the case elsewhere, the parish map takes us back at least to the mid-eleventh century. It can hardly take us much further. Two striking facts emerge: first, the most important document for the early history of medieval London, apart from FitzStephen's *Description*, is the map of the parish boundaries, as they were *c.* 1676, and as they were in 1907; and second, if we wish to penetrate to the heart of the story of London's growth in the Middle Ages into a great city, that it is on the eleventh century that our eyes must be focused.

[1] Cf. FitzStephen, *MB*, vol. iii, p. 11.

[2] *Journal of the British Archaeological Association*, New Series, vol. xxxviii, 1932, pp. 316–33. Since this chapter was written, Dr Alan Rogers has published his 'Parish boundaries and Urban History: Two Case Studies', ib., Third Series, vol. xxxv, 1972, pp. 46–64; the comparative studies are of great interest, although some of the general statements seem to need modification in the light of the exceptionally full evidence for London.

Epilogue

Writing in the thirteenth century, but looking back to the eleventh, Snorri Sturluson described in the Icelandic *Heimskringla* a tale of a French cripple who could only crawl on hands and knees; of how he dreamed of a noble visitor who advised him to go to St Olaf's church in London to be cured. He awoke, and made for London:

> . . . Eventually he reached London Bridge, and there he asked the townspeople if they could tell him where St Olaf's church was; but they all replied that there were so many churches in London that they could not possibly know to whom each of them was dedicated. A little later, however, a stranger came up to him and asked him where he was going. The cripple told him, and the man then said, 'Let us go to St Olaf's church together, then, for I know the way.' They made their way across the bridge and along the street which led to St Olaf's church [in Southwark]. When they came to the lichgate the stranger stepped across the threshold of the gate; but the cripple rolled himself over it, and stood up at once, completely cured. When he looked about him, his companion had vanished.[1]

[1] *King Harold's Saga*, trans. M. Magnusson and H. Pálsson, Harmondsworth, 1966, pp. 105–6 (we owe this reference to Mr W. Kellaway).

7

On Streets and Wards

THE CHANGING PATTERN OF HAGAS AND PALACES

IN THE history of the city parishes, the eleventh century was the age of growth, the twelfth of consolidation. The eleventh saw the appearance of numerous churches related to the private interests of individuals, of groups of neighbours, of small communities of Viking settlers. In some areas more densely settled these formed into recognizable parishes already in the eleventh century; in most the formation of the parish map was still in flux in the twelfth century. By 1200 it was virtually complete – though not yet so immune to change as it later became; by 1666 the pattern was so firmly set that five score of tiny parochial jurisdictions could survive the disappearance of more than half the churches. It was not until 1907 that Parliament eventually laid the axe to the root of the tree, and hacked away the majority of these ancient parishes.[1]

The wards still flourish, and define the temporal divisions of the City, as they did in the twelfth and thirteenth centuries. Like the parishes, they represent order imposing itself on chaos, the conflict of City government with local rights and self-help. Thus we have two stories to tell, a story of rights and government, and a story of boundaries and streets and houses; and they must be told together, for only thus can any progress be made and any sense disentangled from a complex tale.

It is notorious that the makers of 'Domesday Book' failed to record the City of London. Whether it was because the details came to hand too late, or because they shirked an awkward task, we cannot now tell. The omission is in either case eloquent testimony to the difficulty of the task. Domesday attempts to reduce the facts of tenure to statistics, and for all the fascinating variety of its details on towns, it never mastered the problem of

[1] See pp. 123, 147.

describing them. The reason for this is neatly illustrated in Mr David Johnson's study of *Southwark and the City*:[1]

> Fifteen houses appurtenant to the manor of Walkhampstead were described as being in London or Southwark. Eustace, Count of Boulogne, the lord of this manor, is known to have held the court of his honour at his soke[2] of Aldersgate in the City and to this court, presumably, the men of his *hagae* in Southwark were summoned. This same Eustace was also lord of Oxted in Surrey, an example which shows still more clearly the manorial origin of sokes. One house in Southwark worth twopence a year, six serfs, and nine bordars were attached to this manor. In other words, these urban tenants were regarded as belonging to the society of the parent manor and as being under the jurisdiction of their own lord. This illuminates the entry in 'Domesday Book' which states that a man who committed an offence in the street was subject to the king's justice unless he escaped elsewhere (to one of the *hagae*) when he would have to defend himself before the lord who held sake and soke, a jurisdiction which might extend over men or land.

Boroughs were never, even in the time of Domesday, simply a bundle of complicated rights held by lords or lesser men in the countryside around: they were facts, in law, society and economics too. The confusion in Domesday reflects the way in which such towns were originally settled, and the structure of even the most advanced towns of the early Middle Ages. Pavia, for example, was the capital of the Lombard kings from the sixth century to the ninth, and had a more continuous prosperity than any other north Italian town.[3] The presence of the king explains why here, in spite of frequent destruction and change, the structure of the old Roman streets was more fully preserved than in most towns even in Italy: they were *viae publicae*, the king's highways. A similar doctrine was to preserve the pattern of streets in English towns as it was revived or as it emerged in the tenth and eleventh centuries, although in no known case did this have any significant relation to a Roman town plan. But even in Pavia the layout of houses in these early centuries followed no sort of pattern. 'The records of sales and gifts,' Professor Bullough writes, 'show that like the churches they [the private houses and their associated structures] were more often

[1] London, 1969, p. 14.
[2] I.e. centre of jurisdiction; for the various meanings of 'soke' see p. 156.
[3] D. A. Bullough, 'Urban Change in early medieval Italy: the example of Pavia'.

The Wards of London

KEY

1 Farringdon (Within and Without)

2 Castle Baynard

3 Aldersgate

4 Cripplegate

5 Bread Street

6 Queenhithe

7 Bassishaw

8 Cheap

9 Cordwainer

10 Vintry

11 Coleman Street

12 Walbrook

13 Dowgate

14 Broad Street

15 Cornhill

16 Langbourn

17 Candlewick

18 Bridge

19 Bishopsgate

20 Lime Street

21 Billingsgate

22 Aldgate

23 Tower

24 Portsoken

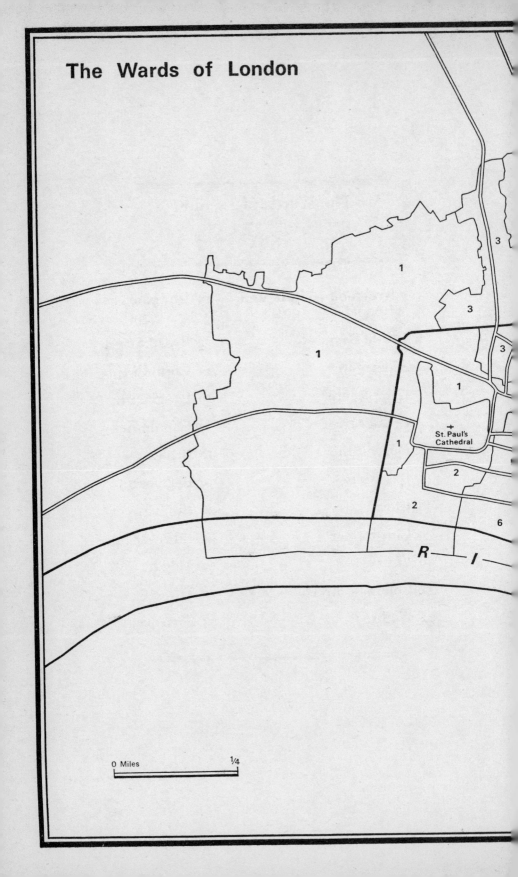

The Wards of London

1

3

3

3

1

1

+
St. Paul's
Cathedral

2

2

6

R — I —

0 Miles   ¼

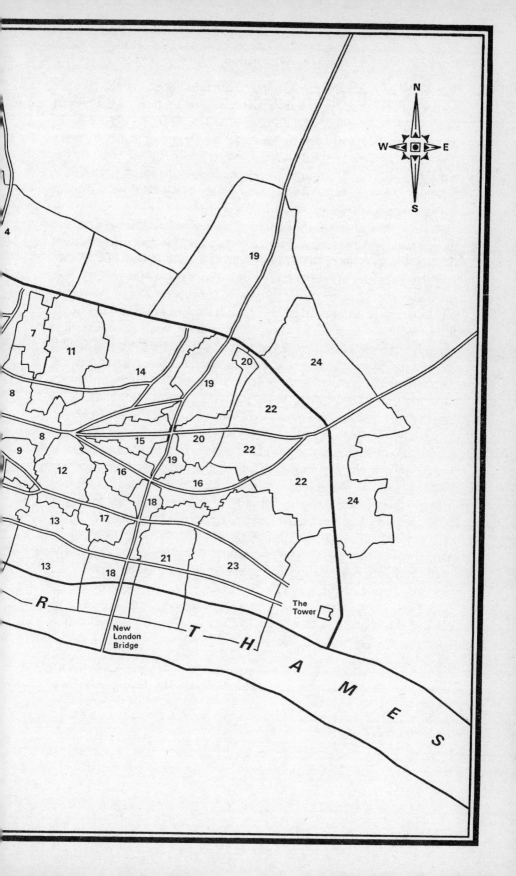

distributed haphazardly throughout the rectangles formed by the network of *viae publicae* than aligned along the edges of the streets – the normal siting of their later medieval successors and probably of their Roman predecessors. Most had their own enclosure (hedge or wall) and were surrounded by a patch of land on which vegetables could be grown. In the ninth and early tenth centuries there were in addition many plots free of buildings. Access to 'courts' and empty plots was provided by paths that were *communia vicinorum*.[1]

In a similar way – though it occurred somewhat later, and at first on a smaller scale and even more chaotically – we may visualize the growth of the hagas in London: of enclosures representing little enclaves, of City property belonging to a community, a manor or a man in the country. The enclosures, or hagas, or even *burhs*, have impinged in a most interesting way on the place-names of the City. Thus Bassishaw Ward and Basinghall Street recall the haga of the men of Basingstoke, a name of very high antiquity.[2] Bassishaw is a small but central ward, adjacent to the Guild-hall and to Aldermanbury, and the one case within the walls where parish and ward were virtually identical. It may well be that the ward still re-presents the shape of the haga, though its jagged edges can hardly reflect the first enclosure put into the space by the men of Basingstoke – these reveal, very likely, the shape it took when the local housing schemes developed in our period.[3] Of similar age is Lothbury, the *burh* or fortified enclosure of Lotha's folk. Lotha is a form of Hlothere, the name of an early Kentish king (673–85), but not recorded in later times; evidently, again, we have here a name of high antiquity.[4] Finally if we could tell the history of Aldermanbury, a great slice of London's past would be revealed to us. It is not the name of a ward, nor the origin of a ward; its parish is ap-parently no earlier than the twelfth century; it was not even a street name until the fourteenth century. But it is evidently an ancient district. Its situation suggests that it lay in the heart of the most populous part of the early City. To the south-west is St Paul's Cathedral and the meeting-place of the folkmoot, where St Paul's Cross later stood.[5] Immediately to

[1] Bullough, p. 106.

[2] Ekwall, p. 94.

[3] The angles in the boundaries in this part of the City, both of wards and parishes, suggest that small plots of land, houses and tenements have played their part in forming the precise line of the boundaries. Some of the lines further east in the City are less jagged, suggesting less complete settlement when they were fixed.

[4] Ekwall, pp. 196–7.

[5] See p. 249.

the west is St Alban Wood Street, the oldest church in this part of the
City, so far as the record goes; to the east, Bassishaw and Lothbury. And
who can say what the significance may be of the siting of the Guildhall
where Bassishaw and Cheap and Cripplegate (Aldermanbury's ward) now
meet?

But it is the name which lends Aldermanbury its fascination. Down to
the reign of Cnut an alderman, ealdorman, was the headman of a shire, a
leading noble; from then on the Danish Jarl, earl, replaced the title.
'Alderman', however, survived in its more general sense of a headman of
a ward (first recorded in 1111) or of a guild;[1] and so to the leading men of
any city, as it has survived to the present day. That the leading men of a
city should carry the same title as an earl may seem not so surprising or
inappropriate in the twentieth century; in the eleventh or twelfth it is
much more remarkable. This is one of a variety of pieces of evidence
which suggest that the transition took place in London; that it was in the
City that the head men first came to be called aldermen. The conversion
clearly belongs to an age when the language of the city was still predominantly English, and the memory of the noble ealdorman was still
fresh. We may suppose in general terms that it was applied to city magnates
some while before its first recorded occurrence in 1111, that is, in the
eleventh century. It is possible that Aldermanbury, the *burh* of the
alderman, hides some part of this story. In any event, it is to the wards
and the aldermen that we must now turn.

The hagas and *burhs* and sokes spread and flourished and had by the
time of Domesday laid a chaotic pattern on the City within the walls. But
they were always at war with the fact of the City – with the fact that
London was a place in its own right, with its own life. In due course the
hagas and *burhs* became bundles of houses and gardens; rents scattered
over the face of the town replaced the enclosure as units of property;
and the outlying manor failed to keep its grip on the City tenant. Already
in the 1180s 'Glanvill' presents what is evidently his rationalization of
established custom when he says: 'If any villein stays peaceably for a year
and a day in a privileged town and is admitted as a citizen into their

---

[1] The first clear use of 'alderman' for a ward is in 1111 (see discussion in Beavan,
vol. i, p. 363); for a guild in 1179–80 (p. 280); Brihtmaer of Gracechurch (mid-eleventh
century) was called 'senator' in a document of 1098–1108, and this probably, though not
certainly, translates 'alderman' (Tait, p. 266 n.). The use of 'ealdorman' for the head-man
of a shire was gradually superseded by 'eorl' in the early and mid-eleventh century.

commune, that is to say, their guild, he is thereby freed from villeinage.'[1] The precise meaning of this rigmarole is very obscure, and guilds and communes must engage us in a later chapter. But it is evident enough on the surface of the text that it reflects a world in which town and village were clean different things. Between the pride of hagas which was the nucleus of London's settlement, no doubt, in the time of Alfred, and the fully settled City of Henry II's time, the 'sokes' provide a transition. They sometimes started as hagas; they were not, however, in themselves areas of jurisdiction, still less of property, but bundles of rights;[2] and it was because these bundles were so diverse, so diffuse and so complex that London defeated the makers of Domesday.

Elusive as the sokes may be, they were a vital part of London's history in this period, and still form a substantial area of research. Some of them undoubtedly had a solid territorial base, and were treated as areas in the documents of the twelfth and thirteenth centuries. Unfortunately, the swiftly changing pattern of landholding has left little certain trace of these. Where a direct identification between soke and parish could be made – as by the late thirteenth-century jury which identified the parish of St Andrew by the Wardrobe with the soke of Robert FitzWalter,[3] lord of the honour which at one time had included Baynard's Castle – we may be tolerably sure that the saying incorporated both genuine tradition and a desperate plastering of the cracks. The queen's soke in the early twelfth century included both the Queenhithe and the soke of Aldgate, where Queen Matilda founded Holy Trinity Priory.[4] There is little reason to suppose, however, that either was ancient, though if not both must have

[1] Glanvill, ed. G. D. G. Hall, NMT, 1965, p. 58.

[2] Page, in his interesting discussion of the sokes (pp. 127–58) too readily assumed that the leading sokes were distinct areas of land. Doubtless many of them originated in hagas and plots on which great men built their town houses. But a soke was a bundle of jurisdiction, or rights; it involved a court, however slight or occasional, to which tenants owed suit. It was in the nature of a growing city in which no single lord or small group had dominant proprietary claims, that in course of time, granted much development, buying, selling, exchange and usurpation, these rights were often scattered higgledy piggledy over the face of the City. Page attempted to identify some of the early sokes with wards and parishes; only in the case of the Portsoken can any such identity be proved, and even that changed its shape in later times, when the Liberty of the Tower was in part cut out of it. Some of his other suggestions may indeed be correct, but cogent early evidence is lacking. The importance of the sokes is well explained in Stenton, pp. 14–15.

[3] *Placita de quo warranto*, p. 472.

[4] *Cart. Aldgate*, no. 11; Bateson, pp. 483–4.

been in the king's gift about 1100. Thus in the present state of learning the sokes have little to contribute to the study of London's topography. This needs a firm statement, for William Page thought otherwise; but his reconstructions were highly conjectural, and need ruthless criticism before the element of truth beneath them, which may yet prove large, can be discerned.

In the early eleventh century it seems that the king's palace[1] and the town houses of many great men actually lay within the City walls. Some, perhaps a large number, had moved out into the suburbs by the late twelfth, and so their personal grip on areas of the City had weakened. The move of the king's palace to Westminster in the time of Edward the Confessor began the process which spread the great men's houses over a large area. We do not know its full extent, though doubtless we ought to look as far afield as Tottenham, where an official of the king of Scots (or his son) had his London house in the twelfth century.[2] But its heart was the river, the great highway of London. Along the Strand, in the twelfth and thirteenth centuries, bishops and nobles began the building of houses which left the Savoy as a permanent mark on the physiognomy of London. The Bishop of Winchester had a manor in Southwark, and the whole south bank lay within his diocese.[3] It was natural that he should build his palace a little to the west of the old Borough on his own land not far from Westminster. If the Archbishop of Canterbury rode to London, he naturally stayed the last night of his journey on his own territory, spiritual and temporal, at Croydon. If one draws a straight line from Croydon to Westminster, it runs through the narrow corridor of the old parish of Lambeth, and impinges on the river approximately where Lambeth Palace now stands. Down to the last decade of the twelfth century, the bishops or monks of Rochester Cathedral were lords of Lambeth.[4] From the time of St Anselm (1093–1109) they not infrequently gave hospitality to the archbishops. But when Hubert Walter enjoyed the unique combination of offices of Archbishop of Canterbury, Papal Legate and Royal Justiciar, in the days of an absentee king, as he did from 1195 to 1198, then a more permanent headquarters on the river seemed essential. Indeed,

[1] See p. 111.

[2] *Early Scottish Charters*, ed. A. C. Lawrie, Glasgow, 1905, no. 53.

[3] Johnson, *Southwark and the City*, p. 25.

[4] *VCH Surrey*, vol. iv, pp. 44 ff.; the history of Lambeth, and the ambiguity of tenure, is discussed in Brooke, 'Lambeth and London in the eleventh and twelfth centuries' (see p. 364 n.).

he and his predecessor seem already to have conceived the idea of establishing their metropolitan headquarters in a great church at Lambeth, with the bishops of the province as the chapter and a special stall for the king.[1] Not unnaturally the monks of Canterbury objected to the erosion of their rights and privileges, and fought the issue tooth and nail to and from the court of Westminster and of Rome; and in the end Rome sustained them. But when the dust had settled, a more modest chapel was rising on the banks of the Thames at Lambeth which still survives as the nucleus of the palace we know today; and Lambeth Palace symbolizes, not only the place of the Church in medieval government and the supreme importance of the primate's office, but also the relation of the Thames, the great thoroughfare for heavy goods and weighty potentates, to Westminster and the City, the crucial fact on which London's topography is based.

The Rivers and Bridges

The major elements in the City's plan depend on the waterways, the bridges, the wall and the gates; only when we have grasped them securely can we come to terms with wards and streets. Across the Thames from Roman times – though not perhaps continuously – ran the bridge which defined London's original situation.[2] In the late twelfth century, about 1176, the great stone bridge was begun some distance to the west, and the wooden bridge was dismantled when the stone bridge was complete, a generation later; it was this massive structure of stone, often repaired and built over, which is well known from the fifteenth-century miniature and the seventeenth-century panoramas, London Bridge as it was until 1831.

The line of the Thames below and above the bridge formed the Port of London, with wharves at many points along the water-front – especially at Billingsgate and Botolph's wharf below the bridge, Dowgate, Queenhithe and Paul's wharf above.[3] About 1160 the French poet Thomas described in his *Tristran* how the hero's friend Caerdin sailed into the Thames on an errand to Ysolt, disguised as a merchant. He carried with

---

[1] Ibid.; *Epistolae Cantuarienses*, ed. W. Stubbs, Rolls Series, London, 1865, pp. xxxvii ff., xcii ff. There has been some difference of opinion whether the archbishops' design was in truth so grandiose; at least a substantial collegiate church was intended.

[2] See p. 109 and n.

[3] See map, pp. 173–5; Stenton, p. 37 (E. Jeffries Davis and M. B. Honeybourne); Honeybourne, in *LTR*, vol. xxii, 1965, pp. 29–30.

him 'silken wares worked in rare colours, and rich plate from Tours, wine of Poitou, and birds of the chase from Spain . . . He sails up-river with his merchandise and within the mouth, outside the entry to the port, has anchored his ship in a haven. Then, in his boat, he goes straight up to London beneath the bridge, and there displays his wares, unfolds and spreads his silks. London is a very noble city; there is none better in Christendom or any of higher worth, of greater renown, or better furnished with well-to-do people. For they much love honour and munificence and bear themselves very gaily. London is the mainstay of England . . . At the foot of its wall there flows the Thames, by which merchandise comes from every land where Christian merchants go.'[1]

Apart from the Thames, the waterways which affected medieval London were three: the Tyburn, the Holborn and the Walbrook, all minor streams.[2] The Tyburn flowed down past the site of Bond Street Tube station, and at Marble Arch a police station has replaced the famous gibbet called Tyburn Tree, which stood there until the spread of the aristocracy into the West End compelled its removal and renaming. The Tyburn flowed into the Thames in two channels which made Westminster in early days an island, the isle of Thorney, as it is described in early histories of the abbey. The Holborn flowed from Hampstead Heath down through the little valley which provided a natural western frontier for the Roman city, into a small estuary and so to the Thames. The estuary was known in the Middle Ages as the Fleet. The Fleet and the Holborn have suffered the final indignity, and been consigned to sewers. But the valley through which they flowed is still clearly marked, and their names are preserved in two of the main streets out of the City, Holborn and Fleet Street.[3] The Walbrook has entirely disappeared and has to be reconstructed (in its lower course) entirely from the boundaries of wards and parishes known to march with it, confirmed by archaeological traces.[4] In Roman times it divided the City into two, and some considerable remains of its influence survived into the medieval City. The pattern of the streets

[1] The *Tristran* of Thomas, trans. A. T. Hatto, in Gottfried von Strassburg, *Tristan*, Penguin Classics, 1960, pp. 345–6.

[2] Stenton, pp. 37–8 (as above); *Place-Names of Middlesex*, pp. 4, 6–7; cf. Ekwall, pp. 192 ff.; H. R. Ormsby, *London on the Thames*, London, 1924, esp. p. 83 (map of Tyburn); N. J. Barton, *Lost rivers of London*, London, 1962.

[3] Cf. Ekwall, pp. 88, 192–3.

[4] Cf. Merrifield, *Roman City of London*, pp. 86–9; cf. pp. 141, 260, 269; Grimes, pp. 92 ff.

still divided, and in a measure still divides today, at the Walbrook, with those to the west centred in the western market, the West Cheap, Cheapside, stretching out towards Newgate and Aldersgate, and those to the east round Eastcheap, which sits above the Bridge. But its most conspicuous influence on the map was the Moor. After the departure of the Romans there was no civic authority with the resources and power to keep the Moor drained or the Walbrook flowing freely, though it survived in some form for many centuries. Thus the meadow-lands north of the wall became a large bog, whose name survives in Moorfields and Moorgate.

THE ROMAN LEGACY: ROADS, GATES AND WALLS

Moorgate, however, was an addition to the company of gates made in the fifteenth century; otherwise the wall and the gates were the outstanding examples of continuity in the City's history. For the most part, their names are as obscure as their history is clear. Ludgate, Newgate, Cripplegate, Bishopsgate and Aldgate were on the site of the Roman gates, and all save Cripplegate – the north gate of the Roman fort which preceded the development of the City – led out to Roman or pre-Roman roads to the west and north and north-east.[1] To the west from Ludgate ran a Roman road of uncertain destiny: modern Fleet Street and Strand are its medieval successors showing a much more marked tendency to follow the river bank round to Westminster. From Newgate ran the main road to the west, not at first on the course of any modern street, but presently picking up the thread of Holborn, High Holborn and Oxford Street; and its junction at Marble Arch, where the Edgware Road runs north-west straight along the ancient line of Watling Street, and the Bayswater Road carries straight on to the west, is very clear. From Aldersgate two roads, probably pre-Roman, meandered north along the shallow ridges, until they converged to clamber up Highgate Hill, whose 400 feet make it one of the highest eminences in northern London. The great width of Highgate North Hill still represents the sprawl which a medieval high road needed to allow horses and drivers to recover from a stiff climb and search for a track in the spreading mud. From Bishopsgate ran the Ermine Street, the old north road, and from Aldgate the eastern road to Colchester. This leaves only the postern gate, by the Tower, the hatch or wicket, which gave its name to Hatch Street, later Hog Street, which the nineteenth century (for obvious

[1] On the gates and early road pattern see Grimes, esp. chap. II; Merrifield; Ekwall, p. 36. On roads outside London, see Grimes, p. 44.

reasons) preferred to call Royal Mint Street; the hatch was evidently a medieval gate, but its early history was quite obscure.[1]

So too are the names of the ancient gates. Bishopsgate is the one exception: it sat in land belonging to the bishop.[2] Billingsgate, the water gate, is probably the most ancient element in the history of London's wharves. Aldgate and Newgate in early Saxon time were the east and west gates; the east became (so it seems) the 'ale gate' shortly before or after the Norman Conquest; the west gate 'new' doubtless at some moment when it was rebuilt. One Ealdred had given his name to Aldersgate before the year 1000. That is all that we can say with confidence. But the vital fact emerges that the structure of Roman walls and gates remained to define the shape and topography of the City until the eighteenth century. At the western end the Normans built two castles, Montfichet's and Castle Baynard, to defend the City and to watch it;[3] and to the east they built the Tower. When the westerly castles disappeared in the thirteenth century, they rebuilt the western wall to enclose their space; but this only began in the third quarter of the century. On the east the extension of the Tower in the late twelfth century began the breaching of the Roman line; this was completed, likewise, in Edward I's time, when the full *enceinte* with concentric walls and moats was brought to its final extent. Otherwise, the wall lay on its Roman foundations, so far as we know, throughout its length. Most medieval cities which grew to any size burst out of their Roman walls and built a larger *enceinte*. A few, like Trier and Rome, were of such large extent in Roman times that the medieval city, for many centuries, could not comprehend the whole area it had covered.[4] Rare are the cases in which a medieval city fitted its Roman walls. On the Continent there is an additional reason for this; a reason well illustrated by the walls of Lucca. Here the visitor may still see, and wander round, the great bastions and moats of a sixteenth-century fortification; the kind of *enceinte* which many great continental cities acquire in the age of cannon, and which one can study in innumerable cases from sixteenth- or seventeenth-century maps and panoramas, rarely on the ground.[5] Kings and governments in England were sufficiently powerful, and most of the country

[1] Ekwall, pp. 92–3.
[2] Harben, p. 75.
[3] See pp. 214–15.
[4] For Trier, see Ganshof, map 34, and pp. 24, 42n.; for Rome, above, p. 6 n.
[5] See J. R. Hale, in *Europe in the late Middle Ages*, ed. Hale, J. R. L. Highfield and B. Smalley, London, 1965, pp. 466–94.

sufficiently peaceful, for such tremendous fortification to be either needless or forbidden. The walls and gates survived, party because it was still reckoned possible they might be needed for defence; mainly to curb the smugglers. The numerous dues and customs continued to be gathered at the gates of many an English walled city down to the eighteenth century; freer trade and the stage coach were their downfall.[1]

Yet the walls of the old city have never in recorded history marked the City's frontier. This runs up to the bars in all the main roads out of the City; runs west a considerable distance until it meets the City of Westminster; is at various points remarkably irregular, and has been in late medieval times made even more so by the large slices cut out of the City by the Liberty of the Tower and the Liberty of the Rolls.[2] These apart, it seems clear from a glance at the map that the City boundaries represent, in the main at least, the area over which the City had spilt when they were drawn; that they represent a spreading City with suburbs. Beyond that point, the history of the City's boundaries must also be seen as the history of the wards.

THE WARDS

There are now twenty-six wards in the City of London; and they remain units of some electoral and administrative significance. Of these, 'Bridge Ward Without', the borough of Southwark, only came into the City's hands in the sixteenth century.[3] This was the end of a long process. The borough of Southwark had always been an outwork of the City, which owed its significance to the Bridge and its wealth to London. But private sokes and public shire boundaries kept it for many centuries formally distinct from the City. The building of the stone bridge brought it nearer, for it was a civic enterprise which brought City men to the edge of Southwark, and involved the purchase of much key property on the south bank, which was administered under the City fathers by the Bridge House Trust; and it presumably improved communications across the river.[4] Finally, in the fifteenth and sixteenth centuries, the City won

---

[1] See W. G. Bell, F. Cottrill and C. Spon, *London Wall through Eighteen Centuries*, London, 1937. See Plates 23–4.

[2] For the western boundary in particular, see p. 169. On the bars, first recorded in thirteenth–fourteenth centuries, see Harben, pp. 8, 303, 570.

[3] Johnson, *Southwark and the City*, part III.

[4] Ib., pp. 124 ff.; Honeybourne in *Studies in London History*, pp. 29 ff.

administrative control of the borough, and the degree of union which still persists, incomplete though it is and incomprehensible to anyone not versed in the bypaths of English legal history, became established.

Before 1550 there were twenty-five wards, and before 1394 there were twenty-four. In the latter year the large, unwieldy ward of Farringdon was formally divided into Farringdon Within and Farringdon Without. From the end of the thirteenth century the wards were beginning to acquire their modern names, and a few go back much further than that. But the normal practice in the twelfth and thirteenth centuries had been to label each ward with a man's name – the name of its head man, its alderman for the time being; when the alderman changed, so did the ward's name. This practice records a fact of real significance in the history of the wards: the close links between their functions and the aldermen who led them and represented them in the early councils of the City.[1] But it also makes identification of wards and of their history extremely difficult. None the less, it is possible to penetrate a fair depth into their history and the secrets of their formation, thanks above all to two vital documents of great fascination. The earlier is the list of St Paul's properties and rents *c.* 1127, which divides them – not, like later rentals, into their parishes – but (in the main at least) into wards; and the second is the perambulation of 'purprestures' made in 1246.[2] In this enquiry it is peculiarly important to approach the unknown through the known, and it is with 1246 that we must start.

On St Hilary's day and the day after, and on the Sunday following, and on the Tuesday and Wednesday before the Conversion of St Paul, in the thirtieth year of the King Henry the son of King John – that is, by our reckoning, 13–14, 21, 23 and 24 January 1246 – a team of Royal justices perambulated the streets of the City to investigate and take note of

---

[1] See below; on the aldermen, see Beavan.

[2] The list of *c.* 1127 was edited by H. W. C. Davis in *Tout Essays*, pp. 45–59, with text on pp. 55–9 from St Paul's Cathedral Library, Liber L, ff. 47–50v (not entirely accurately, but the only substantial error is the omission on p. 58, para. 22, after the 'Terra Wluardi . . .' of 'Terra uxoris Radulfi iij solidos in festo sancti Pauli reddit, et est longitudinis lxxxxiii pedum, latitudinis in fronte iuxta viam xxx pedum'). Davis, pp. 46–7 dated it with fair probability to the vacancy of the see, i.e. to *c.* 1127, not, as he said, 1128, with outside limits 1123 × 32 (cf. Le Neve, p. 1). The phrase 'Terra episcopi Dunelmensis quam tenet Helyas' (p. 56) presumably refers to Ranulf Flambard and his son (cf. Le Neve, p. 77), and Flambard died in 1128, which perhaps confirms Davis's date, although his successor was not consecrated until 1133. The purprestures of 1246 are in *Eyre*, pp. 136–53.

obstructions, or 'purprestures' built on the king's highway. Approximately twenty wards seem to be represented in the list, some by a long tale of obstructions, some by only one item; and there are good reasons for thinking that the full twenty-four were then in existence.[1] What is especially significant about this document is that it is possible to check the extent of some of the wards with its help. It opens in the ward of 'Henry of Frowyk without', which we can quickly recognize as Farringdon Without.[2] In this and a few other wards purprestures were numerous, and we can even trace the route of their perambulation. We start at the western limit of the ward and of the city, just inside the Temple Bar, in Fleet Street. Opposite the New Temple they found a forge in the king's highway, for which the Knights Templar were paying a rent: 'let it be taken into the king's hand'. Opposite Shoe Lane the knights had another forge, rather smaller, which was assigned to the same fate. Then they moved on and looked down into the Fleet, where the Templars had their mill. Twelve elders of the neighbourhood were collected with the alderman of the ward to give evidence as to what had happened twenty years before, at the eyre of 1226. Then, as now, complaint was made against the Templars that they had obstructed a watergate leading to their millrace (doubtless to increase the force of water turning their wheels), and had furthermore planted willow trees upon and beyond the bank, and so narrowed the channel in which ships had of old been wont to pass. All this makes an interesting comment on the effect of such proceedings, but the investigation in 1246 apparently had more effect: 'It is amended,' is the terse conclusion of the record.

Next the justices looked at a house which projected seven feet into Fleet Street beside the Fleet Bridge, 'well and truly built'; here the justices were lenient and offered 12*d* fine as the alternative to demolition. But no such alternative was offered to Stephen of Cheshunt, tanner, when they passed north, skirting the Fleet, into 'Newgate Street', as Snowhill is called in the record.[3] Here at the corner of Seacoal Lane they found a wall

---

[1] *Eyre*, pp. 136 ff. The survey of *c.* 1127 specifically names twenty wards (most of which cannot now be certainly identified), and includes three or four other paragraphs which may represent areas already wards. See below pp. 166–7; cf. Stenton, p. 10 and n. For other evidence, see Beavan.

[2] Although the alderman's name should probably be Laurence; cf. *Eyre*, p. 34; Beavan, vol. i, p. 372. The details in *Eyre*, pp. 137 ff., leave no doubt as to the identification of the ward. (Farringdon was a single ward at this time; the formal division into 'Within' and 'Without' came in 1394.)

[3] As the context makes clear; the name Snow Hill ('Snore' Hill originally) is already recorded, however, in Henry III's reign and may be older (cf. Ekwall, pp. 29–30).

which the tanner had built, narrowing the entry to the lane. This they ordered to be demolished. And so north to the Smithfield bar, then back, via Holborn Bridge, where another tanner had built a great purpresture near the Fleet, opposite the Dominican Friars, in their original home in Holborn.[1]

Back from Holborn Bridge past St Sepulchre's, where they found a horse-enclosure in the king's highway, through Newgate, where the modest beginnings of the famous prison could already be seen, to Farringdon Ward Within: here they soon entered the broad highway of Newgate Street, which contained the first of the string of food markets which ran on along the West Cheap to where the Bank now stands: the meat market, or Shambles.

The justices sought for purprestures; we ask, first and foremost, whether the wards in which they wandered had already achieved their modern shape. To this no complete answer is possible, but the beginning of an answer is to be found in Farringdon, Within and Without.[2] We find the identity of the Farringdons in 1246 and today is as closely confirmed as such a record could be expected to confirm it. For Farringdon Within has an ungainly shape. It runs right down Newgate, through a narrow funnel between the liberty of St Martin le Grand, near which a lady called Wymarca stabled her horses, and the precinct of St Paul's; and to the corner of West Cheap and Friday Street, where Richard Abel had set the steps of two cellars to the nuisance of passers-by. In this area it spreads in all directions, including south along Old Change, 'the street of St Augustine leading to the gate of St Paul's', where Margaret Blund had a chamber jutting into the road, 'to the great nuisance of the passers-by'.[3] The other part of Farringdon Within is a long arm running down from

---

[1] The Dominicans were in Holborn from 1221 till after 1275, when they moved to 'Blackfriars' (KH, p. 217); A. W. Clapham in *Archaeologia*, vol. lxiii, 1912, pp. 57–84 W. A. Hinnebusch, *The Early English Friars Preachers*, Rome, 1951, chap. II. The sites of religious houses were worked out by Miss Honeybourne in her M.A. thesis, University of London (see her note in Stenton, pp. 39–40, with other references, and esp. for the friars, *LTR*, vol. xxii, 1965, pp. 32–3, and references). The sites of the friaries are all of later date than this book, but they are relatively well documented (esp. the Franciscans, see Honeybourne, *LTR*, vol. xvi, 1932, pp. 9–51) and extremely helpful in defining the changes which took place in the shape of the City in the thirteenth century.

[2] Then, as now, the line of the wall made the difference between 'Within' and 'Without'.

[3] *Eyre*, pp. 139–40.

Newgate just inside the wall, and marching at its southern end, in a somewhat haphazard way, with Castle Baynard ward. Here Master Peter of Newport, Archdeacon of London, a leading figure of the cathedral chapter later to be promoted Dean, had built a stone wall facing Castle Baynard, and the aldermen of both wards – Robert, son of John and Laurence of Frowyk – gathered the men of the neighbourhood to give evidence about the wall. 'They say that the said wall is well built but the pillars supporting it stand in the king's highway. The archdeacon offered half a mark to the king but was not listened to. The pillars are to remain rendering 6*d* a year to the king.'[1]

No other ward produces quite this quantity of evidence and for many there is little indeed. But there is enough to suggest quite strongly that the pattern in all parts of the City, and in some areas the detail of the later ward boundaries, was already marked out in 1246. Since the boundaries shown by Ogilby *c*. 1676 have many jagged edges, like the parish boundaries, we must suppose that their crystallization and formation were determined by property boundaries, and minor shifts may well have occurred in the later Middle Ages. There was no event quite equivalent to the reception of canon law in the twelfth century to fossilize the ward boundaries; and they may have been more susceptible than parishes to later changes.[2] But there are strong reasons for supposing that their number had become fixed even earlier than the parishes.

In or about 1127 the canons of St Paul's took stock of their City properties, defined them by wards and measured them, so that we know the precise areas of some of their houses and messuages. Unfortunately there is no single case in which we can be entirely confident that we have identified the property on the ground.[3] The wards, as in 1246, are mostly named from their aldermen; and this gives us the earliest list of aldermen and a most interesting cross-section of the City patriciate. A few wards had

[1] *Eyre*, p. 140; cf. Le Neve, pp. 7, 11, 24, 56.

[2] But from the moment when aldermen were elected by a recognized group of fellow-citizens, and even before that (in all probability), when suitors first gathered to the wardmote, some degree of definition was needed. Unfortunately we cannot be at all precise when these events happened, and the crystallization of the institutions may have been spread over several generations.

[3] In contrast to Canterbury and Winchester (see W. Urry, *Canterbury under the Angevin Kings*, London, 1967; and the work of D. Keene for the Winchester Research Unit, forthcoming). Doubtless future work will be able to make such identifications for late medieval London, but the extent of modern rebuilding makes London a much less favourable case for such study.

already found their later names – Cheap ('Fori') and Aldgate: another, 'Brocesgange', has tempted the unwary to identify it with Walbrook, but as all the properties ran down to the Thames, if a later equivalent must be found, Vintry or Dowgate are better candidates. The chief interest of the survey, however, is that it provides us with evidence of perhaps twenty-two or twenty-three wards.[1] Since the property was not in its nature evenly distributed over the face of the City, we could not expect to find every ward represented; and it is tolerably clear that the list supports the view that there were already approximately twenty-four wards or so *c.* 1127.

The ward was (at least by the thirteenth century) a military, judicial and administrative unit; the equivalent within the City of the hundred without;[2] a purely civil unit. In theory, there is no reason why its boundaries should march with the boundaries of ecclesiastical parishes. But in practice civil and ecclesiastical boundaries were often in the Middle Ages affected by the same pressures, and for various reasons it was found convenient to assimilate them. Thus, in particular, many archdeaconries were approximately equivalent to shires. Where they differ, there is commonly some significant historical circumstance to explain the difference. Thus the boundaries of the sees of St Asaph and Chester–Coventry did not conform with the frontier of England and Wales between the time of Edward I and the 1920s, but revealed a situation at some early date when a Welsh prince had carved a frontier deep into Shropshire.[3] The medieval archdeaconries of Worcester and Gloucester were formed in the twelfth century and conformed to the shape of those shires – save where the see of Worcester overlapped them, since its own boundaries were those of the Hwicce some

[1] See above, p.163 n. The doubtful paras. are 1 (land some of it 'iuxta forum', which could be the ward of Cheap, which is, however, para. 8); 2 (beyond the Fleet, evidently part at least of Farringdon); 5, Vicus Judeorum (possibly Coleman St Ward); 7 (Aldermanbury, i.e. within Cripplegate Ward: cf. Ekwall, p. 195). This suggests that two or three more wards than the twenty listed may be included, but the paragraphing is arbitrary and may mislead. See also J. Tait, *LTR*, vol. xv, 1931, pp. 1–3.

[2] Stenton, p. 10; M. Weinbaum, in *Aus Sozial- und Wirtschaftsgeschichte : Gedächtnisschrift für G. von Below*, Stuttgart, 1928, pp. 105–14. There is a useful general account of the early history of the wards in *Calendar of the Plea and Memoranda Rolls . . . 1413–37*, ed. A. H. Thomas, Cambridge, 1943, pp. xxx–xli. The wardmotes were evidently in existence well before the word first occurs, as an error for 'vadimonia' in the early thirteenth-century text of the charter of Henry I (see Brooke, Keir and Reynolds, p. 576).

[3] See Brooke in *Flintshire Hist. Soc.*, 1964, pp. 42 ff.; corrected by O. E. Jones in his MA Thesis 'At extual and historical study of Llyfr Coch Asaph' (University of Wales, 1968), who suggests a twelfth-century date.

centuries before the shire boundaries were fixed.[1] The rural deaneries of the diocese of Chichester roughly correspond to the boundaries of the rapes; such differences as there are seem to indicate that the deaneries were formed very soon after the Norman Conquest, when there is reason to suppose that the coincidence would have been exact.[2] The shape of some of the wards is even stranger and more puzzling than that of the parishes; and of none more than the Farringdons, whose general conformation, as we have seen, is certainly early. Within the walls, A. H. Thomas saw little indication of any change in the boundaries after the Conquest.[3]

There are distinct correspondences between ward and parish boundaries in the City; but what hits the eye is how frequently they differed. Some of the differences reflect their different functions. The parishes would have been too small to support the functions of a hundred court, too small to supply 'watch and ward' to police a gate or a main thoroughfare. The parishes respected the wall; the wards, on the whole, did not. The reason for this is plain: the prime function of many wards was to protect a gate into the City. Thus Bishopsgate, Aldersgate and Cripplegate wards each lapped round their gates, and included a substantial area within, and the whole faubourg without. Farringdon, far and away the largest, included two gates, Newgate and Ludgate, and the whole western suburb. The only exception is Aldgate,[4] the ward whose name seems to have been attached to its gate earlier than any other, and yet had no space beyond it. The explanation seems to be that the Portsoken was established before the ward.

A glance at the map suggests that the wards were established before the faubourgs carried any great number of folk; and the very unequal size of the wards suggests that they were fixed at a time when the City was very unevenly settled. The Portsoken gives us a more specific clue.[5] This was the area of the soke of the Cnihtengild, who also had rights, it seems, within the walls. The Cnihtengild was formed, so far as the evidence goes, in the time of Edgar. We may reckon that the formation of the wards, at least in the eastern part of the City, took place later than the 970s.

The map also seems to tell us that wards and parishes grew up together.

[1] See pp. 197 ff.
[2] See W. Hudson in *Sussex Archaeological Collections*, vol. lv, 1912, pp. 108–22.
[3] Thomas (p. 167 n.), p. xxxiii.
[4] See p. 318.
[5] See p. 96 and n. For the rights of the Cnihtengild, see *Cart. Aldgate*, nos 109, 871 ff., 960 ff.

If we reckon that the parish boundaries began to be formed in the eleventh century and achieved their full pattern in the twelfth, we may reckon that the ward boundaries were fixed at some period roughly in the middle of this process, or perhaps a little earlier. If the wards were entirely stable before the parish boundaries began to take their final shape, or vice versa, we should expect much closer coincidence between the two: the divergences are eloquent testimony that in some measure they grew up together.

It is indeed quite likely that when they began to take shape there was more coincidence between the wards and a number of parishes more modest than the ultimate total of nearly one hundred. Yet the later development of the parishes makes it clear that when the wards were fixed the parishes had sufficient life already not to be unduly constrained by these comparatively parvenu boundaries.

The tendency of this line of thought is to place the formation of wards fairly early in the long period of time over which parishes were formed. The document of *c.* 1127 shows the wards firmly established.[1] The shape of some wards, when compared with the final form of the parishes, seems also to show that the ward boundaries are older. The smaller the units, the more jagged their edges, the more we may presume that they represent areas of the City fully settled, with property rights established and respected. Both sets of boundaries show an intra-mural City far more occupied than the suburbs; both show a concentration of folk and houses in the west and south. But the large area and the impressionistic outline of the wards of Aldgate and Tower are eloquent of a time when the City was conspicuously less developed in this region than in the areas round Cheapside or Basinghall Street – the one area, apart from the Portsoken, where ward and parish had virtually identical frontiers. Most striking of all is the enormous extent of Farringdon Without the Wall. The boundary of the City itself at this western end seems first to have acquired something like its present shape in about 1000, when the frontier of Westminster retreated to somewhere near the Holborn and Temple Bars.[2] At that time St Andrew's church was an ancient wooden building; St Bride's (if it existed at all) was a modest cemetery chapel. The extension of the churches and the development of the suburb went on apace in the eleventh century; but there were still large areas unsettled in the early twelfth; of this the formation of the large precinct of St Bartholomew's, which still left ample

---

[1] Later surveys usually defined properties by parishes; thus the survey of *c.* 1127 strongly suggests that the wards were longer and more clearly established at that date.

[2] See M. B. Honeybourne, in *LTR*, vol. xix, 1948, pp. 16–17; and below, p. 319.

space for the great horse and cattle markets at Smithfield, is clear witness. Yet the open ground within the walls must have been much reduced by 1100. When the religious houses of the City began to proliferate in the early twelfth century, only Holy Trinity was placed inside the walls – significantly, in the largest intra-mural ward, of Aldgate, the ward which was neighbour to that in which the Conqueror had placed his Tower. True, in a wooden city fire and purchase could quickly clear large spaces; and the friars and the nuns of St Helen's and some small hospitals were to join St Paul's and Holy Trinity within the walls in later times. But the large precincts were all set round the periphery, from the New Temple round to St Katharine's.[1]

WARDS AND ALDERMEN

We may be tolerably confident that the wards grew up in the eleventh century, though their remote origin may be older; we may conjecture that the ward boundaries still represent something of the pattern of London in the first half of the eleventh century. But what were the wards in these early days? – apparently hundreds in miniature, with hundred courts and hundredal jurisdiction, competing with and often confused with the rights of sokes, as in the countryside without. As to when their headmen came to be called aldermen, or when the aldermen acquired the important status already visible in the early twelfth century, we cannot tell. But we may note that the wards were beginning to take shape at about the epoch when the title alderman was dropping from the headmen of the shires. In some sense it clearly represents a transfer to the towns of what had been a nobleman's title.

We have moved into the world of conjecture. But some speculation on this theme is necessary, for the alderman represents on the small scale the way in which City government first emerged on the large; in the origin of the aldermen we may see in miniature the origin of the sheriffs. It has been disputed whether the title alderman was first applied to the headman of a ward or of a guild. To this we can offer no clear answer, though if it were the case that the head man of the Cnihtengild and of the Portsoken was established as early as any of the other aldermen, then we could say that in origin there was no difference.[2]

[1] See map, pp. 173–5, and pp. 328–37.
[2] See p. 168; at least from the moment that the Cnihtengild handed over its rights to Holy Trinity, the Prior exercised the jurisdiction as alderman of the Portsoken (though first so named in 1290: Beavan, vol. i, p. 180), as well as lord of its other properties.

STREETS, MARKETS AND QUARTERS

As we accompanied the royal justices on their hunt for purprestures, we encountered a number of significant street-names and occupations. It is remarkable how many names have been stable in the City since the twelfth century and how clearly we can plot the establishment of spaces and places dedicated to particular trades and crafts. It is necessary to keep a fairly close watch on chronology in such an exercise, since markets and trades can shift. In Winchester the excavation of 'Tanner Street' has revealed that it was surrendered at quite an early date to the fullers and dyers;[1] and in London the fish market was moved in the late twelfth century, so that 'Fish Street' – of which there were two at the best of times – is ambiguous, and one soon became 'Old Fish Street'.[2] Nor must we expect clear segregation of this trade from that, or rich from poor. At its northern end Aldermanbury, the alderman's home, meets Addle Street, not the Addle Street south of St Paul's where the Ætheling, the Old English prince, once lived, but the street of dung.[3] Both names go back to the earliest stratum of London names, and both reveal basic elements in the City's character. London indeed was one of the first European cities to have suburbs and segregated quarters; and it already could claim a 'west end' in the twelfth century. This, however, was due to the attraction of Westminster, which spread out new large houses along the strand or bank of the river and in Holborn; the Strand first meets us as a roadway when the Templars completed their establishment between the Strand and the river in 1185.[4]

Within the City walls the first and most conspicuous fact which the map reveals is the crucial importance of the food markets. These had their

[1] M. Biddle in *Antiquaries Journal*, vol. xlviii, 1968, pp. 266–7; vol. xlix, 1969, pp. 304–5, 310–12. There is an interesting general study of streets in G. Bebbington, *London street-names*, London, 1972.

[2] See Ekwall, pp. 72–5. The evidence of *Eyre*, p. 140, no. 369, makes it certain that one of the streets called Fish Street ran past the church of St Mary Magdalene, and so confirms the possibility discussed by Ekwall that Old Fish Street was the former name for Old Change. This establishes that Old Fish Street and Friday Street ran parallel to one another into the part of West Cheap where the fishmarket lay, and makes it probable that Friday Street as well as Old Fish Street did not themselves contain the fishmarkets) but led to it (St Paul's Cathedral A18/1430, *HMC*, p. 19, refers to the 'antiquam piscatoriam' in West Cheap). Bread Street likewise no doubt led to that part of West Cheap where the bakers' stalls were gathered.

[3] On the two Addle Sts. see Ekwall, pp. 55, 81, 102.

[4] See pp. 231, 232.

centres in the two Cheaps of West and East; and the activities of the Cheaps were evidently, in a very broad and general sense, orientated to land and sea respectively.[1] The East Cheap was the smaller of the two, and linked the wards of Candlewick and Bridge and Billingsgate; and from the Bridge came to it Fish Street. Doubtless fish and meat were landed and sold here from early times; but it is a curious and interesting fact that the fish market next St Paul's, an element in the western Cheap, is recorded long before that nearer to the river and the sea;[2] whereas the oldest element in the eastern Cheap was the trade of the candle-wrights or chandlers, who gave the name to the great street later Candlewick, now Cannon Street[3] – and yet the greatest centre of candle-burning must always have been in St Paul's.

These facts remind us that the space between the cheaps was never large, that a candle-wick might reach St Paul's after walking only 500 yards; and it also underlines the crucial importance of the West Cheap. The justices of 1246 passed within the walls through Newgate, and almost immediately came upon the stalls of the butchers in the Shambles. 'All the stalls of the butchers are to be numbered and it is to be asked who holds them and by what service and of whom. Let there be a discussion' – or, as the Latin more succinctly puts it, 'Loquendum'.[4] A curious discussion forms the very last item in the Eyre, in which the citizens tried to claim that King Richard I had granted the stalls to the citizens with the shrievalty.[5] Whatever came of this piece of shadow-boxing, the stalls remained, and the Shambles formed the first element in a continuous chain of markets running to the 'Stocksmarket', where the Bank of England now stands. Beyond the Shambles, at the corner of St Paul's Churchyard, lay the corn market, under the eye of St Michael 'le Querne'. Here is the centre of the old city, where St Paul presided over its spiritual welfare, his churchyard provided the space for the great assembly of the Folkmoot, and the corn market the staff of temporal life. In the late Middle Ages the meeting of God and Mammon was represented by Paternoster Row, the

[1] For early references, see Ekwall, pp. 182 ff. The siting of the two markets is extremely interesting. Each formed a centre for an ancient division of the City, west and east of the Walbrook; and the line of Westcheap was evidently designed to be accessible primarily to traffic coming from Newgate, Aldersgate and Cripplegate, whereas Eastcheap is nearer to the Bridge and the Thames.

[2] See above, p. 171 n.

[3] Ekwall, p. 79.

[4] *Eyre*, p. 139, no. 360.

[5] *Eyre*, p. 153, no. 486.

London c. 1200

NOTES

Streets

Only those streets which we have clear reason to believe existed appear on the map. There were in fact many more but the contemporary custom of referring to them often as 'via regia', 'via regalis' or simply 'venella' makes identification extremely difficult. Where names are known they have been given in their twelfth-century form but with modernized spelling.

City Boundary

The boundary of the City has been equated with the present one, which follows the extra-mural ward boundaries. Two liberties, that of the Rolls in the west and the Tower in the east, developed after 1200 and have slightly reduced the area under City jurisdiction.

River Frontage

The river came to a higher level in the twelfth century than at the present day. An approximate position has been shown.

Three churches omitted from the map on pp. 124–5 are marked here: St Andrew Holborn, St Dunstan in the West, and St Bride by Fleet Street.

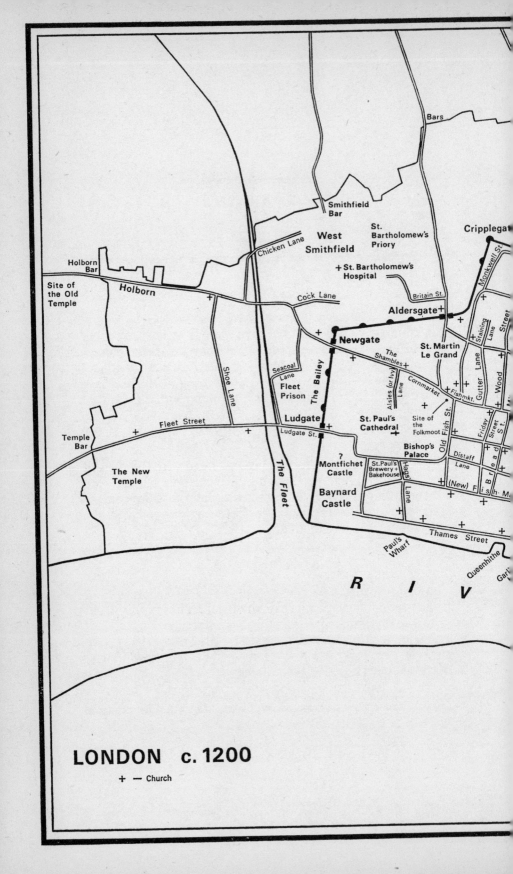

Smithfield
Bar

West
Smithfield

St. Bartholomew's
Priory

Cripplega

Chicken Lane

Monkwell St.

Holborn
Bar

Site of
the Old
Temple

+ St. Bartholomew's
Hospital

Holborn

Cock Lane

Britain St.

Aldersgate +

Newgate

St. Martin
Le Grand

Staining

Lane

Street

The
Shambles

Wood

Seacoal
Lane

Aisles (or Ivy) Lane

Cornmarket

Gutter

Lane

Shoe Lane

Fleet
Prison

The Bailey

Fishmkt.

Fish St.

Fleet Street

Ludgate

St. Paul's
Cathedral

Site of
the
Folkmoot

Old Fish St.

Friday

Street

St.

Temple
Bar

Ludgate St.

Bishop's
Palace

Distaff
Lane

B r i e a d

The New
Temple

The Fleet

?
Montfichet
Castle

St. Paul's
Brewery +
Bakehouse

(New)

F i s h. M

Baynard
Castle

Hags' Lane

Thames Street

Paul's
Wharf

Queenhithe

Gar

R   I   V

LONDON c. 1200

+ — Church

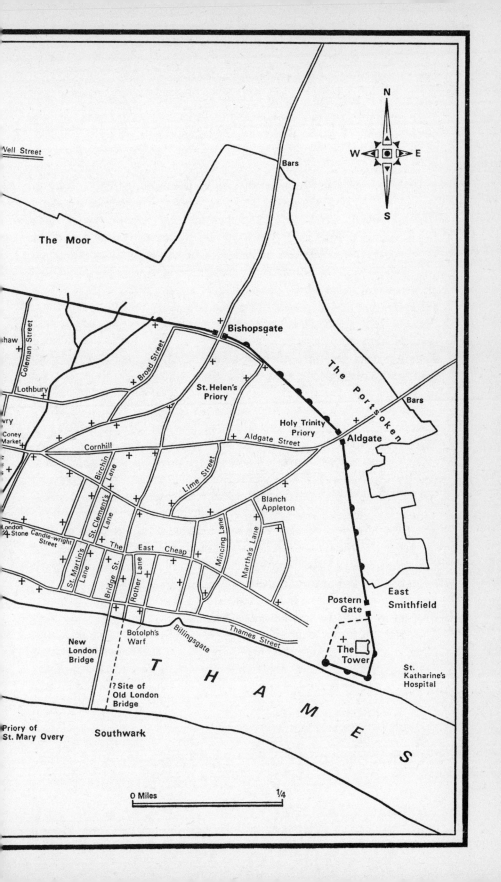

Vell Street

The Moor

N
W E
S

Bars

shaw

Coleman Street

Lothbury

Bishopsgate

Broad Street

The Portsoken

St. Helen's
Priory

Bars

vry

Coney
Market

Cornhill

Birchin Lane

St. Clement's Lane

Holy Trinity
Priory

Aldgate

Aldgate Street

Lime Street

Blanch
Appleton

London
Stone

Candle-wright
Street

St. Martin's
Lane

The

East Cheap

Bridge St.

Rother Lane

Mincing Lane

Martha's Lane

East
Smithfield

Postern
Gate

New
London
Bridge

Botolph's
Warf

Billingsgate

Thames Street

The
Tower

St.
Katharine's
Hospital

?Site of
Old London
Bridge

T H A M E S

Priory of
St. Mary Overy

Southwark

O Miles   ¼

street of the rosary makers or paternosterers.[1] In early times, and down to the fourteenth century, the churchyard linked the corn market to the northeast and the cathedral brewery and bakehouse to the south, which in its turn lay by a street running straight down to Paul's Wharf on the river.

The brewery and bakehouse were strange antique institutions whose survival provides a key to much that is important in the City's history in this period.[2] In earlier centuries wealthy churches, like kings and princes, lived off the food-farms provided by their manors. From the laws of King Ine of Wessex, of the late seventh century, we have a list of the sort of items which a royal estate of ten hides might be expected to produce, so as to feed the royal household for 'one night': honey, bread, ale, 'two full-grown cows or ten wethers', geese, hens, cheeses, butter, salmon, fodder and eels[3] – and we can imagine these items trundling in carts, or marching, through Newgate and Aldersgate, and being spread along the line of food markets from the Shambles to the Poultry. By the time of the Norman Conquest most such farms had been commuted into money, though no doubt much payment in kind, much direct supply took place. But the food-farms from the manors of St Paul's Cathedral continued to be paid in kind at least down to the mid-fourteenth century. The produce of the manors was brought from the estates in Essex and Hertfordshire and Middlesex – and a few even further off – and converted into beer in the cathedral brewery and into bread in the bakehouse. The produce was then equally divided between the thirty major canons, each of whom received, week by week, a gargantuan issue of this rather basic provender.[4]

At first sight this seems a bewildering mixture of the old world and the new. The thirty major canons, each with individual incomes based on their 'prebends', are the result of reorganization and expansion after the Norman Conquest; by that date the food-farm was an old-fashioned instrument. Furthermore, from the start some of the canons were non-resident, and very soon many of the canons ceased to be resident most of the time; resident in the Close and the cathedral, that is, for many of them were royal servants and not infrequent visitors to Westminster, or men with other reasons for making their home in the City, and so not wholly non-resident. Yet few of these could personally have eaten the loaves or drunk the beer; and from the Norman Conquest on, if not before, a well-bred

[1] Ekwall, pp. 168–9.
[2] See pp. 340, 352 ff.
[3] *EHD*, vol. i, ed. D. Whitelock, London, 1953, p. 371.
[4] *HSP*, pp. 60 ff.

canon would in any event prefer French wine to English beer. All manner of complex issues may be involved in this single problem; but the large fact to which it bears witness is that if you did not consume bread and ale it was easy to sell them; the food market was the heart of the life of London.

After the Shambles, the Quern; and after the Quern the opening of the older Old Fish Street – now Old Change, followed closely by Friday Street: it may be that fishmongers lived in these streets, even that fish was sold there; but the convergence on to Cheapside of Friday Street, Bread Street and Milk Street seems to signify that Friday's fish, and bread and milk, were sold in the market where these streets impinged upon it.[1] Before Milk Street there opens on the left Wood Street, an ancient throughfare linking the Cheap with Cripplegate, part of it on the line of the central road in the Roman fort of Cripplegate – and so the oldest street in the City. Here, evidently, the timber-sellers lived. After Bread Street, one passed between Honey Lane and St Mary-le-Bow, where the Dean of Arches provided wills for the aged and annulled the marriages of the not-so-aged, to the area first named in 1246 the Drapery and the Mercery, past Old Jewry to the Poultry market.[2] Off the Poultry ran Coneyhope Lane, which represented a small district – or rather, probably, a market-place of considerably greater extent than modern Poultry – the Coney Market, where rabbits and other honorary poultry were sold.[3] And finally, beyond the Poultry, the wool church in the market-place where wool was sold, and cheating shopkeepers in later times enclosed in the Stocks, the centre of the City from which the whole system of its roads, then as now, revolved.

We have explored Cheapside, the West Cheap, at some length, because it speaks so eloquently of the close link between the making of a great town in this age and the trade in foodstuffs and other basic necessities of life, on which recent students of early medieval towns have come so strongly to insist.

[1] See above, p. 171 n.

[2] For Drapery and Mercery, see *Eyre*, pp. 140–1, nos. 370, 372. For Old Jewry, see below.

[3] For Coneyhope see Ekwall, pp. 150–1: '*Cuningchep* must mean "rabbit-market".' The attempt by H. G. Richardson and G. O. Sayles, *Law and Legislation from Æthelberht to Magna Carta*, Edinburgh, 1966, p. 10 n., to derive it from 'king's market' is philologically impossible, since 'Cuning' could not be used for king in the twelfth century (we are indebted to Mr J. McN. Dodgson for confirmation of this point).

FOREIGN SETTLEMENTS

We have from time to time emphasized that London remained in many ways an English city after the Norman Conquest; but it was also, and always, cosmopolitan. The full flavour of this must be tasted when we study London's trade. But already, in our study of the churches, we have met the Vikings, and in our perambulation with the justices, we have encountered the Jewry. If we walked along the wharves from Billingsgate to Paul's Wharf, we should meet also the Flemish, Norman and German elements in London's trading population.[1] The Scandinavian element must have been large in the eleventh century, when the Scandinavian trade was the most flourishing in western Europe; its imprint is clear on churches scattered over the face of the City, and especially in the western suburb; its mark is on the City's institutions, especially on the name of the Husting. Archaeological evidence confirms that London had a strong Viking element in it in the eleventh century; but it has left no mark on the lists of moneyers before the reign of Cnut, nor on the street-names of the twelfth and thirteenth centuries.[2] These are predominantly English, with a few French (but most of the French are known to be of much later date) and no Viking names at all. Some of the English names look clearly more ancient than 1100; but for the most part it seems that the City streets received their present names in the twelfth and thirteenth centuries, when English was the language chiefly spoken there. A large number are recorded already in the twelfth century, and in general terms it is reasonable to suppose that bakers and dairymen passed along Bread Street and Milk Street, and conies went their way to the Coney Market, in the twelfth century.

The mark of Normans and Flemings on churches and streets is slight. Compared with St Olaf, St Vedast of Arras and St Audoen of Rouen have a modest place in the list of churches.[3] Yet in all probability they had a large place in the City's life in the late eleventh and twelfth centuries. According to the charters of Edward the Confessor and William the Conqueror to St Peter of Ghent the Confessor gave to St Peter's a portion of Warmansacre, with its shops and stalls and wharves and wharfage. Unfortunately this early testimony of the Flemish presence in London was forged in Westminster long after the Confessor and the Conqueror were

---

[1] See pp. 265 ff.
[2] See Ekwall, esp. p. 19.
[3] See pp. 141–2.

dead.¹ But at least we can say that it was a firm tradition by the mid-twelfth century that St Peter's had acquired its wharf a century before; and the same (broadly speaking) is true of the Germans. The men of Cologne had acquired their Hanse by the mid-twelfth century, and tradition had it the men of the emperor already had privileges in the Confessor's time.² So assuredly had the Normans.

But the Norman Conquest began the true growth of Flemish and French influence, especially of the former. The reasons for this are partly political; but in the main we are seeing here the edge of a massive re-orientation in the trade of London and with it of England. From being an outpost of the Scandinavian trade-routes the City became the centre of Flemish commercial enterprise; for London was the largest port in the world of Flemish commerce in this age, and also the midway point between the English sheep whom the Flemish clothiers fleeced and the English folk whom they clothed, and the growing industrial towns of Flanders. The men of Rouen already had Dowgate from the Confessor's time: the Norman link naturally tightened after the Conquest.

The Jewry

The Jewry seems to have been an element wholly new in the reign of William I, which owed its strong hold in England to the moderate patronage of the Conqueror, and the generous assistance of William Rufus and Henry I. Rufus enjoyed shocking intolerant churchmen by giving patronage and aid to 'infidel' Jews;³ above all he valued them for their help in financing his armies of knights. It is a bold man who asserts with confidence that there were no Jews before 1066, nor any left remaining after the expulsion of 1290. But no one doubts that these two centuries mark the age of medieval Jewry in this country. Old Jewry and St Lawrence Jewry still mark the centre of their London quarter; and the Eyre shows us rich Jews living there and blocking, or trying to block up lanes to extend their property behind St Mary Colechurch and near the Coney-hope;⁴ also as far to the north-west as the prosperous quarter near

¹ Sawyer, no. 1002 and references; Thorpe, *Diplomatarium*, pp. 357–61; for the name, see Ekwall, p. 38.

² See pp. 266 ff.

³ Eadmer, pp. 99–101; on the Jews see below, pp. 222–7 and H. G. Richardson, *English Jewry under Angevin Kings*.

⁴ *Eyre*, pp. 143–4.

Cripplegate. The London Jewry was the chief centre of Jewry in England, and one of the chief centres of finance and moneylending in London.

Epilogue

Our perambulation of London has led us far from the happy visions of William FitzStephen; yet his rhapsody must always be in our minds as we tour the City. To balance it, at the conclusion of our study of London's topography in the eleventh and twelfth centuries, let us hear the un-flattering account of London's place among the English towns which Richard of Devizes, a Winchester monk of the late twelfth century, put into the mouth of a French Jew, advising a young protégé about to travel.[1] The Jew assumes that one can live only in a town and passes in review all the English cities that he (or Richard) knew:

> If, therefore, you arrive in the neighbourhood of Canterbury or if, indeed, you pass through it, your journey will be wasted. There is a whole collection of men there who have been abandoned by their lately deified leader, I know not whom, who was high priest of the men of Canterbury, who now, through lack of bread and of work, die in the open day in the broad streets.[2] Rochester and Chichester are mere hamlets, and there is no reason why they should be called cities, except for the bishops' seats.
>
> Oxford scarcely sustains, much less satisfies, her own men. Exeter refreshes both men and beasts with the same provender. Bath, placed or, rather, dumped down in the midst of the valleys, in an exceedingly heavy air and sulphureous vapour, is at the gates of hell. Neither should you choose a seat in the Marches, Worcester, Chester, or Hereford, because of the Welsh, who are prodigal of the lives of others. York is full of Scotsmen, filthy and treacherous creatures scarcely men. The region of Ely stinks perpetually from the surround-ing fens. In Durham, Norwich, and Lincoln there are very few people of your sort amongst the powerful, and you will hear almost no one speaking French. At Bristol there is no one who is not or has not been a soapmaker, and every Frenchman loves soap-makers as he does a dung-heap. Outside the cities, every market-place, village, or town

[1] Richard of Devizes, *Chronicle*, ed. J. T. Appleby, NMT, 1963, pp. 64–7.
[2] This is a reference to the plight of the monks of Canterbury (whose deified leader was of course Thomas Becket) in dispute with Archbishops Baldwin and Hubert Walter (see pp. 157–8).

has inhabitants both ignorant and boorish. Moreover, for such qualities always look on Cornishmen as we in France consider our Flemings. In other respects, that country is most blessed with the dews of heaven and with richness of soil. In each locality there are some good men, but there are fewer by far in all of them put together than in one city, Winchester. That city is in those parts the Jerusalem of the Jews; in that city alone do they enjoy perpetual peace [a reminder that the passage was written in the 1190s, very shortly after the massacres which accompanied the preaching of the Third Crusade in London and York]. That city is a school for those who want to live and fare well. There they breed men; there you can have plenty of bread and wine for nothing.

And he enlarges on the virtues of the monks, the citizens and the city:

There is one vice there and one alone, which is by custom greatly indulged in. I would say, with all due respect to the learned men and to the Jews, that the people of Winchester lie like sentries. Indeed, nowhere else under heaven are so many false rumours made up so easily as there; otherwise they are truthful in all things.

But for London he has no good word:

I do not at all like that city. All sorts of men crowd together there from every country under the heavens. Each race brings its own vices and its own customs to the city. No one lives in it without falling into some sort of crime. Every quarter of it abounds in grave obscenities. The greater a rascal a man is, the better a man he is accounted . . . Whatever evil or malicious thing that can be found in any part of the world, you will find in that one city. Do not associate with the crowds of pimps; do not mingle with the throngs in eating-houses; avoid dice and gambling, the theatre and the tavern. You will meet with more braggarts there than in all France; the number of parasites is infinite. Actors, jesters, smooth-skinned lads, Moors, flatterers, pretty boys, effeminates, pederasts, singing and dancing girls, quacks, belly-dancers, sorceresses, extortioners, night-wanderers, magicians, mimes, beggars, buffoons: all this tribe fill all the houses. Therefore, if you do not want to dwell with evil-doers, do not live in London. I do not speak against learned or religious men, or against Jews: however, because of their living amidst evil people, I believe they are less perfect there than elsewhere.

This vision of the teeming life of the twelfth-century city – though its phrases may owe as much to Horace's *Satires* on ancient Rome as to Richard of Devizes' knowledge of the London of his day – none the less fairly reflects in a general sense the reverse of FitzStephen's coin. Between them we can come to grips with a lively, exciting, squalid, yet attractive, even splendid, medieval city.

Part III

Society, Trade and Government

8

On Sheriffs and the Money Market

SHERIFFS AND CONSULS

MUCH OF London's history is written into the title of its leading officers. From the dawn of recorded time – in this case, the early eleventh century – London's chief 'magistrates' were royal reeves. By the late twelfth century it had become established custom that two sheriffs were elected or appointed each year to manage the affairs of London and Middlesex under the King's aegis (see p. 234); they were sheriffs like the sheriffs of other shires, and yet with a difference. The difference became even more marked in the last decade of the twelfth century, when the sheriff was joined by a new official, a single head or representative of the community of the City, who came to carry the title recently popular in leading French towns of 'mayor'.[1] The sheriffs were royal officials still, yet also civic officials, superior to the mayor in the antiquity of their function and in wearing the mantle of a royal office; inferior to the mayor since they could not claim to represent the City in the measure that he did, nor any longer preside at its crucial assemblies and meetings. Beyond 1200 lay the growth of the infinitely complex, yet wonderfully lasting and adaptable institutions of the City as we know them still. To understand the origin of the shrievalty it is more important to understand the institutions of those early centuries in which it lived and moved and had its being, than what the office later became. And these institutions (if we are really to grasp the essence of the matter) include not only the shrievalty elsewhere in England, and similar institutions else-

[1] See below, pp. 237–8.

where in Europe, but vicars and good men and consuls in the Mediterranean lands. For the London sheriffs adapted themselves between 1000 and 1200 to changes in the nature of their city, of its life and quality and livelihood and population and governments, which had analogies all over western Christendom.

The circumstances of English towns, and the special relation of London to the shrievalty, have always seemed to most English historians – naturally given in any event to insularity – to be so different from any continental parallels known to them, that for the most part the history of English towns has been written as if the Continent scarcely existed. Scarcely, for there are obscure and fascinating hints in James Tait's *Medieval English Borough* of a rich and deep learning about continental towns which he was reluctant to reveal.[1] Its significance is understood, but never expounded. Yet it is essential to see London in a wide European setting: partly because the cities of Western Europe lived and grew in a common world, and partly because the flow of pilgrims, litigants and merchants who knew the Italian cities at first hand steadily increased as the eleventh century turned into the twelfth and the twelfth into the thirteenth.

The wide context helps a little, too, to overcome the slender nature of the evidence which afflicts us everywhere in the early stages of this process, though it carries with it the danger of making too much of the analogies. But the real danger in recent years has been to make too little of the similarities, too much of the differences. Richard of Devizes cried out hysterically when the commune of London was sworn in 1191: 'a commune is the tumult of the people, the terror of the realm, the tepidity of the priesthood'[2] – he was summarizing the history of Europe in the eleventh and twelfth centuries, as it appeared to a conservative-minded churchman, to a monk living in Winchester Cathedral priory with a city lapping round him.

In the eleventh century even the greatest of north Italian cities had acknowledged the supremacy of the emperor; when not engaged in riots that is, and in burning his palaces or chasing out his representatives. But we can observe that some great change was in the wind when the Emperor Henry IV granted to Pisa, in 1081, a privilege which 'provided that any future nomination of a marquis of Tuscany would require the assent of

---

[1] Tait, pp. 221, 255, 264: in each case a substantial and important generalization not discussed or documented.

[2] Richard of Devizes, *Chronicle*, ed. J. T. Appleby, NMT, 1963, p. 49. But cf. Reynolds, 'Rulers of London', p. 343.

twelve Pisans to be elected in the *commune colloquium*'.[1] About the same
time (*c.* 1080–5) we first find the word 'consul' attached to the leading men
of an Italian city, again at Pisa. The appearance of the word consul is
commonly reckoned the outward and visible sign of the formation of civic
institutions in Italy; the symbol of the communes. One has to tread warily
here: these early communes were not the fully fledged mercantile oligar-
chies which flourished in the thirteenth century; and the process is fully
as obscure in its way as it is in England.[2] But we pass through certain
well-defined stages. First, the town revived as a place where people wished
to live. In the Italian cities of the eleventh century the nobles of the
country round mingled with merchants and craftsmen; all the elements in
the population are needed to explain the process of growth, and between
the lesser nobility and the merchant no clear lines were drawn. Commercial prosperity early revealed to some Italian cities, most notably to
Pisa and Genoa, that the political strait-jacket of marquises and emperors
was at variance with the interests of a people whose empire lay on the seas
and the trade routes.[3] Furthermore, the old aristocracy of northern Italy
in fair measure withered away, and the emperor, however dominant and
domineering on occasion, spent most of his time the other side of the Alps.
From the 1080s on increasing self-consciousness among the 'good men' of
the cities led to the formation of groups of consuls who in the long run took
over the management of the city. Pisa came first, in the 1080s; many
others followed in the next generation. But they were no more independent
officials in the first place than the aldermen of London. In some cases a
local count kept watch over their activities on the emperor's or the
marquess's behalf; far more often it was the local bishop. For this reason
the story of Italian municipal independence has often been described as the
process by which the citizens wrested power from the hands of their
bishops, as an anti-episcopal, anti-clerical movement of secularization.

[1] Waley, p. 56; on Pisa see esp. G. Volpe, *Studi sulle istituzioni comunali di Pisa*, rev.
edn, with introduction by C. Violante, including a bibliographical survey, Pisa, 1970.
[2] See pp. 77 ff., and a general survey in Waley, chap. 2; Y. Renouard, *Les Hommes
d'affaires italiens au moyen âge*, 2nd edn, Paris, 1969; A. Sapori, *Le Marchand italien
au moyen âge*, Paris, 1952; J. Lestocquoy, *La Vie sociale et économique à Arras du XIIe
au XVe siècle*, Arras, 1941; *idem, Les Villes de Flandre et de l'Italie sous le gouvernement
des patriciens*, Paris, 1952; cf. A. B. Hibbert in *Past and Present*, no. 3, 1953, pp.
15–27.
[3] See pp. 66 ff; on Genoese trade see brief bibliography in Renouard, *Les Villes
d'Italie*, p. 565, and esp. R. Doehaerd, *Les Relations commerciales entre Gênes, la Belgique
et l'Outremont . . . aux XIIIe et XIVe siècles*, 3 vols, Brussels–Rome, 1941.

Conflict no doubt there was; but conflict was the stuff of life of medieval cities.[1] 'A commune is the tumult of the people' was a saying echoed in every corner of Europe in the twelfth and thirteenth centuries; faction and conflict were in the end to be the undoing of the republican governments of most Italian cities.[2] Anti-clericalism there was too; and it is no chance that the cities of north Italy were often major centres of the heretical movements of the late twelfth century. But the ousting of the bishop was a slow and gradual process, and often quite incomplete. In all cities the bishop remained a figure of great importance – all the more so because virtually every Italian city had a bishop and a cathedral. In some cases he was reduced to secular impotence by violent means, in others by more subtle processes. In early days the leading consuls were commonly (in part at least) nobles of the *contado* who came increasingly to make their home in their local metropolis; commonly the bishops were men of the same breed.[3] Their relations were sometimes adapted in the peace or the Armageddon of family conclaves; in all cases the shifting relationship was part of a complex social change not the subject of this chapter, but vital in the end to its understanding.

The cathedral and the splendid Romanesque churches frequently survive to this day as symbols of the piety, unity and wealth of Italian cities in this age. If we visited eleventh-century London – even more the City of the early or mid-twelfth – we should be impressed by the size and splendour of St Paul's. We should perhaps be even more impressed by the welter of tiny churches in which the citizens worshipped, and baptized their babies. The relation of bishop and civic community is well summed up in a story that St Francis' companions delighted to tell about Assisi in the saint's dying months, in 1226:[4]

During the time that he lay ill, and after he had composed these Praises [the Canticle of Brother Sun], the bishop of Assisi of the day

[1] Waley, chap. 5.

[2] Waley, chaps 5, 6; the famous stories of riots in Cologne in 1074 and in Laon in 1112 show that these characteristics were not confined to Italy (Lampert of Hersfeld, *Annales*, in *Opera*, ed. O. Holder Egger, Hanover and Leipzig, 1894, pp. 185 ff.; Guibert de Nogent, *De vita sua*, lib. iii, *passim*, ed. G. Bourgin, Paris, 1907, pp. 176 ff., Migne, *Patrol*, *Lat.*, vol. clvi, coll. 907 ff., esp. 921–2).

[3] Somewhat more remotely, all the bishops of London of the late twelfth and thirteenth centuries had some earlier connection with the chapter of St Paul's; this was no longer the case after 1338 (*HSP*, pp. 42–3).

[4] *Scripta Leonis*, etc., ed. and trans. R. B. Brooke, pp. 166–71.

excommunicated the podestà of Assisi. The podestà had been angry with the bishop and had had it forcefully and diligently proclaimed through the city of Assisi that no one was to sell anything to him or buy anything from him, or make any contract with him. And so they had a great mutual dislike of each other. Although St Francis was so ill, he was much concerned about them, especially as no one, lay or religious, was intervening to restore peace and concord. He said to his companions: 'It is great shame to us, the servants of God, that the bishop and podestà hate each other so much, and no one intervenes to make peace and concord between them.' So he made on this account a verse in those Praises, thus:

> Be praised my Lord
> For those who pardon for thy Love
> And bear infirmity and tribulation.
> Blessed are they who uphold peace
> For by thee, O most High, they shall be crowned.

The dying saint sent a companion to gather the podestà and the city fathers to the Piazza del Vescovado, and two more to sing the Canticle in the presence of bishop and podestà; the quarrelsome potentates were duly made to feel ashamed of themselves. As they sang the podestà stood entranced with folded arms; then he threw himself at the bishop's feet; and the bishop took him up and said: 'My office requires me to be humble, but as I am by nature quick-tempered, you must make allowances for me.' The friars were astonished at their success, and the other witnesses regarded it as a great miracle. No doubt there were many such quarrels not so readily allayed by the prestige of a dying saint.

The office of podestà is more obviously analogous to the mayoralty and we shall return to it anon. Immediately, however, it shows comparisons and analogies which can stir us to ponder on the whole system of town government in England in the Middle Ages. Most of the early podestà were imperial representatives. But sometimes already in the mid-twelfth century, very commonly in the later twelfth century, the podestà, the potestas, the authority, was a leading citizen chosen to act as effective chairman of the tumultuous assemblies and committees which had sprung up to govern or to spread anarchy in the Italian cities.[1] In due course, sometimes quickly, sometimes after a long interval, in many cities he ceased to be – what the mayor, his equivalent in northern Europe,

[1] See pp. 239–42.

was becoming and was to remain – the representative of the governing oligarchy, and became an arbiter between the warring factions. In many cities the office came to be held normally by a citizen from another city, and only for a year. Eminent men made a profession of it, and went from city to city umpiring the civic tug-of-war in each in turn. This endemic faction was in part due to the concentration of all political and social life into the cities. The nobles of the *contado* built towers as symbols of their status within the city to protect them from fires and their neighbour's swords, partly because civic life, at peace or war, had become congenial and fashionable, partly because the cities were in any case assuming control increasingly over their *contadini*. The cities ceased to be islands of social and political and economic activity in a countryside ruled by its petty nobility. Italy became, like ancient Greece, a land of city-states, in which petty nobility and stout burghers, merchants, craftsmen, professional men, and clergy, ruled together in tumultuous discord.

Midway between Pisa and London lies Toulouse, which makes an interesting comparison, since it has something of Italy in it, something of the north, and since it lay for a time within the Angevin realm.[1] In the eleventh century it was firmly under the control of the count of Toulouse. His viscount, his reeve as one would say in England, for the whole district, was also his vicar in the town. It was in this age that it first became, once again, a notable place and one of the great cities of Europe. In the twelfth century the post of vicar came increasingly to be a full-time civic office, though still under the count's control; but in the early thirteenth century the good men turned chaptermen turned consuls finally took over, the office of vicar declined, the count was forced to make terms with his leading city, and the consuls began extending their authority out into the contado. This kind of story, even more than Richard of Devizes' hysterical outburst, explains why the English kings, though very well aware of the value of the City of London, and of all cities, to them, and frequently dependent on the city fathers for their solvency, or at least their liquidity, looked with a jealous and suspicious eye on the City's pretentions to independence.

The vicar of the count of Toulouse is the nearest analogy one could hope to find, or wish to find, outside England and its immediate continental neighbourhood,[2] to the Sheriff of London; and to the sheriff we may now

---

[1] J. H. Mundy, *Liberty and Political Power in Toulouse 1050–1230*, New York, 1954; P. Wolff, *Histoire de Toulouse*, Toulouse, 1958, chap. III.

[2] For the more immediate colleagues of the sheriff nearer home, see pp. 199 ff.

at last turn our gaze. The origin of the office must be sought in the tenth and early eleventh centuries, though in some form or other it may be much older than that. Anglo-Saxon officials, even the greatest, have a way of disappearing as one turns the microscope upon them. Every local official was called a reeve, and in the last two generations of the Old English Kingdom every central official was liable to be called a staller. That is all that we know for certain. Yet if we wish to penetrate the history of London's government in the eleventh century, we must try to go behind this statement to the practical situation which it hides.

THE SHERIFFS OF LONDON AND MIDDLESEX: ORIGIN AND PREHISTORY

In July 1141 Geoffrey de Mandeville won from the Empress Matilda the grant of a wonderful collection of titles, which were confirmed later in the year, in slightly different form, by King Stephen.[1] He was confirmed, along with his ancestral estates, with the earldom of Essex, the custody of the Tower of London, the shrievalties of London and Middlesex (for a farm of £300), of Essex and of Hertfordshire, as his grandfather had held them, together with the justiceships of these three shires; and much else beside. Thus he held all the offices in local government north of the Thames in the shires surrounding London and in the City itself; and as if this was not enough, the Empress conceded that neither she, nor her husband nor her sons would make 'any peace or agreement with the burgesses of London, save with the grant and approval of Earl Geoffrey, since they are his mortal enemies'. The earl notoriously played a crucial role in the political history of his day.[2]

What concerns us now are first, the concentration of offices he held, and the historical tradition concerning his grandfather; and second, the statement in the charter that he, like his grandfather, had London and Middlesex to farm for £300.

Down to the reign of Henry II the offices of earl, local justiciar and sheriff formed the secular hierarchy in local government; Geoffrey could only have extended his power by becoming Bishop of London as well. He had monopolized every link between London, and the counties near her, and the crown. Furthermore he claimed that the shrievalty at least was his by inheritance from his grandfather Geoffrey de Mandeville I, who

[1] *Regesta*, iii, nos. 274-6; cf. pp. 37, 217-18.
[2] See pp. 37 ff.

was of the generation of the Norman Conquest.[1] Perhaps already, and certainly in the time of Earl Geoffrey's son, Earl William (1166–89), the doctrine seems to have been held that their ancestor, Geoffrey I, had been granted the inheritance of Esgar or Ansgar the Staller along with his office, and on this account was Sheriff of London and Middlesex.[2]

In William's time, probably in the 1170s or early 1180s, one of the canons of Waltham in Essex – later Waltham Abbey – wrote an account of the traditions of their church from the discovery of their miraculous cross in the early eleventh century down to the mid-twelfth century.[3] The secular potentates who figure largely in the story are Tofi the Proud, an eminent Danish thegn of Cnut's time who died early in the reign of Edward the Confessor, his son Athelstan, his grandson Ansgar; and Earls Geoffrey and William. In the account of Athelstan, it is said that he lost his father's estates, save those which pertained to the staller's office, which Earl William held when the book was written. The passage was at one time taken to be a claim that Geoffrey de Mandeville I had succeeded Ansgar as staller, and therefore that the office of Sheriff of London and Middlesex was the equivalent of that of staller. But Miss Florence Harmer rightly objected that it was really more probable, not that the offices had any identity, but that Geoffrey had acquired Ansgar's lands, a doctrine amply confirmed (at least in general outline) by 'Domesday Book'.[4] But we have not disposed of Geoffrey's hereditary pretensions, for it is clear that if we take the canons to have meant simply this, they propounded a doctrine as misleading as the view that a staller and a sheriff were the same: namely that certain very large estates were attached to the office of staller. Nothing is less probable.[5] There is no evidence before 1066 for the identity of a sheriff and a staller and indeed the staller is almost the only official who was never called a 'reeve' or any variant of the word; and yet it remains beyond question that Ansgar had authority in London over a long period.

[1] On Geoffrey de Mandeville I, see Round, *GM*, pp. 37–8, 439.

[2] *Chron. Waltham*, p. 13 (quoted Round, *GM*, p. 37 n.); see below.

[3] The *Chron. Waltham* was ed. W. Stubbs in 1861; pp. 6 ff. relate to Tofi the Proud, p. 13 to his descendants, Athelstan and Esgar or Ansgar.

[4] Harmer, pp. 51–2 n.

[5] There is no other evidence that estates were attached to such offices in pre-Conquest times. On the office of staller, see L. M. Larson, *The King's Household in England before the Norman Conquest*, Madison, 1904, pp. 147 ff.; Harmer, pp. 50 ff.

REEVES AND STALLERS

Ansgar was addressed as one in authority in London in a writ of Edward the Confessor issued early in his reign (1042–4), in which the king confirmed to Westminster Abbey the wharf which the abbey had been given by Ulf the Portreeve and Cynegyth his wife.[1] Over twenty years later we meet him in the vivid account in Guy of Amiens' *Carmen* of the preparations of London for a siege in the weeks following the Battle of Hastings. It is made clear that the affairs of the City and of the eminent members of the *Witan* who had gathered in London were directed by Ansgar, even though he was severely wounded and had to be carried in a litter.[2] London was not the only sphere of Ansgar's duties; and the stallers were sent on roving commissions like Carolingian *missi*. Nor was Ansgar the only staller with authority in London in this age. It was probably in the period 1044–6, shortly before rebelling against the king, that Osgod Clapa was addressed with the Bishop of London, Ulf the sheriff and the thegns of Middlesex. Osgod was a colleague of Ansgar's grandfather, Tofi the Proud – indeed he was his father-in-law.[3] When Tofi married Osgod's daughter, evidently his second wife, in 1042, King Harthacnut died in his cups at the wedding feast in Osgod's house in Lambeth.[4]

But the most interesting feature of the writ addressed to Osgod is the name of Ulf the Sheriff of Middlesex for this is the first named sheriff of Middlesex, and he bears the same name as the first known portreeve of the City. The next reference to a portreeve (also very early in the Confessor's reign) is to one 'Wulfgar', a name at the time almost identical to 'Ulf' and very likely the same person.[5] Soon after we meet Leofstan and Aelfsige, portreeves, and Ælfgaet the sheriff,[6] and it is clear that there were at least two or them at a time. Tantalizing like all the evidence about Anglo-Saxon administration, such fragments provide us with all the evidence we have. If Ulf the sheriff was also Ulf the portreeve then the possibility of a combination between the offices goes back at least to the early 1040s.

---

[1] Harmer, no. 75, p. 342.

[2] *Carmen*, pp. 44–5.

[3] Harmer, p. 344, no. 7 (cf. p. 497; 'the outside limits would be 1044–51'). Chronologically, the relationship of Osgod and Tofi is puzzling; presumably Tofi was advanced in years at the time of the marriage.

[4] Florence of Worcester, vol. i, p. 196.

[5] See Appendix II.

[6] See Appendix II.

Exactly the same problem meets us after the Conquest: the first Norman portreeve[1] and the first Norman sheriff were both called Geoffrey – the latter evidently the first Geoffrey de Mandeville.[2] Were they the same man? It is very likely that they were, and it has been commonly assumed so: we are never likely to have proof.

The sheriff was 'the reeve of the shire'; but both reeve and shire were in origin more modest affairs than they had become in the days of Ulf and Tofi the Proud. The reeve was a great man's servant, and his title survived in the later Middle Ages attached to the lowliest of officials, the head of a peasant community in a village; meanwhile, in the tenth, eleventh and twelfth centuries the sheriff mounted until he became himself a great man with a team of officials at his beck and call. By a similar change the humble *maire* of a French village handed his title to the Mayor of Rouen and London in the late twelfth century; but the process was very different.[3] The mayor was a new creation provided with an old title; the sheriff evolved. The first step in his progress was the appearance, far back at the dawn of Anglo-Saxon royal administration, of the king's reeve.[4] From a small centre of administration, a royal village with an estate surrounding or based upon it which provided the king with his farm, his food-rent, the king's reeve looked after the king's interest in the neighbourhood. He was governor of the estate, farmer of the royal revenues, whether corn and honey or silver, and convenor and president of the court in which the king's peace was enforced and other high matters attended to. In due course it was laid down that his court met monthly; and in due course again we find that it is growing into the court of the hundred. That is to say, as the Old English Hundred emerges into the light of day, we can

[1] The evidence for the identification is the coincidence of a name not unduly common and the close link between the offices, which can be presumed even though the evidence that they could be identical is all of later date.

[2] It is clear enough, as Round showed (*GM*, pp. 353-4; cf. Harmer, p. 50), that the offices of portreeve and sheriff became merged in early Norman times, and quite possible that this had been anticipated in pre-Conquest times. But it is very hard to prove precisely when it first happened, or the identity in particular cases. Both before and after the Conquest there are 'reeves' who cannot be shown to have held both offices. Thus the identity of name, and the absence of any evidence from addresses in writs to contradict the identification, make it likely, but not certain, that Geoffrey de Mandeville I, the sheriff, was also Geoffrey the portreeve. See Appendix II for details.

[3] See pp. 236 ff.

[4] On the king's reeve, see Harmer, p. 49 and n. 3; H. M. Chadwick, *Studies on Anglo-Saxon Institutions*, Cambridge, 1905, pp. 228-39; Morris, pp. 9 ff. See Liebermann, vol. i, p. 11, for a reference to a King's reeve in London in 685-6.

discern that in many cases its jurisdiction has grown out of an old royal vill, and its head man is an old royal reeve. Likewise the 'scir' or shire is an ancient word for a district; and it was commonly used in the ninth and tenth centuries – as for many centuries to come in Yorkshire and in Gloucestershire, in such areas as 'Howdenshire' and 'Winchcombeshire'[1] – for districts much smaller than the shire as we know it. But in the tenth century the shire emerged, and there appeared at its head, beside the bishop and the alderman, a king's reeve of special eminence, the sheriff. The stages of this development are exceedingly unclear; and the difficulty of tracing the line of change is enhanced by the Anglo-Saxon practice of using a single word to cover a variety of men and institutions. The reeve was an official; the king's reeve a royal official. The sheriff emerges in the tenth and eleventh centuries as the summit of this hierarchy of service; but by his side there also appears, as boroughs struggle into life, the reeve of the borough, commonly the 'portreeve'.[2] It is clear that the portreeve was sometimes a person distinct from, and presumably inferior to, the shire-reeve; there is evidence of a reeve of London distinct from the sheriff as late as the 1110s and 1120s. The documents seem in a conspiracy to baffle us, for most of our evidence consists of writs addressed to officials of the shire court, whose offices are often not specified (see p. 371); and the vagueness of the labels used in late Old English times leaves us guessing as to whether the portreeve and the sheriff could or could not be the same man, as to the relation between the Sheriff of Middlesex and the portreeve of London. There is no reason to think it impossible that one man could hold both offices, no reason to suppose that any attempt was made to distinguish different office-holders by these titles. Thus when we meet sheriff and portreeve shortly before the Conquest and shortly after bearing the same name – Ulf in both roles before 1066 and Geoffrey after – there is a slight balance of probability that in each case we have to do with one man. But Ulf was not a rare name in eleventh-century England, and Geoffrey was one of the commonest names among the Normans; and it appears that the offices could be sometimes distinct.

These thoughts enable us to carry the history of the office back several generations before Ulf, and to consider the meaning of the famous decree of the reign of Athelstan (925–39), 'the ordinance which the bishops and

[1] For the variety of uses of *scir* and their history, see esp. A. H. Smith, *English Place-Name Elements*, pt. ii = English Place-Name Soc. vol. xxvi, Cambridge, 1956, p. 110.

[2] See Harmer, p. 50 and references cited in nn. 2–4.

the reeves who belong to London have agreed to and confirmed with pledges in our peace-guild, both nobles and *ceorls* [earls and churls].'[1] London had lain for many centuries on a boundary of one sort or another, and this in large measure conditioned its history before the Conquest. Here already, before it had become again a great city, we see how important a place it can hold in administration. Whatever the precise nature of the peace-guild, it seems to have been a large community, similar to the gatherings which swore to the peace of God in France and Germany a hundred years later, and yet in its way more sophisticated. For it has precise rules, and organizes police jurisdiction of a primitive kind over an area not only wider than a shire, but wider than a bishopric.[2] It is formed of a group of leaders in the home counties, and it seems to be trying to organize the king's peace and decent security in a substantial area. The effort which may be implied here to find a unit of administration between shire and kingdom did not bear fruit, but the idea that London could be the centre of a group of shires surrounding it reappears in the time of Henry I and Stephen.[3] Meanwhile the full emergence of the hierarchy whose heirs were Ulf and Geoffrey can be seen in the king's addendum to the ordinance: 'Eleventhly, Athelstan commands his bishops and his ealdormen and all his reeves over all my dominion, that you observe the peace just as I and my councillors have enacted it' – on pain of losing (for the reeve) his office and the king's friendship.[4]

This code lifts the curtain which hides London's administrative history in the tenth century, but only briefly; we cannot inspect a reeve at work, or name him, before the days of Ulf.

A shire court in late Old English times could be presided over by a galaxy of officials: bishop, earl, staller and sheriff.[5] It is noticeable that stallers rarely appear in documents relating to shires outside London and Middlesex, while earls are rare in the metropolis. The only earl known to have had status there was Leofwine, Godwine's son, who appears briefly wielding authority in Middlesex and Hertfordshire in the 1050s or 1060s.[6] He was perhaps the most obscure of King Harold's brothers, and the significance of his earldom is hidden from us; nor do we know how his authority was matched with Ansgar's, since Leofwine fell in the slaughter

---

[1] *EHD*, vol. i, pp. 387–91; Liebermann, vol. i, pp. 173–83.
[2] Since it speaks of both reeves and bishops in the plural.
[3] See below, pp. 203 ff. [4] *EHD*, vol. i, p. 391.
[5] See Harmer, esp. pp. 45 ff., and references cited at p. 45 n. 3.
[6] Harmer, nos. 88–90, p. 567 (earl *c.* 1057–1066: he died at Hastings).

of the royal family at Hastings, before the incident described by Guy of Amiens. There is, indeed, no evidence that he held sway in London; nor did any other earl, so far as the record goes, lay claim to Middlesex.

All this may not be sufficient to prove a firm and tight bond between city and county, though Ulf and Geoffrey certainly hint at a bond of some kind. It is, however, extremely unlikely that Middlesex would ever have become a shire at all but for its link with London. Before we become oppressed by the difficulty of finding clear and firm ground among the shifting names and titles of these early officials, let us grasp two large and hard facts. First of all, the history of the boundaries and frontiers in the neighbourhood of London, in early times and still in the reign of Henry I, points to the key importance of the City itself as a centre of power and (after a fashion) of government. The second fact is that though stallers and sheriffs, like bishops and earls, had varied functions, including the leading of armies and the presiding over local courts, the portreeve's and the sheriff's chief function seems to have been fiscal.[1] What this meant in practical terms is not revealed to us until the Pipe Roll of 1130, when the sheriff's function is clearly unfolded. By then it was his business to handle the royal farms and revenues in his shire, and to bring the proceeds twice yearly, for delivery and audit, to Westminster; thereafter what was surplus to the King's immediate needs was deposited in his treasure-house at Winchester or elsewhere.[2] We cannot be sure how far back these functions go. But we can be certain, from all that we know of the wealth of England, and of the farming of manors in the eleventh century, that the reeves who handled the royal revenues and organized the royal estates in the mid-eleventh century must have been themselves – or had access to – the best experts on estate management and the handling of money of the day.

LONDON AND THE BOUNDARIES OF SHIRES AND SEES

The boundaries in and around London are peculiarly baffling; and the puzzles they raise can perhaps only be resolved by taking note of the continued importance of London throughout early Saxon times, even

[1] See Larson, *King's Household*, pp. 147 ff.; Harmer, pp. 48 ff.; Stenton, *Anglo-Saxon England*, pp. 540 ff.; W. A. Morris, in *EHR*, vol. xxxi, 1916, pp. 20–40, and in *Sheriff*, chap. i; Liebermann, vol. ii, pp. 648 ff.

[2] See *PR 31 Henry I*, passim; Poole, *Exchequer*, chap. vi. On the farm in the eleventh century, R. V. Lennard, *Rural England 1086–1135*, Oxford, 1959, chaps. v–vii. On the treasuries, below, p. 232.

before it became a great city once again.[1] Between the East Saxons and the West Saxons lay a people comparable in name, the Middle Saxons. These are artificial labels – which one presumes to represent the facts of political geography in the seventh and eighth centuries, even though there apparently never was a kingdom of Middlesex – not ancient tribal units. Similarly, the whole of Surrey bears the name 'the southern region' and we look north of the Thames for its northern counterpart. It has already been observed that the boundaries of the medieval diocese of London were almost certainly older than the shire boundaries as we know them, and included Essex, the eastern part of Hertfordshire and Middlesex; London sat in a corner of this comparatively large area. All three sets of boundaries suggest a stage or a situation in which London was the centre of a large and important district. The first two raise a strong presumption that Middlesex is the crumpled fragment of a once larger region.[2] But it is the diocese which seems truly to reflect the historical circumstances which gave rise to these curious units. The bishopric of London began its career as the see of the East Saxon Kingdom, which in its heyday stretched far further west, no doubt, than the later diocese, but before it was formed and established London, and the area to its north and west, came to be overshadowed by the Middle Angles and the rising power of Mercia.

By an interesting paradox, it is the boundaries of the sees that show us now how the kingdoms converged on London. The sees of Wessex converged from the south and west: Winchester embraced Surrey as well as Hampshire, and ran right up to the river, to Southwark, where Winchester House in later times enabled the bishop to stay on his own ground in the metropolis, and where he could lock up the local debtors in his Clink.[3] The see of Salisbury (as it became after the Norman Conquest) ran to the confines of Berkshire. The see of the Middle Angles, alias eastern Mercia, alias Dorchester, or Lincoln, came down into Buckinghamshire and western Hertfordshire. As Wessex turned into the Kingdom of England, the West Saxon interest in Mercian London steadily increased, until the king sat at Westminster and the Earl of Wessex saw his son Earl of Middlesex.

This story carries two evident morals. The first is that London was a

[1] See pp. 16 ff.

[2] See p. 18; Stenton, p. 6.

[3] D. J. Johnson, *Southwark and the City*, p. 25; Stow, vol. ii, p. 56; C. L. Kingsford in *LTR*, vol. xii, pp. 57–60. In what follows we use the word 'justice' rather than its synonym 'justiciar' for the *local* official.

place of great importance and prestige irrespective of the coming and going of kingdoms; that it is only a manner of speaking to call it an 'East Saxon' or a 'Mercian' town in early centuries. The second is that Middlesex was never at any time anything but the territory of London. If it is permissible to generalize from our fragmentary evidence over a number of centuries, the Anglo-Saxons seem to have eschewed tidy patterns in their administrative arrangements. There may have been portreeves separate from the sheriffs, or there may not; in later times there certainly seem to have been two tiers of reeve. There is no way of telling the precise role of the earl in Middlesex and London or the influence wielded by the staller in London. But it is extremely unlikely that at any date Middlesex had a separate jurisdiction from London; and natural to assume that sheriff and portreeve were identical in the eleventh century. But it is an assumption incapable of proof.[1]

NORMAN LONDON: THE SHERIFF AND THE JUSTICE

With the Norman Conquest the staller disappears; but, as if to ensure that our view of local administration should not become simpler and clearer, there appears the local justice instead. This office is clearly documented from the reign of Henry I and Stephen, and withered away in Henry II's time, when his local functions devolved upon the sheriff, and the rest of his judicial functions were absorbed into the work of the itinerant royal justices.[2] It is fairly clear, in fact, that the office, or some equivalent type of sheriff, was already in existence before 1100, how much before we cannot say. If we attempt to construct lists of justices and sheriffs for any of the shires near London, we encounter great difficulties.[3] First of all,

[1] Miss Reynolds, 'Rulers of London', p. 340, points out that there is no cogent and contemporary evidence that the offices of sheriff and portreeve were united before 1128. It seems to us probable (though not demonstrable) that the penumbra of lesser officials who meet us in the documents of the first half of the twelfth century were subordinate to the sheriff; i.e. that an effective union of the offices of sheriff and portreeve had taken place at an earlier date. But precision is impossible.

[2] See Cronne, 'Justiciar'; D. M. Stenton, *English Justice*, pp. 65 ff.

[3] See Appendix II. There are some indications, not systematically gathered, in Morris, *Sheriff*; lists for Stephen's reign of sheriffs and justices in *Regesta*, vol. iii, pp. XXIV-V. From the early years of Henry II virtually complete lists can be compiled from the Pipe Rolls, though even there are hazards not fully mastered in the PRO *List of Sheriffs* (cf. Appendix II).

most of the evidence consists in the addresses of royal writs.[1] It may have been the normal practice to arrange these addresses in strict hierarchy: if all possible officers were taken in, then bishop, earl, justice (or justiciar) and sheriff may appear. But it is far from clear that this was the invariable, or even the normal practice. Furthermore, when the documents specify the offices, they frequently confuse them. Thus the *Chronicle of Abingdon* tells us that Hugh of Buckland, a leading administrator of Henry I's early years, was sheriff not only of Berkshire, but of seven other shires besides. Yet many of the other documents suggest that he was, in some at least, rather justice than sheriff.[2]

The difference is far from clear. But we may presume that the justice was essentially concerned with legal matters, and acted as the King's representative in the courts; and also that he was (in some sense) the superior official, set to keep a watch on the sheriff. It is also clear that the sheriff handled the farm and retained the fiscal administration in his hands.[3] In the Empress' second charter to Geoffrey de Mandeville, from which we started on this enquiry,[4] it is stated that Geoffrey is to have the shrievalty of London and Middlesex for a farm of £300, as his grandfather had held it; also the justiceship of London and Middlesex hereditarily for himself and his heirs and the same combination in Hertfordshire and Essex. This seems to imply that Geoffrey's grandfather was reckoned to have held the shrievalties and not the justiceships, though the matter was immediately confused later in 1141 in the charter of King Stephen, which seems to make both part of his inheritance; and it is fairly improbable in historical fact that Geoffrey I held anything but London and Middlesex. The younger Geoffrey's claim to be a hereditary grand administrator had only a modest substance in it; yet it is of extreme interest, because it draws together the threads of four fundamental elements in the history of Anglo-Norman local administration: the hereditary shrievalty, the grouping of shrievalties, the social and political standing of the London sheriffs and the fixing of the London farm.

It is well known that the Norman shrievalty was not in principle hereditary – and the kings sometimes took the most stringent steps to

---

[1] See esp. *Regesta*, iii, pp. xxiii–vi.

[2] *Chron. Abingdon*, vol. ii, p. 117: 'Hugonis vicecomitis qui non solum Berchescirae, sed etiam aliis VII. sciris praeerat vicecomes.' Cf. Morris, *Sheriff*, p. 52; below, pp. 204–5. In the addresses to charters some officials occur who seem to be justices not confined to particular shires.

[3] See above, p. 197.   [4] See p. 191.

enforce the doctrine – but that it was not infrequently treated as if it were. The classic case is Gloucestershire.[1] In 1067 the shrievalty was apparently in the hands of one Brihtric, whom we may readily identify (as did J. H. Round) with the great thegn, son of Ealfgar, whose large estates formed the base of the honour of Gloucester; and to the lords of the honour of Gloucester, in due hereditary succession, passed the shrievalty. Here is a unique case of tidy succession. For this two special circumstances accounted. Gloucester was a marcher lordship, and a stable power there was highly desirable, even though it never became, like Shropshire (for a time), Cheshire and Durham, a county with special privileges, or a palatinate. The second is that the family of Gloucester, Roger de Pîtres and his brother Durand, and their descendants, were devoted royal servants of proved and unshakeable loyalty, down to the death of Henry I at least. Walter of Gloucester became royal constable and was steadily advanced by good service to Henry I, winning a notable heiress for his son, Milo; and Milo rose to be Earl of Hereford. The last step involved adroit manoeuvring in the anarchy; but the inheritance did not falter until Henry II's reign, after the death of Milo's son, Earl Roger, and his brothers. It no doubt provided the model for the ambitions of Geoffrey de Mandeville. Geoffrey's first charter from the Empress was won at very much the same time as Milo's earldom, also from the Empress.

There are many other cases in which a leading baronial family – still more a family rising 'from the ranks of the aristocracy' for loyal service to one or more of the Norman kings – held a shrievalty through two or three generations. The Normans needed above all effective and loyal service, and they rewarded it; equally they looked with intense suspicion at anyone tempted to play the overmighty subject, or at a hereditary succession which might deprive them of their rights. No doubt it is true, as has long been noticed, that William I was more inclined to hand shrievalties to tenants-in-chief, Henry I more suspicious and also more experimental with different types of men and different types of grouping.[2] In Devon the Conqueror's faithful Baldwin de Clare was followed by his two sons

[1] On Brihtric, Round, *Feudal England*, pp. 423–4; on the rest of the family, and esp. Roger's son Walter and grandson Milo, D. Walker in *Transactions of the Bristol and Gloucestershire Archaeological Society*, vol. lxxvii, 1958–9, pp. 66 ff. and *Camden Miscellany*, vol. xxii, 1964, esp. pp. 4–5; *GF*, pp. 35 ff. Their estate formed the honour of Gloucester, quite distinct from the earldom, held by Robert son of Henry I, and his successors, whose headquarters lay in Bristol and Cardiff castles.

[2] See Morris, *Sheriff*, pp. 76 ff.; Southern, pp. 130 ff.

William and Richard, and Richard extended the family empire into Cornwall. But he was supplanted in 1128.[1] In Essex a Normanized administrator, one of the few to survive from the Confessor's reign, called Robert son of Wimarc, passed his shrievalty to his son Swein; but he did not long survive. In due course the Norman soldier Ralph Bainard, founder of Baynard's Castle in London, replaced him.[2] In Bedfordshire the first Norman Ralph Taillebois was succeeded by his son Ivo. There are several other cases in the reigns of all three Norman kings; but in no other case known did the shrievalty last for more than two generations.

Nor were rising barons the only type of sheriff; and there are a fair number who are simply names to us. Sometimes local evidence reveals that they were men of some importance in their own shires. Thus Picot the Sheriff of Cambridgeshire meets us in the chronicle of Barnwell priory as the pious founder, whose wife Hugolina had so great a devotion to St Giles that she inspired her husband to build the church of St Giles in Cambridge – fragments of their church still survive in a heavy Victorian case – and set a community there which was subsequently moved to Barnwell. If the canons remembered him for his own (or his wife's) devotion to St Giles, the monks of Ely remembered him for his contempt for St Etheldreda.[3] 'Who is this Etheldreda of whom you say that I have usurped her lands?' – a lion, they said he was, a wolf, a sow, a dog; no name was too bad for the rapacious Picot. Thus we learn something of a man of considerable local possessions; however the saints may have viewed him, he seems to have been well regarded by the king, and his family only disappeared from view because his son rebelled against Henry I.[4] Beside the barons were the royal officials. Aiulf the Chamberlain, Sheriff of Dorset from the 1080s until the 1110s and perhaps also of Berkshire, and Warin, his successor in Dorset, who may also have been a fiscal official.[5] Lincolnshire for a time

[1] Round, *Feudal England*, p. 330 n.; L. C. Loyd, *The Origins of Some Anglo-Norman Families*, p. 65; *Regesta*, vol. i, nos. 58–9, 125, 135–6, 378; vol. ii, no. 649 n., 1068, etc.; W. A. Morris in *EHR*, vol. xxxvii, 1922, p. 162; C. H. Walker in ib., p. 71. There was an interlude early in Henry I's reign when Geoffrey de Mandeville I was joint-sheriff (*Regesta*, vol. ii, nos. 633, 649, 662, 773 – one of them may have been justiciar), and Richard appears to have recovered the office briefly in 1135–6 (ib., vol. iii, no. 500).

[2] E. A. Freeman, *Hist. of the Norman Conquest*, vol. iv, Oxford, 1871, pp. 736–8; Gibbs, no. 4 (of uncertain date).

[3] *Chron. Barnwell*, pp. 38 ff.; *Liber Eliensis*, pp. 210–11.

[4] *Chron. Barnwell*, pp. 40–1.

[5] 'Domesday Book', vol. i, p. 82–3 (his tenures); *Regesta*, vol. i, no. 204; vol. ii, nos 544, 573, etc., 1018, 1341, 1367n.; vol. iii, nos. 434, 818.

was ruled by clerics. The justice was the bishop; the sheriff, Osbert the Clerk.[1] How clerkly he was we cannot now tell, and though he appears to have been genuine enough to hold a canonry at St Paul's a later sheriff may have been his son. His appearance under Henry I is in any case interesting evidence of the increasing importance of literacy in shrieval administration.

But the facts to which lists of early sheriffs bear most eloquent testimony are the frequency of change, especially in important centres, and above all in London itself; and the contrary tendency, especially under Henry I, to group shrievalties under a single sheriff or a pair of sheriffs, no doubt in order to provide a framework of more efficient government. Henry I's reign saw two new twists to Norman administration and government: a new emphasis on patronage, and the formation of the institutions of the Exchequer.[2] Both may be in essence or in certain elements older than Henry I's reign; but both became a visible part of the scene in his time. Loyalty had been an acute problem for the two Williams; but to Henry it was a constant nightmare, for from 1106 to 1134 his eldest brother was his prisoner, securely guarded, but an obvious centre for any rebel cause.[3] No king has had to plan and plot to prevent rebellion getting under way more urgently than he. Dr Southern has taught us how skilfully Henry instructed his barons and servants not only that progress and wealth depended on his nod and favour, but that any sign of disloyalty – disfavour however won – led to instant disaster.[4]

In Henry's early years, we may discern in the bewildering pattern two clear elements. In the marches, administration lay, so far as possible, in the hands of trusted viceroys. So far as possible, since a hint of rebellion could destroy a palatinate as happened when the whole Montgomery clan was crushed in 1102, and Shropshire was (in due course) put in the hands of a powerful cleric, Richard de Belmeis, or Beaumais, later Bishop of London (1108–27).[5] The other element in the pattern was the grouping of the shires near the centre. The home counties were gathered, early in Henry's reign, into the hands of a man called Hugh of Buckland. He held

[1] *EHR*, vol. xxx, pp. 280–1; Le Neve, p. 43; *CHJ*, vol. x, p. 124 n. 70; *Regesta*, vol. iii, no. 490. William Torniant, sheriff before Michaelmas 1127, may have been Osbert's son (*PR 31 Henry I*, pp. 109–10; *EHR*, vol. xxxvii, pp. 73–4).

[2] Southern, pp. 130 ff. (209 ff.); see below; Henry I's administration is being studied in detail by Mrs Judith Green.

[3] See p. 32.

[4] Southern, loc. cit.

[5] See J. F. A. Mason in *TRHS*, 5th Series, vol. xiii, 1963, pp. 10–11; *Regesta* vol. ii, nos 765, 823, 900, 1473.

sway in London and Middlesex, Essex, Hertfordshire, Bedfordshire, Berkshire and Buckinghamshire,[1] sometimes as sheriff, sometimes as justice. Whether he still held all these shires when he died in or about 1115 we cannot tell; but his tenure of them was clearly not a momentary or emphemeral thing. A single man, however 'upright and wise',[2] can hardly have had effective control of so large an area; no doubt he worked through deputies. What seems clear, however, is that he was put there to preside over some vital administrative reorganization. London was the centre of his power; his name is significantly mentioned in a treatise on the abacus; and it is possible that he combined his royal offices with that of a canon of St Paul's. Whether he was or was not a canon and a cleric – and it is deplorable that we cannot be sure even of this crucial detail – he seems evidently to have been a master of efficient administration, and, we may be sure, of literate administration. The first use of the principle of the abacus in Exchequer accounting may well date from this time. The system of Exchequer accounting described in the *Dialogus de Scaccario* of Henry II's reign had at its centre a table with a cloth upon it marked out in lines and squares – like a chess-board, *scaccarium*, Exchequer;[3] and upon these squares counters could be laid, so that addition and subtraction, and a sheriff's audit, could be rapidly achieved in the presence of many witnesses. The accounting depended on a sophisticated knowledge of Arabian arithmetic; but once installed and arranged, it could be understood by illiterate witnesses. It was thus a vital bridge between the literate clerks and the illiterate (or still largely illiterate) barons in Henry I's service.

Whatever may be the significance of Hugh of Buckland's reign in the home counties, it illustrates the old link between London and the area surrounding it to the north. To the south lay Surrey, never part of Hugh's

[1] See p. 200. Robinson, *GC*, pp. 154–5 seems to show that Hugh died before Gilbert Crispin, i.e. before 1117 or 1118 (the former is perhaps the more probable: see *Heads*, p. 77). *GC*, p. 154 shows William of Buckland as his successor; but the fact that he built up no lay fee perhaps supports the view that Hugh was a cleric, which is argued in *CHJ*, vol. x, p. 124, n. 70; cf. Le Neve, p. 51. His importance in the Exchequer, and grasp of mathematical detail, are emphasized by the citation of his name in Turchill's treatise on the abacus: Poole, *Exchequer*, pp. 47 ff., esp. p. 49; Haskins in *EHR*, vol. xxvii, 1912, p. 102.

[2] *Chron. Abingdon*, vol. ii, p. 117: 'probi et sapientis viri'.

[3] The Exchequer was based on a chess-board: chess was becoming known in the west in the tenth–eleventh centuries, and won great popularity in the twelfth. On the history of the chess-board see H. J. R. Murray, *A History of Chess*, Oxford, 1913, pp. 756–75; for more recent literature, H. and S. Wichmann, *Chess*, Eng. trans., London, 1964.

empire, but part of a more modest, yet more widely scattered, administrative group. The foundation of Barnwell priory in Cambridge was completed by Picot's successor, Gilbert the Knight, Gilbert of Surrey, who was sheriff of the three shires of Surrey, Cambridgeshire and Huntingdonshire,[1] an odd combination, until it is seen that they formed a narrow ring round Hugh of Buckland's territory.

When Hugh died, his son William appears for a time, or from time to time, to have held a fragment of his authority. When Gilbert died, all his three shires appear to have passed to his nephew Fulchered. But in 1129 and 1130 a new broom appeared again, sweeping clean all the shires which Hugh and Gilbert had ruled. We know the full extent of ground covered by the joint shrievalty of Aubrey de Vere and Richard Basset because of the survival of the single Pipe Roll of 1130.[2] Whether the Pipe Roll is a chance survival or was in itself a significant event we cannot yet be sure; historians have not studied it sufficiently with this question in mind for it to yield all its secrets. But the fact of the Pipe Roll and of this large roving commission are not matters of pure coincidence. It is abundantly clear that these two men dealt with a crisis in Henry's affairs, and also with an administrative reorganization of some significance. The Pipe Roll is the earliest survivor of a type of account which came to be very common in later medieval England. It is not designed to tell king or people whether the kingdom prospers, whether the firm is making a profit or a loss; it is an auditor's account, intended to check the efficiency and honesty of the royal officials. It is the document of a suspicious administration: the enormous effort put into written, audited accounts in this country (and for a long while, in this country alone), reveals two things: the suspicious nature of our kings, and the eagerness of the accounting clerks to provide

---

[1] See Round, *CL*, pp. 121–3; *Regesta*, vol. ii, nos. 659, 851, etc. 1416, 1435 (ranging from 1103 × 6 to 1123 or later). Fulchered, or Fulk, his successor, was apparently sheriff of Surrey by 1126, Round, *CL*, p. 121; certainly by 1127 (*Regesta*, vol. ii, no. 1498); he occurs in 1129, Round, loc. cit.; and was succeeded in 1129–30 by Richard Basset and Aubrey de Vere (*PR 31 Henry I*, pp. 43–4). The narrative describing Gilbert's foundation of Merton Priory has been printed in full by M. L. Colker, in *Studia Monastica*, vol. xii, 1970, 241–71.

[2] See Southern, p. 141 (219) and n. for references; *Complete Peerage*, revised edn, vol. x, pp. 193 ff., esp. 196–7; *VCH Leics.*, vol. i, p. 343; *PR 31 Henry I, passim*, esp. pp. 43 ff., 52 ff., 100 ff. Both of them came of landholding families and Aubrey was tenant-in-chief and royal chamberlain by inheritance; but Richard Basset held comparatively little by his own inheritance (so far as we know) and both owed much to Henry I's favour.

themselves with employment. No doubt there was a political as well as fiscal background.

In 1129–30 the efforts to settle the succession on the Empress Matilda, and her unpopular marriage into Anjou, were recent; political clouds were threatening, and it is interesting to note that the roving commission was not given to clerks, but to barons, albeit barons deeply involved in royal administration. It seems that they were not intended to become permanent sheriffs, but to preside over a temporary phase in the reorganization of their shires; then to retire and leave others to carry on the work they had set on foot.

There is one curious feature of the commission of Aubrey de Vere and Richard Basset. Aubrey had himself been sheriff of London and Middlesex, as well as the king's Master Chamberlain; and this had been a part of Hugh of Buckland's empire. In general, Aubrey's and Richard's commission covered exactly the territory of Hugh and Gilbert the Knight combined. But they were not made sheriffs of London and Middlesex. Aubrey appears indeed to have held this office in the early and mid-1120s but never to have held it with Richard and to have lost it in the late 1120s. In 1125 we meet Aubrey in harness with Roger nephew of Hubert, the founder of another great official dynasty, for he was the father of Gervase of Cornhill.[1] The difference between the dynasties was that Aubrey was by birth a tenant-in-chief, by inheritance a feudal warrior, whereas the Cornhills were London citizens, dealers in land in the country and in the city, dealers in money and probably in merchandise – though, in truth, the categories are not water-tight. By joining Roger with Aubrey in the shrievalty Henry I seems to have been taking a step towards the citizen sheriffs of the next generations, not perhaps for the first time (see p. 234). None the less, the step may have been cautiously taken, and we must be even more cautious in following it. There are many gaps in our list of sheriffs, and earlier experiments may have gone unrecorded; but in any case it seems probable that Roger had a spell as sheriff earlier than this, in the 1110s. We must assume him to have been a citizen, from the history of his family and the little that we know of his own activities, but he may have been much else besides. And we shortly find him supplanted by one Fulchered son of Walter, who is wholly obscure. After Fulchered (who occurs in 1128–9) we pass from darkness into the first half-light before dawn.

---

[1] *Cart. Aldgate*, no. 871, p. 169. On the Cornhill family, see W. R. Powell, 'English Administrative Families in the 12th and 13th centuries' (Oxford, B.Litt. thesis, 1952); S. Reynolds, 'Rulers of London', pp. 346–7 and references.

THE PIPE ROLL AND THE CHARTER OF HENRY I

To the years which follow belong unquestionably the first Pipe Roll, and much less certainly the first of London's major charters. The opening clauses of this remarkable charter runs thus:

> Know that I have granted to my citizens of London the shrievalty of London and Middlesex to farm for £300 by tale, for themselves and their heirs, of me and my heirs; in such fashion that the citizens may place one of themselves, such as they will, as sheriff, and whomsoever of themselves and of whatever quality they will as justice to keep the pleas of my crown and watch over their pleading. And no-one else shall be justiciar over the men of London.[1]

This clause raises a fascinating problem, to which no clear solution has yet been found. If it is authentic, it reveals an act of unaccountable generosity to the City by a king not commonly given to such acts. There is no doubt that the right to choose their own sheriff was conceded for a time at least in 1129–30; the Pipe Roll shows us that the citizens had offered 100 marks ($\frac{2}{3} \times$ £100), and paid £30 down, for the privilege.[2] But the farm was running, as usual in the twelfth century before 1189–90, at over £500. A hundred marks might buy an election, but it could hardly explain an annual remission of £200. All manner of explanations have been offered, of which perhaps the most plausible is that the great fire which occurred at the season of Pentecost in 1133[3] had impoverished many of the citizens and caused the king to cut back the farm; but this is no adequate explanation of what appears to be a grant in perpetuity. It is true that in 1141 the Empress Matilda granted the shrievalty and the farm to Geoffrey de Mandeville for £300 and King Stephen soon after confirmed it.[4] But these were desperate favours to a great baron in conditions of civil war. Yet until quite recently the constitutional history of London in the twelfth century was made to revolve round this awkward clause, and its authenticity was assumed. In consequence, Stephen's relation with the citizens

---

[1] Brooke, Keir and Reynolds, p. 575. What follows is based on art. cit., *passim*.

[2] *PR 31 Henry I*, p. 148; Reynolds, 'Rulers of London', p. 341; Brooke, Keir and Reynolds, pp. 567–8.

[3] Suggested by J. C. Russell, *Dargan Historical Essays* (ed. W. M. Dabney and J. C. Russell, University of New Mexico Publications in History, vol. iv, 1952), pp. 14–16; cf. Brooke, Keir and Reynolds, p. 568 n. 1.

[4] *Regesta*, vol. iii, nos. 275–6.

appeared somewhat confused and paradoxical, and Henry II was generally reckoned to have been mean.[1]

Apart from a tiny writ of William I giving general approval to city custom, the earliest original charters granting important privileges to the City are the twin copies of the charter of Henry II of *c.* 1155.[2] From then on the series is complete. It has been common for English boroughs to treasure the charters on which their rights and liberties depend; yet no series has been preserved with more loving care than those in the Corporation of London Records Office – so well have they been kept that even the seal, the most fragile element in any charter, is usually intact; or at least a substantial fragment has been preserved. But no trace of an original of Henry I's charter has survived, and no copy earlier than the early thirteenth century.[3] There are hints in the formal language of the charter which suggest that a genuine writ of Henry I or Stephen lies behind our surviving texts, and the form of the opening 'protocol' might even lead to the deduction that it is the work of a chancery scribe who worked for both kings and whose career has been traced in some detail from surviving specimens of his handwriting. Yet this hint is not very comforting; for 'scribe xiii', as Mr T. A. M. Bishop christened him,[4] seems to have earned his living in later years as a forger.

We cannot enter deeply into all the elements in this curious puzzle, which has recently been explored by Miss Reynolds and ourselves.[5] It is clear that the greater part of the document faithfully reflects the customs or the pretensions of the City in the later years of Henry I and in the reign of Stephen; it is improbable that the farm of £300 was really conceded by Henry, and doubtful if it was ever more than a temporary concession by Stephen. From the late 1120s on the citizens began to play a part in the financial administration of the City which meant that some of their leaders acted as sheriffs and justices;[6] whether they were chosen by the City fathers or by the king is usually quite obscure between 1130 and 1190 – though it is clear that the City fathers exercised a measure of choice on

[1] Cf. Tait, p. 163; Williams, p. 2, corrected by Reynolds, 'Rulers of London', pp. 343–4.

[2] Corporation of London Records Office, Charters 3a, b; ed. Riley, *Liber Custumarum*, pt. 1, pp. 31–2; cf. Brooke, Keir and Reynolds, pp. 577–8. See **Plate 10**.

[3] See Brooke, Keir and Reynolds, pp. 559 ff., 572 ff.

[4] *Scriptores Regis*, Oxford, 1961, pp. 25, 30, etc., esp. p. 77; cf. *Regesta*, vol. iii, pp. xiii–xiv; vol. iv, pp. 18–19; Brooke, Keir and Reynolds, pp. 563–4.

[5] Brooke, Keir and Reynolds, *passim*.

[6] See pp. 210 ff.; Reynolds, 'Rulers of London', pp. 341 ff., 354.

some occasions and that the king never wholly relinquished his grasp; and it must be evident that even royal nominees could not have exercised jurisdiction over their colleagues unless they were in some measure acceptable to them.

For the rest, the charter opens a window into the traditional life of the City. The citizens do not plead outside the walls and have a variety of liberties from tax; they cannot be compelled to give hospitality to members of the king's household; they are quit of custom throughout the land and its ports; the churches and barons and citizens have their sokes confirmed.[1] The men of London cannot be asked for more than their traditional wergeld of a hundred shillings; their debtors must pay or plead in London. Other clauses release them from the ancient procedure of 'meskennynge' – the breach of a precise verbal formula which led to a fine – in the courts of husting and folkmoot; and laid down that the husting met weekly on a Monday;[2] and the final clause reminds us that the citizens had not been brought into this world for business alone, and also that many of them were by origin or aspiration country gentlemen: it safeguards their hunting rights in the Chilterns and Middlesex and Surrey. Some of this may go a little beyond true custom of the period 1129–33, or it may all derive from an authentic instrument of those years. More probably it is genuine custom incorporated in a charter of *c.* 1141 originally issued in Stephen's name, or in a spurious charter forged about the same time.[3] For secure contemporary evidence of the City's affairs in Henry I's last years we must return to the Pipe Roll.

When the Pipe Roll of 1129–30 was composed four men had recently paid a handsome sum to be relieved of the shrievalty of London and Middlesex. This sum, and the debts they owed, strongly suggest that they found the farm which the sheriffs were bound to pay exorbitant. It stood somewhat above £500 in 1129–30; and it was to be run at this level for most of the reign of Henry II. Early in Richard's reign the citizens bought the reduction of the farm to £300 and the right to farm it themselves; and this was in due course formally confirmed by King John.[4] Yet there is no doubt that the citizen shrievalty and the farm of £300 had been

---

[1] Brooke, Keir and Reynolds, pp. 575–6, cc. 2–5.

[2] Ib., cc. 6–10; cf. p. 250. On 'meskennynge' see *British Borough Charters*, vol. i, pp. 146–8.

[3] Brooke, Keir and Reynolds, esp. pp. 571–2.

[4] Reynolds, 'Rulers of London', pp. 348 ff.; Corporation of London Rec. Office, Charter, 6 a, b, ed. Riley, *Liber Custumarum*, pt i, pp. 249–51.

living issues already in the 1130s and 1140s, and that if we knew the whole story of those decades, the origin of the later shrievalty, and of many of the City's liberties would be bathed in light.

The four sheriffs of the Pipe Roll of 1129–30 were called William Lelutre, Ralph son of Herlewin, William de Balio and Geoffrey Bucherell.[1] William de Balio is wholly obscure, though his name may suggest that he sojourned near the Tower. William Lelutre bears a surname, or nickname, borne by London citizens of moderate note a little later. Geoffrey Bucherell's name suggests that he was a member of one of the families which flourished longest in the City's history, from *c.* 1100 to the mid-thirteenth century. His surname has long intrigued historians, for it has long been supposed to suggest an Italian origin. Bocherelli can indeed be found in Italy in this age, but there is no evidence to connect our Geoffrey or his clan with any known Italians; all the early London Bucherells bore French names, and as with the Buccuintes, who have also been supposed Italian, a more prosaic Norman or French origin is really more probable.[2] Ralph, son of Herlewin was uncle to Gervase of Cornhill, and in all probability brother-in-law of Roger, nephew of Hubert.

The other sheriff of Henry's later years who is of special interest to us is Gilbert Becket, father of Thomas. In December 1170 Thomas Becket, Archbishop of Canterbury, returned from exile, to be greeted, or at any rate met, by Gervase of Cornhill, Sheriff of Kent.[3] It was a piquant encounter of two citizens of London, both brought up in the same world in the 1120s, and much of an age; it is abundantly clear that there had been no love lost between them. We have Becket's own word for it that he regarded Gervase as a private enemy, and Becket's biographers present him as a great and corrupt man of the world, growing fat on the proceeds of usury. He was certainly a man of wealth and power. He held property in Essex, Suffolk and London; some of this he seems to have had by inheritance and marriage, more he probably acquired by purchase, and perhaps by foreclosing on his debtors. He seems to have been sprung from a notable family of London citizens of mixed Norman and English origin.

[1] *PR 31 Henry I*, p. 149; Reynolds, 'Rulers of London', p. 354 and nn. 12–15.

[2] See Reynolds, 'Rulers of London', pp. 339–40 and n. 13. See p. 214.

[3] *MB*, vol. vii, p. 403 (Becket's last letter to the Pope); vol. i, pp. 87, 100 (William of Canterbury); vol. iii, pp. 118–19, 125 (William FitzStephen); vol. iv, p. 68 (Anon. I, probably Roger of Pontigny); William of Canterbury speaks of Gervase 'plus besses et centesimas usuras quam bonum et aequum attendens' (*MB*, vol. i, p. 100). Cf. Richardson, p. 59, n. 1.

We have met his father, Roger nephew of Hubert, citizen and sheriff; and his wife's mother Ingenold was presumably sister to Ralph and so daughter to Herlewin. Gervase married Agnes, who came of wealthy English stock; her father was Edward of Cornhill and her grandfather Edward of Southwark. Gervase himself was justice of London in Stephen's time, sheriff 1155–7 and 1160–1, sheriff of Surrey 1163–82, sheriff also of Kent 1168–74. What is not so clear is in what sense he was a citizen of London, in what sense a great royal administrator and landowner.[1] Clearly his own and his wife's family had a substantial standing in the City. The fact that he took his father-in-law's surname seems to show that he regarded the manor of Cornhill and his city house as the heart of his properties and of his world; and we may reasonably suppose that the moneylending business and the usurious transactions and the fiscal expertise which he practised in his shrievalties had their centre in the City. It has also been suggested that he was a merchant, and it may well be so. But of this there is no evidence.

In 1182 Gervase was succeeded as Sheriff of Surrey by his son Henry, and Gervase himself died either that year or in 1183. For a few years Henry maintained the kind of position his father had held. He was Sheriff of Surrey till his death; Sheriff of London and Middlesex with Richard, son of Reiner, another hereditary magnate of great wealth and influence in the City and the court; in 1191 he was keeper of the exchanges of the realm, that is to say it was his business to organize the exchanges in which coins from overseas, or English coins long in circulation, were gathered to be re-minted; and in the process to supervise the gathering of the new mint tax imposed in the later years of Henry II.[2] A long career in royal administration might have lain before him; but he died in 1192–3. The Cornhills survived as country landholders, and holders of property in the City; in the mid-thirteenth century another Henry of Cornhill was Dean of St Paul's.[3] But none of them was ever sheriff again.

Thus it passes the wit of man to say whether Gervase and Henry of Cornhill were city magnates, landowners and gentry, or royal administrators. It has been suggested that Henry was opposed to the formation of the commune; but there is no evidence for this, and it seems more likely that he and his family had become progressively detached from their civic

---

[1] On Gervase, see Reynolds, 'Rulers of London', pp. 346 ff.; Powell, 'English Administrative Families' (see p. 206 n. 1); Round, *GM*, pp. 304–12.

[2] On the Exchequer and the new mint tax, see *BM Coins*, Allen, pp. lxxxviii ff.

[3] Chancellor 1217–43, Dean, 1243–54: Le Neve, pp. 7, 26, 50, 84, 90.

roots.[1] But we cannot doubt that they were experts in handling city and country property, and in moneylending; and that the family was by tradition a family of Londoners.

So too was the family of Thomas Becket. Gilbert, his father, like Gervase's ancestors, was a Norman of well-to-do family from Rouen, who prospered by dealing in city rents and properties, though not (as William FitzStephen hastens to assure us) a usurer.[2] The emphatic denial shows that this kind of business was common, among men of their type, and was perhaps a hit at Gervase of Cornhill himself. Gilbert Becket had been rich, and his connections included Osbert Huitdeniers, or Eightpence, another rich citizen of the period, justice or perhaps sheriff early in the reign of Stephen.[3] When Gilbert Becket was sheriff is not entirely clear; very likely soon after 1130, for it appears that the great fire of 1133 started in his house and burnt so much of the city that his properties were seriously diminished and he himself reduced to comparative poverty.[4] About 1140 the young Thomas was employed by Osbert Eightpence as sheriff's clerk and had thus his first taste of royal administration. Soon after, he was

[1] See Reynolds, loc. cit.

[2] *MB*, vol. iii, p. 14: 'patre Gileberto, qui et vicecomes aliquando Londoniae fuit, matre Mahalt; civibus Londoniae mediastinis, neque foenerantibus neque officiose negotiantibus, sed de reditibus (*sic*) suis honorifice viventibus'. For his surname and origin, *MB*, vol. iv, p. 81 (cf. Round, *CL*, p. 101); and esp. the fascinating study by R. Foreville, 'Les Origines normandes de la famille Becket . . .'

[3] FitzStephen (p. 14) says that Thomas Becket was 'vicecomitum clericus et rationalis effectus'; Roger of Pontigny (*MB*, vol. iv, p. 8) says that he spent three years working under an eminent citizen of London, 'cognatum suum'; William of Canterbury (vol. i, p. 3) says 'civi vice tabellionis adhaesit'. Edward Grim (vol. ii, p. 361) also says 'about three years' ('fere per triennium'), and tells us that his patron was 'carne propinquus' and named 'Osbernus Octo-nummi' – i.e. Osbert Eightpence, justice (or sheriff: see Reynolds, 'Rulers of London', p. 354 and n. 17).

[4] William of Canterbury (*MB*, vol. i, p. 3) says of Thomas Becket's father 'quem incendia crebra civitatis attenuabant' in a context which suggests a date in the 1130s (i.e. before *c*. 1139–40); Grim says 'frequentibus incendiis caeterisque infaustis incursibus rerum non mediocriter attenuati' (vol. ii, p. 359). The best attested fire of this period is that of Pentecost 1133 (John of Worcester, *Chronicle*, ed. J. R. H. Weaver, Oxford, 1908, pp. 36–7); and it was possibly this fire of which tradition asserted that it started in the house of Gilbert Becket (cf. Russell, p. 15, who lists various annals of the late twelfth–fifteenth century which refer to disastrous fires in 1130–2, esp. two which date it to April, 1132; the *Ann. Bermondsey*, p. 434 associates this with Gilbert Becket. But it is notoriously inaccurate, though partly based on good early Cluniac annals: see *Heads*, pp. 6, 114). See also *Assize of Nuisance*, ed. H. M. Chew and W. Kellaway, p. ix.

transplanted to the court of Theobald, Archbishop of Canterbury, and became one of the leading figures of that brilliant circle. By 1155 he was a great man: royal chancellor, Archdeacon of Canterbury and a pluralist on an ample scale. As chancellor he was notably extravagant and ostentatious. This may have been deliberately fostered to support the new regime of the young King Henry II, and to compensate for the king's comparative indifference to outward show and pageantry. It is very likely that it corresponded to a trait in Becket's own temperament. He delighted to show the ostentation that he might have displayed in another sphere if he had grown up to be a city patrician. But there seems also to have been some element of personal compensation. In 1166 the battle of words, by which a group among the bishops sought to aid the king in the dispute which had driven Becket (now Archbishop of Canterbury) into exile, came to a climax. Gilbert Foliot, Bishop of London, the ring-leader among the bishops, drafted an open letter to Becket taunting him, among other charges, with ingratitude, for he was wholly the king's creation.[1] In his reply to Gilbert, Becket uttered a flood of words so great on his own and the bishop's origin as to raise more than a suspicion that he felt and resented a sense of social inferiority. It is true that Foliot counted an earl and a bishop among his elder relations, but his father was not a tenant-in-chief and it is doubtful if a great distance separated the social standing of the Foliots and Beckets. It is perhaps more likely that it was the stigma of failure and bankruptcy in a highly competitive society which aroused Becket's jealousy of the successful Foliots who had come to settle in his own City of London. We may imagine too that Gervase of Cornhill had looked on Gilbert Becket in his decline much as the successful merchant looked on the unsuccessful in *Vanity Fair*: 'And yet he was a better man than I this day twenty years – a better man I should say, by ten thousand pound.'[2]

GEOFFREY DE MANDEVILLE AND THE FEUDAL ELEMENT IN LONDON SOCIETY

Of the known justices and sheriffs of Stephen's reign, two, Gilbert Proudfoot and John (both probably of the 1140s), are only names to us;[3]

[1] *GFL*, no. 167; cf. *MB*, vol. v, nos 223–4; *GFL*, no. 170.
[2] W. M. Thackeray, *Vanity Fair*, London, 1848, chap. lxi, p. 549.
[3] *Regesta*, vol. iii, no. 530; Reynolds, 'Rulers of London', p. 354 n. 19. See reference cited by Reynolds, p. 354, n. 22. The identification with Gilbert Becket suggested there by C.N.L.B. seem very unlikely, since Gilbert Becket was impoverished by *c*.

four – Gervase of Cornhill, Andrew Buccuinte, Osbert Eightpence and Theodoric, son of Deorman – are known to have been substantial citizens, of whom Gervase was also a royal official, as was William Martel; and one, Geoffrey de Mandeville, was a baron and major political figure. Andrew Buccuinte was a member of one of the notable City dynasties of the century. His son, John, was sheriff 1169–72; another John, perhaps of a collateral branch, was sheriff in 1190–1.[1] A Buccuinte, very possibly Andrew's son, appears with Gervase of Cornhill in the deeds of William Cade the money-lender; and Andrew himself witnessed a number of City deeds of the 1120s and 1130s.[2] The other citizen, Osbert Eightpence, we have already met as Becket's relative and patron.

The tenure of William Martel, king's chamberlain, as justice of London is recorded only in one document, and that of King John's time.[3] But it is an account of the rights and wrongs of fish weirs and fish nets in the Thames from Baynard's Castle to the bridge at Staines of a nature both circumstantial and plausible; and is of special interest for the galaxy of officials and potentates it parades for our inspection. One John Belet had tried, *c.* 1135–6,[4] to build a weir with the support of the justice, William Martel. The constable of Baynard's Castle forbade it on the ground that his master, the lord of Baynard's Castle, had authority over all the fishing in the rivers from his castle to Staines; and he sent to Robert FitzRichard the lord of the castle, who in his turn gathered 'a council of the whole of England' at St Paul's to judge the case. The lord of Baynard's Castle made his claim; a like claim was made by the lord of Montfichet Castle. And the judgement was 'that the lord of Castle Baynard should have the lordship of the water as royal standard bearer and proctor of the whole City even to the bridge of Staines'. Then the king and the great men of the realm sued for John Belet, and Robert FitzRichard made him warden of the waters

---

1139 and died soon after, whereas Gilbert Proudfoot seems to occur as sheriff in 1143 (W. Dugdale, *Monasticon Anglicanum*, edn. of 1817–30, vol. iii, p. 348 = B. M. Cotton MS Claud. D. xiii, f. 24v, as 'William'; for date, see *Heads*, p. 86 and n. 1), and the two surnames seem quite distinct. For Prutfot, Proudfoot, see Reynolds, 'Rulers of London', p. 354, n. 22.

[1] See Reynolds, 'Rulers of London', esp. pp. 355–7; Page, pp. 236–9. Cf. p. 373 n. (the doctrine that they were of Italian origin is extremely doubtful, but not wholly impossible).

[2] See loc. cit.; Round, *CL*, pp. 101–2, 108 ff.

[3] Bateson, pp. 485–6; nor is it certain that he was justice *of London*.

[4] It can be dated not long before the death of Robert FitzRichard (cf. Brooke, Keir and Reynolds, p. 565 n. 24).

under his lordship, and the office passed to his son Robert Belet, who held it – despite rival claims by Gervase of Cornhill, Sheriff of Surrey, and other potentates – until Henry II confiscated it 'on account of a sparrow-hawk which he refused the king'.

One of the many interesting features of this story is that it reminds us of the feudal element in London's government and society: of the power of the lords of Baynard and Montfichet castles, and of the Tower of London itself.

In the years following the Norman Conquest three substantial castles were built to keep London secure and under royal control. Castle Baynard was first in the hands of the baron Ralph Bainard and his successor William; after William's forfeiture in 1110–11, it passed into the hands of Robert FitzRichard, a member of the great family of Clare; and it remained in his family until the thirteenth century. Then it disappeared and the site it had occupied in the corner of the City wall was given over to the peaceful occupation of the Dominican Friars, the Blackfriars, whose name still clings to their old home:[1] and in the fourteenth century Castle Baynard was rebuilt as the more modest fortress whose remains have recently been unearthed a little further east on the banks of the Thames. The most famous of the Clare dynasty was Robert FitzWalter, who in 1215 was the leader of the barons who rebelled against King John and forced him to grant Magna Carta. A generation earlier, Robert's father, Walter FitzRobert, had held an uneasy situation in the City in the great rebellion of 1173–4 against Henry II. According to the chronicler Jordan Fantosme, Henry II, at the height of the rebellion, asked for news of the barons of London. He was told that they were loyal and powerful and under arms – this was very much the same time that William FitzStephen was extolling the strength and splendour of the City militia – but that Gilbert de Montfichet was strengthening his castle, and claiming that the Clares were in alliance with him.[2] The Montfichet challenge came to nothing; the City stood by the king; and it is likely that the charge against the Clares proved false.[3]

[1] On Robert FitzRichard and the early history of Baynard's Castle, see Brooke, Keir and Reynolds, p. 565 n. 24; on the sites of Baynard's Castle, see Stenton, pp. 8–9, 39 and n.; Honeybourne, *LTR*, vol. xxii, 1965, pp. 38–9; cf. FitzStephen, *MB*, vol. iii, p. 3 ('ab occidente duo castella munitissima'), for Blackfriars, see p. 337.

[2] Fantosme, ed. R. Howlett, *Chrons. Stephen* etc., vol. iii, p. 338.

[3] This would indeed be almost certain if we could be sure that the Peter FitzWalter who was 'custos' in 1174–6 was Walter's son and Robert's brother; but this really

In any case, the story illustrates the key importance that still attached to the Norman castles and their lords. A later document shows that the lords of Baynard's Castle had been hereditary leaders of the City militia, and gives a circumstantial and picturesque account of how the host was summoned and led. In 1303 the current Robert Fitzwalter claimed that he and his heirs 'ought to be, and are chief Bannerets of London, in fee for the Castelry, which he and his ancestors had by Castle Baynard, in the said City. In time of war, the said Robert and his heirs ought to serve the City in manner as followeth: that is, the said Robert ought to come, he being the twentieth man of arms on horseback [i.e. with 19 others], covered with cloth, or armour unto the great west door of St Paul's, with his Banner displayed before him, of his arms: and when he is come to the said door, mounted and apparelled, as before is said, the Mayor with his Aldermen, and Sheriffs armed in their arms shall come out of the said church of St Paul, unto the said door with a Banner in his hand, all on foot, which banner shall be gules, the image of St Paul gold, the feet, hands and head, argent, with a sword in the hands of the said image.' And then the banneret announced to the mayor that he was come to do service, and the mayor placed the banner in his hands; and Robert led the militia to Aldgate, stopping if necessary at Holy Trinity Priory to arrange for the defence of the City. Various other details are provided.[1] It is improbable that all this rigmarole really goes back as far as the late twelfth or early thirteenth centuries,[2] at least to the period before there was a mayor. No doubt, however, the tradition that the lord of Baynard's Castle led the City militia had some basis in it, and it serves to underline the importance of the loyalty of Walter FitzRobert in 1173–4 and the close links between the three castellans and the City in the twelfth century and in 1215.

The Tower itself the king normally kept under close personal control, for on the security and loyalty of the Tower's custodian depended his control over the City, and if invasion threatened, his share in the City's defence. By 1100–1 it was in the hands of the powerful tenant-in-chief, William de Mandeville; and later tradition asserted that he held it

---

seems very improbable chronologically. See Reynolds, 'Rulers of London', p. 346: 'unfortunately the genealogy rests on nothing but the coincidence of three common personal names'.

[1] *Liber Custumarum*, pt. 1, pp. 147–51; Stow, vol. i, pp. 62–5, corrected ib. vol. ii, pp. 278–9. Cam, *Eyre*, vol. ii, pp. 178–80.

[2] See Stenton, p. 9; the coats of arms in particular give a thirteenth-century air to the description.

hereditarily, after his father Geoffrey de Mandeville I.[1] There is no doubt that the hereditary claim was part of the attempt by William's son, the famous Geoffrey II, to support his claims for monopoly of royal office in and around the City, and it is singularly improbable that either William I or Rufus would have allowed the Tower to become a hereditary fief. In any event, William's tenure was short; for in 1101 he allowed Henry I's enemy (as he then was) Ranulf Flambard, Bishop of Durham, to escape. William lost heavily, and the Tower presently appears in the hands of Othwer, natural son of Earl Hugh of Chester. It has recently been suggested that Henry I both punished William and retained his loyalty by marrying him to the heiress of Eudo dapifer, who had been the recipient of some of William's losses; and when William died, that his widow was married to Othwer. Othwer 'was apparently on his way to becoming one of the great magnates of the realm when his life was cut short by the disaster of the *White Ship*' in which he was drowned in 1120.[2]

In Henry's later years the Tower was kept by an obscure castellan named Aschuill; then early in Stephen's reign, under circumstances which are hidden from us, it came into the powerful hands of Geoffrey de Mandeville.[3] It may be that Stephen himself, a warrior and baron, with neither the opportunity nor the ability to govern with his uncle's care and cunning, saw advantage in having a great baron hold sway on his behalf in London; or he may simply have succumbed to Geoffrey's importunity. Geoffrey claimed that his grandfather had held the royal offices of London and the neighbourhood and that his right to them was hereditary; in the circumstances this can have been little more than corroborative detail to lend artistic verisimilitude to claims based on power and ambition. In 1141 Stephen was captured at the Battle of Lincoln and many of his supporters changed sides; Geoffrey welcomed the Empress to London, and was soon entangled in her rapid retreat. The Londoners rose against her and him, and in the charter she issued granting him the earldom of Essex, the Tower and the shrievalties and justiceships of London and Middlesex, Essex and Hertfordshire, she observed that the citizens of London were his mortal enemies.

[1] *Regesta*, vol. iii, nos 275–6; C. W. Hollister, in *History*, vol. lviii, 1973, pp. 19 ff.
[2] Hollister, p. 24.
[3] Hollister, pp. 25, 27 (dating Geoffrey's tenure 1137 × 41 to 1143; for the first dates he cites *Regesta*, iii, nos 506, 274). On Geoffrey, see Round, *GM*, *passim*; R. H. C. Davis, 'Geoffrey de Mandeville reconsidered', *EHR*, vol. lxxix, 1964, pp. 299–307; and above, pp. 37–9, 191.

Later in 1141 he returned to his allegiance to Stephen, and was confirmed in his offices. Neither Stephen nor the Empress reckoned that they could side with the rebellious citizens against this great baron; but his power over the City was precarious and brief. In 1143 the king finally quarrelled with him and Geoffrey died in the following year. The relations between Stephen and the City in his later years seem to have been quieter, and although the lords who held the castles played a significant part in the history of the City in the rebellions of 1173–4 and 1215, the attempt to establish feudal control was not resumed.[1]

THE SHERIFFS UNDER HENRY II

It used to be supposed that Henry II looked with notably less favour than his grandfather on the liberties of London: but Miss Reynolds has shown that such a view is groundless.[2] We have no certain evidence before the 1190s that the citizens chose their own sheriffs, but the men who held office under Henry were almost all 'identifiable as City landowners, some as merchants or craftsmen, and a few as aldermen or the fathers of aldermen'. In 1162 – possibly also in 1159 – the new sheriffs took over responsibility for the debts of the old; and this suggests that, hidden behind the documents, there was an arrangement comparable to that at other, lesser, towns, whereby the citizens accepted that the sheriff was their representative when they were allowed to choose him, and so took responsibility for his debts. It looks as if the sheriffs may have been elective 'between *c.* 1157–9 and 1169 at least'. What seems certain is that Henry was not unfavourable to some measures of urban liberty; he might suppress 'communes in Gloucester and York', but 'his attitude to Eu, La Rochelle and Rouen implies that he may have been more pragmatic about urban government'[3] than some contemporary and modern commentators have supposed.

In Stephen's later years we meet two kinds of justice and sheriff: the professional administrator rising from the ranks of the barons in the person of Richard de Lucy, and the entrenched citizenry in the person of Theodoric son of Deorman,[4] a man whose roots were even more deeply sunk in City history than Andrew Buccuinte or Osbert Eightpence. One

---

[1] Above, pp. 39 ff.
[2] 'Rulers of London', pp. 343–4.   [3] Ib. p. 343.
[4] *Regesta*, vol. iii, no. 534; Reynolds, p. 354 and n. 21, who, however, reckons Richard de Lucy already 'justice of more than London'.

of the earliest documents in the Corporation Records Office is a tiny writ of William I restoring a hide of land in Essex to one Deorman, very likely the same.[1] None knows why it is there – the land seems to have passed to Westminster Abbey – but it is a fitting monument to an English citizen and landowner who quickly won Norman favour and whose sons and grandsons figured in the City's history down to the middle of the twelfth century; we shall meet them again among the leading benefactors to the nuns of Clerkenwell, and we shall meet another of Deorman's sons among the canons of St Paul's.[2] Richard de Lucy not unnaturally was a friend of Thomas Becket; London may or not have been a link between them, but they certainly met in the royal court in the late 1150s, when Becket was chancellor and Richard royal justiciar, and in 1162 it was Richard who managed the business of Becket's election as archbishop on the king's behalf. He evidently tried to keep on some terms with the archbishop as the quarrel developed; but in the end it proved impossible and Becket's hand was heavy on him on Whit Sunday 1166 in the abbey church at Vézelay when Becket excommunicated his enemies.[3] Yet clearly Richard never lost his admiration for his former friend, and his last days were spent in retirement at the abbey he himself had founded in the martyr's honour at Lessness, which is in Kent but as near to London as Kent can be, and was apparently the first religious house to be dedicated to St Thomas, save for a Cistercian abbey in Poland.[4]

In Henry II's earliest years Gervase of Cornhill was sheriff, in harness with John, son of Ralph, a shadowy figure who may just possibly have been sheriff for a time already in the 1140s.[5] Although the office of justice rapidly disappeared it was normal for there to be at least two sheriffs at a time; this became a formula in the 1190s. In Henry II's reign, however, there were some rapid changes and experiments such as characterize his imaginative, unpredictable method of government, but may also reflect a balancing of his own and the City's interests.[6] In 1157–9 a committee of sheriffs appears, which included two men whose names recur later in the reign and who were members of leading London dynasties. Reiner, son of

[1] Bishop and Chaplais, no. 16 (pl. XV).
[2] Algar, son of Deorman (Dereman), Le Neve, p. 57.
[3] *MB*, vol. v, no. 198, pp. 392 ff.
[4] KH, p. 164; the Cistercian abbey of St Mary and St Thomas of Canterbury at Sulejów, *c.* 130 km. south-west of Warsaw, was founded in 1177 from Morimond (F. Van der Meer, *Atlas de l'ordre Cistercien*, Amsterdam–Brussels, 1965, p. 298).
[5] Reynolds, 'Rulers of London', p. 342.
[6] Ib. pp. 343–4. On Henry II see now W. L. Warren, *Henry II*, London, 1973.

Berengar was a dynast of the second, perhaps of the third generation; his son Richard was sheriff at the end of the reign[1] and another descendant, perhaps a grandson, was mayor in the 1220s. Brihtmar of Haverhill seems to have been a newcomer of English descent.[2] He certainly prospered exceedingly; he was *custos* with Peter FitzWalter in the years 1174–6 and his son, William of Haverhill, was one of the most eminent citizens of the next generation, and sheriff for two years in 1189–91. Both families seem to follow the common pattern of combining landholding in the home counties with a town house and City property. For the rest, their activities are not documented. One of the colleagues in 1157–9 was Josce the vintner, representative of a trade which greatly prospered in the reign of Henry II.[3] The other two colleagues in the shrievalty are more obscure: Geoffrey 'Bursarius' was probably a financier, and of Richard Viel little is known though his surname is one which recurs with tantalizing frequency in twelfth-century London.[4] What is abundantly clear, however, is that they were all men with a stake in the City, though most, perhaps all of them also had dealings with the crown.

In 1159–60 there is a gap in our information; by 1160–1 Henry reverted from a team of sheriffs to a single officer, and Gervase of Cornhill had his final term.[5] In 1161–2 he was succeeded by Ernald the shield-maker (Scutarius) who had supplied arms to the king and prospered no doubt in the wars and rumours of war in France and elsewhere in Henry's early years; his colleague was Vitalis the clerk, perhaps the man who had served and serviced the sheriff's office in former years, a professional administrator.[6] In 1162 Reiner reappears in the office, now accompanied by the man

[1] Reynolds, 'Rulers of London', pp. 355–7; Page, pp. 244 ff.

[2] At least his name was English, although his son, William, and his grandson, Thomas, had French names; on them see Reynolds, 'Rulers of London', pp. 355–7; Williams, p. 55.

[3] See pp. 265–6; cf. Reynolds, 'Rulers of London', p. 356, n. 6.

[4] Ib., nn. 5, 7, and p. 345 and n. 39. Geoffrey Bursarius frequently occurs in the *PRs* (references ibid) and as a witness in *Wilts., Devonshire and Dorsetshire Portion of the Lewes Cartulary* . . ., ed. W. Budgen and L. F. Salzman, Sussex Record Soc., 1943, p. 49.

[5] Reynolds, p. 356, n. 9, suggests that Gervase may have been sheriff also in 1159–60, or possibly Humphrey Buccuinte.

[6] Doubtless the sheriff's clerk could be a person of considerable importance, though we know little of the clerks – save that Vitalis (who occurs later in *Cart. Clerkenwell*, no. 160) may have risen to be sheriff from being sheriff's clerk, and Thomas Becket learned some of the craft he used as chancellor in this office (see above, pp. 212–13; and for clerks as sheriffs in the time of William II and Henry I, pp. 202–4).

who was to play the leading role in the management of London's farm, and in the government of the City, until near the end of the reign, William, son of Isabel.[1] William, son of Isabel seems to have had some association with the Flemish moneylender William Cade, who dominated the London money market in the late fifties and early sixties; and it is fairly clear that he was a financier as well as dealer in houses and land. Even more closely associated with Cade was John Buccuinte, bearer of a name already well known in London history, who led the syndicate which managed the sheriff's office from 1169–72 and witnessed a number of Cade's bonds and charters in which he was involved.[2]

So the story goes on: sometimes one, sometimes two, sometimes four; sometimes 'custodes', as in 1174–6, when the City was rewarded (one may think) for its loyalty to the king in the great rebellion by the suspension of the farm, for the 'custodes' rendered only what they collected of recognizable royal revenue, not the full sum of the traditional farm.[3] In all these shifts and changes, there were two periods of relative stability, the years 1162–9 of the long rule of Reiner son of Berengar and William son of Isabel, and the later reign of William, son of Isabel alone from 1181–87. But even when the pattern changed, the men were not greatly different.[4] All had some stake in London which can be established by other evidence. Some were merchants, some houseowners, some local landlords with City property, some financiers; and we may suspect that many or most of them pursued all these avocations at one time or another – suspect, for the evidence never tells us the range of a man's activities. One thing is certain: the City farm was important to the king for the money it produced, and the City was doubly important as the chief source of supply of much else besides money to his court. Thus it is no surprise that the sheriffs should be men with a substantial stake in the City, whether they were chosen by the City fathers or by the king;[5] their business was to keep smooth the relations between king and City, to ensure a reasonable money flow. To understand the significance of the office, and the part the sheriffs played in London and London in the kingdom, it is above all necessary to penetrate

[1] See Reynolds, 'Rulers of London', pp. 355–6 and n. 12; Page, p. 254.

[2] For William's relations with Cade, see Jenkinson (1913), p. 227; John witnesses nos iv, vi, vii (Jenkinson [1927], pp. 207–9). On Cade, see below, pp. 227–30. For John Buccuinte, see Reynolds, 'Rulers of London', p. 356 n. 13.

[3] Cf. Tait, pp. 167–8; Reynolds, 'Rulers of London', p. 344.

[4] Cf. Reynolds, pp. 343–4.

[5] See above, p. 218.

as deep as we can into the money market which lay at the centre of the story.

THE MONEY MARKET

1 Jewry[1]

The argument so far has developed the thesis that a close link must be seen between the office and work of the sheriffs of London and the place of London as a monetary centre. This means not only that London was the place where control of the mint was organized and in which the largest group of mints in the country was placed, and therefore in the physical sense the place to which the largest quantity of silver flowed in England in this period; it also means that the City played a crucial part in the money market in the wider commercial sense. When Henry II, as a young duke, planned his invasion of England, he turned to two major financiers of the world in which he then lived. William Trentegeruns, Vicomte of Rouen (though what his thirty 'geruns' were eludes us), had a name and office reminiscent of Osbert Eightpence (Huitdeniers) of London. He was a leading citizen of Rouen, and so remained until his death in 1159. Thereafter his wife continued his business, that is to say, she gathered in the profits of his operations in Southampton and the repayments of Henry's loans.[2] His other, and even more substantial, supporter in the early 1150s was William Cade of St Omer, whose reward was to be that he dominated the London money market until *c.* 1164. Cade, like Trentegeruns, frequently appears in the Pipe Rolls, helping payment by this sheriff and that of large sums of money not readily available, and doubtless increasing his own income in the process. 'By the middle of the century,' wrote H. G. Richardson, 'credit and finance had developed upon a wide, an international scale.'[3] But evidence as to its roots and to the way in which it worked is lamentably scarce. None the less, the existence of the Pipe Rolls gives us a means of inspecting it at work in England, and in London in particular, unique for the period; and it is evidently one of the keys not only to the history of the shrievalty and of administration in London, but of the City's economy and, in a measure, of its social structure.

The money market in twelfth-century London was ruled by three types of men: by the richer Jews of London, by the Christian usurers of whom

[1] What follows is based chiefly on Richardson (but see p. 225 n.); and see above, pp. 179 ff.

[2] Richardson, pp. 50 ff.   [3] Richardson, p. 50.

Cade was the most eminent, and the Knights Templars. They mobilized credit in a variety of different ways, and overcame the extreme inflexibility of medieval currency; they provided rich men with ready money, poor men with the cash to survive; in the process they enriched themselves, and, as some of their enrichment was at other folk's expense, and more appeared to be, they waxed unpopular. In 1290 Edward I expelled the Jews; in 1312 the Order of Knights Templars was suppressed by the Pope, under pressure from the French king; in the same epoch the Cahorsins – the Christian usurers who had taken over the work of Cade and his associates – were a byword for greed and cruelty. No doubt there were cruel money-lenders in the twelfth and thirteenth centuries, as in every age; but we need have equally little doubt that the general reputation of these folk was thoroughly unfair, and in large measure based both on misunderstanding of how interest worked (a very proper misunderstanding, a cynic might observe, in a Christian society formally dedicated to condemn all interest as usury) and of the part the moneylenders played in fructifying the economy. It seems clear that the real measure of economic progress that we can observe in the twelfth century, by which men's choice of what they could buy and what they could do was greatly increased, owed much to the men who developed credit, banking and the money market; and it is also clear that in the twelfth century at least this was widely recognized. This did not save the Jewish communities of several English cities from falling victim to murder and riot when the crude zeal of the crusades, and the cruder hate and envy of the Christian mob, attacked them.[1] This first occurred, on any significant scale, in 1189; the period from the Norman Conquest until then was one of relative quiet and real prosperity in English Jewry. From 1189 on, persecution hardened; until a government no longer interested in Jewish financial support bowed to the clamour of religious and irreligious alike and started to issue the anti-Jewish legislation of the 1270s and 1280s, culminating in the Expulsion.

The Jewish community seems to have been a creation of the Norman kings.[2] They were familiar with the comparatively modest Jewry of Rouen; they doubtless knew that the Jews had techniques for handling money rarely equalled at that time among Christians, and the Jews as a ducal, or royal, possession, could be used or ignored for ducal or royal purposes. They were protected by William I and allowed or encouraged to settle in London; they were favoured by William II, always in need of stores of

[1] See p. 48.
[2] See Richardson, chap. i, pp. 1 ff.

money and delighted to shock the churchmen about him by showing favour to non-Christians. But it was probably Henry I who really grasped the value of the Jews to his government, and the emergence of the London Jewry as a major financial power seems to date from his reign.

Before the coming of the Jews the English businessmen of the eleventh century had been pre-eminent in the organization of the profits of farming and the handling of coin. 'The Jew was a town-dweller,' as H. G. Richardson observed in the book which has done more than any other in recent years to elucidate both the money market and the share of the Jews in developing it in twelfth-century England. 'Whatever his occupation, he was not an agriculturalist and, except as a source of profit, agricultural land had no interest for him.'[1] By tradition and necessity, the Jews were specialists, not solely in moneylending as used sometimes to be said, but in trade and industry and in all the operations proper to a medieval town save agriculture: by necessity, since they were forbidden to hold land – in England they were virtually royal serfs or royal chattels, without rights save such as he graciously allowed them – and the suspicion of one exclusive religious system for its only local rival created a number of taboos set on the Jews by the Church. For centuries the Jews had been the leading long-distance merchants of Christendom and Islam;[2] and thus they had inherited an understanding of how trade worked over long distances, of how to make and use the large profits which only luxury trade could bring in the early Middle Ages, above all, of how to arrange credit. By the eleventh century their pre-eminence in trade was gone, and they were coming to be more involved in moneylending. It has often been alleged that they benefited from having little religious scruple as to interest; and almost equally often replied that Christian usurers like William Cade were able in the twelfth century to practise in the open, and seem not to have been inhibited by any scruple of the kind. No doubt there were many Christians like Cade, and in all probability even more who genuinely believed usury to be a sin, especially when they were the victims of it. The Church tightened the screw on believers and 'infidels' alike, while at the same time its cleverer minds were devising the elaborate system of

[1] Richardson, p. 83.
[2] See the famous description of the Jewish 'Rhadanites' in the ninth-century Arab geographer Ibn Khurradadhbah, quoted in translation in R. S. Lopez and I. W. Raymond, *Medieval Trade in the Mediterranean World*, New York, 1955, pp. 31–3; for modern discussions cf. S. D. Goitein, *A Mediterranean Society*, vol. i, Berkeley and Los Angeles, 1967, p. 418, n. 29.

common sense and casuistry which modified the letter of the law in the late Middle Ages. All that we can say with certainty is that the Jews had inherited an understanding of credit, and of the handling of money, more sophisticated than was normal at the time. They also had links and connections which made it comparatively easy for them to deploy their expertise. The Jew who conversed with Gilbert Crispin, Abbot of Westminster, was French-speaking, but had studied in Mainz; he was evidently known to many of the Jewish communities of northern Europe, and perhaps more widely.[1] Personal knowledge, and the tight loyalties of Jewry in all the major towns, made possible arrangements for cash and credit and exchange not otherwise available; and because the Jewish communities were so readily identifiable – and so vulnerable to legal or illegal vengeance – the Jews were in fact more trustworthy as a group than Christians in matters financial.[2] It need hardly be said that this is not a moral judgement; such would in this context be meaningless. There is abundant evidence that some Jews were trusted and some not; on the whole they were probably much less unpopular before the Third Crusade (1189) than the sensational stories of Jewish ritual murder circulated by a few fanatics at the time might suggest.[3] But they could not escape their origin: they were imported by the Norman kings, presumably as a form of indirect taxation, and like all taxation they were liable to be disliked and evaded; and plausible grounds were found by Christians for claiming the divine sanction for such attitudes.

The Jewish community established in London by the first Norman Kings rapidly spread in the early and mid-twelfth century to many other towns in the island. Richard of Devizes mentions in his imaginary speech[4] about a dozen or fifteen towns which a Jew might visit; and an earlier and more reliable source shows that already in 1159 they had spread extensively in the home counties and the west, and were strongly established at Lincoln.[5] On the whole H. G. Richardson's view has much to commend it, that they were still centred in London in the reign of Henry I, and that settlements elsewhere only got under way in Stephen's reign; they seem to have reached their full extent under Henry II.[6] But they

[1] See pp. 304–5.

[2] Cf. e.g. Richardson, pp. 62–3, 122 ff.

[3] But for the development of anti-semitic feeling in the twelfth century see G. I. Langmuir in *Traditio*, vol. xix, 1963, pp. 183–244 (a critique of Richardson).

[4] See pp. 180–1.

[5] Richardson, chap. 1.

[6] Ib., pp. 2, 11, 23 ff.

always remained closely interconnected. In Henry I's reign the leading member of the London Jewry was the Rabbi Josce from Rouen, whose sons Isaac and Abraham were leading moneylenders and business associates in the middle of the century; Isaac bought a house on Cheapside from Gervase of Cornhill.[1] But in Henry II's later years the most eminent figure in the English Jewry was Aaron of Lincoln, who had a London house indeed and must have made increasing use of it, but whose main headquarters may have remained in Lincoln.[2] In the early years of Henry II's reign Isaac and Abraham were lending money to the king; but it was only in the mid- and late 1170s that he borrowed substantial sums from Jewish moneylenders. Two syndicates were formed, the first about 1175, the second after a mysterious disaster had roused the king's anger against the first in 1177; and it is probably significant that Aaron was only involved in rescuing the first syndicate.[3] For these loans to the king were no doubt a form of taxation, not a source of profit to the Jewry, and the big money was to be made by private lending and by financing better businessmen than kings are wont to be. Richardson has argued that the Pipe Rolls are the tip of the iceberg of royal finance and that they can only show us a proportion even of the king's dealings with moneylenders.[4] This would generally be thought exaggerated: a high proportion of royal revenue in this period seems to be shown in the Pipe Rolls, though evidently not the whole; and the Pipe Rolls are a fair indication of royal needs. They suggest that in his opening years Henry was extravagant and needed help; then recovered remarkably in the 1160s, suffered a crisis in 1173–4 and proceeded from the late 1170s on more smoothly and economically.[5] There is other evidence to confirm this. Government in the early days, under the direction of Thomas Becket as chancellor, showed a panache and extravagance apparently foreign to Henry's natural bent. No doubt a new regime felt the need to impress, and Becket's extravagance may well have had political justification.[6] When he became archbishop Henry was able to

[1] Richardson, pp. 239–40.

[2] Richardson, *passim*, esp. pp. 8, 47, 61–2, 68–70, 74–6 and index s.v. Aaron of Lincoln. See J. W. F. Hill, *Medieval Lincoln*, pp. 220–2: though Aaron retained his house in Lincoln it is likely that his business took him increasingly to London in his last years.

[3] Richardson, pp. 60, 62 ff.

[4] See esp. Richardson, pp. 51–2.

[5] See Richardson, chap. 3, for the chronology of Henry II's borrowing. The lowest figure of revenue is in 1173–4 (ib. p. 66).

[6] For his extravagance and its use, see esp. *MB*, vol. iii, pp. 29–33; also T. A. M. Bishop, *Scriptores Regis*, Oxford, 1961, pp. 9 ff.; *GF*, p. 212.

retrench. But in 1173 the greatest crisis of the reign fell on him, and the rebellion of that year may well have stimulated borrowing on a scale never needed again. The pattern of Henry's borrowing suggests that although the Jews had played little or no part in financing his adventures in the early 1150s, once established on the throne he came to regard them as one of the chief sources of ready money; and it is evident that they were engaged in fructifying the English economy in a diversity of ways. The surviving documents reveal the list of debtors of men like Aaron, and some of the bonds and land transactions in which they were involved.[1] We can see all sorts of men escaping from temporary shortage with their aid; we can see feckless landowners mortgaging their property to Jews; we can also see something of the way in which the Jews who were not inclined to manage country properties, passed on the land acquired in this way and enabled successful rising gentry and religious houses to add field to field and manor to manor. Thus in the early thirteenth century Henry of Braybrooke acquired land at Tolleshunt in Essex by clearing the debts of the holder of the land to two London Jews, Benedict Crespin and Manasses the Scribe.[2] Benedict Crespin is otherwise known as the owner of a substantial property in the City, who was accused in 1246 of having blocked two lanes to make his home behind the Becket house, by that date the hospital of St Thomas of Acon, towards Lothbury, beside the street still called Old Jewry.[3]

The only recorded source of Benedict's wealth is this loan to an impoverished country landlord. No doubt he made loans to merchants too; and it may well be that this aspect of Jewish finance, which is wholly undocumented, was in its day as important as loans to squires and kings. What is certain is that the Jews prospered because they substantially helped the king, the great nobles and the sheriffs to mobilise the inflexible medium of silver coins on which the whole monetary system depended.

2 William Cade

This can be shown with even greater clarity in the case of the leading Christian moneylender of Henry II's early years, William Cade.[4] William

[1] See esp. Richardson, pp. 247 ff.

[2] Richardson, pp. 270 ff.

[3] Richardson, p. 280; cf. *Eyre*, pp. 143–4 (nos 401, 403).

[4] On Cade, see Jenkinson (1913) and Jenkinson (1927). The bonds are PRO E210/ 5196–5203 (facsimiles of some, Jenkinson [1927], facing p. 192, texts of all, pp. 205 ff.); we have checked some of the printed texts with these (see p. 229 n. 2. We are much indebted to Dr Patricia Barnes for help with this.) See **Plate 36**.

Cade was a Flemish cloth merchant and moneylender with the most extensive connections in the western world of his day of any native of northern Europe whose dealings can now be traced. He was a native of St Omer, and continued to live there and have his main headquarters there until his death *c.* 1166. His operations must have involved the help of numerous associates and partners in many countries. His closest partners were his son Eustace and his brother Ernulf.[1] He and they seem to have been frequent visitors in London, where he had a house, and his activities there, and the companions who regularly witnessed his surviving bonds, suggest that he was for a number of years one of the central figures in the London money market. His debtors represented a wide spectrum of English society, from the king to men of quite humble station. They included monasteries, for he was one of the pioneers in what was to become the common practice of Flemish merchants (later Italians) buying the wool clip from Cistercian houses and paying them money in advance on expectation of the harvest.[2] They included bishops and lesser clergy, and several earls and leading barons. They also included a number of sheriffs, for it is evident that when the sheriffs were struggling to pay their dues to the Exchequer, and to manipulate the bundles of talleys and writs and the cartloads of silver coins that were needed to straighten out their affairs twice yearly in the presence of the barons of the Exchequer, the grand master of credit and finance of the age was at hand to help them. 'We get, in fact,' wrote Sir Hilary Jenkinson, who discovered Cade and published his roll of debts and his bonds from the records of the Exchequer in the Public Record Office, 'the picture of a convenient and semi-official Cade waiting on the court, especially when it was engaged in Exchequer business, equally ready to accommodate the king or his debtors or, if necessary, both parties.'[3] This may be exaggerated, but it is a remarkable picture which emerges, of a man called in frequently between the accession of Henry II and 1164, to service the men who worked the Exchequer, king, lords, sheriffs, and the machine itself. It is probable that he had advanced large sums to the young Henry before he became king; it is certain that he was the greatest of the king's creditors in early days, and

[1] Jenkinson (1927), pp. 206–9, nos ii, iii, iv, vi, vii; cf. p. 195. For another brother, Baldwin, see Jenkinson (1913), p. 214. For Eustace see also PRO DL 10/28, ed. C. Johnson and H. Jenkinson, *English Court Hand*, Oxford, 1915, Text, p. 103, Facsimiles, pl. VII (b).

[2] See esp. Jenkinson (1913), p. 221 for his relations with Louth Park Abbey.

[3] Jenkinson (1927), p. 198.

that at least £5,600 was repaid to him between 1155 and his death in 1166.[1] To an early bond, which can be dated to 1157, Reiner,[2] son of Berengar, John Buccuinte and Peter FitzWalter were all witnesses, all three at one time or another sheriffs of London. In 1160 another bond was witnessed by a group of royal officials led by the Bishop of Ely (presiding genius of the Exchequer) and the Earl of Leicester, the royal justiciar; evidently we are at the Exchequer board.[3] Even more evidently are we there in the latest of the surviving bonds to which we can attach a date. At the Michaelmas audit in 1165 the Sheriff of Oxfordshire, Roger d'Oilli, produced a writ from the king ordering him to pay a hundred marks from his farm to William Cade, the king's creditor.[4] Cade's bond shows in fact that the sheriff did nothing of the kind. He executed a bond with Cade in 1163 by which he acknowledged a debt to the financier to the tune of 109 marks, and he pledged a piece of property for its safe repayment, as well as calling to his aid as pledges his bishop, Robert de Chesney of Lincoln, and the bishop's nephew, Gilbert Foliot, recently translated to the see of London. The witnesses consisted of the barons of the Exchequer and included two men who appear so often in Cade's company that we may assume them to be his business associates, Peter FitzWalter and John Buccuinte.[5] If we wring out every scrap of evidence we can from the bonds and from the list of debtors, we shall be inclined to think that he was also associated with the two most notable figures in the administration of London in this age, William, son of Isabel and Gervase of Cornhill, though other explanations of their presence could be found.[6] Even so, it is clear that the new reign meant that money had to burgeon in a way it had not been accustomed to do in Stephen's later years; and that William Cade was one of the instruments in the process.

FitzStephen's account of Becket's splendour and extravagence as chancellor is a striking illustration of why large sums were needed in Henry II's early years; and one is tempted to ask whether Cade was associated with Becket. FitzStephen acquits Thomas' father of usury and strongly implies (contrary to contemporary rumour) that Becket paid no

[1] See Richardson, p. 52; cf. Jenkinson (1913), pp. 215 f., 219 f.

[2] 'Reinaldo' in Jenkinson (1927), p. 207, no. iv; 'Rein', in the MS (E210/5197).

[3] Jenkinson (1927), pp. 205–6, no. i.

[4] *PR 11 Henry II*, p. 72; Jenkinson (1927), pp. 198, 208, no. vi; **Plate 36.**

[5] Jenkinson (1927), pp. 207–9, nos iv, vi, vii (Peter FitzWalter occurs as Cade's debtor, Jenkinson (1913), p. 227).

[6] Jenkinson (1913), p. 227; for Gervase, cf. Round, *CDF*, nos 1380–2.

cash to become chancellor;[1] and it is hardly surprising that none of Becket's biographers mentions the eminent moneylender, for usury was a sin and on the way to becoming a crime. At the same time it is clear from Cade's bonds that in his heyday he was perfectly respectable and treated so by three bishops simultaneously at Michaelmas 1163. One of these was Gilbert Foliot, soon to become Becket's enemy. None of this suggests any association between the usurer and the chancellor, yet it is hard to believe that they had not met, and when in England Becket would have been a leading figure at the Exchequer board when Cade was there.[2]

Becket was abroad from 1158 to 1162, which helps to explain why he is not witness to any surviving bond. But at Michaelmas 1163 he was facing the first serious trial of strength; within the next few months he fell rapidly into disgrace. And so, by a curious chance, did Cade; for this one may infer from the fact that royal borrowings abruptly ceased, and when Cade died in 1166 Henry promptly seized his assets in England, and inherited bonds worth about £5,000.[3] Becket undoubtedly had friends at St Omer, since he headed thither when he had to flee from England late in 1164, as had his close associate John of Salisbury some months earlier.[4] Thus we may have hints that Cade had been associated both with Becket himself and with men who were to prove his enemies. They do not suffice to give any serious indication that Cade's fall from favour was due to personal association with the archbishop; but a link there doubtless was. For when Henry confiscated Cade's bonds – for whatever legal reason – he was parading his independence of the moneylenders, and this was (as we have seen) due to a new economical phase in which Becket's departure from the chancery may well have played a part. Although in the 1170s, in a time of crisis, Henry was to be much beholden to Jewish financiers, he seems to have succeeded on the whole for most of the rest of his reign in keeping clear of large-scale borrowing. 'When the king needs money,' wrote H. G. Richardson, 'he takes it in the form of tax' – though tax is doubtless a kindly description of Henry's methods.[5]

[1] *MB*, vol. iii, p. 18; but cf. D. Knowles, *The Historian and Character and other essays*, Cambridge, 1963, p. 106 and n.; *GF*, p. 171 and n.

[2] For the chancellor's place at the Exchequer, see *Dialogus de Scaccario*, ed. C. Johnson, NMT, 1950, pp. 18–19.

[3] Jenkinson (1913), p. 211.

[4] See *MB*, vol. ii, p. 400; vol. iii, pp. 71, 313, 329, etc.; vol. v, p. 96 (John of Salisbury).

[5] Richardson, p. 63.

3 The Knights Templars[1]

The absence of borrowing and usury made appropriate the use of the Knights Templars as bankers in his later years; for they were the third large group of experts in handling bullion and credit to play a part in the London money market, and in their transactions, in this period at least, usury seems to have played no part. The Templars were founded in the 1110s to protect pilgrims to the Holy Land, and in the course of the 1120s they became a religious Order of Knights with an austere Rule similar to that of the Cistercians. In 1128 they first came to England, and in the years which followed they rapidly established themselves and made the London 'Temple' their headquarters. They settled first in Holborn, but as their resources, recruits and visitors grew, the site proved much too small. Doubtless they looked with envy at the ample precinct enjoyed by their colleagues and rivals, the Hospitallers, in Clerkenwell;[2] from early in the reign of Henry II, certainly by 1161, they had acquired the large site by the river, just outside the City wall, which still bears the name Temple (Plates 44–7). There they flourished until 1312, when the Pope suppressed the Order under urgent pressure from the French king, not unsupported by the English. They had managed the financial affairs of the French king for several generations, and Philip IV wished to nationalize his treasury; no doubt this is a superficial statement of a complex issue and a human tragedy but it illustrates the key part the Templars had played in national and in international finance in the twelfth and thirteenth centuries. In London they had lived in some splendour in the strongly guarded precinct surrounding the fine church with its circular nave dedicated by the patriarch of Jerusalem in 1185 – at the same time that he dedicated the very similar church of the Hospitallers in Clerkenwell; in this as in other affairs the two Orders, though rivals and sometimes deadly rivals, were very similar, and it may well be that the Hospitallers were almost as much involved in finance as the Templars.

Henry II was associated with the Knights of the Temple already in the 1160s, when he began to give out that he was planning a Crusade.[3]

---

[1] See pp. 331–2; and on the Templars and their English houses and lands, especially Lees; for the extent of the Temple, cf. Ogilby's Map of *c.* 1676; cf. also Stow, vol. ii, pp. 47 ff., 365.

[2] See pp. 331–2.

[3] Cf. *GF*, p. 173 and n. 1; R. C. Smail in *TRHS*, 5th Series, vol. xix, 1969, pp. 12 ff.

Whether his scheme was ever sincere, we do not know, but in the end he crusaded only with his purse. A part of his penance for Becket's murder – after swearing that he was in no way involved – was to give the Templars sufficient money to pay for 200 knights for a year in the Holy Land.[1] This grand gesture clearly reveals some of the reasons why the Templars were international financiers in the twelfth century, and why they did not need to engage in moneylending in their early years to grow and stay rich. Henry II gave them cash in England; this they gathered at the Temple and hoarded there. But they could not hoard it indefinitely, for its purpose was to maintain knights several thousand miles further east. Henry also gave them land at one time and another; and innumerable lesser men, wishing to support the Crusade, or pay their penance without the grim exertion of a long pilgrimage to Jerusalem, paid their contributions too. All this had to be transported over greater distances than any English merchant considered trading (so far as we know) at this time. Further-more, many of the Temple's benefactors were small landholders without any great supply of ready cash; sometimes no doubt short of cash.[2] These men gave or sold small plots of land, not a commodity readily convertible into crusading knights on active service in the East. Thus the Templars rapidly became experts in land-management (which the Jews were not), banking, credit, long-distance transport and trade. One special asset they enjoyed was their military strength: the convoy needed by every large merchant enterprise was ready-made for the Templars. The money transported the knights to the east, and the knights escorted the money. Little wonder that Henry II was impressed by their efficiency as bankers and the security of their banks. These facts, and the extreme convenience of the New Temple, determined him to use it as a treasury in his later years. It rapidly became one of the king's chief treasuries, a rival to the old storehouse at Winchester, until the royal treasuries were concentrated at Westminster in the thirteenth century.[3]

Thus the royal court, the royal Exchequer, the sheriffs of England and especially of London, mingled in the London money market; and London was already a major financial centre, partly because it was also the home of

[1] *MB*, vol. vii, p. 521; cf. Smail, p. 140 n. 3.

[2] But the Templar records (as normal in the twelfth century) never reveal hidden usury in their acquisitions.

[3] See R. A. Brown in *Studies presented to Sir Hilary Jenkinson*, London, 1957, pp. 35–49, esp. p. 43 and n. 9; A. Sandys in *Essays . . . presented to T. F. Tout*, pp. 147–62, esp. p. 151.

a leading branch office of the firm of Cade, Brothers and Sons, of the rich London Jewry, and of the Knights Templars. But these were not simply causes and effects: they had grown together. William Cade's London office, the Jews and the Templars prospered in London partly because the royal court was often there; and we have seen how closely their prosperity was linked with royal finance. It is doubtful, however, whether Cade and the Jews prospered directly through royal finance; kings were not reliable borrowers, nor could deep usury commonly be extracted from them. But their courts and Exchequers provided ample opportunities and access to rich profits, as Cade's bonds with unfortunate sheriffs amply show. Likewise the Templars, to whom Henry II was himself a major asset, found that the king helped them in indirect ways as well, above all by setting the fashion in preparing for a Crusade and paying for not going on it. His son and successor, Richard I, by mortgaging every asset in his kingdom for the Third Crusade and then absenting himself for years on end, laid financial and political foundations for the formation of London's commune and the institution of the mayor.

9

On the Mayor[1]

DOWN TO the death of Henry II the normal situation was for the shrievalty to be in the hands of one or more of a group of men with a strong stake in the City. Some of the arrangements were short-lived, some lasted for as much as seven years at a time, but there is a certain stability in a pattern which gives us Reiner, son of Berengar and William, son of Isabel as sheriffs from 1162–9, William son of Isabel in 1176–7 and 1178–87, and Richard son of Reiner with Henry of Cornhill son of Gervase, from 1187–9.[2] The early years of Richard I signal a change, and from 1190–1 until the early 1220s an ever clearer pattern, and a new one, emerges. It is from this point that the tradition began that there should always be two, and never less or more than two, sheriffs of London. Furthermore, in this generation, it is exceedingly rare for any sheriff to hold office twice. Parts at least of the list of sheriffs from 1190–1220 is like a roll-call of the City patriciate. William of Haverhill, John Buccuinte, Nicholas Duket, Peter son of Neuelon, Roger le Duc, Roger FitzAlan – and so it goes on. Nicholas Duket alone occurs twice; one or two sheriffs of the 1170s and 1180s reappear.[3] But it is abundantly clear, from the list alone, that a tradition had been established, almost in a moment of time in the opening years of Richard's I's reign, that the office of sheriff should rotate among the leading City fathers.

[1] The fundamental existing studies are by Round, in *Archaeological Journal*, vol. i, 1893, pp. 247–63; and *The Antiquary*, vol. xv, 1887, pp. 107–11; see also Page, pp. 249 ff.; Williams, pp. 29 ff.; Reynolds, 'Rulers of London', p. 349.

[2] See pp. 218–22.

[3] See pp. 373–4. William son of Isabel was sheriff 1193–4, but his identity with the sheriff of Henry II's reign cannot be certain; John Buccuinte, sheriff 1190–1, is possibly to be identified with the sheriff of 1169–72 (cf. Reynolds, 'Rulers of London', pp. 355–7 and nn. 13, 30).

The rotation was almost perfect for nearly thirty years. From 1218–19, however, John Viel, a member of what appears to have been an old established shrieval family,[1] embarked on a two-year term; in 1220 the current Richard Reiner did the same, and then passed onto the mayoralty in 1222. But in spite of breaches of this kind, common in the 1220s, occasional later, it has been the tradition since 1190, broadly speaking, that sheriffs are elected in pairs and that a man holds office once only.

The Pipe Roll which reveals the sheriffs of 1190–1 to us does so thus: 'The citizens of London – William of Haverhill and John Buccuinte for them – render account of £300 blank for this year.'[2] From 1190–1, the farm which had run at about £520–£530 for many years, was restored to the figure of £300 which the citizens claimed to be traditional, and which Geoffrey de Mandeville had in fact enjoyed in 1141.[3] Thus the farm that was in these sheriffs' hands may have made the office a position of some emolument as well as of dignity and eminence; and this is perhaps a part of the reason for the new tradition. It could be interpreted doubtless in the opposite sense – that the office was a chore which none was prepared to endure for more than a year. But the eminence of these early names, and the part the shrievalty played in the city's *cursus honorum*, strongly suggest that it had become an honour to be shared among the oligarchy.[4] In the mid-1190s there were serious riots in the City, and a party emerged under the famous, or notorious, William Longbeard, set on improving the lot of men of lesser substance in a City dominated by a small oligarchy of great wealth. This confirms the impression given by the list of sheriffs: that a small band, approximately the size of the body of aldermen,[5] entered into power in the City and held the reins of government in its hands.

Of special interest is the coincidence of this new arrangement for the shrievalty with the inauguration of the commune and the first appearance

[1] See p. 220 and n.

[2] Cited, Round, *CL*, pp. 233–4; cf. Reynolds, 'Rulers of London', pp. 348–9.

[3] See p. 207; Reynolds, p. 348.

[4] On the nature of the 'governing class' in the period, see Reynolds, 'Rulers of London', pp. 349–50, 352–3.

[5] Not necessarily, however, consisting of aldermen: Miss Reynolds, 'Rulers of London', p. 345, shows how few of the London citizens can be definitely identified, or have been so far identified, as aldermen: 'less than fifty . . . in the middle and later years of the century'. But the fixing of the number of sheriffs at two, which would allow for circulation among all the citizens of aldermanic rank (if such was the practice) in twelve years or so is suggestive.

of the Mayor. The commune was allowed to show its face in October 1191, though it may have been formed in 1189 or 1190; the farm of the City had meanwhile been lowered from over £500 to £300 at Michaelmas 1190. The mayor 'first meets us in the spring of 1193'.[1]

These last words are from J. H. Round's famous essay on the Commune and he went on to print for the first time the oath of 1193:[2]

> The oath of the commune of the time of King Richard, when he was a prisoner in Germany. (The adherents of the commune swear) that they will bear faith to their lord King Richard for his life and limbs and earthly honour against all men and women who can live or die; that they will preserve his peace and help to preserve it, that they will keep the commune and be obedient to the Mayor of the City of London and to the *échevins* of the same commune, in faith to the king, that they will follow and keep the decisions of the Mayor and *échevins* and other good men [probi homines] who will be with them, saving the honour of God and of Holy Church, the faith of their lord King Richard, and saving at all points the liberties of the city of London ...

The words 'Mayor and *échevins*' suggest a very radical break with the past, for no such officials appear in any London record before the 1190s; and there is no doubt that they represent a vital stage in London's history. The words themselves, as Round pointed out, established that the commune had been set up on a French model, and more particularly suggested the influence of Rouen,[3] the capital of Normandy. The titles were French; but this is not to say that the officials themselves were foreign or exotic. None the less, it is of obvious and genuine significance that the old, royal officials, the sheriffs and king's chamberlain, are not mentioned. Through all the vicissitudes of the City's history, from the 1190s to the present day, one consistent thread has run: the City's own representative, its leading magistrate, the man who is set between the government of the City and the kingdom, has been the mayor, or, as he has been called since the fifteenth century, the Lord Mayor.

[1] Round, *CL*, p. 235; cf. p. 256.
[2] Ib. pp. 235–6; **Plate 37**.
[3] See below, pp. 243–4; Round, *CL*, pp. 237, 248 ff. For the date, see Reynolds, 'Rulers of London', p. 350 and n. 66.

MAYOR AND PODESTÀ IN FRANCE AND ITALY

To understand the origin of the office we must forget all, or almost all, that we know of its role in more recent times. Only thus can we avoid taking the mayoralty for granted, or reading into its early history anachronisms, duties and privileges of later times. In the twelfth-century context, what was a mayor? The first thing to say is that the title was somewhat new-fangled. Literally, it means the chief or headman of a community; and it had anciently been used, both of the grand vizier of the Frankish kingdom, 'the mayor of the palace', and the much more humble head man of a village community, 'the mayor of the vill'.[1] The variety of use in France by the twelfth century is bewildering. A mayor, *maior*, could be the formal head of the group of échevins, *scabini*, who were the nucleus, or rulers, of the sworn commune; or he could be the much more informal head of a group or committee, the leader, as we should say, the chairman. Indeed, the modern words chairman and president have many of the same ambiguities; but the analogy must not be carried to any distance, for medieval government was rarely at all comparable to modern committee government – anyway so early as this – and the *maior* could also be an official of quite a different kind, the bailiff of a king or great lord, either for any large estate, or for a village. There is thus a fundamental ambiguity about the word in its twelfth-century uses, which means that we can never recapture the precise overtones of those who pronounced it. The mayor could be a great man of the world, or the estate officer of a tiny rural community; he could be, in early days usually was, the lord's representative, an official, a man of the establishment; or he could be the chairman of a city oligarchy, of a commune, even in some circumstances, as conservative observers might have thought of him, the chairman of a revolutionary committee.

In the north of France and in Flanders, to which English townsfolk looked for the immediate precedents for their own experiments in civic freedom or reform, the managing groups of officials or citizens were called 'échevins' or 'jurés' (*scabini* or *iurati*).[2] By a heroic simplification,

---

[1] *Novum Glossarium Mediae Latinitatis*, Fasc. Ma, ed. F. Blatt, Copenhagen, 1959, cols. 47–50, esp. *magnus* IIB3, mayor of forests etc., and mayor who was also a peasant cultivator, ninth century and later; IIB4, head of commune, citing texts of 1181, 1186 (see below); IIB5 *maior domus* and *palatii*; see also J. F. Niermeyer, *Mediae Latinitatis Lexicon Minus*, fasc. 7, Leiden, 1959, pp. 627–9.

[2] For this development see A. Luchaire, *Les Communes françaises*, edn of Paris, 1911, pp. 173 ff., esp. 175–6; Giry, vol. ii, pp. 234 ff. (index) and references; G. Bourgin,

one might say that the échevins were in origin estate officials converted into city fathers, the jurés from the start city magnates; both became legal, administrative and, in a sense, political leaders in their communities. In many cases, especially in the north and west of France, the échevins either became or were from their first recorded appearance, civic officials, respectable in the eyes of the commune as well as of the feudal overlord. In Flanders the development was more complex. The échevins remained officials of the count of Flanders; the mayor, where he appeared, was their chairman or leader. The leading citizens, however, came increasingly to be represented by the jurés, and in due course they tended to choose two leaders, provosts or masters, *magistri*, to whom in later centuries the 'burgi magistri', *burgomeister*, were heirs. Thus at Liège a mayor appears in the 1180s among the échevins, but by then the rulers of the civic community were coming increasingly to be the council of jurés with their two masters, who by the fifteenth century had become *burgomeister*; at Tournai, already by 1167, thirty jurés were established with two provosts. Midway between Liège and Rouen stands Soissons, where we have earliest evidence of a communal mayor.[1] Here, unlike most of the towns of the north and east of France, the mayor was from his first appearance head of the jurés, leader in the commune, rather than a royal official. In the neighbourhood of Soissons there were estate mayors, officials of the local lords; but in the city there was no such dual authority as in the Flemish towns. In Liège and Tournai one can still trace the characteristic division of many medieval towns of the Continent into the

---

La commune de Soissons, Paris, 1908, pp. 67–8, 105–6, 420–2 (Louis VI, 1136), 424–8 (= *Acta Phil. Augusti*, vol. i, no. 35, Philip II, 1181), 431: A. de Belfort, *Archives de la Maison-Dieu de Châteaudun*, Paris-Châteaudun, 1881, p. 21 (1186); P. Rolland, *Les Origines de la commune de Tournai*, Brussels, 1931, pp. 104–5, 199 ff., 203 ff.; J. Gilissen in *La Ville*, vol. i, pp. 554 ff., 570 f.; H. Van Werveke, *Gand*, Brussels, 1946, pp. 32 ff.; G. Kurth, *La Cité de Liège au moyen âge*, Brussels-Liège, 1909, vol. i, pp. 92–3; F. Vercauteren, *Luttes sociales à Liège*, Brussels, 1943, p. 21. For Henry II's relations with towns, see Reynolds, 'Rulers of London', pp. 343–4; J. Boussard, *Le Gouvernement d'Henri II Plantegenêt*, Paris, 1956, pp. 167 ff. (English), 181 ff. (Norman towns).

J.-F. Lemarignier in two important papers, *Revue du moyen âge latin*, vol. iv, 1948, pp. 191–6, and *Revue du Nord*, vol. xl, 1958, pp. 319–21, has shown evidence for a close relationship in the development of towns in Flanders and Normandy, esp. (in the second paper) in the use of the title 'échevins'. It may well be that Flanders played a more important part in the development of the title mayor than can at present be shown: cf. the occurrence of a mayor of a guild in Arras in 1111 (*Actes des comtes de Flandre, 1071–1128*, ed. F. Vercauteren, Brussels, 1938, no. 52).

[1] See preceding note.

castrum, the old fortified centre, and the *burgus*, the burghers' town – a division still visible in the physiognomy of many cities from Ghent to Krakow. This made a separation between two ruling groups, mayor and échevins, and provosts or masters and jurés, reasonable and tolerable. But in the long run even in such divided cities, and in the short run in cities not so divided, a single authority was likely to be needed.

Lootus, the mayor of Soissons, meets us in a document of 1136, in which peace was made at the instance of King Louis VI in the presence of the king and of the mayor 'and other jurés'. It is noticeable that in the charters of Louis VII (1137–80) no reference is ever made to the officials of Soissons; they first reappear at the opening of the reign of Philip Augustus, in his charter of 1181 – once again, as mayor and jurés. This example should teach us not to expect the title mayor to become formal too quickly, and not to assume without further enquiry either that the mayor is in origin a royal official or a communal leader. Yet when we first meet mayor and échevins in Rouen in the 1170s, the mayor is clearly respectable in the eyes both of his overlord Henry II, Duke of Normandy and King of England, and of his colleagues the citizens: he is the man to whom the oath of the commune is made.[1]

The commune was essentially a sworn confederation: a sworn conspiracy to its enemies, a sworn gathering of friends and colleagues to those within. The idea of the sworn commune had grown up in every part of Europe in the eleventh and twelfth centuries; and what is new and remarkable both in Italy and in parts of France in the second half of the twelfth century is that a single magistrate came to be regarded as the necessary president, ruler, guide or umpire of the commune.

In Italy and the south of France this official was usually called the podestà, a title as vague and portentous in its origin as that of mayor.[2] The podestà was the *potestas*, the power, the authority. In numerous Italian communes of north and central Italy in the 1150s and 1160s such independent government as the citizens had managed to establish lay primarily in the hands either of groups of consuls or of single magistrates. Commonly indeed, over a long period stretching in some cases from the 1130s or 1140s to the early thirteenth century, the consuls were presided over by a single magistrate, or else rule by a group alternated with

[1] For the French mayor, see above, pp. 237–8 n., esp. references in Giry, Luchaire.
[2] What follows is based on Waley, chap. 3; Fonseca, pp. 47–57 (E. Cristiani, et al.); V. Franchini, *Saggio di ricerche su l'instituto del podestà nei comuni medievali*, Bologna, 1912; Hanauer, art. cit. (p. 243 n.).

government under a single head.[1] These leading consuls, or consuls' rivals, were called by a variety of titles, of which at first 'rectors' was the more popular, but soon 'podestà' eclipsed all others. The office only became common in the heyday of the Emperor Frederick Barbarossa, who appointed podestà as imperial representatives in several cities during his years of effective control. It is a nice question whether one should consider the office as essentially an imperial creation; or take more note of the fact that it developed and flourished in its characteristic form in cities which had effectively shaken off the imperial lordship. Indeed, there was evidently a middle stage when podestà were acting as a kind of intermediary between emperor and commune in the long negotiations which led to the peace treaties of 1177 and 1183.[2] In the long run the podestà became a civic official; and it is highly likely that the significance of these movements was observed from afar, even in England and France. For the fortunes of Henry II and Thomas Becket, Thomas of London, greatly depended on the emperor's adventures among the Italian cities in the 1160s and both parties watched his campaigns there with the closest attention.[3]

In all of these cities there were wider groups of *boni homines*, equivalent to the *probi homines* of the London commune,[4] the largest group of men reckoned worth consideration by the citizen oligarchy. In some there were highly organized guilds and crafts, already by the end of the twelfth century, sometimes spreading power and faction more widely and deeply in the population. In most Italian cities the early podestà were citizens or feudal nobles of the *contado*; and so far as we can discern the obscure origins of the institution, they often arose to put in a better frame the troubled relations between the city and the outside powers imperial or papal.

In due course however, the podestà in Italy came to acquire a characteristic rarely to be found in northern Europe: he came commonly to be an annually elected umpire drawn from another city. This reflected the exceptional independence and exceptionally factious nature of Italian city politics in the twelfth and thirteenth centuries. The families of Romeo

---

[1] See esp. Cristiani in Fonseca, loc. cit.; Franchini, pp. 57 ff., head consul (at Siena, 1151), rector, occasionally podestà in the mid-century; also 73 ff., 77 ff. on other cases of 'il dittatore' and rectors. See also below, p. 243, n. 2.

[2] For the podestà under Frederick I, Franchini, pp. 44 ff., with list on p. 46 n.

[3] See e.g. *MB*, vol. v, pp. 90, 377, 385, 432–3, vol. vi, pp. 227–9, 235, 240–1, 402–5, etc.

[4] See p. 236.

and Juliet lived under the later signoria, and they had to accept the authority of the Duke of Verona; their predecessors in the golden age which saw the building and adornment of San Zeno Maggiore would have trusted no native superior to be an objective judge, and so a succession of eminent citizens and feudatories from other cities and *contadi* came to rule over them.[1] It was not an easy task: in 1195 an eminent Pistoian attempting to exert control as podestà of Bologna, lost both his job and his teeth.[2]

The towns of France and Flanders were closer to London than Genoa or Bologna, and it is in the north of France that we shall find the immediate source for the title and function of the mayor. It would be quite false, however, to suppose that the citizens of London in the late twelfth century had a narrow horizon bounded by the frontiers of Normandy or even of France. It was a cosmopolitan age, in which natives of England felt more in tune or in touch with – or a part of – a wider world than perhaps at any other time in the Middle Ages. The king to whom the members of the commune swore faith, Richard I, spent his reign settling the affairs of Sicily, Cyprus and Jerusalem, when not in prison in Germany or at war in France. Nearer home the visit of the Patriarch Heraclius to London in 1185 symbolized the links between London and his own Jerusalem, at the opposite ends of the accessible world; and he blessed these links by consecrating the churches of both the Templars and Hospitallers in London.[3]

In or about 1189, the year of Richard's accession, there died in the close of St Paul's a canon of some intellectual pretension, Master David of London.[4] In the 1160s he had been a student, perhaps a doctor at Bologna; and in that period of his life he had acted as guardian to other English students there, including two of the archdeacons of the diocese of London. Through the chapter of St Paul's, throughout the century, flowed men who knew France and Italy well; and not only there, for several of the canons of Holy Trinity had studied abroad, and no doubt Thomas Becket was not the only citizen's son to study at Paris and Bologna. In these circles, the affairs of the Italian cities had been observed from near

[1] *Verona e il suo territorio*, vol. ii, pt. ii, esp. pp. 256 ff., 265 ff.

[2] Waley, p. 72.

[3] See Lees, pp. lvi-lvii; B. M. Cotton MS Nero E. v.i, f. 3 (we owe this reference to Dr M. Gervers).

[4] Le Neve, p. 30; Z. N. Brooke, 'The Register of Master David', pp. 227-45, esp. p. 239.

and far with close interest. It would be absurd to suppose that there was no communication between Thomas or David of London and their like and some at least of the men who formed the commune. It would be pleasant to go further, and to assert that some of the City fathers of the 1190s had visited Italy. It is highly likely that they had; but it cannot be proved.[1]

The lack of evidence does not prove lack of contact. The documents from which one might hope to find such evidence are scarce in the twelfth century: Italian notarial deeds were normally witnessed by men who had settled in the cities, not by visitors, and the same is true of English charters. The documents which reveal trade in later periods – as we shall see – do not exist for the most part in the twelfth. None the less, it is likely that it is more than chance that Genoa should provide the most significant exception, for in the late twelfth century she had captured and held the most cosmopolitan trading fields in western Europe, and she was, of all the major Italian cities, the one with the strongest links north of the Alps.

These facts give a special piquancy to a passage in the Genoese annals relating to the year 1190 (the year before London's commune was recognized) quoted by Dr Waley as a characteristic sample of the way in which cities referred to the origin of their podestà. It was not only external pressures and the needs of diplomacy which made the single governor a necessity, but:

> Civil discords and hateful conspiracies and divisions had arisen in the city on account of the mutual envy of the many men who greatly wished to hold office as consuls of the commune. So the *sapientes* and councillors of the city met and decided that from the following year the consulate of the commune should come to an end and they almost all agreed that they should have a podestà.[2]

Be the link far or near, this must be accepted as an interesting commentary on the reasons why the City of London, from the same epoch, established as its leading officials two sheriffs who changed annually so

[1] See p. 271.
[2] Waley, p. 66, citing the *Annali Genovesi*, ed. L. T. Belgrano and C. Imperiale, Fonti per la Storia d'Italia, vol. ii, Genoa, 1901, p. 36: 'Unde contigit quod sapientes et consiliarii ciuitatis conuenerunt in unum, et de communi consilio statuerunt ut consulatus comunis in futuro anno cessaret, et de habenda potestate fuerunt omnes fere concordes.'

that all the leading citizens could have their turn, and a mayor who presided alone over their quarrels for twenty years.

There can be no suggestion here of direct imitation; we have inference, not evidence, on which to work, and the mayoralty and podestàship were not in their origin all that alike. The podestà normally held office for a year, and was rarely renewed; the first mayor of London held office for life. So far as the name and pattern of the office is concerned, we must follow Round and look to Rouen.[1] But it has been quite insufficiently appreciated that all these institutions grew up in a world used to taking long views, a world cosmopolitan in its culture; and that the mayoralty and podestàship were children together.

The first known podestà were established in Lombardy and Emilia *c.* 1130–50: it is not impossible that the institution is somewhat older, but no certain trace can be found.[2] The earliest known mayor appears briefly in Soissons in 1136; the next of which we have documentary witness are in Rouen and La Rochelle in the mid-1170s.[3] It cannot now be established that Soissons was the first town in the north, or Rouen and La Rochelle in the west of France, to have mayors, nor when these officers were first appointed or elected. This matters little. The title was ancient; its informal use was natural and may have been widespread. Soissons may or may not be close to its origin among the communes; Rouen and La Rochelle and the 1170s may be assumed, with rather more confidence, to be near in place and time to its first recognition in the territories ruled by Henry II. In the 1180s Soissons was joined by Châteaudun,[4] and at the turn of the century mayors appear in many north and central French towns. That is all that is certain.

It is indeed quite likely that the mayor of Rouen was the first Norman mayor, and first in the Angevin empire; and that his colleague at La Rochelle was appointed in direct imitation. For it is evident that the liberties of La Rochelle – themselves to become a model for Poitou – were already in the 1170s imitated from the *Établissements* of Rouen; and the date suggests that Henry's charter to Rouen of *c.* 1174–5, was, like that for La Rochelle, a reward for loyalty and aid in the great rebellion

---

[1] Round, *Archaeological Journal*, vol. 1, pp. 256–60; *CL*, p. 244; see below.

[2] Cf. above, p. 239. Franchini, pp. 293 ff., esp. pp. 318–20, 329 ff., and 152, 333 on Siena; G. Hanauer in *Mitteilungen des Instituts für österreich. Geschichtsforschung*, vol. xxiii (1902), pp. 376–426, esp. pp. 377 ff. Some of Hanauer's dates are too early; the status of some officials of the mid-twelfth century is very hard to determine.

[3] See above, pp. 237–8 and 237 n. 2.

[4] Ibid.

of 1173–4.[1] Rouen had received recognition of its commune (*communio*) from Henry's father, Duke Geoffrey, when he conquered Normandy and made a treaty with citizens *c*. 1144–5.[2] This was confirmed, implicitly at least, by the young Henry, as duke, in 1150–1.[3] In the mid-1170s (1173–8) a terse confirmation of the city's rights was granted; and as this approximately coincides with the first naming of Bartholomew Fergant as mayor of Rouen, it is quite likely that his establishment as head of the commune belongs to the same epoch.[4]

At first sight it must seem strange that the title 'mayor' spread in the territories of two of the strongest monarchies of the late twelfth century, those of Henry II and his sons and of Philip II, Augustus, King of France. This may, however, provide a clue to the title itself. Both kings may have been impressed by the need, so clearly shown in Frederick Barbarossa's adventures in Italy, for a clearly defined *power*, a stable authority, with whom to deal in handling the affairs of their cities. But any title such as rector or podestà must carry too much the implication of Italian freedom and faction. In the context of the twelfth-century *maior* had a pleasant ambiguity about it; for what could be more modest than to suggest that that the head of the commune of Rouen – or of the City of London – was a peasant patriarch, equivalent in standing, in the face of the king-duke, to the head man of a village?

This aspect of the title may well have commended itself to Henry and Philip. But Bartholomew Fergant and his colleagues no doubt saw other implications in the title mayor, and some among whom they moved had doubtless heard of the title Mayor of the Palace which Charlemagne's father had borne till he became king. Hence, in 1251, the head of the household of the English queen was given (for a brief space) the title *majorissa*, mayoress.[5]

---

[1] Cf. Giry, vol. i, chap. v, esp. pp. 63 ff., 67 ff.; Boussard, pp. 183 ff., esp. 188 n. 3 on the date of the *Établissements*; Round, *CL*, p. 251.

[2] As is made clear in Duke Henry's charter of 1150–1, *Regesta*, vol. iii, no. 729 – see editors' note.

[3] Ib.; also D-B, vol. i, no. 14*; Round, *CDF*, no. 109.

[4] D-B, vol. ii, no. 526; Round, *CDF*, no. 110. Bartholomew first occurs as mayor in *CDF*, nos 29, 34 (and see p. xxiv). No. 29 is dated *c*. 1170 × 81 in *Heads*, p. 164 n. 1. No. 34 is part of a series of charters, nos 32–4, seemingly of *c*. 1175 (1174 × 6 or 1179 × 80 are the outside limits, between the consecration of the Bishops of Winchester and Ely and the last departure of the young King Henry from England; cf. Eyton, index, s.v. England, King Henry II, Henry son of). (An Osbert Fergant occurs in London *c*. 1200: Gibbs, no. 251.)

[5] R. E. Latham, *Revised Medieval Latin Word-List*, London, 1965, p. 286.

As with the podestà, so with the mayor, it is an easy temptation to read later ideas back into the origin of the title. There is, however, sufficient evidence to show that in origin there was great variety in the status of the mayor in northern France. Some were mayors by election, some seem to have had an office for life which might become hereditary – or at least a mayor might hope to designate his successor; in some the mayor was securely a sole magistrate, in others one of a pair.[1] The varieties of election and appointment survived for many generations; only in England did the tradition soon become established that mayors should be annually elected. But this was not established until some years had passed after the death of Henry FitzAilwin in 1212.

London's reward for standing by the king in 1173–4 was two years of rule by *custodes* which meant, in effect, a sharp reduction in the farm.[2] It was short-lived, and the fact that Rouen might be supposed to have made more lasting gains in the mid 1170s may well have caused some jealousy. In 1190–1 the citizens of London were able to bargain and bribe once more: civil war and the king's long absence gave the government a strong incentive for accepting a reasonable settlement. The commune was allowed, the farm reduced; London, like Rouen, received a mayor.

THE FIRST MAYOR OF LONDON

Since Round's penetrating studies of these events, it has been doubted if Henry FitzAilwin was appointed or elected Mayor before 1193.[3] For Round showed that even after the granting of the commune, he appears in documents without the title mayor. He thus deduced that the statement of the late-thirteenth-century alderman and chronicler, Arnald FitzThedmar, that Henry FitzAilwin had been elected at or soon after the accession of Richard I in 1189–90, must be wrong.[4] The issue has never been entirely settled, and some scepticism has occasionally been observed as to Round's argument; for ourselves, we were first distinctly made aware of the difficulty of accepting it by Miss Susan Reynolds some years ago.[5] Although FitzThedmar's statement cannot be entirely ac-

[1] See references on p. 237–8 n.
[2] See p. 221.
[3] But see Reynolds, 'Rulers of London', pp. 348–9.
[4] *LAL*, p. 1.
[5] See Reynolds, loc. cit., for criticism of Round's dating of the early history of the commune.

cepted, and there are errors in this section of the book, his details on the dates of mayors and sheriffs are for the most part exceedingly reliable. Moreover, the absence of the title in documents of the early 1190s may not be so remarkable as it appears at first sight. It may well be that Henry FitzAilwin's position was informal at first; and it is most unlikely that it was confirmed either by the regents or the king.[1] So novel a title can hardly have carried the prestige or official connotation we are inclined to attribute to it as soon as it appeared. As late as the 1120s, even so long-established and prestigious a title as 'earl' could be omitted from royal writs;[2] under these circumstances the omission of 'mayor' in the 1190s can hardly be regarded as decisive evidence. What does seem clear is that the events of Richard's imprisonment and the help that Henry FitzAilwin gave to the government in collecting money for his ransom, made the open use of the title safe, respectable and generally accepted.[3]

For nearly twenty years, through the riots of the mid-1190s and the troubled relations of the City and King John, down to 1212,[4] when he died, the City of London enjoyed the presidency of Henry FitzAilwin. He must have been a remarkable man; and it is sad that we know very little of him as a person, or indeed of his family history. He has been provided by various scholars with a genealogy tracing his ancestry back to the Conquest; he has been thought to be descended from English thegns or citizens or both. But in truth his father's name, Ailwin or Æthelwine, was exceedingly common in English-speaking London, and he cannot be certainly identified.[5]

The name is English; that is beyond doubt. We may therefore assume that Henry's place in the London oligarchy was in part due to his roots

---

[1] See pp. 45–7.

[2] *Early Yorks. Charters*, vol. viii, ed. C. T. Clay, Yorks. Archaeol. Soc. Record Series, 1949, pp. 46–7.

[3] See pp. 45 ff. It spread rapidly to other English towns: see the list of a dozen in Tait, p. 291 n. 4, starting with Winchester (by 1200) and working through Exeter (by 1205), Lincoln (by 1206), to Barnstaple, Oxford, Lynn, York, Northampton, Beverley, Bristol, Grimsby, and Newcastle-upon-Tyne – the last by 1216.

[4] *LAL*, pp. 1, 3; cf. Reynolds, 'Rulers of London', p. 349 and n. 62.

[5] See ibid. for Ailwin son of Leofstan, the most promising candidate – there is no doubt that Henry is to be identified with Henry, son of Ailwin, son of Leofstan who fined for land, with his brother Alan, in *PR 11 Henry II*, p. 18 – *13 Henry II*, p. 154 (Essex and Herts.), and who occurs as mayor in Public Record Office, E40/2507 (*Cat. of Ancient Deeds*, vol. ii, p. 88). Cf. *Cart. Aldgate*, no. 1024, and esp. Corporation of London, Bridge House Deeds F35, B95, with seal of Henry, son of Ailwin, son of Leofstan.

in the old and established population of the City; and it is reasonable to suppose that his standing both as citizen and local landowner was hereditary. It has been plausibly suggested that Ailwin's father was Leofstan the 'doomsman', reeve or sheriff in the reign of Henry I.[1] He lived near London Stone and held land in Hertfordshire, Kent and Surrey;[2] the combination suggests a man of similar status to Gervase of Cornhill, though Henry never rose high in the royal service. He was a Londoner, acceptable to the government, of assured position among his fellow citizens. Of his wife, we know only that her name was Margaret, and of his children, not much more than that four sons were called Peter, Alan, Thomas and Richard.[3] Peter indeed married into the gentry: his wife Isabel, daughter of Bartholomew de Chennay, was buried at Bermondsey Priory to which Peter himself was a benefactor.[4] Clearly the next generation were men of substance like Henry, though none succeeded to his standing in the City. It was his friend and close associate Roger FitzAlan, who succeeded as mayor, though only briefly (1212–14).[5] The length of Henry's reign, and his succession by a close colleague, suggests a very strong hold on the reins of power and the affection of his fellow oligarchs. Perhaps there was substance in the famous jibe attributed to a dissident citizen that the mayor was a quasi-regal figure in the City – 'may the Londoners never have any king but the mayor'.[6]

What is abundantly clear is that Henry must have been well established as a figure of the City patriciate before the 1190s, and that he must have been conspicuous for diplomatic skill to have survived so long in so tricky an office. He was an alderman at least by 1168, and so an elder statesman by 1191,[7] though probably not an old man, since he lived and ruled till 1212.

[1] Reynolds, ibid., and p. 354 n. 3.

[2] *LAL*, p. 1; PR, *ut sup*.

[3] Page, p. 251; *LAL*, introd., pp. ii ff., esp. vi ff.

[4] Ibid. p. vi.

[5] *LAL*, pp. 3–4; see Appendix III. He has been supposed a nephew of Henry, but the evidence consists solely in the coincidence of the not uncommon name Alan (for: Page, pp. 251–2; Williams, p. 5; against: Reynolds, p. 349 and n. 63). It could be added that the names Peter, Alan and Richard occur in both families (cf. Page, pp. 251–2). But the evidence of relationship is stubbornly circumstantial.

[6] '. . . dixit: "quecumque eat uel ueniat, quod nunquam habeant Lond' alium regem quam Majorem Lond' "' (*Rotuli Curiae Regis*, vol. i, pp. 69 f., 95, cf. pp. xi ff.).

[7] Reynolds, 'Rulers of London', p. 349.

It is also clear that he was an oligarch. It is highly probable that his rule as mayor witnessed the coming of age of the Court of Aldermen, though it would be anachronistic to insist on any such title so early as this.[1] The rioters and rebels of the mid-1190s were expressing disappointment that the new commune, inaugurated with great enthusiasm, and heralded no doubt by men of very various opinions as the dawn of a new era of independence and grandeur, had not in any conspicuous way benefited the poorer sections of the community.[2] For reign by sheriffs under royal control the City had exchanged a tight oligarchy of the established citizens. The arrangements were very different; but the men much the same. Liberty in the Middle Ages often meant privilege, and in this case it must so have appeared to those outside the counsels of the échevins and good men. Indeed, the late twelfth century was evidently a period when the rights of entry to citizenship, and the privileges of various classes of citizen, were undergoing new scrutiny, and many ordinary folk, and many not so ordinary, presumably lost status and privilege in the process.[3] One can well understand how it could be that the decade of the commune was also the most riotous recorded in the twelfth century in London. This makes Henry FitzAilwin's long survival the more impressive, and underlines the interest of the constitutional experiments over which he presided.

COURTS AND COUNCILS

It may well be that 'presided' is not quite the right word, for there is a deep and ineradicable mystery attaching to these constitutional experiments. Some kind of council of leading men had very probably guided the affairs of the City for generations before the advent of Henry Fitz-Ailwin. In 1087–8 the Bishop of Durham claimed to have checked any tendency to rebellion in the City by bringing 'the twelve better citizens of the City' to the king – 'meliores . . . xii . . . cives', says the text;[4] but as there is no definite article in Latin we cannot be absolutely certain that these were an established twelve, and not just a chance collection of leading men. In the course of the early twelfth century, at latest, the

[1] Reynolds, p. 350; Tait, pp. 265 ff.
[2] See pp. 48–9.
[3] See pp. 252–3.
[4] Symeon of Durham, *Opera omnia*, ed. T. Arnold, Rolls Series, London, 1882–5, vol. i, p. 189; cf. Tait, pp. 265–6.

growing importance of civic affairs must have involved meetings of aldermen from time to time. At least they must have met regularly at the Court of Husting, the central formal law court and meeting place of the City fathers.

The most ancient court of the City was presumably the folkmoot, the general gathering of all the folk of London, which was a formal gathering summoned by the ringing of the bell at St Paul's three times a year; twelfth- or thirteenth-century tradition believed indeed (perhaps rightly) that the folkmoot was older than St Paul's, attributing it at latest to the time of King Arthur.[1] By the early thirteenth century it was held three times a year only, at Michaelmas to acknowledge the new sheriff or sheriffs; at Christmas to ensure that the keeping of the wards, that is to say the police duties of the city, were catered for; and at Midsummer to remind the citizens of the fire precautions.[2] But long before this, serious business had been transmitted to a smaller, more frequent assembly, which bore the name of the Husting.[3] This was the shire court of London, as the wardmotes were to become its hundred courts. The name of the Husting is its most remarkable feature, for it is a Viking word, representing the 'house thing', the basic assembly of the Scandinavian world. Other evidence of Viking influence in London is mainly of the eleventh century: the age of St Olaf and of his cult; and of the Ringerike tombstone found in St Paul's churchyard (see Plate 30); the age of Cnut and his immediate successors.[4] But the Husting is evidently much older than that, for in a document of the second half of the tenth century otherwise unconnected with the City there is reference to two cups of silver weighing twelve marks, 'by the weight of the husting of London'.[5] It very much looks, as Stenton observed, as if the Danes who were settled in London in Alfred's time were its founders; and if so the Hustings is a monument not only to Scandinavian influence in the early centuries of London's formation as a city, but also to the epoch in which the formation of the medieval city really began.[6]

[1] Stenton, p. 10; Liebermann, vol. i, p. 655 (the *Leges Edwardi Confessoris*, treating of the folkmoot as a national moot).

[2] Bateson, p. 502, cf. Stenton, pp. 10–11.

[3] Stenton, pp. 11–12.

[4] See pp. 21 ff., 261 ff.

[5] Stenton, p. 11 and n. 3 defends the early date of the reference, which is not, however, certain. It next occurs in a probably authentic document of 1032 (ibid.; see Sawyer, no. 1465 for references).

[6] See chap. 3.

In the charter attributed to Henry 1, which certainly reflects London custom of the second quarter of the twelfth century, the king is made to grant that the Husting be held every Monday.[1] It is evident that it already had a substantial quantity of business to transact; the disputes, the lawsuits, and the royal instructions and writs which came before every shire court were presumably its business, and also the multifarious problems of the largest commercial centre in the kingdom. An important measure of length settled, it would seem, about 1100 was the foot of Canon Algar son of Deorman at the base of a column in St Paul's.[2] The weights in which precious metals of the kingdom were measured had needed to be fixed in a more refined and commonly accepted way long before, and it is evident that the Husting in early days, as in later, had been the place where this happened.

Before the advent of the mayor it was no doubt the business of one of the sheriffs or the justice to preside at the Husting; and even before 1190 there are quite a number of surviving references to cases settled there or transactions witnessed there. From the accession of Henry FitzAilwin it is presumed that the mayor presided. Of this in early days, there is little precise evidence; but already in the 1190s, there are documents witnessed by the mayor in the Husting,[3] and by the early thirteenth century it was coming to be the common practice for the mayor and the sheriffs and a group of leading citizens to witness deeds with a common form and a formality which suggests that this was done at meetings of the Husting; it is evident that the mayor was presiding with the sheriffs to his hand.[4] All the circumstances make clear that from the early years of Richard I, the sheriffs had assumed a position of authority and dignity much below their standing in the reign of Henry II. Later on the regular meetings of the Husting were found insufficient to cope with the volume of business in the central city courts. Its business steadily increased owing

[1] See p. 209.

[2] See P. Grierson, *English linear measures: an essay in origins*, Stenton Lecture, Reading, 1972, pp. 17–18; J. G. Nichols in the *Gentlemen's Magazine*, New Series, vol. xxxviii, 1852, pt. 2, pp. 276–7; Le Neve, p. 57 (we are indebted to Dr Greenway for advice on the identity of Algar).

[3] See e.g. Gibbs, no. 110 (1193–4, though it is not entirely clear that the mayor was witness at the Husting).

[4] See e.g. *Cart. Colchester*, vol. ii, pp. 297–8 (1193–4); British Mus. Harl. MS 4015, ff. 83v–4 (1196–7), and 78 (1200–1); Westminster Abbey Domesday Cart., f. 491r–v (1201–2); etc. – they become relatively more numerous in Henry's later years.

(it seems) to a vast increase in litigation, and it was doubtless partly for this reason that actions concerning foreign merchants, and some other cases, were in due course transferred to the mayor's court.[1]

The mayor's court was in existence by 1220, and may well have grown up during the long reign of Henry FitzAilwin.[2] In due course the mayor's court came to replace the Husting as the normal place for legal proceedings; the Husting, like the shire court elsewhere, gradually and gracefully subsided, as its jurisdiction was eroded on the one hand by the newly developing royal courts, on the other hand by a group of lesser courts which eventually replaced it. The charter of Henry I had specifically stated that crown pleas were to be heard before the citizens' justice alone; and whatever the origin of that remarkable document we have no evidence that its terms were breached for a while even after the local justices disappeared in the reign of Henry II. The story of London's relations with the royal justices must wait for another volume, for we have little evidence on the matter before 1221.[3] Then and in 1226 commissions were issued to justices to hold eyres for crown pleas in the Tower; and the records of the next eyre, that of 1244, actually survive to provide us with much vital information about London's early customs and topography, and that side of its social life which criminal records are inclined to reveal.[4] For the legal historian the eyre of 1244 and the eyre of 1321 are the foundation for any study of London's share in the history of law.[5] What goes before is but fragments, fascinating and tantalizing. Nor is it until the late thirteenth and fourteenth centuries, that we have any clear notion of how the structure of law or courts worked. Wardmotes there must have been in the twelfth century, presumably regulating under the alderman's eye the police and tax arrangements of the ward; they may go back even to the eleventh century.

We must avoid trying to read more than necessary, however, of the conditions of the thirteenth and fourteenth centuries back into the twelfth,

[1] See A. H. Thomas's introds to *Early Mayor's Court Rolls*, pp. xiii-xlv, and *Cal. Plea and Memoranda Rolls, 1364-81*.

[2] On its early history, see Cam, *Eyre*, vol. i, p. lv; ib. pp. li ff. on the courts in general.

[3] See *Eyre*, pp. ix ff.; Cam, *Eyre*, vol. i, pp. lx ff. and *passim*.

[4] Well over one-third of the entries in *Eyre* deal with homicide, other crimes apart, so that we cannot look to it for a balanced picture of social life; but its information is exceedingly valuable, and helps to balance the rosy view of FitzStephen in his description.

[5] *Eyre*; and Cam, *Eyre*, esp. vol. i, introd.

since it is clear that the age of Henry FitzAilwin saw many experiments and innovations. It is in this light that we should view the various references to elections of twenty-four of twenty-five councillors which meet us in the early 1200s.[1] They may have been a check on the existing oligarchical arrangements or a diplomatic way of giving them respectability. In all probability there was an element of both. For it seems that Henry FitzAilwin's achievement – or at least the achievement of his mayoralty – was to preserve traditional oligarchic government through an epoch of threatened revolution and change. One great change he himself represented: the establishment of the mayor. But beside him on all important occasions sat the sheriffs, bearing an ancient title and preserving traditional forms of administration, members themselves of families well entrenched in the citizen throng. It is very striking indeed that this was the age in which the ancient traditions and customs of London were codified: that active legal antiquarians were behind the spurious collections of the laws of Edward the Confessor and William the Conqueror which emanated from London in the second half of the twelfth century, and the genuine collections of customs enshrined in the famous law-book now divided between the British Museum and the John Rylands Library in Manchester.[2]

MAYOR AND CITIZENS

It was also the age which saw, for the first time, an attempt to define the qualifications for a man to call himself a citizen of London. This is a very remarkable fact. Hitherto the men of London and the citizens had received privileges without any specification as to who they were.[3] The same is true of every city and town in Europe of which we have contemporary information: the rights of citizens were being restricted in the late

[1] Specific references to such elections occur in 1200–1 (25: *LAL*, p. 2: 'Hoc anno fuerunt xxv. electi de discretioribus Civitatis, et jurati pro consulendo Civitatem una cum Maiore') and 1206 (24: Page, p. 282–3; 'to reform abuses which had been committed by default of those *qui hucusque fuerunt superiores*' – thus summary, with comment on these experiments, in Reynolds, 'Rulers of London', p. 350; cf. also Tait, chap. x, esp. pp. 266–70). It is possible that a similar group lie behind the phrases 'skivini' and 'probi homines' of *c*. 1193, although it is possible, even likely, that the former were simply the aldermen.

[2] See p. 51.

[3] See esp. A. H. Thomas in *Calendar of Early Mayor's Court Rolls . . . 1298–1307*, pp. xiii ff.

twelfth and early thirteenth centuries by a variety of definitions which
excluded many who could easily have claimed them in an earlier generation.[1] To put it another way, as the privileges of citizen bodies become
more clearly defined, as their grouping together in the communal bond
becomes more permanent, so there is an understandable urge to determine with precision to whom the privileges belong. But to pursue this
argument to the point of justifying all the work of definition which went
on would be special pleading. There can be little doubt that the cities of
the twelfth century were freer in the use of their privileges than those of
the thirteenth; that in the few political rights which citizens had in most
cities and the very numerous commercial opportunities, there was much
less restriction in 1150 than in 1250 or 1300. All this is intelligible, but it
also helps to explain why many citizens and would-be citizens felt restive
under the rule of Henry FitzAilwin.

Supposing, at the end of this enquiry, we should ask whether Henry
FitzAilwin was first and foremost the servant of the City or of the king,
whether he was elected by the citizens or appointed by the king, whether
he imagined himself to be mayor by election or hereditary office-holder,
we might hope to look for an answer in three directions. First, we should
expect analogies from other towns in England and on the Continent to
help. It is just these questions, however, on which analogies fail us, for
they point to all the possibilities. A mayor at the turn of the twelfth and
thirteenth centuries could be elective or hereditary, could be king's man
or citizens' man.[2] Nor are the political circumstances much more helpful,
for the moment of his first election or appointment is precisely the most
uncertain fact in his career as mayor. We may be sure that it bore some
relation to the recognition of the commune in 1191, and we may be sure
that it was acceptable to both Richard and John, for without royal favour
he could hardly have survived. We may be tolerably sure too that he was
acceptable to that part of the oligarchy which he represented; he seems
to have been exceptionally secure in the support of his colleagues. All the
indications are that his rule was a golden age for the oligarchs, much less
congenial to the rank and file. Thus the political circumstances strongly
suggest that he was both the king's man and the citizens'; and to this

[1] See e.g. Waley, pp. 102 ff.
[2] See Giry, vol. i, pp. 78, 143; vol. ii, pp. 4 ff.; A. Luchaire, *Les Communes françaises*
(edn of Paris, 1911), pp. 154 ff. – for the varieties of status and appointment or election
in France established in or before the early thirteenth century.

extent – though not himself an ex-sheriff – in the tradition of the men who had served as sheriffs in the reign of Henry II.

Our third type of evidence is the witness lists in which Mayor Henry's name appears, and these are perhaps the most interesting and revealing. Long ago, William Page observed how often Henry was accompanied by Roger FitzAlan, who ultimately succeeded him, and he suggested that Roger was Henry's nephew.[1] We have seen how slender is the evidence for relationship, but a close association between the two men does seem probable. Out of slightly over 115 charters which we have noticed in which Henry witnesses as mayor,[2] nearly seventy also contain the name of Roger FitzAlan (*c.* 69); the next most frequent witnesses are Thomas of Haverhill and his father William (*c.* 56 and 41) and Alan FitzPeter (*c.* 53). Most of the names which occur very commonly were of men who were at one time or another sheriffs; exceptions are the brothers William and Henry, sons of Reiner (*c.* 25 and 20). The conditions which led to their presence in these witness lists are very imperfectly known; but the figures are suggestive, or at least teasing. Roger FitzAlan's score is far and away the highest, whereas most of his successors as mayor had not been frequent witnesses to his charters. No doubt one or two of them were younger men; but there is an intriguing contrast between the occurrences, on the one hand, of Serlo the mercer, the mayor of Runnymede, who held office in 1214–15 and 1218–22 (4), James the Alderman (4), and Solomon of Basing (1), mayors in 1217–18, and, on the other hand, of William Hardel, who replaced Serlo for a time after Runnymede, who had witnessed eight documents of Henry's mayoralty.

Other aspects of these charters deserve our attention. There is, for instance, a group securely dated before Michaelmas 1196, and thus early in Henry's reign, in which Roger son of Reinfred appears in the mayor's company.[3] In 1196 Roger died, and no special pattern attached to the

---

[1] Page, pp. 251–2; see above, p. 242 (and esp. Reynolds, 'Rulers of London', p. 349, who detected the slender nature of the evidence).

[2] This is based on a count taken from our notes: i.e. from printed sources, and from documents in the Public Record Office, British Museum, Guildhall Records Office, St Bartholomew's and Westminster Abbey. G.K. is preparing an article on the documents of Henry FitzAilwin's mayoralty.

[3] *Cart. Clerkenwell*, nos 56, 62–3, 82, 109 (1193–6), 238–40 (1194). The number of documents is not so impressive as it seems, for the first five all deal with the gifts of Henry Foliot and his family, the last three with a single transaction; and all come from a single archive. No. 238 (13 March 1194) was printed by Round (*Home Counties Mag.*, vol. i, pp. 63–4) as the first securely dated document witnessed by Henry as

next five years or so. In later years it becomes increasingly common for the sheriffs to witness immediately after the mayor, and this long continued to be the norm. But in one charter of 1211–12 in the *Cartulary of St Mary's Clerkenwell*, the editor observed that Roger FitzAlan witnessed between the mayor and the sheriffs.[1]

These facts suggest two reflections as to Henry FitzAilwin's rule. First of all, Roger, son of Reinfred was an important royal justice, a man with a considerable stake in and near the City, and the brother of Walter of Coutances, Archbishop of Rouen.[2] In spite of his name, Walter was a Cornishman; but he had close links in Coutances, and he and his brother made their way by faithful service to Henry II, so that Walter rose to be head of the royal chancery, Bishop of Lincoln and Archbishop of Rouen (1184–1207), Roger, who was a layman, to be a baron and a leading royal justice. When Richard I set off on crusade in 1189–90, he left William de Longchamp, Bishop of Ely, chancellor and papal legate, in control.[3] But his administration was unpopular, and he failed to keep Richard's brother John in check. When news of the intrigues and manoeuvres, and threat of civil war, filtered through to Richard, he sent Walter of Coutances from Sicily to be royal justiciar, and with secret instructions to keep peace and a fair balance between chancellor and prince, but to sack the chancellor if his position was untenable. Walter proceeded to carry out these instructions, and to remove the chancellor, with remarkable adroitness. He subsequently failed in his turn to keep John in check, and Richard (now a prisoner in the Emperor's keeping) sent Hubert Walter to replace him. Hubert Walter became archbishop and justiciar, subsequently legate and chancellor, and undoubtedly proved the most successful administrator of the age. But in the crucial years 1191–3, and for a time after Hubert's arrival in 1193, Walter of Coutances played a role which was both loyal and adroit, if not at all points successful. In all this Roger, son of Reinfred was his able supporter; and Roger remained a leading

mayor, and these references remain in sum suggestive of a link in the early years of his period of office.

[1] *Cart. Clerkenwell*, no. 252. But there are other cases (e.g. Gibbs, no. 106) in which the sheriffs take a still lower place.

[2] On Walter, see p. 273 and reference; *DNB*, s.v. Coutances; for Roger's death, *Cart. Clerkenwell*, no. 104 n.; *Recueil des Historiens des Gaules et de la France*, vol. xxiii, p. 359 n. 15 (d. 11 February), which establishes his relationship to Walter; cf. ib. pp. 352, 362–3, 369 for the family.

[3] The fullest accounts of these events are still Stubbs, introd. to Howden, vol. iii, and Round, *CL*, chap. x.

royal justice until his death in 1196. Meanwhile, Henry FitzAilwin made his debut in the spring of 1193 as one of the men entrusted by Hubert Walter with handling the money for King Richard's ransom. His colleagues were the Bishop of London, who was also royal treasurer, and two barons known to have had no love for John.[1] Henry FitzAilwin appears here as a king's man, but also as the leading figure in the City community; a man to be trusted to handle coin in large quantities. His association with Roger, son of Reinfred suggests the further possibility that favour and trust between him and Walter of Coutances, 'The Pilate of Rouen' as his enemies called him, lay behind his rise to power in the City. The commune was recognized in October 1191 at the moment that Walter of Coutances was revealing to the sharp-eyed that the government lay in his hands – not in Longchamp's and not in John's. It is reasonably certain that Henry FitzAilwin took his title in the knowledge that Rouen had a mayor; and it may well be that Henry secured the mayoralty and held it fast in his early years by association with the Archbishop of Rouen and his powerful brother.

At the other end of his career as mayor, Dr Hassall suggested that Henry's successor may have witnessed after the mayor and before the sheriffs in 1211–12 for some reason connected with his succession. A single witness list must not be the basis for too much conjecture;[2] but it is possible from their long and close association that Roger was Henry's chosen successor. Henry may well have supposed himself to have founded a stable dynasty. If so, he was wrong, for Roger FitzAlan held office for only two years. The events which followed are quite obscure. We may assume that the rise and fall of mayors in the next decade depended on the favour both of the ruling oligarchs and the king or royal government, commonly of both; but also that the principle of election quickly won.[3] In the autumn of 1214 Serlo the mercer was elected mayor, and in 1215, after the searing experience of resistance and rebellion, after London had supported and aided its standard-bearer, Robert FitzWalter, 'Marshal of the Army of God and Holy Church', to a peaceful victory on the field of Runnymede, William Hardel succeeded.[4] But the victory of 1215 was

---

[1] Howden, vol. iii, p. 212.

[2] And see p. 255 n. 1.

[3] It seems likely that the principle of annual election had been established by 1215 (cf. Reynolds, 'Rulers of London', p. 349; see p. 375); there may even have been formal elections in Henry FitzAilwin's time, but there is no evidence of this.

[4] See pp. 55–6, and Appendix III; *LAL*, pp. 4–5.

followed by the civil war of 1216 and by John's death, and under circumstances which we cannot now reconstruct, James the Alderman held
office from Easter to Trinity 1217. In May 1217 Solomon of Basing took
the reins, and in October Serlo the mercer came back into the mayoral
office. The City fathers seem to have grown weary of rapid change and
uncertain direction, and for five years Serlo remained mayor, to be followed
by Richard Reiner, a leading patrician of at least the third generation,
mayor for another five years. For some time to come terms of four, five
and seven years became the norm; but no one since Henry FitzAilwin
has held the mayoralty for life.

10

Trade and Crafts

LONDON'S TRADE: INTRODUCTION – THE FUR TRADE

'THE ARAB proffers gold, the Sabaean spice and incense; arms the Scythian. Thy rich soil, O Babylon, gives oil from the fertile palm trees, and the Nile precious stones; the Chinese send garments of purple silk, the French their wines; the Norse and Russians vair, gris and sable.' Thus, or more or less thus, for the Latin doggerel is untranslatable, William FitzStephen sang the trade of London, 'from every people which is under Heaven'.[1] We know that the verses were meant to be impressionistic, and that the impression was not meant to be too deeply soiled by the smell of the market. We can doubt now how much geography he really knew, for it was a cliche that gold came from Arabia, as Guy of Amiens had said when describing the crown with which William the Conqueror was crowned in 1066. 'Arabia provided gold, Nilus gems from the river; Greece inspired a smith skilled in the art as he who . . . created Solomon's wondrous and befitting diadem' – and the author goes on to list the jewels of the crown.[2] Nor can we tell whether he knew where China was (however vaguely), or supposed, with Lucan, that it lay at the source of the Nile, so that the silks (he may have supposed) came down that river, along with the gems, to Cairo, or Babylon as it was called in the medieval west, there to join the olive-oil. But when all allowance has been made for rhetoric, exaggeration and absurdity, it is not a bad index of the luxury trade of London in the mid-twelfth century. He knew at least that the chief source of gold was Islam, that spices, silks and precious stones – the rarer of them – came via Islam,[3] that olive-oil came from the Medi-

---

[1] *MB*, vol. iii, p. 7.
[2] *Carmen*, p. 49.
[3] Cf. (in general) *Cambridge Economic History*, vol. ii, esp. p. 281 (R. S. Lopez).

terranean. They were not carried by English merchants and perhaps men like FitzStephen knew little of their true origin. With wine it was a different story, and with furs as well. 'French wine' meant wines of the Paris region, of Poitou, and of Bordeaux, a part, but a vital part of the wine trade into England.[1] That belongs to the last phase of our story, the commercial revolution of the twelfth century. The furs go back into the mists of time.

The history of the fur trade is a fascinating illustration of the interplay between sense and fashion.[2] In cold climates fur wraps and coats or cloaks are exceedingly practical; yet the fur trade has long been a luxury trade, with the most obscure and abstruse commanding the highest prices. Many of the furs most prized in the later Middle Ages came from the far north, and FitzStephen associated them with two countries on the old Viking trade routes, Russia and Norway. No doubt in the early centuries of this book Viking traders, and Slav and Viking trappers, accounted for many of the furs sold on the London market. But such indications as we have as to the specialized luxury fur trade of the twelfth century suggest that it reflected new-fangled fashions and the rising living standards characteristic of that age.

The flow of comment from ascetic churchmen, especially from those who came from overseas, enables us in a measure to trace the growth of these fashions. In 1127 an English church council at Westminster passed sumptuary legislation against the excesses of abbesses and nuns: they were not to wear garments more precious than those of lambs' wool or of black cat's fur. But when, in 1138, the austere French Cluniac monk Alberic, recently consecrated Cardinal Bishop of Ostia and sent to England as papal legate, presided over another similar council at Westminster, he and the English bishops found it necessary to be much more specific. 'By papal authority we forbid that nuns wear furs of vair, gris, sable, marten, ermine or beaver, put on gold rings, or twist or make up their hair. Any found to have broken the decree will be excommunicated.'[3] Most of the evidence as to the nature of these furs and their origin is later

---

[1] See pp. 265-6.

[2] What follows is mainly based on E. M. Veale, *The English Fur Trade in the Later Middle Ages*, Oxford, 1966, to which we are much indebted.

[3] Council of Westminster, 1127, c. 11; Council of Westminster, 1138, c. 15 (new edn by M. Brett and C. N. L. Brooke in *Councils and Synods*, vol. i, forthcoming; see meanwhile D. Wilkins, *Concilia Magnae Britanniae . . .*, vol. i, London, 1737, pp. 410-11, 413-16).

than 1138; yet the words used, and reasonable deduction from the subsequent history of the fur trade, can tell us much about the world of fashion of this age. The beaver is reckoned to have been common throughout western Europe in the later Middle Ages, and fur-bearing animals such as stoats and squirrels were obviously well known in England. Yet the precise names used in this list suggest that some of the more recondite and expensive types of fur which are recorded in the thirteenth and fourteenth centuries were already well established and in fashion. Then the products of the weasel family were perhaps the most admired of all, the sable, the rich brown or black-skinned marten of the far north of Europe, and the ermine, made from the winter fur of pure white of the northern stoat. 'Richard I was willing to pay as much as £13 for a fur of ermine and four sable skins, £12 to have two ermine linings sent overseas to him from England' – from London indeed – 'and treasured squirrel skins sufficiently to see that those taken from his enemies were reserved for his use'.[1] The other furs apart from the beaver in the list drawn up at Westminster in December 1138, as the English nuns, in London and elsewhere, prepared to keep themselves warm at Christmastide, were from the red squirrel: the vair or variegated fur of alternate grey and white, and the gris, or grey fur, both derived from the winter coat of the squirrel in the far north of Europe, precisely as FitzStephen says, in Scandinavia and Russia.[2] The use of these words indicates that discrimination between different shades of squirrel skin, and preference of those from furthest away, was already well understood by 1138. But it is doubtful if it had been long established in this precise form. All these words, except beaver, are derived from French, or from Latin words which seem likely to have been coined in a French-speaking milieu. Vair and gris tell their own story. 'Ermine' is of an etymology wholly obscure, not made easier by the fact that in the eleventh century the word seems to have shifted from one animal to another. Sable is the most interesting. It is one of the few words, like slave, which Old Slavonic has given to all the languages of western Europe. Though definitely Slav in origin, it may come to the west via Magyar; and, unlike slave, it apparently did not come to England before the Norman Conquest.[3] It has been suggested that the love of costly furs spread from the royal court, and was due to the queens

---

[1] Veale, p. 17.

[2] Veale, pp. 30, 223 ff., 228, and index, s.v. furs.

[3] See *Oxford English Dict.*, s.v. ermine, gris, sable, vair; Bosworth, Supplement, p. 525, Enlarged Addenda, p. 40.

who came from Aquitaine and Provence. No doubt they played their part in the story of English fashion; but the devotion to northern marten and squirrel skins is evidently earlier than the arrival of the first Queen Eleanor in 1154. One is tempted to associate it rather with St Margaret, Queen of Scotland, the old English princess brought up in Hungary, noted for her fondness for luxurious dress as well as for all works of piety, or her daughter, Henry I's Queen Matilda, who inherited her mother's piety and may well have inherited her mother's devotion to fashion.[1] In any event, the knowledge of these animals and the colour of their fur came not from English or Norman queens but from Russian and Norse trappers, and Viking traders.

The furs from Norway and Russia remind us of the beginning of our story, of the great trade routes and the traders of the ninth, tenth and eleventh centuries; the French wine of its end, of the change of direction in English trade in the twelfth century. But the fur trade and the wine trade were not in origin or essence luxury trades. Both could have been provided from English skins and vineyards, and the nuns ought to have worn 'pilches' (*pellicia*), ordinary skins of sheep or goats, to keep out the winter cold.[2] None the less the profusion of animals with a charming fur and of timber and of slaves in the areas in which the Vikings operated as traders and pirates made these the main victims of their traffic – for piracy and trade were partners in their callings, and have always been so where slaves and wild animals were the chief commodities of commerce. And these facts also show that it is an error to draw too sharp a distinction between trade in 'luxuries' and trade in the necessities of life.

OVERSEAS TRADE: THE VIKINGS

In a subject so central to London's history, and yet so obscure, a clear definition of the lines of enquiry is especially needed. Let us fashion a tool, then refine it if we can. Let us say at the outset that from the seventh to the ninth century England and London lay in the Frisian sphere of trade, from the ninth to the eleventh in the Viking commercial world, in the eleventh and twelfth and in the German, Flemish and French – pre-

---

[1] See the Life of St Margaret in *Acta Sanctorum Bollandiana*, June, vol. ii (edn of 1867), p. 326; see p. 316 for a contemporary account of Matilda's dislike of the nun's veil.

[2] Cf. texts cited above, p. 259 n. 3; Orderic Vitalis, ed. M. Chibnall, vol. iv, OMT, 1973, p. 324 and n.

dominantly Flemish and French, owing to the Norman Conquest and the Angevin inheritance and Aquitanian marriage of Henry II – and that Italy was looming on the horizon when our book closes.

The age when Friesland, where Holland and Germany now meet, and Frisian merchants provided the pivot of north European trade[1] is the most obscure. Bede tells of a Northumbrian warrior sold as a slave in 679 to a Frisian in London who carried him off to the Continent; and we may conjecture that the Frisians had played their part in transporting the English slaves whom Gregory the Great met in the market at Rome nearly a century earlier.[2] In the eighth century there is a little evidence of Frisians engaged in England as in other western European countries in trade in cloth, slaves and luxury goods, though the tiny trickle of surviving documents literally interpreted might suggest that there were as many English traders in the Frankish empire, especially in the north of what we call France, as Frisians in England; and also that after 679 there is very little evidence of them in London.[3] Yet we have every reason to suppose that among the many nations who came there the merchants of Quentavic (near Étaples) and Duurstede (near Utrecht), well placed for trading into England by the Thames, were represented.

Gold and silver and coins and most kinds of goods moved, from hand to hand and from country to country by a variety of different methods in the Dark Ages. Gift exchange, normal among primitive peoples, was developed on a grandiose scale by all the barbarian peoples who had access to the wealth of the Roman empire; and this tradition was preserved by the Vikings, the last heirs to many barbarian traditions. Wealth of all kinds came too to professional soldiers who hired themselves out as mercenaries, whether in the armies of Rome in the fourth, fifth or sixth centuries, or in the armies of Europe and Byzantium later on. Trade could carry goods long distances, for the Jewish merchants of the eighth and ninth centuries travelled from China to many parts of western Europe; and the Vikings in their turn plied between Russia, the Byzantine empire, the frontiers of Islam, western Europe, Greenland and North America.[4] Finally, goods passed by loot and piracy.

[1] For what follows, see W. Levison, *England and the Continent in the Eighth Century*, Oxford, 1946, pp. 5 ff. On Duurstede and Quentavic, see Ennen, esp. pp. 56 ff.; Levison, loc. cit.

[2] Bede, *Hist. Eccl.*, bk iv, c. 22; bk ii, c. 1 (ed. B. Colgrave and R. A. B. Mynors, OMT, 1969, pp. 400–5, 132–5; cf. Levison, p. 8 and n. 4).

[3] See Levison, loc. cit.; and for the later slave trade, below, p. 264.

[4] On the Jewish merchants, see p. 224 and n. 2.

It has been earnestly debated by economic historians which of these methods accounts for the movement which took place, especially in the Viking world.[1] No one doubts that the Vikings began with plunder and piracy and ended as traders. The problem is: when did they begin to be traders and cease to be pirates? These are undoubtedly separate questions, and the recent tendency has been to say that they were all the time both traders and pirates. It is true that one can live by plunder in a world without trade. But the Viking world was not so simple or primitive as that. Pirates, it is argued, can only thrive where there is a thriving trade on which to prey; and the commodities on which their trade depended, silver, slaves, furs, were in fair measure stolen. Of the furs we have already spoken; in a sense a fur must be an object of theft from the animal which originally wore it. But the Vikings no doubt sometimes paid a good price to the trappers, sometimes failed to pay any price at all, and sometimes were themselves the trappers. That the fur trade greatly interested them is evident from their sagas and from the value they attached to Greenland, which was a principal source for furs, especially in the eleventh and twelfth centuries, before the Russian trade routes became really prolific, and outrivalled those to the far west.[2]

The slave trade is characteristic of Viking endeavour, since it combined war, piracy and long-distance trade, and has left a minimal trace in the records. The researches of Professor Verlinden and others have shown how profuse was the flow of slaves into southern Europe in the early and mid-Middle Ages.[3] The slave trade was always frowned on by the Church, but never forbidden;[4] and the result is that it seems to have carried on very actively without being extensively recorded in contemporary literature. An unusual exception is Ireland, where *ancillae*, female slaves, passed as currency in the early Middle Ages.[5] On the surface, it was alleged that the slaves were non-Christian; hence the word slave, that is 'Slav', which covered slaves from any source being carried south by the traders, for

---

[1] See P. Sawyer, *Age of the Vikings*, 2nd edn, London, 1971; P. G. Foote and D. M. Wilson, *The Viking Achievement*, London, 1970, chap. 6.

[2] See Sawyer, chaps 5, 8.

[3] See esp. C. Verlinden, *L'Esclavage dans l'Europe médiévale*, vol. i, Bruges, 1955.

[4] Verlinden, vol. i, pp. 99–101, 291 ff., 803 ff., and *passim*. The enslavement of Christians was in principle forbidden and the freeing of slaves commended as a good work; but the institutions as a whole was not condemned, and enslavement of Christians seems not to have been uncommon in countries where slavery remained a normal institution.

[5] See K. Hughes, *The Church in early Irish Society*, London, 1966, p. 134 n.

Slavs were supposed to be pagan and therefore were not protected by the Church. In point of fact we simply cannot tell what proportion of the slaves really came from the Slav world, nor in any period on what scale the movement took place. In the seventh and eighth centuries the English had a certain notoriety for enslaving one another – or even selling the surplus stock from their own families; and a beautiful Saxon maiden called Balthild rose to be queen to the Merovingian King Clovis II. After a career of power politics and violence she died a nun, in the odour of sanctity; and thus the slave market had brought her to two careers, as queen and saint, normally open only to princesses among her own Anglo-Saxon folk.[1]

Between the fifth and the eleventh centuries we know that the slave trade between England and Ireland was active; and in the early eleventh century we are clearly seeing the backwash of the Viking trade which had dominated the western seas for 200 years when we observe the foundation of Bristol.[2] Later in the century St Wulfstan went to Bristol to preach against the traffic;[3] and at much the same time the settlement of the Normans, which speeded the tendency for household slaves to disappear and unfree peasants to multiply, helped to bring the trade to an end. It was the characteristic trade of the Vikings, not because they were more inhumane than the other peoples with whom they mingled, but because they were experts both in adventure and in violence in an age in which piracy and trade were widely regarded as part of a single enterprise.

The part the slave trade played in London is hidden from us. Granted the direction of the trade – from the east and north, in a great arc west and south down the coasts of western Europe to Spain, to the Mediterranean and to western Islam – it is a reasonable conjecture that London was a a major centre of it in the tenth and eleventh centuries, and it may even in its day have played the role that the Liverpool slave market played in the eighteenth century. But all this is conjecture; what is clear is that the Viking traders who gave the City's central institution the name of 'Husting' in the tenth century and inspired the dedication of St Bride in the tenth or eleventh and of the six churches of St Olaf in the eleventh and

---

[1] Levison, pp. 9–10, and references there cited.

[2] See E. M. Carus-Wilson in *Historic Towns*, vol. ii, forthcoming. For a sidelight on the trade in England and Normandy, cf. Warner of Rouen's *Maiuht* (early eleventh century), cited in P. Dronke, *Poetic Individuality in the Middle Ages*, Oxford, 1970, pp. 76, 81 ff.

[3] William of Malmesbury, *Vita Wulfstani*, ed. R. R. Darlington, pp. 43–4.

early twelfth, played an important part in the formation of the City and the pattern of its civic life and trade in the period between the rise of Alfredian London and the early twelfth century.[1] In this epoch the overseas trade of England, and particularly London, was a part of the great crescent of Viking trade. In early days this had started in the east in Russia, and even after the decline of the Russian trade and the fall of Birka in the late tenth century it still embraced the frontiers of Islam and Byzantium,[2] the Slav lands bordering on Germany along the Baltic, Scandinavia itself, the British Isles, with trading centres in the Viking towns of Ireland and northern England, Normandy, Greenland and parts of North America.

FRENCH MERCHANTS

This is not to say that the Vikings ever had a monopoly of the overseas trade. Even apart from the involvement of native English seamen and merchants, who no doubt formed a substantial nucleus of the *Burhwaru*[3] who elected Edmund Ironside and Cnut in the early eleventh century, there were already French and German merchants in noticeable quantities in the mid-eleventh century.

Already about the year 1000, in the reign of Ethelred II, royal edicts regulated the tolls for the men of Ponthieu, Normandy, Flanders and the Île de France, and above all for the men of Rouen bringing wine and large fish.[4] The wine and fish were still remembered when the young Duke Henry confirmed to his citizens of Rouen their privileges in 1150-1. Those who belonged to the guild merchant were free of all tolls in London save these; and the citizens of Rouen were to keep 'the port of Dowgate', that is, one of the major hithes in the City, as they had had it in the time of King Edward.[5] This important confirmation was, in 1150-1, perfectly valueless, because Duke Henry's writ did not run in London. Small wonder that the citizens of Rouen played their part in financing his adventures in England, and his early years as king. Throughout the twelfth century, down to the loss of Normandy in the opening years of

---

[1] See pp. 139-42.

[2] See Sawyer, chap. 8.

[3] See p. 23.

[4] IV Ethelred II, ed. Liebermann, vol. i, pp. 232-7; ed. and trans. A. J. Robertson, *Laws*, pp. 71 ff.

[5] *Regesta*, vol. iii, no. 729.

the thirteenth, the wine which came from Rouen was an important element in London's trade. Even Queen Eleanor's son John, who from a child had the best Bordeaux and La Rochelle could offer, valued the wine which came from Rouen – that is, in effect, the wine of the Paris region little prized today – sufficiently to exempt from his charter to Rouen his own prisage: he was to have, for his own drinking and to give away but not for resale, two barrels at his own selection for every wine-ship, one from before, one from behind the mast; but he paid compensation for it.[1]

GERMAN MERCHANTS

Trade with Rouen no doubt received a fillip from the Norman Conquest, but was well established long before; and we may suppose that Dowgate was the site of the Norman wharf even before the Confessor's day. None the less, the foreign traders most conspicuous in the documents of the eleventh and early twelfth centuries are the Germans.[2]

Writing about 1125, and possibly a little out of date in some of his information, the chronicler William of Malmesbury describes London as bursting with wealth and merchants, coming from every land and especially from Germany.[3]

As far back as Ethelred II, the same code which introduces us to the

---

[1] On the wine trade, see Carus-Wilson, chap. 7. R. Dion, *Histoire de la vigne et du vin en France des origines au xixe siècle*, Paris, 1959, pp. 337 ff., 357 ff. (on La Rochelle and the wines of Poitou), 365 ff., esp. 357, 372 (on Bordeaux), suggests that the rise of the Bordeaux wines was delayed by the influence of La Rochelle, and that down to the loss of Normandy and Poitou in the first decade of the thirteenth century wines from the north and especially from Poitou predominated; only in the thirteenth century did Bordeaux come to the fore in the English wine trade. But the evidence is not substantial, and is somewhat negative, and seems to attribute more influence to La Rochelle than really seems probable in the conditions of the twelfth century. We may accept that Poitevin wines had an important share of the market in the twelfth century, and that Bordeaux greatly benefited from the disasters of John's reign, without denying Bordeaux and her vineyards a place earlier. Cf. *Hist. Bordeaux*, vol. ii, pp. 246 ff.; and the studies of Y. Renouard and Dr Margery James noted in Carus-Wilson, p. xii.

[2] On trade with Germany, see Weinbaum, 'Stahlhof und Deutsche Gildhalle'; Lappenberg; *Hansisches Urkundenbuch*, vols ii–iii. On twelfth-century London trade in general, J. de Sturler in *Revue de l'Univ. de Bruxelles*, vol. xlii, 1936–7, pp. 61–77.

[3] William of Malmesbury, *Gesta Pontificum*, ed. N. E. S. A. Hamilton, Rolls Series, London, 1870, p. 140: 'Opima civium divitiis, constipata negotiatorum ex omni terra et maxime ex Germania venientium commertiis . . .'

merchants of Rouen, says that the men of the Emperor who came in their ships were entitled to the same privileges as the English.[1] In the eleventh century the merchants of the Rhineland seem to have played a leading part in western European trade; those of the southern Rhineland were coming to overtake the Vikings as entrepreneurs for goods from further east. There is a statement of the custom of German merchants in London of uncertain date, but probably reflecting the circumstances of the eleventh century, that tells us the commodities they brought and some of the places they came from.[2] First of all, they brought wine, and it seems likely that the English taste for Hock preceded by a century their dedication to Claret, although the name Hock is nothing like so venerable and the German wines, the 'Rhenish', were eclipsed by the French in the twelfth and thirteenth centuries;[3] in the thirteenth and fourteenth centuries little German wine came to England. They also brought cups of gold, silver and precious workmanship, some of the wares so marvellously described in the early twelfth century by the German monk-craftsman Theophilus.[4] They brought luxury cloth and linen from Constantinople and nearer home, from Regensburg, via Mainz, from which also came coats of mail. Finally they brought spices, pepper and cumin, and wax and fustian; and when local harvests failed, boatloads of grain.[5] Special privileges were accorded to the men from Mainz and Cologne; on the men of the coastlands, for some reason not explained, restrictions were placed. The men of Tiel, Bremen and Antwerp 'shall not pass London Bridge unless they will be ruled by the law of London'. But evidently it was the men of Cologne who formed the backbone of the German colony in England from the eleventh century for many to come.[6]

In the twelfth century the German merchants were expanding their activities in London while the Danes were contracting theirs, and we are

[1] See p. 265.

[2] British Museum Add. MS 14252, ff. 99v-101; Bateson, pp. 495 ff.; cf. *Lib. Cust.*, vol. i, pp. 61-3. Some of the details, e.g. reference to the king's chamberlain, suggest a date after 1066; but it seems to reflect regulations and trading conditions earlier than Henry II's time (cf. Bateson, p. 495), and the clear indication that Scandinavian trade is still important suggests an early date. It is curious that the document is in French, and it may well be translated from a Latin original.

[3] See pp. 265-6 and n.

[4] Theophilus, *De diversis artibus*, ed. and trans. C. R. Dodwell, NMT, 1961, esp. bk iii; cf. C. Brooke, *Twelfth Century Renaissance*, London, 1969, pp. 106 ff.

[5] Bateson, pp. 499 ff.

[6] Bateson, p. 498.

told that the Germans had by 1225 taken over the holdings of the Danes in the parish of St Clement Danes, and the upkeep of Bishopsgate. But their main headquarters had long been in the Guildhall of the men of Cologne near Dowgate, first mentioned in the reign of Henry II.[1] This later developed into another hall for merchants from all the German cities. Cologne was always the leader, but Bremen and Münster came in under her wing in the thirteenth century; and others followed. As the Hanseatic League based on the great Baltic ports of Germany grew in wealth and power in the thirteenth and fourtheenth centuries, the whole area became the centre of the Hanse in London, the 'Steelyard'.[2]

FLEMISH MERCHANTS

Although the Germans are better documented, the most substantial and the most crucial links already in the eleventh century were probably those with Flanders. In Ethelred's law of *c.* 1000 there is mention already of the men of Flanders, especially those of Huy, Liège and Nivelle. Already in the early eleventh century English cheese was appreciated in the market of Arras; by 1200 it was a significant element in the diet of the men of Bruges.[3] But it was in the eleventh century that Flanders became a major economic power. The flowering of Flemish industry and the rise of the Flemish towns in the eleventh and twelfth centuries were dependent on their proximity to England. Wool and cheese were not the only commodities bought by the Flemings: cattle, hides, lead and tin were also in demand. Nor was trade the only link. Edward the Confessor's

[1] See M. B. Honeybourne in *LTR*, vol. xxii, 1965, pp. 69–75 and references cited there, p. 69 n. 3, esp. Weinbaum, 'Stahlhof und Deutsche Gildhalle'; Lappenberg, pp. 3–5 (the charter of Henry II attributed to 1157 is undated and probably of the 1170s); Cam., *Eyre*, vol. i, pp. lxxiv-v, cxxviii, cxxxiv.

[2] The problem has been discussed whether there was originally one or two guild-halls – one for the men of Cologne, one for the rest of the German traders. The evidence is inconclusive, but a single hall (no doubt many times altered and adapted) seems the more likely answer. (We are particularly indebted for the advice of Professor E. M. Carus-Wilson on this problem.)

Cannon Street Station now occupies the site of the Steelyard.

[3] See J. Lestocquoy, *Les dynasties bourgeoises d'Arras*, Arras, 1945, p. 27. On Anglo-Flemish trade, see P. Grierson, 'The relations between England and Flanders before the Norman Conquest', *TRHS*, 4th Series, vol. xxiii, 1941, pp. 71–112 (repr. in *Essays in Medieval History*, ed. R. W. Southern, London, 1968, pp. 61–92), esp. repr. pp. 86 ff.; G. G. Dept, 'Les marchands flamands et le roi d'Angleterre (1154–1216)', *Revue du Nord*, vol. xii, 1926, pp. 303–24, esp. p. 303 for period before 1154.

court included some Flemings as well as many Germans; William the Conqueror's wife was a Flemish princess of Anglo-Saxon descent.[1] In the twelfth century Flemish mercenaries played a part in the civil wars of Stephen's reign. But at the heart of Anglo-Flemish relations lay the fundamental relationship between English wool and Flemish cloth. While some of the Flemish towns, such as Arras and Ypres, had a considerable prehistory, some, like Bruges, were virtually new towns in the eleventh century.[2]

Between 1000 and 1150 Flemish cloth production developed so strongly that it far outran the local supplies of wool, and this was only possible because large flocks of English sheep lay near enough to hand. It was also possible only because the population of western Europe prepared to buy Flemish cloth increased with some rapidity in the same epoch; in the thirteenth century Flemish cloth even conquered the English market and put some traditional sectors of the local cloth industry almost out of business.[3]

But in the eleventh and twelfth centuries, so it has been argued, the balance of trade was for the most part in England's favour; indeed, it seems likely that it was so, and that the strong interest of the Flemish merchants in London and England at large lay in buying wool;[4] but substantial evidence still eludes us. Thus it would seem that the basis of William Cade's vast fortune had lain in his activities as a wool merchant, though his operations in his later years seem to have been much more extensive as a moneylender. That Cade, a Flemish merchant and financier based on St-Omer, should be prepared to support the young Duke Henry in his attempt on the English throne in the early 1150s is hardly surpris-

[1] For these links, see Grierson, art. cit.

[2] The name is first mentioned in 892, and is thought to be Old English (= bridge) in origin; if so, it is a striking anticipation of later links. See M. Gysseling, *Toponymisch Woordenboek . . .*, vol. i, p. 195, following a suggestion of the late A. H. Smith, and correcting Gysseling in *Bulletin de la Commission Royale de Toponymie et de Dialectologie*, vol. xviii, 1944, pp. 69–79. But its period of growth came in the eleventh century, so far as can be seen.

[3] See esp. E. Miller, in *EcHR*, 2nd Series, vol. xviii, 1965, pp. 64–82; E. M. Carus-Wilson, Ford lectures (forthcoming).

[4] See esp. P. Sawyer, 'The wealth of England in the eleventh century', *TRHS*, vol. xv, 1965, pp. 145–64, esp. pp. 161 ff.; *Cambridge Economic History*, vol. ii, pp. 367 ff. (E. M. Carus-Wilson). For the English wool trade and woollen industry see Carus-Wilson, op. cit. (preceding note), and her *Medieval Merchant Venturers*, 2nd edn, London, 1967, esp. chaps. iv, v, and bibliographical survey on pp. xi f.

ing; nor that an early charter of Henry II after he had succeeded to the throne granted privileges to the citizens of St-Omer.[1] They may have lodgings in London 'at their will and choice', may sell without view of justice or sheriff, and in general had considerable freedom of movement in English markets. William Cade's dealings in the London money market illustrate the opportunities and the importance it had for Flemish merchants. Perhaps the most substantial compliment the Flemings paid to London was to call an important trading association of the Flemish towns the 'Hanse of London'.[2] This association was formed in the twelfth or thirteenth centuries for the protection of mutual interest among the leading merchants of a number of Flemish cities. It was a temporary association, and short-lived; but the name which it acquired in the course of the thirteenth century bore witness to the centre of their common interests. London was one of the mercantile capitals of Flanders.

England and the Mediterranean

In the main, too, the Flemish towns acted as a frontier beyond which English merchants did not penetrate, save into the west and south of France, and in due course to Spain and Portugal. Far and away the best indication of the range of trade and traders coming into southern Europe in the twelfth and thirteenth centuries are the notarial registers of Genoa.[3] They go back earlier, and are for our purposes much more revealing and much fuller, than any surviving registers from other Italian cities – and nothing of the kind survives for any northern town in our period. Furthermore, of all the Italian cities, Genoa had the most extensive trade in

[1] Round, *CDF*, no. 1352, of 1155–8.

[2] See H. Pirenne, 'La hanse flamande de Londres', in *Les Villes*, vol. ii, pp. 157–84, who, however, probably exaggerated the duration and significance of this short-lived alliance.

[3] Genoa, Archivio di Stato, Cartolari Notarili Genovesi, in which G. K. has made an extensive search without finding any certain trace of Londoners save for those noted by R. L. Reynolds in *EcHR*, 1st Series, vol. iv, 1932–4, pp. 317–23 (and see next note); although the name 'Bucuct', 'Bucucius', 'Bucontius' the (first two as surnames of men called Hugh and William) could conceivably be relatives of the Buccuintes (see p. 214); Notai Ignoti, busta 1, doc. XIII, no. 78; doc. XVI, no. 21. There is an inventory of the Cartolari in *Pubblicazioni degli Archivi di Stato*, vol. xxii, Rome, 1956 (see esp. p. xvii for last of those published); and a group of scholars has put together and edited the work of some of the major scribes in *Notai Liguri del Secolo XII* (e del XIII), 8 vols in 9, Genoa, 1938–61.

western and north-western Europe in this age. Some direct links with England and with London in particular, it undoubtedly had. The studies of Professor Reynolds and Professor Doehaerd have revealed a flourishing English colony at Genoa in the period *c.* 1170–1227.[1] In early years this community was presided over by a rich man called Robert of London, who had settled in Genoa with his family, and whose daughter he married under Genoese law to a young English associate. Yet it is also clear that he and his friends were still in touch with London, and at least one of the community, Jordan of London, may be linked to the leading citizen of London, Jordan de Turri – of the Tower – not infrequently found in company with the first Mayor of London, Henry FitzAilwin, towards the end of the century.[2] The community in 1170 was quite large, and its occupations varied. By the early thirteenth century the evidence suggests that the group had contracted; and it is noticeable that at this time its leading members were all goldsmiths, expert craftsmen who had found Genoa a city of special opportunity where their craft was valued.

Compared to the Londoners, the Flemings in Genoa were legion. Most of them were cloth merchants, especially from Arras, led by the numerous members of the clan 'Stanfort', not named after the English cloth town Stamford in Lincolnshire, but after a tiny hamlet near Arras.[3] Flemish merchants came in large numbers to Genoa, and Genoese merchants went north, at least as far as the Champagne fairs. No doubt much English wool, disguised as Flemish cloth, was sold in the markets of Genoa; but the Genoese records suggest that bulk trade was not carried directly to Genoa by English merchants nor directly between England and Italy at all.[4]

In luxury goods, and objects of craft and cult, the story may be different.

[1] Reynolds, art. cit.; R. Doeheard, *Les Relations commerciales entre Gênes, la Belgique et l'Outremer . . . au xiiie et xive siècles*, 3 vols, Brussels, Rome, 1941, vol. i, pp. 162, 176–8.

[2] He might even be identified with him, since the surname 'de Turri' occurs among his associates in Genoa; but this seems hardly probable. Jordan de Turri occurs with Henry FitzAilwin among the leading citizens witnessing, e.g. Westminster Abbey Domesday (Muniment Bk 11), ff. 483v-4, 484r-v; St Paul's A9/465 (*HMC*, *9th Report*, p. 10a); Brit. Mus. Add. Charter 1046; *Cart. Colchester*, vol. ii, pp. 297-8; Brit. Mus. Harl. MS 4015, ff. 33v-4; Gibbs, no. 110; *Cart. Clerkenwell*, no. 243.

[3] Doeheard, vol. i, p. 153 n.; *Notai Liguri del secolo XII*, vol. ii, pt i, nos. 230, 355 etc.; vol. v, pt i, nos. 183, 185, 250, 396, 526, etc. On the word *stamfort*, however, cf. Carus-Wilson, p. 213 n. 1 and in *Cambridge Economic History*, vol. ii, pp. 374-5.

[4] See Doeheard, vol. i, pp. 186 ff., 212 ff.

Far and away the most substantial evidence of the luxury trade in the twelfth and thirteenth centuries is to be found in the inventories of ecclesiastical treasuries, and of these none is more evocative than the inventories of St Paul's Cathedral of 1245 and later.[1] Where the objects were made is rarely revealed, but these lists are a vivid indication of what was once available, or at any rate visible, in London – once, for alas not a single item is known now to exist. They vary from small objects like the box in which Bishop Gilbert (presumably Foliot, 1163–87) carried chrism, 'a chrismatory lined with wood, covered with silver leaves and images in relief . . .'; through the two candelabra of Richard of Stortford, canon and dignitary in the late twelfth century, adorned with trefoils and men riding lions, weighing 4⅔ lb.; to the great shrine of St Eorcenweald (or Erkenwald), presumably made for his translation in the mid-twelfth century, with images, with 130 precious stones ('as is said') and angels at either end. Among the more remarkable objects were the legacies of Bishop Richard FitzNeal (1189–98), once royal treasurer, including a cope of purple samite, embroidered with leopards and flowers (if this was correctly identified); his reliquary, wood covered with silver gilt, accoutred with stones made to look like carbuncles and sapphires, with some hairs of the Blessed Virgin within and another little box containing St Vincent's tooth; and two pastoral staffs, one with a volute of silver gilt ending in an angel, the other of horn ending in a dragon's head, from which issued a vine encircling a lion. Noticeably brief is the list of carpets, on which a letter of Gilbert Foliot's provides an interesting commentary: he sent a carpet as a gift to the Pope (1163–81), apologizing that it was neither large nor round (as apparently the Pope had wished); for carpets were not made in London, but were brought from overseas, and this was the best that could be found 'by diligent search in every part of our city'.

Already in the mid-twelfth century Henry of Blois, Bishop of Winchester, disappointed of his aims in the papal Curia, had compensated himself by buying old statues and transporting them home; and in the Henry of Blois Psalter in the British Museum two pages showing exceptional Byzantine influence are living witnesses that he acquired not only ancient statues but more modern Byzantine artefacts, doubtless from Sicily and south Italy.[2] These may have come to him as gifts from an-

[1] The earliest inventory, of 1245, is ed. W. S. Simpson in *Archaeologia*, vol. l, 1887, pp. 439–524 (see esp. pp. 468 ff.); Gilbert Foliot's carpet is described in *GFL*, no. 247.
[2] See G. Zarnecki, *Later English Romanesque Sculpture*, London, 1953, p. 30; Brooke, *Twelfth Century Renaissance*, pp. 149 ff. and plates 117–18.

other disappointed visitor to the Curia, William, Archbishop of York, Henry's nephew and the future St William of York, who visited friends and relations in the Norman kingdom in south Italy in 1147–8. Among the objects he brought home may very likely be counted the fine ivory casket still preserved in York Minster, and made in the Norman kingdom in the eleventh or twelfth century.[1] Painted ivory boxes and other objects were characteristic products of Moslem craftsmen in Sicily, which had been a Moslem island until the 1060s. The boxes were probably for the most part secular in origin, and some of them have Arabic inscriptions which prove them to have been bridal caskets.[2] These however could not be read by Christian purchasers, and they became fashionable in northern Europe in the twelfth and thirteenth centuries as reliquaries. Over 200 ivories from this school and this period are known to survive, scattered over western Europe; but only two of those now preserved in England are at all likely to have been here in the Middle Ages. This does not suggest a very active trade between the Norman kingdom of Sicily and England, although the general destruction of church ornaments at the Reformation may partly or largely account for the dearth.

Nor are they necessarily objects of trade, for the box at York may well have come as a gift from St William. But the other box, now at Bodmin in Cornwall, was almost certainly the one bought by Walter of Coutances, head of Henry II's chancery, to help in the dramatic rescue of the bones of St Petroc, stolen from Bodmin Priory in 1176–7 (**Plate 38**). Early in 1177 the prior of Bodmin won the aid of Walter, who was a Cornishman with Norman and Breton connections, to obtain royal writs to secure the bones' return from the Breton monastery to which they had been taken. And Walter went out of the royal court, very likely (though not certainly) at Westminster, and found a pedlar offering an ivory box for sale just the right size for the purpose.[3] Thus the reliquary at Bodmin is very likely a virtually unique representative of the luxury trade of twelfth-century London.

We cannot tell how the box came to England, nor how exceptional a visitor it was. There was much coming and going between England and the Mediterranean in the twelfth century, but there is very little precise

---

[1] See R. Pinder-Wilson and C. N. L. Brooke, 'The Reliquary of St Petroc and the Ivories of Norman Sicily', *Archaeologia*, vol. 104, 1973, pp. 261–305.

[2] Art. cit.

[3] Art. cit., pp. 266–7, and references there cited. Walter of Coutances was later Archbishop of Rouen: see p. 255.

evidence of English merchants in the south or of Italian merchants in England. The colony of English citizens in Genoa suggested to us that it might be worth looking into the records of other Italian cities for evidence of links with England and London. An extensive preliminary survey has failed to produce any result during the period of this book.[1] The records of other cities are for the most part less rich and less rewarding than Genoa's, and it may be that the record hides much activity from us. But there seems little hope of establishing the extent to which England and Italy were in direct commercial contact in the twelfth century.

By the late thirteenth century merchants of Rome, Lucca and Siena had established themselves in England, and the men of Cahors had replaced the Flemings and the Jews as the leading moneylenders. But these represented a new pattern of financial relationships. The Cahorsins were internationally famous by the mid-thirteenth century as financiers, and enjoyed the benefits of the links between the court of Henry III and southern France. The Italian merchants came to England in the first instance as papal bankers; and it was the enormously increased scale of papal taxation in the thirteenth century which gave them their opportunities, which they took to the point that, in the mid- and late thirteenth century, they were competing with the Flemings for the English wool clip. Already in the twelfth century there had been felt a need for men who could transport money to Rome, indeed to the eastern Mediterranean. Transport to the Holy Land had naturally been the vocation of the Knights Templars, and had helped them to find their career as bankers and financiers, which made them rich and powerful in the twelfth and thirteenth centuries, and destroyed them in the fourteenth.[2]

Money on its way to Rome was no doubt carried by many suitors and pilgrims; but the regular payment of Peter's Pence seems to have been performed by Flemings.[3] In the mid-twelfth century it was being sent from England to the Abbot of St-Bertin, just outside St-Omer. That he sent it in the hands of Flemish merchants is suggested by the contretemps which occurred when, in the course of the dispute with Thomas Becket, Henry II stopped payment. Eight Flemish merchants came to London on behalf of the Pope, and Gilbert Foliot, the Bishop of London, kept

---

[1] See pp. 67, 270.
[2] See pp. 231–3.
[3] See John of Salisbury, *Letters*, ed. W. J. Millor *et al.*, vol. i, NMT, 1955, p. 19 n. 2; W. E. Lunt, *Financial Relations of the Papacy with England to 1327*, Cambridge, Mass., 1939, pp. 3–84, esp. p. 52.

them for a few days in the hope that the royal licence to export the money he had collected would arrive.[1] In the end the merchants had to go without the money, though it appears that payments were presently resumed.

CONDITIONS OF INTERNATIONAL TRADE IN THE ELEVENTH AND TWELFTH CENTURIES

No doubt the dearth of literary evidence on English trade in the eleventh and twelfth centuries tends to make the activity of English merchants seem less extensive and less substantial than it was. Yet it is unlikely that the main lines of the picture which have emerged are wrongly drawn. In the eleventh century England was still in the main a part of the Viking world of commerce, spread all over nothern Europe, with limbs far to the south and west; and trade with Norway remained of great importance throughout the twelfth and thirteenth centuries. But already English trade was involved with its neighbours on the Continent, especially with Germany, and increasingly with Flanders and Normandy. After the accession of Henry II and his queen, Duchess of Aquitaine in her own right, the link with central and southern France and particularly with the region of Bordeaux became of great importance, and the Poitou and Bordeaux wine trade a major element in English trade. Although there were English merchants plying further afield, and links spread all over the known world, the normal lines of communication were now running between London and the Rhineland and Flanders, south into Normandy and to Bordeaux; but beyond Cologne and Mainz, Bruges and Arras, the markets of Champagne and the vineyards of Aquitaine the direct links grew much slighter.[2]

One of the major lessons taught by the study of Anglo-Flemish relations in the eleventh and twelfth centuries is that the condition for major economic change in this period was growing specialization in Flanders; and this presupposes the growth of a large population in the Flemish towns which did not grow their own food nor even the wool they wove and dyed. The argument in economic history frequently moves in a circle. The growth of towns in western Europe in this period was made

---

[1] *GFL*, nos 155 (p. 206), 156, 168, 177-9. The merchants had made a loan of 300 marks to the Pope on the expectation of Peter's Pence. In no. 179 Foliot suggests to the Pope an alternative method of payment, by the meeting of messengers in Rouen.

[2] See above, p. 266 n.

possible by growing markets and trade: the markets made the towns prosperous and enabled them to carry larger populations. But the markets could only prosper if there were larger populations able to buy the goods. From this circle we cannot entirely escape; it is better to admit so much than arbitrarily to determine cause and effect where a variety of co-operant factors were at work together. The Flemish towns show the argument at its most circular. They became centres of industry un-paralleled in Europe at the time, and only paralleled in Italy in the late Middle Ages. This assumes a rapid growth in the hinterland and further south of markets for Flemish cloth, which could rapidly pay for the bread and meat the artisans ate and the cloth they wove. If we wish to get beyond these statements to the way in which the change was wrought, and how the Flemish economy worked, we have to study the crafts of the Flemish cities, how they grew and how they were organized.[1]

The Crafts and Markets of London

Our subject is London, not Flanders; but the lesson applies there too. The growth of London as a city in the eleventh and twelfth centuries proved by the evidence of topography, presupposes that food could be provided for the population, and also that its markets were sufficiently active to provide them with occupation, and a proportion of the citizens with wealth. Before we lay out the pattern of trade, it is wise to examine the crafts of the city, to see the inner structure of her markets.

A full map of the quarters where the London craftsmen lived, and the markets pertaining to them, cannot be drawn until a later period.[2] But a little early evidence and the street-names help to show that although there were some shifts and rearrangements the pattern was on the whole remarkably stable. In early days it seems that the main craft centres were oriented round the great West Cheap, now Cheapside, and in the areas between the West Cheap and the Thames. The great quantities of meat needed to feed the growing population were walked or carried through Newgate and Cripplegate and Aldersgate into the western part of the long market, to the Shambles, where the butchers had the stalls on which they sold meat to the great convenience of hungry citizens, and

---

[1] See *Cambridge Economic History*, vol. ii, pp. 367 ff. (E. M. Carus-Wilson); G. de Poerck, *La Draperie médiévale en Flandre et en Artois*, 3 vols, Bruges, 1951; and Pirenne's many studies, esp. in *La Ville*.

[2] See meanwhile Unwin, p. 34.

washed the remnants down the drain which ran to the Thames and was in 1246 in need of repair and much 'to the nuisance of the houses of the dean and chapter'.[1] Beyond the Shambles lay the fish market, where fish was brought from the Thames wharves up Old Fish Street (now Old Change) and Friday Street to the stalls in Cheap.[2] As the other stalls in Cheap expanded and the nostrils of their users grew more delicate the fish market was moved nearer the Thames, and seems to have been installed in the mid- and late thirteenth century in a new fish market in what is now unfortunately called Old Fish Street, at the south end of Friday Street.[3] Meanwhile fish was also creeping up from London Bridge so the Eastcheap, so that what is now called Fish Street runs from London Bridge to the market. But the fishmongers continued to live near their old quarters by the Thames, and there in a much later age the Fishmongers' Hall was built.

Beyond Friday Street lie Bread Street and Milk Street, and at the head of Bread Street, or near by, already about 1140 we have record of the Pantry, the centre of the baker's craft.[4] Thus men catered for the basic needs of life, and in dozens of ale-houses ale-wives brewed beer, that is for those who did not draw it from the ancient brewery of St Paul's.[5] By the twelfth century men of any substance reckoned wine a necessity, and the area still known as the Vintry had acquired that name already well before 1244.[6]

Men cannot live by bread alone, and the long line of the West Cheap had many other stalls than the food stalls. In the parish of St Vedast the Lorimers, or men who made harness for horses, already plied their business, and since St Vedast gave his name to Foster Lane and the saddlers were established where Foster Lane debouches on the Cheap in the later Middle Ages, we may suppose that these two related crafts grew up there together.[7] At the corner of Friday Street, on its east side, where the Goldsmiths Row was placed in later times, was already to be found the 'Aurifabria', the goldsmiths' quarter. Further east were the cordwainers,

---

[1] *Eyre*, p. 153, no. 485.

[2] See pp. 171 ff.

[3] See p. 171. Curiously little complaint, however, was made of stench in *London Assize of Nuisance 1301–1431* (ed. H. Chew and W. Kellaway: see pp. xxiv f.).

[4] *HMC 9th Report*, p. 28a (St Paul's A25/257). For these streets see Ekwall, pp. 72 ff.

[5] See *HSP*, pp. 60 ff., 363.

[6] St Paul's Cathedral A12/143; St Bartholomew's, St Martin Vintry deeds, 1268; *Eyre*, nos 208, 284.

[7] St Paul's Cathedral, MS W.D. 12, f. 3 (Lorimeria in the parish of St Vedast).

who gave their name in the end to a whole ward, and were certainly established near St Mary-le-Bow by the early thirteenth century. Opposite the Mercers' Hall and St Thomas of Acon beside it, lay the Mercery, first recorded in 1246, but doubtless older.[1] At that time the mercers had a market in the Mercery already, and the drapery was beside or near it. In due course the rivalry of drapers and mercers, and the expansion of their business, led the drapers to seek pastures new in Candlewick Street (now Cannon Street) and St Swithin's Lane, among the candlewrights or chandlers.[2]

THE GUILDS

These various groups and crafts were later to form the guilds and companies which have been the core and backbone of the City and the basis of its government since the fourteenth century.[3] These have been from early days of two very different types: the guilds of great merchants, as the mercers, drapers and pepperers became in the thirteenth century, and the guilds of less wealthy crafts, such as the weavers and bakers. For whatever reasons, whether to preserve declining trade, support standards of workmanship, or merely to express the convivial and spiritual brotherhood of men of like persuasion, the craft guilds of the late Middle Ages established closed shops and tight rules round their various avocations. Because of this fondness for rules and regulations, and because many of the livery companies which grew out of them are still flourishing, the later guilds are extremely well documented. By the same token their predecessors, the guilds and craftsmen of the twelfth and early thirteenth centuries, have left little trace. Partly this seems wholly natural to us, accustomed to find all elements in civic life ill-documented before the mid-thirteenth century. But it has in recent years often been argued that it was also because there was much greater freedom to ply a trade and move from town to town in the twelfth century than later. The statutes of

---

[1] For *aurifabria*, St Bartholomew's Hospital, Cok's Cartulary, f. 246; for the site, see the charter in *Cart. Clerkenwell*, no. 350, of 1238–9, placing it at the corner of Friday Street and Cheapside. The Corveiseria (Cordwainery) occurs in the early thirteenth-century, Canterbury Cathedral Reg. K, p. 1; see also *Eyre*, no. 212, p. 87; Ekwall, pp. 79–80; for the Mercery, *Eyre*, p. 141, no. 372 (and see p. 177).

[2] *Eyre*, pp. 140–1, nos 370, 372; Unwin, p. 34, shows their later site. Cf. Ekwall, p. 79, for the history of Cannon St. Cf. J. Dummelow, *The Wax Chandlers of London*, London and Chichester, 1973.

[3] On their history, see esp. Unwin.

towns and guilds, which survive from about 1200 on, grow increasingly restrictive and pernickety as the generations pass.[1] None the less, guilds played their part already in the twelfth century, and they attracted unfavourable notice from the king, who fined the more conspicuous from time to time, so that they impinge on the Pipe Rolls of the royal Exchequer.

Thus we know that the weavers of London, like those of Winchester and other towns, had formed a guild by 1130.[2] This strongly suggests that they already found it necessary to organize in defence of their common interest in the face of entrepreneurs who had come in the late eleventh and early twelfth centuries to dominate the complex processes of the clothing industry.[3] These men were sometimes the dyers, who controlled the finishing processes and the marketing. But of the fullers and dyers the London records have almost nothing to tell us, and of the weavers not much more.

The first substantial list of guilds comes from the Pipe Roll of 1179–80; by then there were nineteen to attract the king's attention, and doubtless a number more which had already paid for their licence.[4] The Bakers first appear in 1155–6, and the Fishmongers, though not recorded until the thirteenth century, may well go back deep into the twelfth.[5] At some date unknown, but very likely in the twelfth century, the Saddlers established a lien with the canons of St Martin-le-Grand, for mutual support and comfort. The Saddlers visited St Martin's and there paid their dues, and the canons prayed for their earthly and heavenly success.[6] The list of guilds of 1179–80 introduces us to a number more, and arranges them in rough order of wealth. They ranged from the guild of Goldsmiths, of which Ralph Flael was alderman, which was fined 45 marks (£30), to the guild of Odo Vigil, which paid a modest 6s 8d. It is immediately clear

[1] See A. Hibbert in *Cambridge Econ. Hist.*, vol. iii, pp. 161 ff.; cf. Carus-Wilson, pp. 235 ff.

[2] *PR 31 Henry I*, pp. 144–5; Carus-Wilson, pp. 225 ff. On the history of the weavers, see F. Consitt, *The London Weavers' Company*, vol. i, Oxford, 1933.

[3] Carus-Wilson, loc. cit., and chap. v in general.

[4] *PR 26 Henry II*, pp. 153–4; Unwin, chap. iv, esp. p. 48 (not entirely accurate).

[5] *PR 2 Henry II*, p. 4; Unwin, pp. 36 ff.; S. Thrupp, *A Short History of the Worshipful Company of Bakers of London*, London, 1933, pp. 1 ff.

[6] See the curious draft agreement in a twelfth-century hand preserved among the muniments of St Martin's in Westminster Abbey (facsimile in J. W. Sherwell, *History of the Guild of Saddlers of the City of London*, London, 1937, 3rd edn, 1956, plate 1, trans., p. 4).

that the guilds represented groups of many different kinds and purposes and standards of living, and were linked only by their desire to form little companies for mutual comfort and protection, or for good works; and that each was identified by a leading member, the 'alderman'.[1]

Much ink has been spilt to little purpose in the attempt to define a guild. If we ask what bound together the Frith Guild of the tenth century, the Cnihtengild of the tenth and eleventh,[2] and the charitable, social and craft guilds of the list of 1179–80, it is a little as if we should ask for a definition of a committee in the twentieth century, or of a fellowship of an Oxford or Cambridge college in any age. We are all familiar with in-stitutions whose nature is perfectly clear to those who live in or near them, perfectly obscure to anyone else. Such were the medieval guilds; and the matter is not made easier for us by the inveterate habit of calling any group a 'guild'. In the late twelfth century, Walter Map and his friend Gerald of Wales were doubtless echoing a joke that they had often en-joyed together when Walter described in one of his tales a large building 'such . . . as the English have as drinking houses, one in each parish, called in English *Ghildhus*', and Gerald referred to the London Guildhall as a notable drinking house.[3] That this could be more than a joke is evident from a solemn reference (if such it is) in the Winton Domesday to the citizens of Winchester drinking their guild, and to the undoubtedly serious description in the *Life of St Christina of Markyate* of the guild merchant at Huntingdon as 'a very great and famous feast for merchants'.[4] Evidently the great feast was already regarded as a crucial part of a guild's activities. But it can only have been one of many; and these early guilds, like the later, bear every sign of having an element of social concern, for mutual self-help and prayers, as well as conviviality, in them.

The guild merchant or 'hanse' was also the vehicle for market prileges; and here the difficulty of definition is most acute. For sometimes the guild merchant seems little more than a vehicle, sometimes it seems a very

[1] Unwin, pp. 47 ff.

[2] See pp. 195–6; and on the origins of guilds, esp. E. Coornaert in *Revue historique*, vol. cxcix, 1948, pp. 22–55, 208–43, which contains a wide-ranging comparative study, and is of especial interest for the eleventh-twelfth-century guilds in Germany, France and the Low Countries.

[3] Map, *De nugis curialium*, dist. ii, c. 12 (ed. M. R. James, p. 75; trans. James, p. 82); Giraldus, vol. iv, pp. 404–5.

[4] Winton Domesday in 'Domesday Book', vol. iv, p. 531 (cf. Gross, *Gild Merchant*, vol. i, pp. 183–8; *Life of St Christina of Markyate*, ed. and trans. C. H. Talbot, Oxford, 1959, pp. 48–9. Cf. Coornaert's phrase 'culte de l'ivresse', art. cit., p. 241.

active and precisely defined group of men engaged in far more than organizing market privileges – sometimes it is almost identical with a town council. But nearly every town which had market privileges, and exemptions from toll, had a guild merchant to administer and protect them. There are, however, several exceptions, of which London is the most conspicuous. It is commonly said that London's market privileges were so extensive they could not be – or did not need to be – confined within the purview of a single guild.[1] We are bound to confess that this is an explanation which is not entirely clear to us, for it seems essentially to restate the problem without solving it. And the problem itself is made all the more obscure by the fact that the central building which enshrines London's civic institutions and privileges is the Guildhall, and has been so named since at latest the twelfth century.[2] In other towns the guild merchant drank their guild in the town hall, and so it was called the Guildhall; what manner of guild the citizens of London drank in theirs seems to be an impenetrable mystery. That they had privileges, and administered them, and knew how to manipulate a patrician oligarchy, is abundantly clear from the events of the years 1189–1212.

The guilds of 1179–80 are the mixture of craft, charitable and neighbourhood guilds which we might meet in any later age; the list suggests, however, either that a number of crafts were not yet in any real measure organized, or that they escaped tax either by being exceptionally respectable or so disreputable no cognisance could be taken of them. The list sounds reputable indeed. It starts with the goldsmiths, who paid the handsome fine of forty-five marks; next a thirty mark guild identified solely by Goscelin the alderman; then the guild of St Lazarus, doubtless supporting hospitals and good works, as were no less than five guilds of 'Bridge'. The largest communal effort in late twelfth-century London was the rebuilding of the Bridge, begun in the 1170s, completed in or about 1209.[3] Three of these guilds were of some substance, led by

[1] Cf. Gross, *Gild Merchant*, vol. i, pp. 20 ff.; Unwin, p. 60; C. G. Crump in *EHR*, vol. xviii, 1903, p. 315, showed that there is a reference to a guild merchant in 1252, but the reference probably reflects bureaucratic habit not a current institution.

[2] The first reference to the Guildhall seems to be the mysterious 'terra Gialle' in the St Paul's survey of *c*. 1127 (*Tout Essays*, p. 57); the form was certainly in use in the thirteenth century, and the identification was accepted by Round (*GM*, p. 436) and Stenton (p. 12n.). The next earliest reference is that in Giraldus cited in p. 280 n. 3 above. See C. Barron, 'Medieval Guildhall of London', 1974.

[3] See pp. 109–10.

Aylwin Fink, a leading moneyer,[1] Peter FitzAlan and Robert de Bosco (fifteen, fifteen and ten marks), two of modest resources, led by men called Cook and Cooper, and paying each a mark. Three other craft guilds appear in the list; the Pepperers (sixteen marks), representing the long-distance trade in spices which was later, and probably already, an important element in London's luxury trade, a group of humble cloth-workers whose status and function is not clear, and the Butchers (each a mark); nearby in the same roll the weavers appear, paying £12 for their right to form a guild.

THE GREAT MERCHANTS

Of the aldermen of the period 1200–1250 analysed by Professor Gwyn Williams, the majority of those whose original or chief occupation is known were drapers, mercers, vintners, goldsmiths and pepperers, in that order.[2] These terms have a spurious air of precision: the majority of the aldermen were not given a precise occupation in the records largely because they were (so far as we can tell) rarely specialists in this period. All the indications are that this would have been even more clearly the case in the twelfth century. The hereditary element among the leading citizens and those who rose partly by prospering in the royal service, had a large investment in land;[3] many doubtless lived partly or mainly, like Gilbert Becket, on city rents; a certain number were moneylenders. But if we could penetrate the mercantile element among the leading citizens – the men who were merchants some, most or all the time – we should doubtless find the same trades predominant already then.

Long distance trade in luxuries no doubt represented a small proportion of the bulk of London's trade and may not have been a large proportion of its value. But in early medieval trade in general it undoubtedly played a part out of proportion to its scale owing to the enterprise, the distances involved, and the contacts which it brought. In the early Middle Ages, long distance trade mainly in spices and silks and luxuries of this kind had given the Jews the opportunity to acquire and preserve a tradition of commercial expertise rare in the western world. The men who carried mercery and spices from the far and middle east to the far west

[1] See *PR 14 Henry II*, p. *5–22 Henry II*, p. 14; also D. F. Allen, pp. 82–4 and index.

[2] Williams, p. 319.

[3] See e.g. pp. 210–11, 247.

were in the spearhead of commercial advance in the twelfth century. In a similar way, the goldsmiths had an importance beyond the scale of their craft. Already in the eleventh century – and very likely long before – the goldsmiths of London were noted for their skill.[1] The presence of London goldsmiths in Genoa in the early thirteenth century shows that the craft itself had a reputation far afield, and the goldsmiths were outstandingly the most prosperous of the guilds of 1179–80.[2] But what set them apart from their fellows was their control of the mint and the dies from which money was cut; William, son of Otto, hereditary goldsmith whose family ran the mint in the twelfth and thirteenth centuries, was the central figure in a profession of great wealth as well as of great importance to the economy of the country at large.[3]

TRADE AND THE COURT

The proximity of London to Westminster, the part both played in government and the frequent visits of the royal court were essential to London's prosperity and especially important to us; for it is from the records of the Exchequer and Chancery that most of our evidence comes; royal payments in the Pipe Rolls of the twelfth and early thirteen centuries, and from about 1200 royal orders in the Chancery rolls. In the earliest Pipe Roll of 1129–30 many purchases are recorded. In that year wine and its transport cost £45, pepper, cumin, ginger, towels, basins and royal shirts £24, and substantial sums were paid for cloth, for fish, oil, nuts and unguents.[4] From Henry II's time and later there is copious evidence, though of a very miscellaneous character, for what the Pipe Rolls essentially show is the method of payment, not a comprehensive picture of royal purchases. Nonetheless it is helpful as indicating the quantities spent on armaments, on luxury costume, for the king as well as for the queen, and on wine. It reminds us that beeswax had to be provided for the royal chapel, and by that token the more for candles in every church in the City; and oil for lamps besides, as well as more durable materials to build and adorn the churches. Expensive presents appear of fine cloth, orphrey and scarlet and the like. They remind us of the many types of goods carried through London, as well as those imported for use

[1] *Chron. Waltham*, p. 34.
[2] Reynolds, *Econ. Hist. Rev.*, 1st Series, vol. iv, 1932–4, pp. 317–23; above, p. 279.
[3] See pp. 93–4.
[4] *PR 31 Henry I*, pp. 143 ff., esp. 144.

there or exported from its markets. They remind us that the substance of London's trade in the twelfth century probably lay in cloth, wine and food – and stone and timber.

The Building Trades

The frequent fires, and the comparative wealth of the citizens, meant that the City saw a constant activity in building and rebuilding; and a few stone houses, and a throng of stone churches, meant the passage of many shiploads of stone. What survives of Edward the Confessor's abbey and of William II's hall at Westminster are visible evidence of the shiploads of stone from Caen, and cartloads from nearer home; so too the White Tower. In the Temple Church we see the consequence of new fashions in the late twelfth century, especially for Purbeck marble from Dorset, even more profuse in the new Westminster Abbey of the mid-thirteenth century. Stone survives as a monument of the heaviest of the heavy carrying trades; no doubt the carrying of timber was an even more frequent sight in the twelfth century. One of the miracles wrought in St Bartholomew's was on a timber merchant called Spillman who plied (it seems) between Northamptonshire and London:[1] he must stand as a rare witness of a trade evidently of great importance which has left little record.

Wool and Cloth

The orders of the Chancery rolls show that the king looked to London for ample supplies of 'burrel', cheap cloth.[2] It was to Beverley, Lincoln, Stamford and the other towns of the eastern plains that the king, and lesser men, looked for fine cloth; scarlet of Stamford was being sought by the merchants of Spain and Italy in the thirteenth century, and perhaps before. But although the scarlets and others passed through London, were worn in London and carried in London ships, they were not made there in significant quantities. It was the chief centre for cheap cloth. This no doubt acounts for a major crisis in industrial relations recorded in the reign of John.

The weavers had already been organized in 1130; but the City fathers of the late twelfth and early thirteenth centuries showed disapproval of their organization. In 1202 the citizens of London paid sixty marks for

[1] St Bartholomew's *FB*, pp. 40–1 (Webb).
[2] See Carus-Wilson, pp. 213 f., and for what follows, pp. 211 ff.

the total destruction of the guild of weavers by royal charter.[1] The 'citizens' meant the rich oligarchy, which included the men who organized the cloth trade, against whom the Weavers' Guild, acting evidently as a kind of trade union, had attempted to organize itself. Here again we have a very clear illustration of the way in which the Commune, that is the patrician oligarchy, feathered its nest at the expense of the poorer citizens, who were losing their earlier rights and privileges. This is spelt out for us by the remarkable ordinances of this period which tried to control the weavers, and their colleagues the fullers, in a group of English cloth towns. The ordinances belong to the late twelfth century, or about 1200, and relate to Winchester, Marlborough, Oxford and Beverley.[2] There is some variety between them, but obviously collusion too, and the general theme is that the weavers and fullers are not free citizens with civic privileges, and can only become so by abjuring their crafts and paying a large fine; and that the weavers and fullers are not permitted to organize the selling of their wares. These rules survive in the London legal collection of the early thirteenth century, and glosses are added to two of them stating that the laws apply to, or are derived from, the privilege and custom of London, 'as it is said'.[3] The last clause, twice repeated, suggests that it was in fact the citizens of London who were searching for precedents for suppressing the aspirations of their weavers; and it is abundantly clear that the cloth industry in London was a substantial affair managed by a group of capitalist entrepreneurs with a powerful lobby among the ruling oligarchs. But it is likely that throughout the period the quantity of raw wool being exported went far beyond the cloth manufactured in London,[4] and that it was met by a very substantial inflow of dye-stuffs, especially of woad.[5]

[1] *Rotuli de oblatis et finibus*, pp. 185–6; *Cal. Letter Book C*, p. 55: the citizens paid 60 marks 'pro gilda telaria delenda'.

[2] The laws of the weavers and fullers of Winchester, Marlborough, Oxford and Beverley are recorded in the London law book of the early thirteenth-century in British Museum Add. MS 14252, f. 111 (printed in *Beverley Town Documents*, ed. A. F. Leach, Selden Soc., vol. xiv, 1900, pp. 134–5; cf. *Liber Cust.*, vol. i, p. 130). Cf. Carus-Wilson, pp. 235 ff.

[3] Brit. Mus. Add. MS 14252, f. 111 (ut sup.): 'si cum il dient'.

[4] No statistics can be provided before the late thirteenth century: see Williams, pp. 110–11, 149 ff.; E. M. Carus-Wilson and O. Coleman, *England's Export Trade 1275–1547*, Oxford, 1963.

[5] Carus-Wilson, pp. 216 ff.; idem, in *Revue du Nord*, vol. xxxv, 1953, pp. 89–105.

FOOD AND DRINK

It remains to talk of food and drink. We have explored the markets of the West Cheap, which reveal to us one of the fundamental economic changes of the period. In 900 or 1000 a tiny percentage of the population of England lived in towns, and so the large majority grew at least a part of what they fed on. Surpluses there were, to feed those who fought and those who prayed but did not till the fields; and surpluses to supply the growing markets. But these markets could only grow on a very substantial scale when the 'drones' themselves became more numerous. The way in which this happened is imperfectly known; we are back at the circular argument. But at least we can see that those who fought increased in numbers, and the households which served them grew substantially; and that those who prayed grew out of all recognition.[1] The difference that London's growth made to the food market can indeed best be imagined by considering the contribution of the religious, for they alone can be in any measure quantified. A count of the religious may exaggerate the effect a little, since the twelfth century was the golden age of such foundations; but there is no reason to suppose the scale is false. St Paul and St Peter were there before the mid-eleventh century, but both only became the heads of major communities then or later; most of the religious houses were founded in the twelfth century. In 1000 two or three dozen clergy would account for all the jobs we can attach them to, though the number may have been a little more than we realize. By 1200 there were at least 300 monks, nuns and knights under religion in London, Westminster and Southwark; there were the canons of St Paul's, and even if many were not resident, or only occasionally resident, there were thirty households amply provided by the food farms established in the late eleventh century; there were canons in St Martin's and parish priests in a hundred parish churches; and this leaves out of all account the servants and the lesser folk attached to every community.[2] In the hospitals, by 1100, there must have been at least another hundred or so permanent inmates, apart from the occasional visitors and the sick. These are not huge figures, but they represent a really substantial advance; and they help us to understand why the food markets became increasingly important, how it could be that virtually every manor in 'Domesday Book' could envisage selling some surplus and paying a rent.

[1] See KH, esp. pp. 488 ff.
[2] See KH, *passim*, for the figures on which this is based.

The poor drank beer, and some ascetics would accept the water from the wells of Haliwell and Clerkenwell and the like as a substitute for beer or fruit juice.[1] But the men of substance drank wine; and it is evident that the demands for wine greatly expanded the vats and cellars and resources of the Vintry in the eleventh and twelfth centuries. From the middle of the twelfth century the wine from La Rochelle and (perhaps a little later) from Bordeaux came flooding in,[2] to add to 'the drunkenness of fools', which even FitzStephen recognized to be characteristic of London, and gladden the hearts of the wise; by the early thirteenth century, especially after King John had lost Poitou, the wines of Bordeaux ruled the English market and dominated rich men's tables in every English city, especially, one may suppose, in Bristol and London through which it chiefly flowed. It replaced the Rhenish and the north French, which came henceforth in slender quantities; and it was itself in due course supplemented by the sweet wines of the Mediterranean and the south, Malmsey or Madeira or what you will; and the white wines of southern Spain which grew up into Sack or Sherry and the red wines of Portugal which eventually gave us Port. The history of wine in the twelfth and thirteenth centuries is of continuous expansion; the number of wine drinkers, and perhaps their capacity, seems steadily to have increased; though some of this was undoubtedly at the expense of the native English vineyards which went sharply into decline when faced by Claret.

The city of Bristol had been founded in the early eleventh century in some, perhaps in large, measure for the slave-trade; in the mid-twelfth century it found a new vocation as the route by which French wine entered the west. Needless to say there is far more to Bristol's trade than that, but these were apparently the crucial commodities.[3] They were not so crucial, we may reckon, in London, but the growth of the wine trade was undoubtedly a major element in London's prosperity from the arrival of Queen Eleanor on. The Pipe Rolls and the Close Rolls often make thirsty reading, and show us that whatever else a royal court might sometimes lack, wine was in plentiful supply, even when Henry II was in economical mood.

Bristol's is a miniature of the story of London. We began in the Viking age, and found the slave-trade to be the core of the Viking commercial

---

[1] On wells, see *MB*, vol. iii, pp. 3–4; on wine, beer and water in the monastic diet, see Knowles, *Monastic Order*, pp. 464–5.

[2] See p. 266 n.

[3] See E. M. Carus-Wilson in *Historic Towns*, vol. ii, forthcoming.

enterprise, a traffic demanding just that mixture of piracy and trade in which they excelled. We saw that London's place in the commercial world was gradually swung round on its axis; that the Germans ousted the Danes from their halls and their holdings, and the French came too, before and after the Conquest. London proved once again the value of its site as the Flemish connection became increasingly vital both to London and to Flanders. The final turn on the axis came when England entered the orbit of the southern wine trade, and the wines of Bordeaux flowed from the Garonne to the Thames.[1]

Epilogue

Thus we can trace a pattern of a kind, though the picture is made up of fragments. But ever and anon the sources light up a merchant, or a rich man enjoying the fruits of merchandise. Thus the Song of Tristran gave us a brief and vivid glimpse of merchant furling his sails in the Port of London.[2] Thus too FitzStephen gives us much vivid help; and as we began with him, so we shall end:

> One day they rode together through the streets of London [he wrote, to illustrate the intimacy of Becket as chancellor and King Henry II]. It was a harsh winter's day, and from afar the king espied an old man coming, poor, and in a costume worn and thin. He said to the chancellor: 'Do you see him?' 'Yes, I see him.' 'How poor, how weak, how meanly clad he is! Would it not be a great deed of charity to give him a thick, warm cloak?' 'Huge indeed,' said the chancellor, 'and to such a work of mercy, my dear king, you should set your mind and eye.' The poor man came up; the king stopped his horse, so did the chancellor. Gently the king accosted the man, and asked if he would like to have a good cloak.
>
> The poor man, not knowing who they were, thought he was making a joke, and not in earnest. Said the king to the chancellor, 'Surely yours shall be this huge work of charity'; and he threw his arms over the chancellor's hood and strove to pull off the splendid new cloak of scarlet and gris which the chancellor was wearing – and which the chancellor struggled to hold onto. Thus they shook each other mightily and shouted, and the rich men and knights who were following them came rushing up in astonishment to know why they

[1] See p. 266 and n.   [2] See pp. 158–90.

had suddenly fallen to struggling with one another. Neither spoke; both were intent on their wrestling, so that at times it seemed as if they might fall together. The chancellor resisted a while, then allowed the king the victory: he bent his head and the king lifted off the cloak and gave it to the poor man. Then the king was the first to tell his companions the story: all laughed loudly, and some offered the chancellor their cloaks and scarves. The old, poor man went off with the chancellor's cloak, enriched and made happy beyond his dreams, giving thanks to God.[1]

[1] *MB*, vol. iii, pp. 24–5 (cited Veale, p. 17).

Part IV

Church and Society

11

Monasteries and
Hospitals

1 WESTMINSTER ABBEY

Edward the Confessor

IN THE second half of the twelfth century William FitzStephen could
count thirteen conventual churches and 126 lesser churches, all or most of
them parish churches. We have argued that the pattern of parishes was the
product above all of the eleventh and twelfth centuries; and that the formation of this mighty battalion of tiny churches was especially characteristic
of London and a few other English cities of the age; and that the churches
great and small form, with the wards and their boundaries, the crucial
evidence for the formation of the new city in this era.

The thirteen conventual churches, and many more which were added
in the two generations after FitzStephen wrote, reflect the religious
sentiment of high society in Europe at large between the mid-eleventh and
the mid-thirteenth centuries; and they reflect in a quite remarkable way
the social attitudes of the leading men of London over these two centuries.

The parishes reveal the age of the missionary church in the English
towns;[1] although they flourished exceedingly in the late eleventh and
twelfth centuries, they already belonged to an era passing out of fashion,
the pre-Gregorian, unreformed church of the tenth and early eleventh
centuries. From the tenth century on monastic reforms, with their centres
in Lorraine, Burgundy and England, spread over western Europe a
monasticism of new and lofty prestige; and in the mid-eleventh century,
partly inspired by the monasticism of Cluny, Gorze and Glastonbury, the
Papacy itself became the centre of ecclesiastical reform. The sentiment of

[1] Chap. 6; Brooke in *Studies in Church History*, vol. vi, pp. 59–83.

the reformers was monastic and ascetic; they tried to enforce the laws of celibacy, to separate the clergy from the crowd. The tiny churches of London represented everything of which they disapproved: the close intimacy of cleric and layman, and lay proprietorship of churches.

So far as the record goes, this monastic movement seriously impinged on London and its neighbourhood when Edward the Confessor converted Westminster Abbey from a small and struggling community into a great royal abbey.[1] His new foundation represented continental fashions in monasticism; though hardly the new ideas of papal reform, for which Edward seems to have cared little; or perhaps one should say he had not heard of them. If so, he was a little deaf, but it is intelligible that a man no longer young when he became king in 1042, and already king for seven years when the new doctrines were first publicly demonstrated north of the Alps by Pope Leo IX in 1049, should see no incompatibility between harbouring the notorious pluralist Archbishop Stigand, often condemned by the Papacy, and winning a reputation for piety by his pious works, by his visions and his miracles, and by immense expenditure on the new abbey church at Westminster.[2]

Armitage Robinson, himself a former Dean of Westminster, wrote:

There was a pretty rivalry in medieval times between the great abbeys of Westminster and Glastonbury, not unlike the contest for historical precedence between the universities of Oxford and Cambridge which produced less reputable forgeries at a later time . . . Westminster might at first be content to go back to King Sebert in 604; for the great minster at Glastonbury was known to have been built by King Ina [Ine] a century later. But the Glastonbury monks discovered that King Lucius had been left out of account, and they claimed a visit from the missionaries of Pope Eleutherus in 166. Westminster on enquiry discovered that their church also had been founded in the days

---

[1] On Westminster Abbey, see Dom Hugh Aveling, in E. Carpenter (ed.), *A House of Kings*, 1966, pp. 3–84; J. Armitage Robinson, *Flete's History of Westminster Abbey* (including, pp. 2 ff., a summary and criticism of the foundation legends by Sulcard and others), 1909, and *Gilbert Crispin*, 1911; Goscelin's *Vita S. Wulsini*, ed. C. H. Talbot, *Revue Bénédictine*, vol. lxix, 1959, pp. 68–85; *Vita Ædwardi Regis*, ed. F. Barlow, NMT, 1962. On the foundation, see Harmer, pp. 286 ff.; on the abbots, *Heads*, pp. 76–7.

[2] Barlow, *Vita Ædwardi*, esp. pp. 44 ff.; cf. Barlow, *Edward the Confessor*, for a penetrating investigation of Edward and his reign. On Edward and Westminster, see Aveling (n. 1), pp. 6 ff.

of King Lucius, though after the Diocletian persecution it was turned for a while into a Temple of Apollo. Glastonbury, while insisting on 166 as her own date, allowed that Westminster followed quickly in 169; but presently she made a bolder bid for antiquity and took over the legend of Joseph of Arimathaea and the Holy Grail, and so settled her date once and for all as the thirty-first year after the Passion of the Lord and fifteenth after the Assumption of the glorious Virgin. It was vain for Westminster to plead that the blessed Peter himself had left the gate of Heaven and come down to consecrate his new church with his own apostolic hands. For when St David came with his seven bishops thinking to consecrate the church of Glastonbury, the Lord Himself appeared to him in a vision by night and told him that He the Great High Priest had long ago dedicated the little church of wattles to the honour of His Ever-Virgin Mother.[1]

Westminster Abbey in the eleventh and twelfth centuries was the home of many legends, and the factory[2] in which innumerable forged charters were made. The result is that the true lineaments of its early history can hardly be discerned. In the days of Pope Eleutherus, and for many centuries after, the site of the abbey was an island in the Thames liable to floods; although Westminster had a river crossing in Roman times, and a modest settlement, it seems likely that it was almost entirely deserted in the early Middle Ages, until the great Mercian King Offa in the eighth century planted a small church here, with the idea of founding a monastery.[3] No doubt Offa had in mind the assertion of Mercian supremacy in the neighbourhood of London, and he was in any case a prodigious builder of churches. It is likely, however, that he died without founding the monastic community he seems to have intended, and there is no clear record of any abbey at Westminster before the establishment by St

---

[1] J. Armitage Robinson, *Somerset Historical Essays*, pp. 1–2.

[2] The phrase was used by James Tait, in his paper on one of the Coventry forgeries, now known to have been composed by the Westminster forgers (*Essays in History presented to R. L. Poole*, ed. H. W. C. Davis, Oxford, 1927, pp. 158–9 n.); on the Westminster forgers see Bishop and Chaplais, pp. xx ff.; Chaplais.

[3] A grant by Offa, dated 785, spurious in its present form but very likely based on genuine tradition, seems to be the earliest evidence of the abbey's existence to which any sort of credence can be given (Birch, no. 245; Sawyer, no. 124; see Harmer, pp. 500–1).

Dunstan of St Wulfsige, a native of London, as first abbot in or about 958-9.[1] Wulfsige presently departed to be Bishop of Sherborne, and his successors are only names to us; it is clear, indeed, that it was a small and struggling affair until taken in hand by the Confessor.

Edward is said to have had a special devotion to St Peter. Among his first recorded acts was a promise to confirm the English possessions of St Peter at Ghent if ever he should become king; and among the last events of his reign as king one of the most congenial must have been the consecration of the great abbey church of St Peter at Westminster on Christmas Day 1065.[2] It was the first great church built in England according to the new Romanesque fashion, an enormous church with a single vista, and no longer the conglomerate of chapels strung together which mark the character of the few major churches of pre-Conquest England whose physiognomy is known, such as Winchester Cathedral or St Augustine's Abbey, Canterbury.[3] Fragmentary remains, contemporary descriptions, and the stylized representation in the Bayeux Tapestry, enable us to form some notion of the Confessor's abbey. It is likely enough that it was modelled on Jumièges, now the most impressive monastic ruin of this age in Normandy; and thus far reflects the Confessor's continental upbringing and affection for the land and people of his mother, Queen Emma, an affection, one is bound to think, he did not feel for Emma herself.[4] We may also suppose that it reflects a clear conception of the abbey's function.

As a boy, he may have visited the French king's private monastery of Saint-Denis; in later life, he was certainly aware of it.[5] The more substantial of the two surviving fragments of Edward's genuine great seal belongs to, and was once attached to, a writ granting the manor of Taynton in Oxfordshire to Saint-Denis, a grant probably not unconnected with Edward's gratitude to his physician, Baldwin, monk of Saint-Denis,

[1] See *Heads*, p. 76, and Goscelin's Life of St Wulfsige, ed. C. H. Talbot, *Revue Bénédictine*, vol. lxix, 1959, pp. 68 ff. (not entirely reliable, but the main lines of Wulfsige's career seem confirmed by other evidence).

[2] Round, *CDF*, no. 1374, doubtless spurious, but reflecting tradition at Ghent; Barlow, *Edward the Confessor*, pp. 244 ff.

[3] For Edward's church, see Barlow, *Edward the Confessor*, pp. 229 ff., and references cited p. 231, n. 4; for Winchester Cathedral, M. Biddle, *The Old Minster*, Winchester, 1970, with plan on p. 82; for St Augustine's Canterbury, A. W. Clapham, *English Romanesque Architecture before the Conquest*, Oxford, 1930, pp. 149–52.

[4] Cf. Barlow, *Edward the Confessor*, pp. 76 ff.

[5] See Bishop and Chaplais, no. 20 and plate XVIII; Harmer, pp. 243 ff., no. 55.

whom he later made Abbot of Bury St Edmunds.[1] Unquestionably Westminster was intended as a burial church, a mausoleum of kings; possibly also in Edward's own lifetime the idea of it as a coronation church was born; the idea that Harold should be crowned there was evidently conceived before the Confessor was quite dead; in any case the choice of the abbey for the anointing and coronation of kings of doubtful title, Harold and William I, naturally suggested itself in view of the abbey's intimate link with Edward, the symbol of legitimacy. After the twelfth-century forgers had indelibly impressed upon the records that only in their abbey could a successor to St Edward be legitimately crowned, its place in the ceremonial of the monarchy was firmly established;[2] in 1163 this tradition became venerable when the recently canonized Confessor was translated into a splendid shrine in the centre of his own church, and a century later it was canonized when Henry III rebuilt both church and shrine at enormous expense, and reintroduced the English language into the royal line by calling his eldest son Edward.[3]

Quite early in Edward the Confessor's reign, in or soon after 1044, Robert, Abbot of Jumièges, was given the bishopric of London; and it may well be that the idea of an abbey similar in design to Jumièges was worked out between Robert and the king in the years which followed. Robert was clearly a favourite adviser, and for a brief spell in 1051–2 Archbishop of Canterbury.[4] When Earl Godwine and his family went into exile in 1051 Robert was one of those who benefited from Edward's personal rule; but his enjoyment of the archbishopric was short, for on Godwine's return the next year he fled to Normandy. It may be that it was Edward's surrender to Godwine, and the flight of Robert, which inspired his schemes for Westminster, as compensation for defeat and disillusionment. Hitherto, as far as we know, the king's palace when he visited London was within the walls, where he lay at the mercy of the London mob. From now on, no English king stayed in London within the walls for any length of time, and a decision of fundamental moment for London's history was taken.

The abbey of Saint-Denis, like Westminster, lay at a short distance from the kingdom's greatest city. But Saint-Denis differed from Edward's abbey in two respects. First of all, though fully as much the king's

---

[1] See *Heads*, p. 32 and references.

[2] See p. 369.

[3] On Henry III and Westminster, see Colvin, vol. i, chap. IV, esp. part 4, pp. 130 ff. On the translation of 1163, see F. Barlow, *Edward the Confessor*, pp. 325–7.

[4] See pp. 25–6.

possession, his private monastery, in the German phrase, his *Eigenkloster*, and in that respect Edward's chief model, Saint-Denis was not at the same time a centre of government: no great palace grew up about it. Paris itself was already on the way to becoming the one European city apart from the Pope's and St Peter's capital city of Rome, which was truly a capital in the modern, political sense of the term.[1] Although the French king, like the English, was peripatetic, and his government travelled with him, his demesne was so small, and his city so large, that Paris became in a quite special sense his home long before Westminster was a seat of government to anything like the same degree. Thus the royal palaces lay always in the heart of Paris, whereas Saint-Denis lay at a short distance outside its walls. Westminster seems to have been designed as palace as well as *Eigenkloster* from the start, though its buildings at first were of wood. Here an ageing king could settle at a safe distance from the teeming city; close to the river which was the centre of the city's communications with the world, far enough from London to sleep undisturbed at night. He was not quite so intimate with London as was the Count of Flanders when he visited Bruges, and lived in his house in the *castrum*, with one of his favourite *Eigenkirchen*, or proprietary churches, St Donatian's collegiate church, within its bounds, adjacent to the rapidly growing town on which a fair share of his wealth depended.[2] Nor was he so intimate with his city as the first Norman Bishop of Chester with his, for the latter planted his cathedral in the church of St John immediately outside the City walls, perhaps to place a stout wall between himself and the vassals of the Norman earl, perhaps because St John's was his own property and so convenient for the purpose.[3] A nearer analogy to Edward's selection of Westminster was the choice of the first bishops of Llandaff and St Asaph, who planted their cathedrals in villages at almost exactly the same distance from two of the greatest Norman castles of south and north Wales, Cardiff and Rhuddlan, as is Westminster from London:[4] near enough to be in touch, but no so close as to be under the constant eye of, or to be always identified with, the Norman conquerors. Thus Edward seems to have chosen

[1] On Paris in the eleventh and twelfth centuries, see A. Friedmann, *Paris: ses rues, ses paroisses du moyen âge à la Révolution*, Paris, 1959.

[2] See Galbert of Bruges, ed. Ross, pp. xvi (plan), 51 ff., 318 ff. (note on St Donatian by J. Mertens).

[3] See Brooke in *Studia Gratiana*, vol. xii, 1967, p. 54.

[4] Ibid., and references cited n. 37, esp. to *Journal of Flintshire Historical Society*, 1964, pp. 32–45.

8. St Petroc's reliquary: twelfth-century painted ivory casket, Islamic work from Sicily or southern Italy, probably sold in Westminster in 1177, now in Bodmin parish church (*see p. 273*)

9. Twelfth-century hanging bronze lamp from All Hallows' Lombard Street, now in the Guildhall Museum

40-41.
Mid-twelfth-century
capital from the cloister
of Westminster Abbey,
c. 1140, showing the
judgement of Solomon.
See G. Zarnecki, *Later
English Romanesque
Sculpture*, London,
1953, p. 8

The crypt of St Mary-le-Bow, late eleventh century, showing the scale of a major parish church (before restoration) (*see p. 137*)

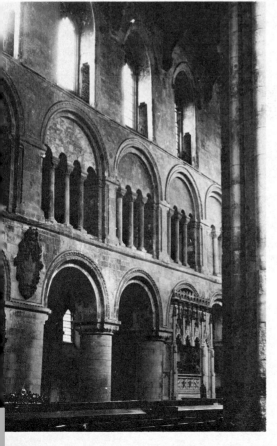

43. The choir of the priory (now parish) church of St Bartholomew Smithfield, mid-twelfth century (*see pp. 325–8*)

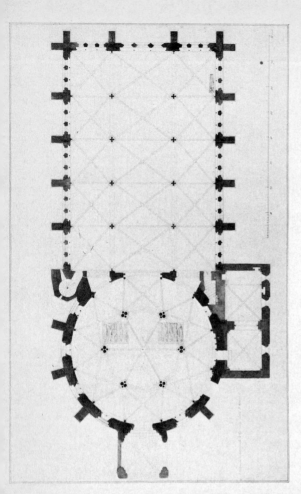

THE TEMPLE CHURCH: BEGUN WHEN
THE NEW SITE WAS ACQUIRED IN
THE EARLY 1160s, CONSECRATED IN
1185; THE ORIGINAL ROTUNDA SUR-
VIVES, MUCH RESTORED AFTER SERIOUS
DAMAGE IN 1941; THE CHOIR WAS
ENLARGED AND REBUILT IN EARLY
THIRTEENTH CENTURY (*see pp. 231-3
& 331-2*)

44. Plan of the Temple Church (from
     an original in the Society of Anti-
     quaries)

45. Richly sculpted Romanesque west
     door, from an early-nineteenth-
     century engraving (from an original
     in the Society of Antiquaries)

...he rotunda, one of ten known ...ves of this shape built in England ... the twelfth century; six of them ...ere for Templar houses

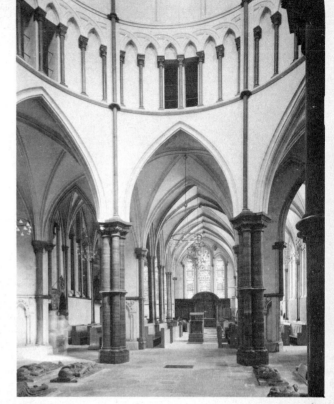

The priory church of the Knights Hospitallers: the crypt of St John's, Clerkenwell; the western part is from the original church begun in the 1140s, the eastern of the extension consecrated in 1185. This church also had a nave rotunda, whose line can still be traced in the street outside the church (*see p. 332*)

48. Panorama of London by J. C. Visscher, 1616: this detail shows St Paul's after the removal of the spire but before Inigo Jones began remodelling the exterior

49. After the fire of 1666, a drawing by T. Wyck showing the south transept and the nave, from the site of the choir

The Norman nave, early twelfth century in design, though not completed until late in the century; engraving by Hollar for W. Dugdale, *History of St Paul's Cathedral*, 1658

Ralph de Diceto's Chronicle: a detail from the copy which Dean Ralph presented to St Paul's, now Lambeth Palace Library MS 8, f. 57r. The pastoral staff draws attention to the passage beside it describing the ordination of Richard de Belmeis II (later bishop 1152–62) as deacon, because he was Archdeacon of Middlesex, in St Paul's in December 1138 and the election of Theobald as Archbishop of Canterbury. In the right-hand column the Empress is expelled from London in 1141

52. Water-colour by C. A. Buckler after a drawing by his grandfather J. Buckler, British Museum Addit. MS 37121, no. 26; the priory church is authentically presented here, though the setting has been surprisingly countrified

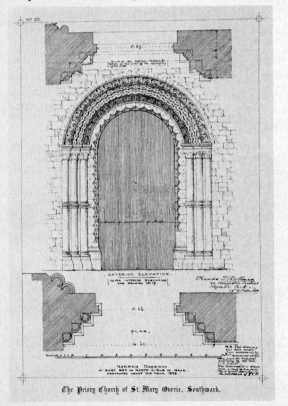

ST MARY OVERY, THE PRIORY CHURCH, SOUTHWARK CATHEDRAL, BEFORE RESTORATION (*see p. 314*)

53. A Norman door, twelfth century, detroyed *c.* 1839; this plate is from FDollmann, *The Priory of St Mary OvLondon, 1881, Plate 20, redrawn froearlier drawing

Westminster deliberately because it was near, but not too near, his metropolis.

In the mid-eleventh century, the abbey church of Saint-Denis, though venerable, was not of great size nor a mirror of the fashion of its age; that it was to become when Abbot Suger, the friend of Louis VI and the regent of Louis VII, began the rebuilding of his church in the incipient Gothic style, a rebuilding which was to give it a high place among the most celebrated buildings of its age.[1] Edward looked to Normandy and to the new fashion of his own day; and built a large basilica in which the trappings and symbols of kingship would be visible to all who came. The circlet of royal tombs which surround him now in the abbey faithfully follow his wish that the abbey should be a symbol of his kingship, a royal mausoleum. All of them are of the style and fashion of later centuries, above all of the thirteenth: Edward has become a saint, his tomb a shrine, an event which would no doubt have caused him great astonishment; and he would probably have been equally surprised by the screens and enclosures which hide his tomb and his successors' from the common view of visitors to the nave. No doubt he had expected that on suitable festivals, especially St Peter's day, the citizens of London would take advantage of the mid-summer weather to visit St Peter's home, and find within it the dazzling symbols of divine regality. Thus in his later years, condemned to accept that other men fought his battles and (in some respects) governed in his name, the ageing king prepared, like Napoleon on St Helena, to carry on his work beyond the grave.[2] Edward's posthumous career gave him a success more remarkable than any he achieved in his life.

Before 1066, Edward was a cosmopolitan figure who made a moderate success of kingship, but failed in a king's first duty: he left a disputed succession and a kingdom open to invasion and disaster. After the Norman Conquest he became, first of all the symbol of respectability, and especially of all things English; his successors tumbled over one another to claim that they ruled as his legitimate heirs, that their chief and only object was to preserve his good laws, to revive the golden age of his rule. The monks of Westminster prayed and plotted that he might become a saint, that his bones might be relics, their church a centre of pilgrimage; and they found a ready ally in the middle of the twelfth century (after several disappointments) in the young and brilliant King Henry II.

[1] See E. Panofsky, *Abbot Suger on the Abbey Church of St-Denis*, Princeton, 1946.
[2] For a rather different view, see Barlow, *Edward the Confessor*, p. 229 ff.

1066–1215

Between the time of St Wulfsige and the days of Edward the Confessor, the abbey seems to have been a modest and small but effective representative of the monasticism of Glastonbury and Abingdon, of Dunstan and Ethelwold and the *Regularis Concordia*. From the days of the Confessor's Abbot Edwin (*c.* 1049–*c.* 1071)[1] it embraced the Norman monasticism willed for it by Edward; and under the direct patronage of a series of kings who for all their faults were (with the single exception of William Rufus) patrons and founders of monasteries, one or two of them on a princely scale, it might seem set for a distinguished and inspiring career.[2] Unfortunately, we have no documents to reveal to us the quality of the interior life of the abbey, and a fitful record only of its fortunes between 1066 and 1216. Yet what we know reveals many examples of the tensions caused by the inward and the outward-looking traditions in medieval monasticism – especially troublesome to a large house set within a royal palace on the edge of a great city; and it also shows the ups and downs to which the chances of royal patronage subjected it.

The core of Norman monasticism before 1050 lay in the abbeys of Fécamp, Bernay and Jumièges.[3] Fécamp enjoyed the immediate inspiration of St William of Dijon, the Italian monk who transformed the monastic observance of Burgundy and Normandy in the early eleventh century under the influence of Cluny. William himself ruled at Fécamp until 1028, at Bernay till his death in 1031, by which date his disciples had long ruled Jumièges. In the spiritual life, Fécamp was supreme, especially under William's successor, John or Jeannelin, one of the notable spiritual writers and directors of the century – famous especially for his devout verses and prayers. In architecture Jumièges was then, and still is, the chief monument of mid-eleventh century Norman monasticism. From

[1] *Heads*, p. 76.
[2] Cf. Knowles, *Monastic Order*, pp. 72, 96, etc.; on the Norman kings as patrons, Brooke in *Il monachesimo e la riforma ecclesiastica*, Milan, 1971, pp. 125–44.
[3] Knowles, chapter V; A. Wilmart, *Auteurs spirituels et textes dévots du moyen âge latin*, Paris, 1932, pp. 101–25, 126–37; J. Leclercq and J. P. Bonnes, *Un Maître de la vie spirituelle au xie siècle, Jean de Fécamp*, Paris, 1946, and the series of volumes commemorating *Jumièges* and *Fécamp* which have appeared in recent years, especially L. Musset's paper in *L'Abbaye bénédictine de Fécamp*, vol. i, Fécamp, 1959, pp. 67–79, on John of Fécamp as an administrator, which explains why the Conqueror might look to him as a source of able managers as well as for spiritual leaders.

Jumièges came Robert, Bishop of London, whose abbey was the model for Edward's Westminster; and it was natural that William I should turn to Jumièges for a new abbot when Edwin died *c.* 1071. But Abbot Geoffrey proved incapable, and was soon returned to Normandy, on the advice (as Westminster tradition asserted) of Archbishop Lanfranc.[1] The Conqueror turned next to John of Fécamp and asked for his help in securing a former monk of Fécamp, one Vitalis, who had already been for some years a notably successful abbot of Bernay. Vitalis ruled Westminster effectively until his death *c.* 1085, when he was succeeded by perhaps the most interesting man to hold the office in the whole period. Gilbert Crispin[2] was a disciple of two archbishops of Canterbury, Lanfranc and Anselm, and won golden opinions from them both; he had been a monk of their Norman home at Bec, later a monk of Canterbury Cathedral (moved there on Lanfranc's insistence to the great sorrow of Anselm, then Abbot of Bec), finally, from *c.* 1085 until his death at a considerable age in 1117–18, Abbot of Westminster. Thereafter the abbey seems to have fallen on evil days. Abbot Herbert (1121–*c.* 1136), though a disciple of Gilbert Crispin, failed to maintain effective discipline and smooth external relations; the revenues declined, and the art of forgery was first effectively practised among his clerks and monks.[3] His successor, Gervase of Blois, King Stephen's illegitimate son, seems to have been even worse; and under him the factory of forgery flourished as never before or after. But the central figure in the abbey's story in the middle of the century was neither of the abbots, but the strange, picturesque, dishonest, dedicated prior, Osbert de Clare, whose letters are our chief source for many aspects of the religious history of the period between the death of Gilbert Crispin and the accession of Henry II.[4]

In 1157 or 1158 Gervase was deposed; Osbert had already been exiled from the abbey. The new abbot was Master Laurence, a man of learning who has left behind him a volume of sermons, the only important monument to Westminster's *scriptorium* between the departure of Osbert and the end of the century.[5] Laurence was also an able and experienced ecclesiastical administrator and politician, who became abbot after a very short

---

[1] *Heads*, p. 76 and references.

[2] See below, pp. 302–6.

[3] On Herbert and Gervase, see *Heads*, p. 77, and references; esp. Chaplais.

[4] See below, pp. 306–10.

[5] *Heads*, p. 77; Robinson, *Flete*, pp. 91–4, 143; F. E. Croydon in *Mediaeval and Renaissance Studies*, vol. ii, 1950, pp. 169–71.

career as a monk of St Albans; though his monasticism cannot have been deeply rooted, he succeeded in restoring the fortune of the abbey by administrative skill and diplomacy, and by taking speedy advantage of the diplomatic situation to win the canonization of Edward the Confessor: a papal schism and a complaisant king gave Laurence advantages Osbert had never enjoyed, and in 1161 Edward was canonized.[1] Thereafter Westminster was ruled by a series of monks from its own community till the turn of the century, effective, so far as we know, but little more than names to us. If we wish to penetrate beneath the surface of this tale, we must look more closely at the two crucial figures of Gilbert Crispin and Osbert de Clare.

Gilbert Crispin

Gilbert is a fair representative of Norman monasticism at its most attractive; he lives for us in his own writings and in the letters of St Anselm. He came of a line of Norman nobles and warriors. His parents, William Crispin and Eva de Montfort, were devoted to the Abbey of Bec, and Gilbert, their younger son, was placed there as a monk while still a small boy. On his deathbed, William Crispin himself was clothed as a monk, and Eva settled down to live a life of dedicated widowhood with two friends in the abbey precinct. She was regarded as a mother to the monks, and Abbot Anselm, who was by no means addicted to female society, referred to himself as her eldest son; she was long remembered at Bec for her austerity, kindness and rich gifts, and there is a pleasantly human touch in her last recorded act, which was to appear to one of the monks after her death to tell him that she had been assigned a penance 'because I loved small dogs and other objects of this kind, which men despise'.[2]

The monasticism of Bec lives for us above all in three documents of exceptional quality: in the life of the founder and first abbot, the shrewd, austere, kindly ex-knight Herluin, written by Gilbert himself; in the letters of Herluin's successor, St Anselm, and in Eadmer's *Life* of Anselm; and its mode of life, with all that was reckoned best in the observance of the Norman and other leading French houses of the day, was enshrined in the Constitutions which Herluin's prior, Lanfranc, drew up when he

---

[1] Barlow, *Edward the Confessor*, pp. 277–84, 309 ff.; Z. N. Brooke in *Essays in History presented to R. L. Poole*, pp. 235–6.

[2] Robinson, *Gilbert Crispin (GC)*, esp. pp. 14–16, and 16n.

became Archbishop of Canterbury for use in his Cathedral priory, and in other communities in England inclined to listen to his directions.[1] It was a monasticism with the quiet, regular routine in church, chapter-house and cloister at its heart; ruled by an abbot intimate with his community, not, as later, the head of a separate establishment with his own hall and chamber. The abbot and the whole community slept in the common dormitory, and had no privacy save on occasions in the special parlours set aside for conversation. Silence was the norm; speech and conversation the exception, at least in theory. But Lanfranc's Constitutions are practical instruments, and he allows more than the usual times for conversation – doubtless not for gossip, but for the practical things of life, and to plan the crafts and other manual tasks of the cloister and domestic buildings. Eadmer's *Life* shows that Anselm not only used the daily chapter, but also the dining-room, for addressing his monks, and the spiritual conversation of the refectory is indeed the stuff of which Eadmer's picture of the saint is made.[2] Lanfranc portrays a monasticism essentially inward-looking, though not exclusively so: the almoner, for instance, is shown visiting the sick and doing good works about the town. In any case, Herluin's *Life* shows that even in the Bec of Gilbert Crispin's youth, far removed from great cities, external relations played a vital part in the life of the community. In the end its prosperity depended on the friendship of well-to-do men like William Crispin, and from quite early days they made ends meet by setting up a school in which the great Italian scholar Lanfranc taught the young of the neighbourhood as well as Gilbert Crispin and the other boys of the cloister.[3] In 1063 Lanfranc left Bec to be Abbot of Saint-Étienne at Caen, en route for Canterbury (1070–89), and Gilbert must then have been in his teens; with Anselm, the other great Italian scholar to whom Bec owes its fame, Gilbert was intimate. In the 1070s Gilbert was himself teaching the young monks, and about 1080 Lanfranc carried him off to help him build up the community in Canterbury Cathedral Priory, much to Anselm's sorrow. Anselm's letters are full of tears and friendship; but there is a note of special intimacy in his exchanges

[1] *Decreta Lanfranci* (*The Monastic Constitutions of Lanfranc*), ed. and trans. D. Knowles, NMT, 1951; 2nd ed. (Latin only), *Corpus Consuetudinum Monasticarum*, vol. iii, Siegburg, 1967.

[2] Eadmer, *Life of St Anselm*, ed. and trans. R. W. Southern, NMT, 1962, repr. OMT, 1972; Southern, *St Anselm and his Biographer*, Cambridge, 1963, esp. pp. 332–3.

[3] Robinson, *GC*, pp. 96–7; on Lanfranc, see A. J. MacDonald, *Lanfranc*, Oxford, 1926 (a new biography by Dr M. Gibson is nearing completion).

with Gilbert: a real friendship and sympathy which are reflected also in Gilbert's writings.

Of these, the most interesting are his *Life of Herluin* and his *Dialogue between a Christian and a Jew*.[1] In the former he showed his devotion to Bec and to its early traditions of observance as well as to its school and its great teachers. We may be sure that Bec was the model for the life Gilbert attempted to instil at Westminster in his long rule from *c*. 1085 to *c*. 1117. In the winter of 1092–3 Gilbert was visited by Anselm, still Abbot of Bec; and in their conversations, it would seem, was born both the *Dialogue* and the idea which issued in Anselm's most famous book, the *Cur Deus homo*. The latter is a justification and explanation of the Incarnation and Redemption; and it is celebrated for marking the first step away from a legalistic interpretation of Redemption such as had been fashionable since the time of St Augustine, to a more humane and human viewpoint. In Bec tradition, Herluin was remembered for his devoutness, Lanfranc for his wisdom, Anselm for gentleness; and the gentle friendship with which he inspired his close disciples is amply testified in Eadmer's *Life*.[2] To those less close, Anselm must have seemed remote and austere, and his writings reveal a philosopher's detachment, and a love of ethereal logic. The *Cur Deus homo* is partly inspired by the thought that the Incarnation must be justified in the eyes of non-Christians, and this, in practical terms, meant the Jew; but beyond the first inspiration, the practical concern seems only slightly to affect Anselm's book. It is much more consistently present in Gilbert's *Dialogue*.

Before the Conquest there seem to have been few or no Jews in England;[3] the flourishing community which lived in the neighbourhood of St Lawrence Jewry and the street still called Old Jewry in the heart of the City was mainly the result of the Conquest. Their first arrival is the background to Gilbert's *Dialogue*. A learned Jew, educated in Mainz, had come to the London Jewry; and he had met and explained to Gilbert the Jewish viewpoint. A discussion of notable moderation ensued. The lot of the Jew was never secure or comfortable in medieval Christendom; and the preaching of the First Crusade in the 1090s was to unleash upon them

---

[1] The Life is in Robinson, *GC*, pp. 87–110, followed by *De simoniacis*; pp. 60 ff. summarise the *Disputation*, which is ed. in full by B. Blumencranz, 1956; his other *Disputation* (with 'a Heathen') was ed. C. C. J. Webb in *Mediaeval and Renaissance Studies*, vol. iii, 1954, pp. 55–77. On him see Southern, *St Anselm and his Biographer*, pp. 205–6.

[2] Cf. above, p. 303, and n. 2.   [3] See pp. 222–7.

ferocious persecution. It was not that the Pope intended to touch the
Jews – far from it; but his initiative gave practical encouragement to a
popular crusading doctrine far cruder than his, which taught that 'the
infidel were cattle for the slaughter and their removal a good work – and
the riff-raff of the Crusades practised this among the 'infidels' in Europe,
that is, among the Jews, before setting off to seek the Moslems.[1] Amid the
hysteria of the Crusades, the calm voice of Anselm was heard preaching
that a life of prayer at home was a better road to Heaven than a life of war
abroad;[2] and Gilbert, in turn, shows a kindly and humane attitude to his
Jewish friend, and a moderate tone towards his doctrine, which was
commonly absent from Christian–Jewish relations in this age. No doubt
there was more such tolerance in the religious and mercantile world of the
day than the record shows us; yet we may still feel that Gilbert's abbey
was (as in a measure the Confessor had intended) a haven of peace and
quiet away from the storm and stress of the City.

In one passage in the *Dialogue* the Jew cites current themes in Romanesque art – a crucifixion with sun and moon personified, and a Christ in
Majesty, with symbols of the evangelists at the four corners. 'These
images the Christians sculpt and work in metal and paint when and where
they can, and they adore and worship them, though God's law altogether
forbids it.' This objection, observed Armitage Robinson, 'may even have
been suggested by a "Majesty" in Gilbert's new refectory'.[3] Christ in
Majesty was to be one of the commonest themes in the art of the day,
sculpted on tympana at Moissac and countless other churches, common too
in paintings in books, once common, doubtless, in wall paintings too,
though most have disappeared. Yet this passage was written, in all
probability, twenty years or so before the tympanum at Moissac was made,
at a time when English churches were notable for their austerity and the
absence of sculpture. The fragments of capitals which survive from
Norman Westminster suggest that the completed buildings were not
wholly lacking in ornament. But they come from the cloister and are of the
mid-twelfth century.[4]

In any event the passage reminds us that owing to the constant presence
of craftsmen and masons even Westminster Abbey was not quite so peace-

---

[1] On the popular doctrine of the Crusade, see Brooke, *Europe in the Central Middle Ages*, London, 1964, pp. 356–65.

[2] See Southern, *St Anselm and his Biographer*, pp. 122–3.   [3] Robinson, *GC*, p. 65.

[4] Lethaby, *Westminster Abbey reexamined*, pp. 22–37; the richer Romanesque capitals are *c.* 1140: **Plates 40–1.**

ful as Abbot Gilbert may have wished. The choir of the abbey church was probably complete when Edward the Confessor died; the undercroft and dormitory, of which substantial parts still remain, may also have been under way. It is likely that the dormitory was completed by Abbot Vitalis, and in Gilbert's time the refectory and the abbot's chamber, the 'locutorium', where conversation was allowed, and where, perhaps, such dialogues as this could take place. But the masons and carpenters must have made the abbey buildings unquiet through much of Gilbert's time, and beyond. Then the main structure was little altered until the advent of Henry III.[1]

Osbert de Clare

Gilbert Crispin represents medieval Westminster Abbey at its best; Osbert de Clare is an equally faithful mirror of a more ambivalent attitude and life.[2] In him tragedy and comedy were oddly mingled, in his mind there was a similar confusion of devotion and chicanery. He was a man of imagination and ability, who was recognized as a leader among his fellow-monks. He was twice prior, and once nearly abbot; but he was evidently difficult and cantankerous, and sat too loosely in his allegiance to his royal patrons to be a suitable abbot from their viewpoint. It was not that he was openly disloyal or rebellious, but simply that the world for him centred too exclusively in the abbey and its traditions, and in the customs of the Old English Church, to make him a comfortable associate of Norman kings. He was not in any ordinary sense dishonest. But it was no uncommon thing for a dedicated monk in this period to feel that his world was bounded by the walls of the monastery; to see everything outside as in a measure unreal. Thus he devoted his great energies to serving the cult of the abbey's chief founder, Edward the Confessor, and to the protection of the abbey's privileges.

It was doubtless from Gilbert Crispin that Osbert learned respect for St Anselm and his circle of disciples. In many ways he was like Eadmer, the Canterbury monk who became St Anselm's confidant and biographer. Both were faithful and devoted monks, wholly absorbed in the traditional, cosmopolitan, Anglo-Norman monasticism of their day. Both were also

---

[1] Colvin, vol. i, chap. IV, pt 4 for Henry III's work.

[2] On Osbert see J. Armitage Robinson in Osbert of Clare, *Letters*, ed. E. W. Williamson, Oxford, 1929, pp. 1–20; see also the letters, and on Osbert's involvement in forgery, Chaplais; cf. Brooke, *Medieval Church and Society*, London, 1971, pp. 107 ff.

Englishmen by birth, devoted to the traditions of their native land – a devotion which seems altogether more natural and healthy in Eadmer, born before the Norman conquest, than in Osbert, who died almost a century after it. Anselm and his circle believed that human salvation lay within the walls of monasteries, and there is something strange about Eadmer's account of the royal court: he speaks with astonishing disrespect, for instance, about Henry I's Queen Matilda, though he wrote when she was the reigning queen and widely regarded as a model of piety. Osbert, writing in the abbey and the precinct of the Palace of Westminster, commiserates in one of his letters with an eminent clerk of the royal chancery, Robert de Sigillo, for living 'in the Babylonish furnace', by which he means the royal court.[1] Robert paid some attention to this point of view, for when the royal Chancery fell into chaos early in Stephen's reign, he escaped to become a monk of Reading, only to return to Osbert's neighbourhood as Bishop of London in 1141, an office doubtless in Osbert's eyes as redolent of hell as the court itself;[2] for his best energies were devoted to securing and enlarging the privileges of his abbey, which he reckoned to include exemption from the bishop's jurisdiction.

Robert's consecration as bishop closed a long vacancy in the see of London, which at one time was nearly filled by the Abbot of Bury St Edmunds, the younger Anselm, the old archbishop's nephew. The younger Anselm was a man somewhat similar in character to Osbert: devoted but ambiguous. His greatest devotion was to the Blessed Virgin, and he was one of the central figures in the diffusion of the Feast of the Conception of the Virgin, an Old English tradition fostered in the circles in which Anselm, Eadmer and Osbert moved in the early twelfth century.[3] This was one notably English cause to which Osbert gave himself freely; another was the movement to secure the canonization of Edward the Confessor. If he lacked nothing in devotion, he lacked a great deal evidently in tact, and it is ironical how rapidly the canonization was achieved by others after he himself had toiled so long to little purpose.

His *Life of St Edward* is a verbose, rhetorical work of little originality. It shows indeed a certain freedom to adapt, if not invent; but this is nothing unusual in such works at this date, and Osbert was no freer as a hagiographer than his eminent successor St Ailred of Rievaulx, who wrote

---

[1] Osbert of Clare, *Letters*, p. 75, no. 10.

[2] See p. 38.

[3] E. Bishop, *Liturgica Historica*, Oxford, 1918, pp. 238–59; cf. Southern, *St Anselm and his Biographer*, pp. 290 ff.

the official *Life* for the canonization.[1] Osbert had a vision of a kind not uncommon at this date. To him the abbey was the centre of the world, a place where God had chosen especially to dwell, a heavenly gate in the midst of Babylon. The abbey was a very grand royal chapel; and from this two consequences (in Osbert's eyes) must inevitably flow. Harold and William I and Henry I had all been crowned there; no English king might be validly crowned elsewhere, a stipulation he would would have regarded as even more important than Eadmer's that only the Archbishop of Canterbury might perform the ceremony. The second point was that it was both a royal chapel and St Peter's special home – consecrated (so legend had it) by Peter himself. No mere bishop could intrude; like most ancient foundations, it must enjoy the privilege of exemption.[2]

To Osbert and his colleagues, such arguments were entirely cogent and required no further proof. Unfortunately they lived in a world in which written evidence for legal claims was becoming increasingly necessary. If Edward were to be canonized, if exemption was to be enforced, the Pope must be convinced; if the coronation privilege was to be effective, the king and the great men who arranged the ceremony must be taught to take it entirely for granted. The *Life* of King Edward was written to help forward the canonization, and a magnificent series of papal and royal documents to convince pope and king of the abbey's rights. All these documents were forgeries, the product of a school of forgers which was providing such testimony for a number of old established Benedictine houses in England and on the Continent, the greatest of its kind of the age.[3] There is no doubt, furthermore, that Westminster was its centre. It produced royal and papal charters, papal bulls of great portentousness, royal charters of enormous size, and royal writs of extreme sophistication. Most of the larger forgeries have long been recognized as such; some of the writs were so cleverly forged that they deceived scholars until very recent years. The final proof that some were forged followed from the discovery that spurious seal matrices for Edward the Confessor and his two successors had been used (and presumably made) in the abbey in the mid-twelfth century.[4] These seals are in some cases attached to documents written in hands which Dr Pierre Chaplais has identified as those of two clerks who

[1] On the lives of Edward the Confessor by Osbert and Ailred, see Barlow, *Vita Ædwardi*, pp. 124 ff.

[2] Knowles, *Monastic Order*, chap. XXXIII, esp. p. 589 and n. 2.

[3] Chaplais; Brooke, *Medieval Church and Society*, pp. 106 ff.; A. Morey and C. N. L. Brooke, *GF*, pp. 139 ff.

[4] Bishop and Chaplais, pp. xix ff.; Chaplais (on whose paper what follows is based).

served Abbots Herbert and Gervase. But the style of the great charters with which the forgers filled out the rather scanty muniments of the abbey – and saved St Edward's face by making up for his lamentable failure to produce an adequate supply of charters for his favourite abbey – is the style of Osbert de Clare; and Dr Chaplais has shown, by intricate source criticism, that he was their author. Thus the Westminster forgeries were the result of a nefarious alliance between the devout monk and the expert clerk, an alliance entirely characteristic of the age.

'Lo, how the hope of the just man who loveth was not deprived of its effect,' wrote Eadmer, when describing the discovery of the papal privileges which established that the Archbishop of Canterbury should be primate of all Britain.[1] Eadmer was one of the most distinguished historians of his age, the humble and dedicated disciple of St Anselm, although it is almost certain that he knew all or most of them had just been forged. He was a man faithful to truth as he saw it, but wholly absorbed in loyalty to his community, to his cathedral and its saints. It was the same spirit which led the heroic, devoted, obstinate, pathetic Osbert to provide his abbey with splendid privileges in the names of St Dunstan, King Edgar, a galaxy of popes and kings, and a box full of charters of Edward the Confessor himself.

Osbert quarrelled both with Abbot Herbert and with Abbot Gervase – with the latter particularly, whom he found too little dedicated to his abbey, and whom he rightly (it seems) thought a worthless abbot. Yet all three agreed to advance the work of forgery, if they agreed in nothing else; and we must conclude that there was corruption in the abbey in the middle of the century. We touch here a deep layer in the monastic sentiment of the twelfth century, and we must not think we have understood it too easily. Osbert was first appointed prior, and Herbert almoner, by Gilbert Crispin, and there are copious indications that Gilbert was not wrong in seeing important qualities of monastic leadership in Osbert de Clare.

Where Osbert failed, Master Laurence, with the king's aid, and a sheaf of letters from numerous influential ecclesiastics, won the canonization of Edward the Confessor. Thus was the shrine of English monarchy, old and new, prepared for the ministrations of Henry III; and after Laurence's time, we know little of the inner life of the abbey, little of its intellectual life – with a brief interval in the heyday of Abbot, Archbishop and Cardinal Langham in the fourteenth century – though many books could

[1] *Historia Novorum*, ed. M. Rule, Rolls Series, 1884, p. 261; cf. Southern, 'The Canterbury Forgeries'.

be filled with the housekeeping and estate management of the second richest abbey in the land.[1]

11 St Martin le Grand

Westminster Abbey was the shrine of kingship, the royal chapel where king and people met, a powerful symbol. The street-name St Martin le Grand within the City walls is all that survives of the other religious house which began, or grew, late in Edward the Confessor's reign, and was to be the outward sign of such relationship as existed between the royal court and the City. It was also a royal chapel, and round it there nestled, as at Westminster, a precinct which provided shelter for the fugitive – a privileged sanctuary.[2] It contained a church, with stalls for a group of canons and a dean; and it remained throughout the Middle Ages a modest haven of royal power within the City, but usually a remote one, for the king visited it rarely, and its dean and canons hardly more often. The dean was invariably an eminent ecclesiastic high in royal favour, usually a civil servant; and the canons often men of the same kidney. It was as it were a rehearsal for the grander chapels of St Stephen at Westminster and St George at Windsor, founded by Edward III to be chantries for his family and to attract handsome ecclesiastical revenues into the pockets of his clerical servants. It is likely enough that some such purpose was in the mind of the founder of St Martin's. He was a royal clerk, landowner and land-agent called Ingelric, a canon of St Paul's who flourished in the later years of Edward the Confessor and early Norman times. His origin is obscure, but the name seems German, and it is likely that he was one of the many wandering scholars, or foreign adventurers, who flocked to Edward's court from France and Germany. Such were Leofric, founder of

[1] On Simon Langham, see D. Knowles, *Religious Orders in England*, ii, Cambridge, 1955, pp. 54–6. On Westminster in the later Middle Ages, Carpenter (see p. 294 n. 1); E. H. Pearce, *The Monks of Westminster*, Cambridge, 1916; and the studies of Miss B. Harvey, esp. *Documents Illustrating the Rule of Walter de Wenlok, Abbot of Westminster, 1283–1307*, Camden 4th Series, 1965. See also J. Armitage Robinson and M. R. James, *The Manuscripts of Westminster Abbey*, London, 1909.

[2] On royal chapels in general, see J. H. Denton, *English Royal Free Chapels*, Manchester, 1970; on St Martin le Grand, Denton, pp. 28–40; R. H. C. Davis in *LTR*, forthcoming. On its precinct, M. B. Honeybourne, *Journal of the British Archaeological Assoc.*, new series, vol. xxxviii, 1933, pp. 316–33; cf. I. D. Thornley, ib. pp. 293–315. On Ingelric, and Albert of Lorraine, see Round, *CL*, pp. 28 ff.; Barlow, *Edward the Confessor*, p. 157 and references; Le Neve, pp. 59, 89.

Exeter Cathedral, Herman, founder of Salisbury, or Albert of Lorraine, royal clerk and Domesday landholder, canon of St Paul's and a City magnate.[1]

The founder of St Martin's evidently enjoyed royal patronage, and presumably also had important connections in the City. St Martin's was one of those collegiate churches in which the revenues were conveniently divided between a dean, usually absentee, and more modestly endowed canons. After Ingelric's death, the deanship is first found in the hands of a man called Fulcher, evidently a Norman, and most probably to be identified with the brother of Ranulf Flambard, who died Bishop-elect of Lisieux in 1102–3.[2] Fulcher may have been technically an absentee, but as a royal clerk and canon of St Paul's (if correctly identified) he would have been a fairly frequent visitor to London, and doubtless St Martin provided him with comfortable lodging when he came. Such too his successor doubtless enjoyed: Roger, Bishop of Salisbury, the rich, ostentatious minister of Henry I, who built for himself (among other palaces and more modest dwellings) a cathedral at Salisbury, and at Devizes one of the largest castles in Europe with a new town at its gate as a pleasant appendage. St Martin attracted the rich; for when Roger fell, like Lucifer, early in Stephen's reign, the deanery passed to another bishop given to pluralism reminiscent of the days of Edward the Confessor, Henry of Blois, Bishop of Winchester, the king's brother and for a time (1139–43) the Pope's legate. St Martin's added to Henry's enormous pile of wealth, with which he rescued the great abbey of Cluny (where he had once been a monk) from penury, built Wolvesey castle and a posse of other palaces, and gave rich treasures to his cathedral. St Martin also, doubtless provided Henry with a town house, though he probably already had lodging enough in Southwark, within his own diocese.

By the time of Henry's death it had become firmly established (for several centuries to come) that a bishop might not hold deaneries *in commendam*, and although many of St Martin's deans became bishops, they passed the church on to other ambitious young men a little way behind them on the same path. In the late twelfth century we find as

---

[1] See preceding note.

[2] On the deans, see Le Neve, p. 89 (Ingelric); Round, *CL*, p. 116 (Fulcher); ibid. and E. J. Kealey, *Roger of Salisbury*, Berkeley, Los Angeles, London, 1972, pp. 73 ff. (Roger); *Regesta*, vol. iii, nos 529, 532, 547, 549, 552 (Henry); Westminster Abbey Muniment Book 5 (cartulary of St Martin's), f. 10v (Geoffrey, Henry's successor); Le Neve, pp. 2n., 47–8 (Godfrey and William).

dean the justiciar's son, Godfrey de Lucy, on the eve of becoming Bishop of Winchester; and another great royal clerk, William of Ste-Mère-Église, followed Godfrey, and held the deanery until 1199, when he rose to be Bishop of London.

The inner life of the church and precinct is much more obscure. For a moment, in Stephen's reign, the veil is lifted, and we can see a small group of canons, with close links in the royal Chancery, feathering their nest, or (as they may have thought) doing faithful service to St Martin. At their centre was a remarkable man called Peter the Scribe, who is first known to us as a chancery clerk of Henry I about 1130. He passed into Stephen's service in about 1135; but after Stephen's capture and imprisonment in 1141 he went over to the Empress Matilda. From about 1145 to about 1147 he seems to have been a resident canon at St Martin's, and the number of royal writs he wrote for his own college is intriguing. Then he passed into the service of Theobald, Archbishop of Canterbury, and wrote numerous charters for him, as well as for others. 'Whether the charters which he wrote for the college,' observed Professors Cronne and Davis, 'were really authorized by the relevant authorities is a question which we cannot answer. Nor are we ever likely to know whether Henry II really authorized the four charters for Christ Church, Canterbury which [the same man] wrote when he was in the archbishop's service; nor whether [the] Prior . . . [of Canterbury] really authorized the charter which [he] wrote in favour of Peter the Scribe.'[1]

Ingelric was a priest, a royal clerk, a landowner and (presumably) a land-agent; St Martin's remained an office in which the business of the royal court and its clerks, the business of managing land and the larger life of the City met. In the intellectual, spiritual or social life of the City it is not known to have played a part in any way comparable to that of the two Augustinian houses founded in the reign of Henry I, Holy Trinity, Aldgate and St Bartholomew's, Smithfield.

III THE PRIORIES OF BERMONDSEY, SOUTHWARK AND HOLY TRINITY, ALDGATE

Bermondsey

The first monastic house founded near enough to impinge on London after the Norman Conquest was the Cluniac Priory of Bermondsey. Its origin

[1] *Regesta*, vol. iii, p. xv; Davis, *LTR*, forthcoming.

and early history are obscure; but it seems to have been founded out of an unexplained alliance between William Rufus and a citizen of London called Alwin Cild, in 1089.[1] Rufus was not at all inclined to spend his resources on religious foundations; rather he was a cheerful blasphemer who regarded their endowments as property which had been alienated by the foolish indulgence of his predecessors, and which should be enjoyed to the full when the happy departure of an abbot or a prior gave him the opportunity. Yet it seems clear that the manor of Bermondsey was his, and that he gave it to enable the foundation of Bermondsey to take place. We may presume that he sold it, or his rights in it, for a handsome sum, and that Bermondsey's founder was a man of considerable wealth. But a date so near the great rebellion of 1088, and not long after Rufus's accession in 1087, may also remind us that he owed his victory over the rebels, and his secure grip on the throne, in part at least to the aid of well-to-do Englishmen; his share in this foundation may conceivably have been part of his thank-offering to God and man. In due course the priory came to form one of the main centres of Cluniac influence – no doubt enhanced by its position near the City – and in the twelfth century it lost several of its priors to more eminent positions.[2] In 1148 Prior Clarembald left to help King Stephen found Faversham Abbey, where he was subsequently buried; he was soon after followed by Prior Roger, who became Abbot of St Ouen at Rouen (1157), and by Adam, who became Abbot of Evesham (1161); and the story was taken up again later in the century, when Abingdon, Faversham (again), and Glastonbury abbeys received abbots from Bermondsey – continuous witness to Cluniac prestige and influence among the Benedictines, and to royal favour and royal interest in Bermondsey.

But for all this we know little of it. The monastic buildings and the church have disappeared; and although excavation shows that it had a large and ample church from early days, only foundations survive.[3] Its early annals can be reconstructed, largely, however, from the muddle and confusion of their fifteenth-century successor; most of its charters are

---

[1] See *Heads*, pp. 6, 114: the fifteenth-century annals are unreliable, though based on good sources. For the date we have ample confirmation; Alwin Cild's involvement depends wholly on the annals. On Bermondsey see Rose Graham, *English Ecclesiastical Studies*, London, 1929, pp. 121 ff.; Grimes, pp. 210-17 (on the excavation of the priory); a full study, including a reconstitution of the lost cartulary, is being undertaken by Miss Janet Foster.

[2] *Heads*, pp. 114-15.

[3] Grimes, pp. 210 ff.

lost; and the only book from its twelfth-century library which can be identified with any plausibility is a fine copy of the works of St Isidore now in the British Museum.[1]

St Mary Overy, Southwark (Plates 52–3)

Apart from Westminster Abbey, the most conspicuous conventual church of medieval London today is the priory church of St Mary Overy – over the water, in Southwark, now Southwark Cathedral. Granted that nave and tower are of the nineteenth century, what remains is a noble fragment, in marked contrast to the other house of Augustinian canons, founded in the first decade of the twelfth century, Holy Trinity Aldgate, which is totally lost. The choir is of the thirteenth century, reflecting a period of prosperity in the house's fortunes. Although it had a fine Norman doorway which survived until the nineteenth century, its origins in the twelfth century were probably more modest. In 1106 the ancient minster church of Southwark was revived and provided with a community of canons; in the years that followed they became canons regular under the Rule of St Augustine.[2] This may have been due to French influence, or to the neighbourhood of the houses at Aldgate and Merton founded soon after St Mary Overy, but regular from their inception. All that we know for sure is that the first prior bore an English name, Algod (1106–30). In contrast, the priory within Aldgate is one of the best documented houses in the land.

Holy Trinity, Aldgate and Queen Matilda

The buildings of religious communities within the area of modern London have had little chance of survival. There are obvious exceptions. Westminster Abbey has never lost many of its privileges, even though some

---

[1] British Museum Royal MS. 11. B. vii; cf. N. R. Ker, *Medieval Libraries of Great Britain*, 2nd edn, London, 1964, p. 9. The *ex libris*, however, is apparently fourteenth century.

[2] J. C. Dickinson, *Origins of the Austin Canons*, pp. 119–20. See *Heads*, pp. 183–4 for references and dates, and for the early priors; there are accounts of the priory (now Southwark Cathedral) in *VCH London*, vol. i, pp. 480–4; *VCH Surrey*, vol. ii, pp. 107–12. KH, p. 174, query Dickinson's view and suggest that it may have had a French community of regulars from 1106. But the first prior had an English name.

departed at the Dissolution; and for different reasons St Bartholomew's Priory and the Temple Church fared better than many. Bermondsey Priory and many others disappeared, leaving hardly a trace. Especially is this true of the greatest religious house within the walls, Holy Trinity, Aldgate. But happily its documents, like those of St Bartholomew, fared relatively well.

It is striking how often Henry I and Queen Matilda meet us in this story. Matilda was the queen who gave her title to the Queenhithe; she it was too who founded the leper hospital of St Giles 'in the Fields' of Holborn; above all, she was the foundress of Holy Trinity, Aldgate. The great wharf, the leper hospital, the house of canons regular: this combination more than hints at a broad concern for the social welfare of the City, and may serve to indicate to us something of the manner in which Henry I set about securing the loyalty and continued prosperity of his most valuable possession.[1]

'Good Queen Maud' lived in the tradition of her house as a pious lady devoted to good works. We have no reason to doubt that this fairly represents one side of her. If we deduced that she was a pious nonentity, we should err: Henry would hardly have made her his regent if it were so; nor is this quite what we should expect from the daughter of St Margaret of Scotland – Queen Margaret, devoted wife of the savage Malcolm, a lady who also enjoyed the most cosmopolitan learning, piety and fashion of her age.[2]

Matilda had been brought up among the aristocratic English ladies who gathered under the wing of her aunt Christina in the royal abbeys of Romsey and Wilton.[3] There they were educated by the redoubtable Christina in learning and religious devotions, and protected, as Matilda herself subsequently observed, from the lust of the Normans. What was quite unclear was whether they were, or were intended to become, nuns in the full and formal sense. King Malcolm, meanwhile, had made it clear that his young daughter was not meant to be a nun. He found her in a black veil and removed it. When he was gone, Christina put it on again; but when her back was turned, so Matilda herself later asserted, she tore it off and jumped upon it.

[1] See pp. 32, 99 f.
[2] See the Life in *Acta Sanctorum Bollandiana*, June, vol. ii (edn of 1867), pp. 324 ff., esp. p. 326; see above, p. 261.
[3] Southern, *St Anselm and his Biographer*, pp. 183 ff.; cf. *Heads*, p. 219; Orderic, ed. and trans. M. Chibnall, OMT, vol. iv, 1973, pp. 272–3 and n.

In 1100 Henry succeeded to the throne, and instantly announced his intention of marrying Matilda. We can hardly doubt that he had longed for the opportunity to win the throne, and had planned the aftermath of his usurpation. A part of the aftermath was to be his marriage to Edith-Matilda. He had remained a bachelor, not out of affection for that state, if we may judge from the number of his children, but to ensure the highest prize in the marriage market. To marry after he had won the throne meant that his legitimate children would all be born 'in the purple' as Henry himself had been born, unlike Robert or William, his elder brothers; and this probably played some part in his very determined, if rather eccentric, notion of legitimate monarchic succession.[1] William the Conqueror had married his Matilda after defying the Church's ban – imposed owing to some mysterious ground of consanguinity – for several years. It is the more surprising that Henry should have entered a marriage on which the Church might frown. But he was very determined, and we may be sure his grounds were strong. The historian Eadmer gives us an extremely lively account of the debate in a council summoned by Anselm to judge the matter – quoting, as he claims, 'the maiden's exact words' about how she had viewed and treated the veil.[2] The council decided, and Anselm (who had withdrawn to leave his colleagues to arrive at their own conclusion) accepted and confirmed their findings, and blessed the marriage.

She was, as Eadmer notes, 'the daughter of Malcolm . . . and Margaret, who is known to have sprung from the seed of the English kings . . . She was daughter of Edward, son of King Edmund, the son of King Ethelred, the son of the most glorious King Edgar.'[3] No one lays so careful emphasis on legitimate succession as a usurper – especially one who lived between the fear that his own throne will be seized and the fear that he will not be able to pass it on to his own heirs. In 1100 Henry's elder brother Robert was returning from the Crusade, with a wife newly wed. After many imminent dangers Robert was defeated and captured at Tinchebrai in 1106. But he lived until 1134, and died only a year before Henry; and, though he was closely guarded, his presence was a constant threat to Henry's throne. This made Henry particularly anxious to find grounds for supporting his own claims; even more anxious to find every means, by

---

[1] See Brooke, *Saxon and Norman Kings*, London, 1963, esp. pp. 195–6.
[2] Eadmer, *Historia Novorum*, ed. M. Rule, Rolls Series, 1884, pp. 122, 125.
[3] Eadmer, *Hist. Novorum*, p. 121.

policy, bribery and fear, to bind his followers to his own cause.[1] But the same motives, and his intimacy with Matilda, also brought out a very different quality in this savage, ruthless man – his fondness for founding and aiding religious houses.

We may take the maiden's word for it that she had no vocation to be a nun; at least that any such thoughts would not survive the dazzling prospect of being queen. She evidently had ability and drive, and the little that we know of her reveals some of St Margaret's quality – her strength of mind, her ability, her fondness for some of the pleasures of the world, and her piety. One cannot but suspect that her lot was in some ways a sorry one. It is clear that she had an intense devotion to St Anselm – 'daughter of Archbishop Anselm' as she subscribed one of her husband's charters when Anselm was about to be driven into exile for his refusal to allow royal investiture of bishops – and the centre of her life henceforth lay in the court and in the schemes of a husband who was unfaithful to her. Her letters to Anselm are aflame with a spiritual daughter's eagerness, to the point that a note of artificiality has been found in them, and Anselm himself seems to have been suspicious of her.[2] When he was in exile she wrote gushing letters to him, and tried to gain credit for saving something from the sequestration of his estates. To all her approaches Anselm returned a guarded or a cold answer: 'he seems . . . to have been singularly difficult to please'.[3] Henry I was a master of intrigue, and it certainly looks as if Anselm suspected the queen of acting on her husband's behalf. Nor is it unlikely that there was some truth in this. He was very reluctant to surrender to Anselm, equally reluctant to lose his allegiance. Either way dangers were obvious to him, and he steered a devious course between them. There could be nothing surprising in his taking advantage of his wife's attachment to Anselm to use her to bind the archbishop to him; and there are evident hints in her letters that she 'tempered her enthusiasm with a strong mixture of prudence', as R. W. Southern has said; and even that 'they are full of sophistication and political wariness'.[4] Yet the devotion seems undoubtedly genuine, and she was manifestly a pious woman given to good works.

Both these elements are implied in the story told by the annalist of Holy Trinity, Aldgate. First of all, it is noteworthy that Matilda not Henry

[1] See p. 203.
[2] Southern, *St Anselm and his Biographer*, p. 191.
[3] Ib., p. 192.
[4] Ib., p. 191.

founded the house; yet the land and the opportunity must have been of Henry's providing. It was founded in a church built 'long ago' by one Syred, and dedicated to the Holy Cross and St Mary Magdalene, and in the church and the area round it the canons of the church of Holy Cross at Waltham had substantial rights.[1] They were bought out by Matilda – no doubt with Henry's help – and the large area within Aldgate where the canons of Holy Trinity were settled became the core of the 'queen's soke'. There is no reason to suppose that it had been a queen's soke before Matilda; just as there is no reason to suppose that the large and important wharf formerly called (so it seems) after Alfred's son-in-law Ethelred's hithe began to change its name before her time.[2]

When Matilda married Henry, the Norman Conquest was less than thirty-five years old. The great English landholders and bishops had all departed, and Normans or Frenchmen stood securely on all the tenurial peaks. But in the towns, and especially in London, the English still survived in important positions, and London was still particularly regarded as holding one of the keys to the royal succession. Matilda was descended from Edgar, and Alfred, from Woden, Noah and Adam – much more closely linked to the Old English royal house than Henry, though he too came of Alfred's stock, and Woden's and Adam's. In 1066 the citizens of London had rallied to Matilda's uncle, Edgar the Atheling; no doubt Henry hoped that they would rally to the niece in like fashion, and at least prefer her to his feckless elder brother. The substantial rights with which she was endowed in the City can hardly be coincidence.[3]

The role of St Margaret's daughter naturally involved some concern for

[1] What follows is based on the chronicle which prefaces the cartulary of Holy Trinity Aldgate (*Cart. Aldgate*, ed. Hodgett, pp. 223–33; cf. Dickinson, *Origins of the Austin Canons*, pp. 99 ff.; *Heads*, pp. 173–4). The chronicle is of the fifteenth century in its present form, but evidently based on early materials and good tradition.

[2] Queenhithe was still called Æthe(l)red's hythe in the early and mid-twelfth century (*Regesta*, vol. iii, nos. 90, 501–4, some of them not earlier than 1147, and no. 90 is of 1153–4); but it seems that the hythe became *de facto* the queen's with Matilda (*Cart. Aldgate*, pp. 192–3; *Regesta*, iii, no. 502; below, p. 334). In a charter of 1151–2 it is described as 'Edredeshede now called Ripa Regine anglice Quenhyth' (*Cart. Aldgate*, p. 193, no. 977). The identification of Ethelred was suggested by Page (pp. 130 f.; cf. Ekwall, pp. 35–6), but is not certain.

[3] It may not be entirely due to coincidence that her chancellor, Bernard, was set to do a similar task of reconciliation in Wales, as Bishop of St Davids; in this he seems to have succeeded beyond his patron's wishes (see Brooke in *Studies in the early British Church*, ed. N. K. Chadwick, Cambridge, 1958, pp. 215 ff.).

the bodily, mental and spiritual welfare of her fellow-citizens. The annalist of Holy Trinity describes the horror with which her brother David detected her in the act of washing the feet of lepers in her own chamber.[1] David was no mere worldling: later, as king of the Scots, he was to found over a dozen monastic houses and spread the fashions of London and Paris among the lowlands of Scotland; the family resemblance to Margaret and Matilda is evident enough. David was struck by the horror and the danger involved in letting lepers into one's own house, and the degradation of so humble a task. Nor can we blame him. A similar horror played a crucial part a century later in the conversion of St Francis; yet even after his conversion Francis on one occasion rebuked a simple friar who brought lepers to dine with his community.[2] Francis ended by eating from the leper's dish as an act of penance; David kissed their feet, if the annalist is to be believed.

The concern of Matilda for the welfare of lepers is undoubted. She acquired a substantial site just outside the City boundary, beyond the Holborn bar, and there laid the foundations of the hospital of St Giles in the Fields.[3] It had to be apart from human habitation, but near enough to the City to offer refuge to its lepers, and to attract the alms of the faithful. This was one of the earliest – perhaps indeed the earliest of all – English leper hospitals; its foundation signifies an important epoch in medieval attitudes to social welfare.[4] The foundation of hospitals was coming to be a recognized element in the work of pious benefactors. At this date many monasteries already included hospices of some kind for travellers and for the old; as time passed more and more separate hospitals were built for a wide variety of social purposes: to provide for orphans, widows, old folk of both sexes, for the sick and for lepers. Leper houses were in their nature specialist institutions; other hospitals often catered for a variety of other needs; they were rarely solely or mainly hospitals in the modern sense; more commonly almshouses, although many catered for the poor and the sick as well. In due course hospitals became increasingly specialized centres of social welfare; and hospitality, in the broadest sense, less and

---

[1] *Cart. Aldgate*, pp. 223–4.

[2] *Scripta Leonis* etc., ed. R. B. Brooke, OMT, 1970, pp. 124–7.

[3] KH, p. 365; *VCH Middlesex*, vol. i, pp. 206–10.

[4] R. M. Clay, *Medieval Hospitals of England*, London, 1909; and there is much material in KH, pp. 310–410. But the subject deserves more study than it has received. For the wider context, see B. Tierney, *Medieval Poor Law*, Berkeley and Los Angeles, 1959. See below, pp. 333–6.

less a function of monastic communities. But in early days their social function was often more inherent in their general working. We shall presently see how St Bartholomew's Priory and Hospital, founded in 1123 as part of a single idea, rapidly became two almost separate houses; their common origin is characteristic of the early twelfth century in which they were born.

We have strayed far, it might seem, from our stated purpose: to found the priory of Holy Trinity within Aldgate. Yet all that has been said is necessary to understand the significance of that event. It was to be the only major religious house within the City walls until the coming of the friars; and the prior of Holy Trinity had a special place in the life of the City, since he was alderman of the Portsoken – a place denied to the bishop or the dean and canons of St Paul's (except to an occasional individual like Ralph, son of Algod). The priory was founded in 1107–8, at about the time of Anselm's return from exile, and we could assume that this was no coincidence, even if the annalist had not told us very specifically that Matilda took Anselm's advice before embarking on her foundation.[1]

Anselm, the old Benedictine, advised Matilda to found a house of canons regular, following the customs recently established in a large number of continental houses, but hitherto only in one or two in England. The Austin Canons followed the current version of the Rule of St Augustine, a document of exemplary piety and vagueness, which has been in the course of the centuries the basis of many religious orders, of canons, friars and nuns. From the mid-eleventh century the papal reformers had strenuously encouraged the conversion of groups and communities of secular clerks and canons into regular canons, canons dedicated to the common life under a Rule; and in the late eleventh century a norm had come to be established: a group of customs widely disseminated over western Christendom had come to be added to the Rule, and so a common, monastic way of life established.[2]

To the question, what distinguished a monk from a canon? – it is vital to realize that the twelfth century had no clearer answer than a modern schoolboy. In early twelfth-century Flanders a book was written to explain

[1] *Cart. Aldgate*, pp. 223 ff.

[2] Dickinson, *Origins of the Austin Canons*; on the history of the Rule of St Augustine, see now L. Verheijen, *La Règle de S. Augustin*, 2 vols, Paris, 1967. See also *La vita comune del clero nei secoli XI e XII*, 2 vols, Milan, 1962.

to educated people what the differences were between different orders.[1] The author distinguished four basic types of monks and canons regular: monks who live in towns – or otherwise among the people – and monks who live remote from humankind; and canons who live in and far from towns. It is clear that canons and monks covered the spectrum of the regular life. Henry's and Matilda's foundations were mostly in towns or otherwise close to the flow of humanity. Holy Trinity, Aldgate, Henry's Cirencester and most of his numerous lesser Augustinian houses were in towns; his great Benedictine foundation at Reading was also in a town.[2] A former royal clerk was one of the founders of the remote house of Llanthony in Monmouthshire, famed in its early days for both asceticism and learning. Henry and Matilda suggested to the founder that they might take the priory in hand and endow it richly: this he refused, wishing poverty and obscurity to be its marks; so they turned their attention elsewhere. The next step in their pilgrimage is obscure, but it seems that they planned to enlarge the modest Cluniac house at Montacute in Somerset and make a rich abbey out of it; perhaps too they schemed to bring over as first abbot Henry's favourite nephew, his namesake Henry of Blois, then a monk in the great house of Cluny, whose church Henry was rebuilding for his own and his nephew's glory. For some reason the scheme for Montacute fell through; and in the end, after Matilda's death, Henry endowed Reading Abbey with substantial wealth, and Henry of Blois even more richly by making him Abbot of Glastonbury and Bishop of Winchester. After Matilda's death and the disaster of the *White Ship* in 1120, in which his only legitimate son was drowned, Henry's foundations became more numerous and lavish; but we need not doubt that his interest in founding religious houses, like David of Scotland's, owed much to the inspiration of Matilda.

Although both monks and canons covered the spectrum of the religious life, and although the differences could be as obscure in the twelfth century as today, none the less some differences were clearly visible to Anselm and Matilda when they chose the way of life suitable for Holy Trinity, Aldgate. The Augustinian was to become the most popular order with patrons and founders in the mid- and late twelfth century; but that it hardly was in 1107. Anselm was a Benedictine, and although it seems

[1] *Libellus de diversis ordinibus . . .*, ed. G. Constable and B. Smith, OMT, 1972; the author also treats of hermits and secular canons.

[2] Brooke in *Il Monachesimo e la riforma ecclesiastica*, Milan, 1971, pp. 136 ff. for Henry I as patron.

commonly to have been taken for granted that monks, like canons, might live close to the world, and even engage in pastoral work, we may presume that Anselm himself regarded spiritual exercises, prayer, intellectual and craft work as the essence of their life; more practical and worldly tasks being more fitted for men not called monks. That is to say, among monks of a contemplative and observant turn of mind, the canons seemed more fitted for pastoral and practical work in the world. In course of time pastoral and practical work became increasingly frowned on, even for canons.

But the original distinction is clearly illustrated in Canterbury itself at the turn of the eleventh and twelfth centuries. In 1084–5 Lanfranc had founded a hospital on the towns edge to be served by canons living a regular life.[1] In due course, presumably under Anselm, the way of life of the canons came to follow the specific arrangements we call Augustinian. This was probably not so, or not distinctly so, in early days, for when the founder of St Botolph's Priory on the edge of Colchester turned to Anselm for advice towards the close of the 1090s, he sent one of his canons with a letter of introduction to the prior of Mont-Saint-Éloi near Chartres, to learn the Rule and customs of the Austin canons.[2] On this ground, and the frankly partisan and misleading statements of the Holy Trinity annalist, St Botolph's is reckoned the first Augustinian house and the fountain head of the Order in England. Clearly, the new way of life was in the wind, and already spreading; and we may accept that Anselm's initiative, intended to provide a basis for an observant French community, played an important part in the development of the canons regular in England. But already, and swiftly, founders were learning the benefit of communities who could be expected to engage in social and parish work, in tending the sick and coping with some of the many problems attendant on growing towns. The large town was a new experience in northern Europe in the eleventh and twelfth centuries; the canons had the task of

[1] *Cartulary of the priory of St Gregory, Canterbury*, ed. A. M. Woodcock (Mrs Erskine), Camden 3rd Series, vol. lxxxvii, 1956, pp. ix ff.

[2] I.e., the current version of the rule of St Augustine and the customs attached to it which had grown up among the Augustinian canons in the previous two generations. See Dickinson, *Origins of the Austin Canons*, esp. pp. 98 ff. The Aldgate chronicler (*Cart.*, pp. 224 ff.) was trying to establish that St Botolph's Colchester and Holy Trinity were the *fons et origo* of the whole Augustinian movement in England. This was evidently an exaggeration, though (as Dr Dickinson argues, perhaps slightly beyond what would be generally agreed) not far wrong.

mitigating the less happy side of this movement, much as had the friars a century later.

Brother Norman, a Kentish man, was chosen to go to Mont-Saint-Éloi, and after his return he was chosen again to be first prior of Matilda's new foundation. He seems to have been a fervent exponent of Augustinian observance, a practical administrator and a notable organizer of charity. He was Matilda's confessor, and helped to plan all her charitable works. His cloister was not remote from the world. In one of the rare glimpses of an Augustinian house in a town of early days, the annalist describes how a procession of pious men and women was accustomed to wind round the cloister on Sundays.[1] Matilda no doubt intended her foundation to be tolerably prosperous; but she may well have shared her husband's talent for generosity on the cheap: a religious house founded in London could expect to grow fat on the offerings and endowments of city men of large and moderate means. In due course the canons received ample endowments from many sources, most notably the lands and rights of the Cnihtengild, potentially of considerable value.[2] However this may be, there were often in the early stages of the best planned foundations moments of dearth, and the story is told how the pious women in the procession were horrified to see table cloths in the refectory, but no bread, and hastened to remedy this defect.

Unfortunately the annalist fails to describe any further the function of Holy Trinity in its early days. We may be sure, from the choice of Order and from the situation – as well as from what we have elicited about the queen – that charity in the best twelfth-century sense, that is to say organized social relief, was a major part of its original purpose. The only aspect of this on which we are informed is its school. William FitzStephen tells us that in the 1170s there were three major schools, as well as many lesser ones, in London; and an early fourteenth century glossator identified these as St Paul's, St Martin le Grand and Holy Trinity.[3] No doubt something of what we should attribute to the primary and secondary stages of education went on there; and perhaps a little more before the crystallization of Oxford (and later Cambridge) as sole centres of higher educa-

---

[1] *Cart. Aldgate*, p. 228.

[2] See pp. 96–8.

[3] H. E. Butler, in Stenton, p. 34 (note to line 82) pointed out that the three churches with schools are only named in the copy of FitzStephen's *Description* in the Liber Custumarum in the Guildhall; the names are clearly an interpolation, though he left them in his translation. Cf. C. L. Kingsford in *EHR*, vol. xxxviii, 1923, pp. 613–14.

tion in the country at the turn of the twelfth and thirteenth centuries. The Augustinians were not specifically a learned order; such things did not exist in the Middle Ages. But many Augustinian houses acquired a reputation for learning and notable libraries in the twelfth century; and in this respect remote Llanthony had more in common with the large city communities of Holy Trinity, or St Frideswide's in Oxford, or Alexander Nequam's home at Cirencester.[1] Norman himself had been a schoolman, and had studied under Anselm – possibly the saint, more probably the famous theologian Anselm of Laon; and before his death Norman was joined in London by the greatest of Anselm's Laon pupils, the biblical scholar Gilbert the Universal, who was Bishop of London from 1128 to 1134. Later in the century, Holy Trinity enjoyed its most notable period of learning under Prior Peter of Cornwall, who has been rescued from the obscurity of his ponderous writings in two well-known papers by R. W. Hunt.[2]

'Precipuus doctor inter omnes doctores Anglicos,' says the pious annalist of Holy Trinity, and not without reason. His writings reveal a man concerned to gather and disseminate knowledge, a man who, though without a trace of originality of mind, was a learned teacher in a circle of clerics noted for learning and practical ability. His *Pantheologus* contains dedicatory epistles to Ralph de Haute Rive, nephew of the Bishop of London, Gilbert Foliot, Master of the schools of St Paul's itself, and later Archdeacon of Colchester and crusader; to Henry of Northampton, Peter's teacher, also a canon of St Paul's and a man of parts – a practising lawyer, founder of a hospital in Northampton; and to Godfrey de Lucy, son of the royal justiciar, fellow-student of Peter's at Master Henry's feet (presumably, though not certainly, at St Paul's), later Bishop of Winchester.[3] Of the rest of the priory's library only the faintest traces survive;[4] but Peter's works reveal a wide, encyclopedic knowledge of the theological deposit of the age.

The most interesting of Peter's works is his *Disputation against Symon the Jew*, a dialogue between Peter and Symon which ended (unlike the

---

[1] See references in N. R. Ker, *Medieval Libraries of Great Britain*, London, 2nd edn, 1964, pp. 51–2, 108–12 (Lanthony in Gloucester, but the nucleus of the library was doubtless made at the mother house in Monmouthshire), 119–20, 123, etc.; R. W. Hunt, 'English Learning' and 'The Disputation of Peter of Cornwall'.

[2] Hunt, arts. cit.

[3] Le Neve, pp. 19, 26, 32, 49; 37; 47; *GF*, pp. 274, 282, 279.

[4] Ker, *Medieval Libraries*, p. 123.

Dialogue of Gilbert Crispin) with Symon's conversion; we leave him happily installed as a canon at Holy Trinity. This was, from Peter's point of view, a thoroughly satisfactory ending.[1] Thus we should expect a moderate and reasonable tone; and if we take into view the tradition of such disputations as it developed in many parts of Christendom in the twelfth century, we may judge Peter's to be reasonably moderate. It is neither so liberal nor so interesting as Gilbert Crispin's; but Gilbert's moderation was quite exceptional. Nor does Peter show any evidence of having studied Hebrew, unlike another, and greater, English Augustinian, Andrew of St Victor and Wigmore.[2] He can 'make offensive references to Jewish beliefs and customs';[3] but he shows none of the persistent rancour which had come to inspire some of the other *Disputations* written shortly before. Peter's was the last of its kind. The thirteenth century was to see the foundation of the House for Converted Jews – on the site now occupied by the Public Record Office – but it was also to see their forcible expulsion.

IV THE PRIORY AND HOSPITAL OF ST BARTHOLOMEW

The practical aspect of the canons regular, and the tradition of social work so clearly revealed in very early days at Canterbury, is shown most clearly of all in St Bartholomew's.[4] In course of time hospital and priory were separated – not entirely, or for all purposes, but sufficiently to give the hospital an independent existence, and so to survive the disappearance of the priory at the Dissolution of the Monasteries, and almost by a miracle, after a period of eclipse, to survive altogether the rapacity of Henry VIII.

The separation of priory and hospital reflects the development of canons regular in the twelfth century to the point at which they had become so little involved in the world, save in the administration of their own estates and properties, that they were virtually indistinguishable from

[1] Hunt, 'The Disputation of Peter of Cornwall', p. 152.

[2] See *Heads*, p. 190 for references, esp. to B. Smalley, *Study of the Bible in the Middle Ages*, 2nd edn, Oxford, 1952, pp. 112–85.

[3] Hunt, 'The Disputation of Peter of Cornwall', p. 152.

[4] On the history of St Bartholomew's see Norman Moore; St Bartholomew's *FB*; E. A. Webb, *The Records of St Bartholomew's*; and Denton (p. 310 n.), pp. 77 ff.; on its foundation, esp. the recent study of N. Kerling, in *Guildhall Miscellany*, vol. iv, no. 3, 1972, pp. 137–48. Dr Kerling suggests that the hospital was founded before the priory; this may indeed be so, but no doubt they became in Rahere's eyes part of a single enterprise.

monks. Yet it is clear that priory and hospital were equally inherent in the foundation enjoined on Canon Rahere by St Bartholomew in the early twelfth century.

The *Foundation Book* of St Bartholomew's is a document of equal interest to and greater authority than the annals of Holy Trinity; in all essentials it is a work of the second half of the twelfth century.[1] Rahere, the founder, is described as a hanger-on at the royal court, a sort of courtly parasite; doubtless this reflects his own self-depreciation, passed on to his community after his conversion. It is likely enough that he was a royal clerk, that is to say a man of clerical profession who had obtained some work and some patronage in the royal court; and his name may indicate that he was of foreign (perhaps German) origin. In any event it is probable that he had acquired considerable wealth, as many highly placed clerks did in the late eleventh and early twelfth centuries, and a canonry at St Paul's.[2] In course of time he became dissatisfied with a worldly life, and worried too, one may suppose from the sequel, with the condition of the London sick and poor, and the squalor of some areas in the City's neighbourhood.

In or before 1123 Rahere's conversion was speeded and directed by a vision of St Bartholomew. The apostle (in his dream or vision) seemed to him to be giving instructions of a very precise character. 'I . . . have chosen a spot in the suburb of London at Smithfield where, in my name, thou shalt found a Church'. The spot in question lay on the edge of the great horse market of Smithfield, and there is an interesting contrast between the view of it taken by Bartholomew and Rahere and their historian, and by William FitzStephen, not wholly due, one may think, to the foundation of 'Barts'. FitzStephen describes a large open field to which every Friday earls, barons, knights and a throng of citizens came to witness the noble spectacle of a horse fair and horse racing – 'everything in flux, as Heraclitus thought'[3] – with the rustic cattle market carefully penned to one side, pigs, cows, oxen and mares in foal. It is the teeming activity and the better side of life which attracted FitzStephen's eye. On

[1] Dr Kerling, art. cit., points out that it was written after the separation of hospital and priory, and it gives somewhat tendentious support to the priory's point of view. None the less it evidently enshrines good tradition, and is a prospectus for the hospital as well as a justification for the priory.

[2] Le Neve, p. 38; the identification is made very probable by the extreme rarity of the name in this country (see also Dr Greenway's comment, loc. cit.).

[3] *MB*, iii, 6–7. On 'Bartholomew Fair', see references in Stew, vol. ii, p. 361.

the edge of the great market and horse fair lay a space, so the *Foundation Book* assures us, frequently flooded, a region abounding in filthy water and mud, with an area above the water-line set aside for gibbets and the execution of other punishments.[1] Rahere determined to replace this sordid place on the edge of the City with Bartholomew's Church, Priory and Hospital, and won the assent and support of the king in the enterprise. The area he had obtained for his precinct was indeed very substantial, and indicates how large the open space on this side of the City must have been, and also, perhaps, the resources on which Rahere could draw. He was helped by other citizens in his good work of clearing the site, raising funds and building the church. Most notable of his helpers were the English Alfuine (Ælfwine), who had already revealed his piety and attachment to the new cults of the conquerors by building the church of St Giles, Cripplegate, and by a fellow clerk, Geoffrey Constable, who seems to have been a protégé of the great Bishop Roger of Salisbury, and was to succeed Rahere as canon of St Paul's and prebendary of Chamberlainwood, and was the owner of substantial house property in London.[2] Rahere was evidently expert in gaining helpers and the endowments of his foundation grew rapidly; even after the separation of hospital and priory at the turn of the century the priory was comparatively rich, and remained so until the dissolution. The choir of the priory church, of the mid- or late twelfth century, is the most substantial single monument of twelfth-century London, and a notable witness to Rahere's success (**Plate 43**).

The *Foundation Book* of St Bartholomew's is a sort of prospectus. Many a church, great and small, and many a saint's life, produced such guides or prospectuses in the twelfth century. The most elaborate were the guide-books to Rome and Jerusalem and the pilgrim guide to St James, Santiago de Compostela.[3] The guide to St James describes Compostela itself and the other shrines one may pass on the way, with some useful hints on the places where one may be well fed, and where poisoned. But the guidebook proper is only a part of a larger whole, including for instance a corpus of miracles which God had performed in St James's honour and on behalf of his pilgrims. St Bartholomew's *Foundation Book* is only to a very limited

[1] St Bartholomew's *FB*, p. 13 (Webb), 12 (Moore).
[2] Le Neve, p. 38; *Regesta*, iii, no. 317. On Geoffrey Constable, see also E. J. Kealey *Roger of Salisbury*, p. 237: Geoffrey seems very probably a protégé of Bishop Roger.
[3] See p.117 ; for the pilgrim guide, see J. Vieillard, *Le guide du pélerin de Saint-Jacques de Compostelle*, 2nd edn, Macon, 1950; but cf. C. Hohler in *Journ. Warburg and Courtauld Inst.*, vol. xxxv (1972), pp. 31–80 for doubts about its authenticity.

extent a guidebook: it describes the site of the priory and hospital in telling the history of its foundation. But it resembles the pilgrim guide in being mainly a collection of miracles. In brief, it is the prospectus of a hospital whose chief physician was the apostle himself. It recounts numerous cases in which sick men and women turned their thoughts and prayers to Bartholomew and his church, and were cured. Thus far, it might be an advertisement for a modern clinic; but no further, for a hospital was not solely an institution for the sick, nor was Bartholomew's healing solely of a clinical nature, nor were his miracles acts of healing alone. That is to say, neither the saint nor his foundation was a specialist. Healing was part of their trade, the part which has survived in the heart of Smithfield to this day. But Bartholomew's function was to help all in need; and several of the miracle stories concern merchants and sailors who were saved from shipwreck by prayers or vows to St Bartholomew. In a general way, the stories reflect a great mercantile community; one of the most touching concerns the epileptic son of a stone and timber merchant plying between London and the Northamptonshire quarry town of Barnack.[1] Others remind us how close and constant had become the relations with Flanders and the Flemings by the days of Rahere and St Bartholomew's London home.

It is clear from the *Foundation Book* and the copious early charters that the affairs of God and men were both equally the concern of those who lived in Bartholomew's Church and precinct. As time passed, the practical work fell increasingly on the hospital, which became gradually separated from the priory.[2] The second prior, Thomas (1144–74), appointed a layman, evidently a businessman dedicated to good works, called Adam the Merchant, as Warden or Master of the Hospital; and although a lay appointment to this office was abnormal in the Middle Ages, it reveals the nature of the task as it appeared in the foundation's early days.

v THE NUNS AND KNIGHTS

St Bartholomew's Hospital cared for the poor and the sick; and we may well suppose that Adam the Merchant was not the only city man to take to a life of pious usefulness. The religious houses also, at least from the time when St Wulfsige became monk and abbot at Westminster, provided

[1] St Bartholomew's *FB*, pp. 40–1 (Webb), 47 (Moore); on Barnack, see Beresford and St Joseph, *Medieval England*, pp. 232–4.
[2] Kerling, art. cit. For the priors, see *Heads*, p. 174.

homes and vocations for numerous citizens, as well as for men and women from further afield. The special function of the houses of nuns was to provide homes for the daughters of well-to-do citizens.

The priory of St John the Baptist of Holywell, or Haliwell, in Shore-ditch[1] was founded by the prebendary of Holywell or Finsbury, Robert, son of Generann, in the early or mid-twelfth century. About the time of its foundation an ecclesiastical council at Westminster condemned the wearing by nuns of rich furs;[2] but it is doubtful if the nuns of Haliwell were seriously tempted to such misdemeanours in early years, since it is clear that the house was still very poor when, in the 1160s, Bishop Gilbert Foliot wrote to his uncle the Bishop of Lincoln asking his aid for it.[3]

'The resources of the house called Haliwell have perhaps come to your knowledge, as these things get about. For the site is narrow and small, so that the whole space is confined within three acres. Twenty sisters veiled and consecrated to God occupy this place, earnestly following the holy office and serving the Lord according to the Rule' – probably the Rule of St Augustine. For food and clothing, the bishop tells us, they depended then mainly on the church of Dunton, which was in Bedfordshire and in the diocese of Lincoln, and which had been given them by Master Roger of Dunton, evidently the rector. Their possession was threatened, and with it their livelihood, for the space 'which the sisters inhabit is sufficient indeed to provide for their burial, but not for their life'. Hence Gilbert Foliot's moving plea for the nuns in their suit, which seems to have been successful. We may suspect that the bishop exaggerated their plight, for it is hard to believe that none of their later endowments save this church had come their way. But the interesting point which emerges is that the founder, Canon Robert, had provided the site and little else. Haliwell later became relatively prosperous; it attracted numerous small gifts from pious Londoners, and numerous gifts too from substantial or moderately substantial citizens or folk of the neighbouring shires who had daughters to spare and a mind to see them in a convent. Though convents were forbidden to demand 'dowries' with their nuns, it is evident that it was a

[1] On Haliwell, see *VCH* Middlesex, vol. i, pp. 174 ff. (J. L. Kirby); KH, p. 281. Robert son of Generannus was canon of St Paul's and prebendary of Finsbury from before 1115 to after 1162 (Le Neve, p. 49). On its slender documentary gleanings, see G. R. C. Davis, *Medieval Cartularies of Great Britain*, London, 1958, p. 68.

[2] See p. 259.

[3] *GFL*, p. 245, no. 172.

common, if not normal, practice, especially among the poorer houses, which could scarcely have lived without them.[1]

In the end Haliwell became relatively prosperous. To put the matter somewhat crudely, when the assessments which were to be the prelude to the last act in the history of these houses were made *c*. 1535, St Helen's Bishopsgate, the Benedictine house whose church still stands, which was founded soon after 1200, was reckoned worth £320 per annum; the Poor Clares of the Minories (founded in 1293–4) £318; Haliwell followed with £294; the other Augustinian house at Clerkenwell £262; and the most famous house of nuns in the ambience of the City, Stratford-at-Bow, came lowest in the table with £108.[2] But even Stratford, immortalized in the lines by which Chaucer defined his prioress's speech:

> And Frensh she spak ful faire and fetisly,
> After the scole of Stratford atte Bowe,
> For Frensh of Paris was to hir unknowe,[3]

was better off than most convents of nuns in the country. The richest convent was Shaftesbury, with an income assessed at £1,166; and the ancient abbey of Barking, founded by St Eorcenweald in the seventh century, where in the 1170s a sister of Thomas Becket and a daughter of Henry II were abbesses, was not far behind with £862.[4] But these came from the small group of exceptionally rich, old Benedictine houses. Among the rank and file, Haliwell, Clerkenwell and St Helen's ranked among the most prosperous.

The motives for founding houses of nuns in the twelfth and thirteenth centuries were both temporal and spiritual. The tiny house at Kilburn was established by the Abbot of Westminster on his own territory in 1139 to provide permanent quarters for three devout anchoresses. This reflects the more spiritual element in twelfth-century convent-making: the world of St Christina of Markyate and the holy ladies of the Ancren Riwle and

[1] On this, and all topics related to nunneries, see Eileen Power, *Medieval English Nunneries*, pp. 16 ff. (the book was primarily concerned with the period *c*. 1275 to 1535, but has much of value in it for earlier centuries).

[2] The figures are conveniently laid out, with much other valuable information, in KH, pp. 253–89. Kilburn, mentioned below, had an income of £74 in 1535. To the houses here described should perhaps be added the shadowy convent which was replaced by the Elsing Spital *c*. 1329–32 (KH, pp. 288, 372); but there is no evidence that it existed in the period of this book.

[3] *Canterbury Tales*, Prologue, ll. 124–6.

[4] *Heads*, p. 208; *VCH Essex*, vol. ii, pp. 115–22.

the Ancren Wisse.¹ But whatever inspired Robert, son of Generann, Jordan of Bricett, and William, son of William the Goldsmith, founders of Haliwell, Clerkenwell and St Helen's, the original endowments were modest, the expectations proportionally and reasonably high. The founders represent the three groups from which one might expect to find resources coming to aid in religious foundations of this kind: wealthy clerics, well-to-do country gentry and lesser barons, and rich citizens. For Haliwell and St Helen's we can name few other benefactors of early days, but we know from the result that they were numerous, and by their aid the City convents flourished.² Stratford and Kilburn lay only a few miles further off, but yet too far to profit much from the benevolence of London's citizens. For Clerkenwell we have a cartulary of the early thirteenth century which is a rich source of information on how such projects were financed and endowed, and one of our best sources of City deeds in the twelfth century.³

Jordan of Bricett was a Suffolk landholder of moderate means, with a substantial holding in Clerkenwell, strong piety and a special interest in the crusading movement. His first and most notable foundation was the Hospital of St John of Jerusalem, whose precinct he provided in Clerkenwell, a little to the north of Smithfield, together with some other land.⁴ The precinct can be clearly traced, from the Gatehouse to the church, where a twelfth-century crypt still stands; and even if St John's Street now pushes rudely through the midst of the Hospitallers' courtyard, the shape of the court can still be readily imagined. In founding the house of Hospitallers, Jordan very likely knew that he was laying a foundation on which others would build; and so it proved, for many with a zeal for the Crusades, and many more who wished to evade the call of the Cross without damage to their conscience, gave land and money and rent. We have already studied the Knights of the Hospital and the Temple in another

¹ On Kilburn, see *VCH Middlesex*, vol. i, pp. 178–82; on Christina, *The Life of Christina of Markyate*, ed. and trans. C. H. Talbot, Oxford, 1959, and *The St Albans Psalter*, ed. O. Pächt, C. R. Dodwell and F. Wormald, London, 1960.

² On St Helen's, *VCH London*, vol. i, pp. 457–61; *Heads*, p. 215; *RCHM, London*, iv, pp. 19–24.   ³ *Cart. Clerkenwell*, ed. W. O. Hassall.

⁴ See KH, pp. 304–5; *VCH Middlesex*, vol. i, pp. 193–200 (H.M. Chew); *RCHM, London*, vol. ii, pp. 16 ff. The early documents are in the great Hospitaller cartulary, British Museum, Cotton MS. Nero E. vi, which is being edited by Dr Michael Gervers, who has kindly discussed the early history of the Order in England with us. On Jordan, see W. O. Hassall in *Genealogists' Magazine*, vol. ix, 1940–6, pp. 585–7: on its buildings, Hassall in *LMAS*, new series, vol. viii, 1938–40, pp. 234 ff.

context.[1] The Templars rapidly became great bankers as well as soldiers; and we may suppose by analogy that the Hospitallers were not far behind. We have little evidence of the activities save as landowners, but the record of the property acquired, now enshrined in their immense fifteenth-century cartulary in the British Museum, is impressive. We may assume from the scale of the precinct and of the church that the headquarters of the Order in England lay in Clerkenwell, then as later; and the crypt bears witness to the growing prosperity of the institution first formed by Jordan of Bricett in the 1140s. The crypt reveals two stages of building, one mid-twelfth century, followed by a substantial extension towards the end of the century, which was probably the building consecrated, along with the New Temple, by the patriarch of Jerusalem on his visit to London in 1185 (**Plate 47**).[2]

The other house in Clerkenwell founded by Jordan of Bricett had a similar success, though on a much more modest scale. The precinct lay immediately north of the Hospitallers', and was in fact considerably larger; but it has disappeared leaving little evidence of its existence, save in the site of the parish church of St James.[3] The remains of the convent were removed in the late eighteenth century, when James Carr built the present church to replace the part of the convent church which had served the parish since the later Middle Ages. The early list of benefactors shows how well placed the house was to gather gifts; also perhaps how successful the founder and his heirs were in organizing an appeal. Though some of the 'gifts' may hide purchases and exchanges, there is little doubt that most were in fact donations.[4] The list includes a few great men, bishops of London and earls of Essex; numerous gentry and local landholders in Essex and Middlesex; and a few citizens of London, more as time went on. They start with Rose, the wife or widow of Osbert Eightpence, the justice or sheriff distantly connected with Thomas Becket, and include

---

[1] See pp. 231–3 and references cited.

[2] Lees, pp. lvi–lvii; M. Gervers in *Actes du xxiie Congrès International d'histoire de l'art*, Budapest, 1972, p. 364.

[3] Pevsner, *London*, vol. ii, p. 112; see esp. W. O. Hassall in *LMAS*, new series, vol. viii = vol. xiv (1938–40), pp. 234–82, for the history of the precinct. On the history of the parish church, see *Cart. Clerkenwell*, p. vii; *RCHM, London*, vol. ii, p. 16.

[4] The basic form of twelfth–thirteenth-century grants normally makes it impossible to tell the true nature of the transaction, even when a pious motive is stated, unless there is other evidence. But the motives stated in some of these documents are circumstantial, and support the natural inference from the kind of pattern they suggest, that the endowment was built up by a host of minor gifts for obits etc. and as 'dowries'.

his sister Agnes Becket.[1] Characteristic entries are grants by Constantine and his brothers, the sons of Alulf, confirming and completing the gift of a substantial stone house in the parish of All Hallows Bread Street or the slightly later grant by Andrew son of Peter son of Nevelun of a rent in Milk Street for a pittance to the nuns to ensure that they remembered the anniversary of his brother Ralph who was buried in their midst.[2] Andrew Nevelun had a cellar in the parish of St James, and in or about 1198 John of St James confirmed to the nuns the cellar which lay between Andrew's and his own, which had been given with his sister Juliana – that is, when she became a nun.[3] In 1238–9 the executors of the will of a goldsmith, Henry of Edmonton, arranged for the payment of a rent of two shillings on a shop at the corner of Friday Street and Cheapside, on the east side, in the Goldsmiths' quarter, half for providing his daughter Matilda, nun of Clerkenwell, with clothes, and the other half to perform the same service for Marsilia, nun at Stratford.[4] For the daughter of well-to-do parents in the twelfth or thirteenth centuries there was little alternative by way of vocation apart from marriage or the convent. The cartulary of St Mary's Clerkenwell shows something of the way in which provision was made for the religious. But it leaves one large question unanswered. In and about London, as everywhere in England, there was far more provision for male religious than for women – and this in contrast, for example, to the situation in Germany, at least in the thirteenth century. The reasons for this no doubt lay deep in social custom and religious sentiment; but they are at present quite obscure to us.

VI HOSPITALS[5]

Holy Trinity and St Bartholomew's have revealed to us something of the pattern of social welfare in twelfth-century London; and at St Bartholomew's we have seen a great hospital formed under the wing of a religious house, and then growing up to independence. In a sense, the distinction

[1] *Cart. Clerkenwell*, nos 6, 10, 257, etc.
[2] *Cart.*, nos 254, 252.
[3] *Cart.*, no. 258.   [4] *Cart.*, no. 350.
[5] On hospitals see R. M. Clay, *Medieval Hospitals in England*, London, 1909, and the quantity of valuable evidence in KH, pp. 310–410; on St Bartholomew's, above, pp. 325–8. Many of these hospitals have been studied by Miss M. B. Honeybourne in *VCH Middlesex*, vol. i, pp. 204 ff. and *LMAS*, vol. xxi, 1963–7, pp. 3–61 (on the leper hospitals). For an interesting comparison, see J. H. Mundy, 'Hospitals and leprosaries in 12th- and early 13th-century Toulouse'.

is false: hospitals were religious houses in their own right, and sometimes had within them small communities of canons and nuns. But in the course of the twelfth century the distinction between the guest house or alms-houses attached to a priory or abbey – the outward sign of its 'hospitality' – and the institution specially dedicated to social welfare became clearer and more visible. Some element of specialization became increasingly necessary. It is generally supposed that leprosy became much commoner in the West as a result of the Crusades and closer links with the East; however this may be, the establishment of separate leper hospitals became common in the twelfth century; in London, Queen Matilda led the way with St Giles in the Fields, immediately outside the Holborn Bar.[1] But the main demand seems still to have been for provision for the old and for the poor. Her successor, Stephen's Queen Matilda, in the late 1140s estab-lished St Katharine's Hospital by the Tower, endowed largely with some of the profits of the Queenhithe; it was in some sort of dependence on Holy Trinity until it was wrenched from the canons' grasp after a fierce, not to say passionate onslaught by Queen Eleanor of Provence in the mid-thirteenth century.[2] St Katharine's was an old people's home, for both men and women, with special provision for thirteen poor folk.

In the late twelfth century the pace intensified: in London, as every-where in England, the late twelfth and early thirteenth centuries saw a large number of hospitals founded. South of the river St Bartholomew's established a second leper house at some date unknown; and the first St Thomas's was established, perhaps (if the tradition is correct), by Becket himself, certainly within a few years of his death.[3] It lay originally within the precinct of St Mary Overy, and its function was to care for the poor and sick. In 1213-15, after a major fire, Peter des Roches, Bishop of Winchester, refounded it a little further west – the first of its several travels. Though its site has altered, it remains, after St Bartholomew's, the most notable monument in modern London to twelfth-century ideas of welfare.

Later in the same century another house was raised to Becket's memory, the hospital of St Mary and St Thomas of Acre – St Thomas of 'Acon' – founded about 1190 by Becket's sister Agnes and her husband in a family

---

[1] Honeybourne in art. cit., pp. 20 ff. and *VCH Middlesex*, vol. i, pp. 206–10.
[2] C. Jamison, *The History of the Royal Hospital of St Katherine*, London, etc., 1952.
[3] *VCH Surrey*, vol. ii, pp. 119–24; *VCH London*, vol. i, pp. 538 ff.; *Chartulary*, ed. L. Drucker (1932); for the earliest document, *GFL*, no. 452 (probably before *c*. 1180). According to tradition it was originally dedicated to the Holy Trinity.

house in Cheapside beside the Mercery.[1] The house may indeed have been the one in which Thomas himself was born. The hospital was the mother house of a tiny military order, the knights of St Thomas of Acre, whose history and precise purpose are quite obscure. It had offshoots at Berkhamsted and perhaps at Doncaster; and as the crusading movement waned, it became a normal hospital with a small community of Augustinian canons serving the poor and sick. About the same time a hospice was established at St Paul's by the learned and beneficent canon Henry of Northampton[2] and, soon after, the substantial 'New Hospital' of St Mary without Bishopsgate was founded by a citizen, Walter Brown, and his wife. In the same epoch a group of small hospitals sprang up in the villages around London.[3]

The various experiments in providing hospitals under the wing of religious houses or of the cathedral, some run by canons, some by knights, some by laymen, reflect the variety of approach which is so noticeable a feature of twelfth-century society and social welfare. The second half of the twelfth century saw a marked increase in the sophistication of the Church's law, canon law, and the exploration of every aspect of the Church's obligations. Since the payment of tithes had begun to be obligatory in the eighth and ninth centuries the Church's hierarchy had come increasingly to accept its duty to organize poor relief and the other aspects of welfare which had been the first purpose of exacting tithe.[4] By the twelfth century tithes had largely been diverted to support the clergy, and many of them alienated in practice to support laymen and monks, or absentee rectors. A great rationalization of the tithing system was set in motion, and, although there was much compromise and prevarication, a certain basic logic was sketched out. But not without cost: what had been

[1] See KH, pp. 372–3; *VCH London*, vol. i, pp. 491–5; J. Watney, *Some account of the Hospital of St Thomas of Acon*, London, 1892, esp. pp. 237. On the 'order', see KH, p. 372, cf. pp. 325 and (on the other houses), 314, 319, 342, 355.

[2] See p. 324 and *GF*, p. 283; KH, p. 374.

[3] For the new hospital see *VCH London*, vol. i, pp. 530–5; others were at Bermondsey (one *c.* 1170 or later, another in 1213: KH, pp. 314, 342); Southwark (?twelfth century, KH, pp. 333, 393); Westminster, St James (twelfth century, KH, pp. 336, 402; *VCH London*, vol. i, pp. 542–6) and St Mary Rouncivall (before 1231, possibly very early thirteenth century, KH, pp. 336, 402). St James's was a leper hospital. It is possible that there were other hospitals, not recorded, and the history of some of these is extremely obscure. We have omitted the second hospital in Holborn listed in KH, pp. 323, 365, since its early history seems totally unknown.

[4] See esp. G. Constable, *Monastic Tithes from their Origins to the Twelfth Century*, Cambridge, 1964; B. Tierney, *Medieval Poor Law*, Berkeley and Los Angeles, 1959.

originally a welfare tax became primarily a tax to support clergy present and absent; the vicar on the spot was now guaranteed a minimum wage, but the larger share of the tithes, in the majority of cases, went either to a religious house or to a member of the upper clergy who was normally engaged in the service of king or Pope or bishop, or at a university. In the process it was, however, firmly established that a proportion of the tithe was intended to be for the relief of poverty; and the canon lawyers laid down the rules in a world in which organized charity was coming to be seen as increasingly necessary, not only to help the rich to heaven, but to relieve poverty and need, to deal with the old and the sick, to educate the young and care for orphans. In village communities there had always been a tradition of mutual help stemming from the days when a village community had little but its own harvest to rely on, and everyone depended on the common effort. Even though the English economy was far removed from the subsistence level by the twelfth century the tradition of mutual help continued, and was of the essence of village life. In the newly formed urban communities such traditions had to be fostered in a much more self-conscious manner, and although the numerous parish churches no doubt provided a basis for social work in eleventh- and twelfth-century London, so large a town was the natural breeding ground for other schemes for social welfare too. The parish churches were small and most of them quite poor: thus the need for larger and more effective centres was evident, and from this it followed that London should play a key part in the development of hospitals in the twelfth century.

The hospital was a place where some might live and others visit. No doubt the brothers or sisters who ran it could go out into the streets and visit the sick at home, but essentially a hospital was a self-contained house, looking after its own. Between the parish clergy and the hospitals a gap existed, and the progressive impoverishment of many of the churches in the thirteenth century must have made this increasingly evident. In the first half of the thirteenth century, all over western Christendom, a major effort to fill this gap was made by the new Orders of Friars. Their inspiration was religious and their message primarily spiritual. But their founders had very definite practical aims too, and their achievement in early days faithfully reflects the area of territory reckoned to be covered by the welfare Church. The first and greatest of these Orders were the Dominicans and Franciscans, both of whom came to England in the early 1220s.[1]

[1] D. Knowles, *Religious Orders in England*, vol. i, Cambridge, 1948, chaps xii, xiv; W. A. Hinnebusch, *The early English Friars Preacher*, chap. 2; C. L. Kingsford,

The Dominicans first settled in London in or shortly after 1221, and soon established a house in Holborn, which was moved in the late thirteenth century to the area still known as Blackfriars. In their Holborn Priory, in 1224, they gave hospitality to the first group of Franciscans to land in England. Then, for a brief period, the Franciscans lived in tiny cells with herb-gardens between them in a plot on Cornhill; but in 1225–7 they were granted the site in the angle between Newgate Street and Stynkyng Lane where their large church and ample buildings subsequently grew. The donor was the eminent patrician and ex-sheriff Josce, son of Peter; and soon after his own son became a friar.[1] The lane acquired its salubrious name, no doubt, from the Shambles, the meat market, in the main street near by. The Franciscans set themselves, here as elsewhere, to cleanse the atmosphere, to provide proper drainage and plumbing, as well as to cleanse the souls of the citizens of London; and in the building of their aqueduct they had notable help from the local alderman, Henry of Frowyk.[2] To these two tasks we must leave them, for they lie outside our scope; but the friars carried on, in new paths, and with a new spiritual drive mingled with a sense of material welfare equally novel, the twelfth-century tradition of social and religious welfare which has been the main theme of this chapter.

The Grey Friars of London, British Society of Franciscan Studies, 1915 (see esp. map facing p. 52); A. R. Martin, *Franciscan Architecture in England*, ib., 1937, pp. 176–204. Thomas of Eccleston, *De adventu fratrum minorum in Angliam*, ed. A. G. Little, Manchester, 1951.

[1] Thomas of Eccleston, p. 21.

[2] Ibid; Henry of Frowyk appears as alderman of what later became the wards of Farringdon within and without in *Eyre*, no. 350, p. 137. The editors reasonably queried whether there was confusion here with Laurence of Frowyk, who seems to occur as alderman in no. 366. Perhaps the most likely explanation is that Henry had been alderman and was succeeded by Laurence before the date of this record, 1246.

12

London and the Kingdom: the Chapter of St Paul's

SINCE ITS foundation by Bishop Mellitus in the early seventh century, the cathedral church of St Paul, the Apostle of the Gentiles and Roman martyr, has played many parts in London's history. It has always been a dominating physical, spiritual and psychological fact. However small Mellitus' cathedral and its Anglo-Saxon successors may have been, they were in all probability the most imposing permanent buildings in the City before the Norman Conquest. In the mid-eleventh century the chief rival, the royal palace, was moved to Westminster, and after the Conquest Bishop Maurice and his successors raised an enormous building which would not only make the Norman presence felt, as well as the Apostle's, but give the City a church which could rival and subdue even the Confessor's abbey at Westminster.[1] Paul had reasserted himself in the presence of Peter. From then on Paul's has been the largest building in the City, and for much of its life, in many men's view, the most beautiful. The Normans rebuilt it from end to end, and the tremendous nave survived into the seventeenth century, to be drawn by Hollar. The choir was rebuilt on the most splendid scale in the thirteenth and early fourteenth centuries, and the 'new Work' was completed in the 1310s; a generation later the chapter house, one of the cradles of perpendicular architecture and the only part of the medieval cathedral of which any trace can be seen today, was added. Above the junction of Norman nave and Gothic choir rose the great spire, begun in the 1220s, which remained until the sixteenth century the centre of the vista of the City. It became

[1] See *HSP*; G. H. Cook, *Old St Paul's Cathedral*, London, 1955; **Plates 48–50**. The chief sources of our knowledge of old St Paul's are Hollar's engravings in W. Dugdale, *History of St Paul's Cathedral in London*, London, 1658.

unsafe and was felled in the sixteenth century, so that it is missing from the panoramas of the late sixteenth and early seventeenth centuries; but by the mercy of providence it survived until 1561, and can be seen in all its beauty in the earliest of these views of the City which survives.[1]

Long before the Reformation the Cathedral had ceased to be the centre of the life of the City. It is true that its nave remained the largest public hall and free shelter, so that Bishop Braybrooke (at the end of the fourteenth century) had to publish stern injunctions against those who played ball games and shot the pigeons,[2] and doubtless generations of deans and vergers overturned the tables of the money-changers there, or failed to do so. It is also true that it remained a great ceremonial centre, where kings were welcomed on peaceful occasions; where the City levies massed under their banners in times of war. It remained a symbol of the City and the kingdom; after the Great Fire Wren was able to build the Baroque masterpiece we enjoy today. But in the late Middle Ages Paul's was ruled by a small clique of resident canons, who kept the world at bay; and although its physical presence must be felt at any time, and although it has remained into the twentieth century a mighty symbol, represented for recent generations in the famous pictures of St Paul's in the great fire of 1940, a history of London can be written at most times since 1313 (when Bishop Ralph Baldock, who finished the New Work, died) which virtually ignores it.

THE PRE-CONQUEST CHAPTER

Before 1066 its history is obscure. Even so, it can lay claim to a continuity through the Conquest beyond what any other English cathedral could pretend. A rule of the tenth or early eleventh centuries, based on the communal life of canons of Carolingian times (as summarized in the *Institutio Canonicorum* of Aachen of 816–17), survived through the vicissitudes of the Norman Conquest and reorganization and many revisions of the constitution, to be enshrined and preserved in the definitive constitutions of Ralph Baldock of c. 1300.[3] It provided for a communal life with its centre in the Opus Dei, the services of the cathedral. But it also

[1] By A. Van den Wyngaerde, London Topographical Soc., 1944.

[2] See *HSP*, pp. 88–9.

[3] *Registrum Statutorum . . . Cathedralis S. Pauli Londinensis*, ed. W. S. Simpson, London, 1873, esp. pp. 38 ff.; see *HSP*, pp. 12–15, with extracts on pp. 14–15, from which the quotations which follow are taken.

presupposed a measure of independence among the canons, the beginning of those separate incomes which grew into the post-Conquest prebends. It defended established authority:

> You shall consider that Paul is the superior of you all by his calling in teaching and preaching; and while Paul provides for you in temporal things, while you are nourished by Paul's food and drink – when you go out from Paul's chapter, never cease the rest of the day to obey his saving exhortation ['The superior power is ordained of God']. He carries a sword not without cause: for he is God's minister, an avenger to execute wrath on him who doeth evil.

Finally, there is a hint of the spirit which brought St Paul's and the City close together in the eleventh century:

> There are some who can wear a worldly habit, and yet not have a worldly mind . . . Reflect on this when you cannot give up all those things which are of the world: do well what you have to do outside in the world, but let your zeal be within, impatient for the things that are eternal . . . To accomplish this we have our aid, 'the mediator of God and men', through whom we shall gain all things speedily, if we burn with a true love towards Him.

The Age of Bishop Maurice (1085–1107)

The estates which supported Paul and his chapter, bishop and canons, before the eleventh century, lay spread across the diocese, from west Middlesex up to the Essex coast, with a few outliers, such as Caddington in Bedfordshire. Before the Norman Conquest, it had already been determined, more or less, which of these estates supported the bishop, which the chapter. 'Domesday Book' shows us some canons squatting on bishop's land and chapter land: Engelbric or Ingelric held of the bishop in Stepney, and Gueri and Durand divided Twyford (Middlesex) between them.[1] At the time of Domesday, Maurice, the former royal chancellor, was recently installed as bishop. He was to preside over the reorganization of the chapter lands and the formation of the prebends, and to start the rebuilding of the cathedral. Evidently his work was well begun and half done; or else he proceeded with reorganization in too high-handed a manner, and possibly reserved chapter moneys for his building enterprise.

---

[1] 'Domesday Book', vol. i, p. 126b; cf. Gibbs, pp. xxii ff.

On his deathbed in 1107 he took counsel with his friend Herbert Losinga, Bishop of Norwich, the worldly prelate converted by the influence of St Anselm, who had been similarly engaged in reorganizing and building at Norwich. As a result he issued a writ to the dean, archdeacons and canons of St Paul's. 'I repent of the evil deeds I have done, and especially against the Church of St Paul and against yourselves. Wherefore I beg you to forgive me what I have done unjustly against you, on the condition that you may hold henceforth the rights which you possessed on the day I was enthroned your bishop, in the customs of your church, its statutes, elections and power of granting prebends and establishing manors.'[1] But Maurice's humility and repentance could not disguise the fact that the chapter and the cathedral wore a different dress in 1107 from 1086; a new era had dawned.

For us, it is a new dawn indeed; for out of the twilight of pre-Conquest Paul's we are delivered into the best documented cathedral chapter of the twelfth century in Christendom. Chance has preserved for us a unique list of canons, for every prebend, which though not perfect in every detail, enables us to reconstruct virtually the whole of the chapter from *c.* 1090 on.[2] Nothing of the kind exists elsewhere in England; virtually no continental parallel is known. There were thirty prebends from that time on, thirty canons and thirty stalls. It must have been very rare – if it ever happened – that all thirty were present on any single occasion. This was probably never quite the intention of Maurice and his colleagues; none the less they doubtless believed themselves to be founding or developing a religious community of a kind.[3]

The papal reformers of the mid-eleventh century had longed to see all clergy, or as many as possible, gathered into regular communities, living and worshipping together, and holding all their goods, like the Apostles, in common. Out of this movement came not only a vast increase in the numbers of monks and monasteries, but the communities and orders which we know as 'canons regular', who lived a communal life according to the Rule of St Augustine. But secular canons did not immediately

[1] Gibbs, no. 59; on Herbert Losinga, see B. Dodwell in *TRHS*, 5th Series, vol. vii, 1957, pp. 1–18.

[2] For the results, see Le Neve (by Diana Greenway); and, on the prebendal catalogue, Brooke in *Cambridge Historical Journal* (*CHJ*), vol. x, 1951, pp. 113; Le Neve, *Fasti . . . 1300–1541*, vol. v, 1963 (by Joyce Horn), p. 73.

[3] On the secular cathedrals in this period, and in general, see K. Edwards, *English Secular Cathedrals in the Middle Ages*, 2nd edn, Manchester, 1967.

disappear; indeed they never disappeared. They simply became more secular, or more obviously secular. In the Anglo-Norman world, they flourished as never before or since; and if we glance at the lists of the canons of St Paul's we can see why. At St Martin-le-Grand in the reign of the Confessor, Ingelric the Priest, very likely the same as the Engelbric, canon of St Paul's, whom we have recently met, established an institution which was to be a model for many to come.[1] It provided masses for the living and the dead; a haven of refuge for the oppressed, and for those pursued by the sheriffs of London. It provided above all a handsome income out of ecclesiastical endowments and landed properties for Ingelric the priest for so long as he should continue dean – an office happily unprovided with duties of any kind; and a not so handsome, but not wholly negligible, income for other secular canons besides. That is to say, it put a pious face on an institution providing incomes for the king's friends and servants.

THE CITY AND THE CLOSE

There was, from the start, an element of St Martin's in St Paul's, both in the person of Ingelric and possibly of others, and of some of their friends at court. By the fourteenth century a great part of the chapter consisted of civil servants, active or retired. But in the late eleventh and twelfth centuries it represented a far wider spectrum of the church of the day.

Of the first generation of canons, roughly half bore English or Viking names, roughly half Norman or French.[2] We may take this figure, with all allowances made, as a faithful reflection of how the balance of influence worked between the two nations in a city which preserved a strongly English element, and in a cathedral which had been ruled by Norman or French bishops since *c.* 1044. Some of the names are particularly intriguing. Quintilian, Prebendary of Ealdland and Archdeacon of Colchester, reflects in his name the first beginnings of the twelfth-century renaissance, as perhaps also his son, with the equally unusual name of Cyprian. The first Prebendary of Oxgate was called Arthur, a reminder that a very different aspect of that renaissance was scattering hints of its presence about Europe in the late eleventh century, even as far as the famous bas-relief of Arthur on Modena Cathedral.[3]

---

[1] See above, pp. 310 ff.   [2] Brooke, in *CHJ*, vol. x, 1951, pp. 121–2.
[3] Le Neve, pp. 18, 45, 67 (cf. Brooke, *Twelfth Century Renaissance*, London, 1969, pl. 1, pp. 12, 208).

For the history of London, perhaps the most interesting name of all in the first generation is Ralph, son of Algod, Prebendary of Rugmere, who drew his income from the western part of the parish of St Pancras, just east of where the London Zoo now stands, called Rugmere, the 'wood-cock's pool'.[1] The combination of a French name and an English father is symptomatic of the generation born soon after the Norman Conquest, of English citizens wishing to win for their children a respectable place in the new regime. The prebendal list shows us that Ralph was a married canon – a respectably married canon, we may reasonably say, as were many in his generation, for he is one of seven or eight who passed on their prebends to their sons, an interesting commentary on the relation between the papal reform – at whose heart lay the campaign for celibacy – and the rise of the Anglo-Norman chapters, at whose centre, in the first generations at least, was a solid nucleus of married canons.

It is a happy circumstance that the prebendal list shows Ralph's son to have been called William, for this sets beyond all reasonable doubt the identification of Canon Ralph with 'Raulf', son of Algot, who is named with his whole family in the list of those who had confraternity with the monks of Durham of the day: Ralph, son of Algod 'and his brother Edmund [presumably the first prebendary of Chiswick] and Maud his concubine and Thomas his son and William, and Ralph's mother Leo-verun',[2] which reveals to us that both Ralph's parents had English names, but his own and his wife's and his children's were all French. It would be interesting to know what language was spoken at the canon's house.

Nor is this all. For Ralph, son of Algod heads two lists of eminent citizens, one of the surviving members of the Cnihtengild in 1125, and one of the witnesses of a major settlement relating to Holy Trinity Priory and the lands it had received from the Cnihtengild in 1137. Between those dates the first list of London wards names him an alderman.[3]

[1] *PN Middlesex*, p. 142. On Ralph, see Le Neve, p. 74, cf. pp. 40–1. He had a brother called Edmund who may also have been a canon.

[2] *Liber Vitae* of Durham, ed. A. H. Thompson, Surtees Society, vol. cxxxvi, 1923, f. 42+.

[3] See Le Neve, p. 74. It is natural to identify the alderman of *c.* 1127 (*Essays . . . presented to T. F. Tout*, p. 59) with the leading burgess who heads the list of witnesses of 1125 (*Cart. Aldgate*, p. 168), and to identify him further with the Ralph son of Algod who heads the similar document of 1137 (ib., p. 190; Round, *CL*, p. 101). In the later document Ralph son of Algod is followed by Randulf or Ralph, canon (not chancellor, as Round) of St Paul's. This may be Ralph of Langford, soon after to be dean (Le Neve, pp. 5, 30), and a nephew of the former bishop, Richard de Belmeis I. In any

The list of 1137 has a French and Norman element in it (as we should expect) and includes Gilbert Becket; his more famous son, Thomas, later parson of St Mary-le-Strand and Prebendary of Reculversland, was ultimately to join St Paul among the City's patron saints. It also names Theodoric, son of Deorman. Theodoric was probably the son of an eminent London citizen and so the brother of Algar, Deorman's son, first Prebendary of Islington; Deorman himself gave the land in Islington for the prebend, and his grandson Bertram gave more land in Islington to the nuns of Clerkenwell.[1] Nor were these links confined to the first generation.

Arthur's successor as Prebendary of Oxgate was Nicholas Crocemannus, perhaps the crutch-man, but more probably the cross-man, founder of a dynasty of canons and aldermen. His sons included Nicholas, a friend of Becket, who was Archdeacon of London from *c.* 1158 for about thirty years, and Master Richard, Prebendary of Sneating; his daughter married Geoffrey Lutre (a well-known city name) and bore him Master Nicholas and Master John of London, both canons of St Paul's, and Simon of Aldermanbury, a leading citizen of the late twelfth century.[2]

THE CLOSE AND THE COURT

If Ralph, son of Algod reveals the links of cathedral and City most extensively – and the worldly interests of some members of the chapter – it is the union of chapter and royal court which appears in the list for Consumpta-per-Mare, the prebend which is supposed to have sunk into the sea by Walton-on-Naze in Essex before 1066.[3] However this story may be, the income of the prebend was slight, and there must have been other attractions, financial and spiritual, to explain a remarkable list of names.

---

event the order of witnesses is much more intelligible if Ralph son of Algod was also a cleric, and it may well be that the original of the list read 'canonicis'. In view of the unusual collocation of names, the presumption is that all these references are to one man. His identity with the Ralph of the Durham *Liber Vitae* is confirmed by other evidence that he had a brother called Edmund and a son called William (Le Neve, pp. 40–1, 75), and this in its turn shows the canon to have been a family man with a stake in the world. All this amounts to probability, though not to proof. See Round *CL*, p. 102; Brooke, in *CHJ*, vol. x, 1951, pp. 122–3.

[1] Le Neve, p. 57.; *CHJ*, vol. x, p. 123 n.; Gibbs, p. xxii n.; *Cart. Clerkenwell*, nos 160, 162.

[2] Le Neve, p. 67; *CHJ*, vol. x, p. 123 n.; *GF*, p. 285; Gibbs, nos 138–40, 143; Round, *CL*, p. 254.

[3] Le Neve, p. 42, n. 6.

It starts with the eminent Lotharingian scholar and royal servant, Robert, who introduced into England Arabian arithmetic and the principle out of which the Exchequer was to grow, and rose to be Bishop of Hereford in the Conqueror's later years.[1] Another colleague of Bishop Maurice followed, in the person of William Giffard, royal chancellor under Rufus, Bishop of Winchester under Henry I.[2] When William went to Winchester, the prebend welcomed in his place Osbern, the king's chaplain, possibly a brother of Ranulf Flambard, the notorious minister of Rufus whose family battened on many chapter prebends, possibly also Henry I's sheriff in Lincolnshire.[3] After Osbern came Thurstan of Bayeux, whose father Anger or Anskar, and brother Audoen, were also canons and royal chaplains.[4] Thurstan was elected Archbishop of York in 1114, but to the great annoyance of his royal master refused to be consecrated until he had successfully asserted his see's independence from the primacy of Canterbury. In his later years Thurstan of Bayeux was to play a leading part in the resettlement of monastic Yorkshire, and showed as shrewd a spiritual as temporal understanding of the movements of his day. He is remembered above all as the founder of Fountains Abbey, though he himself ended his days in the less heroic cloister of the Cluniac priory at Pontefract. His prebend, meanwhile, had fallen to Ranulf Patin, member of a well-known City family which gave its name to St Mary Pattins, who was succeeded in his turn by two relatives of the eminent Bishop Gilbert Foliot, and they by Alexander of Swereford, the Exchequer clerk of Henry III's early years who compiled the 'Red Book' of the Exchequer. Thus Consumpta shows us a cross-section of the types of men we may expect to meet in the chapter of St Paul's in the twelfth century.

The Family of Richard de Belmeis

The shape of the chapter received a new orientation with the arrival of Bishop Richard I de Belmeis, or Beaumais, ultimately from Beaumais-sur-

---

[1] Le Neve, p. 42; *CHJ*, vol. x, p. 122 and n.; W. H. Stevenson in *EHR*, vol. xxii, 1907, pp. 72 ff.

[2] Le Neve, p. 42; ib. vol. ii, p. 85.

[3] Le Neve, p. 43; *CHJ*, vol. x, pp. 124, 130 nn. But the attempt (ib. pp. 129 ff.) to make Flambard himself dean of St Paul's must be said to have failed: see Le Neve, pp. 97 ff.

[4] Le Neve, pp. 36, 43; *CHJ*, vol. x, 124 and n.; D. Nicholl, *Thurstan, Archbishop of York*, York, 1964. For his dates, Le Neve, p. 43.

Dive, in 1108. Beaumais is in the Hiesmois, in Calvados, and the Belmeis came to England under the aegis of the Vicomte of the Hiesmois, Roger of Montgomery, Earl of Shrewsbury.[1] Somehow the Belmeis survived the fall of the house of Montgomery-Bellême in 1102, and prospered in the ruin of their masters, for presently we find Richard as Sheriff of Shropshire, and he and his brother Walter building up properties there. Richard had found such favour with the king that he was rewarded by promotion to the bishopric of London in 1108; and all the indications are that he was a man of great practical ability, a good family man, but of a thoroughly secular disposition. The extent of his family is remarkable. Later in the century, his nephew Richard de Belmeis II, after holding other offices in the cathedral and diocese, was bishop, 1152–62; and his successor, the well-known Bishop Gilbert Foliot, 1163–87, was also related to the Belmeis clan. Soon after his accession – as soon as the office fell vacant – Richard de Belmeis I appointed his nephew, William de Mareni, as dean; William's successor was Ralph of Langford, brother of Richard de Belmeis II, and he was succeeded in his turn by another de Mareni, Hugh, who had already had a spell as Archdeacon of London. And so the story goes on. The family fortunes were based on a Richard, and the name survived in generation after generation; in the second generation two Richards, brothers, appear, both archdeacons, one of them later Bishop Richard II; in the third generation, two more Richards, 'Rufus' and 'Junior', well-to-do canons. Richard Junior became Prebend of Holborn *c.* 1167, after the death of Richard, Archdeacon of Essex, brother of Richard de Belmeis II; it is likely that Richard Junior was his son. If so, this was the last recorded case of a prebend passing directly from father to son.[2] The campaign for celibacy had had substantial effect, at least in driving underground the old practice of hereditary succession; it had certainly not abolished it even among the higher clergy, and it is possible that Richard Junior himself left a son. But he did not succeed to the prebend of Holborn, and when Richard Junior died in 1214, the last of the Belmeis to sit in the chapter had departed.

It is significant that Richard Junior succeeded to his father's prebend in (or *c.*) 1167, for at that date his more distant relative, Gilbert Foliot,

[1] Le Neve, p. 1 (and for the family, *passim*); W. Stubbs, introd. to Diceto, vol. i, pp. xxi–xxix; *GF*, pp. 43–7, 204–6, 271 ff.; *HSP*, pp. 22 ff.

[2] Le Neve, p. 53; *GF*, pp. 272, 280. On the continuance of clerical marriage, however, see M. Cheney in *EHR*, vol. lxxxii, 1967, p. 761.

had recently become bishop.[1] However he may have been related to the Belmeis, he was very close to them in his nepotism. He had been an austere Cluniac monk, and had no addiction to the married life of the Belmeis. But he is an excellent example of the transference from sons to nephews characteristic of this period, an observation attributed by Gerald of Wales to Pope Alexander III (1159–81), and by the Pope to the devil.[2] To every vacant archdeaconry and to several canonries he presented a nephew or some other relation; at least eight out of the twenty-eight or so canons collated in his time were his relations, and probably more. The most important appointment, or election, of his reign, was the promotion of the Archdeacon of Middlesex, Ralph de Diceto, to the deanery in 1180. Diceto is well known not only as a reforming dean but as the author of an important chronicle; and in his study of the chapter and the man, in his introduction to the chronicle, William Stubbs reckoned it hardly credible that Ralph was not somehow related to the Belmeis and the Foliots.[3] Perhaps he was right. No evidence for the link has ever been found, but we have every reason to suppose that the ramifications of these powerful, inter-connected families went beyond our present knowledge.

THE RECRUITMENT OF THE CHAPTER: THE SHARES OF BISHOP, POPE AND KING

Bishop Maurice's deathbed repentance in 1107 shows that in his time the canons reckoned to have some say in the appointment of their colleagues; the hereditary canons of the early twelfth century point the same way. The people we meet in the chapter in the mid-twelfth century strongly suggest that little came of this right or tradition, whichever it was, but that the chief influence on recruitment at this time was the bishop's. In the long run the chapter's rights became effectively reduced to the election of the bishop and the dean, in which cases, however, they were often, perhaps normally, ruled by higher powers. There are distinct indications that already in the late twelfth century even the bishop's influence was beginning to be eroded by king and Pope.[4] First one, then two or three, papal chaplains appear; we have distinct evidence at London that the first papal

---

[1] On him see *GF*, *GFL* (*GF*, chap. ii for Foliot's family connections, with corrections by Sir C. Clay in *Antiquaries Journ.*, vol. xlvii, 1967, p. 124).

[2] Giraldus, *Opera*, vol. ii, p. 304.

[3] Diceto, vol. i, pp. xxvi–xxix (**Plate 51**).

[4] *GF*, pp. 209 ff.; *HSP*, pp. 44, 51 ff.

provision occurred as early as the 1150s. It was not until the fourteenth century that provision played a major part in recruiting the chapter, but the papal infiltration – doubtless here, as elsewhere, inspired by a host of would-be beneficiaries – was under way. Direct royal patronage during vacancies, or indirect, by pressure on bishop and chapter, came in the end to be the predominant influence. How it was exercised in the twelfth century, we do not know; we only know the result. In the last decade of the century, when Ralph de Diceto, 'the good dean',[1] presided over the cathedral and the close, the bishop was the eminent civil servant and former royal treasurer, Richard FitzNeal or Richard of Ely, a late representative of an ecclesiastical dynasty even more powerful than the Belmeis, which descended from Roger, Bishop of Salisbury, Henry I's chancellor and justiciar. A royal clerk called Brand sat in the prebend of Brownswood, to which he gave his name.[2] Richard's younger relative, and successor as king's treasurer, William of Ely, sat in the stall of Caddington Minor, where he was to be succeeded by the eminent lawyer, Dean Martin of Pattishall. Another Richard of Ely sat in Cantlers (the prebend of Kentish Town), where he was succeeded by Peter of Ste-Mère-Église and Peter by William de Fauconberg – just as Bishop Richard was succeeded by William of Ste-Mère-Église and he by Eustace de Fauconberg.[3] But otherwise it is their connections in the royal service not their nephews who are in evidence. None of them was a pater familias after the fashion of Richard de Belmeis I, or an uncle on the scale of Gilbert Foliot. At Chamberlainwood sat Richard de Camera, nephew of Osbert de Camera, an earlier canon; both took their name, in all probability, from the royal chamber, and were household officials; Richard, like Brand, probably

---

[1] See *GF*, p. 206.

[2] Le Neve, p. 29 n. 4, 30, and cf. p. 27 n. There has been some confusion about the origins of the names Broomesbury and Brondesbury. But it seems likely that the former was named after Roger Brun (mid-twelfth century) and the latter after Brand, who received the prebend *c*. 1190 (cf. *PN Middlesex*, pp. 122, 161). Most of the names of the prebends are genuine place-names; all the cases of a canon's name and 'bury' or 'land' or 'wood' seem to be of the mid- or late twelfth-century: Chamberlainwood, from Richard de Camera; Mapesbury, from Walter Map; Reculverland, from Hugh of Reculver (*PN Middlesex*, pp. 161–2; *PN Essex*, p. 230; Le Neve, pp. 38–9, 59–60, 73–4). It is possible that the practice sprang from a joke of Walter Map's (see p. 349). Cantlers has been thought to derive from Roger de Cantilupe (mid-thirteenth century), but it seems to us much more probable that it is an older name connected with the root from which Kentish Town comes (cf. *PN Middlesex*, p. 141).

[3] Le Neve, pp. 2, 37.

left his name to the prebend. Ralph of Ely sat at Chiswick, which had been Richard FitzNeal's own prebend in former times. His successor was to be Alan, clerk of Pope Innocent III, possibly the famous canonist, Master Alanus.[1] A nephew of Gilbert Foliot, one Gilbert Banastre, still held Consumpta, where (as we have observed) the exchequer official Alexander of Swereford sat after him. The stall of Ealdland was held by a nephew of Pope Celestine III (1191–8), called Laurence; his successor was a member of the family of Oxgate, John, grandson of Canon Nicholas Crocemannus, son of Simon of Aldermanbury. John in his turn was followed by the saintly Roger Niger, Archdeacon of Colchester, later bishop (1229–41). As we press on through the lists we shall find another Foliot (also a royal justice) at Neasden, and another at Newington; the last generation of Belmeis still at Holborn and Twyford; another royal official presently succeeding Richard Ruffus at Twyford; another of the Crocemannus clan at Weldland. Royal patronage at this time seems, on the whole, to have proceeded by indirect methods which naturally led to the promotion of royal officials who were also bishops' relatives; and it is noticeable that virtually all the royal officials who became bishops in this period – virtually all the bishops, indeed – had been canons of St Paul's, or in some way connected with the cathedral.

WALTER MAP, THE NON-RESIDENT CANON

Perhaps the most interesting name in the lists at the end of the twelfth century is Master Walter Map, the learned satirist and royal clerk. He is one of a group of canons of this age whose names have lived on in their prebends. Thus Roger Brun is remembered in Broomesbury, Brand in Brownswood, Richard de Camera in Chamberlainwood, Hugh of Reculver in Reculversland, Walter Map in Mapesbury.[2] Map's *burh*, or fortified manor, sounds very grand; and we may conjecture that it originated in a joke. Map was the offspring of well-to-do border folk, half-Welsh, half-English; he had won early patronage both from Gilbert Foliot, when he was Bishop of Hereford, and from King Henry. 'He was dear and acceptable to the king,' writes Map about himself, 'not for his own merits, but for those of his forebears who had been faithful and useful to the king, both before his accession and after it.'[3] Under the aegis of king and bishop he added

[1] Le Neve, pp. 41–2, and *passim* for what follows.
[2] See p. 348 n.
[3] *De nugis curialium*, dist. v, c. 6, ed. M. R. James, Oxford, 1914, p. 246; trans. M. R. James, Cymmrodorion Record Series, no. ix, 1923, p. 270 (a new edn of James's

church to church and prebend to prebend; much of his time was spent as a
royal clerk. But it was commonly not a full-time occupation under Henry
II, and we may suppose that Map had time to spare for his benefices,
even for his castle in Willesden; and perhaps rather especially for his stall
in St Paul's, since royal business must have brought him often to London.
Nor did he necessarily neglect it in later life, when he retired from the
court, and took up residence in the diocese of Lincoln. He was successively
chancellor and precentor of Lincoln Cathedral and Archdeacon of Oxford.
His humour is exceedingly broad, and at times obscene; yet with a strong
moral undertow; and he took the precaution of not putting his *De nugis
curialium* into circulation. It survived by what is almost a miracle, and
only came to be read in the nineteenth century. It is clear that he was
famous in his own day as a wit; his friend Gerald of Wales confirms what
Map himself evidently intends us to believe.[1] But he was also a man of
great learning, as the innumerable references and quotations and hidden
echoes of the *De nugis* reveal; and of some pastoral gifts, or St Hugh of
Lincoln would not have made him an archdeacon. At Oxford, indeed, he
was in a centre already more noted for its learning than London – though
the schools of St Paul's were far from negligible. But Map valued his
prebend in St Paul's: he tells the story of how Geoffrey 'Plantagenet',
Henry II's illegitimate son, with whom Map was always bickering, tried
to get the prebend, which he himself had formerly held, back from Map;
and he valued it sufficiently to leave his name on it.

Ralph de Diceto and Residence

Walter Map was clearly one of the men who can help us to understand the
motives at work in the inner counsels of the chapter of St Paul's, when
Dean Ralph de Diceto promulgated his statute of residence in or about
1192.[2] In it he recognized that full residence by most canons was not to be
expected. It was a turning-point in the history of the secular chapters.
The Anglo-Norman chapters had been founded or refounded in the late
eleventh century as spiritual clubs, ecclesiastical counterparts to the

---

text and translation is in preparation for OMT: what follows is based on C. N. L.
Brooke's contribution to the introduction; cf. Le Neve, p. 60; *GF*, p. 283; Le Neve,
vol. for Lincoln, forthcoming).

[1] Giraldus, *Opera*, esp. vol. iv, pp. 219 ff.

[2] Diceto, vol. ii, pp. lxix–lxxiii; for the date see *GF*, p. 271 n.; cf. Le Neve, p. xiv.
The context is discussed in *HSP*, pp. 51 ff.

earliest guilds; as we have seen, there was even some overlap between the membership of the chapter of St Paul's and of the Cnihtengild. They were intended to be religious communities of a kind, but also to attract revenues and provide pensions for men engaged in the business of the Church in the world – civil servants, bishops' chaplains, and so forth. If we could penetrate behind this final phrase to the realities of life in the City in the days of Bishop Maurice, we should very likely find a lively intercourse between chapter and City. In the late Middle Ages this tended to decline. A sharp distinction came to be drawn between a small group of canons who lived in the close and performed the work of 'residence' – and also enjoyed the revenues and perquisites attached to residence – and the larger chapter, the non-residents, whose link with the cathedral became increasingly honorary. In the nineteenth century the split was finally consecrated by the abolition of the prebends. The names survive, and the stalls can still be distinguished in Wren's choir. But their holders are either canons 'residentiary', that is, the effective chapter, or honorary canons. This is the split which Ralph de Diceto attempted to prevent *c.* 1192; a split which was already on its way, and is in its essence clearly revealed by a spurious statute fathered on him in the fourteenth century.

The essence of his genuine statute is the attempt to regulate the distribution of the common fund of the chapter according to the length of time a canon was actually present in the close. As a statute of residence it 'appears at first reading a very lax affair'.[1] Residence for a bare three months can, in the extreme case, qualify a man to regard himself as a resident canon. In the various attempts made in other cathedrals to preserve the show of a large residentiary community, no one seems to have thought of going to this extreme. St Paul's Cathedral and the bishopric were not exceptionally well endowed; the Bishop of London must often have looked with envy at his neighbour of Winchester, who commanded the income (in modern equivalent) of a multi-millionaire, the paradise of great financiers, from Henry of Blois to William of Wykeham and Cardinal Beaufort. The result was that although the prebends were (in comparison with some other cathedrals) far from princely, the common fund was not unduly substantial either. What St Paul's could offer was unequalled opportunity for enlarging one's income by other work; or, to put it another way, a canonry provided a pleasant addition to one's income, a dignified stall, a place in society, and perhaps a house in the City. Furthermore, the brewery and

[1] *GF*, p. 193.

the bakehouse converted the food farms from the common manors into bread and beer, which could help to provide a household with basic necessities of life.

The Chapter Economy

In the reorganization of the manors after the Norman Conquest, the canons retained most of their more distant manors in common, and divided up estates in what is now North London to make the individual 'manors' or prebends of the thirty canons. The great manor of Willesden, with Twyford attached, was broken into eight prebends; and many of the rest speak for themselves: to give them their original names, or their true modern equivalents, we find, moving east, St Pancras, Tottenham Court (at the top of Tottenham Court Road), Finsbury, Islington, Holborn and 'Port Pool' (now Grays Inn Road); Moorfields; we find Old Street and Hoxton and Wenlock's Barn in Shoreditch. Not far away are Chiswick, and Brownswood in Hornsey (near Finsbury Park); more remote were Reculversland and Ealdland (the 'old land') in Tillingham, Consumpta and Sneating on the Essex coast, and Caddington in Bedfordshire.[1]

The prebends themselves produced rents and sometimes food and fuel for their canons; but chiefly a not very substantial money income. The regular payment of this income must have involved the canons either in administration themselves, or in arranging with someone who was expert in handling rents or running small farms to raise their income for them. Similar problems arose for the community at large on the manors which supplied the food farms. A succession of charters, culminating in a series of surveys, enables us to see how these manors were 'farmed' over the years. A good example is the group of manors of Belchamp St Paul's and the Sokens, outlying manors in Essex, farther from the cathedral than most. Whoever farmed the Sokens either used a good bailiff or was himself an expert in estate management. The organization of rents and farms of this kind must have been one of the largest and most profitable professions in England; but in the centuries before Walter of Henley and his colleagues wrote their treatises – that is, before the late thirteenth century – one of the most obscure. 'There can be little doubt,' wrote J. H. Round, 'that the

---

[1] See *PN Middlesex*, pp. 113–15, 122, 124, 140–3, 147, 159–63; *PN Essex*, pp. 229–30, 341, 355.

canons of St Paul's were as closely connected . . . with secular life in London as they were with farming in Essex.'[1] But in some cases there was no essential distinction between them. We have met the ubiquitous Ralph, son of Algod, husband, father, prebendary and alderman; we meet him again as an early 'farmer' of Belchamp. Evidently his wealth and position were based in part at least on estate management. In this field he had many colleagues, secular and ecclesiastical. His successor was a layman, the bishop's steward, William of Ockendon; and on William's death the farm of Belchamp fell to Richard Rufus, Archdeacon of Essex.[2]

It is interesting to compare Richard Rufus with a secular contemporary not wholly unconnected with the chapter, Gilbert Becket, Thomas Becket's father. William FitzStephen assures us that he was a citizen who lived honourably off his rents, not engaging in usury or lowly commerce, but evidently a house-agent.[3] Richard Rufus' talents lay in managing country estates; but he also had his troubles. When William of Ockendon, bishop's steward and farmer of the Sokens, died, the archdeacon offered twenty marks (£13 6s 8d) to the canons to let him take over the Sokens.[4] At this date, probably owing to the disorders of Stephen's reign, the manor of Belchamp languished, and could not be induced to provide its annual rents. Thus the canons had difficulty in finding a farmer. So they pardoned Richard Rufus his twenty marks, on condition that he took over Belchamp at the old farm; but the next year he complained (as farmers will) that he was ruined; and begged for a rearrangement. When this was complete, the agreement had attached to it a very precise statement of the rents in money and kind which Richard was due to pay them, and the stock of the manor, including the mill wheels and the sheep, the geese and the capons, the granaries and boon-works, into which the archdeacon had entered. The document vividly evokes a world in which archdeacons cared for the bodies of the chapter as well as for the souls of the people of Essex; and when we read the inventory of sheep (400 less four), the twenty geese, twenty hens, five cocks, five capons – as well as the horse of Leofstan the priest – we have a little insight into the methods by which the Shambles

[1] *CL*, p. 102.

[2] Hale, pp. 1 f., 111, 114 ff., 129, 152 (list of farms). On the farming system, see *HSP*, pp. 60 ff., esp. 62; R. V. Lennard, *Rural England* (p. 197 n.), pp. 130 ff., esp. 131–2.

[3] See p. 212.

[4] Hale, pp. 125–6, 129 ff.

and the stalls by the Woolchurch were provided; as well as the sinews of the brewery and home fires in the close.

Nor need we feel undue sorrow at the archdeacon's ruin, for it is most improbable that he starved. When he died in 1167, the Canon Richard Rufus of the next generation, very likely the archdeacon's son, took over these manors evidently in a prosperous state, and proceeded to climb on his father's shoulders to such good purpose that he accumulated other manors besides. The success of this generation of farmers was such that the canons evidently determined to have a monopoly of farming their own manors; and in due course it became a perquisite of the canons residentiary to receive the offer of a vacant manor to farm for their own benefit.[1] From time to time in the late Middle Ages we find a residentiary canon evidently organizing a prosperous estate management business from the cathedral close. Richard Rufus I and II seem to have been pioneers in this enterprise.

Soon after his election in 1180, even though it was still midwinter, Dean Ralph de Diceto set out with two other experienced canons to perambulate the manors and churches and to see how the chapter's affairs were being conducted.[2] They began at Caddington in Bedfordshire on 8 January 1181, were at Belchamp and Wickham St Paul's on the 15th and 16th, took shelter in the church of Kirby-le-Soken to study the Sokens on the 18th, worked south and west into Middlesex, and concluded their business at Sutton in Chiswick on the 30th. At some manors the farmers at this date were clergy, at some laymen; at a few a clerical farmer already had a secular bailiff. What is striking about the list, apart from the ubiquity of Richard Rufus II, is the number of archdeacons. Oddly enough, we start with two archdeacons in no way connected with St Paul's: the archdeacons of Canterbury, Herbert Poore, and of Bedford, Nicholas de Sigillo, farmed the most northerly of the manors, in Bedfordshire, Hertfordshire and north-eastern Essex.[3] In Middlesex we are nearer home. William, Archdeacon of Gloucester, farmer of Drayton, came from Northolt and was Prebendary of Neasden; and the farmer of Sutton in Chiswick was the prebendary of Oxgate in Willesden, Nicholas, Archdeacon of London.[4]

---

[1] *HSP*, pp. 60 ff., esp. 62.

[2] Hale, pp. 109 ff.

[3] Hale, pp. 110 ff.; Le Neve, *Fasti . . . 1066-1300*, vol. ii, p. 14; and vol. for Lincoln, forthcoming (by Diana Greenway).

[4] Hale, p. 112; Le Neve, pp. 64, 68, cf. p. 9; *Fasti . . . 1066-1300*, vol. ii, pp. 100, 107.

All this helps us a little to understand Walter Map's account of his household, how it was provided for and fed. He says of his servants:

They would go into the streets and lanes and say I had sent them to .compel travellers to come in. The servants in the house received the guests with the greatest respect, said that I was most anxious to see them, and hoped they would come often. Then they would run to me and announce that guests had arrived, men of good position, and made me welcome them, in no wise desiring to do so. Then they made meat and drink fly, and gorged themselves to any extent in my presence . . . and actually compelled the high and the humble, willing and reluctant, to make away with all the provisions, feigning to do this exclusively to increase my reputation; correctly enough, according to the Lord's teaching, they took no thought for the morrow, for they turned everything out of doors. When I charged them with being drunk, they swore they were not drunk, but only happy, and that I was a hard man to blame them for the pains they had been glad to take in my honour. When I came back from church in the morning, I would find a huge fire, and guests of yesterday (who I hoped had gone) sitting round it. My servants would whisper to me: 'Dinner will be wanted. They think there isn't an inn for a long distance: they don't know what they'll find there. Better throw the handle after the axe: you've begun well; end well too. Don't you be anxious: God hasn't given away everything yet. You are but spending what you have. Trust in the Lord; it's common talk that they'll make you a bishop . . .'

And he goes on to complain that nephews are even worse than servants.[1] Map was never made a bishop, though he twice came near it; and he stands as the example of the well-to-do prosperous higher ecclesiastic whom one might find among the canons, resident or occasionally resident, in the close at St Paul's.

St Paul's as an Intellectual Centre

There is no doubt that Map had a worldly element in him; no doubt too that he loved to put on a more worldly face than he always reflected in his inner life. He was a man of considerable learning, and so he lived out his

[1] *De nugis*, dist. i, c. 10, ed. James (see p. 349 n. 3), p. 11; trans. James, pp. 10–11.

later years in Lincoln and Oxford rather than in London. Not that London
was negligible in the intellectual world: there was a stream of notable
scholars and teachers in the close right through the century, from the first
master of the schools, Durand, to Gilbert Foliot (whose scholarship
Map himself much admired), Ralph de Diceto, Master David the canonist
and others towards the end.¹ Throughout the century, not without up-
heavals, it had preserved its breadth and variety, its local connections
combined with a certain cosmopolitan flavour.

After the death of Richard de Belmeis I in 1127, old corruption and the
Belmeis connection were firmly entrenched. It may have been to bring
new blood, or in the hope of making London and its cathedral a real
intellectual centre, or for some other motive now hidden from us, that
Henry I made one of his strangest appointments in bringing Gilbert the
Universal, a professor from Auxerre, to the see in 1127–8. He came with
a vast store of learning, and a small team of nephews. He was the leading
pupil of Anselm of Laon, one of the authors of the *Glossa Ordinaria* to the
Bible, a scholar of great eminence. His nephews and protégés were
interested in unusual things, like mythology, and more common things,
like the legends of saints.² His nephew, Arcoid, had something in common
with another cosmopolitan figure of the age, Anselm, Abbot of Bury,
nephew of St Anselm of Canterbury, and like his uncle an Italian deeply
interested in English traditions. Arcoid and Anselm indeed seem to have
been friends, and to have shared an interest in the English devotion to the
Conception of the Blessed Virgin, which Norman and continental piety
was inclined to view with suspicion. After his uncle's death Arcoid
revived the cult of St Eorcenweald (Erkenwald), most saintly of London
early bishops, and wrote his life. We can see from reading it that he had
little help and encouragement from the locals, for the best that he could
do is Bede and water. But he succeeded in inspiring the translation of the
saint to a new and costly shrine. He also succeeded in rousing a party to
propose the election of Abbot Anselm as Bishop Gilbert's successor. This
stirred the anger of the Belmeis clan, led by the dean, who appealed to

¹ Le Neve, pp. 25–6; *GF*, pp. 275–6; Diceto, *passim*; Z. N. Brooke, 'The Register
of Master David'; Eleanor Rathbone, 'The Influence of Bishops and of Members of
Cathedral Bodies in the Intellectual Life of England, 1066–1216', London Ph.D.
thesis, 1935.
² On Gilbert and his circle, see Le Neve, pp. 1, 27, 86; B. Smalley in *Recherches de
théologie ancienne et médiévale*, vol. vii, 1935, pp. 235–62, esp. pp. 238–41; E. Rathbone
in *Mediaeval and Renaissance Studies*, vol. i, 1943, pp. 35–8; cf. *CHJ*, vol. x, p. 126 n.
80.

Rome.[1] The Pope took counsel with the doyen of the ex-canons of St Paul's, Thurstan, Archbishop of York, who had no use for Anselm; and the papal legate, observing that a valid election could not be held without a lead from the dean, whose right it was to give the first vote, sent Anselm on his way. In the event, during the brief supremacy of the Empress Matilda in 1141, a strange concatenation of circumstances brought Robert de Sigillo to the episcopal throne. He represented old corruption in a sense, in that he had a son, who presently found himself installed as a canon.[2] But Robert, an eminent royal administrator, had grown weary of the failing royal service of Stephen's reign, and become a monk at Reading, where his old master, King Henry I, was buried; and as bishop he favoured what can be now obscurely glimpsed as an ascetic movement in the chapter. The hereditary element did not entirely disappear, but it was almost driven underground. Celibacy came to the fore; the Belmeis had quite a struggle to hold their own. When Robert died, the Pope was petitioned by their opponents to provide another monk as bishop. To this the Pope at first concurred; at least, he ordered the canons to elect a man of learning and sound character, 'clad in the habit of religion'.[3] But the Belmeis were again in the ascendant, and the Pope had presently to claim that a secular canon, or any tonsured clerk, was within the definition, which caused John of Salisbury to wonder if the Pope was afraid the Londoners would choose a layman. In the event, Richard de Belmeis II was elected; but the fires of discord burnt on. When he died, a happier compromise was found, and an eminent monk, who was also a relation of the Belmeis, succeeded in the person of Gilbert Foliot. His reign was to have its troubles – troubles without, since his early years were deeply occupied with his bitter struggle against Thomas Becket, culminating in the final humiliation of Foliot when he was cured of an illness at the martyr's intercession; and there are hints that his relations with his chapter were not always easy.

In 1179 or 1180 the last Belmeis dean, Hugh de Mareni, was gathered to his fathers, and Gilbert prepared to choose a successor. Doubtless the canons expected that the Belmeis would be followed by a Foliot; and the canonist Master David, though a protégé of Gilbert, prepared for a fight. Under the newly forming customs such as an expert in canon law might be

---

[1] Diceto, vol. i, pp. 248 ff.

[2] Le Neve, p. 62; *GF*, p. 283.

[3] John of Salisbury, *Historia Pontificalis*, ed. and trans. M. Chibnall, NMT, 1956, p. 88; *GFL*, pp. 137 ff.

reckoned to understand, it was becoming the rule in many cathedrals that deans, like bishops, should be elected by the canons – however much of a formality it might be. Gilbert Foliot got wind of the intrigue to hold an election which was not a formality, and bitterly complained. But the outcome seems to have been a compromise; for Ralph de Diceto, though firmly entrenched in the chapter under both Belmeis and Foliot patronage, and evidently an archdeacon trusted and liked by his bishop, and possibly even a distant relative, was apparently not a nephew of Gilbert.[1] From 1180 for a space we have a chapter united and at peace, under a dean of great prestige; and Diceto rewarded the old bishop when he wrote of the Becket crisis in his chronicle probably not long after his election as dean, by softening the harsh edge of other men's condemnation of Gilbert Foliot's role, and omitting much that might have been uncongenial to him. The chapter in their turn rewarded the 'good dean' by preserving the magnificent copy of his own chronicle which he gave them as if it were a relic, in the treasury; it may be studied still, though it has gone across the river to Lambeth.[2]

THE CHAPTER IN THE LATE TWELFTH CENTURY

Diceto preserved, and for a time in his statute of residence consecrated, a view of the cathedral chapter which summed up its function in the eleventh and twelfth centuries, but gave it a role it could not play indefinitely. It was an institution of the unspecialized church of the eleventh century. Just as priest and people met in close intimacy in the tiny parish churches of the eleventh century – and no doubt in equally tiny taverns later in the day – so in close and cathedral married canons little different from the City men among whom they moved and had their being brought up their families, gathered their rents, farmed their manors. They were experts or amateurs of many aspects of the life of their day and their City. They included royal servants and chaplains; but even they were not full-time 'administrators', and many men called 'royal clerks' in the twelfth century were only on a temporary or part-time secondment to the court. Thus the Walter Maps of this world could reckon to spend weeks and even months in their town houses; and thus the chapter could hope to see something of the cosmopolitan figures who adorned its prebends: men

---

[1] See above, p. 347.

[2] Lambeth Palace Library MS 8; cf. Diceto, vol. i, pp. lxxxviii ff.; and ii, p. ix for the date of composition (starting *c.* 1180 or a bit later). **Plate 51.**

like Peter of Blois, Archdeacon of London *c.* 1201–12, an eminent literary figure who had served in many courts, or William of Ely, the royal treasurer, who occasionally witnessed the cathedral's charters.[1]

A gathering of the chapter at the very end of our period, such as that which witnessed a surviving charter of 1212–14,[2] contained a number of career canons and ecclesiastical administrators, led by the Dean, Alard of Burnham, a sprinkling of royal clerks and men with some link with the City (such as Henry 'de Civitate'), and for the rest looks like a palimpsest showing the patronage of successive bishops – one Belmeis (Richard Junior), and protégés of Bishops Gilbert Foliot, Richard of Ely and William of Ste-Mère-Église. In course of time more papal chaplains, and far more royal servants, appear in the lists; and by the fourteenth century the chapter's links with the royal court seem to have been far closer than its links with the City. But the City fathers never ignored or (so far as we can tell) despised St Paul's, and certainly not in the thirteenth century. The old cathedral was a monument to two main periods of building: the Norman age, and the age of Ralph Baldock, canon, archdeacon, dean and bishop (*c.* 1278–1313) and his immediate successors. We may be sure that the citizens of London, who had largely ignored Westminster Abbey, lent a hand in paying for the 'New Work'. Nor were there ever lacking bonds of interest between St Paul's and the City. Yet perhaps it is true to say that it never played so essential a role in the life of the City in all its aspects as in the days of Ralph, son of Algod, in the early twelfth century.

[1] See Le Neve, pp. 10, 35, 56; J. Armitage Robinson, *Somerset Hist. Essays*, London, 1921, chap. v; Southern, *Medieval Humanism*, chap. 7; H. G. Richardson in *TRHS*, 4th Series, vol. xv, 1932, pp. 45–90. Peter of Blois and William of Ely witnessed numerous St Paul's charters: see e.g. Gibbs, index, s.v. Blois, Ely.

[2] Gibbs, no. 263 (for the date, cf. Le Neve, pp. 10, 66).

13

Epilogue

AT THE end of the fourth century a line of walls, which in great part still survives, was built to define the boundary of the greatest city in Christendom, from the Golden Horn to the Sea of Marmora:

Should the zeal of the Emperor to adorn the city continue [wrote the orator Themistius a few years before in anticipation of this event], a wider circuit will be required, and the question will arise whether the city added to Constantinople by Theodosius is not more splendid than the city which Constantine added to Byzantium . . . No longer is the vacant ground in the city more extensive than that occupied by buildings; nor are we cultivating more territory within our walls than we inhabit; the beauty of the city is not as heretofore scattered over it in patches, but covers the whole area like a robe woven to the very fringe. The city gleams with gold and porphyry . . . Were Constantine to see the capital he founded, he would behold a glorious and splendid scene, not a bare and empty void; he would find it fair, not with apparent but with real beauty.[1]

In comparison with fourth-century Constantinople, London of the eleventh and twelfth must seem modest and provincial. Yet William FitzStephen's panegyric describes a similar delight in the end and product of a similar epoch in London's history. Students of textbooks have often observed that the English middle class has risen in every century of its history; and there is a danger that the City of London will develop a similar tendency to levitation. In his admirable *Medieval London*, Professor

---

[1] Themistius, quoted in R. Liddell, *Byzantium and Istanbul*, London, 1956, pp. 25–6; freely rendered from *Oratio*, 18, Teubner edition, ed. G. Downey, Leipzig, 1965, vol. i, pp. 322, 321. We owe this reference to the kind help of Dr and Mrs J. B. Hall.

Gwynn Williams has argued that the thirteenth century witnessed a great extension in population, wealth and importance; that London, aspiring in the 1190s to be a commune, had by 1300 become a capital.[1] It has been the argument of this book that the crucial stage in the creation of the City had already taken place before 1190; but this is not intended to belittle or to deny the achievements of the age which followed. The thirteenth century saw the intensification of wealth and population, and new directions in the development of London's own government and its place in the English realm. All that we have tried modestly to say is that the foundations were laid in the period between Alfred and Henry II, especially in the eleventh and twelfth centuries.

First of all, London became a city once again, as it had been under the Romans. However one defines its standing in the world in the centuries between, it is impossible in the present state of knowledge to regard it as a great centre of population. It had been a shell of walls capable of defence, and 'a mart of many peoples, coming by sea and land'; from the early seventh century a cathedral city too. Such was the London of the Dark Ages; never deserted, never forgotten, but hardly a city. From Alfred's time on it revived: how fast, or in what precise way, we cannot tell. We can be sure that some of the familiar street-plan, especially in the western part of the City, dates from Alfred's day or from his immediate successors'. In the tenth century the King of Wessex finally became the King of England, and any doubts that had lingered whether London was to be an East Saxon, Mercian, West Saxon or Viking city ceased to have any meaning. It became the greatest of English cities; and in the early eleventh century the *Burhwaru* of London played a part in king-making.[2]

In the conversion of London from a shell to a city, in the present state of knowledge, the eleventh century seems to have been the most crucial. First of all, it saw the establishment of a host of local communities within the City: it may be that the pattern of wards and parishes was not fixed until the twelfth century, but the crochet-work which created the two large nets – the boundaries of wards and parishes – which divided the City from the twelfth century to the twentieth was well under way in the eleventh century. This means that the whole city was coming to be settled. Evidently the western half was still the more densely occupied and the areas round the Cheaps of West and East the most prosperous. There was plenty of space and opportunity for change: the Normans could carve

[1] See p. 101, and Williams, esp. chaps I, XII.
[2] See p. 23.

spaces at both ends for the Tower and the other castles; Queen Matilda could set aside a substantial precinct within the eastern wall, by Aldgate, for her priory. But the great ring of religious houses and hospitals founded in the twelfth and early thirteenth centuries lay outside the walls, outlining the area occupied by the citizens, the barons of London.

The ecclesiastical pattern reveals and reflects the history of the City at large. It has been of special importance in this book, because the materials for ecclesiastical history are much more copious than for secular history in this period; and because the churches large and small reflect the aspirations of the citizens in a creative age. The present life and the next were linked in a bond which most of us today find difficult to grasp. The difference between earthly and heavenly treasure had been somewhat emphatically stated in the Gospels, and this was an incentive to use the most powerful medium of currency exchange known in the eleventh and twelfth centuries – the box or plate in which one placed offerings to the Church. The semi-circle of religious houses, the numerous hospitals and the 126 parish churches bore eloquent witness to the concern of the citizens to make use of their wealth in this exchange: to their understanding that it was not easy for the rich to enter heaven, nor indeed, in the doctrine of the day, for anyone to escape the pains of hell; but also to the contemporary notion that earthly treasure, however it might differ from heavenly, was convertible. Those who contribute to the guild of clergy formed to complete the rebuilding of St Paul's, said Gilbert Foliot, shall have remitted thirty days of penance; similarly those who helped to repair London Bridge, and those who helped to raise St Thomas's Hospital in Southwark as a monument to the Blessed Martyr.[1] By this means the parish churches, the monasteries, the hospital and the Bridge were built; and though only faint visible traces remain today of any but a very few of the churches, we know enough to plot them on the map and to reconstruct with their help the pattern of settlement and the growth of the City in prosperity in this world and the next.

The formation of the parish churches seems to have been mainly the contribution of the eleventh century;[2] it also witnessed two events crucial to London's future: the move of the king to Westminster and the Norman Conquest. From the time when Edward the Confessor began to rebuild the abbey and to found his palace, London steadily became a town with two centres. The traveller today who crosses Waterloo Bridge can see in the

[1] *GFL*, nos 418, 452.
[2] See chap. 6 and esp. pp. 128 ff., 143.

middle distance on either hand the dome of St Paul's and the Palace of Westminster. The conflict which catches his eye is between Wren and Pugin; but this can remind us of an older rivalry between City and government, between a commercial capital in the City and the political capital of quite a different empire in Westminster. If London had not been for many centuries a great port, it is reasonably certain that the traveller would see nothing of consequence made by the hands of man as he crossed the Thames; the foundations of London, as of almost all great towns, have been securely laid in commerce, in gold and silver. But equally, if Great Britain had been an inward-looking island, her political capital would hardly have been set in so unlikely a place as Westminster. The Romans were city dwellers, and needed a great city for their headquarters with reasonably convenient access to Gaul and Italy; their sailors and their practical men of affairs settled in London. They might have chosen St Albans or Colchester, but we can see quite clearly in the shape of the English rivers and ancient roads today why they did not. Edward the Confessor, by creating Westminster as a possible political headquarters, was innocent of any notion of a political capital as we know it. Such an idea was scarcely conceived in his day, save perhaps in Rome. But an idle, ageing king might well conceive a palace more durable, more often occupied, than his predecessors had imagined; and so there is a sense in which Westminster in Edward's last years was the embryo of a capital, even if the palace, like early Washington, was built of wood.[1]

The Norman kings were far more active than Edward, and always on the move; none the less, London and Westminster rapidly became a centre in their English dominions more important to them even than to Edward. For once again, as in Roman times, England was part of an empire whose main focus of interest lay on the Continent. William the Conqueror was a Norman who won England by conquest; Henry II was lord of half of France as well as of England; Richard I was Duke of Aquitaine turned King of England, as it were unexpectedly, owing to his elder brother's early death. No doubt all these men, and the rest of the line, accepted that the title King of the English was the chief basis of their greatness and of their power; but they spent more time on the Continent, and to have a centre of English life so near the Continent suited them much as it had suited the Romans.

Westminster as a stable basis of government first emerged, however,

[1] See pp. 294 ff.

in the rule of Archbishop Hubert Walter in the 1190s. He was Archbishop of Canterbury, and at various times papal legate, justiciar and royal chancellor; the effective head of a very efficient government while Richard I was absent on adventures in France. 'A medieval archbishop, riding from palace to palace, was on his own ground when he came [from Canterbury] to Croydon; for Croydon, though in Surrey which was then in the diocese of Winchester, was and is a peculiar of Canterbury. If a straight line was drawn from the archbishop's former palace at Croydon to the king's palace at Westminster, it ran through the long, narrow corridor which was the old parish of Lambeth, and it fell into the Thames,' where Lambeth Palace now stands. 'It could indeed be made to run a little further east, but then it would have encountered the Clink, the palace and the prison of the Bishop of Winchester.'[1] In the mid-1190s Hubert Walter bought the part of Lambeth which lay near the river, from the monks of Rochester, to whom it had belonged. He was confirming a tradition already venerable, for a hundred years before Archbishop Anselm had started the practice of staying in the comparative quiet of Lambeth, as honoured guest of the monks and Bishop of Rochester, when he was compelled to wait on the king at Westminster or do business in the City. As time passed it became increasingly obvious that a palace opposite Westminster would be highly convenient 'for an archbishop who had often to be near the king, and equally often at a safe distance from the monks of Canterbury'.[2] Hubert had inherited a scheme for building an elaborate collegiate church, certainly to rival and perhaps intended to replace Canterbury Cathedral as the centre of his province, in or near where the palace now stands. This scheme was defeated by an alliance between the monks and the Pope, and he contented himself with a palace. When Richard was absent, Hubert Walter and his colleagues began to form larger institutions of government and administration with something approaching a permanent head-quarters in Westminster. Although it was only in the thirteenth century that Westminster became a capital in the modern sense, the change was foreshadowed in these events of the 1190s.

Thus the last decade of the twelfth century saw a major step forward in the development both of Westminster and of the City. The formation of

---

[1] These quotations come from a lecture on 'Lambeth and London in the eleventh and twelfth centuries' delivered by C.N.L.B. in May 1972 and published in the *Report of the Friends of Lambeth Palace Library for 1972* (1973), pp. 11–23, esp. p. 12. See also above, pp. 157–8; Stubbs in *Epistolae Cantuarienses*, pp. xcii ff.

[2] Brooke, art. cit., p. 19.

the commune and the establishment of Henry FitzAilwin as mayor represented the coming of age of the City as an institution. The oligarchy of rich patricians had a grip on the City between the early 1190s and the 1220s which was as securely based as it was ever to be in later centuries.[1] When Constantine, son of Alulf was hanged in 1222, a shock was administered to the oligarchs which they were never likely to forget: for all the difficulties and disputes both with their poorer colleagues and with King John, there is a sense in which the period from 1191 to 1220 or so saw the oligarchy more firmly in control of London than they were to be for several generations. This must be in a fair measure attributed to the shrewdness and skill of Henry FitzAilwin. But it also reflected a situation in which a stable and organized machinery of government was coming into being in Westminster, glad to have an equally organized government in the City with which to deal. Between them there were powerful tensions, and a strong bond of common interest. From that day forward for many centuries the history of London has had at its centre a string of elastic, stretched and twisted between a hand at Westminster and a hand in the City of London.

[1] See chap. 9.

Appendix I

Pre-Conquest Charters relating to London

See p. 86. Full references to MSS, printed editions and commentaries are given in Sawyer.

1 GENERAL

Sawyer no.	Date	Theme
86	?733	Æthelbald, King of Mercia, grants Mildred, Abbess of Minster-in-Thanet, toll of one ship (i.e., free access to) London (*cf.* no. 98 below; also nos 87–8, 91, 98, 143: similar grants of toll, but without specific mention of London). Probably authentic.
88	734	Æthelbald, King of Mercia, grants Eadwulf, Bishop of Rochester, toll of one ship in London, confirmed by Berhtwulf, King of Mercia, *c.* 845 (now also in *Anglo-Saxon Charters*, vol. i, no. 2). Probably authentic.
98	743–45	Æthelbald, King of Mercia, grants Bishop Milred and St Peter's, Worcester, toll of two ships in London. Probably authentic.

(Nos 100, 106, 119, 132, show grants in Middlesex by Mercian kings, Æthelbald and Offa; cf. below, part 2, no. 65. Grants attributed to Offa and Ecgfrith in Hertfordshire are nos 124, 150[?], 151; 124, 151 are of doubtful authenticity, 150 may not refer to Hertfordshire. Offa grants land in Kent in nos 123, 125, etc.; in Surrey in no. 127.)

133	790	Offa, King of Mercia, grants privileges for land in London, etc., to St-Denis, Paris. Spurious, but probably with a genuine base.
208	857	Burgred, King of Mercia, grants land at *Ceolmundingchaga* in London, not far from the west gate, to Alhwine, Bishop (of Worcester). Probably authentic, at least in base. Cf. Ekwall, p. 37.
346	889	Alfred, King of the English and Saxons, and Ethelred, *subregulus et patricius Merciorum*, grant land in London *aet*

Sawyer no.	*Date*	*Theme*

Hwaetmundes stane to Waerferth, Bishop of Worcester. Of doubtful authenticity, possibly genuine in substance. Cf. Ekwall, pp. 37–8.

940   **1006–12**   King Ethelred II grants privileges at a wharf in London, a bequest to Chertsey Abbey by Wulfstan, priest. Doubtful.

1002   **1044**   King Edward (the Confessor) confirms and grants lands and privileges, including the grant of *Wermanecher* (variously spelt), with the wharf, rights and customs, in London to St Peter's Ghent. Mid-twelfth-century forgery by the Westminster forgers. Cf. Ekwall, p. 38.

1096   **1058–66**   Writ of King Edward (the Confessor) granting sake and soke, etc. in London to Wulfwold, Abbot of Chertsey. Genuine. Harmer, no. 43.

1103   **1042–44**   Writ of King Edward (the Confessor) granting the guild of English *cnihtas* sake and soke, etc. Genuine. Harmer, no. 51; and see pp. 96–8.

1142   **1053–66**   Writ of King Edward (the Confessor) granting Staines, Middlesex, and land in London called *Staeninghaga* and the soke of thirty-five hides, etc. to Westminster Abbey. Possibly based on an authentic writ. Harmer, no. 98. Cf. Ekwall, pp. 123–4.

1234   **1052–70**   Brihtmaer of Gracechurch grants reversion of land and All Hallows Church to Christ Church, Canterbury. Genuine. *Anglo-Saxon Charters*, ed. A. J. Robertson, Cambridge, 1939, no. 116. See p. 135.

1246   **677**   Bishop Eorconweald of the East Saxons grants privileges and lands to Barking Abbey, including land 'iuxta Lundoniam unius manentis data a Uulfhario rege . . . supra vicum Lundoniae data a Queonguyda uxore . . . [Æðelb]aldi x manentium' (Birch, no. 87). Probably spurious, but incorporating early material.

1488   **1003–4**   Will of Archbishop Ælfric, including a bequest of land at London to St Albans Abbey. Authentic. *Anglo-Saxon Wills*, ed. D. Whitelock, Cambridge, 1930, no. 18.

1489   **1035–40**   Will of Bishop Ælfric, including the bequest of a messuage in London to 'St Peter's' (Westminster). Authentic. Whitelock, no. 26.

1497   **Tenth century**   Will of Æthelgifu, including a bequest of a haga in London. Authentic. *The Will of Æthelgifu*, ed. D. Whitelock *et al.*, Roxburghe Club, 1968, esp. pp. 10–11.

1526   **942–c. 951**   Will of Bishop Theodred, including a bequest of money in London. Authentic. Whitelock (as no. 1488), no. 1.

1628   **898–9**   Grant by Alfred, etc., to the Archbishop of Canterbury and the Bishop of Worcester of land at Ætheredes hyd (Queenhithe): cf. Ekwall, pp. 35–6, 38–9 and n.

Sawyer no.	Date	Theme
1809	Tenth century, second half	Grant by Æthelgifu, *comitissa*, to Ramsey Abbey, with reference to the weight of the Husting of London (see p. 249). Probably authentic. 'Et duos cyphos argenteos de xii marcis ad pondus Hustingiae Londoniensis ad serviendum fratribus in refectorio . . .' (Birch, no. 1060.)

2 CHARTERS FOR ST PAUL'S OR THE BISHOPRIC

Sawyer, no. 65, is a copy of *c.* late eighth century of a charter by Swaefred, King of Essex, and Pæogthath, *comes*, to Bishop Waldhere, with Mercian confirmations by Kings Cenred and Ceolred (not certainly genuine). The rest of the St Paul's charters survive either in Bodl. MS James 23, or in the St Paul's cartularies and parallel sources. The latter, Sawyer, nos 5, 337, 452–3, 908, 941, 945, 978, 992, 1056, 1104, 1495 (see below) are mostly doubtful or spurious. The material in James 23 (ed.) Gibbs, pp. 1–8, contain a great deal of authentic material, often in very abbreviated form: cf. especially Sawyer, nos 371(2), 1783–96; Gibbs, p. 2, n. 2, and Stenton in ib., pp. ii–iv. Sawyer, no. 483, is a grant to Bishop Theodred preserved in the muniments of Bury St Edmunds; Theodred was a notable benefactor to the church which preceded the abbey. St Paul's, or the bishop, also figures in wills: Sawyer, nos 1483, 1486, 1494, 1495 (doubtful), 1501, 1526 (see above).

3 CHARTERS FOR WESTMINSTER ABBEY

There is some evidence of forgery at or for Westminster in the tenth and eleventh centuries (see especially Sawyer nos 1450, 1126), and it was undertaken there on the grand scale in the mid-twelfth by a group of forgers with Prior Osbert de Clare and two of the abbot's clerks at its centre, both for Westminster and for a number of other houses (see especially Chaplais; Bishop and Chaplais, pp. xix ff.; *GF*, chap. viii). It is thus a peculiarly delicate task to distinguish the genuine from the false in Westminster documents, and in particular to discern the element of truth in an altered or fabricated document. For the greater number of the mid-éleventh-century documents, there is a thorough foundation in Harmer.

The Westminster charters and writs, etc., are Sawyer, nos 124, 645, 670 (cf. 1450), 774, 894, 903, 1011, 1031, 1030–41, 1043, 1117–50, 1293, 1295, 1450 (expanded version of 670), 1451, 1487, 1489 (doubtfully referring to Westminster), 1522.

Of these the last three are wills and present no problem of authenticity; also probably authentic in whole or part are 645, 670, 903, 1031, 1119, 1121 (?embellished), 1125, 1127–8, 1129 (?expanded), 1131–2, 1135 (?embellished), 1139, 1142 (?expanded), 1143, 1451 and 1146, 1148–50 appear to have some authentic material in them. Of more doubtful authenticity are 124 (Offa's charter, which may well, however, enshrine at least a measure of genuine tradition), 894, 1117–18, 1120, 1122, 1126, 1133, 1136, 1144, 1295, 1450, and the following seem undoubtedly the product of the mid-twelfth-century forgers: nos 774, 1011, 1039–41, 1043, 1124, 1134, 1137–8, 1140–1, 1293– although even with these, it seems likely (as Miss Harmer thought) that nos 1134, 1140–1 are spurious copies of basically genuine writs. The status of nos 1123 (which has been defended), 1130, 1147 seems wholly uncertain.

4 OTHER HOUSES

A full survey of early charters for houses with some relation to London should also take some note of St Eorconweald's foundations, Chertsey and Barking, although their intimate link with the bishopric belongs to an earlier epoch than the period of this book; and also of charters for Waltham Abbey and others which refer to Lambeth and other places near enough to London to fall into our purview. Such a survey can hardly hope to be complete, but it would include: *Chertsey*, Sawyer, nos 69, 127, 285, 353, 420, 752, 940 (see above), 1035 and the others listed in Sawyer, p. 497, of which only no. 1508, a will with passing reference to Chertsey, seems evidently genuine; there is an interesting link with St Paul's forgeries in nos 752, 1035; *Barking*, nos 1171 (authentic eighth-cent. original), 1246, 1248, 1483, 1486, 1494, 1531: the last four are authentic wills, 1246, 1248 spurious, at least in their present form; *Waltham*, Sawyer, no. 1036, is a spurious charter for the secular minster (later abbey), including grant of land in Lambeth.

Appendix II

The Sheriffs and Justices of London and Middlesex, *c.* 1030 - 1216

A draft of this had been prepared when Miss Reynolds' 'Rulers of London . . .' appeared in 1972; with her kind permission we reproduce her list from 1100, which forms her Tables 1-2, pp. 354-7, and refer the reader to her notes for the evidence. The only difference of substance is that we reject the identification of Gilbert Prutfot and Gilbert Becket, which had been suggested by C.N.L.B., and have suggested a rough date for Gilbert Becket's period of office (see p. 212, n. 4); we include two doubtful cases, William Martel and Richard de Lucy, rejected by Miss Reynolds.

We include officials called portreeves in the documents, and stallers with a known connection with London, but officials addressed in writs without their office being specified only if there is other reason to suppose that they were sheriffs: for the chamberlains and other officials, see p. 374.

Athelstan (Adelstan), staller, son of Tovi le Prude, staller, and father of Esgar, staller (see below), occurs, probably in the 1030s or early 1040s, in *Chron. Waltham*, p. 13. The source, however, is late, and insufficient to establish that the office was hereditary or that Athelstan had authority in London.

Ulf, sheriff, occurs 1042-4 (referred to in the past, though presumably still living), and as portreeve, 1044-6 (Harmer, nos 75, 77; cf. pp. 50, 52; and above, p. 193).

Wulfgar, portreeve, occurs 1042-4 (Harmer, no. 51); also referred to as portreeve temp. Edward the Confessor and as 'principalis gubernator civitatis Lundon'', in *Cart. Aldgate*, no. 1072 (fifteenth century). The name is very similar to Ulf, and it is possible that he was the same man.

Esgar (Easgar, Ansgardus), staller, occurs 1042-4: addressed in Harmer, no. 75, as one with authority in London; still in authority in London in late 1066, when referred to as head of the London citizens and organizer of its defences after the Battle of Hastings (*Carmen*, pp. 44-5). According to the *Liber Eliensis* (ed. E. O. Blake, Camden 3rd Series, vol. xcii, 1962, p. 165), he died in prison. See ib., p. 165n.; Harmer, pp. 560-1.

Osgod Clapa, staller (see Harmer, p. 569); addressed as one with authority in London in Harmer, no. 77, prob. 1044–6. He was outlawed in 1046, and died in 1054 (*ASC* C,D).

Leofstan, portreeve, occurs 1051–66 (Harmer, no. 105); *c.* 1054 (*Anglo-Saxon Charters*, ed. A. J. Robertson, Cambridge, 1939, no. 116); 1065–6 (Harmer, no. 106). See Harmer, no. 567. The 'Alestan', reeve of London, who occurs *c.* 1066 (*VCH Kent* vol. iii, p. 208) may be a corruption of Leofstan.

Ælfsige, portreeve, occurs with Leofstan, 1051–66, 1065–6 (Harmer, nos 105–6).

Ælfgaet, sheriff, occurs 1051–66, 1057–66 (prob. 1057–66: Harmer, nos 86–7).

Gosfregth, portreeve, addressed in William I's writ of *c.* 1067 (*Regesta*, vol. i, no. 15 = Bishop and Chaplais, no. 15); Gosfregth, or Goisfredus, Sheriff (of London) in Regesta, i, no. 265, 1070–87 ('apparently genuine', Harmer, p. 179); and Geoffrey de Mandeville, whose grandson claimed that he was hereditary justice and Sheriff of London and Middlesex, as well as Sheriff of Essex and Hertfordshire, occurs *c.* 1076, perhaps as Sheriff of Middlesex, and 1087–8, 1087–1100, perhaps as justice of London and Middlesex (*Regesta*, vol. iii, no. 275, vol. i, nos 93, 306, 444, vol. ii, p. 406; see pp. 191 ff.) and M. Brett in *Councils and Synods*, vol. i, forthcoming – for date of vol. i, no. 93): it has commonly been assumed that these are all one man, although it is possible that the references are two or three, for Geoffrey was a common name (see p. 194).

Ralph Baynard, ?sheriff, occurs 1075–85 (*Regesta*, vol. i, no. 211).

Hugh of Buckland, ?justice, occurs between 1100 and 1115 (see p. 204; for the rest of the list, see Reynolds, 'Rulers of London', pp. 354–7).

Roger de Valognes, justice or sheriff, occurs 1100–7 (*Regesta*, vol. ii, no. 556, with Bishop Maurice), ?1114–15.

Leofstan, reeve or sheriff, occurs *c.* 1108, 1114–15.

Rainer the reeve, ?also sheriff, occurs ?1111.

Aubrey de Vere, sheriff, occurs 1120–2, ?1125, etc. (see p. 206).

Roger nephew of Hubert, sheriff, occurs ?1114–15, 1125.

Robert de Berquereola, ?reeve, ?mid-temp. Henry I.

William of Eynesford, sheriff, occurs 1113–31.

Ralph FitzEverard, sheriff occurs before 1128.

Fulchered son of Walter, sheriff, 1128–9.

Eustace, sheriff, occurs 1128–9.

William Lelutre, Geoffrey Bucherell, Ralph, son of Herlewin, and *William de Balio*, sheriff, 1129–30.

William Martel (?not local) justice, occurs *c.* 1135–6 (see p. 214); cf. *Regesta*, vol. iii, no. 524.

Andrew Buccuinte, justice, occurs 1135–9.

Gilbert Becket, sheriff, before *c.* 1139 (see p. 212, n.).

Osbert Eightpence, ?justice, occurs 1139–41.

Geoffrey de Mandeville, Earl of Essex, justice and sheriff, 1141–*c.* 1143.

John, sheriff, occurs 1135–52.

Gervase of Cornhill, justice, occurs 1135–47 (and see below).

Gilbert Prutfot, Proudfoot, sheriff, occurs prob. 1143 (see pp. 213–14, n. 3).

(?) *Richard de Lucy* and *Theodoric son of Deorman*, justices, occur 1143–52 (*Regesta*, vol. iii, no. 534: see p. 218).

Ranulf, sheriff, occurs mid-twelfth century (*Cart. Colchester,* vol. ii, p. 294, with John, son of Andrew Buccuinte and Walter, brother of the archdeacon, i.e., de Belmeis; see Le Neve, pp. 65–6).

(From early in Henry II's reign the local justice disappears, and the dates of *sheriffs* can usually be more firmly established from the Pipe Rolls; what follows is based on Reynolds, pp. 355–7.)

John son of Ralph, 1154–5

Gregory, ?1155.

Gervase of Cornhill and *John son of Ralph,* 1155–7.

Reiner son of Berengar, Geoffrey bursarius, Josce the vintner, Richard Vetulus and *Brihtmar of Haverhill,* 1157–9.

? 1159–60 (see Reynolds, p. 356, n. 9: possibly Gervase of Cornhill or Humphrey Buccuinte).

Gervase of Cornhill, 1160–1.

Ernald scutarius and *Vitalis the clerk,* 1161–2.

Reiner, son of Berengar and *William, son of Isabel,* 1162–9.

John Buccuinte, Baldwin Crisp, David of Cornhill and *Roger Blund,* 1169–72.

Ralph Goldsmith, Ralph the vintner, Andrew Bucherell, Alard, 1172–4.

Brihtmar of Haverhill and *Peter FitzWalter (custodes),* 1174–6.

William, son of Isabel, 1176–7.

Waleran, John, son of Nigel, Michael de Valence, 1177–8.

William, son of Isabel, Ernulf Bucel, 1178–9.

William, son of Isabel, Reginald le Viel (Vetulus), 1179–81.

William, son of Isabel, 1181–7.

Henry of Cornhill, Richard, son of Reiner, 1187–9.

John son of Herlicun, Roger le Duc, William of Haverhill, 1189–90.

William of Haverhill, John Buccuinte, 1190–1.

Nicholas Duket, Peter (son of Neuelon), 1191–2.

Roger le Duc, Roger FitzAlan, 1192–3.

William, son of Isabel, William, son of Alulf, 1193–4.

Robert Besant, Jukel, 1194–5.

Godard of Antioch, Robert, son of Durand, 1195–6.

Nicholas Duket, Robert Blund, 1196–7.

Constantine, son of Alulf, Robert le Bel, 1197–8.

Arnold, son of Alulf, Richard Blund, 1198–9.

Roger de Deserto, James the alderman, 1199–1200.

Simon of Aldermanbury, William, son of Alice, 1200–1.

Norman Blund, John de Caiho, 1201–2.

Walter Brun, William Chamberlain, 1202–3.

Thomas of Haverhill, Hamo Brand, 1203–4.

Richard of Winchester, John Waleram, 1204–5.

John, son of Elinand, Edmund, son of Gerard, 1205–6.

Henry of St Albans, Serlo the mercer, 1206–7.

William Hardel, Robert of Winchester, 1207–8.

Peter le Duc, Thomas the alderman, 1208–9.

Peter Neuelun (Neuelon), William Blund, 1209–10.
Adam of Whitby (de Whitebi), Stephen le Gras, 1210–11.
Josce son of Peter, John de Garlande, 1211–12.
Constantine the younger, Ralph Helyland, 1212–13.
Martin, son of Alice, Peter Bat, 1213–14.
Solomon of Basing, Hugh of Basing, 1214–15.
Andrew Neuelun (Neuelon), John Travers, 1215–16.

A full list of important London officials would include the king's chamberlains for London, on whom see the account by W. Kellaway in *Studies in London History*, pp. 76–7, and 76 n. 6 for the distinct office of City Chamberlain, first recorded in 1237. The following seem to have been the earliest recorded king's chamberlains: *William,* occurs before 1106 to 1120–2 (*Regesta*, vol. ii, nos 769, 898 [?], 1377; cf. L. F. Rushbrook Williams in *EHR* vol. xxviii, 1913, pp. 719–30); *Fulchered,* occurs 1129, 1130–1 (Round, *CL*, pp. 121–4); *William,* occurs 1137 (ib., p. 101) – who may, however, be the same as the first William, or not king's chamberlain.

Other office-holders of the late eleventh century or early twelfth, some of whom may have been sheriffs or portreeves, are:

R. del Parc or *Delpare,* occ. with Geoffrey de Mandeville I, Gibbs, no. 14; *Regesta*, vol. i, no. 444 = *Cart. Aldgate*, no. 873. He was reeve according to B. M. Harl. Roll C.8.

Ralph de Marceio and *Vluric (Wulfric) of Holborn,* occur 1094–7, Gibbs, no. 13.

Ordgar, occurs in a group of officials of 1114–15 (*Regesta*, vol. ii, no. 898 n.).

Otto the goldsmith may possibly be addressed in ib. no. 898 (before 1115) in virtue of his financial office (see pp. 93–4).

W. Bainard and *William de Mandeville* were addressed in writs of 1100–1, and 1100–6 respectively, possibly as castellans of Baynard's Castle and the Tower (*Regesta*, vol. ii, nos 532, 769).

Appendix III

The Mayors of London,
c. 1191 - 1227

We have discussed above, pp. 245–6, the date of appointment (or election) of the first mayor: the *Liber de Antiquis Legibus* (p. 1) suggests 1189–90; the earliest firm evidence is 1193; following Miss Reynolds, we prefer a date *c.* 1191, in spite of the difficulties put forward by Round. Whether it was reckoned an elective office at first is not clear; Henry FitzAilwin seems to have held office for life, but he may have been formally re-elected. Henry's death in the autumn and the precedent set by shrieval appointments and elections (at Michaelmas) may suggest that Roger FitzAlan and his successors took office about the same time of year. It is possible that informal arrangements were made in early days, and that it was only after John's charter of 9 May 1215 (*Rotuli Chartarum*, Record Commission, vol. i, p. 207) that a fixed scheme for annual arrangements came into force. It may be significant that the earliest evidence for election on Sts Simon's and Jude's day is in 1216 (*LAL*, p. 176). But this is in a list of mayors written *c.* 1264 or later, and anachronism is possible. 28 October remained the day until 1346 (*Cal. Letter Book F*, p. 304, *G*, p. 198 and n.); from then until the sixteenth century 13 October was usual, and this probably explains the statement in *Cart. Aldgate*, no. 1073, that even the first mayor had been elected on St Edward the Confessor's day (i.e. Translation, 13 October). Thus the date of election of the early mayors is far from clear, although the idea of an election on 28 October, approximately a month after the election of the sheriffs, may go back at least to 1216 if not earlier.

The London chronicles give a variety of notes on the early mayors; but the only one evidently a serious authority, and undoubtedly the most accurate, is the *Liber de Antiquis Legibus*, on which the following list is based, allowance being made for dislocation in its years.[1] The annals, pp. 1 ff. (= MS., ff. 63v ff.) are accompanied by a

---

[1] Arnald FitzThedmar evidently had annal and chronicle material before him, and lists of sheriffs and mayors, such as survive in other chronicles, and reconciled them imperfectly. His formula is to give a year of grace and the names of two sheriffs at the opening of each annal; in fact the sheriffs are those elected at Michaelmas in that year but the annals which follow (when they run to length, as they do consistently from the 1240s) are those of the calendar year mentioned. It seems evident that the reconciliation of shrieval and calendar years was imperfect down to 1217, for although the sheriffs are all correctly dated on this principle, some of the events which follow belong to the

list giving length of mayoralty in years, but not dates, in Arnald FitzThedmar's hand (f. 63 = pp. 175–7). The annals give: Henry FitzAilwin ?1189–90 (with the sheriffs for 1188–9, but in the context of events of 1189–90; cf. Reynolds, 'Rulers of London', p. 349), until his death in 1212, 'usque ad finem vite sue, scilicet fere per viginti quinque annos'. There is no reason to doubt that he was mayor until his death: the dates of his occurrences will be laid out in a forthcoming paper by G. Keir (see p. 245 n.). He died 19 September 1212 (Annals of Merton, ed. M. Tyson in *Surrey Arch. Coll.*, vol. xxxvi, 1925, p. 47). Roger FitzAlan succeeded and was mayor for a year (*LAL*, pp. 3, 175); but it seems that his term of office did not end until 1214 in fact (the late chron. in B. M. Cotton Jul. B. i, f. 4v, gives him a year and a bit), since the first mayoralty of Serlo the mercer is made to begin in 1214–15 (i.e. presumably at the end of 1214: see below); this lasted a year (list) and he was succeeded by William Hardel in 1215–16 (annals), also for a year (list). That Serlo was mayor in 1214–15 is confirmed by B. M. Harl. MS 4015, f. 55; and William Hardel occurs in 1216–17 (PRO E40/1476; *Catalogue of Ancient Deeds*, vol. i, 1890, p. 167); furthermore, William Hardel is named by annals of Southwark and Merton as the mayor who did homage to Prince Louis on 2 June 1216 (Tyson, art. cit., pp. 50–1: see p. 56). James the alderman was mayor from Easter to Holy Trinity (Pentecost, list, *LAL*, p. 175), i.e. 1217, and was then deposed, and succeeded by Solomon of Basing the same day (annals, *LAL*, p. 4). That James the alderman was mayor in 1216–17 is confirmed by Gibbs, no. 211. Solomon was succeeded by Serlo the Mercer at the end of 1217, and he lasted for five years, i.e. until 1222 (cf. *LAL*, p. 5).

These details suggest the following list:

Henry FitzAilwin c. 1191–1212, d. 19 Sept.

Roger FitzAlan 1212–14.

Serlo the mercer 1214–15 (and so presumably the Mayor at the time of Magna Carta).
William Hardel 1215–17.

James the alderman Easter–Trinity (or Whitsun) 1217 (i.e. *c.* 26 March–*c.* 14 or 21 May).

Solomon of Basing May–?October 1217.

Serlo the mercer 1217–22

From then on, the dates in *LAL* are clear, and seem correct, and Serlo's successor was:

Richard Reiner, 1222–7.

---

year of grace, some to the next year – i.e. to the shrieval year. The death of Henry FitzAilwin is correctly given as 1212, and Serlo's elections in 1214 and 1217; but also under 1214 (for 1215) the baronial entry into London, and under 1216 (for 1217) the mayoralties of James the alderman and Solomon. Documentary evidence confirms the dates given in the text, though it is possible that Roger FitzAlan was succeeded by Serlo in 1213 – this, however, would do more violence to *LAL* than seems necessary.

Confusion between shrieval years and years of grace also seems implicit in the difference between annals and list. By what is perhaps only a slip, Roger FitzAlan is given one year only in the list (p. 175); James's terms end at Pentecost – very little different from Trinity, but probably sufficient to confirm that the list is from an independent source; Serlo's second election is given as Sts Simon and Jude, 1216. The day may be right (see text); the year must be too early.

Appendix IV

Coin Hoards and the London Mint

This Appendix is based on notes generously provided by Mr B. H. I. H. Stewart, which seemed to us so useful and interesting an account of the current state of research that they should be reproduced fairly fully here, with our grateful thanks: the form (and errors) are ours.

HOARDS

This is based on R. H. M. Dolley, 'Coin hoards from the London area', *LMAS*, vol. xx, 1959–61, pp. 37–50, correcting and amplifying the entries in J. D. A. Thompson, *Inventory of British Coin Hoards A.D. 600–1500*, London, 1956. The first column gives the number of the hoard in Thompson, the second the approximate date of deposit, the third the place where it was discovered. Information is often very scanty about hoards discovered e.g. in the era of railway building in the nineteenth century. We omit the lead 'stycas' sometimes attributed to the ninth century, since they are probably forgeries:

Thompson no.	Date	Place and content
366	c. 842	Middle Temple (cf. C. S. S. Lyons in *BNJ*, vol. xxxvii, pp. 219 ff. About 120 coins, two eighth cent., the rest c. 800–40).
—	c. 870	Wandsworth (small hoard: Dolley, p. 43).
256	c. 875	Waterloo (?railway) Bridge (approx. 100).
—	c. 890	Bucklersbury (at least sixty, pennies of Alfred; Dolley, p. 41 and n. 20).
—	c. 945	Threadneedle Street (small; Dolley, p. 41 and nn. 21–2).
—	c. 1000	Honey Lane (eight pennies of Ethelred II; ib. and nn. 23–4).
249	c. 1015	St Martin le Grand (over sixty; cf. Dolley, p. 39).
244	c. 1062–3	Gracechurch Street (c. sixty; Dolley, p. 38).
255	c. 1066	Walbrook (c. 6,000 coins, including one Byzantine, one German and one Danish = perhaps a moneyer's hoard; cf. Dolley, p. 40).
250	c. 1075	St Mary at Hill (probably 'several hundred', possibly dating from the revolt of 1075, Dolley, pp. 39–40).

Thompson no.	Date	Place and content
(255)	*c.* 1075	Walbrook (2) (small hoard: Dolley, p. 40).
246	*c.* 1170	London Bridge (cf. C. E. Blunt, F. Elmore Jones and P. H. Robinson, in *BNJ*, vol. xxxvii, 1968, pp. 35–42, esp. p. 41).
251	*c.* 1190	St Thomas's Hospital (28 Henry II pennies, 1 ?Richard I).
—	?*c.* 1209	(26 pennies, two cut halfpennies of John, Dolley, in *BNJ*, vol. xxxvi, 1967, pp. 193–5).

THE LONDON MINT, 800–1216

In the eighth and early ninth centuries, London is never named on coins certainly Mercian. But a Mercian mint which has been presumed to be in London was active late in Offa's time (d. 796) and under Coenwulf (796–821); in this period (i.e. 796–839) mints have been identified as at Canterbury (two), Rochester, somewhere in East Anglia, London and Winchester. The London mint is named only in 829–30, under the supremacy of Egbert of Wessex (C. E. Blunt, C. S. S. Lyon and B. H. I. H. Stewart in *BNJ*, vol. xxxii, 1963, pp. 1–74, esp. pp. 5–8, 30–36, 36–43; cf. C. E. Blunt in *AS Coins*, pp. 43–4; Blunt and Dolley, ib., p. 83 and n. 16, for Egbert's coin; for solidus of (?)London, temp. Offa or Coenwulf, see H. E. Pagan in *BNJ*, vol. xxxiv, 1965, pp. 8–10). See **Plate 190**.

The assumption that London was a Mercian city in the eighth and ninth centuries is not as securely based as is sometimes asserted (see p. 92 n.): the only firm foundations at present seem to be a small number of Charters of Æthelbald, Offa and Burgred (852–74), and under these circumstances there is a danger that the argument for the site of the mint will move in a circle. But the studies cited above, confirmed by H. E. Pagan's work on Burgred's coins ('Coinage in the age of Burgred', *BNJ*, vol. xxxiv, 1965, pp. 11–27) undoubtedly help to support the case for both the siting of the Mercian mint in London and for Mercian predominance there. This has long been assumed to be the explanation of Alfred's grant of the recaptured city to the ealdorman of Mercia (p. 15).

H. E. Pagan discusses a London coin of the period before 851 (p. 12); suggests that the London mint flourished under Burgred in the late 860s and until 874 (pp. 13–14), and argues for some continuity, and no major break, through the period of Alfred's reign (on Alfred's relations with Burgred and Ceolwulf, and this continuity, Pagan, pp. 14, 26–7). Thus although there is comparatively little evidence for the London mint in the mid-ninth century, it undoubtedly grew or revived in the last third (see also C. S. S. Lyon in *BNJ*, vol. xxxvii, 1968, pp. 225–6, 228, 230, 233–4). The issue of the last Portrait-type penny of Alfred, carrying the monogram of 'Londonia', is associated with the events of 886 by Blunt and Dolley in *AS Coins*, pp. 82–3, who point out that Alfred may have been imitating his grandfather, Egbert (see above). **Plate 20**.

The London mint was probably important from Alfred to Edgar, though few coins bear its name; in Athelstan's decree (II Athelstan, *c.* 14.2) it is the largest mint, with eight moneyers, followed by Canterbury with seven and Winchester with six. From the 970s it was no doubt consistently the largest of the mints. This is most dramatically revealed in the catalogues of the Stockholm and Copenhagen collections for Ethelred II and Cnut, shown in the following table: the numbers, for Stockholm, are those in

B. E. Hildebrand, *Anglo-Saxon Coins in the Royal Swedish Cabinet of Medals at Stockholm all found in Sweden*, new ed., Stockholm, 1881; for Copenhagen, from *Sylloge*, vols 7, 13–15. Cf. also *BM Coins*, Grueber, vol. ii, pp. 313–15, 326–7, 397–416 (for Edward the Confessor); V. J. Butler in *BNJ*, vol. xxx, 1960–1, pp. 221–26.

	LONDON	LINCOLN	YORK	WINCHESTER
Ethelred II				
Stockholm	2019–3021	1619–2018	607–1012	4029–4343
Copenhagen	635–975 (with five additions)	517–634	221–327	1323–1442
Cnut				
Stockholm	1849–2858	1463–1848	431–873	3656–3866
Copenhagen	1946–3084	1509–1945	494–928	3995–4210, 4219–20

In late Anglo-Saxon and early Norman times London remained one of the very few mints at which coining took place in most months of the year.

It has been shown that *dies* were probably cut at several centres, including London, from the 970s. The chief centre in Ethelred II's middle years seems to have been in Winchester; in his later years (d. 1016) in London. But variety continued down to *c.* 1030, and Winchester was still important late in Cnut's reign (d. 1035). From then on London appears to have been predominant, and is noted as such in 'Domesday Book'. See esp. C. S. S. Lyon in H. R. Mossop, *The Lincoln Mint, c. 890–1279*, Newcastle, 1970, pp. 11 ff.; Lyon in *BNJ*, vol. xxxix, 1970, pp. 200 ff. discusses the evidence of an experimental coin of the 990s, of which fragments were discovered in Bergen by R. H. M. Dolley, and which reveals the importance of London as a die-centre. See also H. R. Loyn in *AS Coins*, p. 124, etc. Links between London and other mints were also evidently due to the secondment or travels of London moneyers: e.g. B. H. I. H. Stewart has adduced evidence of moneyers working for London, Hertford and Southwark (or combinations of the three) under Ethelred II (*NC*, 7th Series, vol. xi, 1971, p. 241); C. S. S. Lyon has revealed the activities of a London moneyer (as it seems) who travelled to Cissbury, Stamford and the unidentified 'Gothaburh' in the west country (*BNJ*, vol. xxxix, 1970, pp. 202–3).

The list of known moneyers is particularly striking evidence for continuity of Old English names in London (*BM Coins*, Brooke, *passim*; and cf. Allen); and the names of moneyers have much to teach us. Philological analysis, revealing, e.g. the German element, has been begun for Edgar's reign by O. von Feilitzen and C. E. Blunt in *England before the Conquest*, ed. P. Clemoes and K. Hughes, Cambridge, 1971, pp. 183–214; but it is only with Ethelred II's reign that the consistent appearance of mint-names makes the evidence for geographical distribution really revealing. Mrs V. J. Smart's study of 'Moneyers of the late Anglo-Saxon coinage, 973–1016', in *Commentationes de nummis saeculorum IX–XI in Suecia repertis*, vol. ii, Stockholm, 1968, pp. 191–276, esp. pp. 250–5, 258–9, is a major contribution to social history: her analysis shows that virtually all the London moneyers bore English names; in Lincoln and Chester a fair proportion bore Scandinavian; in York a large preponderance were Scandinavian. With all allowances made for the danger of arguing from the language of a name to the origin of its bearer, this is striking evidence both for Viking settlement (at a certain level of society) in York and its absence in London.

For the London mint under the Norman kings, see *BM Coins*, Brooke, esp. vol. i, pp. ccxx ff., and under Henry II, *BM Coins*, Allen, esp. pp. cxliv–cxlviii; on the exchanges, pp. lxviii ff., lxxxix–xcii. The reign of Henry II saw an increasing preponderance of the London mint, with reduction of local mints, which continued after 1180, except at the recoinages of 1205, 1247 etc. (For the reign of John, we await the outcome of Mr Stewart's recent researches.) The Pipe Rolls of 1179–80 and 1204–5 show the arrangements to set the London mint going in advance of recoinages, before the reopening of provincial mints; the new exchange system meant that small mints were not needed to raise revenue, and this helped to enhance the position of the London mint still further.

Three additional points illustrate the significance of the London mint in the eleventh-twelfth centuries. Relationship between London and forgery of coins is discussed in *BM Coins*, Brooke, vol. i, pp. cxlix ff.; see also B. H. I. H. Stewart in *BNJ*, vol. xxviii, 1956–7, pp. 190–1, on the activity of the moneyers Ælfsi and Wulfwine (and a possible link with Thetford).

Henry I granted the Abbot of Reading the use and profits of the London moneyer Edgar 'as if he were at Reading'. 'This was because such a privilege in the Metropolis was far more valuable than if it had been restricted to the rural conditions then surrounding the new monastery,' wrote W. J. Andrew (cited Stewart, *NC*, 7th Series, vol. xii, 1972, p. 168; see also Andrew's monograph on Henry I's coins, *NC*, 4th Series, vol. i, 1901; see pp. 371–8 for Reading, pp. 273–316 for the London mint). But Andrew's attempt to identify Edgar's successor in Stephen's reign was not successful: see Stewart, 'Stefanus R', *NC*, ut supra, pp. 167–75, with much useful material on Stephen's coins.

Brooke, *BM Coins*, vol. i, pp. lxxi ff., had already shown that no irregular or baronial issues of the 1140s could be associated with London.

Bibliography and List of Abbreviated References

Manuscript sources are not listed here: see pp. xvi, chap. 4, 270; printed books and articles referred to in the notes are included, save for a few used only once and not otherwise relevant to the history of London, or of European towns in the period. Thus this is a guide to our references, not a *catalogue raisonnée* either of the literature of the subject or of all the works we have consulted. But we hope it is, in practice, a *corpus* of useful work on the subject.

Abbaye bénédictine de Fécamp, L', vol. i, Fécamp, 1959.
Acta Philippi Augusti, ed. E. Berger and H.-F. Delaborde, vol. i, Paris, 1916.
Addyman P. V., and Hill, D. H., 'Saxon Southampton: a review of the evidence', *Proceedings of the Hants Field Club*, vol. xxv, 1968, pp. 61–93; xxvi, 1969, pp. 61–96.
Adigard des Gautries, J., *Les Noms de personnes scandinaves en Normandie de 911 à 1066*, Nomina Germanica, vol. ii, Lund, 1954.
Alfred's Orosius, ed. H. Sweet, Early English Text Soc., pt. i, 1873.
Allen, D.F.: *see BM Coins.*
Andrew, W. J., 'A numismatic History of the Reign of Henry I', *NC*, 4th Series, vol. i, 1901, *passim* (pp. 273–316 on the London mint).
Anglo-Saxon Charters, vol. i: Charters of Rochester, ed. A. Campbell, British Academy, London, 1973.
Ann.: Annals.
Ann. Mon.: Annales Monastici, ed. H. R. Luard, 5 vols, Rolls Series, 1864–9.
Annali Genovesi, ed. L. T. Belgrano and C. Imperiale, Fonti per la Storia d'Italia, vol. ii, Genoa, 1901.
Aprato, G., *Bologna, complesso di S. Stefano*, Tesori d'Arte Cristiana, Bologna, 1966.
'Archaeological Finds in the City of London, 1963–4', '. . . 1965–6', '. . . 1966–8' (by P. R. V. Marsden, and staff of the Guildhall Museum), *LMAS*, vols xxi, pt. 3, 1967, pp. 189–221; xxii, pt. 1, 1968, pp.1–17, pt. 2, 1969, pp. 1–26 (part of a long and useful series).
ASC: Anglo-Saxon Chronicle (the MSS are numbered A, C, D, E etc. and dates corrected as in the translation by D. Whitelock *et alii*, London, 1961; also in *EHD*, vol. i; some quotations from trans. G. Garmonsway, rev. edn, London, 1960. For the text, see *Two of the Saxon Chronicles Parallel*, ed. J. Earle and C. Plummer, 2 vols, Oxford, 1892–9).
AS Charters: Anglo-Saxon Charters, ed. A. J. Robertson, Cambridge, 1956.

AS Coins: Anglo-Saxon Coins: Studies presented to F. M. Stenton on the occasion of his 80th birthday, 17 May 1960, ed. R. H. M. Dolley, London, 1961.

Ashdown, M., *English and Norse Documents*, Cambridge, 1930.

Asser's Life of King Alfred, ed. W. H. Stevenson, Oxford, 1904, rev. edn with introd. by D. Whitelock, 1959.

Baker, T., *Medieval London*, London, 1970.

Barlow, *Edward the Confessor*: Barlow, F., *Edward the Confessor*, London, 1970.

Barlow, F., *The English Church 1000–1066: a constitutional history*, London, 1963.

Barlow, *Vita Ædwardi: Vita Ædwardi regis: The Life of King Edward . . .*, NMT, 1962.

Barsali, I. B., *Guida di Lucca*, 2nd edn, Lucca, 1970.

Bately, Janet M., 'King Alfred and the Old English translation of Orosius', *Anglia*, vol. lxxxviii, 1970, pp. 433–60.

Bateson: Bateson, M., 'A London Municipal Collection of the reign of John', *EHR*, vol. xvii, 1902, pp. 480–511, 707–30.

Beavan: Beavan, A. B., *The Aldermen of the City of London*, 2 vols, London, 1908–13.

Bebbington, G., *London Street Names*, London, 1972.

Bede's Ecclesiastical History of the English People, ed. and trans. B. Colgrave and R. A. B. Mynors, OMT, 1969.

Belfort, A. de, *Archives de la Maison-Dieu de Châteaudun*, Paris–Châteaudun, 1881.

Bell, W. G., Cottrill, F. and Spon, C., *London Wall through Eighteen Centuries*, London, 1937.

Beresford, M. W., *New Towns of the Middle Ages: town plantation in England, Wales and Gascony*, London, 1967.

Beresford and St Joseph: Beresford, M. W., and St Joseph, J. K. S., *Medieval England, an Aerial Survey*, Cambridge, 1958.

Beverley Town Documents, ed. A. F. Leach, Selden Society, vol. xiv, 1900.

Bibliography of British and Irish Municipal History, ed. G. H. Martin and S. McIntyre, vol. i, Leicester, 1972.

Biddle, M. and R. N. Quirk, 'Excavations near Winchester Cathedral, 1961', *Archaeological Journal*, vol. cxix, 1964 for 1962, pp. 150–94. (First Interim Report).

Biddle, M., 'Excavations at Winchester, 1962–3', '. . . 1964', '. . . 1965', '. . . 1966', '. . . 1967', '. . . 1968', '. . . 1969', '. . . 1970', *Antiquaries Journal*, vols xliv, 1964, pp. 188–219; xlv, 1965, pp. 230–64; xlvi, 1966, pp. 308–32; xlvii, 1967, pp. 251–79; xlviii, 1968, pp. 250–84; xlix, 1969, pp. 295–329; l, 1970, pp. 277–326; lii, 1972, pp. 93–131. (Second – Ninth Interim Reports.)

Biddle, M., *The Old Minster*, Winchester, 1970.

Biddle, M., and Hill, D., 'Late Saxon Planned Towns', *Antiquaries Journal*, vol. li, 1971, pp. 70–85.

Biddle, M.: see also *Future of London's Past.*

Birch: Birch, W. de G., *Cartularium Saxonicum*, 3 vols, London, 1885–93 (Index, 1899).

Birch, W. de G., *The Historical Charters and Constitutional Documents of the City of London*, rev. edn, London, 1887.

Bishop, E., *Liturgica Historica*, Oxford, 1918.

Bishop, T. A. M., *Scriptores Regis*, Oxford, 1961.

Bishop and Chaplais: *Facsimiles of English Royal Writs to A.D. 1100, presented to Vivian Hunter Galbraith*, ed. T. A. M. Bishop and P. Chaplais, Oxford, 1957.

Blumenkranz, B., 'La *Disputatio Judei cum Christiano* de Gilbert Crispin, Abbé de Westminster', *Revue du moyen âge latin*, vol. iv, 1948, pp. 237–52.

Blunt, C. E., 'The coinage of Offa', *AS Coins*, pp. 39–62.

Blunt, C. E., Jones, F. Elmore and Robinson, P. H., 'On some hoards of the time of Stephen', *BNJ*, vol. xxxvii, 1968, pp. 35–42.

Blunt, C. E., Lyon, C. S. S., and Stewart, B. H. I. H., 'The coinage of southern England, 796–840', *BNJ*, vol. xxxii, 1963, pp. 1–74.

BM Coins, Allen: D. F. Allen, *A Catalogue of the English Coins in the British Museum: The Cross-and-Crosslets ('Tealby') Type of Henry II*, London, 1951.

BM Coins, Brooke: Brooke, G. C., *A Catalogue of the English Coins in the British Museum: The Norman Kings*, 2 vols, London, 1916.

BM Coins, Grueber: H. A. Grueber and C. F. Keary, *A Catalogue of English Coins in the British Museum: Anglo-Saxon Series*, vol. ii, 1893.

BNJ: British Numismatic Journal.

Boniface, St, *Epistolae*, ed. M. Tangl, *Die Briefe des heiligen Bonifatius und Lullus*, Berlin, 1916 (= *Monumenta Germaniae Historica, Epistolae selectae*, vol. i).

Borman, C. de, *Les Echevins de la souveraine justice de Liège*, 2 vols, Liège, 1892–99.

Bosworth, I, II (= *Supplement*), III (= *Enlarged Addenda*): J. Bosworth, *An Anglo-Saxon Dictionary*, ed. T. N. Toller, Oxford, 1898; *Supplement*, by T. N. Toller, Oxford, 1928; *Enlarged Addenda and Corrigenda*, by A. Campbell, Oxford, 1972.

Bourgin, G., *La Commune de Soissons . . .*, Paris, 1908 (Bibliothèque de l'Ecole des Hautes Etudes, Sciences Hist. et Philol., vol. clxvii).

Boussard, J., *Le Gouvernement d'Henri II Plantegenêt*, Paris, 1956.

Boyd, C., *Tithes and Parishes in Medieval Italy*, Ithaca, 1952.

Braunfels, W., *Mittelalterliche Stadtbaukunst in der Toskana*, 3rd edn, Berlin, 1966.

British Borough Charters: British Borough Charters, vol. i, *1042–1216*, ed. A. Ballard, Cambridge, 1913.

Broodbank, Sir J. G., *History of the Port of London*, 2 vols, London, 1921.

Brooke, C. N. L., 'The Composition of the Chapter of St Paul's 1086–1163', *CHJ*, vol. x, no. 2, 1951, pp. 111–32.

Brooke, C. N. L., 'Historical Writing in England between 850 and 1150', in *La Storiografia Altomedievale*, Spoleto, 1970, vol. i, pp. 223–47.

Brooke, C. N. L., 'The missionary at home: the Church in the Towns, 1000–1250', in *The Mission of the Church and the Propagation of the Faith – Studies in Church History*, vol. vi, ed. G. J. Cuming, Cambridge, 1970, pp. 59–83.

Brooke, C. N. L., *The Saxon and Norman Kings*, London, 1963.

Brooke, C. N. L., *Time the Archsatirist*, London, 1968.

Brooke, C. N. L., *The Twelfth Century Renaissance*, London, 1969 (1970).

Brooke, Keir and Reynolds: Brooke, C. N. L., Keir, G., and Reynolds, S., 'Henry I's Charter for the City of London', *Journal of the Society of Archivists*, vol. iv, 1973, pp. 558–78.

Brooke, R. B. (ed. and trans.), *Scripta Leonis, Rufini et Angeli, Sociorum S. Francisci*, OMT, 1970.

Brooke, Z. N., 'The Register of Master David': Brooke, Z. N., 'The Register of Master David of London and the part he played in the Becket crisis', in *Essays in History presented to R. L. Poole*, pp. 227–45.

Brooks, N. P., 'Excavations at Wallingford Castle, 1965: An Interim Report', *Berkshire Archaeological Journal*, vol. lxii, 1965–6, pp. 17–21.

Brooks, N. P., 'The Unidentified Forts of the Burghal Hidage', *Medieval Archaeology*, vol. viii, 1964, pp. 74–88 (with supplement by M. Gelling, pp. 89–90).

Brown, R. A., '"The Treasury" of the later twelfth century', in *Studies presented to Sir Hilary Jenkinson*, ed. J. Conway Davies, London, 1957, pp. 35–49.

Bullough: Bullough, D. A., 'Urban Change in early medieval Italy: the Example of Pavia', *Papers of the British School at Rome*, vol. xxxiv, 1966, pp. 82–130.

Cal. Letter-Book C, F, G: Calendar of Letter-Books preserved among the Archives of the Corporation of the City of London..., Letter Book C, F, G, ed. R. R. Sharpe, London, 1901, 1904, 1905.

Calendar of Early Mayor's Court Rolls preserved among the Archives of the Corporation of the City of London ... AD 1298–1307 ed. A. H. Thomas, Cambridge, 1924.

Calendar of Plea and Memoranda Rolls ... AD 1364–1381, and 1413–37, ed. A. H. Thomas, Cambridge, 1929, 1943.

Calendar of the Patent Rolls preserved in the Public Record Office, Henry VI, vols i–vi (vol. v, 1446–52), London, 1901–10.

Cam, *Eyre: The Eyre of London, 14 Edward II, 1321*, ed. H. M. Cam, 2 vols, Selden Society, vols lxxxv–vi, 1968–9.

Cam, H. M., *Liberties and Communities in Medieval England*, Cambridge, 1944.

Cambridge Economic History, vols i–iii, ed. J. H. Clapham, E. Power, M. M. Postan, E. E. Rich, and E. Miller, Cambridge, 1941–63.

Carmen: The Carmen de Hastingae Proelio of Guy Bishop of Amiens, ed. C. Morton and H. Muntz, OMT, 1972.

Carpenter, E. ed., *A House of Kings: The History of Westminster Abbey*, London, 1966: Part I, 'Westminster Abbey – the beginnings to 1474', by Dom H. Aveling, pp. 3–84.

Cart. Aldgate: The Cartulary of Holy Trinity Aldgate, ed. G. A. J. Hodgett, LRS, vol. vii, 1971.

Cart. Clerkenwell: The Cartulary of St Mary, Clerkenwell, ed. W. O. Hassall, Camden 3rd Series, vol. lxxi, 1949.

Cart. Colchester: Cartularium monasterii S. Johannis Baptiste de Colecestria, ed. S. A. Moore, 2 vols, Roxburghe Club, 1897.

Cartulary of the Priory of St Gregory, Canterbury, ed. A. M. Woodcock (Mrs Erskine), Camden 3rd Series, vol. xxxvii, 1956.

Carus-Wilson: Carus-Wilson, E. M., *Medieval Merchant Venturers*, 2nd edn, London, 1967.

Carus-Wilson, E. M., 'La guède française en Angleterre: un grand commerce du moyen âge', *Revue du Nord*, vol. xxxv, 1953, pp. 89–105.

Carus-Wilson, E. M., and Coleman, O., *England's Export Trade 1275–1547*, Oxford, 1963.

Cate, William A., 'St Mary of Westcheap, London, called Newchurch', *Journal of the British Archaeological Association*, New Series, vol. xxv, 1919, pp. 83–110.

Cattaneo, E., 'Il battistero in Italia dopo il Mille', *Miscellanea Gilles Gerard Meersseman*, = *Italia Sacra*, vols xv–xvi, Padua, 1970, vol. i, pp. 171–95.

Chadwick, H. M., *Studies on Anglo-Saxon Institutions*, Cambridge, 1905.

Chadwick, O., 'The Evidence of Dedications in the Early History of the Welsh Church', in H. M. Chadwick *et allii*, *Studies in Early British History*, Cambridge, 1954, pp. 173–88.

Chaplais: Chaplais, P., 'The Original Charters of Herbert and Gervase abbots of Westminster (1121–1157)', in *A Medieval Miscellany for Doris Mary Stenton*, ed. P. M. Barnes and C. F. Slade, Pipe Roll Society, New Series vol. xxxvi, London, 1961, pp. 89–110.

Cheney, C. R., *Hubert Walter*, London, 1967.

Cheney, C. R., 'The Twenty-Five Barons of Magna Carta', *Bulletin of the John Rylands Library*, vol. l, 1967–8, pp. 280–307.

Cheney, M. G., 'Master Geoffrey de Lucy, an early chancellor of the university of Oxford', *EHR*, vol. lxxxii, 1967, pp. 750–63.

CHJ: Cambridge Historical Journal.

Christie, H., 'Old Oslo', *Medieval Archaeology*, vol. x, 1966, pp. 45–58.

Christina of Markyate, The Life of, ed. and trans. C. H. Talbot, Oxford, 1959.

Chron. Abingdon: Chronicon Monasterii de Abingdon, ed. J. Stevenson, 2 vols, Rolls Series, 1858.

Chron. Barnwell: Liber Memorandorum ecclesie de Bernewelle, ed. J. W. Clark, Cambridge, 1907.

Chron. Jordan Fantosme, in *Chrons. Stephen etc.*, vol. iii.

Chron. Waltham: The Foundation of Waltham Abbey: The Tract De inventione sanctae crucis nostrae in Monte Acuto et de ductione ejusdem apud Waltham, ed. W. Stubbs, Oxford and London, 1861.

Chronicles of . . . Edward I and Edward II, ed. W. Stubbs, 2 vols, Rolls Series, 1882–3.

Chrons. Stephen etc.: Chronicles of the Reigns of Stephen, Henry II and Richard I, ed. R. Howlett, 4 vols, Rolls Series, 1884–9.

Città nel alto medioevo, La, Spoleto, 1959 = Settimane di Studio del Centro Italiano di Studi sull'Alto Medioevo, vol. vi.

Clapham, A. W., *English Romanesque Architecture before the Conquest, . . . after the Conquest*, Oxford, 1930, 1934.

Clapham, A. W., 'On the Topography of the Dominican Priory of London', *Archaeologia*, vol. lxiii, 1912, pp. 57–84.

Clapham, A. W., 'Three mediaeval hospitals of London', *Transactions of St Paul's Ecclesiological Society*, vol. vii, 1911–15, pp. 153–60.

Clarke, M. V., *The Medieval City State*, London, 1926.

Claude, D., *Topographie und Verfassung der Städte Bourges und Poitiers bis in das 11. Jahrhundert*, Lübeck-Hamburg, 1960.

Clay, R. M., *Medieval Hospitals of England*, London, 1909.

Colker, M. L. 'Latin texts concerning Gilbert, founder of Merton Priory', *Studia Monastica*, vol. xii, 1970, pp. 241–71.

Colvin: Colvin, H. M. (ed.), *The King's Works*, vols i– , London, 1963– .

Complete Peerage: The Complete Peerage by G. E. C., revised edn by V. Gibbs, H. A. Doubleday, Lord Howard de Walden, G. H. White and R. S. Lea, London, 1910–59.

Consitt, F., *The London Weavers' Company*, vol. i, Oxford, 1933.

Constable, G., *Monastic Tithes from their Origins to the Twelfth Century*, Cambridge, 1964.

Cook, G. H., *Old St Paul's Cathedral*, London, 1955.

Coornaert, E., 'Les ghildes médiévales (Ve–XIVe siècles)', *Revue historique*, vol. cxcix, 1948, pp. 22–55, 208–43.

Cronne, 'Justiciar': Cronne, H. A., 'The Office of Local Justiciar in England under the Norman Kings', *University of Birmingham Historical Journal*, vol. vi, no. 1, 1958, pp. 18–38.

Croydon, F. E., 'Abbot Laurence of Westminster and Hugh of St Victor', *Mediaeval and Renaissance Studies*, vol. ii, 1950, pp. 169–71.

Crump, C. G., 'London and the Gild Merchant', *EHR*, vol. xviii, 1903, p. 315.

Cunliffe, B., 'Excavations at Portchester Castle, Hants, 1966–1968', *Antiquaries Journal*, vol. xlix, 1969, pp. 62–74.

Dändliker, K., *Geschichte der Stadt und des Kantons Zürich*, vol. i (to 1400), Zürich, 1908.

Darlington and Howgego: Darlington, I., and Howgego, J., *Printed Maps of London circa 1553–1850*, London, 1964.

Davidsohn, R., *Geschichte von Florenz*, 4 vols, Berlin, 1896–1925.

Davis, G. R. C., *Medieval Cartularies of Great Britain*, London, 1958.

Davis, H. W. C., 'London lands and liberties of St Paul's, 1066–1135', *Essays in Medieval History presented to T. F. Tout*, pp. 45–59.

Davis, H. W. C., 'Some documents of the Anarchy', in *Essays in History presented to R. L. Poole*, pp. 168–89.

Davis, R. H. C., 'Alfred the Great: Propaganda and Truth', *History*, vol. lvi, 1971, pp. 169–82.

Davis, R. H. C., 'Geoffrey de Mandeville reconsidered', *EHR*, vol. lxxix, 1964, pp. 299–307.

Davis, R. H. C., *King Stephen*, London, 1967.

Davis, R. H. C., 'An Oxford Charter of 1191 and the beginnings of municipal freedom', *Oxoniensia*, vol. xxxiii, 1968, pp. 53–65.

Dawson, G., 'Roman London Bridge', 'London Bridge – a rejoinder', and 'The Saxon London Bridge', *London Archaeologist*, vol. i, nos 5, 7, 1969–70, pp. 114–17, 156–60; no. 10, 1971, p. 224; no. 14, 1972, pp. 330–2.

D-B: *Recueil des actes de Henri II . . . concernant les provinces françaises et les affaires de France*, Introduction and 3 vols, ed. L. Delisle and E. Berger, Académie des Inscriptions et Belles Lettres, Chartes et Diplômes, Paris, 1909–27.

Deck, S., *La Ville d'Eu . . . (1151–1475)*, Paris, 1924 (Bibliothèque de l'Ecole des Hautes Etudes, vol. ccxliii).

Decreta Lanfranci (The Monastic Constitutions of Lanfranc), ed. and trans. D. Knowles, NMT, 1951; 2nd edn (text only), *Corpus Consuetudinum Monasticarum*, vol. iii, Siegburg, 1967.

Denholm-Young, R., 'Eudo Dapifer's Honour of Walbrook', *EHR*, vol. xlvi, 1931, pp. 623–9.

Denton, J. H., *English Royal Free Chapels 1100–1300*, Manchester, 1970.

Denton, W., *Records of St Giles Cripplegate*, London, 1883.

Dept, G. G., 'Les Marchands flamands et le roi d'Angleterre', *Revue du Nord*, vol. xii, 1926, pp. 303–24.

Dialogus de Scaccario, ed. C. Johnson, NMT, 1950.

Diceto: *Radulfi de Diceto decani Londoniensis opera historica . . .*, ed. W. Stubbs, 2 vols, Rolls Series, 1876.

Dickins, B., 'The cult of St. Olave in the British Isles', *Saga-Book of the Viking Society for Northern Research*, vol. xii, 1937–54, pt ii, 1940, pp. 53–80.

Dickinson, *Origins of the Austin Canons*: Dickinson, J. C., *The Origins of the Austin Canons and their Introduction into England*, London, 1950.

Dion, R., *Histoire de la vigne et du vin en France des origines au XIXe siècle*, Paris, 1959.

DNB: *Dictionary of National Biography*, ed. L. Stephen and S. Lee, 66 vols, London, 1885–1901, repr. 22 vols, Oxford, 1921–2.

Dodgson, *see PN Cheshire*.

Doehaerd, R., *Les Relations commerciales entre Gênes, la Belgique et l'Outremont . . . au XIIIe et XIVe siècles*, 3 vols, Brussels, Rome, 1941.

Dolley, R. H. M., 'Coin Hoards from the London area', *LMAS*, vol. xx, 1959–61, pp. 37–50

Dolley, R. H. M., *The Norman Conquest and the English Coinage*, London, 1966.

Dolley, R. H. M., 'Two unpublished hoards of late Saxon pence in the Guildhall Museum', *BNJ*, vol. xxvii, 1953, pp. 212–13.

Dolley, R. H. M., *see also* under *AS Coins*, *Sylloge*, and Appendix IV.

Dolley, R. H. M., and Blunt, C. E., 'The Chronology of the Coins of Ælfred the Great, 871–899', in *AS Coins*, pp. 77–95.

Dolley, R. H. M. and Metcalf, D. M., 'The Reform of the English Coinage under Eadgar', in *AS Coins*, pp. 136–68.

Dollinger, P., Wolff, P. and Guenée, S., *Bibliographie d'histoire des villes de France*, Paris, 1967.

Domesday Book: Liber Censualis vocatus Domesday-Book, 4 vols, Record Commission, 1783–1816.

Douglas, D. C., *William the Conqueror*, London, 1964.

Dronke, P., *Poetic Individuality in the Middle Ages*, Oxford, 1970.

Duby, G., *L'Economie rurale et la vie des campagnes dans l'occident médiéval*, Paris, 1962; Eng. trans. by C. Postan, London, 1968.

Dugdale, W., *History of St Paul's Cathedral in London*, London, 1658; also edns of 1714–16, 1818.

Dummelow, J., *The Wax Chandlers of London*, London and Chichester, 1973.

Eadmer: Eadmer, *Historia Novorum in Anglia . . .*, ed. M. Rule, Rolls Series, 1884.

Eadmer, *Life of St Anselm*, ed. and trans. R. W. Southern, NMT, 1962, repr. OMT, 1972.

Early Yorkshire Charters, vol. viii, ed. Sir C. T. Clay, Yorks Archaeologica Society, Record Series, Extra Series, vol. vi, 1949.

Edwards, K., *The English Secular Cathedrals in the Middle Ages*, 2nd edn, Manchester, 1967.

Egloff, E., *Der Standort des Monasteriums Ludwigs des Deutschen in Zürich*, Zürich, n.d. (1949).

EHD: English Historical Documents, ed. D. C. Douglas, vols i, *c.* 500–1042, ed. D. Whitelock, London, 1955; ii, 1042–1189, ed. D. C. Douglas and G. W. Greenaway, London, 1953.

EHR: English Historical Review.

Ekwall: Ekwall, E., *Street-Names of the City of London*, Oxford, 1954 (cited from corrected repr., 1965).

Ekwall, E., *Early London Personal Names*, Lund, 1947.

Ekwall, E., *Studies on the Population of Medieval London*, Stockholm, 1956.

Encomium Emmae reginae, ed. and trans. A. Campbell, Camden 3rd Series, vol. lxxii, 1949.

Ennen: Ennen, E., *Frühgeschichte der Europäischen Stadt*, Bonn, 1953.

Epistolae Cantuarienses, ed. W. Stubbs, in *Chronicles and Memorials of the Reign of Richard I*, vol. ii, Rolls Series, 1865.

Erdmann, C., 'Die Burgenordnung Heinrichs I', *Deutsches Archiv für Geschichte des Mittelalters*, vol. vi, 1943, pp. 59–101.

Essays in History presented to Reginald Lane Poole, ed. H. W. C. Davis, Oxford, 1927.

Essays in Medieval History presented to Thomas Frederick Tout, ed. A. G. Little and F. M. Powicke, Manchester, 1925.

Eyre: The London Eyre of 1244, ed. Helena M. Chew and Martin Weinbaum, LRS, vol. vi, 1970.

Farrer, W., 'The Sheriffs of Lincolnshire and Yorkshire, 1066–1130', *EHR*, vol. xxx, 1915, pp. 277–85.

Fasoli, G., *Dalla 'civitas' al comune nell'Italia settentrionale*, Bologna, 1969.

Feilitzen, O. von, and Blunt, C. E., 'Personal names on the coinage of Edgar', in *England Before the Conquest: Studies in Primary Sources presented to Dorothy Whitelock*, ed. P. Clemoes and K. Hughes, Cambridge, 1971, pp. 183–214.

Fiumi, E., *Storia economica e sociale di San Gimignano*, Florence, 1961.

Flenley, R. (ed.), *Six Town Chronicles of England*, Oxford, 1911.

Florence of Worcester: Florence of Worcester, *Chronica ex chronicis*, ed. B. Thorpe, 2 vols, English Historical Society, London, 1848–9.

Folz, R., *Le Souvenir et la légende de Charlemagne dans l'empire germanique médiéval*, Paris, 1950.

Fonseca: Fonseca, C. D. ed., *I problemi della civiltà comunale*: Atti del Congresso Storico Internazionale per l'VIIIo Centenario della prima Lege Lombarda (Bergamo, 1967), Bergamo, 1972.

Foote, P. G., and Wilson, D. M., *The Viking Achievement*, London, 1970.

Foreville, R., 'Les origines normandes de la famille Becket et le culte de saint Thomas en Normandie', in *Mélanges offerts à Pierre Andrieu-Guitrancourt = Année Canonique*, vol. xvii, 1973, pp. 433–78.

Franchini: Franchini, V., *Saggio di ricerche su l'instituto del podestà nei comuni medievali*, Bologna, 1912.

Frere, S., *Britannia*, London, 1967.

Friedmann, A., *Paris: ses rues, ses paroisses du moyen âge à la Révolution*, Paris, 1959.

Future of London's Past: M. Biddle, D. Hudson, with C. Heighway, *The Future of London's Past*, Worcester, 1973.

Galbert, Galbert of Bruges: Galbert of Bruges, *The Murder of Charles the Good, Count of Flanders*, trans. J. B. Ross, rev. edn, New York etc., 1967.

Galbraith, V. H., *The Making of Domesday Book*, Oxford, 1961.

Galbraith, V. H., 'Notes on the career of Samson, Bishop of Worcester (1096–1112)', *EHR*, vol. lxxxii, 1967, pp. 86–101.

Ganshof: Ganshof, F. L., *Etude sur le développement des villes entre Loire et Rhin au moyen âge*, Paris–Brussels, 1943.

Genova, Storia di, vols ii–iii, Milan, 1941.

Geoffrey of Monmouth, *Historia Regum Britanniae*, ed. A. Griscom, New York, 1929.

Gervase of Canterbury, *Historical Works*, ed. W. Stubbs, 2 vols, Rolls Series, 1879–80.

Gervers, M., 'Rotundae Anglicanae', in *Actes du XXIIe Congrès International d'Histoire de l'Art* (Budapest, 1969), Budapest, 1972, pp. 359–76.

Gesta Henrici II: Gesta Henrici secundi Benedicti abbatis, ed. W. Stubbs, 2 vols, Rolls Series, 1867.

Gesta Stephani, ed. and trans. K. R. Potter, NMT, 1955.

GF: Morey, A. and Brooke, C. N. L., *Gilbert Foliot and his Letters*, Cambridge, 1965.

GFL : The Letters and Charters of Gilbert Foliot . . ., ed. A. Morey and C. N. L. Brooke, Cambridge, 1967.

Gibbs: *Early Charters of the Cathedral Church of St Paul, London*, ed. M. Gibbs, Camden Third Series, vol. lviii, 1939.

Gilbert Crispin, *Disputatio Iudei et Christiani* . . ., ed. B. Blumenkranz, *Stromata Patristica et Mediaevalia*, ed. C. Mohrmann and J. Quasten, vol. iii, Utrecht-Antwerp, 1956.

Gilbert Crispin, *Disputatio Christiani cum gentili*, ed. C. C. J. Webb, in *Mediaeval and Renaissance Studies*, vol. iii, 1954, pp. 55–77.

Gilbert Crispin, *see also* Robinson, J. Armitage.

Giraldus, *Opera : Giraldi Cambrensis Opera*, ed. J. S. Brewer, J. F. Dimock and G. F. Warner, 8 vols, Rolls Series, 1861–91.

Giry: Giry, A., *Les Etablissements de Rouen*, 2 vols, Paris, 1883–5 (Bibliothèque de l'Ecole des Hautes Etudes, Sciences philol. et hist., vols lv, lix).

Giry, A., *Histoire de la ville de Saint-Omer et de ses institutions jusqu'au XIVe siècle*, Paris, 1877.

Glanvill: *Tractatus de legibus et consuetudinibus regni Anglie qui Glanvilla vocatur*, ed. and trans. G. D. G. Hall, NMT, 1965.

Godfrey, W. H., 'Recent Discoveries at the Temple, London . . .' *Archaeologia*, vol. xcv, 1953, pp. 123–40.

Goscelin, *Vita S. Wulsini*, ed. C. H. Talbot, *Revue Bénédictine*, vol. lxix, 1959, pp. 68–85.

Graham, R., *English Ecclesiastical Studies*, London, 1929.

Gregorovius, F., *History of the City of Rome in the Middle Ages*, Eng. trans., 2nd edn., 8 vols, London, 1900–2.

Gregory, Master, *De mirabilibus urbis Rome*, ed. R. Valentini and G. Zucchetti, *Codice topografico della città di Roma*, vol. iii, Fonti per la Storia d'Italia, Rome, 1946.

Grierson, P., *English Linear Measure : an essay in origins*, Stenton Lecture, 1971, Reading, 1972.

Grierson, P., 'The relations between England and Flanders before the Norman Conquest', *TRHS*, 4th Series, vol. xxiii, 1941, pp. 71–112, repr. in *Essays in Medieval History*, ed. R. W. Southern, London, 1968, pp. 61–92.

Grierson, P., 'Sterling', in *AS Coins*, pp. 266–83.

Grierson, P., 'The Volume of Anglo-Saxon Coinage', *Economic History Review*, 2nd Series, vol. xx, 1967, pp. 153–60.

Grimes: Grimes, W. F., *The Excavation of Roman and Mediaeval London*, London, 1968.

Gross, C., *The Gild Merchant*, 2 vols, Oxford, 1890.

Guibert de Nogent, *De vita sua (Histoire de sa vie)*, ed. G. Bourgin, Paris, 1907; Eng. trans. by J. F. Benton, *Self and Society* . . ., New York, etc., 1970.

Gysseling, M., 'Etymologie van Brugge', *Bulletin de la Commission Royale de Toponymie et de Dialectologie*, vol. xviii, 1944, pp. 69–79.

Gysseling, M., *Toponymisch Woordenboek van België, Nederland, Luxemburg, Noord-Frankrijk en West-Duitsland (vóór 1226)*, 2 vols, 1960.

Haddan, A. W., and Stubbs, W., *Councils and Ecclesiastical Documents*, vol. iii, Oxford, 1871.

Hale: *The Domesday of St Paul's . . .*, ed. W. H. Hale, Camden Soc., 1858.

Hale, J. R., 'The early development of the Bastion: an Italian chronology, *c.* 1450–*c.* 1534', in *Europe in the Late Middle Ages*, ed. J. R. Hale, J. R. L. Highfield and B. Smalley, London, 1965, pp. 466–94.

Hanauer, G., 'Das Berufspodestat im dreizehnten Jahrhundert', *Mitteilungen des Institut für österreich. Geschichtsforschung*, vol. xxiii (1902), pp. 376–426.

Hansisches Urkundenbuch, ed. K. Höhlbaum, vols i–iii, Halle, 1882–6.

Harben: Harben, H. A., *A Dictionary of London*, London, 1918.

Harmer: Harmer, F. E., *Anglo-Saxon Writs*, Manchester, 1952.

Harvey, B., *Documents illustrating the rule of Walter de Wenlok, abbot of Westminster, 1283–1307*, Camden 4th Series, vol. ii, 1965.

Harvey, S., 'The knight and the knight's fees in England', *Past and Present*, no. 49, Nov. 1970, pp. 3–43.

Haskins, C. H., 'The Abacus and the King's Curia', *EHR*, vol. xxvii, 1912, pp. 101–6.

Haskins, C. H., 'William Cade', *EHR*, vol. xxviii, 1913, pp. 730–1.

Haslam, J., 'Medieval Streets in London', *London Archaeologist*, vol. ii, no. 1, 1972, pp. 3–8.

Hassall, W. O., 'The conventual buildings of St Mary, Clerkenwell', *LMAS*, New Series, vol. viii (= vol. xiv), 1938–40, pp. 234–8.

Hassall, W. O., 'The Family of Jordan de Briset', *Genealogists' Magazine*, vol. ix, 1940–6, pp. 585–7 (= no. 15, pp. 21–3).

Heads: The Heads of Religious Houses, England and Wales, 940–1216, ed. D. Knowles, C. N. L. Brooke and V. C. M. London, Cambridge, 1972.

Henry of Huntingdon, *Historia Anglorum*, ed. T. Arnold, Rolls Series, 1879.

Hibbert, A. B., 'The origins of the medieval town patriciate', *Past and Present*, no. 3, 1953, pp. 15–27.

Hildebrand, B. E., *Anglo-Saxon Coins in the Royal Swedish Cabinet of Medals at Stockholm all found in Sweden*, new edn, Stockholm, 1881.

Hill, D., 'The Burghal Hidage: the establishment of a text', *Medieval Archaeology*, vol. xiii, 1969, pp. 84—92.

Hill, J. W. F., *Medieval Lincoln*, Cambridge, 1948.

Hinnebusch, W. A., *The Early English Friars Preachers*, Rome, 1951.

Hist. Bordeaux, vols ii, iii: *Histoire de Bordeaux*, vol. ii, C. Higounet, *Bordeaux pendant le haut moyen âge*; vol. iii, Y. Renouard *et al.*, *Bordeaux sous les rois d'Angleterre*, Bordeaux, 1963, 1965.

Historic Towns, vol. i, ed. M. D. Lobel, with maps by W. H. Johns, Oxford, 1969.

HMC, 9th Report: Royal Commission on Historical Manuscripts, Appendix to the Ninth Report, 1883–4, vol. i, pp. 1–72 (H. C. Maxwell-Lyte on St Paul's Cathedral MSS).

Hohler, C., 'Kings and Castles: Court Life in Peace and War', in *Flowering of the Middle Ages*, ed. J. Evans, London, 1966, pp. 133–78.

Hohler, C., 'A note on Jacobus', *Journal of the Warburg and Courtauld Institutes*, vol. xxxv, 1972, pp. 31–80.

Hollister, C. Warren, 'The misfortunes of the Mandevilles', *History*, vol. lviii, 1973, pp. 18–28.

Holmes, M., 'An unrecorded map of London', *Archaeologia*, vol. c, 1966, pp. 105–28.

Holmes, U. T., Jr., *Daily Living in the Twelfth Century*, Madison, 1952.

Holt, J. C., *Magna Carta*, Cambridge, 1965.

Home, G., *Old London Bridge*, London, 1931.

Honeybourne, M. B., 'The Fleet and its neighbourhood in early and medieval times', *LTR*, vol. xix, 1947, pp. 13–87.

Honeybourne, M. B., 'The Leper Houses of the London area', *LMAS*, vol. xxi, 1963–7, pp. 3–61.

Honeybourne, M. B., maps of London under Henry II, see Stenton, and Richard II, London Topographical Society, Publication no. 93, 1960.

Honeybourne, M. B., 'Norman London', *London and Middlesex Historian*, no. 3, Oct. 1966, pp. 9–15.

Honeybourne, M. B., 'The Pre-Norman Bridge of London', *Studies in London History*, pp. 17–39.

Honeybourne, M. B., 'The Reconstructed Map of London under Richard II', *LTR*, vol. xxii, 1965, pp. 29–76.

Honeybourne, M. B., 'The Sanctuary Boundaries and Environs of Westminster Abbey and the College of St Martin-le-Grand', *Journal of the British Archaeological Association*, New Series, vol. xxxviii, 1933, pp. 316–33.

Honeybourne, M. B., *A short account of the Church of St James, Garlickhythe*, E.C.4, 1951.

Howden: *Chronica Rogeri de Houedene*, ed. W. Stubbs, 4 vols, Rolls Series, 1868–71.

HSP: *A History of St Paul's Cathedral*, ed. W. R. Matthews and W. M. Atkins, London, 1957 (chap. i, to 1485, by C. N. L. Brooke, pp. 1–99, 361–5).

Hughes, K., *The Church in early Irish society*, London, 1966.

Hunt, 'Disputation of Peter of Cornwall': Hunt, R. W., 'The Disputation of Peter of Cornwall against Symon the Jew', in *Studies in Medieval History presented to F. M. Powicke*, ed. R. W. Hunt, W. A. Pantin and R. W. Southern, Oxford, 1948, pp. 143–56.

Hunt, 'English learning': Hunt, R. W., 'English learning in the late Twelfth Century', *TRHS*, 4th Series, vol. xix, 1936, pp. 19–42; repr. in *Essays in Medieval History*, ed. R. W. Southern, London, 1968, pp. 106–28.

Hyde, J. K., 'Medieval Descriptions of Cities', *Bulletin of the John Rylands Lib.*, vol. xlviii, 1966, pp. 308–40.

Hyde, J. K., *Society and Politics in Medieval Italy*, London, 1973.

James, M. K., *Studies in the Medieval Wine Trade*, Oxford, 1971.

Jamison, C., *The History of the Royal Hospital of St Katharine, London . . .*, London, 1952.

Jenkinson (1913): Jenkinson, H., 'William Cade, a financier of the Twelfth Century', *EHR*, vol. xxviii, 1913, pp. 209–27, with supplement on pp. 731–2.

Jenkinson (1927): Jenkinson, H., 'A money-lender's bonds of the Twelfth Century', in *Essays in History presented to R. L. Poole*, pp. 190–210.

Jesson, M., and Hill, D. (eds), *The Iron Age and its Hill Forts: Papers presented to Sir Mortimer Wheeler . . .*, Southampton, 1971.

Johansen, P., 'Die Kaufmanskirche im Ostseegebiet' in *Studien zu den Anfängen des europäischen Städeswesens*, Vorträge und Forschungen, ed. T. Mayer, Lindau-Constance, 1958, pp. 499–525.

John of Salisbury, *Historia Pontificalis*, ed. and trans. M. Chibnall, NMT, 1956.

John of Salisbury, *Letters*, vol. i, ed. and trans. W. J. Millor, H. E. Butler and C. N. L. Brooke, NMT 1955.

Johnson, A. H., *The History of the Worshipful Company of the Drapers of London*, 4 vols, Oxford, 1914–22.

Johnson, C. and Jenkinson, H., *English Court Hand*, 2 vols, text and facsimiles, Oxford, 1915.

Johnson, D. J., *Southwark and the City*, London, 1969.

Jones, F. Elmore, and Blunt, C. E., 'A remarkable parcel of Norman pennies in Moscow', *BNJ*, vol. xxxvi, 1967, pp. 86–92.

Jones, O. E., 'A textual and historical study of Llyfr Coch Asaph', Wales M.A. thesis, 1968.

Jones, P. E., and Judges, A. V., 'London population in the late seventeenth century', *Economic History Review*, 1st Series, vol. vi, 1935–6, pp. 45–63.

Jones, P. E., and Smith R., *A Guide to the Records in the Corporation of London Records Office and the Guildhall Library Muniment Room*, London, 1951.

Kealey, E. J., *Roger of Salisbury, Viceroy of England*, Berkeley, Los Angeles, London, 1972.

Ker, N. R., *Medieval Libraries of Great Britain*, 2nd edn, London, 1964.

Kerling, N. J. M., 'The Foundation of St Bartholomew's Hospital in West Smithfield, London', *Guildhall Miscellany*, vol. iv, no. 3, Oct. 1972, pp. 137–48.

KH: Knowles, D., and Hadcock, R. N., *Medieval Religious Houses, England and Wales*, 2nd edn, London, 1971.

Kingsford, C. L., *Chronicles of London*, Oxford, 1905.

Kingsford, C. L., *English Historical Literature of the Fifteenth Century*, Oxford, 1913.

Kingsford, C. L., *The Grey Friars of London*, British Society of Franciscan Studies, vol. vi, Aberdeen, 1915.

Kingsford, C. L., 'Historical Notes on mediaeval London Houses', *LTR*, vols x, 1916, pp. 44–144; xi, 1917, pp. 28–81; xii, 1920, pp. 1–66.

Kissan, B. W., 'An early list of London Properties', *LMAS*, New Series, vol. viii, 1940, pp. 57–69.

Knowles, D., *The Episcopal Colleagues of Archbishop Thomas Becket*, Cambridge, 1951.

Knowles, D., *The Historian and Character and Other Essays*, Cambridge, 1963.

Knowles, *MO, Monastic Order*: D. Knowles, *The Monastic Order in England*, Cambridge, 1940, 2nd edn (pagination unaltered), 1963.

Knowles, *RO* : D. Knowles, *The Religious Orders in England*, 3 vols, Cambridge, 1948–59.

Kurth, G., *La Cité de Liège au moyen-âge*, 3 vols, Brussels–Liège, 1909–10.

Kurze, D., *Pfarrerwahlen im Mittelalter : Ein Beitrag zur Geschichte der Gemeinde des Niederkirchenwesens*, Cologne:Graz, 1966.

LAL : Liber de antiquis legibus, ed. T. Stapleton, Camden Society Old Series, vol. xxxiv, 1846.

Lamperti monachi Hersfeldensis Opera, ed. O. Holder-Egger, Hannover-Leipzig, 1894.

Langmuir, G. I., 'The Jews and the archives of Angevin England: reflections on medieval anti-semitism', *Traditio*, vol. xix, 1963, pp. 183–244.

Lappenberg, J. M., *Urkundliche Geschichte des Hansischen Stahlhofes zu London*, Hamburg, 1851.

Largiadèr, A., *Geschichte von Stadt und Landschaft Zürich*, 2 vols, Erlenbach-Zürich, 1945.

Larson, L. M., *The King's Household in England before the Norman Conquest*, Madison, 1904.

Latham: Latham, R. E., *Revised Medieval Latin Word-List*, London, 1965.

Latouche, R., 'La commune du Mans (1070)', *Mélanges d'histoire du moyen âge dediés à la mémoire de Louis Halphen*, Paris, 1951, pp. 377–82.

Lavedan, P., *Histoire de l'urbanisme*, 3 vols, Paris, 1926–52.

Lavedan, P., *Les Villes françaises*, Paris, 1960.

Lees: *Records of The Templars in England . . .*, ed. B. A. Lees, British Academy, London, 1935.

Lemarignier, J.-F., 'Notes sur les échevins dans les établissements de Rouen . . .', *Revue du Nord*, vol. xl, 1958, pp. 319–21.

Lemarignier, J.-F., 'L'origine de Lille and de Caen', *Revue du moyen âge latin*, vol. iv, 1948, pp. 191–6.

Le Neve: Le Neve, J., *Fasti Ecclesiae Anglicanae, 1066–1300*, vol. i, St Paul's, London, ed. D. E. Greenway, London, 1968.

Le Neve, J. *Fasti . . . 1066–1300*, vol. ii, ed. D. E. Greenway, Monastic Cathedrals, 1971.

Le Neve, J., *Fasti . . . 1300–1541*, vol. v, St Paul's, London, ed. J. M. Horn, 1963.

Lennard, R. V., *Rural England 1086–1135*, Oxford, 1959.

Lestocquoy, J., *Les Dynasties bourgeoises d'Arras du XIe au XVe siècle*, Arras, 1945.

Lestocquoy, J., *Les Villes de Flandre et d'Italie sous le gouvernement des patriciens*, Paris, 1952.

Lethaby, W. R., *Westminster Abbey and the King's Craftsmen*, London, 1906.

Lethaby, W. R., *Westminster Abbey re-examined*, London, 1925.

Lévi-Provençal, E., *Histoire de l'Espagne musulmane*, vol. iii, Paris, 1967.

Levison, W., *England and the Continent in the Eighth Century*, Oxford, 1946.

Levison, W., 'St Alban and St Albans', *Antiquity*, vol. xv, 1941, pp. 337–59.

Libellus de diuersis ordinibus . . ., ed. and trans. G. Constable and B. Smith, OMT, 1972.

Liber Cust.: Munimenta Gildhallae Londoniensis . . ., ed. H. T. Riley, 3 vols in 4, Rolls Series, 1849–62, vol. ii, pts 1, 2, *Liber Custumarum.*

Liber Eliensis, ed. E. O. Blake, Camden 3rd Series, vol. xcii, 1962.

Liber Vitae ecclesiae Dunelmensis, facs. ed. A. H. Thompson, Surtees Society, vol. cxxxvi, 1923.

Liebermann: *Die Gesetze der Angelsachsen*, ed. F. Liebermann, 3 vols, Halle, 1903–16.

Liebermann, F., 'A contemporary Manuscript of the "Leges Anglorum Londoniis collectae" ', *EHR*, vol. xxviii, 1913, pp. 732–45.

Liebeschütz, H., *Mediaeval Humanism in the Life and writings of John of Salisbury*, London, 1951.

Liggins, E. M., 'The authorship of the Old English *Orosius*', *Anglia*, vol. lxxxviii, 1970, pp. 289–322.

Lipman, V. D., 'The anatomy of Medieval Anglo-Jewry', *Transactions of the Jewish Historical Society of England*, vol. xxi, 1968, pp. 64–77.

Llewellyn, P., *Rome in the Dark Ages*, London, 1971.

LMAS: Transactions of the London and Middlesex Archaeological Society.

London Assize of Nuisance 1301–1431, ed. H. M. Chew and W. Kellaway, LRS, vol. x, 1973 for 1974.

London Inhabitants within the Walls, 1695, with introd. by D. V. Glass, LRS, 1966.

Lopez, R. S. and Raymond, I. W. (eds), *Medieval Trade in the Mediterranean World*, New York, 1955.

Loyd, L. C., *The Origins of some Anglo-Norman Families*, ed. C. T. Clay and D. C. Douglas, Publications of the Harleian Society, vol. ciii, Leeds, 1951.

Loyn, H. R., 'Boroughs and Mints, A.D 900–1066', in *AS Coins*, pp. 122–35.

Loyn, H. R., 'The term *Ealdorman* in the translations prepared at the time of King Alfred', *EHR*, vol. lxviii, 1953, pp. 513–25.

Loyn, H. R., 'Towns in late Anglo-Saxon England: the evidence and some possible lines of enquiry', in *England before the Norman Conquest: Studies in Primary Sources presented to Dorothy Whitelock*, Cambridge, 1971, pp. 115–28.

LRS: London Record Society.

LTR: London Topographical Record.

Luchaire, A., *Les Communes françaises à l'époque des Capétiens directs*, nouv. edn, Paris, 1911.

Lunt, W. E., *Financial Relations of the Papacy with England to 1327*, Cambridge, Mass., 1939.

Lyon, C. S. S., 'Historical Problems of Anglo-Saxon Coinage – (2) The Ninth Century – Offa to Alfred', and '. . . – (4) The Viking Age', *BNJ*, vols xxxvii, 1968, pp. 216–38; xxxix, 1970, pp. 193–204.

McInnes, E. M., 'St Thomas' Hospital, London, and its archives', *Journal of the Society of Archivists*, vol. i, 1955–9, pp. 277–82.

McKisack, M., 'London and the succession to the crown during the Middle

Ages', in *Studies in Medieval History presented to F. M. Powicke*, Oxford, 1948, pp. 76–89.

Map, *see* Walter.

Martin, A. R., *Franciscan Architecture in England*, British Society of Franciscan Studies, 1937, pp. 176–204.

Martin, G. H., 'The Registration of Deeds of Title in the Medieval Borough', in *The Study of Medieval Records: essays in honour of Kathleen Major*, Oxford, 1971, pp. 151–73; and see *Bibliography*.

Mason, J. F. A., 'Roger de Montgomery and his sons (1067–1102)', *TRHS*, 5th Series, vol. xiii, 1963, pp. 1–28.

Matthew Paris, *Abbreviatio Chronicorum*, in *Historia Anglorum*, ed. F. Madden, vol. iii, Rolls Series, 1869.

Matthew Paris, *Gesta abbatum S. Albani*, ed. H. T. Riley, in *Gesta*, Rolls Series, vol. i, 1867.

MB: Materials for the History of Thomas Becket, Archbishop of Canterbury ..., ed. J. C. Robertson and J. B. Sheppard, 7 vols, Rolls Series, London, 1875–85.

Merrifield: Merrifield, R. B., *The Roman City of London*, London, 1965.

Merrifield, R. B., 'Roman London Bridge: Further Observations on its site', *London Archaeologist*, vol. i, 1970, pp. 186–7.

MGH, Epistolae Selectae, vol. i: *see* Boniface.

Milano, Storia di, vols iii, iv, Fondazione Treccani degli Alfieri, Milan, 1954.

Miller, E., 'The fortunes of the English Textile industry in the Thirteenth Century', *Economic History Review*, 2nd Series, vol. xviii, 1965, pp. 64–82.

Mittellateinisches Wörterbuch, ed. O. Prinz and J. Schneider, vols i– , Munich, 1959– .

Il Monachesimo e la riforma ecclesiastica (1049–1122), Miscellanea del Centro di Studi Medioevali, vol. vi, Milan, 1971.

Morris: Morris, W. A., *The Medieval English Sheriff to 1300*, Manchester, 1927.

Morris, W. A., 'The Sheriffs and the administrative system of Henry I', *EHR*, vol. xxxvii, 1922, pp. 161–72.

Mossop, H. R., *The Lincoln Mint c. 890–1279*, Newcastle, 1970.

Mundy, J., 'Hospitals and leprosaries in 12th and early 13th century Toulouse', in *Essays in Medieval Life and Thought, presented in honor of Austin Patterson Evans*, New York, 1955, pp. 181–205.

Mundy, J., *Liberty and Political Power in Toulouse, 1050–1230*, New York, 1954.

Murray, H. J. R., *A History of Chess*, Oxford, 1913.

Myres, J. N. L., 'Some Thoughts on the Topography of Saxon London', *Antiquity*, vol. viii, 1934, pp. 437–42 (and see Wheeler, R. E. M.).

NC: Numismatic Chronicle.

Nelson, J., 'The problem of King Alfred's royal anointing', *Journ. of Ecclesiastical History*, vol. xviii, 1967, pp. 145–63.

Nicholl, D., *Thurstan, Archbishop of York*, York, 1964.

Nichols, J. G., 'The foot of St Paul's. The King's iron elne', *Gentleman's Magazine*, New Series, vol. xxxviii, 1852, pt 2, pp. 276–7.

Niermeyer, J. F., *Mediae Latinitatis Lexicon Minus*, Leiden, 1954–64.

NMT: Nelson's Medieval Texts.

Norman Moore: Moore, Sir Norman, *The History of St Bartholomew's Hospital*, 2 vols, London, 1918.

North, J. J., *English Hammered Coinage*, vol. i, London, 1963.

Notai Liguri del Secolo XII (e del XIII), R. Deputazione di Storia Patria per la Liguria, later Società ligure di Storia Patria, 8 vols in 9, Genoa, 1938–61.

Novum Glossarium Mediae Latinitatis, Fasc. Ma, ed. F. Blatt, Copenhagen, 1959.

O'Donovan, M. A., 'The Vatican hoard of Anglo-Saxon pennies', *BNJ*, vol. xxxiii, 1964, pp. 7–29.

OMT: Oxford Medieval Texts.

Orderic Vitalis, *Ecclesiastical History*, ed. and trans. M. Chibnall, vols ii–iv, OMT, 1968–73.

Ormsby, H. R., *London on the Thames*, London, 1924.

Osbert of Clare, *Letters*, ed. E. W. Williamson, Oxford, 1929 (with 'A sketch of Osbert's career' by J. Armitage Robinson, pp. 1–20).

Oxford English Dictionary, Oxford, 1888–1928.

Pagan, H. E., 'A third gold coin of Mercia', *BNJ*, vol. xxxiv, 1965, pp. 8–10.

Page: Page, W., *London, its Origin and Early Development*, London, 1923.

Panofsky, E., *Abbot Suger on the Abbey Church of Saint-Denis*, Princeton, 1946.

Paris, *see* Matthew.

Partner, P., *The Lands of St Peter*, London, 1972.

Pearce, A., *The History of the Butchers' Company*, London, 1929.

Pearce, E. H., *The Monks of Westminster*, Cambridge, 1916.

[Pegge, S.], *FitzStephen's Description of the City of London*, London, 1772.

Petit-Dutaillis, C., *Les Communes françaises: caractères et évolution des origines au XVIIIe siècle*, Paris, 1947.

Petit-Dutaillis, C., *Studies and Notes supplementary to Stubbs's Constitutional History*, vol. i, Manchester, 1908.

Pevsner, N., *London*, 2 vols, The Buildings of England, Harmondsworth, vol. i, cited from 2nd edn, 1962, ii, 1st edn, 1952.

Pinder-Wilson, R. H., and Brooke, C. N. L., 'The Reliquary of St Petroc and the ivories of Norman Sicily', *Archaeologia*, vol. civ, 1973, pp. 261–305.

Pirenne, *Les Villes*: Pirenne, H., *Les Villes et les institutions urbaines*, 2nd edn, 2 vols, Paris–Brussels, 1939.

Placita de quo warranto, Record Commission, 1818.

PN Cheshire: Dodgson, J. M., *The Place-Names of Cheshire*, 5 vols, Cambridge, 1971– .

PN Essex: P. H. Reaney, *The Place-Names of Essex*, Cambridge, 1935.

PN Herts: Gover, J. E. B., Mawer, A. and Stenton, F. M., *The Place-Names of Hertfordshire*, Cambridge, 1938.

PN Middlesex: Gover, J. E. B., Mawer, A. and Stenton, F. M., *The Place-Names of Middlesex*, Cambridge, 1942.

Poerck, G. de, *La Draperie médiévale en Flandre et en Artois*, 3 vols, Bruges, 1951.

Poole, R. L., *The Exchequer in the Twelfth Century*, Oxford, 1912.

Powell, W. R., 'English administrative families in the twelfth and thirteenth centuries, with special reference to the Cornhill family', Oxford B.Litt. Thesis, 1952.

Power, Eileen, *Medieval English Nunneries, c. 1275 to 1535*, Cambridge, 1922.

PR : Pipe Rolls, cited by the regnal year, *31 Henry I, 2–4 Henry II and 1 Richard I*, ed. J. Hunter (1833, 1844, the first two repr. 1929, 1931), the rest in the Pipe Roll Society, London, 1884– .

Pubblicazioni degli Archivi di Stato (Ministero dell' Interno), vol. xxii, Rome, 1956: *Archivio di Stato di Genova, Cartolari Notarili Genovesi (1–149)*, Inventario, vol. i, pt. 1.

Rahtz, P. A., and Musty, J. W. G., 'Excavations at Old Sarum, 1957', *Wiltshire Archaeological and Natural History Magazine*, vol. lvii, 1958–60, pp. 353–70.

Rajna, P., 'Strade, pellegrinaggi e ospizi nell'Italia del Medioevo', *Atti della Società italiana per il progresso delle scienze*, vol. v, Rome, 1911, pp. 99–118.

Rathbone, E., 'The Influence of Bishops and of members of Cathedral bodies in the intellectual life of England, 1066–1216', London Ph.D. thesis, 1935.

Rathbone, E., 'Master Alberic of London, "Mythographus tertius Vaticanus"', *Mediaeval and Renaissance Studies*, vol. i, 1943, pp. 35–8.

RCHM : Royal Commission on Historical Monuments, esp. *London*, vols ii, iv, 1925, 1929.

Reaney, *see PN Essex*.

Recueil des historiens des Gaules et de la France, ed. M. Bouquet *et al.*, nouv. édn, ed. L. Delisle, 24 vols, Paris, 1869–1904.

Regesta : Regesta Regum Anglo-Normannorum, ed. H. W. C. Davis, vol. i, ed. H. W. C. Davis and R. J. Whitwell, Oxford, 1913; ii, ed. C. Johnson and H. A. Cronne, 1956; iii–iv, ed. H. A. Cronne and R. H. C. Davis, 1968–9.

Reg. Malmesbury : Registrum Malmesburiense, ed. J. S. Brewer and C. T. Martin, 2 vols, Rolls Series, 1879–80.

Registrum statutorum et consuetudinum ecclesiae cathedralis sancti Pauli Londinensis, ed. W. S. Simpson, London, 1873.

Renouard, Y., *Histoire de Florence*, 2nd edn, Paris, 1967.

Renouard, Y., *Les Hommes d'affaires italiens du moyen âge*, Paris, 1949, cited from nouv. édn, 1968.

Renouard, Y., *Les Villes d'Italie de la fin du Xe siècle au début du XIVe siècle*, nouv. édn by P. Braunstein, 2 vols, Paris, 1969.

Reynolds, R. L., 'Some English settlers in Genoa in the late twelfth century', *Economic History Review*, 1st Series, vol. iv, 1932–4, pp. 317–23.

Reynolds, 'Rulers of London': Reynolds, Susan, 'The Rulers of London in the Twelfth Century', *History*, vol. lvii, 1972, pp. 337–57.

Richard of Devizes, *Chronicle*, ed. and trans. J. T. Appleby, NMT, 1963.

Richardson: Richardson, H. G., *The English Jewry under Angevin Kings*, London, 1960.

Richardson, H. G., and Sayles, G. O., *The Governance of Mediaeval England from the Conquest to Magna Carta*, Edinburgh, 1963.

Richardson, H. G., and Sayles, G. O. *Law and legislation from Æthelberht to Magna Carta*, Edinburgh, 1966.

Rigold, S. E., 'The trail of the Easterlings', *BNJ*, vol. xxvi, 1949–51, pp. 31–55.

Robertson, *Laws*: Robertson, A. J. (ed. and trans.), *The Laws of the Kings of England from Edmund to Henry I*, Cambridge, 1925.

Robinson, *GC*: Robinson, J. Armitage, *Gilbert Crispin abbot of Westminster*, Cambridge, 1911.

Robinson, *Flete: Flete's History of Westminster Abbey*, ed. J. Armitage Robinson, Cambridge, 1909.

Robinson, J. Armitage, *Somerset Historical Essays*, British Academy, London, 1921.

Robinson, J. Armitage, and James, M. R., *The Manuscripts of Westminster Abbey*, London, 1909.

Roger of Wendover, *Flores historiarum*, ed. H. G. Hewlett, 3 vols, Rolls Series, 1886–9.

Rogers, A., 'Parish boundaries and urban history: two case studies', *Journ. of the British Archaeol. Assoc.*, 3rd Series, vol. xxxv, 1972, pp. 46–64.

Rolland, P., *Les Origines de la commune de Tournai*, Brussels, 1931.

Roth, C., *A History of the Jews in England*, 3rd edn, Oxford, 1964.

Rotuli Curiae Regis, ed. Sir F. Palgrave, 2 vols, Record Commission, 1835.

Rotuli de oblatis et finibus . . ., ed. T. D. Hardy, Record Commission, 1835.

Round, *CDF: Calendar of Documents preserved in France illustrative of the History of Great Britain and Ireland*, vol. i, AD 918–1206, London, 1899.

Round, *CL*: Round, J. H., *The Commune of London and other studies*, Westminster, 1899.

Round, *GM*: Round, J. H., *Geoffrey de Mandeville: A Study of the Anarchy*, London, 1892.

Round, J. H., 'The debtors of William Cade', *EHR*, vol. xxviii, 1913, pp. 522–7.

Round, J. H., 'The first Mayor of London', *The Antiquary*, vol. xv, 1887, pp. 107–11.

Round, J. H., 'London notes', *Homes Counties Magazine*, vol. i, 1899, pp. 62–5.

Round, J. H., 'The origin of the Mayoralty of London', *Archaeological Journ.*, vol. l, 1893, pp. 247–63.

Russell, J. C., 'The date of Henry I's charter for London', in *Dargan Historical Essays*, ed. W. M. Dabney and J. C. Russell, University of New Mexico Publications in History, vol. iv, 1952, pp. 9–16.

St Albans Psalter, The, ed. O. Pächt, C. R. Dodwell and F. Wormald, London, 1960.

St Bartholomew's *FB: The Book of the Foundation of St Bartholomew's Church in London*, Middle English trans. ed. Sir Norman Moore, Early English Text Society, Original Series, vol. clxiii, 1923 (Moore); also cited from modern Eng. trans. by H. H. King and W. Barnard for E. A. Webb's *Records . . .*, and separately, ed. E. A. Webb, London, 1923 (Webb, by page of separate edn).

St Margaret (of Scotland), Life of: *Acta Sanctorum Bollandiana*, June, vol. ii, cited by edn of 1867.

Sandys, Agnes, 'The financial and administrative importance of the London Temple in the Thirteenth Century', in *Essays in Medieval History presented to T. F. Tout*, Manchester, 1925, pp. 147–62.

Sapori, A., *Le Marchand italien au moyen âge*, Paris, 1952.

Sawyer: Sawyer, P. H., *Anglo-Saxon Charters: an annotated list and bibliography*, London, 1968.

Sawyer, P. H., *The Age of the Vikings*, 2nd edn, London, 1971.

Sawyer, P. H., 'The wealth of England in the Eleventh Century', *TRHS*, 5th Series, vol. xv, 1965, pp. 145–64.

Scullard, H. H., *The Etruscan Cities and Rome*, London, 1967.

Sheppard: Sheppard, F., *London, 1808–1870: The Infernal Wen*, History of London, vol. (vii), London, 1971.

Sherwell, J. W., *The history of the Guild of Saddlers of the City of London*, London, 1937, 3rd edn, 1956.

Simpson, W. Sparrow, 'The inventories of the Cathedral Church of St Paul, London, dated respectively 1245 and 1402 . . .', *Archaeologia*, vol. l, 1887, pp. 439–524.

Simpson, W. Sparrow, 'Visitations of certain churches in the City of London in the patronage of St Paul's Cathedral Church, between the years 1138 and 1250', *Archaeologia*, vol. lv, 1897, pp. 283–300.

Sims, J. M., *London and Middlesex published records: a handlist*, LRS, 1970.

Smalley, B., 'Gilbertus Universalis, Bishop of London (1128–34), and the Problem of the "Glossa Ordinaria"', *Recherches de théologie ancienne et médiévale*, vol. vii, 1935, pp. 235–62.

Smalley, B., *The Study of the Bible in the Middle Ages*, 2nd edn, Oxford, 1952.

Smart, Veronica J., 'Moneyers of the late Anglo-Saxon coinage, 973–1016', in *Commentationes de nummis saeculorum IX–XI in Suecia repertis*, vol. ii, Stockholm, 1968, pp. 191–276.

Smith, A. H., *English Place-Name Elements*, 2 parts, Cambridge, 1956.

Smith, H. L., *The History of East London from the Earliest Times to the End of the Eighteenth Century*, London, 1939.

Southern, R. W., 'The Canterbury Forgeries', *EHR*, vol. lxxiii, 1958, pp. 193–226.

Southern: Southern, R. W., 'The place of Henry I in English history', *Proceedings of the British Academy*, vol. xlviii, 1962, pp. 127–69; repr. in *Medieval Humanism and other studies*, Oxford, 1970, chap. 11, cited by art. with pages of repr. in brackets.

Southern, R. W., *St Anselm and his Biographer*, Cambridge, 1963.

Stenton, D. M., *English Justice between the Norman Conquest and the Great Charter, 1066–1215*, Memoirs of the American Philosophical Society, vol. lx, Philadelphia, 1964.

Stenton: Stenton, Sir Frank M., *Norman London, an essay*, cited from the rev. edn, Historical Association, London, 1934, with a trans. of William FitzStephen's *Description* by H. E. Butler, and a Map of London under

Henry II by M. B. Honeybourne, annotated by E. Jeffries Davis. Sir F. Stenton's text was again rev. and repr. in *Social Life in Early England*, ed. G. Barraclough, London, 1960, pp. 179–207, and in *Preparatory to Anglo-Saxon England*, ed. D. M. Stenton, Oxford, 1970, pp. 23–47.

Stenton, F. M., *Anglo-Saxon England*, Oxford, 1943 (3rd edn, 1971).

Stenton, F. M., *The First Century of English Feudalism*, 2nd edn, Oxford, 1961.

Stephenson, C., *Borough and Town: A Study of Urban Origins in England*, Cambridge, Mass., 1933.

Stevenson, W. H., 'A contemporary description of the Domesday Survey', *EHR*, vol. xxii, 1907, pp. 72–84.

Stewart, B. H. I. H., 'The early coins of Ethelred II's Crux Issue with right-facing bust', *NC*, 7th Series, vol. xi, 1971, pp. 237–42.

Stewart, B. H. I. H., 'A new Norman forger', *BNJ*, vol. xxviii, 1955–7, pp. 190–1.

Stewart, B. H. I. H., 'Second thoughts on medieval die-output', *NC*, 7th Series, vol. iv, 1964, pp. 293–303.

Stewart, B. H. I. H., 'Stefanus R', *NC*, 7th Series, vol. xii, 1972, pp. 167–75.

Stow: Stow, J., *A Survey of London*, ed. C. L. Kingsford, 2 vols, Oxford, 1908, cited from the corrected repr. of 1971; edns of 1598, 1603 also used.

Stubbs, W., *Select Charters . . .*, 9th edn, ed. H. W. C. Davis, Oxford, 1913.

Studies in London History: Studies in London History presented to Philip Edmund Jones, ed. A. E. J. Hollaender and W. Kellaway, London, 1969.

Studies in Medieval History presented to Frederick Maurice Powicke, ed. R. W. Hunt, W. A. Pantin and R. W. Southern, Oxford, 1948.

Sturler, J. de, 'Le port de Londres au XIIe siècle', *Revue de l'Université de Bruxelles*, vol. xlii, 1936–7, pp. 61–77.

Sylloge: Sylloge of Coins of the British Isles, publ. by British Academy, London, 1958– . The following vols are cited: 7, 13–15, *Royal Collection of Coins and Medals, National Museum, Copenhagen*, vols ii, iiia–c, ed. G. Galster, 1966, 1970; [11] *Royal Coin Cabinet. Stockholm, The Anglo-Norman Coins*, ed. M. Dolley, F. Elmore Jones and C. S. S. Lyons, London–Stockholm, 1969.

Tait: Tait, James, *The Medieval English Borough: Studies in its Origins and Constitutional History*, Manchester, 1936.

Tait, J., 'An alleged charter of William the Conqueror', in *Essays in History presented to R. L. Poole*, pp. 151–67.

Tait, J., 'Two unknown names of early London wards', *LTR*, vol. xv, 1931, pp. 1–3.

Tatlock, J. S. P., *The legendary history of Britain*, University of California, Berkeley and Los Angeles, 1950.

Taylor, H. M. and J., *Anglo-Saxon Architecture*, 2 vols, Cambridge, 1965.

Theophilus, *De diuersis artibus*, ed. and trans. C. R. Dodwell, NMT, 1961.

Thomas, *Tristran*, cited from Eng. trans. A. T. Hatto in Gottfried von Strassburg, *Tristan*, Penguin Classics, Harmondsworth, 1960.

Thomas de Celano, *Vitae S. Francisci*, ed. in *Analecta Franciscana*, vol. x, Quaracchi, 1926–41.

Thompson, J. D. A., *Inventory of British Coin Hoards AD 600–1500*, London, 1956.

Thorpe, *Diplomatarium: Diplomatarium Anglicum aevi saxonici*, ed. B. Thorpe, London, 1865.

Thrupp, S. L., 'Medieval Gilds reconsidered', *Journal of Economic History*, vol. ii, 1942, pp. 164–73.

Thrupp, S. L., *The Merchant Class of medieval London, 1300–1500*, Chicago, 1948.

Thrupp, S. L., *A short history of the Worshipful Company of Bakers of London*, London, 1933.

Tierney, B., *Medieval Poor Law*, University of California, Berkeley and Los Angeles, 1959.

To God and the Bridge. Catalogue of Exhibition in the Guildhall Art Gallery, 16 June–28 Sept. 1972.

Tolaini, E., *Forma Pisarum*, Pisa, 1967.

Tout Essays: see *Essays in Medieval History presented to T. F. Tout . . .*

TRHS: *Transactions of the Royal Historical Society*.

Tyson, M., 'The Annals of Southwark and Merton', *Surrey Archaeol. Collections*, vol. xxxvi, 1925, pp. 24–51.

Unwin: Unwin, G., *The Gilds and Companies of London*, London, 1908 (4th edn, 1963).

Urkundenbuch der Stadt und Landschaft Zürich, ed. J. Escher and P. Schweizer, vol. i, Zürich, 1888

Urry, W., *Canterbury under the Angevin Kings*, London, 1967.

Valuation of Norwich, The, ed. W. E. Lunt, Oxford, 1926.

Van Houtte, J. A., 'The rise and decline of the market of Bruges', *Economic History Review*, 2nd Series, vol. xix, 1966, pp. 29–43.

Van Werveke, H., *Gand: esquisse d'histoire sociale*, Brussels, 1946.

Vaughan, R., *Matthew Paris*, Cambridge, 1958.

VCH: *Victoria History of the Counties of England*.

Veale: Veale, E. M., *The English Fur Trade in the later Middle Ages*, Oxford, 1966.

Verbruggen, J. F., 'Note sur le sens des mots castrum, castellum, et quelques autres expressions qui désignent les fortifications', *Revue belge de philologie et d'histoire*, vol. xxviii, 1950, pp. 147–55.

Vercauteren, F. (ed.), *Actes des comtes de Flandre, 1071–1128*, Brussels, 1938.

Vercauteren, F., *Luttes sociales à Liège, XIIIme et XIVme siècles*, Brussels, 1943.

Verheijen, L., *La règle de S. Augustin*, 2 vols, Paris, 1967.

Verhulst, A. E., 'Les Origines et l'histoire ancienne de Bruges (IXe–XIIe siècle)', *Moyen Âge*, vol. lxvi, 1960, pp. 37–63.

Verlinden, C., *L'esclavage dans l'Europe médiévale*, vol. i, Bruges, 1955.

Verona e il suo territorio, Istituto per gli Studi Storici Veronesi, vol. i– , 1960– , esp. vol. ii, 1964.

Versus de Verona, Versus de Mediolano Civitate, ed. G. B. Pighi, Bologna, 1960.

Ville, La, Société Jean Bodin, vols i, ii (=vols vi, vii of the Société), Brussels, 1954–5.

Vita comune del clero nei secoli XI e XII, La, Miscellanea del Centro di Studi Medioevali, vol. iii, Milan, 1962.

Volpe, G., *Studi sulle istituzioni comunali a Pisa*, Pisa, 1902, rev. edn with introd. by C. Violante, 1970.

Waley: Waley, D., *The Italian City-Republics*, London, 1969.

Walker, C. H., 'Sheriffs in the Pipe Roll of 31 Henry I', *EHR*, vol. xxxvii, 1922, pp. 67–79.

Walter of Coventry, *Memoriale*, ed. W. Stubbs, 2 vols, Rolls Series, 1872–3.

Walter Map, *De nugis curialium*, ed. M. R. James, Oxford, 1914; Eng. trans. by M. R. James, Cymmrodorion Record Society, 1923.

Warren, W. L., *Henry II*, London, 1973.

Watney, J., *Some Account of the Hospital of St Thomas of Acon, in the Cheap, London . . .*, London, 1892.

Watson, A. G., *The Manuscripts of Henry Savile of Banke*, London, 1969.

Webb, E. A., *The Records of St Bartholomew's*, 2 vols, London, 1921.

Weinbaum, M., *London unter Eduard I. und II.*, 2 vols, Stuttgart, 1933.

Weinbaum, M., 'Londons Aldermänner und Warde im 12–14 Jahrhundert', *Aus Sozial- und Wirtschaftsgeschichte: Gedächtnisschrift für Georg von Below*, Stuttgart, 1928, pp. 105–14.

Weinbaum, M., 'Stahlhof und Deutsche Gildhalle zu London', *Hansischen Geschichtsblättern*, vol. xxxiii, 1928, pp. 45–65.

Weinbaum, M., *Verfassungsgeschichte Londons, 1066–1268*, Beihefte zur Vierteljahrschrift für Sozial- und Wirtschaftsgeschichte, vol. xv, Stuttgart, 1929.

Weiner, A., 'Early commercial intercourse between England and Germany', *Economica*, no. ii, 1922, pp. 127–48.

Wheeler, Sir R. E. M., 'London and the Grim's Ditches', *Antiquaries Journ.*, vol. xiv, 1934, pp. 254–63.

Wheeler, Sir R. E. M., *London and the Saxons*, London Museum, 1935.

Wheeler, Sir R. E. M., *London and the Vikings*, London Museum, 1927.

Wheeler, Sir R. E. M., 'The topography of Saxon London' and 'Mr Myres on Saxon London: a reply', *Antiquity*, vol. viii, 1934, pp. 290–302, 443–7 (see Myres).

Whitelock, D., 'The conversion of the eastern Danelaw', in *Saga-Book of the Viking Soc. for Northern Research*, vol. xii, 1937–45, pp. 159–76.

Whitelock, D., 'The Prose of Alfred's reign', in *Continuations and Beginnings*, ed. E. G. Stanley, London, 1966, pp. 67–103.

Wichmann, H. and S., *Chess*, Eng. trans., London, 1964.

Will of Æthelgifu, The, ed. D. Whitelock *et al.*, Roxburghe Club, 1968.

William of Malmesbury, *Historia novella*, ed. and trans. K. R. Potter, NMT, 1955.

William of Malmesbury, *Vita Wulfstani*, ed. R. R. Darlington, Camden 3rd Series, vol. xl, 1928.

William of Newburgh, *Historia rerum Anglicarum*, in *Chrons. Stephen etc.*, vols i, ii.

William of Poitiers, *Gesta Guillelmi*, ed. R. Foreville, Paris, 1952.

Williams: Williams, G., *Medieval London, from Commune to Capital*, London, cited from corr. repr., 1970.

Williams, L. F. Rushbrook, 'William the Chamberlain and Luton Church', *EHR*, vol. xxviii, 1913, pp. 719–30.

Wilmart, A., *Auteurs spirituels et textes dévots du moyen âge latin*, Paris, 1932.

Wilts, Devonshire and Dorset portion of the Lewes Cartulary, with London and Essex documents from the Surrey portion, ed. W. Budgen and L. F. Salzman, Sussex Rec. Soc., 1943.

Wolff, P., *Histoire de Toulouse*, Toulouse, 1958.

Wormald, F., *English Kalendars before AD 1100*, Henry Bradshaw Soc., London, 1934.

Yvon, J., 'Esterlins à la Croix Courte dans les tresors français de la fin du xiie et de la première moitié du XIIIe siècle', *BNJ*, vol. xxxix, 1970, pp. 24-60.

Zarnecki, G., *Later English Romanesque Sculpture*, London, 1953.

Index

Where names occur both in text and notes, only page numbers are normally given; where in notes only, 'n.' is given. Persons are indexed under Christian names, unless they have a recognizable surname; thus Thomas Becket is under Becket, William de Longchamp under William. King, by itself, signifies King of England; mayors and sheriffs are of London (or London and Middlesex) unless otherwise stated.

Entries for places within London are gathered under LONDON: some cross-references are given to avoid ambiguities.

c. = canon
p. = prebendary
r. = river
s. = sheriff

Harold Hardrada, King of Norway, 27
Harthacnut, King, 25
Hassall, W. O., 256
Hastings, Battle of, 14, 27, 28, 193, 197, 371
Haverhill family, 41
Hedeby, 61
Helyland, Ralph, s., 374
Henry I, King: 32–3, 36, 38, 66, 83, 97, 99–
  100, 127, 201, 315–17; and Archbishop
  Thurstan, 345; and Bishop of London, 356;
  chancery, 348; charter for London, 52, 54,
  87, 207–10, 250–1; and City, 207–10;
  coins, 93; and Jews, 179, 224–6, 247; and
  Holy Trinity Aldgate, 146 n., 315–17;
  laws, 34, 40, 51–2, 54; and Reading, 357;
  and sheriffs and shires, 196, 202–3, 205,
  220 n., 250–1; and Tower, 317
Henry II, King: 45, 84–5, 267 n., 361; and
  Angevin Empire, 363; and Becket, 213,
  240, 288–9; and Cade, 227–30, 269; chancery, 273, *and see* Becket; charter for London, 208, Pl. 10; coins, 380, Pl. 21; and
  communes, 237–8 n., 239, 243–4; court,
  274, court purchases, 283; as Duke of
  Normandy, 222; and Jews, 225–7; and
  justices, 199; and Knights Templars, 231–
  3; and London, 40–5, 156, 208; and Map,
  349–50; and monasteries, 67; and Peter's
  Pence, 274; rebellion of 1173–4, 215; and
  Rouen, 265; and St-Omer, 270; and
  sheriffs, 218–22, 234, farm, 209; and Westminster Abbey, 301; and wine trade, 275;
  his sons, 350
Henry, King, son of Henry II, 42–3, 244 n.
Henry III, King: 56, 163, 164 n.; clerk of,
  345; and Westminster Abbey, 128, 297,
  306, 309
Henry VIII, King, 16, 147, 325
Henry I, King of Germany, the Fowler, 62
Henry IV, King of Germany, Emperor, 186,
  255
Henry de Civitate, c. St Paul's, 359
Henry of Blois, Bishop of Winchester: 36–7,
  351; Abbot of Glastonbury, 321, Dean of
  St Martin le Grand, 311; and works of art,
  272–3
Henry of Braybrooke, 227
Henry of Cornhill, son of Gervase, s., also of
  Surrey, 46, 79 n., 211, 234
Henry of Cornhill, Dean of St Paul's, 211
Henry of Frowyk, alderman, 164, 337
Henry of Northampton, Master, c. St Paul's,
  324, 335
Henry of St Albans, s., 373
Henry, son of Reiner, 254
Heraclitus, 326

Heraclius, Patriarch of Jerusalem, 241
Herbert, Abbot of Westminster, 301, 309
Hereford: 180; bishopric, 16; bishops, *see*
  Foliot, Robert of Lorraine; earls of, *see*
  Milo, Roger
heretics, 188
Herlewin, *see* Ralph
Herluin, Abbot of Bec, 302–3
Herman, Bishop of Salisbury, 311
Hertford, Hertfordshire: 17, 176, 198, 200,
  247; earldom, 196; justices and sheriffs,
  shire, 191, 203, 217
Hiesmois, Vicomte of, 346
Hlothere, Lothar, Old English name, 154
Hock, 267
Hodges, P., 139–40
Hogenberg, map by, 1–11, 13, Pl. 6
Hollar, W., engravings by, 81, 338, Pl. 50
Holy Land: 271; *and see* Crusades
Holywell, *see* London
Honeybourne, M. J., xiii, 89, 109–10, 122 n.,
  130 n., 147, 333
Horace, 118, 182
hospitals: 81; *and see* London
Howdenshire, Yorks, 195
Hubert, 138
Hugh, St, Bishop of Lincoln, 350
Hugh, Earl of Chester, 217
Hugh de Mareni, Archdeacon of London,
  Dean of St Paul's, 346, 357
Hugh le Noreis, 132
Hugh of Basing, s., 374
Hugh of Buckland, s. and justice, also of
  various other shires, ?c. of St Paul's, 200,
  204–6, 372
Hugh of Reculver, c. St Paul's, p. Reculvers-
  land, 349
Hugolina, 202
Huitdeniers, *see* Eightpence
Hull, 76
Humber, r., 18
Hundred, 194
Hungary, 261
Hunt, R. W., 324
Huntingdon, 89, 280
husting: xx; *and see* London, courts
Huy, 268
Hwicce, 16, 167

Ibn Khurradadhbah, 224 n.
Ine, Ina, King of Wessex, 176, 294
Ingelric, ?=Engelbric, c. of St Paul's, Dean
  St Martin le Grand, 310–11, 340, 342
Ingenold, mother of Roger, nephew of Hubert,
  211
Innocent II, Pope, 357